KENNAN

KENNAN

A Life between Worlds

FRANK COSTIGLIOLA

PRINCETON UNIVERSITY PRESS

PRINCETON *&* OXFORD

Published by Princeton University Press
41 William Street, Princeton, New Jersey 08540
99 Banbury Road, Oxford OX2 6JX

press.princeton.edu

Library of Congress Cataloging-in-Publication Data

Names: Costigliola, Frank, 1946– author.
Title: Kennan : a life between worlds / Frank Costigliola.
Description: Princeton : Princeton University Press, [2023] |
    Includes bibliographical references and index.
Identifiers: LCCN 2022019150 (print) | LCCN 2022019151 (ebook) |
    ISBN 9780691165400 (hardback) | ISBN 9780691189307 (ebook)
Subjects: LCSH: Kennan, George F. (George Frost), 1904–2005. |
    Ambassadors—United States—Biography. | Historians—United States—
    Biography. | United States—Foreign relations—1945–1989. | United States—
    Foreign relations—Soviet Union. | Soviet Union—Foreign relations—
    United States. | BISAC: BIOGRAPHY & AUTOBIOGRAPHY / Political |
    POLITICAL SCIENCE / History & Theory
Classification: LCC E748.K374 C67 2023 (print) | LCC E748.K374 (ebook) |
    DDC 327.73047—dc23/eng/20220623
LC record available at https://lccn.loc.gov/2022019150
LC ebook record available at https://lccn.loc.gov/2022019151

British Library Cataloging-in-Publication Data is available

Editorial: Priya Nelson, Barbara Shi
Jacket Design: Heather Hansen
Production: Danielle Amatucci
Publicity: James Schneider, Kate Farquhar-Thomson

Jacket Credit: Photo by Trygves Skramstad, Faedrelandsvennen

This book has been composed in Arno Pro and Kepler Std.

Printed on acid-free paper. ∞

Printed in the United States of America

10 9 8 7 6 5 4 3 2 1

To the dear friends who have inspired and improved my work over the years: Lloyd Gardner, Richard Immerman, Ara Keys, Mel Leffler, Emily Rosenberg, and Andy Rotter. That most of them were influenced by Walt LaFeber is yet another testament to his impact.

TABLE OF CONTENTS

ACKNOWLEDGMENTS

MY DILEMMA IS that while George F. Kennan animates this book, he was lousy at writing acknowledgments. Creativity came natural to Kennan. Whether he was composing with his precise cursive, the clickety-click of his stadium-seating typewriter, or a colored pencil in his sketch pad, Kennan's imagination sparkled. The glow dulled, however, when it came to thanking those who had helped him write his many books. Nor did the wit that conjured playful rhymes on birthdays or talking-animal stories for children enliven his formulaic thank-yous to those who had assisted him in various archives. Nevertheless, Kennan never neglected acknowledging the Institute for Advanced Study in Princeton, his intellectual home during his half-century as a historian.

That unique institution lives up to its unofficial motto, "In paradise there are no excuses." This book originated in 2009–2010, my idyllic year at the Institute for Advanced Study. Learning of my curiosity about Kennan, IAS faculty member Nicola Di Cosmo invited me to give an "After Hours Conversation" on the famed diplomat-historian.

It all then came together. The long-sequestered Kennan papers, housed just a walk away in Princeton University's Seeley G. Mudd library, had recently opened for research by ordinary historians. I plunged into the voluminous Kennan diary, the letters, and the reveal-ing interviews done by John Lewis Gaddis, then writing his authorized biography. I was hooked by the distinction of Kennan's writing and thinking, the quirkiness of his personality, and the turmoil of his inner life. Enhancing the allure were the extant traces of someone who had died only a few years earlier. I found some of Kennan's books in a used book shop in Princeton. I visited his grave site. The informal seminar sparked an invitation to write about Kennan's years at the Institute for the *Institute Letter*. I got to talk with his former friends, including the physicist Freeman Dyson and the historian John Lukacs. Mary Acheson Bundy, neighbor of George and Annelise, shared not only her own memories, but also the perspective of her father, Dean Acheson, Kennan's former boss in the State Department. I walked amid the towering trees of the 600-acre Institute Woods, where Kennan had spent many an afternoon, striding along the trails or hand sawing firewood. (He was engrossed in cutting up fallen tree limbs when the blizzard of 1978 hit.) An invitation by Director Peter Goddard to return to the Institute for a summer the following year enabled me to put together a proposal to edit the Kennan diaries. The publication of the *Kennan Diaries* (2014) drew me in further, as did an article in the *Journal of American History* (2016). A fellowship from the University of Connecticut Humanities Institute provided needed time for writing. Throughout this journey, and even down to today, I have remained intrigued by the challenge of understanding the thoughts, feelings, and actions of a flawed genius who cared almost too much.

Many people have aided my efforts to comprehend Kennan. As the dedication of the book attests, Lloyd Gardner, Richard Immerman, Ara Keys, Mel Leffler, Emily Rosenberg, and Andy Rotter, all brilliant scholars, have read the manuscript and have offered invaluable suggestions. Often I would send them a snippet or even a whole chapter and get it back that very day with incisive comments. David A. Mayers and Dick Brown also gave me the benefit of their reading.

Multiple interviews with Grace Kennan Warnecke, Joan Kennan, Christopher Kennan, and Wendy Kennan afforded a deeper look at their father's inner world, his daily routines, and their life as a family. I enjoyed my many lunches and telephone calls with Grace. Joan graciously invited my wife and me to the Kennan farm in East Berlin, Pennsylvania. There I saw the third floor office where Kennan did his writing, the workshop he had built, and the trees he had planted. Also during this visit to the farm, Wayne Lau hared memories of East Berlin's famous resident. Chris Kennan tooled his motorcycle over to Storrs and, over a two-day period, we talked about his father. Chris also clarified some issues in subsequent emails. I appreciate Wendy's conversations over the telephone and regret her passing. Grace, Joan, and Chris all granted use of previously unpublished photographs. Doug James, the son of Kennan's cousin and best friend, Charlie, shared crucial information about the maternal side of Kennan's family as well as the riveting interview he did with Kennan in 2003. John Lewis Gaddis mused about Kennan over a lunch at his home in New Haven. Betsy Barrett shared her moving reminiscences. Bill Riley, Terrie Bramley, Simki Mattern Kuznick, and Marcus Padulchick provided important details. Nancy and Gene Hotchkiss relayed vivid memories of their Uncle George.

Somewhere there should be acknowledged how much Gene's mother, Jeanette Kennan Hotchkiss, did for her brother George and his family. Nettie mothered her needy younger brother, remained his confidant for decades, and shared his ambitions as a writer. At times during World War II, she squeezed into her packed, though loving, household young Grace and Joanie while their parents remained in Europe. After the war, she on occasion also shouldered child care for Christopher and Wendy.

Invaluable for anyone doing research on Kennan are the interviews conducted by John Lewis Gaddis not only with George and Annelise, but also with George's siblings and some two dozen of his associates. Gaddis generously deposited these transcripts as well as the further revealing aural recordings in the Mudd Library. Mudd also houses the interviews done by Joan Kennan with her father and his siblings in the early 1970s.

I appreciate the memories of Kennan shared with me by Stephen Arbogast, Bart Gellman, and Anders Stephanson. I also learned much from exchanges with the late Bob Silvers and Stephen F. Cohen.

In addition to reminiscences, this book draws heavily from archival documents. I have benefited enormously from the consistently helpful, highly competent work of Dan Linke, archivist at Mudd Library, and his staff, particularly Christa Cleeton. I thank also the staff at Yale's Sterling Library, the Harry S. Truman Presidential Library, and the University of Connecticut's Babbidge Library. John Lamberton Harper, Anders Stephanson, and John Crawford shared some important documents.

Like many historians from the former colonies, I have been awed and aided by the brisk efficiency of the National Archives in Kew, England.

Among the treasures of the National Archives in College Park, Maryland, is archivist extraordinaire David Langbart. David commands unparalleled familiarity with the scope as well as the nooks and crannies of the archive's vast holdings of U.S. State Department records. He decoded the log of outgoing despatches from both the Berlin Consulate and the Moscow Embassy so that I could track down the myriad, diverse reports written by Kennan in the 1920s and 1930s. He filled my inbox with scans of Kennan documents from other scattered files. This book owes much to him.

Also going beyond the call of duty was Erica Mosner, archivist at the Shelby White and Leon Levy Archives Center at the Institute for Advanced Study. Along with Marcia Tucker, Erica combed the Archives Center for documents on Kennan. She also discovered, in a random file, the photograph that graces the cover of this book.

For permission to use that image, I thank the photographer, Trygve Skramstad, and the *Fædrelandsvennen* newspaper as well as Grace Kennan Warnecke and Elisabeth Eide, who helped me find Mr. Skramstad in Norway.

A key aspect of my first chapter, the strange story of why young George, despite his sizable inheritance, believed he had to pinch pennies, owes everything to the sleuthing of attorney Ed Ehrlich. Ed dug through the archives of the Milwaukee County Probate Court to find the monthly financial accounting submitted by George's father, Kent Kennan, as well as the wills of George's mother and grandparents.

My own finances were aided by research grants from the University of Connecticut. The Institute for Advanced Study, the National Endowment for the Humanities, and the University of Connecticut History Department. My thanks to History Department heads Chris Clark and Mark Healey for facilitating my scholarship.

I am also indebted to a group of indefatigable research assistants: Megan Dawson, Rohit Kandala, Julie Leighton, Lauren Stauffer, and Gabrielle Westcott.

In addition to the friends and co-workers already mentioned, other historians have offered support and inspiration over the years. I thank in particular History Department colleagues Bob Gross, Brendan Kane, Brad Simpson, Nina Dayton, Ken Gouwens, Nancy Shoemaker, Fakhreddin Azimi, Helen Rozwadowski, Fiona Vernal, Sylvia Schafer, and Charles Lansing. Peter Baldwin took me to task when I needed it.

My fellow SHAFR-ites are too numerous to list here. But I cannot refrain from acknowledging the valued comradeship of Bob Brigham, Doug Little, Bob Hannigan, Bob and Margie Van Meter, Jeff Engel, David Mayers, Kristin Hoganson, Ryan Irwin, Mike Hogan, Peter Hahn, Randall Woods, Petra Goedde, Anne Foster, Mark Stoler, Michael Donoghue, Tom Paterson, Paul Kramer, Catherine Forslund, David Engerman, and the late Geoff Smith and Marty Sherwin. Molly Hite helped me understand the intellectual importance of analyzing not just the stories of history, but also how those stories are constructed.

In producing this book I have been shepherded along by the sure touch of my agent Andrew Wiley and my Princeton University Press editors Eric Crahan and Priya Nelson. Production manager Christine Marra averted a crisis, while editorial assistant Barbara Shi demonstrated initiative in many areas, including the baking of cherry pie. Bob Bettendorf skillfully oversaw the publicity for this book.

I hope that someday my granddaughters Aviva and Elana Tarsky will find this book of some interest. The determination and achievements of my daughter, Jennifer Nancy Costigliola, continue to inspire me.

Finally, I owe the largest debt to my D.D., Diann Bertucci. Not only does she come through with rescue remedies of various kinds, but she has managed to retain good cheer morning after morning as I greet her with yet another fascinating tidbit about George F. Kennan.

Dunhamtown Farm
Storrs, CT
April 2022

PREFACE

THE GREATEST tragedy in the life of George F. Kennan arose from his most famous success. As the author of the "long telegram" and the "X" article in 1946–1947, Kennan urged that the United States contain the expansion of the Soviet Union. Thereafter, he could not shake his association with the vastly more militarized version of containment pursued by the United States throughout the Cold War. Kennan also failed in what became his central mission from 1950 onward. With the Kremlin contained, Kennan sought desperately to get Washington to negotiate with Moscow to defuse the threat of nuclear war. Despite their bluster, the Soviets repeatedly signaled their openness to such diplomacy.

Kennan remains a largely unsung hero for his persistent efforts to ease the Cold War long before the collapse of the Soviet Union in 1991. Indeed, the story of Kennan's life demands that we rethink the Cold War as an era of possibilities for dialogue and diplomacy, not the inevitable series of confrontations and crises we came to see. As early as February 1948, the author of containment was already musing about talks with the Kremlin to reduce tensions over defeated Germany. He helped initiate the negotiations that would end the Korean War. In 1952 as ambassador to Moscow, Kennan tried so hard to jump-start diplomacy that he instead set off an explosion that wrecked his mission. His BBC radio broadcasts in 1957 calling for a mutual U.S.-Soviet military pullback from Europe inspired a groundswell of public support that shook the Cold War establishment. In 1961–1962, as ambassador to Belgrade, he opened a diplomatic back channel to the Kremlin in hopes of easing the Berlin crisis. Kennan's February 1966 televised testimony against the Vietnam War, and his critiquing the containment doctrine justifying it, helped make such opposition respectable. In the 1970s–1980s, he became a leading voice calling for an end to the nuclear arms race and a sharp reduction in suicidal weaponry.

Even after the collapse of the Soviet Union in 1991, Kennan, now in his nineties, did not rest. Having helped instigate one cold war with Russia in the 1940s, he tried in the 1990s to head off another such conflict. In his public writings and in conversations with the White House, he warned that expanding the NATO alliance into the former domains of the Soviet Union would incite nationalism and militarism in Russia, doom its infant democracy, and poison relations with the West, effectively restarting the Cold War. Though honored, Kennan was not heeded. As he predicted, the enlargement of NATO to the border of Ukraine would spark fury in Moscow, contributing to Russian leader Vladimir Putin's decisions to attack Ukraine in 2014 and to launch a brutal full-scale invasion in 2022.

Kennan's role as both the author of containment and the critic of its implementation reflected not a contradiction, but rather a sophisticated intelligence. His thinking blended keen emotions with keen reasoning.

Though Washington insiders could not deny Kennan's brilliance, they tried to limit his influence. Kennan would remain contained by his own containment doctrine. This was so not only because he had sold the approach so effectively that it would forever be associated with his name, but also because most leaders in government dismissed his urging that they advance from restraining the Soviets to negotiating with them. Dorothy Fosdick, an influential foreign policy adviser in Washington from the 1940s to the 1980s and the only woman on Kennan's Policy Planning Staff, later recalled that "we from time to time debated whether it might not be a good idea to bring [Kennan] back into government as a way to make him more sensible. The 'containment' George was the George I respected as a public official, not the later one."[1]

This book aims to liberate Kennan from containment by exploring the full range of his political ideas as well as the connections between those beliefs and his feelings. Kennan's love for the people and culture of Russia intensified his fury at the Stalinist repression that, in the 1930s–1950s, prohibited contact between Soviet citizens and foreigners such as himself. He opposed Soviet expansion after World War II in part because it extended the domain of such secret police–dominated regimes. And yet his love for what he regarded as the essence of Russia also bled into a measure of sympathy for the dilemmas of Soviet leaders. He understood their point of view in struggles with Washington. He even felt on occasion more Russian than American.

What Kennan imagined as the wondrous mystery of eternal Russia appealed to deep-seated elements of his personality. Scarred by the loneliness he had endured as a motherless child, he longed for some enveloping maternal warmth. Also impelling him was a recurring desire to flee, somehow and somewhere, from the boredom and duty of his regimented daily life.

His life pivoted not only from America to Russia, but between other worlds as well. He navigated between his own era of the twentieth century, and the eighteenth and nineteenth centuries, in which he would have felt more comfortable, or so he believed. Living in Milwaukee, Princeton, Riga, and Berlin from the 1910s to the early 1930s, he absorbed ugly biases he never could totally shake. And so in subsequent decades he would toggle between brilliant perception and blinkered prejudice. In his last years, dissatisfied with his limited influence in his own era, Kennan tried to shape the history written about him so that future generations would be receptive to his ideas and his life story.

In still other ways, he stood betwixt and between. As a boy who had lost his mother at the age of two months, young George had to negotiate between maternal relatives who doted on him and his father, whom they despised. At class-conscious Princeton University, he pinched pennies, unaware of the extent of his inherited wealth. After getting engaged to a daughter of Washington insiders, he found himself cast aside and humiliated. He responded by throwing himself into his work in the State Department, where he rose faster than anyone else in his age cohort. Nevertheless, here too, Kennan remained an outsider. He had chosen to study Russian language and history in Berlin, and he oriented himself toward Central and Eastern Europe. These choices seemed odd to the in-crowd in the State Department, who valued Paris and London as the foreign capitals normative in culture and central to diplomacy. For them, Berlin and points east figured as problem-causing and "other."

Even in the late 1940s, when his influence in Washington and Washington's influence around the world were rising meteorically, Kennan retained a degree of independence. Although he owed much to such powerful benefactors as Secretary of Defense James V. Forrestal, he operated largely on his own terms. As founding director of the Policy Planning Staff in the State Department, the forty-three-year-old conducted staff meetings like a self-assured professor running a seminar. He alone crafted the influential policy papers for Secretary of State George C. Marshall, whose office adjoined his own. Kennan maintained a "certain aloofness in his personal relationships," explained a former member of the Planning Staff. "And this was true in his attitude toward foreign relations, too." He favored "a dignity" in "dealing with foreign countries, not try to become too intimate with them; we get into trouble doing that."[2] With regard to relations with the people of Russia, however, Kennan did seek such intimacy, at least for himself.

George and his wife, Annelise, also kept some distance from the fashionable Georgetown set. Though they attended dinners and cocktail parties during the week, weekends they reserved for their 252-acre farm in East Berlin, Pennsylvania. Visiting diplomats could talk foreign policy with Kennan, but they had to do so while installing a trough in the pigsty, laying the foundation for a workshop, or otherwise making themselves useful.

The devotion to the farm reflected Kennan's love of nature, his yearning for roots, and his element of Russian sensibility. The farm "satisfies all my irrational demands for solidity and security," he explained to his sister after buying the property in 1942. "It was just like the 'Cherry Orchard' without the orchard."[3] The reference to the play by Anton Chekhov expressed George's reverence for the wisdom of this favorite Russian writer.

Kennan shared Chekhov's root-and-branch critique of industrialism. The Russian argued that the basic problem of modern society was not that factory workers were exploited by capitalist titans—or by Communist

Party bosses—but rather that machine production itself exploited people and alienated them from each other and from nature. The tragic error of industrialism and of its twin, urbanization, bore much of the responsibility for the ills of contemporary society, Kennan believed. America needed a "policy to prevent the plundering of the natural treasures and the beauties of our own country," he declared years before the modern environmental movement took off in the 1970s.[4]

Kennan also favored personal rather than automatic interaction in matters large and small, whether it pertained to having operators rather than computers place telephone calls, or having porters rather than do-it-yourself baggage carts move luggage. As for transportation, Kennan believed that commuting by train encouraged a clustered community around the station, while the automobile furthered alienation by dispersing the population. In contrast to ships, transoceanic airplanes deprived the traveler of a gradual and graceful adjustment to the destination. He condemned advertising as lying. Often elusive and reclusive, he despised commercialization, declined to use a computer, and disdained other technological gadgets. Quirky yet wise, he remained difficult to understand.

"My father had a deep emotional life that was very regimented and repressed," Christopher Kennan concluded. "There was a lot that he did not say."[5] Regimenting his feelings was a response that young George had mastered in the stern household of his father and stepmother, where proper English was mandatory and mentioning that puppies were born was deemed vulgar. Those parents had their sensitive, well-mannered son skip a grade so that they could send him off to a military boarding school for problem boys. Slender and underage, George was bullied when starting out at St. John's, but toughened himself enough to survive and even thrive. He would forever after retain an inner, distinctly masculine, regimenting voice that sounded much like the ironhanded disciplinarian of the school, "Duke" Smyth.

"Repressed" was a term that George in his twenties and early thirties became familiar with as he absorbed the theories of Sigmund Freud. Kennan believed that the lives of men (he simply assumed the masculine gender was normative) were unavoidably wrenched by the struggle between Eros and Civilization. While Eros in the form of sexual free-dom, art, adventure, wonder, mystery, and strong emotion would always entice him, Civilization as family, study, duty, achievement, and cold rationality would usually claim him, at least for a while. He saw the chal-lenge as balancing these two forces. While unchecked Eros led to chaos, unrelieved Civilization deadened the spirit.

With regard to international relations, Kennan emphasized reining in runaway emotions. He regarded containment as a means to check the offensive brashness of the Soviet Union after its stunning victory over Nazi Germany. He would likewise seek to calm Cold War hysteria in the United States. As a junior diplomat, Kennan had admitted that "any demonstration of mass emotion always gives me a sinking sensation at the pit of the stomach." He saw such feeling as "a revelation of the hope-less mixture of stupidity and good intentions" that was the fate of humanity.[6]

And yet in a fragment penned late in life on "'my' Russians," he ex-cused emotional intensity. Juxtaposed against the "wild, primitive bru-tality" of the Russians was their "most touching tenderness in personal relations." With "their moral earnestness, their courage and endurance, and their . . . faith, they put all us Westerners to shame." He extolled the Russians as "emotionally, intellectually, and aesthetically one of the world's potentially greatest peoples."[7]

Despite his edging into the world of Russia, Kennan remained an American. And though he lived in Eastern and Central Europe for most of the two decades before 1946, summered in Norway, and mused in old age about retreating to rural Scotland, he remained in the United States for most of his 101 years.

That life span, from 1904 to 2005, encompassed a huge chunk of U.S. history. When Theodore Roosevelt, the president in 1904, was born in 1858, the oldest Americans had come into the world as subjects of the British Empire. George's father had accompanied his father on cam-paigns during the Civil War. At the time of Kennan's death, there lived Americans who, barring some global calamity, would survive into the twenty-second century.

Technology and international politics changed during Kennan's life in ways that often he did not find comfortable. At the 1904 St. Louis World's Fair, held to celebrate the centennial of the Louisiana Purchase, visitors marveled at an early radio device, the x-ray machine, and an incubator for infants. One hundred and forty models of gasoline, steam, and electric automobiles vied for attention, as did airships that could barely fly. In a tribute to America's imperial expansion, the fair exhibited not only the defeated Apache leader Geronimo but also the supposedly primitive Igorots of the Philippines. A week before George was born on February 16, Japan humiliated Russia with a surprise attack on the Russian fleet at Port Arthur in Manchuria. Russia's defeat in that war would trigger the aborted revolution of 1905, the eventual overthrow of the czar, and the rise of the Bolsheviks in 1917.

Much had happened by the time of Kennan's death on March 17, 2005. The Bolsheviks in Russia had been cast aside, as had the militarists in Japan. China, the helpless victim of their rivalry, had risen to wealth and power. George's close friend J. Robert Oppenheimer, the atomic physicist and director of the Institute for Advanced Study, also born in 1904, had already been gone for nearly four decades. Over the course of Kennan's life, spending by the U.S. government ballooned from less than a billion dollars a year to $2.5 trillion dollars, while the population more than tripled from 82 million to 296 million. By instinct a conservative, Kennan regarded the expanded spending, especially on advanced weaponry, as wasteful. Reluctant to see Anglo-Saxons such as himself pass into minority status and worried about the environmental and social impact of crowding, he deplored the increase in the number of people.

Whole scenes and cultures that Kennan knew well would disappear during his lifetime. Always partial to trains, he marveled in the 1920s at the "five layers of gleaming rails and thundering wheels!" converging at Pennsylvania Station in New York City. He also admired the roomy and sturdy Russian-built cars on the rails in Estonia. On an uneventful trip in that Baltic nation, Kennan observed in the carriage with him "a couple of Jews, some natty Latvian officers," and others who remained unaware that they were unfortunate enough to live in what a future historian would term the "bloodlands."[8] The unrelenting killing of the Second World War would also incinerate Hamburg, the vibrant and gritty city that Kennan idolized as "a goddess." There he could hear a "multisonic, buzzing song in which all hope and all fear of humankind finds its expression." That melody, however, would be drowned out by the roar of the firestorm ignited by the Allies' incendiary bombs.[9] Visiting the burnt-out shell of Hamburg after the war would turn Kennan against nearly all war.

His opposition to most wars, along with his skepticism about American empire, industrialism, and globalization, set Kennan at odds with Cold War America, while making him newly relevant in our own time. It is Kennan's oddity, his penchant for thinking otherwise, that renders his voice important. This lyric mourner of a bygone age, this lover of Russia and permanent visitor to America, this faultfinder of modern and postmodern society, offers a skewed yet discerning critique of what most simply accept. Although often painfully estranged, Kennan never gave up for long on America, or on Russia. Nor did he abandon hope of mutually beneficial relations between the people of these two rivals. As someone who longed for inclusion but seldom found it, and as a thinker who felt and thought too deeply for comfort, it was fitting that Kennan often referred to himself as "bewildered." His was a life between worlds. We owe it to ourselves to try to understand him.

KENNAN

INTRODUCTION

THE FAMOUS "X"—the anonymous strategist who burst on the scene in 1946–1947 with a plan for blocking, even besting, the seemingly unstoppable Soviet Union—was soon identified as George Frost Kennan. The once obscure diplomat quickly rose to become America's top Russian expert and the founding director of the State Department's Policy Planning Staff. Later, as an establishment icon dressed in an old-fashioned, three-piece suit with a heavy gold watch chain, Kennan would remain associated with the containment doctrine until his death at 101.

Given this thumbnail sketch, how to account for Kennan's "blubbering" while watching a performance of Anton Chekhov's *The Cherry Orchard* because the play stirred up "my Russian self" which was "much more genuine than the American one"?[1] Even as the strategist championed rational realism in foreign policy, powerful emotions coursed through his personal and professional life. Though widely respected and honored by presidents and the public, Kennan judged his career a failure because he had been dropped as a pilot of U.S. foreign policy. A success at helping initiate the Cold War, he fizzled in trying to end it. In his mid-nineties, he warned that expanding NATO eastward threatened democracy in Russia and renewed hostility with Moscow. This pioneering, even radical, environmentalist pointed to the machine as the root cause of economic exploitation and environmental depredation. A devoted family man, Kennan repeatedly strayed from his marriage despite the ensuing guilt. He viewed himself as a scion of an earlier time cast astray in a twentieth-century world. Indeed, the abandoned child would remain the foundational story of his life.

FIGURE 1. Deep currents flowed below Kennan's immaculate
exterior. (Courtesy of Joan E. Kennan.)

February through April were always difficult months for Kennan. It
was not the weather; he loved the cold and early spring. But he hated
revisiting the agony that had beset his mother, Florence James Kennan,
from shortly after he was born on February 16, 1904, to her death from
a burst appendix on April 19 of the same year. As a young boy, he suffered that pain partly out of the mistaken belief that she had died from
the complications of his birth. As an adult, Kennan year after year would
take sick or succumb to depression during those dark months. He
would die on March 17, 2005.

Two years earlier, so crippled by arthritis that he could barely walk,
he was lying in bed in his Hodge Road house in Princeton, New Jersey,
and talking with Doug James, the son of his cousin and childhood best

friend, Charlie. Kennan was trying to put his long life into context. What accounted for his persistent longing for succor and intimacy? Reflecting on his mother, he lamented that he had been "torn away from her breast." The violation was so abrupt and final that it "affected me for life. Subconsciously, this was a trauma for myself and for her." Kennan, who regarded Freudian theory as settled science, blamed his restless quest for sexual intimacy as an adult on this rupture of maternal intimacy as an infant. What he referred to as "my weakness" stemmed from "the shock of what happened to me" as an infant.[2]

Kennan's lifelong yearning for deep familiarity and closeness, for union with some wondrous mystery and beauty, went far beyond sex, however. Long before he became America's foremost strategist on the Soviet Union during the pivotal years of the early Cold War, Kennan invested his desires in the people and culture of Russia. As both the rational strategist mapping out plans for containing and isolating the Soviet Union and the emotional man beset by longing to connect with the Russian people, Kennan was wrenched almost unbearably.

Though flawed in many ways, Kennan shines as an unsung hero of the Cold War. While most people focus on the inflammatory manifestos he penned in 1946 and 1947 that helped ignite the Cold War, they underplay his pivot in the opposite direction soon thereafter. In the four decades from 1949 to the dissolution of the Soviet Union in 1991, Kennan, as U.S. government official and then as public intellectual, devoted his formidable talents to pushing for negotiation and compromise with the Russia that he would always love. His repeated pointing to this and that opportunity for a settlement with Moscow offers an alternate history of the Cold War, one in which that struggle, which always entailed the danger of nuclear Armageddon, might have ended decades earlier and more safely. Why Kennan the Cold Warrior was lauded as the all-wise Grand Strategist and why Kennan the critic of that conflict was often dismissed as a sentimental poet says much about the political culture and emotional sensibility of America. After the Cold War, Kennan presciently argued for bolstering Russia's fragile democracy with a new, European-wide security organization that would replace NATO and mitigate the division between East and West.

As a young boy, George was yanked away not only from his mother but also from a succession of nurses and, most sorrowfully, from "Cousin Grace" Wells, whom he had wanted to call mother. She was a beloved relative of his mother hired to care for George and his three older sisters. After three happy years, Grace had to leave when the children's father, Kossuth "Kent" Kennan, remarried. These breaches scarred him, George would later believe.

The emotional security of young George was shaken further by suspicions of an egregious infidelity committed by his father. Both temperament and training inclined Kennan toward privacy. He praised restraint even more than he practiced it. He regarded public displays of emotion and revelations of intimate secrets as vulgar. While his diary is rife with allusions to his various affairs and his subsequent guilt, he remained elusive as to details. Now, however, in this 2003 interview with Doug James, he opened up for the first time about a shocking scandal.

When Florence Kennan at age forty-four was dying in great pain from a burst appendix, her three young daughters were called in to kiss their feverish mother goodbye. Infant George nursed until almost the end. Florence's brother and sister-in-law—Charlie's parents, Alfred and Nellie James—and Florence's parents all hovered nearby. Conspicuously absent, however, was her husband. "Uncle Alfred and Aunt Nellie suspected my father of being away for no good purpose," George explained. They believed he had "another woman somewhere." Kent, however, would always claim that he had been on a hunting trip. "I should have insisted on talking with my father" about this before he died, the son realized too late. Shyness on both sides and perhaps also this dark suspicion had hampered meaningful communication between George and his father. While "Uncle Alfred and Aunt Nellie were always very nice to me and to my sisters," they never forgave his father.[3] Personality differences, financial tensions, and conflicts over Kent's later decisions to remarry and to send his son off to a military school further poisoned relations between the maternal and paternal sides of young George's family.

Though he would live a long life, Kennan seems never to have gotten over this cratering of his emotional security. Losing his mother as an infant loomed as the defining story of his life, one he felt compelled to tell over and over. He emphasized the loss in his diary and memoir, to his authorized biographer, to his children, to caregivers, and in the final interview of his life. An astute observer of the adult George Kennan was Mary Acheson Bundy, a Princeton friend of the Kennans and the daughter of Kennan's former boss, Dean Acheson. Her own son had suffered trauma when she was quarantined with tuberculosis during his first year. George "liked Mary Bundy a lot," his daughter, Grace, would remember.[4] Looking beyond the shell of George's outward sociability, Mary discerned a "haunting sadness, deep in him. It's an awfully big part of him." She added, "You don't have to go very far, psychologically, to discover that almost everything starts before you even can think."[5]

Kennan did go far, however, when it came to what he regarded as psychological science. He analyzed both his personal life and foreign policy issues in psychological terms. He kept a diary of his dreams, and he suspected that some were communications from an outside source. He had read Freud in a sanatorium in Vienna in 1935 while being treated, though not psychoanalyzed, by a Freudian-minded doctor. He believed that the life patterns of nations paralleled those of individual humans. As America's preeminent strategist on Russia in the 1940s, he diagnosed the Soviet Union as a neurotic, at times psychotic, patient who needed calm management by policy makers such as himself playing the rational doctor. The pervasive influence of Freudian theories in mid-twentieth-century America gave credibility to Kennan's often reductive psychological explanations.[6]

Freud's *Civilization and Its Discontents* had convinced Kennan that "at the center of our psychic construction [is] a libido, the demands of which, as Freud has demonstrated, we ignore at our peril."[7] Warring with the "instinct to reproduce" were the "taboos and penalties" of civilization. If a man—and Kennan nearly always regarded the male gender as normative—was "caught between the cogs of nature and those of society," he would be "rubbed to pieces."[8] More than sexual freedom stood at stake. Kennan regarded the libido as the control switch for vitality and intellectual and esthetic creativity. While inciting chaos, the erotic force also enabled escape from deadly boredom. As a young man, he feared that by upholding "the laws of society," in particular his "dignity as a husband, a father, and an official," he was being forced into "a renunciation of [his] own life."[9]

He would forever view Freud's notion of a dichotomy between Eros and Civilization as framing the dilemmas of his own life. In endeavors ranging from foreign policy to lifestyle, he felt torn between what he called unconventional and conventional solutions. Even though he longed to escape professional duties, and at times broke down in order to break free, he also impressed superiors with his fierce work ethic. He acted on his desire for extramarital affairs, while also reproaching himself and remaining with his wife for nearly three-quarters of a century. As Kennan saw it, Civilization entailed the bourgeois (or Communist) order that kept diplomatic channels humming, trains running, and society functioning. Eros invited not only creativity, but also immersion to the point of a liberating obliteration of self.

This Freudian dilemma loomed so large in Kennan's world view that in 1962, while serving as ambassador to Yugoslavia, he chose it as the topic of his Palm Sunday sermon to the Protestant Church Group in Belgrade. Perhaps because he was feeling battered by the political struggles of his ambassadorship, he lifted the veil on his personal difficulties. He praised Freud's insight about "what slaves we all of us are to our vanity, to the emotional fixations of our early youth . . . and not least to the frequently chaotic and destructive urgings of the sexual instinct." These drives impelled "a real conflict between man's emotional nature and his effort to lead the civilized life." Repressing Eros to satisfy Civilization triggered neurosis. He noted that nations with "the most highly disciplined and orderly and successful civilization" also suffered "the highest rates of mental illness."

In sum, Freud in Kennan's view had applied science to reaffirm original sin. The strategist drew two lessons from the conundrum. First, was the need for personal humility. "Man" was a cracked vessel. Therefore, "no one is entirely wonderful." This view excused sexual and other transgressions as inevitable and understandable. Second, in terms of political arrangements, such utopian ideologies as communism were doomed to excess and ultimate failure.[10]

Kennan took this analysis to heart because it fit his conflicting impulses. He felt both enticed and endangered by the prospect of escaping into a bohemian life or in writing a novel so meaningful that it would consume him. Though he dreamed about a wondrous union with the people of Russia, he remained an American. Despite the prevailing image of Kennan as an impeccably dressed icon of the establishment, as he was viewed by millions in televised Senate hearings questioning the Vietnam War, he remained far more complex. He imputed emotions to nature, empathized with God, and half-believed in fairies.

He ran away from boarding school, imagined running away from Princeton, longed to drop diplomacy to become a deckhand on a tramp steamer, and, as an old man, yearned to abandon his civic and social responsibilities in Princeton for a secluded farm in northern New England. Nevertheless, he had dutifully returned to boarding school, and he never acted on the other fantasies.

Kennan's need to salve the loneliness within him, his efforts to combat the depression that often engulfed him, and his search for mysterious meaning in a quotidian world—all these cravings became entangled in his complex relationship with Russia. He detested the Soviet government that had betrayed the idealism of the Bolshevik Revolution, perpetrated the horrors of the 1930s purges, and extended its police-state rule into Eastern and Central Europe after World War II. Nevertheless, he loved the people and culture of Russia, especially those of the pre-1917 era. His fervor as a Cold Warrior flamed out as early as 1948, only months after publishing his famous "X" article in *Foreign Affairs* and two years after penning his influential long telegram of February 1946. Thereafter, he was most often pushing for negotiations to ease tensions. For decades he sought to get both the United States and the Soviet Union to pull back from their confrontation in Central Europe. After the Cold War, Kennan crusaded against the expansion of NATO into the domains of the former Soviet Union. Even the strategist's ill-advised and regretted support for covert CIA operations in Eastern Europe in the late 1940s was intended to pressure the Soviets into realizing that they were overextended.

Kennan was beguiled by the notion that by immersing himself, somehow, in Russia he might find the wondrous presence that he desired while escaping the Eros versus Civilization dilemma that he dreaded. He saw the land and the people, though not the government, of Russia as appealingly feminine in ways both maternal and erotic. He imagined the Russian people and their government as "a beautiful lady guarded by a jealous lover."[11] In this scenario he figured as the true partner of the beloved. He rhapsodized about the "powerful maternal thighs of the female Slav."[12] He lauded the Russian Church, which idealized the Virgin Mary, for its "tolerant, maternal" influence.[13] Even as a dignified ambassador, he could not refrain from celebrating "the great good earth of Mother Russia . . . exud[ing] her benevolent and maternal warmth" over all. Nor could he ignore the pain that only he, the American emissary flanked by his secret-police minders, was "effectively isolated" from that deep satisfaction.[14] A dream had him "searching for his mother in a crowd of Russian peasants."[15]

A family tie also drew him to Russia. A cousin of his grandfather, George Kennan (1845–1924), had gained fame for travels in czarist Russia and for publicizing the grim penal system in Siberia. Kennan had been named after this relative, and they shared the same birthday. Other coincidences would connect their lives. The younger Kennan, whose own father remained cool and distant, admired the pioneering Russophile as a paternal model. In Moscow, Kennan would be delighted to hear from Mikhail Kalinin, the nominal president, that his forebear's writings on Siberia had been the bible for the revolutionists.[16]

George F. Kennan wanted this complex life story, with the embarrassments smoothed away, to be understood by those who came after him. From age eleven to one hundred, he kept a diary that he expected to be read by others. He mused about publishing his collected works, which by his life's end would amount to over 330 archival boxes. He took great care in choosing his biographer while discouraging aspirants he feared would distort the story.

In his very first interview with his authorized biographer, John Lewis Gaddis, Kennan made sure that the political historian understood three basic elements of his life. Amid an explanation of why Marxism had never appealed to him, he interjected that with regard to "my own lone-liness . . . I was affected neurotically by the absence of a mother." He found Freud more helpful than Marx. Second was his love for the cul-ture and language of Russia, "a source of unending pleasure and wonder to me." Third was how his senses and imagination picked up on the es-thetic qualities of localities. "I read all sorts of mystery and beauty . . . into landscapes and places, and also into music." Every city and land-scape disclosed "not only a different atmosphere but a different sort of music and intonation." He felt "immensely sensitive and responsive" to these sensations.

Kennan was gifted in his ability to reduce to words not only percep-tions that transcended the bounds of sight and sound, but also the feel-ings flowing from such observation. At especially poignant moments in his life, such as when he sought to make rational sense of the horrors of Stalin's purges, or when he imagined communication with his deceased mother or father, he succeeded in translating turbulent feelings into words. It took poetry to really convey what he perceived, he knew, and indeed, "I was part artist." In his younger years, he had dreamed about leaving the Foreign Service and writing a great novel. But "art is open-ended" in its emotional demands, and "I didn't have a balanced enough personal life to have gone into this expression of the emotions without being torn to pieces by it."[17] Achieving a personal life with greater equi-librium required reconciling, somehow, the competing pulls of Eros and Civilization.

What particularly tore Kennan apart was his passion for Russia. A visit to Leningrad in September 1945, only weeks after the end of World War II, demonstrated both the reach of his supersensory perceptions and the elegant prose they could inspire. Though newly arrived in the city, "it was like coming home." He had read so much about this capital of czarist Russia, and he had envisioned it from across the Baltic during his years in Riga, Latvia. He discerned in this dark, damp, and cold city "a strange warmth, a strange intensity, a strange beauty. Giving free rein to his imagination and intuition inspired arguably the most exquisite sentence written by Kennan in his eighty-eight years as a diarist: "I know that in this city, where I have never lived, there has nevertheless, by some strange quirk of fate—a previous life, perhaps?—been deposited a portion of my own capacity to feel and to love, a portion, in other words, of my own life; and that this is something which no American will ever understand and no Russian ever believe."[18] There he stood, between America and Russia, and enveloped for a moment in the wondrous mystery that he pursued all his life.

Nevertheless, while Kennan in his private thoughts mused about a possible previous life in Leningrad, Kennan in his public image as Washington's foremost strategist of the Cold War remained an American, even if a quirky one.

After joining the Foreign Service in 1926 and then rising faster in the ranks than anyone else in his age cohort, Kennan in February 1946 broke into the Washington inner circle with his famous long telegram. This 5,500-word alarm intoned the death of the World War II alliance with Moscow (attempts at further cooperation would amount to appeasement) while explaining how to resist Soviet expansion without going to war. His July 1947 article in Foreign Affairs, attributed to an anonymous "X," spelled out the policy of containment that would forever remain associated with his name. Also couched in alarmist language depicting the Soviet Union as an existential threat, the manifesto nevertheless assured that the Kremlin was not bent on war. The Soviets could be contained by rebuilding the economy and morale of Western Europe and by addressing the weaknesses in U.S. society, faults that had long disturbed Kennan. Although the strategist intended the United States to contain the Soviets using political and economic means rather than military force, he presented the threat in such dire terms that many Americans, understandably, concluded that containment mandated a military buildup. Moreover, while Kennan believed that only a few major industrial areas around the globe—Britain, Western Europe, and Japan—merited Washington's commitment of resources, the long telegram and the "X" article mentioned no such geographical limits. Nor did the administration adhere to such limits when President Harry S. Truman in March 1947 announced the doctrine that the United States would oppose Communist aggression and radical change wherever they occurred. These gaps between what Kennan intended and what he wrote would later grow into a chasm that cast him once again on the wrong side of power.

THE STRATEGIST

But that problem still lay in the future as Kennan in 1946–1947 won acclaim as the Truman administration's premier expert on the Soviet Union. He basked in the glow of attention from such power brokers as Secretary of the Navy (and soon to be the first Secretary of Defense) James V. Forrestal. Thrilled by this newfound respect and feeling of belonging, Kennan swam with the tide of Cold War militancy more than he later would admit. In late summer 1946, after a lecture tour through the western states, the rising star became Deputy Commandant for Foreign Affairs at the National War College in Washington. He read widely, talked with such faculty as the pioneering nuclear strategist Bernard Brodie, and delivered to midlevel military officers fourteen lectures on such topics as "Measures Short of War," "The Soviet Way of Thought and Its Effect on Foreign Policy," and "What Is Policy?" Kennan ascended still higher in May 1947, when Secretary of State George C. Marshall honored him with the dream job of founding director of the State Department's Policy Planning Staff. Little more than two years after Kennan, languishing in bed with a bad cold in far-off Moscow, had dictated the long telegram, he commanded an office next to Secretary Marshall's and a purview that included all of U.S. foreign policy.

Those National War College lectures and a stream of Policy Planning Staff papers constituted a remarkable output from someone now so engaged in influencing others and crafting policies that he had no time or inclination to grumble in his diary. His diary entries for 1946 amount only to notes for lectures on strategy, while 1947 included only a one-page rhyme.

Kennan's policy recommendations reflected his grasp of economics, particularly the economies of scale that would result from the integration of Europe, and the crisis arising from Europe's lack of dollars to buy needed American products. He addressed these concerns with his most significant initiative, the Marshall Plan. With generous aid funded by

U.S. taxpayers, Washington assisted Western Europeans in recovering from wartime devastation while modernizing and integrating their national economies. This was the model that early in World War II he had hoped an enlightened German occupation would implement. He pushed as well for rebuilding the Japanese economy.

Kennan also planned policies to thwart Soviet ambitions, at times using or advocating means more militarized than he would later like to recall. He helped set the CIA on the path of political warfare, an effort that soon got beyond his control and that he would regret.[19] He pushed for psychological warfare and covert military operations within the Soviet bloc, especially in Albania. He worked to sway the crucial 1948 election in Italy with targeted food aid, a letter-writing campaign by Italian Americans, and tours by Hollywood stars. Kennan also prepared to go much further. When it looked as if the Communists might win the election in Italy, he urged militarily reoccupying that nation even if it sparked a civil war. With regard to the Middle East, Latin America, Africa, and much of Asia, Kennan recommended only limited U.S. action. He viewed these areas as dangerously entangling and strategically unimportant.

While taking bold steps, he downplayed the terminology of Grand Strategy. In notes taken in 1946 on a lecture with that title, he penned "Drop the word 'grand.'"[20] Kennan's lectures and his Policy Planning Staff papers would nevertheless become the basis for his reputation as America's Grand Strategist. Grand Strategy envisioned a coordinated, holistic response that mobilized all the tools and resources of government to achieve a specific, doable task or policy. The concept emphasized realistic appraisal of goals and means with a healthy appreciation of unexpected developments and consequences.[21]

Nevertheless, while Kennan's writings and policies from 1946–1948 retain a secure perch in the pantheon of conventional American Grand Strategy, Kennan himself soon trended elsewhere. From the late 1940s onward, he advocated an unconventional strategy that could be categorized, depending on one's outlook, as either more or less "grand." In February 1948, barely six months after his warning in the "X" article about the implacable Soviets, Kennan was already musing about a diplomatic deal with them. That impulse would intensify. Kennan's Plan A for Germany in 1948–1949, which called for negotiating with Moscow to achieve a reunified, neutral, and demilitarized Germany, and his opposition in 1949–1950 to developing the "super" or hydrogen bomb addressed the two core issues of the Cold War: who would control Germany, and how to control nuclear weapons. In both cases, Kennan looked toward containing conflict rather than escalating it. That stance applied also to Eastern and Central Europe. Despite the partisan furor between Secretaries of State Acheson and Dulles over containment versus rollback, both their administrations—and subsequent U.S. policy down to 1989—favored getting the Russians out of the satellite nations. While the thrust of U.S. policy was largely to pressure the Kremlin to withdraw, Kennan wanted to pressure the Russians and then negotiate a joint pullback. His disengagement policy amounted to mutual rollback through diplomacy.

In the context of the Cold War, serious diplomacy remained unconventional. Kennan regarded containment as an if-then proposition. If the Soviets were contained, then they would become amenable to serious negotiations. By contrast, Acheson, Dulles, and other Cold Warriors expected the conflict to continue until Moscow's unconditional surrender. They saw the Cold War as useful in terms of corralling allies and keeping Congress and the public compliant. Kennan's unconventional strategy arguably ranked as grander than that of his opponents in Washington. He sought actual diplomacy, big agreements reached through difficult, extended negotiations, ideally by him talking in Russian with Stalin or a successor.

Viewed through another lens, Kennan favored a strategy less grand than that of conventional policy makers because he was not a big fan of the empire. He judged the United States as too incompetent to manage a formal or informal empire, and the costs as outweighing the benefits. His plowing through Edward Gibbon's *The History of the Decline and Fall of the Roman Empire* while on long transatlantic flights during the war had convinced him that empires invariably frayed and then collapsed.

Throughout the Cold War, the would-be Grand Diplomatist kept pushing for negotiations with Moscow. He urged Acheson to seek

Moscow's help in ending the war in Korea. As ambassador to Moscow in 1952, he ached to initiate serious talks with the Soviets. In his famous Reith lectures in 1957, he laid out a plan for mutual disengagement in Europe. He favored talks to end the crisis over Berlin and to end the war in Vietnam. In the 1970s–1980s, Kennan proposed dramatic reductions in nuclear arms as well as joint U.S.-Russian efforts to address environmental degradation. In the 1990s, he vehemently opposed NATO expansion into the former Soviet bloc, fearing it would trigger yet another Cold War.

The significance of Kennan's unconventional strategy was that it pointed out potential turning points, junctures when Washington and Moscow might have negotiated a lessening of tensions and the nuclear danger. The narrative of Kennan's unsuccessful efforts from 1948 to 1988 to ease the Cold War is the story of what might have been, the diplomacy that could have yielded enormous benefit to the world. Kennan's efforts traced an alternative history of the Cold War, one in which the conflict eased or ended far earlier.

In this context, Kennan's love for Russia, his quest for some mystical connection with Russia—impulses that stemmed in part from the hurt and loneliness in his psyche going back to the loss of his mother—had enormous consequences for policy. His feelings for the Russians impelled him to seek reconnection with the Soviets and to perceive issues also from the Kremlin's perspective. Though he had denigrated diplomacy with the Russians in the long telegram and in the "X" article, he himself could not adhere for long to those restraints. The story of Kennan the unconventional strategist bears as much importance as the better known history of Kennan the conventional Grand Strategist.

Kennan had sought not Moscow's abrupt capitulation in the Cold War, but rather a negotiated compromise. A diplomatist at heart, he venerated the process of patient, secret bargaining by calculating, shrewd professionals. He disdained summit conferences as showy disruptions by bungling amateurs, whether the perceived offender was Franklin D. Roosevelt meeting with Joseph Stalin—and shutting out not only Kennan, but the entire State Department—or Ronald Reagan's conclaves with Mikhail Gorbachev.

In the emerging post–Cold War era, Kennan remained a bit of a Russian nationalist. He feared the breakup of the Soviet Union would destabilize geopolitics and endanger control over nuclear weapons. He thought it unwise for Ukraine to break away from Russia. He believed that not only should reunified Germany disengage from NATO and the Warsaw Pact, but that those two alliances should be replaced by a European-wide security agreement. He envisioned the post–Cold War world as an arena in which the contenders would rely on diplomacy, not war, to settle their inevitable differences. He looked to a concerted international effort to safeguard the natural environment. Kennan wanted the United States to pull back from trying to manage a global informal empire. He believed that such efforts were not only doomed, but also diverted attention and resources from America's pressing domestic problems.

FAMILY AND INNER LIFE

The unconventionality of Kennan's thoughts and feelings coupled with the privacy of his nature did not make it easy to understand him. While still in his twenties, he consigned himself to "intellectual isolation."[22] The problem was not eased by his marriage to Annelise Sorensen. Years later, when asked by his authorized biographer about her role in his life, George replied, "Well, you must realize that she's not a particularly intellectual woman."[23]

Nevertheless, a sense of the inner George Kennan emerges from the day-to-day observations of Annelise and of their four children: Grace, born in 1932, Joan (1936), Christopher (1949), and Wendy (1952). Also pertinent are the observations of the grandchildren. "The shadow of his example still falls over all of us," a grandson testified years after Kennan's death. He added that the four children of George and Annelise, even late in their own lives, "all have their scars."[24] The force of Kennan's personality and the magnitude of his abilities and achievements made it difficult to follow in his footsteps.

Kennan's insatiable curiosity, inherent creativity, and indefatigable work ethic impelled him into fresh ventures. Grace marveled at his "huge appetite for life." He studied medieval architecture while in Russia and modern agriculture for the Pennsylvania farm purchased in 1942. He pursued bird-watching and woodworking. He mastered sailing and celestial navigation on the open seas around Scandinavia aboard the *Nagawicka* and then the *Northwind*. With pulleys and a crowbar he leveraged huge stones into place for steps at the family's Norwegian summer home. As Wendy affirmed, her father was "physically strong, had incredible concentration, and could think through a problem without getting distracted." Christopher marveled that his father knew engineering and "could explain how a steam engine worked." Although color blindness stymied Kennan's painting, he filled many a sketchbook with drawings. A natural musician, he taught himself not only how to read music but also how to play the guitar, piano, cornet, banjo, and French horn. He sang mournful Russian folk songs. He played in a jazz band in military school and in an orchestra at Princeton, for the "Kremlin Krows" ensemble in wartime Moscow, and on the terrace below Wendy's bedroom in Princeton as she fell asleep. He loved ballet, opera, and classical music as well as jazz.[25]

While such recreation helped balance his work ethic, Kennan devoted most of the years after leaving the State Department in 1950 to writing. He would rise at six, eat a breakfast of oatmeal, and then climb the stairs to his office. At the farm in East Berlin, "he wrote on the highest floor in a quest for peace and quiet. A trapdoor closed it off from the rest of the house," Joan recalled. "My father had a simple, homemade table and his old Underwood typewriter—the kind that is rather tall with rows of letter in a 'stadium seating' arrangement. Here he would click and clack for hours in the morning."[26] The office was stuffed with books and old Soviet journals and newspapers. At the Hodge Road house in Princeton, he chose the fourth-floor tower for his academic writing. While the height of the tower offered a panoramic view from all five windows, it also obliged him to lug up firewood for the wood-stove. George used other rooms of the huge house for writing his diary and letters. Whether with writing or with voice, Kennan remained the storyteller.

The imagination that filled the long telegram and the "X" article with exaggerated dangers functioned more benignly to populate stories for young Grace and Joan. He told tales of the pixies Tom and Belle and built a playhouse for a fictitious Uncle Zachariah. He made up stories of animals with names and personalities and acted out their talking to each other. Kennan read aloud to his children from a variety of books ranging from *The Wizard of Oz* to *War and Peace*. Beloved as "Bumpa" by his grandsons, he set aside a private time for each of them at holiday gatherings. He would invite them to his bedroom and ask how and what they were doing. "We all had absolute reverence for him," a grandson recalled. A granddaughter did not, however, come away with such loving memories. Nor could he always find it easy to relate to a younger generation. When a grandson brought his date to Princeton for lunch with the great man, Kennan, upon hearing that the young woman hailed from Utah, responded, "So, what's the soil like there?"[27]

Although he loved his children, George delegated their actual rearing to Annelise. She in turn hired caregivers. Annelise was not a hands-on mother, one daughter remembered. George allowed situations to develop in which neither parent "paid attention to the kids' being unhappy," as Grace later explained. "The welfare and ease of their kids was not of paramount concern." In the summer of 1953, when the family was departing for its annual vacation in Norway, traveling on a freighter to save money, it seemed too much trouble to take along Wendy, then little more than a year old. So the parents left the toddler with a Czech couple who knew little English. By the time the family returned to Princeton, Wendy had lost the ability to speak any language, Grace observed to her dismay. The parents did not make it a point to appear for all the children's birthdays. Nor did they attend Grace's wedding in Washington in the spring of 1958, when George had a fellowship at Oxford. At the reception, the bride, who had been expecting a surprise appearance from her parents, received instead a transatlantic phone call. "I just wept," she recalled. "It was very painful."[28]

Although George and Annelise remained married for nearly three-quarters of a century, grew closer in their last years, and concurred on a traditional division of labor, they were not a tight fit. Mary Acheson Bundy observed a telling detail: "I never heard him say 'we'—it was always 'I.'"[29] George confided to Grace, "It's so painful being with your mother because I can't talk with her." Nevertheless, they made an attractive couple: "He was so smart, and she was so beautiful; she looked like Greta Garbo," the daughter would recall.[30]

As the eldest child, Grace observed the marriage as evolving in three stages. The years 1931 to 1940 proved a time of physical love and establishing a family for the two young daughters. Yet even then, George confided in his diary that "the technique of marriage is nothing more or less than the art of dissimulation."[31] In the second stage, wartime dangers, George's internment by the Germans in the first half of 1942, his heavy responsibilities before and after that ordeal—plus some voluntary separation—kept them often apart. Kennan's rocketing career in 1946–1950 led to further strains, prompting their daughter to "really worry about their getting divorced." Perhaps in retaliation for George's wartime affairs, Annelise had a fling in Lisbon and "a big romance in Moscow," Grace recalled. When the not-yet-famous journalist John Hersey came for tea with her mother in Moscow, the twelve-year-old daughter hung around out of fear that they were more than friends. Then, years later in the third stage, "Father accepted the marriage," though he still "missed having a woman he could talk to." Grace suspected that the arrival of Christopher thirteen years after the previous child reflected efforts to save the marriage.[32]

"You wonder why they got married," Christopher reflected decades later. His mother was "a party girl" who loved the social life, while his father had "this very active and rich inner life which he couldn't share with my mother." Hence he "idolized women who were his intellectual peers." His relationships with such stars as the Prussian aristocrat, anti-Nazi activist, and publisher Marion Dönhoff, and the journalist, novelist, and former wife of Ernest Hemingway Martha Gellhorn amounted to "affairs of the head as much as anything else." Grace saw her father as "very handsome with an almost movie star look." He "flirted with all kinds of women, especially intelligent women."

And yet he could put women down. He could be ruthlessly sarcastic and condescending toward Annelise. He hounded her to lose her Norwegian accent. He continually marveled that Dönhoff had reached such heights though only a woman. When Grace described her serious executive responsibilities running a nonprofit organization in post-Soviet Ukraine, her father enthused: "You're so good, you could be the social secretary of the embassy in Moscow!" That hurt, especially since Grace had aspired to be in effect a first son. Nevertheless, she adored her father as someone "so smart, so prescient." Listening to him, "people knew they were hearing something very different."

Even smart, prescient talk could wear, however. "Dinner time was time to listen to Daddy," Grace recalled. Joan later wished that the children had been allowed to talk more at the table. When their father got rolling at dinner, it would turn into a monologue, Christopher remembered. "Everyone else would shut up." Even though the children would wince at their father's racist or otherwise prejudiced comments, they knew that "he didn't like to be argued with."[33] So they grimaced to themselves, and fled the table as soon as possible—just as George and his siblings had done decades earlier in Milwaukee. Kennan did not limit expostulation to family settings. The Princeton professor and expert on Woodrow Wilson, Arthur S. Link related how at dinner parties, George liked to get up, "put his hands behind his back, walk back and forth, and give you a monologue . . . with everybody else sitting and listening." That Link treasured such occasions as "marvelous" suggests that he was not a regular at the Kennan family dinner table.[34] Although after such a public performance George would privately castigate himself for being so garrulous, his faith in his insights impelled further such presentations.

Both confident in his superior qualifications and shy, Kennan disliked "working the system" to snare some advantage. Christopher observed that his father "felt he was above badgering for power." Similarly, Kennan impressed an East Berlin neighbor as "one of the most humble men he had ever met." When the Lions Club launched a project to plant trees, George was the first one there that Saturday morning, ready with a shovel over his shoulder. And yet he never totally blended in, perhaps by choice. While dressed in regulation farm overalls, he also sported his trademark black beret. As Christopher perceived, while his father could appear "modest in behavior," he retained "a very healthy sense of his importance and abilities."[35]

Always the gracious hostess, Annelise backstopped her husband's career. She ensured organization and tidiness, whether in the Hodge Road house in Princeton, the cramped Moscow hotel room in 1934, or in the capacious Moscow and Belgrade embassies decades later. She almost always had hired help. Her charm did not, however, extend to the servants, who, resenting her imperious tone, often quit.

Aside from their stint in impoverished Riga in the early 1930s, where even a modest U.S. salary went far, the Kennans often struggled to pay the domestic help they considered essential. Annelise also devoted scarce funds to clothes and other things to keep herself attractive. Commenting on a sister whose husband had deserted her, she admonished Grace: "If Aunt Mossik had spent money on hired help and had gotten her hair done, she would not now be divorced." The summer trips to Norway and farm expenses also soaked up cash. Although George's State Department earnings rose steadily with his promotions and though he later received a generous salary from the Institute for Advanced Study, "the family was very worried about money all the time," Grace recalled. She had to work several jobs while at Radcliffe. During the five months in early 1942 when George was interned by the Germans, the State Department cut off his pay with the rationale that he was not working. Annelise, though lacking any visible means of support, rented a house in upscale Bronxville, New York, courtesy, it seems, of Carl Siegesmund, a longtime admirer. Annelise's fretting about money did not extend to feeling impelled to earn it. Apart from a brief period at the Lisbon legation during the war, she never worked. In Moscow in 1944–1946, where the U.S. embassy was hard-pressed for help, she remained the only unemployed wife.[36] These decisions evidently were not disputed by her husband.

As Christopher remembered it, his father, scarred by having lost his inheritance during the Great Depression, remained frugal. He kept part of his savings in gold secured in a vault in New York City. Nevertheless, he donated some of the $50,000 from the Einstein Peace Prize to the local historical society close by the farm. Though he idealized the simple life, most of George and Annelise's friends ranked as Princeton's high society and wealthy. Family finances eased only after 1967, with the publication of George's best-selling *Memoirs, 1925–1950*, as well as other books, the Einstein Peace Prize in 1981, and lucrative lecture fees.[37]

While such family perspectives are necessarily skewed and scattered, they bring into focus a devoted (though not always loyal) husband and a loving (though not always engaged) father. If it was difficult being George F. Kennan, it was also often difficult being a member of his family.

TALENTED YET FRAGILE

As for more distant observers, few could dispute that Kennan was, literally, extraordinary. His impressive talents were exceeded only by his ambitions. Precariously balanced with the abilities and aspirations was what Mary A. Bundy observed as "George's very sensitive and fragile temperament." "He collapsed a lot; he needed understanding," she explained.[38]

Dorothy Fosdick, the only woman on the Policy Planning Staff while Kennan was director, testified that her boss "had a strong messianic streak. I always felt he thought he should have been Secretary of State himself." He felt "superior to everyone around him." In the late 1950s, when he was making waves by calling for negotiations with Moscow, Kennan regarded "himself as a world statesman," Isaiah Berlin recalled. "He said he thought he and [Indian prime minister Jawaharlal] Nehru were perhaps unique figures . . . having a political doctrine to offer to the world."[39]

Kennan had reason to feel superior. William P. "Bill" Bundy, Mary's husband, who was a top State Department official and later editor of *Foreign Affairs*, conceded that his Princeton friend was often "twenty or thirty years ahead of anybody else's thinking."[40] According to the leading historian of the Policy Planning Staff, the work leading to the Marshall Plan, the rebuilding of Japan, the decision to limit aid to Nationalist

China, and outreach to Tito's Yugoslavia after its break with Moscow merited Kennan the title of "America's Global Planner."[41] As a diplomat, he rose to the top rank as director of the Policy Planning Staff; as a historian, he snared what was arguably the nation's most prestigious professorship, at the Institute for Advanced Study.

Elegant writing came easily to Kennan. Bundy commented, "I've never seen anybody whose mind and his pen were so synchronized as his." He remembered waiting for a late train on a "freezing, freezing day, in the barely heated Princeton Junction station. George sat there with yellow paper, pen flowing across the paper . . . just flowing."[42] His books garnered two National Book Awards, two Pulitzers, and a Bancroft prize. The Einstein Peace Prize was only one of many such awards. He could speak both German and Russian like a native. "No American spoke Russian the way George did," recalled the Princeton University political scientist Robert C. Tucker, who also had served in the Moscow embassy. "He speaks an intellectual kind of Russian that really cultured people speak," added his wife, herself a Russian native. While ambassador to Yugoslavia under President John F. Kennedy, Kennan learned Serbo-Croatian, a Slavic language quite different from Russian, well enough to give a public lecture. He also mastered Norwegian and French.

Though he often complained of fatigue, Kennan appeared to others as indefatigable. "He was incapable of just stopping and taking a few hours off," recounted a friend and neighbor. After the long drive to the farm, Kennan would immediately start "the tractor to mow the lawn. Then he'd rush inside and go upstairs to type . . . most of the night." Following an arduous sailing trip in Norway, the exhausted crew lay down, only to "hear a wheelbarrow going back and forth. Here was George building a set of steps."[43] Kennan, who over the years delivered hundreds of talks and labored over each one, would never give a lecture a second time around, a longtime secretary testified. Summing up her boss's approach to life, she marveled: "He never takes the easy way out, even with his bicycle."[44] It was on a heavy, old-fashioned bike lacking gears that he pedaled around Princeton.

Nevertheless, Kennan remained fragile. Fosdick remembered, "He could go into a bad slump when he thought he was not being listened to." In such a crisis, he would take her to lunch "and pour out his heart to me." He explained to her that providing such solace "was a natural role for a woman. Women throughout history had been confidential advisers to monarchs." Fosdick prized her role of confidant/comforter as "a very high compliment." Venturing into pop psychology, she suggested that her boss's "attitude toward women grew out of deep psychological considerations. . . . George had a strong desire to return to the womb."[45]

Kennan always pushed himself hard. Rather than ease up, he broke down. His daughter Wendy recalled that her father was "never able to take a normal vacation. Getting ill was his way of calming himself down."[46] When the strain got too intense, he would collapse, as he did in Moscow in December 1934, while serving as PPS director in 1948, after his controversial Reith broadcasts in 1957, and on other occasions.

Kennan suffered ill health throughout his long life. Scarlet fever contracted his first year in college nearly killed him. His gastrointestinal tract never recovered from the amoebic dysentery he picked up as a twenty-year-old traveling in Italy. He self-diagnosed many of his illnesses as partly psychosomatic. In an informal medical autobiography, he explained that every month or so he suffered from herpes zoster, "preceded, as a rule by a spell of depression, irritability, and sometimes gastro-intestinal discomfort." Ulcers afflicted him throughout his years of service in the State Department. Beginning in 1963, he endured a painful kidney stone. He contracted hepatitis in 1964. In 1966, a "very gnarled, but not cancerous" prostate gland was removed. He had a heart murmur and increasingly painful arthritis in his knees.[47]

Keeping tabs on these physical and psychological ailments was Dr. Frieda Por, a key figure in Kennan's life. She was the Jewish Hungarian doctor who had restored him to health at the Gutenbrunn sanatorium outside Vienna after his December 1934 breakdown in Moscow. A Freudian-minded physician who stressed diet and a holistic approach to a healthy body and mind, Por became the Kennan family doctor after George helped her emigrate to the United States in 1938. They corresponded frequently, he detailing his activities as well as physical and emotional symptoms, and she prescribing remedies and tests for her

"MIP (Most Important Patient)." As Grace observed of her father, Dr. Por "penetrated under his skin as no one else did."[48]

In June 1977, after two weeks of relative relaxation and beautiful weather at the summer home in Kristiansand, Kennan complained to his doctor that aside from the grating of the kidney stone, he suffered "intestinal abnormalities and great tiredness through much of the day." Nevertheless, "I force myself to do two to three hours of stiff physical work daily." Por recommended tests to discover the cause of the tiredness. Though he had not done the tests, he felt rejuvenated by a sailing trip in rough seas to Denmark and back. He proudly detailed how he had been able to "rise at 3:30 A.M., after only 4–5 hours of sleep . . . sail 15 hours straight in beastly weather," eating only a few biscuits and a cup of soup "consumed in the heaving cockpit, with the spray and rain flying—one hand holding on to the cup, the other to the boat," soaked to the skin and all the while wondering "how one is ever to find one's way to a safe place on some shore." He could endure such trials because of the "mysterious effect of challenge and danger" upon the body and the psyche.[49] The ordeal was exhilarating also because it unleashed, as George and Frieda both believed, the creative forces of Eros.

After giving an elaborately formal address in Germany, Kennan again informed Por that he feared a major problem: "liver, gall bladder, bile duct, or what?" From a distance Dr. Por diagnosed lingering worry over his big speech. She prescribed Valium, "an excellent relaxant without being a dope." The patient acknowledged that the "intestinal spasms" were, "as you say, no doubt of psycho-somatic origins." He then listed the ailments: kidney stone, heart murmur, arthritic knees, and tendency to forget names. A problem they had evidently often discussed, "his eye for feminine beauty," had "unfortunately not been dimmed."

While Kennan feared living into old age would reduce him to a "slobbering old vegetable," he endured, despite or maybe because of the hypochondria, until 2005.[50] Nearing 100, he continued campaigning against NATO expansion, which he feared threatened a renewed Cold War, and against the 2003 U.S. invasion of Iraq, which he condemned as yet another doomed and unnecessary intervention.

FIGURE 2. As he aged, Kennan grew even more passionate about nature, especially the waters around the family's summer home near Kristiansand, Norway. (Courtesy of Grace Kennan Warnecke.)

At stake in investigating the inner life of George F. Kennan is understanding the tortured, talented, and ultimately tragic individual who helped instigate the Cold War and then worked unceasingly to end it. While Kennan's ambitions exceeded his abilities, those talents remained extraordinary. A diarist as discerning and elegant as John Quincy Adams, Kennan also ranked with Adams as a perceptive strategist of U.S. foreign policy. Adams and Kennan both understood that for the self-righteous American behemoth, exercising restraint in foreign involvement could pose more of a challenge than exercising power. Kennan liked to quote Adams's famous July 4, 1821, peroration that "America goes not abroad in search of monsters to destroy." In 1946–1947, Kennan painted a portrait of a monster that he thought should be contained, not destroyed. Yet, tragically, he blazoned the beast with such vivid imagery that Americans assumed they had to destroy it. Appalled at the consequences of his scaremongering, Kennan then spent a half century trying to subdue the alarm he had helped provoke.

Kennan shared with John Quincy Adams's grandson, Henry Adams, skepticism about industrialization and admiration for an agrarian republic. They had little truck with the ideological conceits, inflated self-esteem, and worship of commerce that characterized their countrymen. And they shared an ironic, detached style. Although Kennan respected Adams's warning about the force of the dynamo in modern times, his environmentalist critique of technology and the machine had a largely Russian origin. He took to heart Anton Chekhov's view that industrial production amounted to a tragic misunderstanding of how human beings should relate to each other and to nature.

Also like Henry Adams, Kennan felt abandoned in the wrong century. His upbringing reflected the paternal influence of a father born in the middle of the nineteenth century who clung to the habits of an earlier era. On his maternal side, the larger-than-life image of his grandfather, Alfred James, who returned from his swashbuckling, high-seas adventures around the world to build a successful insurance company, also anchored George to an earlier time. Reared with stories of his grandfather, George as a young boy dreamed of going not to Russia, but to sea. The grandfather shone also for having apparently achieved the balance between creativity and order to which the grandson would aspire.

Kennan's distance from the twentieth century afforded him the independence of mind to see beyond the ideological struggle between communism and capitalism that preoccupied most strategists in the half century following World War II. Particularly because he had witnessed Stalinist repression firsthand during the purges of the late 1930s, Kennan hated the Kremlin's hold over the Russian people and its dominance in Eastern Europe. He believed the solution was: first, contain Soviet expansion; then, negotiate a mutual U.S.-Soviet pullback from Germany and the rest of Europe.

Eventually, he predicted, a contained Soviet Union would mellow or even collapse. As early as 1948, Kennan saw possibilities for serious diplomacy with Moscow. Partly because he empathized with the Russian people, he could not help but see international issues also from the perspective of Soviet leaders, regardless of how offensive he regarded their rule. Thus positioned between America and Russia, Kennan repeatedly discerned opportunities for negotiation, particularly to settle the explosive issues of Germany and nuclear weapons. Kennan's Cold War should be understood as a contingent struggle, a conflict surely real and dangerous, but also amenable to easing through determined diplomacy, of which there was little after 1945. Attuned to his own emotional sensibilities, Kennan understood the impact of feelings on international relations, especially with regard to demonstrations of pride and respect.

Kennan's lesson for us, in understanding the Cold War of the twentieth century and in defusing the explosive tensions of the twenty-first century, is that seemingly intractable conflicts may be more susceptible to settlement than it may at first appear. As Kennan put it, sharply opposed positions are just the asking price in the long, necessarily patient process of diplomacy. Kennan would have argued that peace in the twenty-first century requires accepting that Russia, like the United States, has legitimate national interests and, because it indulges in notions of an expansive national mission, it needs to be checked through diplomacy and a balance of power.

Kennan's alienation from his own era and country afforded unique insights, some piercingly perceptive and others just bizarre. Love for Russia wracked his equilibrium while extending his vision. The America that he loved existed, if at all, before his time. In failing miserably at restoring this lost idyll, he offered, ironically, some lessons for postindustrial, postpandemic American society. Throughout his life, Kennan championed physical as well as mental labor, personal rather than anonymous or machine interactions, local sourcing, small farms, other small enterprises, backyard ventures, environmental cleanup, crafting and building things, hand tools, small-scale everything, trains rather than planes and cars, and the arts and technologies lost with the hegemony of the internal combustion engine. While Kennan probably would not feel at home in our era, we could learn much from him.

CHAPTER 1

NOT VERY HAPPY PEOPLE

The Kennan Family, 1904–1925

AS A TODDLER, the motherless child would "lean his head over and hit it gently on the floor and pretend to cry." George's three sisters "would all descend upon him and love him, comfort him. That was all he wanted, poor little thing." But as he grew older, a sister remembered, "if we would try to put our arms around him, he would push us away."[1] Although lifelong patterns of behavior track first years only imperfectly, it seems that early on Kennan figured out how to express his neediness, how to get temporary solace, and how to assert his independence. An enduring lesson was that by inciting alarm, he could get others to act. As he matured, he learned also how to contain and focus the pain from not having a loving mother. Hunger for what could never be helped drive his imagination and fantasies, his quest for transcendent wonder and ultimate meaning, and his search for embracing natural and human environments. His bottomless personal desires would influence his entire life, including his longing for connection with the people and culture of Russia.

Young George blamed himself for the death of his mother, Florence James Kennan, who had actually perished from complications from appendicitis. He assumed, incorrectly, that she had died in the aftermath of his birth. As an adult, he believed that he had been "scarred for life by the loss of his mother shortly after his birth."[2] The death of Florence inflicted both the intermittent melancholy suffered by George and the

FIGURE 3. The adult Kennan would see his life as shaped
by having lost his mother at the age of two months.
(Courtesy of Princeton University Library.)

everyday sadness of his father, Kossuth Kent Kennan. "I don't think the
Kennan family were very happy people," remembered George's oldest
sister, who fled as soon as she could.[3]

Also complicating the life of young George was the tension between
his father, who went by "Kent," and his mother's relatives. Conflicting
temperaments, clashing values, and contrasting approaches to money
set Kent against the wealthy family of his deceased wife. While shy Kent

stumbled in many social settings, the confident Jameses glided through
Milwaukee high society. Florence's mother and father and her brother,
Alfred Farragut James, looked down on Kent as not only awkward, but
also as "probably a scoundrel," a Kennan daughter observed.[4] Forty-four
years old and a widower with an eclectic work history, Kent had seemed
an unworthy match for beautiful, thirty-three-year-old Florence. Her
family had packed her off to Europe in an effort to quash Kent's pursuit.
When the couple nevertheless married on January 24, 1895, the parents
refused to attend the ceremony. Thereafter, Kent, though an attorney,
struggled to support the four children he fathered. His most grievous
sin, however, was not being there to comfort his wife as she lay dying in
great pain.[5] "Your mother made the best of a bad business," Alfred's wife,
Aunt Nellie James, would tell the Kennan children.[6]

Four years after the death of Florence, Kent married Louise Wheeler,
whom the Jameses dismissed as "not our kind."[7] George and his three
sisters also disdained the new stepmother, whom they secretly mocked
as "the kangaroo from Kalamazoo."[8] They sought refuge with the Jameses, who even offered to adopt them. Alfred Farragut and Nellie, backed
by family friends, would be appalled yet again when Kent and the stepmother sent sensitive, well-behaved, thirteen-year-old George to a military school geared toward troublemakers.

George's loneliness arose not only from the death of his mother and
the tension between the families but also from the departure of others.
Kent hired a series of nurses in white uniforms to care for the infant.
Each, for some reason, left the employment of the father. They also left
the infant with an enduring impression. "A woman in a nurse's uniform
has for me a dangerous attraction," George would explain many years
later. The allure stemmed "from the fact that the first mother I had was
probably this nurse with the white uniform."[9] Kent himself would inflict
a wrenching loss. Sister Jeanette, who was two years older than George
and who would long remain his confidant, later recalled that their father
loved babies. With Florence gone, the widower resolved to act as both
parents. "He was *so* maternal," Jeanette remembered. On long-distance
train trips, Kent would go up to the mother of a crying baby and offer
to walk the child up and down the aisle to calm it. A sensitive man who

FIGURE 4. Kossuth Kent Kennan (1851–1933), George's shy, intellectual father. Though a world-class expert on the income tax, he had to rely on his children's inheritance and on boarders to make ends meet. (Courtesy of Princeton University Library.)

FIGURE 5. Florence James Kennan (1862–1904). Images of his lost mother would flit through George's dreams and imagination his entire life. (Courtesy of Princeton University Library.)

could tear up when reading *The Little Match Girl* or when listening to "The Star-Spangled Banner," Kent was also harsh in reining in those feelings. Thus he cuddled and sang to George and Jeanette as infants but then abruptly stopped such open affection. "It finished when we weren't babies any more," Jeanette explained.[10] Kent's usual reserve then took over. Jeanette's son later remembered of his grandfather, "I never saw any warmth in him at all."[11] Kent remained distant from his son also out of fear that showing George love was not manly for either of them. Even more painful for George, however, was that Kent drove away his beloved Cousin Grace.

George's earliest memory was of plaintively asking his sisters, "Why didn't we call Cousin Grace 'mother'?" As an adult, he recalled that Grace had wanted to remain in the household and marry Kent. He wished that union had occurred because "she would have been a wonderful mother."[12] Mary Grace Wells, a twenty-eight-year-old second cousin of Florence James, had studied at the Simmons School and lived in North Adams, Massachusetts. She had come to Milwaukee, probably at the suggestions of the Jameses, to care for the motherless brood: Frances, the eldest, then Constance, Jeanette, and George. Kent paid the governess $50 per month. She lit up the grim household with love and caring. Though she did not spare the hairbrush in punishing George and Jeanette (they labeled their bottoms "the spanking place"), she was kind and knew how to manage children. They quickly came to love her. Grace especially "adored George—he was her baby," a sister recalled. Another remembered that George blossomed "into the most perfect little child. He had blue eyes and golden hair that [Grace] carefully trained into a curl. Oh, he was a lovely little boy!"[13] The Kennan children would sustain lifelong ties with their nanny and render financial support when she was too old to work. George would name his first daughter after her. Decades later, that daughter would affirm that she could tell Cousin Grace anything. Although Grace was receptive to marrying Kent, he was not interested. He probably also resented her familiarity with the Jameses who disdained him. George's sister remembered finding the caregiver in her room in tears and muttering under her breath, "He treats me like dirt under his feet."[14]

This sad drama played out in a thriving city. Milwaukee's population shot up 60 percent from 1900 to 1920. By 1910, Milwaukee approached New York City as the urban center with the highest proportion of foreign-born residents. Immigrants from Germany, Poland, and elsewhere streamed into the city blessed with the best natural harbor on the western shore of Lake Michigan. In addition to the shipping industry, flour milling, beer brewing, and metal fabrication yielded plentiful jobs for workers, potential clients for lawyers such as Kent Kennan, and opportunities for such firms as the Northwestern National Insurance Company of Milwaukee, headed by Alfred Farragut James and before

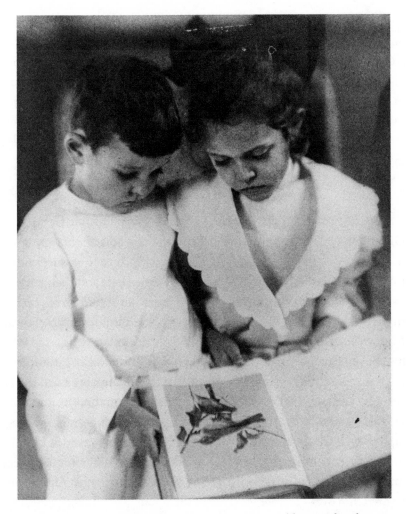

FIGURE 6. Two years older than George, Jeanette would remain his closest confidant for decades. (Courtesy of Princeton University Library.)

him by his father, Alfred James. Although they disagreed on much else, the paternal and maternal sides of George's family concurred on restricting their social interactions to the older, Anglocentric populations of the city. Absent from the reminiscences of both George and his sisters was much reference to the burgeoning German American community in Milwaukee.[15] A mention of neighboring Polish Americans noted that of course the Kennans had nothing to do with them.

The consequences of this segregation amid an increasingly diverse environment would prove lasting. For the rest of his long life, George Kennan would lament the waning dominance of the Anglo-Saxon population that he believed had founded the nation and inspired the best in American society and government. He would deplore immigrants for diluting those values. As a boy, George did become familiar with German language and culture but only through his family's six-month stay in Cassel, Germany.[16]

GEORGE AND THE JAMES FAMILY

Offsetting winter months in the gloomy Kennan household were summers shared with the Jameses on Nagawicka Lake, about thirty miles from Milwaukee. A gaggle of Kennan and James kids and their parents lived in neighboring houses built by Grandfather Alfred James on the three-mile-long lake. George, who would later christen his own boat *Nagawicka*, delighted in swimming, boating, and horsing around with his cousin, Charlie James, and the other kids. The families gathered for the traditional Sunday feast of roast beef or spring lamb prepared by the servants and presided over by Uncle Alfred Farragut and Aunt Nellie. Decades later, at the start of his first interview with his authorized biographer, Kennan stressed that his Uncle Alfred Farragut ranked as "a much more prominent man than my own father, and [was] affluent. I was very much brought up together with his son, my cousin Charlie." Aunt Nellie favored him over his siblings. George spent long periods with the Jameses, whether in Milwaukee, on Nagawicka Lake, or at their fancier summer house in Fox Point. Though his mother's family "were not on good terms with my father, they didn't take it out on me."[17]

Nevertheless, the breach upset George. When his father died in 1933, he fantasized about replaying the Kennan–James tragedy as a happy story, with the family and his own life made whole. He pictured "Father in a Heaven like the country place at Nagawicka . . . with himself no longer only a Kennan and our mother no longer only a James, but both of them full, complete beings, and ourselves as the group of understanding children we should have been." Essential to this paradise—as would be central to his entire life—was nature, with "the breeze coming off the lake on summer afternoons, and the sounds of the grasshoppers and the crickets and frogs and the barking of the dogs across the lake on the long summer nights."[18] In actual life, however, the rift between Kent and the Jameses persisted.

Young George bore the imprint of both families. His grandfather, Alfred James, had run away at the age of thirteen, worked his way east riding the horses that pulled the boats on the Erie Canal, was "shanghaied" onto a whaling ship, crisscrossed the Pacific, and got into a fight that landed him in the brig of a French ship. After many other such exploits, he came home determined to make a fortune in business. He worked his way up to president of the Northwestern National Insurance Company, a Milwaukee-based fire and casualty insurance firm. Though he died only months after George's birth, tales of his adventures inspired the boy's interest in foreign lands and in the sea. At the age of eight, he had implored his father, "Can I join the navy?"[19]

The father had also tried to leverage the link with the elder George Kennan, the famed author on czarist Russia. Though Kent ended up quarreling with the man's jealous wife and had to leave abruptly, a flame flickered. For years, the older George Kennan sent the younger one books on February 16, their shared birth date. That and other coincidences were not lost on a boy inclined toward signs of divine intent, fantasies, and superstition.

Financial dependence flamed the mutual resentment between Kent and the Jameses. George's father was neither lazy, incompetent, or provincial. He had worked his way through Ripon College by rising early to do farm chores. He had taught himself enough engineering to supervise railroad and irrigation construction projects in Montana. Years later, when a hotelkeeper in the area was asked if he remembered Kent Kennan, he replied: "Kennan? He was no man; he was a damned antelope."[20] Based in Basel, Switzerland, he had skirted the Reich's restrictions to recruit German migrants to settle rural lands owned by the Wisconsin Central Railroad. In Europe, he had mastered German and picked up a smattering of Danish, Norwegian, and other tongues. Back home, he taught himself French so that he could read novels in that language. He read the entire Bible several times. Along the way, he had studied and practiced law. He published two respected law books. "Father was a scholar, all the way through," George later affirmed.[21] Most impressive was his status as an internationally recognized advocate for the income tax. In 1897, he was appointed tax commissioner for the state of Wisconsin. His book *Income Taxation* (1910), a global review of practices from New Zealand to the Leeward Islands to Russia, spurred the passage of the Sixteenth Amendment to the U.S. Constitution.[22]

FAMILY FINANCES

While distinguished as an expert on income tax laws, Kent Kennan was, sadly, even more distinctive as a tax lawyer who failed to translate his expertise into income. Instead, he had to draw on his children's inheritance money to make ends meet. As Uncle Alfred Farragut told the Kennan children and no doubt many others, "Kent Kennan is a very good lawyer, [but he] is a very poor businessman."[23]

Kent invested heavily in land around Ashland, Wisconsin, expecting it to grow into a major port. Nearby Duluth boomed instead. He bought into iron mines that later closed. (By contrast, Grandfather Alfred James had made a pile from gold mines in the West.) In the 1920s, Milwaukee boasted many wealthy residents. U.S. income tax rates reached 25 percent for the highest incomes. The state of Wisconsin levied its own income tax. Surely potential clients abounded who would have paid generously for advice from such a respected authority as Kent Kennan. Nevertheless, he never earned much as a tax lawyer.

Uncle Alfred Farragut, whom the Kennan children remembered as kind to them but as nevertheless prone to hold a grudge, probably did not forget Kent's promises when courting his sister. Mindful of her parents' disapproval, Florence had initially turned him down. He responded with poetry and with assurances of a comfortable life. To assuage the parents, who feared Kent was after Florence's money, he told her that he owned $25,000 worth of real estate and could net at least $4,000 a year from his law practice. His repeated declarations of love and the fact that she herself was no longer young encouraged her assent.

In ensuing years the patriarch, Alfred James, and his son, Alfred Farragut, could not fail to see that Kent did not buy a home for his rapidly growing family. Instead, they lived in rented dwellings, including a row house in "Johnson Barracks." Finally, in 1901, Florence's father purchased a house at 309 Cambridge Avenue in Milwaukee and vested ownership in his daughter, not her husband. After she died, title passed to the four Kennan children, with Kent having the right to live there during his lifetime.

That Kent, whom George remembered as a shy and unhappy man, did remain in the house, both before and after Florence died, was telling. Years later, George described 309 Cambridge Avenue as a "dark, strange household." The three-story house, situated on a lot barely thirty feet wide, "was built absolutely the wrong way, with all the windows of the living room almost right up against another house, and the blank side toward an open lawn."[24] Luckily, the neighboring house, owned by Edward and Ida Frost, owned that large lawn, and the Frosts encouraged the children to play there.

Indeed, they became "Uncle Edward" and "Aunt Ida" and installed a private telephone line between the two houses. George's older sister would remember that the Frosts "were just second parents to us, always."[25] This closeness had prompted Florence and Kent to endow George with the middle name Frost. Though roomy with many bedrooms, a butler's pantry, and both a parlor and sitting room, 309 Cambridge Avenue remained gloomy, and it looked odd. When Jeanette as a teenager had a boy drop her off at home, she would pretend that she was going into the neighbor's much nicer house.[26]

Why, then, did Florence's parents choose this particular house? As Jeanette later remarked, "they surely could have afforded to be more generous, for Grandpa James was . . . very well off financially." Tough-minded in many ways, Alfred James probably intended this spacious but sunless house as a message to Kent. The old sailor was in effect saying, "Kent, since you apparently cannot afford to purchase a home for my daughter and the children you are producing, I am buying one for them. But the house is as dark as my opinion of you. A proper provider would secure a more suitable home for his family." Also astute, Kent probably got, and no doubt resented, the message. But he remained at 309 Cambridge Avenue until his death three decades later.

The peculiar house constituted only one strand of the James-dominated financial web in which Kent raised George and his siblings. With the deaths of Florence in April 1904, her father eight months later, and her mother the following July, the four Kennan children inherited $101,075 plus the 309 Cambridge Avenue house and a share in the house on Nagawicka Lake. Invested largely in municipal and railroad bonds and in stock of the James's insurance company, this substantial inheritance yielded some $5,000 income per year. Each of the children would inherit one-fourth of the principal on reaching maturity.[27] The assets were held in trust by the First Trust Company of Wisconsin, with Kent as the guardian. By the terms of the trust, Kent could draw on the income for the children's expenses and to maintain the Cambridge Avenue house and the Nagawicka place. Each year he dutifully submitted to the Milwaukee Probate Court a detailed account of the moneys earned and spent.

These documents offer an intimate view into the Kennan household from 1905 to 1925, when George reached his twenty-first birthday. In 1917, for example, George's monthly allowance grew to $15, his two pairs of shoes totaled $9.50, and 80 cents went to Famous Shoe Hospital. The income of the children paid for property taxes, painting the country house, lamps for the city house, manure for the vegetable garden at Nagawicka, and other ordinary expenses. The children's money also covered repairs and parts for the father's automobile and travel and hotel expenses on the family's vacations. The inheritance would take care of prep school and college expenses. In sum, rather than meeting the expenses of his home and his children out of his earnings, as most of his peers had to do, Kent relied on the income yielded by his children's inheritances from the James family. Moreover, the trust's income often exceeded expenses so that, for instance, Kent was able to save $3,500 in the years leading up to George's going to Princeton in 1921. The father's financial dependence on his own children—and, ultimately on the Jameses—no doubt rankled George's Uncle Alfred Farragut, who had listened to his parents' worry that Kent was interested in Florence only for her money.

George remembered his uncle as quiet though exacting.[28] In view of the taciturn inclinations of both Kent and Alfred Farragut, it seems likely that the shame and resentment from this financial dependence remained largely unspoken even as it smoldered. George would remember his aunt and uncle's family as "very tough" people, "capable of biting in and holding right on."[29]

Much also remained unsaid between George and his father, including an explanation of how the income from the inheritance was being spent and the capital that remained. Years later, when George went to college, not knowing that he had income of his own would add to his difficulties in fitting in at class-conscious Princeton.

THE STEPMOTHER

In early 1908, Kent told his daughters that he was marrying Louise Wheeler, a classics teacher at Ripon College, where he served as a trustee. Cousin Grace would have to go, "and that nearly killed us," Constance later recalled. She and her sisters ran upstairs crying. Cousin Grace was sobbing. Even decades later, memories of their stepmother sparked protests. "She wasn't a motherly person, she didn't like children, and we resented her very much," Constance fumed.[30] George later recalled that Frances hated the woman. Jeanette remained puzzled about what had led Louise to "marry the father of four children, twenty-two years older than herself and far from wealthy, and become the manager of his tall narrow house on Cambridge Avenue." Equally unpromising was his choosing a "spinster school teacher" as a mother. Jeanette remembered that her father and stepmother kept "separate bedrooms, unlike the parents of all my friends."[31] The bedrooms were not even adjoining but rather separated by a sister's bedroom. George hated to hear Louise "speak terribly sharply to my father" and faulted her as incapable of deep affection.[32]

Lifelong consequences likely stemmed from George's dislike for someone he regarded as "a highly nervous woman, thin and uncertain of herself . . . a sissy of a woman," who displayed neither "strength of character or courage."[33] Such vehemence about Louise would later bleed into a generalized misogyny toward women who reminded him of her.

George's sharpest resentment of his stepmother stemmed from her discomfort with biology in general and with male physiology in particular. Upon discovering she was pregnant, Louise "was absolutely mortified." The forty-year-old woman was "so ashamed to tell her mother about it" that she wrote a letter, signed "Your repentant twin," begging her sister to bear the news. Louise was shocked into silence when one of the children asked what a midwife did. She remained too embarrassed to inform them of her own pregnancy, and so the birth of Kent Wheeler Kennan on April 18, 1913, "came as a complete surprise," Jeanette remembered.[34] On another occasion, the stepmother brought George and Jeanette into the parlor, reserved for important matters, to instruct them never to talk at the dinner table about dogs having puppies or cats having kittens.[35] "My stepmother never really understood little boys," Jeanette affirmed.[36]

George and his stepmother clashed over his determined self-identification as a boy. What George would regard as a foundational episode of his early life occurred at the start of first grade. Even decades later, he grew indignant when recalling his "admiration for boys in school who had a fly to piddle." He, by contrast, had "trousers that had no fly." He had to sit down like the girls, and he was ridiculed for it. He had "wanted to be as manly as the others." In retrospect, he deemed it "significant that it did not occur to me to tell my stepmother" about the problem. Instead, "I found a scissors and cut an appropriate slit myself." Also significant was Louise's reaction: she was so shocked and embarrassed that she spanked him.[37] A few years later in Cassel, he was "amazed to see German women . . . take their children's pants down and let them go in the park. And I remember thinking how wonderful it would be if you were that intimate with your mother that you would want to tell her when you had to go."[38] Kennan volunteered this story to his authorized biographer along with what he regarded as the foundational narrative of his life: "I was affected neurotically by the absence of a mother."[39]

In 1912, Kent, now head of the Wisconsin Income Tax Commission, needed to do a bit of research in Germany in preparation for passage of the Sixteenth Amendment. He seized the opportunity to have Louise and the children spend several months in Cassel.

He had chosen Cassel, Jeanette explained, "because he felt the purest German was spoken in that area."[40] Not thrilled with the venture, Louise explained to her mother that it was "a lifelong dream of Kent's to educate his children partially at least on the other side, so I am yielding to what appears to be my duty." She was nervous about the cost of the trip as well as the recent *Titanic* disaster, which "has made us anything but anxious to try sea travel."[41]

George, however, was thrilled at the prospect of crossing the Atlantic. He had always loved being taken to see big ocean liners. His favorite book had stories and pictures of ships. He hoped to join the navy. On the eve of their departure on August 8, Cousin Grace, now living in New Jersey, treated George and Jeanette to a ride in a hansom through Central Park, and then saw them off the next day. On the voyage over, George and Jeanette wandered all over the *President Grant*. In cahoots with a German boy, he scampered into the captain's quarters. Even on the rough crossing back home in January 1913, George enjoyed the voyage. In Cassel, he enrolled in the Henkelsche Privat Vorschule, where he quickly picked up German while studying arithmetic, reading, and writing. The marching of soldiers and cadets to and fro in this garrison town gave credence, at least in his imagination, to talk of an impending war between England and Germany. At Christmastime, George and Jeanette, who had known only the minimalist decoration of their Presbyterian church in Milwaukee, were awed by the cathedral with its great fir trees trimmed with silver balls on either side of the altar, and by the voices of the soldiers and cadets filling that great space. The American children joined in singing the German Christmas carols.

Soon afterward, Louise discovered she was pregnant. She brought George and Jeanette home, leaving the two older girls in a boarding school. Kent was away working on income tax legislation. With their Cambridge Avenue and Nagawicka homes both rented to get needed cash, Louise and Jeanette retreated to her mother's home in Kalamazoo, while George lived, as he often did, with the Jameses. He later reflected that the James family was "in some ways, more important than [my] father's."[42] George celebrated his ninth birthday, February 16, 1913, with cousin Charlie, Uncle Alfred Farragut, and Aunt Nellie.

For the next three years, his life would roll along much the same path: living with his sisters, stepmother, father, and baby "Kentie"; escaping to the Jameses; attending the excellent Milwaukee State Normal Training School, where he got middling grades; playing with friends and running or riding the streetcar around Milwaukee. One day he caught a glimpse of visiting President Woodrow Wilson.

THE JUNEAU PARK FAIRIES

Family life at 309 Cambridge Avenue remained starched. Emotional gloom compounded the darkness from the misplaced windows. The parents "were trying to repress everybody," believed Frances, who rarely returned after fleeing to New York City, and then to Alaska.[43] Though usually bubbly, Jeanette discerned "a certain strain at our house at the dinner table." After supper, everyone fled to their separate rooms. Father "had a way of churning his teeth together so that you could see the inside, sort of suppressing things."[44]

Nevertheless, the house was full of books. George read widely. From Louise, who had taught Latin and Greek, he absorbed a mastery of English grammar that would infuse elegance into his future writing. "The speech in our house was very, very correct," Jeanette remembered.[45] Outside the home, George enthused about the "Preparedness" campaign to get America ready for possible participation in the raging European war. One Saturday, he attended "a meeting of the Junior National Security League, where I heard two very interesting talks." The following week, "we were drilled for an hour and a half by a naval officer."[46]

He seemed happy enough and, aside from this budding interest in national security, quite ordinary. But what were his inner thoughts and inclinations during these preadolescent years? George as a boy and George as an adult offered two different answers. In January 1916, the almost-twelve-year-old began keeping a diary, probably because Jeanette was doing so. Over the next few months, he penned entries that

FIGURE 7. George at seven years old. From the back of the
photograph: "Not so sweet an expression as he usually wears."
(Courtesy of Princeton University Library.)

revealed a physically active, curious boy, smart but not a grind, someone more interested in the discipline of drilling than in flights of fancy. In memoirs written a half-century later, however, Kennan painted a different portrait of his childhood: "In a world that was peculiarly and intimately my own I habitually read special meanings into things, scenes, and places—qualities of wonder, beauty, promise, or horror—for which there were no external evidence." Behind a dark, forbidding entryway, "I never doubted, lay a house of horror—horror unnamed, unmentionable, not to be imagined." Moreover, "the trees in Juneau Park were populated by fairies."[47]

How to square these differing accounts? It was at some cost that the adult Kennan confessed to having lived in a dream world "particularly in childhood but with lessening intensity right on to middle age." When he wrote the memoir in 1966–1967, he had not given up hope of reentering government. He knew that detractors already mocked his mystical bent. Acknowledging this fantasy life took courage, and it evidenced how much these memories meant to him. It seems likely, then, that the safe, unrevealing flatness of the twelve-year-old's diary reflected his caution in baring his inner self to this austere household. Not all could be hidden, however. On the first page of his published memoir, Kennan recalled "dreaming daydreams so intense and satisfying that hours could pass in oblivion of immediate surroundings." Similarly, on the first page of her memoir of childhood with George, Jeanette recalled that "even as a little boy his mind always seemed to be occupied with speculations and ruminations." An aunt admonished him: "Stop thinking, George. Stop thinking now."[48]

Lacking a devoted mother and an expressive father, George depended on the love of his sisters, especially Jeanette. "I could talk more with Jeanette than with almost anyone else in the world."[49] She and her sisters often "got into bed with him, cuddled. But it ended too early for George."[50] Baby "Kentie" Kennan came onto the scene, and "all my maternal instincts which had been satisfied by my relations with George, now found a new object. Somehow George and I drifted apart a little." The two older sisters also focused on the adorable baby.

FIGURE 8. The Kennan family in 1917. From left, Frances, Kossuth Kent,
George, Kent Wheeler, Louise, Constance, Jeanette.
(Courtesy of Princeton University Library.)

Once again, as with the death of his mother, the departure of the
white-uniformed nurses, the pullback from his father, and the firing of
Cousin Grace, George was cast emotionally adrift. To be sure, he was
now older and stronger, he had friends and the Jameses, and he did retain ties with Jeanette. Nevertheless, Kentie's arrival marked the end of
an era. Meanwhile, Louise, whose maternal instinct had remained dormant with the Kennan children, now grew totally absorbed with her
own son. She even took pleasure in nursing him, despite anxiety about
the vulgarity of such physical intimacy.

George's adolescence further alienated his stepmother. Louise
couldn't understand why he ate so much.[51] Watching the stepson mature may have spurred Louise into pushing Kent into deciding that the
boy needed separating from his sisters—and from the household—and
the toughening of an all-male environment.[52]

ST. JOHN'S MILITARY ACADEMY

George's inheritance yielded the money to send George to almost any private school. But for some reason Kent chose for his bright son St. John's Military Academy in Delafield, Wisconsin, not far from Nagawicka Lake. "Uncle Edward and Uncle Alfred were both shocked," Jeanette recalled, at the father's decision to "send this very sensitive youngster to this tough school."[53] "*Why*," the uncles persisted, "send that boy to St. John's?"[54] The school specialized in troubled boys. As Jeanette's son, Gene, who later grew close with Kennan, put it, he "got kicked out of his house. They sent him away to school."[55] While Kent was unwise in choosing St. John's, he was irresponsible in casting the vulnerable boy into that den a year early, after having him skip eighth grade at Milwaukee Normal. The father and stepmother seemed eager to get him out of the house. And so the slender lad of thirteen was, as he later recalled, "tossed into this barracks with a lot of boys who were really little short of criminals, very tough boys indeed."[56]

What counted at St. John's was muscle. Two boys on his floor already ranked as professional boxers. By contrast, George, younger than his peers, remained "so small that I couldn't carry a gun in my first year and had to stride along behind the band with a bugle." Years later, in a puff-piece interview for the academy's history, Kennan cited as his most vivid memory of his first years "the hazing, the escapades, all the things that go on between boys of that age."[57] As his daughter less delicately put it, her father "was terrorized at St. John's." Boys stole the treats sent by his sisters. Learning of George's phobia about serpents, they put snakes down his back.[58] Kennan, however, rose to the challenge: he grew taller, he toughened up, and later in life he even remembered his last two years at St. John's with pleasure.[59]

The caption under his photo in the 1921 yearbook said it all: "Disposition—Vascillating," "Pet Peeve—The Universe." The misspelling had sailed past the book's editors and their faculty mentors. The pet peeve implied that Kennan, feeling out of sync with his environment, did not find much to be happy about at St. John's, despite the rosy glow he would imbue it with in later years.

FIGURE 9. Sensitive, slender, and younger than most of his schoolmates, George at age thirteen was packed away to a military school specializing in problem boys. (Courtesy of Princeton University Library.)

"Vacillating" suggests how he coped. He seems to have both internalized the discipline of St. John's and rebelled against it. Later, in times of great stress, such as his breakdown in Moscow in 1934–1935, inner voices that seemed to harken back to St. John's would articulate these warring impulses. Order at the school rested in the iron grip of the "almost Dickensian headmaster," "Duke" Smythe, "an Episcopal clergyman, with white hair and a white beard and a derby hat and a frock coat and a limp." A boxer in his youth, he employed a heavy hand in controlling six hundred often unruly boys. His punishment could prove indiscriminate. Hearing him bellowing at a cadet, the officer of the day would quickly empty the hallways lest he slam an innocent. The headmaster "commanded a respect among the boys that bordered on terror."[60] George was also impressed with how Duke Smythe wielded both physical discipline and the emotional force of elevated language. He would never forget the majesty of Smythe's intoning at Sunday services the Gospel of St. John: "And the Word was made flesh and dwelt among us, and we beheld his glory, the glory as of the only begotten of the Father, full of grace and truth." That was "the most beautiful sentence in the English language," Kennan marveled.[61] He regarded such eloquence as a model.

Though awed by Smythe, George also rebelled. In his second year, he suffered a sudden bout of appendicitis and was rushed to a Milwaukee hospital for the operation. But "it was during the First World War, and they didn't have good catgut to sew you up with, and the sutures got infected." All that winter, he was running around with "this big bandage on my side, and that was rather depressing."[62] Finally, he ran away and sought refuge back home. Unsympathetic, Kent reprimanded his son and sent him back with a letter authorizing Smythe to punish the runaway any way he saw fit. On the train to St. John's, George hoped for a derailment—anything to avoid discipline from the headmaster. Smythe read the letter, asked the frightened boy why he had run away, and then, to George's amazement, dismissed him with no further punishment.[63] Another time, he ran away to Madison, where Jeanette was at the university.[64]

Though he would graduate ninth in a class of 102, Kennan at times suffered from depression or just discouragement. In his third year, he confessed to Jeanette that his grades were sinking "because I'm lazy, I guess." Something was holding him back from anything "too much like work." Signing the letter, "your loving brother," he hoped she would send more stuffed dates and write soon because "it certainly does seem good to get letters out here."[65]

Before graduating in June 1921, Kennan's mood and performance lifted. He ranked as president and tenor banjo player with the St. John's Syncopators, a jazz band that performed in the mess hall and at silent movies. He remained so blatantly emotional that a satirical daily "schedule" for the school listed "1:10 P.M. Kennan gets a letter and has delirium." As class poet, George graced the class of 1921's yearbook with verse expressing the emphasis on toughness that he had internalized:

> The daily battle fought and won,
> And fitness for a harder run.

Though George ranked as a lieutenant, he had had his fill of the military. Gone was the boyhood dream to join the navy. On his St. John's transcript, the phrase "West Point Course?" was crossed out and penciled above it was "Harvard."[66]

Kennan's highest grade was a 96 in fourth year English. (By contrast, he earned a 78 and a 72 in two semesters of American History.) A young English teacher made a lasting impression by introducing George to Oscar Wilde and to Bernard Shaw, then "frightfully avant-garde." Princeton replaced Harvard once the teacher had him read F. Scott Fitzgerald's *This Side of Paradise*. After graduation, the instructor invited George to Chicago, "and it turned out that he was homosexual." George fled when he made a pass at him. In commenting on this episode, Kennan alluded to the homosexuality at St. John's. "What could you expect? These were boys in ages from 13 to 18 and obviously during this period the sexual powers ripened." He acknowledged that he himself had found an older student attractive, and "I'm sure that had I remained in an all-male environment any longer, I like all of us would have developed homosexual tendencies." But, he affirmed, "it was never in any way natural to me, and the moment I had an interest in women I never had anything like that."[67]

In assessing her brother's experience at St. John's, Jeanette asked herself whether the school had indeed toughened him or had sent him "farther into his own world" of fantasy about Juneau Park fairies and other such mysteries. "The latter seems more plausible," she concluded.[68]

Despite its rigor, St. John's did not prepare him for Princeton. As graduation approached, a kindly dean excused him from classes so that he could study for Princeton's entrance examination. Jeanette dutifully tutored her brother in chemistry, about which she knew nothing—they both crammed from the book. He still failed the test. Then he took the exam again and passed just before the semester began. As the last student admitted to Princeton's class of 1925, George got stuck in housing distant from campus.

PRINCETON

In *Memoirs 1925–1950*, written in 1966–1967, Kennan depicted his Princeton years as grim. He portrayed himself as an oddball, nearly friendless, intellectually unengaged, and swinging helplessly between his "only two moods: awkward aloofness and bubbling enthusiasm." Though arriving with dreams inspired by reading *The Other Side of Paradise*, he had remained "hopelessly and crudely Midwestern."[69]

Much of this picture was a distortion. In the memoir, Kennan tellingly acknowledged that the memory of his Princeton self flickered "only dimly and uncertainly—too uncertainly to permit of confident judgment." He emphasized that not only was it difficult "to picture myself as I was at that time," but "I prefer, in fact, not to try to do so."[70] Perhaps it was reluctance to delve into that phase of his past that dissuaded him from incorporating, or perhaps even reading, a trove of revealing letters written while a student at Princeton. This correspondence, sent mostly to Jeanette, depicts a more complex—and far more positive—experience than what he described in the memoir. While students' letters to the home front tend toward the bright side to ease parental worries, George's letters to his confidante packed such detailed depictions and covered such a wide range of reactions that they, cumulatively, ring true. To be sure, the Midwesterner did feel, especially in his first year, out of place in the eastern prep school–dominated hierarchy of Princeton, where being rich and getting into an exclusive eating club counted almost as much as starring on the football team. Weighing only 130-pounds, a year younger than his peers, lacking athletic talent, easily intimidated, and bearing the imprint of St. John's rather than St. Paul's, Kennan had reason to feel insecure.

Inherited money, the most crucial currency at Princeton, he actually did possess, but he did not know that. Kent had never told him either the extent of his inheritance or the substantial annual income it generated. As a consequence, Kennan hesitated asking his father for money. Rather than smoking cigarettes, "I smoked only a pipe because it was cheaper."[71] He pinched pennies, took odd jobs, and did without. Even Jeanette, who dearly loved her father, believed he had unnecessarily added to her brother's challenges at Princeton. As she later reflected, for George, coming from a "socially unsophisticated family, how different it might have been if he had started off with more money in his pocket and, at least a tuxedo in his wardrobe?"[72]

Despite the difficulties, Kennan at Princeton found himself. He matured into a young adult with growing control over his life. Though self-absorbed and moody as most seventeen- to twenty-one-year-olds are, his outlook expanded beyond the confines of 309 Cambridge Avenue, St. John's, and the Kennan–James feud. While many of his views and attitudes remained sophomoric, they were no longer childish. Significantly, while he would never live again in Milwaukee, he would spend the second half of his life in Princeton.

In the university environment, Kennan's maturing intellect grappled with the emotional trauma of his earliest years. While the pain of not having a loving mother touched him deeply, how he interpreted that loss reflected the intellectual and societal currents swirling around him. He would remember realizing at Princeton that "I was in someway twisted; that the young tree had been bent."[73] Yet he was not yet sure what had damaged the sapling. That came later, in Europe, where he would delve deeply into what he called the science of Sigmund Freud's psychoanalytic theories. Still later, at mid-century, thoughts about his mother were probably also influenced by the pop psychology of "momism," which held that almost every problem in one's personality traced back to the relationship with the mother.[74]

A month after George arrived at school, his father visited. The newly minted Princetonian already assumed a nonchalant, patronizing tone.

Father, he wrote Jeanette, "was more impressed with Princeton than I myself have been. Poor Father, what a hard time he does have." Kent waxed "quite sentimental" in telling his son, "'Make good. I know you will.'" He then "laughed the self-conscious laugh which we all do ourselves." George, now a self-confessed atheist, surmised that his father had read his Bible for solace on the train ride back.[75] By Thanksgiving Day, George was telling himself that "happiness is simply the practice of skillfully kidding oneself along."

Despite the superficial cynicism, he was exploring the dilemmas of thought. "Introspection is like looking through a window into a dark and dirty old shack when you have a myriad of nice views to look at in the other direction." Only months after leaving the Midwest, he breezily generalized about the East. "It's very queer," he informed Jeanette, "everybody here is so satisfied with everything and themselves, and so much more conservative than the people of the west."[76]

Though no Amory Blaine stepping from the pages of *This Side of Paradise*, George had immersed himself in F. Scott Fitzgerald. He would later recall feeling, while a student at Princeton, totally attuned "to language, to atmosphere" as depicted in the novels. "I fully grasped . . . that this was stated in an artistic way, with a *marvelous* sort of restraint and effect. All of this went right into me immediately and became part of me."[77] What pierced him especially were the midwestern origins of Blaine and Nick Carraway and the latter's awareness of nature. Years later, Kennan could still remember reading Carraway, the narrator in *The Great Gatsby*, describe the Christmas trips back from college in the East. When the train, leaving Chicago, "pulled out into the winter night and the real snow, our snow, began to stretch out beside us . . . and the dim lights of small Wisconsin stations moved by, a sharp wild brace came suddenly into the air. We drew in deep breaths of it . . . unutterably aware of our identity."[78] "My identification with this passage was so intense," Kennan later confessed, that "I could not read it without weeping."[79]

For the rest of his life, he would find alluring the wintry cold, snow, and long nights of the Baltic states, Russia, and Norway as well as his native Midwest. It was nature itself that moved him, not only the sharp winds of winter, but also the "sweet smells out of the ground" on "a warm, rainy spring evening." Those smells awakened "all the memories of Nagawicka and all the romance I used to imagine there," he wrote Jeanette. He would always cherish Nagawicka as "a wonderful old place."[80]

George in Princeton could not escape Milwaukee. The tight budget mandated by the father back at 309 Cambridge Avenue crimped the prospects of the son at the class-conscious school. Although probably facetious in complaining that "I haven't been able to afford a postage stamp," George did worry about outlays greater than two cents.[81] As Christmas of his freshman year approached, he lacked the $28 needed for a train ticket back to Milwaukee.

Therefore, according to an oft-cited chestnut from the *Memoirs*, Kennan, "fearing to burden my father," took a job in nearby Trenton delivering mail. On his first day, with his leather bag overstuffed with bundles of letters carefully arranged by address, he fumbled while stepping off a streetcar. The bundles broke and letters spilled onto the snowy street and tracks. Kennan managed to scoop them up, but now the addresses were all mixed up. He worked into the night crisscrossing the slums of Trenton, trying to find streets, knocking on doors to ask directions, and chilling himself. He ended up contracting deadly scarlet fever. The disease displayed itself shortly after New Year's when he was back in Milwaukee. Kent and Louise packed the sisters off to college and isolated George in a third-floor bedroom, to be cared for by a nurse. (He fell in love with her, he later recalled.) "I remained in quarantine until Easter," Kennan recounted in his memoir. By the time he returned to campus, "the academic year was drawing to a close," and friendships among students had already gelled.

Though poignant in making the point of a rough start at Princeton, this woeful tale is problematic in two ways. First, Easter in 1922 occurred on April 16. By March 1, nearly seven weeks earlier, George was already back on campus. (And that was after stopping off in Washington, D.C., where a friend of his father's showed him around town and set up an appointment to meet President Warren G. Harding. When Harding proved tardy, Kennan left.)[82] The spring 1922 semester was not yet nearly over, as George later remembered it, but instead would run well into May. Moreover, with regard to missed work, almost all his professors assured the convalescent, "'Oh, that'll be all right; never mind that.'" And so, "I don't have any work to make up at all," he crowed to Jeanette.[83]

Second, and of greater importance, Kennan really did not have to trudge through snowy Trenton to earn the train fare. He had money—indeed, extra money—in his inheritance account. According to the report Kent submitted to the Milwaukee Probate Court in August 1922, in the first eight months of that year alone, George's trust funds earned $420.15 more in interest and dividends than the total expenses that Kent charged to his son's account. Those charges included tuition and other expenses at Princeton; one-fourth of the taxes, utilities, supplies, and maintenance for 309 Cambridge Avenue and the Nagawicka house; and six weeks at $49/week for Clara Zeitler, "trained nurse for George."[84] The surplus of $420.15 amounted to one-quarter of George's total expenses, and an even higher fraction of what he spent at Princeton. If Kent had not been so stingy with George's money, the freshman certainly could have afforded the $28 train fare at Christmas.

Many years later, George recalled that after Frances, his independent-minded eldest sister, had charged their father with using the inheritance for his own purposes, the latter at Christmastime took out the account books and offered to show them. George replied, "Well, Father, I don't really want to look at them. I'm not worried about that. And I could see that he was very pleased with this." Still loyal to his father's memory, the adult Kennan commented about Frances's accusation, "I can't understand it at all." As a boy, with "no curiosity" about the financial arrangements, he had just "felt that I mustn't make it too hard for my father."[85]

George's worries about money, his efforts to earn money, and the problems caused by a tight budget run like a thick red cord through his correspondence and diary. A year after the Trenton mail debacle, he affirmed, "I'll certainly be working at Trenton this Christmas."[86] Having taught himself to play several instruments, he snared "a very good job" performing for $1.35 an evening with the Freshman Commons Orchestra.[87] He agreed to address five hundred envelopes for a local tailor, even though he felt "doozy" after only the first couple hundred.[88] He managed to attend a prom at a girl's school only by borrowing a tuxedo and wearing the same shirt the next day.[89] On another date, when "asked to stay all night," he caught himself in the midst of explaining that he had to return the tuxedo early the next morning.[90]

In view of his middle-class, midwestern background, George could not expect to be tapped for the most exclusive eating clubs, such as Ivy. (When Ivy inducted only eleven new members, a bitter candidate protested, "Even Jesus Christ took twelve."[91]) Nevertheless, Kennan did find friends, even fans, who liked and respected him. An anonymous angel paid for his ticket and transportation to the Harvard football game. He boasted of his "'ungodly' drag with the powers that be ... even though I haven't enough funds to run around with the elite."[92] His friends included boys "with oodles of money" who "treat me wonderfully, considering my lack of personality." But, he rued, "I just can't go much with their set unless I spend a little more money." He was self-aware enough to know that "if there's one thing that isn't good for me, it is to be alone, and it's a choice of going with them or no one. They are all mighty nice fellows, a lot nicer than I knew at St. John's, but they will go to movies, buy books and magazines, play bridge, and eat and all that."[93]

Hopes of affording the Key and Seal eating club were buoyed when Uncle Alfred Farragut, visiting Princeton with his son Charles, who had been accepted for the following year, offered to pay for George's room, as George wrote to Jeanette, "if I can get a double room (which I easily can) for Charles and myself." While that "would practically offset the expenses of the club," he was "afraid Father won't see it that way." Remaining unclear here was whether George expected his father to object to the club's expense regardless, or whether he feared his father would resent Uncle Alfred Farragut's deploying his wealth at Princeton. In any case, George did room with Charles, and he did remain in Key and Seal, where he worked to offset expenses, until his senior year.[94]

Tight funds did not stop Kennan from throwing himself, totally, into the pandemonium surrounding Princeton's October 28, 1922, football game against the University of Chicago. The historic game, the first such contest to be broadcast nationwide, would ennoble Princeton's "Team of Destiny." George abandoned any self-consciousness as he joined two thousand classmates "shouting, screaming, and praying" for the players as they prepared to depart for Chicago. "When the team finally pulled out there was a yell that fairly shook the earth," he boasted. One of his friends had a good radio set, and a group packed into a room to hear "this thin, almost unintelligible voice" call the plays against "a background of yelling." Following the game required distinguishing the Princeton "'Tiger, tiger, tiger'" from the "Chicago sky-rocket" cheers. "Tiger" yells reached a fever pitch in the last minutes of the game. With Chicago ahead, Howdy Gray of Princeton picked up a fumble and ran forty-two yards for the touchdown. Another touchdown soon followed, and Princeton squeaked out a 21 to 18 victory. Nassau Street erupted into a "mass of crazy-men, hundreds of them, dancing, screaming, waving their arms, and hugging each other." "I was one of them," he proudly told Jeanette. "We swarmed into the dining halls and somebody stood up on a table and led cheers."

Though George seldom got drunk, he made an exception that night. Along about midnight, still going strong, he was roaming the campus, arm in arm with two buddies and singing "Chicago, they can't play ball" to the tune of "Hail, hail, the gang's all here." George was part of the gang and he felt good about it. After welcoming the team back on Sunday by carrying "the poor devils all over campus on our shoulders," he joined other sophomores on Monday afternoon as they painted hapless freshmen with a horrid mixture of "water, flour, eggs, tomatoes, fish, green paint, cement, alabaster, and every other conceivable concoction."[95]

The weekend illustrated that at times George did fit seamlessly into Princeton, despite his meager budget and midwestern background. Moreover, as the administrators of Princeton and other elite schools understood, such seemingly spontaneous, student-inspired torrents of feeling bonded classmates to each other and to the institution. Such emotional ties anchored self-identity for students and hooks for school fundraising. Even though Kennan at Princeton failed to make much of a mark on others, Princeton marked him. However much the mature memoirist disparaged the "bubbling enthusiasm" of his younger self,

FIGURE 10. An undergraduate at Princeton
University. (Courtesy of Orren Jack Turner and
of Christopher Kennan.)

such exuberance and excess remained normal for college boys, especially at elite schools.[96] This was, after all, the heyday of bathtub gin and
flappers.

Nonacademic activities often left little time for studying. At graduation, Kennan ranked 83rd of 219. In only two courses of his senior year
did he earn the highest grade, in Polity 407 and 408. With one being the
highest score and five the lowest, he averaged a four in his history
courses.[97] He boasted of "getting good experience in how to do three
things at one time and skim through exams without studying."[98] Enticed

by nature, the future environmentalist whiled away spring days at the Moses Taylor Pyne estate not far from campus. Though he was supposed to be reading history, he "found it so much more diverting to watch the ducks & fish."[99] On another day he compromised by reading his book while sitting in a tree. In the spring of his junior year, George was crushed when an English professor "informed me that my previous English record was exceedingly poor and that, in effect, I might as well effect the international abolition of armaments as to get into his composition course."[100]

Two of his history professors did make a lasting impression. Joseph C. Green, who later served in the State Department during Kennan's tenure, taught Historical Introduction, nicknamed Hysterical Interruption. The course was no joke, however. Green was rigorous as he stressed the impact of climate, geography, and economics on history—lessons that Kennan would retain. Also influential was Raymond J. Sontag, later an adviser to the State Department, who emphasized the social and cultural elements shaping political developments.

Kennan was probably learning and thinking more outside the classroom than in it. By the second half of his sophomore year, in 1923, he had attained a broader perspective on Princeton's hierarchy. "College honors, important as they may seem at present," he wrote Jeanette, "are fearfully temporal." By four years after graduation, "no matter how important you may have been, your name will be practically unknown" to most students.[101] He had also come to perceive the limits that could close in on even the most ambitious young person. "We all run along with our head in the cloud . . . hoping for some kind of great thing," until the end, when "nothing great has happened at all."[102]

In Kennanish fashion, he theorized about sex more than he indulged in it. To Jeanette, about to get engaged and exploring her own sexuality, he claimed that he was not "much of a prude." How could he be, he argued, considering his "utter lack of religion" or "parental advice," his four years at St. John's, and his "various sojourns in railroad yards, post-offices, [and] cherry-pickers camps"? "I'll be all right," he assured her.[103] He often visited his sister Frances, then an actress living in Greenwich Village. Once Frances brought home her friend, Puritan, "thinking I ought to have a girl." George was evidently more the puritan than she, for not much happened. "I wasn't prepared to go to these lengths yet," he later explained. "I just idealized women so, you know."[104] He also idealized the "Boheme life" of Frances and her friends in New York. "I was absolutely neurotic with excitement of this city and the way they lived," he later recalled. It seemed like "fairyland" to him, "the most exciting place I'd ever seen."[105]

"CONVENTIONALITY" VERSUS "UNCONVENTIONALITY"

The appeal of this freewheeling lifestyle clashed with George's aptitude for order. He was feeling and thinking his way toward a framework that could accommodate these conflicting impulses. He aimed for both freedom and restraint, creativity as well as order, and wanderlust along with responsibility. He would ponder, elaborate, and agonize over such a structure of polarized choices throughout his life. He was, evidently without having yet read Sigmund Freud, edging toward the latter's thesis of an inherent tension between Eros and Civilization. That concept would later become central to how he explained much about himself, including his impulse for extramarital affairs.

Now, in 1923, George framed the battle as between "conventionality" and "Harry Kemp." "My hardest job is to be conventional," he confided to Jeanette. His model for "unconventionality" focused on Kemp, the self-promoting "Hobo Poet," who had recently published a tell-all autobiography, *Tramping on Life*. Kemp's motto, "It's a great life if you have the courage to face it," intrigued Kennan. As a teenager, Kemp had left the Midwest to explore the seven seas, as had George's grandfather. Upon returning, Alfred James had amassed a fortune in business and had founded a dynasty. Kemp, by contrast, had remained footloose, laboring on ore boats and farms, and writing poetry and prose. He had also seduced many women, including, notoriously, the wife of a friend, the social reformer Upton Sinclair.[106] Kemp and the two Sinclairs had made headlines by jointly advocating the institution of trial marriage. Years later, Kennan in Moscow would also advocate such experimental intimacy. Kemp's enthusiasm for outdoor labor and his lyricizing of nature also resonated with Kennan. "Despicable" as Kemp was morally, George wrote his sister, "he had an interesting time."

In pondering how to position himself between conventionality and unconventionality, Kennan found Kemp both appealing and appalling. He admired the man's writing about life with the same zest he had put into living it. He surmised that "self-respect and blood" argued against conventionality. Though George would not admit it in a letter to his sister, he probably envied the aspiring bard's success with women. Yet he also criticized the love-them-and-leave-them attitude as proof that "Harry Kemp believes in selfishness." As for the opposite pole, "my strongest argument for conventionality" is that "it brought me Princeton." Moreover, "Princeton is greater than Harry Kemp by an infinitely long margin," because the Princeton community abhorred selfishness. Then, immediately second-guessing that claim of selflessness, he added, "I'm afraid I'm an idealist."[107] In this battle for George's soul, the safer alternative seemed to have won.

But conventionality held only a tenuous grip. A month later, a friend who was also on a tight budget suddenly left Princeton to ship as a sailor and see the world. That "stirred up what I think must be an inherent wanderlust in me to a dangerous degree—Lord how I wanted to go with him." The daring of his grandfather and of Harry Kemp beckoned him. He was, he told himself, "young, godless," held back by neither a girl nor ambition. Out there shimmered "a world of energy and curiosity." In a pattern repeated throughout his extra-long life, Kennan apprehended his future as dim and short. He should seize the moment while the world remained "colorful and romantic." Within two years, "it will all be drab and meaningless—now is the time to see it." "Penniless and friend-less" seemed "the only way to tackle it." Unconventionality, whether personified by Kemp or by his departed friend, seemed ascendant. Then the heavy hand of conventionality: "But I wouldn't go. I have too much feeling for Father."[108]

A year later, in 1924, he did venture out into a still "colorful and ro-mantic" world—during a summer trip to Europe. Neither "friendless" nor totally "penniless," George benefited from the journey. Neverthe-less, his "feeling for Father," juxtaposed against the latter's inadequate feelings for him, created unnecessary difficulties. The balance sheet of George's inheritance income, about which he knew little, backdropped his adventure.

Though George's income had exceeded expenses every year previously, outlays in 1924 totaled $2,537.97, while income reached only $2,428.36. Kent as guardian had to advance his son's account $109.61, which he would recoup early in 1925. It remains pertinent that Kent, along with his wife and their son, Kent Jr., were living at 309 Cambridge Avenue while he toted up these figures. They had summered on Nagawicka Lake. George's inheritance income covered not only one-quarter of the property taxes on this real estate (the other three-quarters were paid with inheritance money still held for the three Kennan sisters) but also one-fourth the cost of a new roof, and one-fourth of the money for decorating and painting, plumbing repairs, ice, gravel, and other needs. Kent also charged to George's account $400 for the trip to Europe, $1 for the birth certificate for his passport, and—this proved contentious— two American Express Money Orders, for $101.75 and $136.71, sent to his son in Europe.

George kept a journal of his European adventure. Three themes permeate the ninety-six pages of this record. First was money. Finances immediately became tight because he had generously offered to cover the expenses of his impoverished classmate, Constantine Nicholas Michaelas Messolonghitis, whose "uninhibited Greek hedonism was a good foil to my tense Presbyterian anxieties."[109] Though not Anglo-Saxon, the friend qualified as Princetonian. On the trip George grew increasingly anxious about having enough money to eat, to treat the dysentery he contracted, and to make it back home. In Italy, he resolved to go to jail if necessary rather than appeal to his father for further funds.

After sleeping in Central Park to save money, George and Constantine secured third-class passage on the RMS *Berengaria*. The fare, at $97.50 each, not including visas and tips, ate almost half of their meager stash.

Kennan was maturing at a time when racism pervaded American society. Venturing now outside his bubble of largely "Nordic" Milwaukee,

St. John's, and Princeton, he casually—indeed, gleefully—tossed off slurs that make the phrase "ethnic prejudice" seem like a whitewash.

Aboard ship, he exclaimed, "My God! We are with a bunch of deportees! Of all the scurvy, seedy, filthy, low-down, diseased, wrecked, ignorant, miserable human beings that God ever made a bad job on, these wretches hold down first place." Then, for some 250 words packed into a single sentence, he shoveled scorn and contempt in such heaps that he caricatured himself. To be sure, George was consciously honing his skill at descriptive writing and attempting humor. He was also showing how fully he had absorbed Princeton's dictum on distinguishing between those who did and did not belong, whether in the college, American society or the bowels of the *Berengaria*. Exercising a haughtiness worthy of Ivy eating club, he recorded: "There is a one-eyed man; there is some dark-skinned devil in a turban who grins unceasingly; . . . there is a bearded, consumptive old devil who looks like Santa Claus out of a job in Constantinople; there is an infernal Hunyak . . . with hair like a mop & a mouth like a cavern & bla-a-a-a-s, idiotically, under the impression that he is rendering a native song; . . . there are at least a hundred spaggettis [*sic*] who all look alike, with long brown mustaches & several layers of dirt. . . ." On he ranted, until finally coming to "two respectable, civilized, American female school teachers, who don't associate with the vulgars, & to whom Nick & I hope to address ourselves if we can summon the courage."[110]

As for discouraging communication with these lesser beings, Kennan deployed "true Princeton snobbery." He prided himself on having mastered a disciplining behavior that had humiliated him back on his first day at Princeton. The technique entailed "glowering angrily at the culprit by way of preparation, then sticking the main blow by a choice bit of frigid & conclusive civility & finally capping the operation by a return to the pose of wearied indifference."[111]

Landing at Southampton, England, on July 2, "We got quite a shock! The taxis, all following the left-hand side of the street, are the most antiquated, fantastic, ancient hacks I ever imagined." Coming from Prohibition-era America, the boys found every third emporium a saloon, with "some long rigmarole printed on its white plaster." Heading toward London, they took trains and hitched rides, including "in a sort of dog cart" driven by a farmer's wife. George appreciated the pretty waitress at the Express Dairy, who "knew enough to bring great big glasses of water" and was kind enough to "overlook an item or two for us on the bill." They would have to "get a job somehow, despite the unemployment, for we have very little money left above our passage home." They soon spent that reserve. Bereft of funds but not a sense of humor, George irreverently prayed,

> Dear God, who got us in this town
> Without a solitary crown
> For Christ's sake, get us back again
> And make it snappy, God—Amen.[112]

The boys then resolved to "move on to the Continent & to hell with finances." They mused about hitching down to Marseilles and making the U.S. consul there send them home. They found Paris impressive: "It has all the magnificent distances of Washington, the boulevards of Philadelphia, the metropolitan freedom & gaiety of New York (but more so), the time-honored mellowness of London."[113]

Even as Kennan took in Paris, Princeton retained its grip. He was thinking about writing an essay on "'Princeton Democracy.'" He pondered, "What causes the super-sensitiveness which underlies Princeton's stratified society? Is this stratification a good thing? On what is it based?" Continuing this long-distance jaunt down Nassau Street, he sketched an essay about how Princeton had changed from the "'golden nineties.' Has the 'glory that was Princeton' died away?" He arrived at the summer's "pet generality," a dictum that underscored his undiluted Darwinism: "The only virtue is strength, & the only fault weakness."[114]

One evening, George and Constantine treated themselves to a drink of cognac at a fancy bar, then a horse-taxi ride up the Champs-Élysées to the Arc de Triomphe, "a damn fool luxury for two individuals who are just six days from starvation." Then, on July 26, George's oldest sister, Fran, whom he had written from London, came to the rescue with $100 wired through American Express. She assured him, "Don't be afraid to cable Father for money; he is willing to send you all you need." George was not buying it. He imagined that his father, instead, had "gritted his teeth, boiled with rage, & assured her he would send me all I needed." His sister "couldn't have meant better; she couldn't have done worse." The son was so intimidated by this projection of his father's wrath that he predicted that "it will be some time" before he dared visit 309 Cambridge Avenue again. All this anxiety when, in fact, the income on George's inheritance still showed a positive balance.

Moving on to Genoa, the boys hoped to work their way back to America. "If there's anything in this world more discouraging than trying to get a job on a boat I have yet to find it." When they appealed to the U.S. consul to help, he told them they had to wire home for money. "When we go broke we'll go to jail. The consul will then kindly offer to advance the money for a wire; and we, I at any rate, refuse to wire for money." That led to the question of whether the consul had to send them home, "or can he let us stay in jail as long as possible?" Desperate for money to get home, George finally wired his father, but as of July 30, remained unsure whether the funds would arrive "this week (or any other week, for that matter)." Wandering around the city, they talked with some Italian military sentries and exchanged American cigarettes for a canteen of cold water. "They were a coarse, rude, sloppy bunch. But we had a good time talking with them." Through a mix of pidgin English and Italian, the soldiers got across that "they didn't like Italy nor Mussolini, and that they were all coming to America as soon as they might have a chance."[115]

On August 5, "I sent home a cable for money which set me back more than half of our worldly funds." The stress was getting to him. "I had some very terrible & weird dreams not of the usual kind & woke up very much depressed. I dreamed of the family & pondered about it all." Retaining only shards of the vision, he knew only "that it was very sad." The "only possible explanation" for some dreams, he decided, was "some kind of mental telepathy."[116]

He was also suffering "intestinal trouble from this Italian food, & tonight I was really sick—had to spend 4 of our few lire on some castor oil." Despite it all, he had resolved "to be more equable in temper & disposition, by restraining myself when I find myself too congenially inclined, as well as otherwise." By August 8, however, he was "despairing over our financial condition & worrying over my physical condition, which seems to be with me for good, & which is, I suppose, dysentery, or something like that, caused by bad water. Nick kindly informs me that people die from it."[117] Kennan had contracted amoebic dysentery and was suffering loss of blood and high fever.[118] Relapses would trouble him for years.

That day, $130 from his father finally arrived. They hurried by train to Boulogne-sur-Mer in France, where they boarded the SS *Veendam* for the voyage to New York.

George and Constantine's excellent adventure ended as it had begun, with tight money and ample pluck. They walked off the ship with $2.25 each, the proceeds of a British pound they had saved and exchanged on the boat. George decided to "strike out for Schenectady & get some money from Connie," his sister. Subway fare through New York City, a streetcar to Hastings-on-Hudson, and lunch brought him down to $1.60. He hitched to Albany, arriving at about 9:00 P.M. Then a train and a streetcar to Schenectady. He finally found Connie's bungalow at around midnight. She "pretended to be real glad to see me." The next day, after his sister civilized him with "a haircut, a shave, and a pair of garters," he took the trolley to Albany. There he boarded "a terrible old tub by the name of *Fort Orange*" for the trip to New York City. "Here ended, by exhaustion, the account of the European trip of George F. Kennan."[119] Although the journey did little to mitigate George's ethnic prejudices, it did broaden his perspective and give him a taste for foreign travel. Then followed his final year at Princeton.

"I am qualified only to play in an orchestra," a daunted Kennan feared as graduation neared. Yet by 1933, only eight years later, he had risen farther and faster in the Department of State than anyone in his age cohort. He snared the dream job of helping the first U.S. ambassador to the Soviet Union establish formal diplomatic relations.

Although Kennan tended to play it down, connections helped launch his career. His international law professor at Princeton, P. M. Brown, "with whom I have quite a high standing," knew officials in the State Department and had served there himself. The Kennans' Milwaukee neighbor, Uncle Edward Frost, assured George that he would enjoy "re-markably excellent 'pull'" with Frost's friend who ranked as assistant secretary of state. One of the under-secretaries was a fellow alumnus of Key and Seal Club. Finally, George's father knew, probably from his tes-tifying on the income tax amendment years earlier, Senator Cordell Hull of Tennessee, who in 1933 would become President Franklin D. Roosevelt's secretary of state.[120]

————

As George advanced into adulthood, he saw himself as bearing traits passed down from his forebears. He believed he had inherited from his father a passion for detailed investigation and scholarship. He also bore some of the anguish of this "shy and unhappy man." Sharing the same Feb-ruary 16 birth date and a name with the elder George Kennan opened for George a connection that would deepen as he discovered other paral-lels in their lives, including a fascination with Russia. Kennan might have claimed that his later comfort with elites stemmed from his mother's "Victorian gentility . . . quite equal in its dignity, and really in culture, to the New England families." Also in the upper class, at least that of Milwau-kee, was the James family. George believed that he looked much like his Uncle Alfred Farragut, emphasizing "I always admired him greatly."[121] He did not say the same about his own father. Both the unconventional and conventional poles of George's personality could take inspiration from the Harry-Kemp-to-corporate-tycoon life story of his maternal grandfather, Alfred James, the sailor who rose to insurance company president.

Although the death of his mother, the distance maintained by his father, and his stepmother's difficulty in understanding boys all contrib-uted to the emotional neediness of young George, the James family, his sister Jeanette, and Cousin Grace helped fill the gap. Though successful at St. John's and at Princeton, Kennan in his first two decades did not display the driving ambition that would characterize the rest of his life. That striving, while foreshadowed in his admiration for the Jameses, would emerge in full force only with the stimulus in Washington of the State Department and the Hard family.

SEEKING RUSSIA FROM GERMANY, 1926–1933

HOW GEORGE F. KENNAN spent a vacation in the spring of 1931 reveals much about why he rose so rapidly in the State Department. Fueling this ascent were his fierce intelligence and work ethic. These traits emerged in the late 1920s as George responded to the simultaneous challenges of a serious, demanding job and an equally serious, though disastrous, romance. The rising star received a boost from ambitious mentors, men who hitched Kennan's talents to their own agendas. He failed, however, at winning over his prospective father-in-law, the nationally prominent journalist William Hard.

From 1929–1931, Kennan studied Russian language, history, and culture at the University of Berlin under the auspices of a State Department program to train specialists. His local boss was the consul general in Berlin, George S. Messersmith. Messersmith had convinced the penny-pinching State Department to triple the size of his staff.[1] This empire builder aimed to outflank both the legation at Riga, Latvia, Washington's traditional listening post on Soviet Russia, and the U.S. embassy in Berlin by positioning the Berlin consulate as the conduit in relations between America and Russia. Messersmith asked Kennan to devote his March–April 1931 semester break to two official research projects and a third, more covert effort.

Guaranteed to turn heads in the State Department, Kennan's reports zeroed in on key geostrategic and ideological worries. In only weeks,

George completed an eighty-six-page despatch analyzing a pilgrimage to Moscow by German industrialists and their tentative deal to increase exports of machinery to the Soviet Union. As Kennan and Messersmith understood, Washington's perennial nightmare was that Germany might link its technological prowess with Russia's natural resources. That would forge an industrial behemoth that could dominate the world, regardless of whether its ideology was communist, capitalist, or some mix. Kennan's April 21 report, prominently bearing his name, won "a rating of EXCELLENT" from the State Department, which judged the analysis important enough to circulate to the Commerce and Treasury departments.[2]

Seven days later, Messersmith sent off Kennan's second vacation report, which addressed fears of Communist subversion at home. Sifting through an array of sources, Kennan identified the names, statements, and activities of many of the workers and engineers who had abandoned Depression-wracked America to help build a socialist paradise in Russia. Pointing out that under U.S. law Americans who pledged allegiance to another nation could lose their citizenship, Kennan urged the State Department not to renew the passports of such turncoats, to turn a deaf ear to any pleas for assistance, and to prohibit their return to the United States. Though this recommendation met pushback from the State Department on technical grounds, Kennan, still only twenty-seven years old, had again made his voice heard in that vast bureaucracy.[3] His third, more shadowy project initiated what would become a decades-long familiarity with covert activities.[4]

The marathon revealed much about Kennan at this early stage of his career. He was not good at relaxing on vacations. Instead, he would drive himself until he collapsed. Typically, he then sought refuge in a hospital staffed with caring nurses. His budding interests extended into economics, ideology, and geostrategy. Intense in everything he did, Kennan was tackling Russian with instruction both at the university and from private tutors, all of them Russian émigrés. In his spare time he read Russian literature, socialized with a Russian family, and attended theater and other cultural events produced by Russians who had fled Soviet rule. He perfected the pronunciation and absorbed the

George F. Kennan
ST. JOHN'S '21

GRADUATE OF PRINCETON
UNIVERSITY 1925

Foreign Service School at Washington after one year of study.

He ranked 6th in a class of 110 and was selected for immediate duty, and was appointed Vice Consul at Hamburg, Germany. Then shifted to the Consul General's Office at Geneva during the World Economic Conference and the Naval Arms Conference. Aug 1927 served as Executive Officer for the Berlin Consulate General. After this assignment he served as Vice Consul at Hamburg, and then to Tallinn, Esthonia. Promoted to the position of Secretary of Embassy in Riga. 1929 he was selected to study for three years in the Orientalisches Seminar in Berlin – a super-university for study of Near-East problems. 1930 he has been promoted to the position of Consul (unassigned) and is said to be the youngest officer of that rank in the service.

Cast of "Nerves"

Winners of First Place in Dramatic Tournament at Madison

CAST

TED HILL, *Captain, U. S. Air Service*		Rosebush, R.
BOB THATCH JACK COATES	*First Lieutenants*	Fifield, F. T. Bossert, C.
B. C. LANGSTON ARTHUR GREEN PAUL OVERMAN FRANK SMITH	*Second Lieutenants*	Johnston, M. B. Wright, L. H. Stearns, H. S. Weitzman, J. H.
ROOK, *a mess attendant*		Olsen, S.
AN ORDERLY		Peters, I. G.

FIGURE 11. St. John's alumni magazine in the early 1930s. (Courtesy of Princeton University Library.)

perspective of upper-class refugees who mourned the passing of the pre-1917 order.

Kennan was pulled toward Russia by both conventional ambition and unconventional, indeed mystical, attraction. Russian enticed him as "a natural language, in which words sounded as they ought to sound . . . as though one had known it in some dead past and as though the learning of it was some sort of rediscovery."[5] Much of this Russian he learned in German, a language in which he also immersed himself to the point where his dreams became trilingual. Despite the allure of Russian culture, Kennan despised the Soviet government. He mustered sympathy for neither idealistic American radicals seeking a better future in Soviet Russia nor, at this stage, with the Soviet experiment. The enterprising young man grew close with Messersmith, much as he later bonded with other father figures, including Ambassador William C. Bullitt in Moscow, Chargé d'Affaires Alexander Kirk in Berlin, Secretary of the Navy James Forrestal, and Secretary of State George C. Marshall. Indeed, Kennan would continue rising only so long as he had such pull from above.

Years before reaching that plateau in the late 1940s, however, George was painfully dropped, not only by a hoped-for mentor, William Hard, and his accomplished wife, Anne, but also by their daughter, Eleanor, George's fiancée. Making the breakup still worse was the loss of a precious memento from his mother.

ELEANOR HARD

George first met Eleanor in 1926 while in Washington studying for the Foreign Service exam. (He would score 84 out of a 100 on the written and oral examination.) Candidates, decked out in striped trousers, wing-tipped collars, and spats, were expected to circulate in Georgetown's high society, just as they would do in foreign capitals if they made the grade as junior diplomats. Eleanor's parents, nationally known journalists, hosted such luminaries as Senate Foreign Relations Committee chair William E. Borah of Idaho. While George tended to hang back at parties, Eleanor, "not inhibited at all," would urge him, "Come along, come along, don't be so shy; come and meet these people." "This was very good for me," he would later affirm. At one party Eleanor pushed George to meet Joseph C. Grew, a relative of the hosts, undersecretary of state, and head of the Foreign Service oral examining panel. "I've always thought I got in because" of that exclusive gathering, Kennan later recounted.[6] Once again, connections helped smooth his path.

George's feelings for Eleanor "struck deep" for powerful reasons.[7] She was beautiful, popular, and a catch coveted by competitors. (She was considered the "second best ballroom dancer in Washington," Eleanor would later boast.) Sexual attraction between them retained the potency of potential. "Personal purity stood out as a cardinal virtue," George much later remarked in reference to his fiancée. Eleanor would remember that "since George and I were even to the right of most young people, we also preserved the man/woman psychological relationships of the time." Eleanor's tightly knit family also appealed to George. Like the Jameses, the Hards displayed the high achieving, socially at ease sensibility that George's truncated, riven family painfully lacked. A successful journalist, William Hard had started out as a muckraker, penned the "Weekly Washington Letter" for the *Nation*, and had authored five books, including a campaign biography of his friend, Herbert Hoover. Just as he had with Uncle Alfred Farragut, George looked up to William Hard as "a fine man" with "a striking personality." Eleanor would remember that her father ranked as the "first nationally known political commentator on radio, rather like [the 1960s–1970s icon Walter] Cronkite. My mother, too, was a successful professional, publishing both fiction & nonfiction in national mags." Finally, George pursued Eleanor because he was looking for a wife. Before courting her, "he had already proposed to a very attractive young Washington woman," Eleanor later testified.[8]

Seeking feminine succor in a romantic partner marked a departure for George. He had earlier reacted to a slight fever by checking himself into a hospital. That afforded "the only good time since I've been in Washington," he wrote Jeanette. He enthused about his red-headed caregiver from Tennessee, who appealed as "a good nurse despite her extreme youth."[9] Cheered by her "extreme devilment and mischievous energy," he soon recovered from the illness.

With George, Eleanor played the more mature, savvy, take-charge partner. Kennan welcomed her role and, significantly, he interpreted it as verging on maternal. Even decades later, he grew wistful in recalling how "Eleanor took me in hand, showed me how to overcome my over-sensitiveness . . . showed me how my own intelligence and delicacy of feeling could take me far." Through her, he realized "for the first time that I could beat the people I had always envied at their own game." Escaping the fetters of the odd house and odd family back in Milwau-kee, "I could become both respected and powerful—I, too, might some-day make the very pillars of the State Department tremble, as I walked through the ringing corridors." Precisely two decades later, Kennan would indeed become "respected and powerful," with an office next door to the secretary of state and with a mandate to plan the entirety of U.S. foreign policy. Even though he absorbed Eleanor's lesson about pushiness, he lost her.[10]

In 1928, Eleanor's "truly loving" though "ruthless" mother concluded that "GFK would never amount to anything." She destroyed all of George's letters. The mother also "devoted months to undermining our relationship," Eleanor later recounted. That it took months to quash the young woman's feelings for her fiancé, especially when he was far away in Europe on Foreign Service duty, suggests that there was something of substance to destroy.[11]

The breakup that March was excruciating for George. He would re-member his would-be father-in-law as sneering, "Go back to your tea-cups and fancy pants and safe obscurity, and let's hear no more of this."[12] Further humiliating was Hard's cavalier dismissal of the younger man's ambitions as a writer. George had asked the journalist to read an essay he had labored over for months. He had expected a response such as "'you have some promise, but it's got these and these faults.'" Hard, however, never bothered even to look at George's work. Even crueler, Eleanor blithely told George that she had lost his emerald ring, a me-mento from his sainted mother. "That was quite a blow to him," Jeanette remembered many years later.[13] Kennan felt betrayed and bereft.

Nevertheless, still under the spell of what the Hards represented, he made a melodramatic, "last reluctant obeisance" to these "cool, derisive deities who have taken without compensation the best two years of my life." The Hards loomed as "the gods of my own personal Washington." Memories of this time "sear like fire, for in every one of them lies the glow of failure!"[14]

Despite the humiliation, George clung to the philosophy and lifestyle of the Hards. What at Princeton he had labeled "conventional," he now defined as "bürgerlich" or "conservative individualism." This orientation dominated Milwaukee, Princeton, and "the drawing-rooms of north-west Washington." The polar opposite of this convention was bohemian, Harry-Kempian, dreamy "unconventionality." Carried to its Kennanish extreme, the latter meant the "renunciation of all individualistic hopes" and accepting the penalties of being "a queer duck." Unsure which of these two outlooks to choose, Kennan envied the Hards for smoothly integrating both of them. In terms of unconventional credentials, "Mrs. Hard breathed [women's] emancipation," while Mr. Hard's muck-raking made him seem like a "Red." As for Eleanor, she "wrote poetry and patronized queer people." And yet the Hards also ranked "among the very high priests" of conservative individualism. Their conventional ideals represented "America, firm as a rock, amid a world of sin, good, Protestant America, hard-fibered, efficient, moral—accepting material prosperity as the just due of a spotless conscience. On this rock one built one's life." He had internalized the metaphor: to fit in with Eleanor and her family, "one made one's self hard and cold, as the rock was hard and cold." He believed he needed Eleanor to lead him toward success and happiness. He needed her also to ease the loneliness gnawing at him since childhood.

Although Kennan decades later would claim that his "melodramat-ics" over the March 1928 breakup had lasted just three days, he suffered much longer.[15] In the November election pitting the Democratic Al Smith against the Republican Herbert Hoover, whose campaign biog-raphy had been authored by William Hard, George for the first time in his life worked up "real emotion" for a candidate—Smith. He acknowl-edged that despite Hoover's ability, "personal bitterness against his chief backers in Washington"—in other words, the Hard family—"probably plays a large part in my opinions."[16] Five years later, by which time

George himself was long since married, the hurt lingered still. News of Eleanor's wedding flooded him with self-pity. He lashed himself with the humiliating thought that William Hard had forgotten about George's engagement to his daughter. The Hards "all lead a very full, exciting life, with a lot of loose ends which they never have time to collect, and many things which would play large parts in other people's lives, they are gone and forgotten with them in a few days."[17]

In trying to tie up his own "loose ends," Kennan at first swerved toward renunciation. In September 1928, he despaired: "I will probably never be vastly admired; I shall never achieve personal dignity; my wife . . . will doubtless be in no sense ideal"; and "far from becoming wealthy, I will probably effectively lose what money I have." Though never totally escaping this dour perspective, he bounced back. Even when downcast, he retained confidence in his "undeveloped strength, and many potentialities." As to how and where he was to exercise this potential, "I myself have no idea."[18]

LEARNING RUSSIAN

Back in November 1927, Kennan had informed the State Department that he was resigning for "the most urgent and unalterable personal reasons." He did not explain to the department his need to make enough money to support his soon-to-be wife. Department officials surmised the problem was health. Kennan had failed his physical examination in 1926 when applying to the Foreign Service because of low albumin, an indicator of chronic inflammation. He managed to pass a subsequent test. George's superiors noted that "physically he is not very strong and gives the impression of being rather delicate."[19] Nonetheless, not wanting to lose him, the department asked Kennan to reconsider—and then held out a golden opportunity. He was offered three years of fully paid graduate study at a European university in one of the critical languages of the day: Chinese, Japanese, Arabic, or Russian. After being dropped by Eleanor, he accepted. In a nod to the first George Kennan, he chose Russian. Candidates for the program had to undergo a probationary period as consular officials before launching their language study.

From mid-1928 to late 1933, Kennan alternated between Germany and the Baltic countries of Estonia and Latvia. He did his consular work first in Berlin, then in Tallinn (Estonia) and in Riga (Latvia). In the fall of 1929, he began formal study of Russian language, history, and literature at Friedrich Wilhelm University in Berlin. From 1931 to 1933, he served at the Riga listening post on the Soviet Union.

Although still in his probationary period, Kennan in Berlin and in Tallinn threw himself into studying Russian on his own. He so quickly mastered the basics that in October 1929 he would test into the third semester of the four-semester program in Berlin, and this at the head of the class. Even without Eleanor there to "[take] me in hand," he was on track toward becoming "both respected and powerful." (Decades later, Anne Hard would ask her daughter "if she had made a mistake— she was utterly surprised by George's success.")[20] Nevertheless, Kennan being Kennan, he could not escape the lure of the "unconventional," whether that option figured as exiting the State Department to become an expatriate novelist, escaping on a river barge as a deckhand, or exploring the mysteries he glimpsed in the East Prussian twilight, sniffed along the Baltic coast, or heard in the "music" of Hamburg.[21]

"The Russian is going very well," he wrote from Tallinn in October 1928. The language was not easy to master, George explained, since the grammar outdid even German in complexity. Verbs could take as many as fourteen cases, and words could extend to twelve or more syllables. Throughout his language study, Kennan depended on émigrés who had fled the despised Bolsheviks. They would impart values as well as vocabulary. His first tutor, a former czarist army officer, "is very Russian indeed. He loses himself entirely in whatever he happens to be doing at the moment, is a born actor and a born liar . . . is always late and is irresistibly likable." With a light workload as consul, he devoted most of his time to Russian. "I have procured a very fine radio set with which I get Leningrad just as clear as though the speaker were in the room. Moscow comes in more faintly, and I have to sit close to the loudspeaker." He believed that the intricacies of pronunciation made it important to learn Russian by listening as well as reading.[22]

FIGURE 12. George at the Estonian border with the Soviet Union in the late 1920s. (Courtesy of Princeton University Library.)

By January 1929, nine months before he began formal language study in Berlin, Kennan was already progressing with private lessons, living for a time with a Russian family, and spending every spare moment listening to and studying Russian. "I read my Tolstoi now without any difficulty, and I even understood the Russian theatre last night, for the first time," he boasted.[23]

His probation completed, Kennan in October 1929 enrolled at Friedrich Wilhelm University in Berlin. "The Russian course at the Orientalisches Seminar is a terrifically hard course," he informed his family, especially because he was skipping ahead to the fourth semester. He was also reading Russian history on his own, studying Russian literature with a private tutor, and taking supplementary language instruction with yet another tutor. The latter, formerly a famous sociology professor in St. Petersburg, survived as one of those "living tragedies" of the Russian émigré world. He eked out an existence in two "dark and miserable" rented rooms, "smoking vile cigarettes, and doing hack translations for a pittance which wouldn't keep a dog alive in America." Though his mind was slipping, "no amount of poverty can take away the rich, precise pronunciation." Nor was "the beauty of the words" impaired by the sentences trailing "off into an uncertain silence."

Immersed in his German/Russian world, Kennan withdrew completely from the Americans in Berlin and went for days without speaking any English.[24] When William and Anne Hard, in Berlin on a business trip, inquired at the U.S. embassy whether there was anybody here by the name of Kennan, the first officer could not think of anyone. Though the Hards succeeded in locating George through the consulate office, they probably also congratulated themselves on having nixed their daughter's engagement to such a nonentity.[25]

Kennan's weekly schedule:

Monday: 9:00 A.M. Russian language at the Orientalisches Seminar, where "I know quite a bit more than the rest of the class." 5:00 P.M. Lecture on Russian political economy at Hochschule für Politik.

Tuesday: 9:00 A.M. Orientalisches Seminar, then translating from German into Russian with the émigré professor. Afternoon, 2-hour seminar on Russian political economy at the Hochschule.

Wednesday: Private lesson "with a Russian woman who does her best to drill me into a mastery of the Russian accent."

Thursday: 9:00 Orientalisches Seminar, then translation with the émigré professor.

Friday: 9:00 Orientalisches Seminar, then tutor in Russian pronunciation.

Saturday: 2-hour lecture on twentieth century Russian history.

Sunday: Outings with Russian or German friends.

Piled atop all this was extensive homework.[26] For amusement, he indulged in "Russian music, films, & theatre. Tonight I am going to hear *Boris Godunov* for the third time."[27]

A GERMAN VIEW OF RUSSIA

Kennan viewed Russia from Germany's window onto the east. The German Teutonic Knights had colonized the Baltic region, and Germans had developed the Russian economy under the czars. He admired the aristocratic Baltic Germans of Estonia, still a formidable presence despite having lost most of their estates and privileges in the new, Slavic-dominated order. He saw these patricians as possessing "by far the bulk of the culture and breeding—possibly also of the ability" in the struggling new nation. Their resentment, plus the limitations of the "stupid, backward peasants," hobbled the government in Tallinn. Tellingly, Kennan in his unofficial correspondence usually referred to the Estonian capital by its German name, Reval.

Travels in the region reinforced his belief in German superiority. On the train to East Prussia to spend Christmas with German friends, he passed through Lithuania, where the sun gleamed "so beautifully on the snow-covered roofs of the peasant huts that one could almost forget the lice and the filth and the darkness which those huts concealed." Then, crossing into East Prussia, "Germany burst upon you with a suddenness that was almost incredible. A swarm of red-capped officials descended upon the car, checked everything from A to Z. A charwoman shook out the carpets and put much-needed towels in the washrooms. Our names, our baggage, our seats, our passports were carefully 'controlliert,' and in a jiffy we had become parts and parcels of the enormous and ponderous organization which is the German Empire." Moreover, "the speed with which our train was whisked away from the border into East Prussia— so noticeable after we had crawled all day across the Baltic countryside— seemed symbolic of German energy and intensity."[28]

He found in Germany "my second home. I know the people so well, and I have identified myself in so many ways with their culture and their way of thinking that their problems and their struggles become more or less mine as well, and I cannot remain the passive by-stander." He judged the dynamo "a Jekyll-Hyde sort of place—embodying the most dangerous and the most hopeful forces in human nature." How it worked out would shape "all European civilization."[29]

The culture of Weimar Germany during Kennan's residence there effervesced with creativity. Experimental form and perspective enlivened the architecture and craft of the Bauhaus movement, the plays of Bertolt Brecht, and the new modes of expression in film, music, and sexuality. As Kennan recognized, he was in the prime of his life and positioned at "the very vortex of the most intense intellectual and cultural currents of the world." Nevertheless, he suffered, especially on weekends, "a senselessness and a hopelessness and a boredom of infinite profundity."[30] For relief he turned not to Brecht, not to the unconventionality of Weimar, but rather to the ultraconventionality of Count von Bredow.

On many weekends and holidays, Kennan fled Berlin for the East Prussian estate of Ferdinand von Bredow, a nobleman whose heritage traced back to 1251. A die-hard officer from the Great War, von Bredow would be slain in June 1934 for trying to set up a right-wing alternative to Adolf Hitler. In explaining his fondness for the count, Kennan revealed his comfort with aristocracy and his priority on personal rectitude. In bearing and perspective, von Bredow appeared "the true Prussian Junker," easy to condemn for his "militarism, ruthlessness, and general truculence." He proclaimed that the Poles "must be wiped out of existence," and the French "deserve undying hate." Although George had warned von Bredow that a war of revenge meant suicide for Germany, "there was no altering his mind" in welcoming such a rematch. And yet, despite his "blood-thirstiness in political life, this count is one of the kindest men I have ever met, personally." As a lawyer before the war, he had often sided with the underdog. The men who had served under him "would still drop anything they were doing" to "undertake anything from murder to revolution on his behalf." Further, "he reads all the good liberal publications."[31] Like other powerful older men, the count took a shine to Kennan, even lending him his fur coat.[32]

What Kennan found especially appealing about von Bredow was the solidity of his domestic life. For the American homesick for his idealized Wisconsin past and still smarting from his humiliation by the Hards, the von Bredows offered an East Prussian version of the James clan. Like the Jameses, they helped satisfy his need for enveloping family. He often brought his girlfriend from Berlin, Charlotte Böhm, with whom he was briefly engaged. Stopping at the von Bredows on his way to Riga for Christmas in 1930, Kennan recorded in loving detail a scene that had grown familiar and dear. He found "the same ice-cold house with the pictures of the ancestors and the dowry-chests, the same impossible

FIGURE 13. George always enjoyed working outside.
(Courtesy of Princeton University Library.)

featherbed which refused to cover both feet and shoulders simultaneously . . . the same chauvinistic provincial newspapers . . . the same
complaints about the economic situation . . . the same little girls with
hair parted in the middle and braided pigtails hanging over each shoulder, the stout grandmother."[33]

In Riga, too, George had gravitated to German aristocrats. He spent a typical Sunday "with the German Minister, with whom I am becoming very well acquainted; Madame Schieman, wife of the editor of the leading German paper; and a German-Balt girl."[34] Though the weekly letters to his prudish father and stepmother never even hinted at romantic involvement, it seems that he preferred German women. He alluded to his "particular bond" with the German minister's daughter, his partner at all the parties. He was often a guest at their family dinners. When the daughter came to Berlin, he squired her to another "baronial estate not far from Bredow's place."[35] Kennan prized an invitation to the salon of "Madame de Nostiz, who is Berlin's leading diplomatic hostess and a niece of [President Paul von] Hindenburg. One meets a great many prominent people there."[36] While diplomatic duties required such socializing, it was toward German diplomats and journalists that Kennan gravitated. He would do much the same in Moscow after 1933.

Kennan's view of the Russians reflected not only his reading of their literature but also the orientalist assumptions imbibed from his German friends and in his Berlin seminars. He perceived in the Russian character the "childishness, the laziness, the gregariousness, the love of music and dancing and declaiming, the superstition, the imagination, and the loquaciousness" of people close to the earth. These qualities appealed to the "unconventional," Kempian side of his nature.[37] In the Russian soul Kennan would seek the mysteries and wonder that had led him as a child to believe that fairies populated Juneau Park in Milwaukee. For all its frustrating inefficiency, Russia offered a break from the disciplining efficiency of Germany.

MASTERING RUSSIAN

In March 1930, Kennan escaped the routine and gray skies of Berlin and East Prussia with a vacation on the French Riviera—spent at a Russian-run pension. Despite the ramshackle building, miserable food, and incompetence of the proprietor (the woman running the place, "like most Russians, [had] no practical common-sense)," he reveled in the atmosphere. Here in Menton was his "first opportunity to *live*, as it were, in Russian—that is, to talk about the food, the washing, the weather and the garden in the Russian language, without being interrupted by hearing other languages."[38]

In contrast to his former years, when funds appeared to be tight—and unlike subsequent years when money actually was tight—Kennan was living the life of a playboy. He bought a sporty Ford roadster, kept a maid, and subsidized an impoverished family of Russian émigrés. His apartment in a suburb of Berlin was "the nicest I've ever had: three rooms with the most spacious and modern bath-room attached." His large bedroom looked out on the garden while his living room, furnished in dark oak, featured "a very imposing desk, huge carved book-case, and grandmother's clock." A stable three blocks away enabled Kennan to ride horseback every day and out into the country on weekends. The maid brought his breakfast and then a mechanic would deliver his car, washed and greased, so that he could drive into the city.[39] All this was easily affordable on Kennan's annual salary, which climbed to $2,750 in 1929. That sum matched the earnings of the president of Latvia, he noted to his family, "so you can see I rank right up with the Latvian Rockefellers."[40] The next year his pay rose to $3,500.[41]

Such nonstop activity stressed George's precarious health. His most painful ailment was herpes zoster, shingles, which would plague him periodically throughout his life. With good reason, Norwegians called it "hell's fire," "the tortures of the damned," Kennan reported. The agony already extended to "a couple square feet" of his body and was spreading."[42] Relaxing remained difficult.

Typical was an abortive vacation when he felt "so run-down physically and yet so keyed-up nervously" that he could neither work nor play. Unable to ease up, he collapsed. He suffered "a complete physical break-down" and checked himself into a sanatorium in Berlin. This turned out to be "the best thing that could have happened, because . . . it was impossible for me to get any rest of my own accord." "I am very contented here," he wrote from the hospitals, surrounded no doubt by attentive, white-uniformed nurses. "I lead the laziest sort of life, and read at leisure in my 2,000-page volume of Tolstoy's 'War & Peace.'" A month later, he confessed to having lost ten to fifteen pounds since he was last home. Clothes hung on him like sacks. Having never completely recovered from the amoebic dysentery contracted in Genoa years earlier, he now reported "something definitely wrong with my stomach, quite possibly gastric ulcers." Then he suffered another severe cold or grippe.[43]

The pattern persisted. In January 1931, he calculated that since entering the Foreign Service four and a half years previously, "the nearest thing I have had to a real [vacation] was 9 days in a rotten Russian pension on the Riviera." He wrote this while on still another failed break: shivering in a "frigid little room" in a Swiss hotel, "with a raging cold, and a fur coat on for warmth," sneezing, and studying Russian.[44]

Through it all Kennan was mastering Russian. After frenzied study for his final examination from the Orientalisches Seminar—"I am going to have to work harder than I have ever worked in my life," he predicted—he passed with flying colors in July 1930. The examination entailed translating without error a speech by Stalin from Russian to German, then writing, without any dictionary or reference book, an essay on either the "rayonisation of the USSR" or the "the Russian agrarian structure at the time of the Bolshevik Revolution." For his Russian history seminar, he had to deliver two lectures, "both of which, to my own astonishment, were extremely successful." Impressed with his achievements, the State Department promoted Kennan to full consul, making him "by far the youngest man to hold that rank."[45]

"The Russian language comes so naturally (if not easily)," he boasted to an old friend. Moreover, Russian culture, "with its striking points of resemblance to the American, has been a sort of a God-send to me in an intellectual way," particularly as "an exit from the intellectual cul-de-sac into which I had fallen in Germany."[46] Kennan would cling to this fond belief about the supposed affinities between American and Russian culture even during the Cold War.

While focusing on pre-1917 Russia study had rescued Kennan from a dead end, that frontier was also closing as he neared completion of the program. What could now absorb his energies? Though eager to move on to learning about contemporary Russia, he faced roadblocks. When he informed Robert F. Kelley, chief of the Eastern European Division of the State Department and the director of his studies, that a German professor had invited him to collaborate on a study of post-1917 Russia, Kelley warned him not to deviate from the earlier period.[47] Kennan encountered another no when the State Department, citing the nonrecognition policy, denied him permission to visit Russia to research his beloved writer, Anton Chekhov.[48]

Kennan eagerly accepted, then, Messersmith's suggestion that he labor through his spring vacation investigating German efforts to expand exports of heavy machinery. Russia's pressing need for machines to fulfill its Five-Year Plan for industrialization matched, at least in theory, the imperative of Depression-wracked Germany and America for putting the unemployed to work producing such equipment. In the wake of the mission of German industrialists to Moscow in February, Kennan pored through dozens of German and Russian language publications and interviewed leading German industrialists and other experts. His lengthy report both reassured those worried about a dangerous German-Russian connection and cautioned those hoping to boost America's own exports to the Soviet Union. A massive surge in sales would need to overcome Germany's difficulties in financing the trade as well as the Soviets' problems in forgetting their hostility toward the capitalists. Kennan held a similarly ideological view in his study of the supposed disloyalty of Americans working in the Soviet Union. His viewpoint would become more nuanced a few years later when he finally got to go to Russia.[49]

In addition to the two aforementioned studies, Kennan also joined with Messersmith in a covert investigation, apparently focused on Moscow's efforts against anti-Soviet Russian émigrés or with pro-Soviet Americans in Berlin. In a letter to his family on March 19, 1931, Kennan referred to having two distinct areas of work for Messersmith. The second was the "reports which I know are going to receive more attention from the powers-that-be [in Washington] than most consular reports receive." Indeed, he expected that the splash "will have considerable influence on my subsequent position in the service."[50]

This work entailed not open research and analysis, but rather a secret operation "completely on my own with a definite job to do" that could be "done well or terribly botched." He needed "strong nerves, mature judgment and social ability." What Kennan actually did remains shadowy. Nevertheless, this work marked his first encounter with covert activity, an arena in which he would play a key role in Lisbon during World War II and in Washington at the onset of the Cold War.[51] Despite the temporary rush of a packed schedule, Kennan's underlying ennui persisted.

CRISIS AND MARRIAGE

"I am approaching a crisis somewhere in the bottom of my Kennanish character," George confided to Jeanette. "I feel an increasing apathy and aversion to most of the things that have attracted and excited me . . . for the last three or four years." Moreover, "one by one my personal contacts with the Europeans are dropping off." Especially pertinent here was his disillusionment with the Kozhenikov family, Russian émigrés whom he had befriended and was subsidizing with some of his inheritance income. His friend's homosexuality, his patronizing of "hermaphrodite" dancers, the mother's incessant wailing, and perhaps also the daughter's schoolgirl crush on him were exhausting his patience. Although Kennan since childhood had habitually looked for secret, wondrous meanings in ordinary things, he now decided that "I have been looking for things, in the ideas and in the people, which are not there." Moreover, "science," by which he meant psychological theory, had taught him "what a fruitless thing is [striving] for individual happiness."[52]

Kennan resolved to get back to his roots in America. He felt his "puritan origin rising in relentless revolt against the non-puritan influences of the last few years." He dramatized his narrative as "'The Death of the Hypocrite,'—The story of the man who tried to sell his soul and couldn't."[53]

Much of this *Sturm und Drang* arose from unhappiness with the life of a bachelor. The tall, handsome, blue-eyed, smart American with the glamorous job, snazzy Ford roadster, and ample spending money attracted women interested in flirtation, love affairs, and more serious ties. His dutiful, weekly letters to "Family"—that is, to his prudish stepmother as well as to his father and teenage half-brother—remained conspicuously silent about such encounters. George's diary and his correspondence with Jeanette in 1931 reveal a litany of frustrated love affairs and then a sudden marriage on September 11.

DECEMBER 31–JANUARY 1: Costumed in a white Hussar's uniform "with a beaver cap and Wilhelm II moustache," flirting with his "friend Trudy (who is the only woman I should whole-heartedly like to marry, but who is unfortunately already married)." Half-Latvian, half-Russian Trudy, "completely drunk and sweeter than ever (isn't that enough to love a woman for?), talking to me in Russian with the 'thee' and 'thou'"; then "Trudy, leading me up to the buffet table and saying, with a sweeping gesture: 'George, all, all is thine,'" with the consequent "black looks of her husband."[54]

JANUARY 3: Walking along the beach near Riga "with my Russian girl, Renata, who is the nicest of all my girls and naive enough to love me."[55]

MARCH 8: Mourning his "youth sliding gently but firmly away without the compensation of either vice or virtue." While dancing with a woman at a Swiss resort, George's eyes filled with sentimental tears. That softness provoked the disciplining voice of a male authority figure, an internalized Headmaster Smythe or William Hard. "'Do you think [such crying] is manly and proper? Don't you think, really, that there is something unnatural, something positively abnormal'" in such weeping? "'Don't you see that you really don't want a woman at all, as a woman? That you only want a mother to hold your head on her shoulder and dry your dancing-tears and flatter your delicate little egotism and tend to your little physical necessities for you.'" In admonishing himself, he revealed his fantasy of a "mother" who could, somehow, satisfy both his "physical necessities" and his childlike longings. This eroticized maternal figure would remain forever distant and elusive: "'You had better realize that mother is far away and that no one is ever going to understand you.'"[56]

MARCH 22: Meeting Annelise Sorensen, a twenty-year-old Norwegian, the daughter of a prosperous building supply merchant, living in Berlin in order to learn German and shorthand. Though they began dating, the relationship did not immediately become serious, at least for George. He failed to mention Annelise in a letter to Jeanette.

APRIL 28: Musing "perhaps I'll get religion. Perhaps I'll fall in love, for the first time in my young life. Or perhaps I'll get broken on the wheel, like Hemingway and others of the expatriates."

JULY 9: "Plagued by the knowledge that I ought to be getting married to someone or other, this summer, because I am thoroughly sick of a bachelor existence . . . but I don't see when I would ever find energy to pay much attention to a wife if I had one. I could never find time to court a wife, so there's not much I could do about it." Expecting a transfer to a different post, he hoped only that circumstances would enable him to get a cocker spaniel.

JULY 31: In just twenty-two days, that abstract "someone or other" whom he should marry if he could ever find the energy and time materialized into Annelise Sorensen, who displayed "the true Scandinavian simplicity," could remain "silent gracefully," and was "incredibly healthy and equable." "Even I don't make her nervous," he burbled. Moreover, "everyone seems to like her." Despite the enthusiasm, he had already identified a fault that would plague their relationship in later years. "She is neither brilliant nor witty," but, he hastened to add, "she is intelligent and well-educated." Though certainly intelligent, the young woman had not gone to university, and she would develop little interest in the intellectual pursuits that intrigued him.

The couple planned a wedding at her home in near Kristiansand, on the southern coast of Norway. She would go on ahead to break the news to her parents. He would follow a few weeks later and, in recognition of the suddenness of it all, devote a few weeks before the wedding to getting to know his new in-laws.

"We didn't know each other very well," Annelise later recounted. "I never told my parents how little I knew him." When George confided to her "that he was terribly worried about the United States," she "couldn't understand why he was so worried about his own country." Other countries "had so much [more] to worry about." Though the savvy young woman knew that the streets of America were not paved with gold, she appreciated that America boasted far greater wealth than Norway. In Norway, "a job was hard to come by." Though Annelise no doubt loved George, she had to have noticed that her future spouse held a steady, well-paying, prestigious, and indeed glamorous position. She may also have learned about his inheritance. In any case, she was eager to marry him. When her parents objected out of fear that she might go off to America and they would never see her again, "I finally just put my foot down and said that if I heard another sigh from my mother, I was going to scream. And I meant it."[57]

With Annelise already in Norway preparing for the wedding and with George still back in Berlin, the soon-to-be bride evidently worried about hanging on to her catch. Her fiancé had had many girlfriends. Berlin was filled with attractive women. How much holding power did their brief relationship command? Needing to fill out legal forms for the wedding, she admitted to him: "I don't even know when it is your birthday!"[58] Perhaps intending to spark some jealousy, she informed George about her "troubles. It was Leo who made them," she explained. They had been "partly engaged" before she had left for Germany. They had broken it off. "But when I came home, he fell in love with me again." Though she had told him about George, the rejected suitor "got quite crazy and would not give up hope."[59] In another letter, she hoped George would come soon. "I am quite sure about myself, dear, that I want to marry you and to be with you always."[60]

George did arrive in late August. After a family-oriented, traditional Norwegian wedding on September 11, 1931, and then a honeymoon, the couple set up housekeeping in Riga. With domestic necessities hard to come by in the impoverished nation, George asked Jeanette to ship them some necessities, including an electric toaster, nylon stockings, jugs of maple syrup, and two twin beds.

More than compensating for the absence of American consumer products in this former provincial capital of the empire was the atmosphere that allowed George to imagine himself as almost Russian. "The sleigh in which I am sometimes driven to the office in winter—a one-passenger open-air affair, in which the fur-coated passenger sits behind and below the massive figure of the bundled coachman on the box—is right out of Tolstoy." In the surrounding countryside, "all that one sees—the cobbled roads, the swamps and fields, the birch trees and evergreen forests—is the purest Russia. I drink it all in, love it intensely, and feel myself for a time an inhabitant of that older Russia, which I shall never see again in the flesh."[61]

Life in this "comparatively primitive country" also held financial attractions. While Kennan's salary amounted to over $300 a month, he paid the cook only $10 a month and a combination of chauffeur-butler $16. He figured that monthly household expenses would total about $80 a month—this in a place "where a lamb roast costs 8 cents a pound."[62]

The economic crisis that had driven down the cost of a lamb roast to pennies was also depressing households and treasuries around the world. Political tensions mounted and violence ensued. As U.S. private loans to Germany dried up, Berlin balked at paying the hated post–World War I reparations to France and the other victims of Germany's wartime destruction. Communists and Nazis battled in the streets of Germany. Trade shriveled as nations erected barriers against each other.

A week after the Kennans' wedding, Japan seized Manchuria from China. Three days later, Britain abandoned the U.S. dollar–dominated gold standard, focusing instead on economic ties within its empire. The trend toward international disarmament in the 1920s faltered and then reversed. Bitter border disputes festered. Kennan observed that as his train from Latvia to Germany entered Lithuania, the conductor placed a green cloth over the map in the hallway, because it showed Poland as possessing the Vilna province seized from Lithuania. The Treaty of Versailles, which had separated Russia and Germany with a cordon of precariously independent nations, now seemed to many, Kennan among them, a dangerous mistake.

The young diplomat assessed the worsening crisis with beliefs absorbed in childhood, reinforced at Princeton, and honed in Europe. He prioritized the economic needs and geographical prerogatives of Germany and Russia over those of smaller nations. He believed that geography, race, and climate would prevail. While saluting the pluck of the Baltic states in wresting free of Russian control, Kennan believed even if they remained politically independent, they "will have to return someday to the Russian economic system. Geographically, they are as much a part of Russia as New Jersey is of the States." Consequently, "every Russian government, Tsarist or Bolshevik, looks westward to the ice-free port of Tallinn as the end of the Russian railway system."[63]

Indeed, in his imagination, the Baltic nations remained part of Russia. He would later recall that the trains and passengers "seem to be right out of Chekhov." [64] Kennan's emotional attachment to Russia and rational respect for Germany led him to question whether, "despite the great fuss which these new countries make over their self-government, they weren't really considerably better-off under the heavy hands of the German or Russian Imperial Governments."[65]

Visceral disgust fed this skepticism of the smaller nations. Warsaw disgusted him as "very dark and dirty and tawdry." It reeked with "the great eastern-European smell." Kennan trusted scent as the most discerning of the senses. "This smell's real home is Poland." Every "room, every article has it—even the clothes which come back from the wash. It hovers around people and animals and automobiles and churches and dishes; it is simply unavoidable. It is a sort of musty, decayed, sour smell."[66]

George's personal life had also soured. Little more than a year after his hasty wedding, he concluded that "the technique of marriage is nothing more or less than the art of dissimulation." The birth of his daughter, named after Cousin Grace, on June 5, 1932, provided only temporary respite. Though born two weeks before the expected due date, Grace emerged "big and energetic" with "very fat and rosy cheeks." While proud, George also felt the added responsibility. That night he finished off most of a quart of "excellent Victoria Vat whiskey." Only eight days later, the new father complained of "boredom, boredom,

FIGURE 14. The proud father holding his infant daughter,
Grace, in Riga, Latvia, in 1933. (Courtesy of Grace
Kennan Warnecke.)

boredom! Boredom that aches, that crushes, that makes the mind
writhe this way and that in its search for some sort of relief. Boredom
that kills the appetite and saps the energy."[67] If before his marriage he
had tried to sell his soul, but could not, now he despaired that the devil
was no longer interested.

Four strands of frustration knotted together to pull him down: his marriage, a financial calamity, the world crisis, and his inability to get to Russia. In a third person, slightly fictionalized account of his predicament, he wrote that "at first he was unhappy in his marriage." Then he just capitulated and gave up "his own hopes, his own life." Marriage "forced upon him" a "thoroughly bourgeois mode of life," which meant "acceptance of death."[68]

Making matters worse, he could not share with Annelise intimate things about his life that he readily put into letters to Jeanette. While Annelise and daughter, Grace, stabilized his life, like "the leaden centerboard on a sailboat" that kept the vessel "upright and steady in its course," this weight was "not the motive power." Indeed, "if you want to take a chance and go fast before the wind"—in other words, live life fully—the heaviness dragged.[69]

He found monogamy oppressive. Since Princeton, he had defined the basic dilemma as stable order versus creative freedom. Convinced by Freud, he regarded as scientific fact that faithfulness amounted to a "ridiculous and unhealthy ideal." Nevertheless, "order and clarity" demanded such restraint. "Promiscuity was not sinful, it was merely sloppy." Sleeping around led to "confusion and disorder and uncertainty." Kennan valued order. Nonetheless, he could not bring himself to give up on extramarital romance. Such renunciation would "cripple" him. "I would have to live in a sort of vacuum. I would be speechless and dull." He wailed that "to be a diplomat is bitter enough, to be a married one is still bitterer." He reflected that "if his wife had been less dependent on him, he would probably have committed suicide."[70]

CRISIS, DEMOCRACY, AND DICTATORSHIP

Also disheartening was suddenly losing his inheritance. George had entrusted the stocks and bonds he had received from his mother and from his grandparents to Jeanette's husband, Gene, a stockbroker. He had authorized using a small portion for more speculative investments. Gene, however, pledged all of George's assets to buy, on margin, shares in the rickety empire of the Swedish "match-king," Ivar Kreuger. When Kreuger committed suicide or was murdered in March 1932, the house of cards collapsed. (Kreuger once admitted: "I've built my enterprise on the firmest ground that can be found—the foolishness of people.")[71] Annelise later remembered the news of the loss as the only time she had ever seen her husband cry. George found especially painful the rupturing of the last financial link to his mother and her parents: his stock in the Northwestern National Insurance Company, chaired by his grandfather and then his uncle.[72] Trying to control his fury and disappointment, George stressed to Jeanette, still his confidant, that he had never authorized Gene to speculate with his Northwestern stock. "It was just enough to stand between me and starvation if I should lose my job, and just enough so that I could never save it up again, even with thirty years in the foreign service." Gene had "just made a bad mistake," he added, charitably, "as all of us do."[73]

Downcast, he discerned a parallel between his own mental crisis and the world's economic crisis. What had erupted was "not *a* crisis but *the* crisis. Just as in the past, the global economy could find "new markets to absorb the flood of economic expansion," he could always find "new illusions and new hopes to absorb energy and attention." That "was all changing now. The world is at the end of its economic rope. I am at the end of my mental one." Moreover, his inability to discuss serious matters with his wife and the absence of stimulating colleagues in Riga prompted him to despair that "my mental processes will never be understood by anyone else."[74]

Kennan's Marxian analysis of the world Depression reflected his intense study of Russian communism. He concluded that while the Bolsheviks had correctly analyzed the problems of Russia and had pinpointed the weaknesses of world capitalism, their one-size-fits-all ideology remained impractical for most of humanity.

Honing a heartfelt prejudice, Kennan disparaged democracy as hypocritical rule by deceit. He favored instead a Platonic rule by benign, farseeing people such as himself. One night he lay awake wondering "whether a radical, anti-democratic party, a fascist party in essence, could have any success in America." He remained pessimistic about such a development, not because it loomed as a threat, but rather because it seemed out of reach. Spoiled Americans were not inclined to "put the public good before their personal lives." Then again, he mused, there emerged "a real possibility in the naive seriousness of the young generation."[75]

The elitist bolstered his critique of American democracy with an unlikely source, *The Rise of American Civilization* (1927) by the Progressive historians Charles A. and Mary R. Beard. The Beards' magisterial synthesis of American history desacralized the writers of the Constitution by describing how they had established a government favoring their financial holdings and elite rule while limiting democracy. If the Founders had focused on their own self-interest in setting up the republic, the Beards argued, so, too, could current-day reformers alter that system to benefit economic equality and democratic rule. Reading the book while on a trip back to America in 1930, Kennan was astonished to learn of the Founders' "frank abhorrence of democracy." Rather than question that prejudice, however, he embraced it. If the early leaders had disapproved of democracy "for a population predominantly white, Protestant and British," would they "not have turned over in their graves" at the prospect of democratic rule for a nation "containing over ten million negroes, and many more millions of southern Europeans, to whom the democratic principle is completely strange and incomprehensible?"[76]

Reinforcing George's prejudices about the masses was anxiety about his own class status. In the same letter in which he disparaged democracy, he described a visit to his sister, Connie, and her husband in their cookie-cutter house set on a treeless development tract in Rome, New York. The house seemed so clean and neat that it provoked George to Harry-Kempian revolt: "One longs for a trace of human disorder, but there is none." The second eldest daughter of Kent and Florence, Connie had never quite recovered from the death of her mother, her sister Jeanette reflected years later. Educated at Vassar and talented, Connie had nevertheless settled for what George saw as an empty existence, dragged down by "all the failure and despair of middle-class life."

Despite being "endowed with an excellent background"—that is, George's own heritage—his sister had been "sucked back into . . . the niveau of the American mass." That fate might also befall him, he often fretted. Kennan had been driven to Connie's house by friends, "two young aristocrats whose pride and assurance" accentuated his own personal insecurities. Connie greeted them with "an uncertain smile on her face." This scene—the contrast between the self-assured, upper-class friends whose breeding gave them the confidence to which George aspired, and the self-conscious, all too visible despair of his own flesh and blood that Connie represented—"will always be one of the most painful recollections of my life."[77]

Kennan distrusted democracy also because he favored radical solutions not likely to win popular approval. He pinpointed the basic problem of modern civilization as "essentially a biological one." "Inferior races" had proved incapable of dealing with technological progress. "No amount of education and discipline" could improve matters "as long as we allow the unfit to breed copiously and to preserve their young." Even if the fascists and the communists managed to alter the environment, "they will not alter heredity!" In defense of Kennan, such racist, eugenicist views were stock in trade for his generation and social class. Nevertheless, they remain a stain on his record—especially because the Nazis would indeed try to alter heredity. Kennan focused on another problem demanding iron rule, the systemic industrial overproduction that had spawned the Depression. The solution here lay in returning great masses of people to the land as "semi-independent European peasants."[78]

Even as Kennan pondered the potential for dictatorship in America, such rule was becoming the reality in Germany. "*Deutschland erwache!* [Germany awake!]" screamed the slogan on the newspaper he was reading. From his perch in Berlin and then in the German-dominated Baltic nations, the diplomat must have seen the emerging power of Adolf Hitler and the Nazis. Yet he commented little on this drama. Visits to Count von Bredow, who was intriguing with Hitler, slacked off after Kennan left Berlin for Riga. In January 1933, the month in which Hitler became chancellor of Germany, Kennan professed "indifference" as to whether

"Germany woke up or not. It was equally distasteful to him awake or asleep." In any case, he did not "consider the Nazi revolution a real awakening." Instead it was "only a nightmare."[79]

THE ROAD TO RUSSIA

While claiming indifference to the future of Germany, Kennan intently followed developments with Russia. With Franklin D. Roosevelt about to be inaugurated as president in March 1933, the United States might abandon its sixteen-year policy of not recognizing the Soviet Union. "The summer may find us heading for Moscow," an excited Kennan wrote in February.[80] He asked his father to inform his old acquaintance, Secretary of State Hull, "that you have a boy . . . who is serving in Riga as a specialist in Russian matters, and who is supposed to have a good record thus far."[81] Eager anticipation may have pushed him over the edge into exhaustion. On the eve of a long-delayed vacation in Norway, Annelise wrote Jeanette, "You know how hard G. works . . . always straining himself nervously; the result is that for the last 3–4 years his nerves are in a bad state." George would retreat to a sanatorium to calm his nerves.[82]

The cure did not resolve George's never-ending struggle between bourgeois security and bohemian creativity. He appreciated that Annelise, like Eleanor Hard, came from a tight, harmonious family. Reflecting to Jeanette on the differences between the Kennan household and that of Annelise's family, "I drink in all the charm (which we never quite knew) of a permanent home . . . where nastiness and mistrust are unknown." The bourgeois contentment of the Sorensens implicitly challenged the imperative to "go out storming the heights, frazzling one's nerves, beating one's wings" against human limitations. "Comfort and security" seemed so appealing even though they meant accepting "death and oblivion."[83]

By August 1933, Kennan's optimism about going to Russia had curdled into despair. Even though the State Department was preparing for negotiations with visiting Soviet foreign minister Maxim Litvinov, neither Kennan's mentor, Robert F. Kelley, nor his supposed contact, Secretary Hull, asked for Kennan's advice or participation. This was humiliating for someone who had studied so hard and who had developed such expertise. He despaired, "Russia is, to me, a forbidden world, and the iron of this realization has struck so deep that I am becoming indifferent to it, as we become indifferent to all things which we really know we cannot have."[84] But of course, being Kennan, he could not remain indifferent.

With his eighty-one-year-old father ailing, Kennan wrangled permission to come home for a visit. He may have also had in mind the impending talks in Washington. Once in the United States, Kennan was asked by the department to participate, not in the actual diplomacy leading to recognition, but rather in what he resented as the "drone" labor of handling petty details. Fuming about being relegated to the back room as the "government's slave," he also complained about having to live in expensive Washington on a salary suitable instead for Riga. George and Annelise camped out in the Washington apartment of his Milwaukee neighbors, "Uncle" Edward and "Aunt" Ida Frost.[85]

The son did manage to get back to Milwaukee for what proved the final meeting with his father. They remained separated by decades of shyness, unshared feelings, and unspoken confidences. As they talked on a late afternoon in a darkening room, one of Kent's legs slid off the bed until his foot rested on the floor. George could only watch. "I wanted to raise his leg for him onto the bed and make him comfortable, and it now seems symbolic to me that some Kennanish repression made it impossible for me to follow even that little tender impulse."[86] After George left for Washington, Kent, his pneumonia worsening, wrote his son that with the departure, "waves and billows of sadness passed over me . . . that I might never see you again."[87]

On November 27, 1933, three days after his father wrote that letter, an encounter changed Kennan's life forever. He recounted walking through the corridors of the State Department when a friend asked if he knew Bill Bullitt, the newly appointed ambassador to the Soviet Union.

Kennan said, no, he did not. "You ought to," the friend replied, who then brought him to Bullitt's office. Kennan was struck by the emissary's "huge forehead," "engaging smile," and "great vitality" and by his commanding the "easy poise of a cosmopolitan." Bullitt delighted in Kennan's answers to his questions about Russia. "'Do you know Russian?' he asked. I said I did. 'Well enough to interpret?' Yes." Then, "'I am leaving on Monday for Moscow. Could you be ready in time to come along with me?'" "The room rocked around me," Kennan later recalled. "For five straight years I had been preparing to go to the Soviet Union." His intellectual and long-distance study of Russia had stimulated in him "a consuming curiosity to know it in the flesh."[88] The metaphor would prove telling because of the passionate, even sensual impulses that would shape Kennan's encounter with Russia.

George had only two days before joining Bullitt aboard the S.S. *President Harding* on November 29. He rushed up to South Orange, New Jersey, to pay his respects to Cousin Grace and, probably, to enlist her aid in getting supplies, warm clothing, and other necessities. He expected to remain in Moscow for only about a week, and then proceed to his post in Riga, at least for a while. Annelise would accompany him on the ship, and then go to Kristiansand, where her family was caring for infant Grace. Then she would follow him to Riga.[89]

The chance to assist Bullitt and to get, finally, to Russia infused focus into Kennan's seemingly muddled life. The writers he most admired, such as Chekhov and Hemingway, "knew one thing, one country at the most, and were saturated with it." Before this opportunity came along, he, by contrast, had "nothing which hung together, nothing coherent." "Father represented something, but I saw and understood damned little of it." As for the Jameses, they were "complete exceptions. So was St. John's, thank God." His "friends at Princeton, such as they were, were all freaks. And then the Atlantic coast and a glimpse of Washington and finally Europe—Geneva and Hamburg and Berlin and the Baltic." He had wooed "a German girl and a Russian girl and a Norwegian wife." He had lost Eleanor and her family. He saw his "poor life and attention" as "scattered around and wasted like the leaves of a tree." He pinpointed the problem: "I lack material and imagination—coordination, familiar, definite material and constructive imagination—and I lack time."[90]

Russia would provide the material. Kennan's experiences, study, and fantasy would provide the imagination. And his frenzied schedule, interrupted by breakdowns, would provide the time.

CHAPTER 3

THE "MADNESS OF '34"

IT WAS ALL TOO INTENSE. Over the long run, George F. Kennan could neither live in Russia nor live without it. And he was not alone. In the intoxicating, impassioned, and exhausting months of 1933–1935, newly minted Russian experts Charles E. "Chip" Bohlen and Charles W. "Charlie" Thayer, as well as Ambassador William C. Bullitt, experienced, like Kennan, the most gratifying and exciting times of their lives. They bonded on the intensity. The embrace by Joseph Stalin and other Soviet leaders angling for U.S. support against Japan, the engagement with young Russians focused on building a new society, the exhilarating mix of intellectual and sexual stimulation—all this fed their egos and was just plain fun. Sadly, however, it all came crashing down. The nonstop working and partying broke Kennan. As the canary in this coal mine, he suffered a physical and mental collapse on December 12, 1934, precisely a year and a day after he had arrived in Moscow.

Political relations also foundered. Eleven days before Kennan's collapse, the popular Soviet leader Sergei Kirov was assassinated. The violence would metastasize as Stalin, his henchmen, and other Communist Party officials launched the bloody purges of 1935–1938. All the thoughtful, friendly Bolsheviks who had so delighted the Americans were exiled or executed. Meanwhile, the ebbing of Japan's threat to Russia, disputes over World War I era debts, and anger over the proselytizing work of the Communist International soured both Stalin and Bullitt. For Kennan and his Moscow colleagues, the magical "madness of '34," so linked with their vanished youth and the chimera of warm ties with Russia, would forever haunt them as a lost paradise.[1] Mournful resentment over the nasty turn of events after 1934 would, a decade later, fuel Kennan's fervor for the emerging Cold War. As for Bullitt, he suffered such searing disappointment that he would devolve into a right-wing critic not only of the World War II alliance with Russia but also of Kennan, his once-favored protégé.

THIS BENEVOLENT MIASMA

The tragedies that ensued should not, however, erase the story of 1934, a moment that Bohlen decades later termed "the most optimistic year in Soviet history."[2] The great famine resulting from the Soviets' forced collectivization of agriculture had lifted. Living conditions were improving. Washington had finally recognized the Soviet Union, and Moscow was entering the League of Nations. Conflict within the Bolshevik leadership had eased. Such exiles as Karl Radek and Nikolai Bukharin, both of them admired and feted by the Americans, returned to Moscow as influential figures. Stalin reassured a Party congress that "there is nothing more to prove and, it seems, no one to fight."[3] The dictator eased restrictions on contact with foreigners, especially Americans. He invited increased trade. Though brief, the heady interlude of 1934 was real. The moment left a permanent imprint on Kennan as well as on his colleagues.

Amid the rising expectations and excitement all sorts of things appeared possible. Bullitt and his crew set about opening Soviet Russia not only to American diplomacy and business, but also to baseball and polo. They planned to build a gorgeous "Monticello" of an embassy overlooking Moscow. Eager to plunge into a country formerly closed to them by both the State Department and Stalin, Kennan and his friends approached Russia as an exotic, sensual frontier. Here beckoned attractive people passionate about remaking themselves and their country. Here also ruled a brash ideology that branded itself as the antidote to the Depression plaguing the West. Though not sold on Marxism, the Americans also wondered whether that ideology did indeed hold the cure.

Kennan arrived in Moscow in December 1933 as someone bored with his marriage and suffering from the cabin fever of remote Riga. He felt he was drowning in convention. For years he had longed to immerse himself instead in the wondrous novelty of Russia. No wonder, then, that in Moscow he immediately got swept up in the hurry-scurry of late-night parties and crowded city streets.

So jammed, in fact, were the streets of the bustling Soviet capital that one day in 1931 the entire city gridlocked. Not even a horse cart could move. The crisis hastened the start of construction on the Moscow Metro, the "Palace of the People," a marvel of both engineering and esthetics. With technical advisers debating how far down to build the subway, Stalin ordered them to go really deep. Gorgeous mosaics and chandeliers would beautify its stations. During Kennan's initial year in Moscow, the first train moved along the track in a test run. The city clang with other ambitious projects. Audacity soaked through public sentiment as well as official propaganda. Pioneering aviators, "Stalin's eagles," and intrepid arctic explorers gained mass followings. Popular songs proclaimed, "We are taming space and time," and "We were born to make fairy tales come true." A later dissident would recall the heady feeling that it was "both possible and necessary to alter everything: the streets, the houses, the cities, the social order, human souls. And it was not all that difficult."[4] Kennan felt it, "this great intoxicating fog of enthusiasm—this benevolent miasma."[5]

Also eager to experience the great experiment were some fifteen hundred foreign visitors who flocked to Russia each year. The American contingent included the architect Frank Lloyd Wright, the singer-activist Paul Robeson, the Socialist candidate for president Norman Thomas, and the comedian Harpo Marx.

Harpo Marx embodied the creativity unleashed by crossing borders. He came across as both silent and noisy, as the Marx brother who communicated through honks, whistles, and harp. This not-Karl Marx, the American scion of Jewish immigrants, ranked as the first U.S. citizen to perform in Russia after diplomatic recognition. His visit was arranged by a friend, the New York critic Alexander Woollcott, who had appealed to Eleanor Roosevelt. Barriers of language, culture, and ideology melted away in Harpo's triumphant tour across the Soviet Union. In Moscow, laughter from his two-person act was interrupted only when the straight-man heroine herself could not stop laughing. Attending Harpo's performance with Bullitt, a friend of Kennan's observed how "dozens of knives, spoons, forks dropped from his sleeves. Then he took a huge volume of cutlery from inside the actress's dress."[6] Russians delighted also in his unorthodox and yet heavenly playing of the harp.

Crossing borders of a different kind was Bullitt, who both hinted at a bisexual orientation and romanced Missy LeHand, President Franklin D. Roosevelt's live-in personal assistant and purported intimate.[7] As ambassador, Bullitt had ready access to the State Department's official pouch, the secure bag immune from Soviet search and transported by an American carrier. Yet Bullitt had some agenda beyond, and perhaps in conflict with, his official position that prompted an appeal to Harpo. As the performer was leaving Moscow for New York, Bullitt asked him to smuggle out some papers taped to his leg.[8]

Bullitt's expansive personality and a kiss with Stalin set the mood for the U.S.-Soviet honeymoon. Back in 1919, this Yale and Harvard educated, twenty-eight-year-old scion of Philadelphia Mainline society had negotiated a tentative deal with Soviet leader Vladimir Lenin on behalf of President Woodrow Wilson. When the president rejected the arrangement, Bullitt retaliated by damning Wilson's Versailles treaty in testimony before the U.S. Senate. Afterward, Bullitt exiled himself to the Riviera, wrote an expatriate novel, and married Louise Bryant, the widow of Jack Reed, youthful chronicler of the Bolshevik Revolution and one of the few Americans buried in the Kremlin. He collaborated with Sigmund Freud in writing a psychobiography of Woodrow Wilson.[9] Bullitt dazzled Kennan as someone "right out of F. Scott Fitzgerald, young, handsome, urbane, full of charm and enthusiasm." To Kennan, whose self-assurance faded easily, Bullitt glowed as someone "confident in himself, confident of the president's support," confident that he could overcome "Communist suspicion and hostility."[10]

While the yearning to know Russia in the flesh set up Kennan and his compatriots for a roller coaster of excitement and disappointment, it was Stalin and his henchmen who took the Americans for a ride. They launched an all-out charm offensive. When Bullitt arrived on

December 11, 1933, they assigned him to the same apartment he had occupied in July 1914 at the onset of the Great War. They decorated his bedroom with a hand-stitched American flag. Soviet authorities combed museums for the most elegant furniture to place in his apartment. (Weeks later, when no appropriate mantelpiece could be found for a fireplace at Spaso House, the residence of the U.S. ambassador, the Soviets simply ripped one out of their Foreign Office building.)[11]

After the ambassador presented his credentials to Soviet President Mikhail Kalinin, the latter affably remarked that he "and everyone else in Russia" considered President Franklin D. Roosevelt unique among capitalist leaders. Roosevelt "really cared about the welfare of the laboring men and the farmers, and he was not engaged in protecting the vested rights of property." Bullitt no doubt beamed upon hearing from Kalinin that "Lenin had talked to him about me on several occasions, and that he felt as if he were welcoming someone he had known for a long time." When Bullitt asked if he could bring in a plane for traveling around the Soviet Union, Kalinin assured him "there would be no restrictions whatever on my movements."[12] The Soviet president then validated Kennan by telling him that the Bolsheviks had venerated the elder George Kennan's books on the czarist exile system as a "bible." The younger Kennan was so moved that, he later confided to his sister, he nearly fainted.[13]

Bullitt also met a warm welcome from Kliment Voroshilov, commander of the Soviet army and navy. Voroshilov shone as "one of the most charming persons I have ever met," he reported to Roosevelt. During a long talk on the morning of December 20, the Russian chief warned Bullitt that "a Japanese attack was imminent." Consequently, he was "especially anxious to have a full equipment of American military, naval, and air attaches in Moscow." Such a delegation, the ambassador advised FDR, would endow the United States with "really immense influence" over the armed forces of the Soviet Union. Bullitt also stressed that Soviet leaders, themselves "sophisticated" and "vigorous" people, eagerly welcomed contact with Americans of "first-rate intelligence." For instance, the Soviets seemed "delighted by young Kennan who went in with me." Voroshilov invited Bullitt to a Kremlin banquet that very evening.[14]

FIGURE 15. Ambassador Bullitt presenting his credentials to Soviet president
Mikhail Kalinin, with Kennan in the background, December 1933, Moscow.
(Courtesy of Princeton University Library.)

Capping a day of intense talks, this dinner, which extended into the
early morning, would prove the high point of Bullitt's roller-coaster ride.
Escorted through lines of soldiers into a Kremlin palace, the American
was welcomed by the Soviet leadership, including Stalin. To FDR, Bullitt described the Soviet leader as short, "wiry rather than powerful . . .

dressed in a common soldier's uniform" without any decorations. His eyes "are dark brown filled with dark blue." He gave the impression of "shrewd humor." With Lenin, Bullitt had felt in the presence of "a great man"; with Stalin, "I felt I was talking to a wiry Gypsy with roots and emotions beyond my experience."

As the ambassador surveyed the grand room, Foreign Minister Litvinov confided, "This is the whole 'gang' that really runs things—the inside directorate." The Russians encouraged the eager American to feel that he, too, ranked as an insider. He was seated at the center of the table on one side of Madame Voroshilov, with Stalin on the other. The dictator offered the first toast to President Roosevelt, "who dared recognize the Soviet Union" despite domestic criticism. Another toast honored Bullitt, "who comes to us as a new Ambassador but an old friend." As one salutation followed another, the ambassador tried sipping only a few drops, only to be warned that it was insulting not to drink bottoms-up. Alcohol lubricated the male bonding. As Bullitt put it, "everyone at the table got into the mood of a college fraternity banquet." Having warned the Soviets that he would not stay in Moscow if "treated as an outsider," the American was gratified when Litvinov whispered, "Do you realize that everyone at this table has completely forgotten that anyone is here except the members of the inner gang?" Given the bad-boy glamor of the Bolsheviks and Bullitt's own disappointment in 1919, it was heady affirmation to be finally, and so lavishly, accepted by the "gang."

Conversation centered on the expected onslaught by Japan. Stalin introduced the general "who will lead our Army victoriously against Japan when Japan attacks." To win, however, "we need 250,000 tons of steel rails at once" to finish the second line of the railroad to the Soviet Far East. The dictator believed that U.S. railroads were upgrading their track. Appealing to American assumptions of industrial supremacy, Stalin asserted that "your rails are so much heavier than ours that the rails you discard are good enough for us." Bullitt agreed to help arrange the purchase of the old rails. After dinner, Stalin, sitting next to Bullitt, said he wanted him to feel "completely at home in the Soviet Union." In reply to the assurance that the president would use his moral influence to restrain Japan, Stalin asserted that Roosevelt, "is today, in spite of being

FIGURE 16. Kennan found Moscow intensely exciting and exhausting. (Courtesy of Grace Kennan Warnecke.)

the leader of a capitalist nation, one of the most popular men in the Soviet Union."

Stalin was not done wooing Bullitt. He stressed: "I want you to understand that if you want to see me at any time, day or night, you have only to let me know and I will see you at once." That was quite a pledge, since, Bullitt believed, the dictator had refused to meet with the ambassadors of other nations. Then, as Bullitt was leaving, Stalin said, "Is there anything at all in the Soviet Union that you want? Anything?" He confided that while the Soviets would have welcomed any ambassador from Washington, they would have so lavishly honored "no one but yourself." As the dictator probably knew, Bullitt had his heart set on building a lavish U.S. embassy, modeled on Jefferson's Monticello, on a beautiful, wooded bluff with a stunning view of the Moscow River. When the American mentioned this aspiration, the Kremlin chief assured him,

"You shall have it." Then the dictator made his final move: As Bullitt stuck out his hand to say goodbye, "Stalin took my head in his two hands and gave me a large kiss! I swallowed my astonishment, and when he turned up his face for a return kiss, I delivered it." Those were kisses "full on the mouth," the ambassador would still remember decades later.[15]

Bullitt was so excited by his experience that he awoke Kennan in the middle of the night and dictated his report to the president. Roosevelt, picking up on the "fraternity banquet" mood, requested "the real low-down on what happens at your parties with the Russian foreign office at 3 A.M."[16]

On December 21, the day after the party in the Kremlin, Bullitt set off for Washington, where he would arrange for an embassy staff of some forty Americans. Kennan left for Riga. Only three days after arriving back in the Latvian capital, however, Kennan was ordered by the State Department, probably at Bullitt's instigation, to return to Moscow with a single aide.[17] The young star was to arrange for the housing, telephones, local transportation, and other basic needs of the ambassador and his crew, due to arrive on March 1. Agreement on these mundane though vital matters had to be threaded through the equally arcane, though not at all aligned bureaucratic regulations of the Soviet and U.S. governments.

GOING RUSSIAN IN A BIG WAY

While the telegram testified to the State Department's rising faith in Kennan, it also illustrated the bureaucratic pettiness that infuriated him. The U.S. government would pay his transportation and a $9 per diem, but it would neither cover the cost of transporting his family nor make provision for the far higher cost of living in the Soviet capital.[18] Moreover, the directive specified that Kennan, though anxious to stay in Russia, was being assigned to Moscow only temporarily. And even that appointment came without the customary diplomatic rank for such a mission. The minister in Riga had to intervene with the State Department to "respectfully request" that Kennan be allocated $200 for postage and telegrams.[19] The job was "full of dynamite" and "horrified" him,

Kennan wailed, since he would bear the responsibility for negotiating with the Soviets without actually having the "status of a real chargé d'affaires"—or the salary.

Nonetheless, he met the challenge with Kennanish thoroughness. He responded to the State Department telegram by writing two letters to Bullitt. First, he penned a personal note that played on the growing mutual affection and respect between them. He thanked Bullitt for his "doubly kind" Christmas telegram and for "the confidence and responsibility you've given me." In a chatty tone, he related the only-in-Russia story of his train to Riga running over a man. "The pieces were removed, one by one, from under the dining car when I was eating breakfast, and were promptly thrown into a ditch." Kennan moved on to a more serious matter, how "beaten down by the bureaucracy" he had been the previous year. He had to struggle not to sink to the level of "a timid, petty little bureaucrat." Then, Bullitt had invited him to Moscow, and the subsequent weeks "took my breath away." Kennan hinted broadly at his hope their association would continue. To help make that wish a reality, the ambitious diplomat then typed a three-page, single-spaced letter with the names, backgrounds, attributes, and suggested positions of personnel whom Bullitt might choose for his embassy. In asking Kennan to draw up such a list, Bullitt, then still in Moscow, had signaled his faith in the younger man's judgment and knowledge. In carrying through, Kennan was making himself indispensable. Still, he did not know when or if Bullitt would request his permanent appointment to Moscow, and at what rank.[20]

Regarding the temporary job, "the whole arrangement is unsatisfactory," he grumbled to Annelise, who since early December had remained with Grace in Kristiansand. Having not heard from her husband, she had sent him a "scolding letter." He now filled her in on their plight. It remained "absolutely out of the question to try to bring the baby" to Moscow, at least for now. Eighteen-month-old Grace would have to stay with her grandparents in Norway.

George did, however, want Annelise to make the arduous journey to Moscow, half-pleading, "After all, darling, we are man and wife, aren't we?" Marital love notwithstanding, "you'll hate the hotel," he warned, and their apartment would not be ready for months. Nor could he afford her travel costs. Nevertheless, George missed his wife. He probably also had in mind his need for someone to prepare meals and keep house for him. Though he had kept a maid while in Riga and in Berlin, in Moscow his Riga-sized salary made that impossible. He faced the predicament of much work and meager assistance. He suggested that Annelise might "want to help me a little." Relieved at finally hearing from her husband and perhaps worried about leaving him alone in Moscow, Annelise promised to depart immediately. "Of course I'll love to help you so much as I can," she assured him.[21] There remains no evidence, however, that Annelise did do any official work. Annelise did work hard "in keeping house for me in the hotel room," Kennan later acknowledged. She "loyally cooked my meals for me, on a whisky-case behind a screen; and our bedroom served as dining-room, living room and Embassy Chancery as well." As he later put it, "Russia, always partial to intimacy and confusion, had promptly claimed its own."[22] Kennan loved that intimacy, and a part of him liked the confusion as well.

While the telephone buzzed erratically and official visitors and friends trooped in and out of their room in the National Hotel, Kennan rushed around the city preparing for Bullitt and the incoming staff. Forty railroad cars filled with furniture, equipment, and supplies for the Americans' offices and apartments were arriving in Moscow. With Thayer's help, Kennan managed to get the Soviet bureaucracy—astonished by the sheer materialism of these Americans—to clear the mountain of stuff through customs, store it temporarily, and then transport it.[23] After Bullitt arrived on March 1, the pace only quickened. Kennan's duties included preparing forty clean apartments for staff, Spaso House for the ambassador, and office space for embassy work. Then he had to deal with "several thousand cases of furniture, effects, canned goods, liquor, office supplies, etc." that had to be "imported, cleared through Soviet customs, and transported around town" with trucks he had to find. Finally, the newcomers "had to be shown how to live—to shop and to get around town and to amuse themselves." In doing all this, Kennan had to negotiate between "the world's craziest financial system" in Moscow and "the world's craziest system of expenditure control" in Washington.[24]

Notwithstanding the pressure, the rising diplomat felt at home in Moscow. His earlier forebodings evaporated. "I am quite happy here," he wrote Jeanette. In walking the cobbled streets, viewing the historic architecture, and meeting the Bolshevik leaders he had only read about, he was breathing life into what "previously been a world of the imagination."[25] Amid all the hubbub, he could immerse himself in the deliciously real sights, sounds, smells, taste, and touch of Russia. "I like to wander around and see as much as I can." While admiring the cultivated order of pre-1917 Russian literature and music, Kennan was fascinated also by contemporary disorder. There was always a whiff of chaos in the air, whether a "streetcar off the tracks, a wagon with a wheel off and a hundred interested spectators" or "the arrest of a wild child," one of many in the city.[26]

Kennan, who had read widely in Russian literature and history, had also come to know Russia through his lectures, seminars, and informal discussions at the University of Berlin. In many ways, he encountered Russia through Germany. He had absorbed notions of the uninhibited, undisciplined, deeply emotional Russian soul. Russians were supposedly enthusiastic but not steady workers. They tended toward extravagant expenditure, whether in feelings expressed, lives sacrificed, or resources committed. If Russians were given to spontaneity and spirituality, Germans tended be dull and soulless. While Germany embodied the culture of Europe, Russia extended into Asia. This sense of the Soviet Union as in part "Asiatic" evoked powerful Orientalist tropes. As against the Russian inclination toward disorder and creativity stood the German penchant for order and duty.[27] This supposed polarity between Germany and Russia corresponded with Kennan's own internal conflict between duty and creativity, between marriage and sexual freedom, and between convention and resistance to it.

Now, in these first months in Moscow, the overstuffing of his schedule ironically engendered balance in his work. In order to get everything done, he had to both follow the pathways obligated by the bureaucracies of Moscow and Washington and yet also find creative ways to sidestep those staid agencies. Not surprisingly, however, the balance broke down when it came to his health. He pushed himself too hard and fell ill.

George's thirtieth birthday on February 16 found him in bed nursing a cold that had dogged him since leaving New York two months earlier. His aide, Charlie Thayer, loyally stopped by, and they "celebrated by having lunch in his room with waffles made by Mrs. Kennan."[28]

Encouraged by both Bullitt and, to an extent, by Stalin, American diplomats and journalists plunged into the fun. "They had all gone Russian in a big way," Kennan later recalled, and lived a life that approached "the true Bohème." "I loved it." It was as if Harry Kemp, the hobo poet he had admired at Princeton, or his sister Frances's Greenwich Village friends had come to Moscow. Memories of this time remained so vivid that decades later he recounted them in the present tense: "[We are invited to] marvelous Russian-American parties in shabby Moscow apartments, at which nobody cares whether the apartments are shabby or not, or where you put your coats, or what there is to eat and drink— parties that are full of good talk, endless talk, in the Russian manner." Then "we all go out to the great Park of Culture and Rest along the Moscow River and skate . . . under the frozen Russian stars, to the strains of the 'Skater's Waltz' rendered by scratchy loudspeakers somewhere up in the trees." One evening he was hosted at the ballet by Litvinov and his family. On another, "I went to Chekhov's 'Cherry Orchard' with Harpo Marx," who let loose with "solitary, unrestrained gales of laughter." After the performance, George and Harpo met Chekhov's wife backstage. With so much going on, "it was rare that we got to sleep before four or five in the morning."[29]

Like Bullitt, Kennan marveled at seeing Soviet "bigwigs" wisecrack among themselves at a Kremlin dinner. Repression had loosened enough that "the waggish [Bolshevik intellectual Karl] Radek kidded the others" about his forced exile a few years back. "The impression left by those commissars was unforgettable," Kennan later acknowledged. He respected, even envied them as a "tough lot: strong-nerved, lean, ruthlessly competent." They could no more retire than could the sworn members of a Chicago gang. Unlike American politicians, whom Kennan despised, these Party leaders "had no chance to get paunchy and flabby." He romanticized them as rough-hewn figures who steered between convention and chaos, standing up for Russia while defying the capitalist West.[30]

Their expressive, barnyard humor reminded him of an iconic painting by Ilya Repin portraying "those Dnieper Cossacks" of the seventeenth century who, in the name of "vast and holy Russia," had drawn up an inventively obscene rejection of Turkish demands.[31] "The Reply of the Zaporozhian Cossacks to the Sultan Mehmed IV" displays a nearly seven- by twelve-foot tableau of raucous, colorfully arrayed semi-barbarians, each in distinctive costume, and all totally enjoying themselves. While these Cossacks, including a half-naked man in the foreground, are giving free rein to unbridled humor, a conventionally dressed scribe with a restrained smile is reducing the tumult to order with his feather pen. The painting spoke to Kennan. He appreciated that the tricky dynamics of simultaneously respecting and restraining the Russian soul afforded the Party bosses no choice but "playing close to the abysses of political and physical disaster."[32] They had to be tough to modernize a "filthy, sordid country, full of vermin, mud, stench, and disease."[33]

Amid the fervor of 1934, Kennan forged lifelong friendships with Bohlen and Thayer. Bohlen had opted for France rather than Germany in learning his Russian language and pre-1917 culture in the State Department program overseen by Robert F. Kelley. Always more of an insider than Kennan, Bohlen was born into Philadelphia high society and trained in the embassy in Paris, which often set the direction for U.S. policy toward Europe. Yet he was like Kennan in his intensity. Bohlen's fingernails were always bitten to the quick, a friend would recall.[34] He would rise to become President Roosevelt's interpreter at the Tehran and Yalta conferences. Thayer, also a scion of Mainline Philadelphia society, had gone to Russia seeking adventure after graduating from West Point. During those weeks in early 1934 when Kennan was frantically trying to prepare for the ambassador and his entourage, he had hired Thayer as an aide. With no embassy car, Thayer dashed through the snowy Moscow streets on a motorcycle with the flaps of his Russian hat bobbing up and down. For Bohlen and Thayer as for Kennan and Bullitt, 1934 proved unforgettable.

"I have never had more fun or interest in my whole life," Bohlen enthused. "This Embassy . . . is like no other Embassy in the world."[35] Thayer agreed, writing home, "Things have been going along beautifully and I am as usual enjoying myself to the limit."[36] It all seemed very special, and exhausting: "Russia! Russia! There's no place like it on the earth—there isn't emotional space to contain more than one."[37]

A carnivalesque atmosphere heightened the intensity. These young Americans saw in exotic Moscow the opportunity to cross boundaries of ideology, class, sexuality, rank, convention, and nationality—crossings that at other times and places would be serious transgressions. As Bohlen put it, "Everything is topsy-turvy and the most amazing things happen, which could only happen here."[38] At an embassy dinner, George Andreychin, a Macedonian Communist and a friend of Bullitt's who had helped organize the International Workers of the World in the United States, entertained with tales of life in American prisons. Street urchins shouted, "Your health, Comrade Bullitt!" as he sped through the capital. The Soviets seemed enthused about Bullitt and Thayer's promise to introduce polo to the cavalry of the Red Army. The dashing Russian Civil War hero General Semyon Budyonny assured Thayer that "Voroshilov thinks you are a fine young fellow, and Stalin does too."[39]

Irena Charnotskaya, a devoutly Communist, self-educated, and intellectually sophisticated ballerina, "has taken the trio of B[ullitt], B[ohlen] and myself by storm," Thayer recorded. Bullitt admired her as "the cleverest women he has ever met." At dinners extending into the early morning, the three diplomats and the ballerina would delve into "some deep subject of Communist theory or psychology," with Charnotskaya usually winning the arguments. "Her personality is so perfect, so free of ordinary pettiness, that she is by far the greatest advertisement of communism," Thayer affirmed. Various registers of eroticism and appropriation intersected as Bullitt, Bohlen, and Thayer bonded with each other in their shared attraction to this exotic and impressive woman. "[Everyone who sees her has] a strong desire to pat her on the head—without any sexual impulses whatever. We simply cannot keep our hands off her. She has become an acquisition of the Embassy." She slept in a room "which the three of us carefully lock together and then fight violently as to who will keep the key. Each one blindly jealous of the next one. What an Embassy!" The walls of Spaso House resounded with the voice of the ambassador trying to memorize the phrase Charnotskaya had written out for him in Russian: "I am here to establish the closest and most friendly relations between the U.S. and the Soviet Union." (Watch for the speech in the movie theater! Bohlen alerted his mother.) Awestruck, the aide concluded that Soviet propaganda was right: "The young Russians . . . really are in a great many ways a new type of human being."[40]

Bullitt, who had not included any women in the group of forty Americans setting up the embassy, constantly urged his "boys" to mix with the Russians. As a confirmed playboy, Bohlen "eagerly carried out his instructions." In addition to Charnotskaya, "there were usually two or three ballerinas running around the embassy."[41] Other Americans in the embassy also found Russian girlfriends. Though increasingly restive about the bounds of monogamy, Kennan remained characteristically discreet about his own liaisons. Looking back on 1934, Thayer later recalled the "not entirely sane existence we led before with Mrs. and mistresses all together in an alcoholic haze."[42]

Thickening that haze was the fluid sexuality of the boss. Bullitt, married briefly to Louise Bryant, remained for decades close with his homosexual aide, Carmel Offie. The ambassador palled around with Bohlen and Thayer, only to grow jealous at seeing Bohlen become "attached to Thayer with an almost violent affection." Though Bullitt clearly adored Kennan, no evidence suggests that he ever made a pass at him. The ambassador romanced Missy LeHand, in part as a means to get closer to her boss, the president. A pervasive eroticism fueled the excitement and the subsequent frustration and fury of Bullitt and his crew in Moscow.

Illustrating the exuberance laced with excess of Bullitt's honeymoon in Moscow was the Christmas celebration of 1934. This ranked, literally, as a wild party in that the entertainment featured imperfectly trained seals. "Make it good," Bullitt had instructed Charlie Thayer and Irena Wiley, the wife of an embassy official, about the Christmas bash. At first, Irena wanted to install an aquarium atop the marble floor of the gigantic ballroom and then glass it over for dancing. When they could find in

Moscow neither the requisite glass nor the tropical fish, they settled for three seals from the Moscow Circus. The animals did tricks, including playing "The Internationale" on the harmonica. At the apex of the evening, one seal slid across the floor balancing on its nose a small Christmas tree with lighted candles. The other two pranced in with a tray of wine and a bottle of champagne atop their noses. All went well until their trainer, who had been drinking heavily, passed out, and the animals ran amok. Although George was too ill to attend the festivities, Annelise was there and still remembered it decades later.[43]

KENNAN ON COMMUNISM—AND ON CHEKHOV

Far more than Bullitt, Bohlen, or Thayer, Kennan had studied Russia and Russian communism. He was deeply curious about how Marxist-Leninist ideology had affected, and been affected by, traditional Russian culture. With fascination tinged with both horror and awe, Kennan judged Soviet Russia as a vast experiment with "human life in the raw, human life brought down to its fundamentals—good and evil, drunk and sober, loving and quarreling, laughing and weeping." Here basic humanity had grown "more simple and direct, and therefore stronger." He admired ordinary Russians as "unmistakably healthy," not with the health of the pampered Westerner, but rather with the vigor bred of survival of the fittest. However shabby, the Russians on the streets had emerged from the charnel house of the revolution and the civil war. Pride that he had survived the less deadly but nonetheless brutal physical harassments at St. John's may have fed Kennan's empathy with what Russians had endured.[44]

In studying Russian communism and Western capitalism during the worst of the Great Depression, Kennan concluded that both suffered inherent and fatal flaws. Both systems were clinging to a blind, destructive faith in progress through industrialism and the production of ever more goods. Capitalism was rushing toward the precipice because firms competing for market share were aggravating overproduction and unemployment. Communism was heading toward eventual collapse because it ignored the spirituality, individuality, and diversity of

humanity. In these early years, Kennan did not condemn Stalin's dictatorial rule with the fury that drove him beginning with the 1935–1938
purges.

Though cognizant of the Kremlin's sins, Kennan as a Riga-based diplomat had criticized communism's refusal to value individual character,
particularly in terms of the traits that he valued: decency, unselfishness,
and courage. He faulted communism also for its delusion that the victory of the proletariat would do away with the impulse for self-interest.
Once a worker secured steady work, that person would focus on "the
feathering of his own individual little nest."[45] The Communists' goal of
world revolution was naive in its lumping together all proletarians,
thereby ignoring ineradicable differences arising from climate, race, and
geography. Kennan also criticized revolutionary crusaders for cowardly
abandoning "the ship of Western European civilization like a swarm of
rats . . . instead of staying on and trying to keep it afloat." Taking offense
at the claim that Marxist-Leninism had trumped the wisdom of all previous thought, Kennan accused the Communists of insolence, even
blasphemy.[46] In contrast to subsequent years, when he would racialize
Soviet ideology as "semi-Asiatic," he still regarded communism as an
element of the Western tradition, however wayward and irresponsible.
Moreover, the crucial category in his critique remained the individual:
cowardice and insolence ranked as failings of personal character.

Kennan pondered whether communism as practiced in Russia differed, if at all, from state capitalism. He concluded that even if one generously granted that the Communist Party leaders running things did
not constitute a new privileged class monopolizing benefits, the Soviet
system still did not prioritize workers. Instead, the economy lay in thrall
to the Communist doctrine of world revolution. That pursuit antagonized other nations and thereby required diverting massive resources
to the Soviet armed forces.

As for the eventual fate of Russian communism, Kennan in 1932 sent
a report to the State Department that reflected his own inner turmoil,
as well as a just-published book, *Youth in Soviet Russia* by the German
journalist Klaus Meinert. Meinert, who would become a close friend of
Kennan's in Moscow, lauded the "unshakable sense of superiority" and

self-assurance of Soviet youth so enraptured with building a better Russia that they no longer worried about their individual lives.[47] The Soviet system seemed to have created a new type of human being.

Kennan projected onto Russian youth the very issues that haunted him: "questions of sex, children, the family, personal affection, religious and artistic expression." (Significantly, sex ranked first on his list of problems.) Many young Russians, Kennan acknowledged, seemed to have sidestepped such personal issues by focusing instead on the "romance of economic development." The happy consequence was that Soviet youth could escape "the curses of egotism, romanticism, daydreaming, introspection, and perplexity" that "befall the youth of bourgeois countries"—and that had befallen him. (He evidently assumed that "romance" leading to purposeful action differed from "romanticism" leading nowhere.)

Nevertheless, Kennan went on, the "artificial conditions" now inflating the "mental health and happiness" of younger Russians would inevitably falter, no matter what. If economic development succeeded, and Russia evolved into a consumers' paradise with "electronic ice-boxes" and other gadgets for all, the victory and consequent mood of demobilization would force the young Communist to turn "inward and to ask himself for the first time what there really is to live for." If, however, the industrial effort failed, discontent would spread. In either case, "the young Russian will probably be as helpless and miserable as a babe in the woods." Unlike their Western counterparts, Soviet youth supposedly lacked experience with personal responsibility or in thinking for themselves. Nor could they turn to discredited tradition. The resulting introspection and perplexity would crush the superficial self-confidence. And so Russia could turn overnight from "the most morally unified country in the world" to "the worst moral chaos."[48]

Kennan's pat analysis underestimated both the ruthlessness of the Soviet government in repressing dissent and the possibility of producing a Goldilocks–middle-level supply of consumer goods. This 1932 report nevertheless remains significant as Kennan's first argument that the Soviet system contained within itself the seeds of its eventual disintegration. Fifteen years later, his assertion in the "X" article in *Foreign Affairs* that the Soviet Union, if contained, would eventually mellow or collapse would bring him lasting fame.

What Kennan never published in *Foreign Affairs* or anywhere else was the belief, confided in his diary, that Western capitalism also suffered fatal flaws: "overpopulation, overproduction, and intellectual collectivization." By the last he meant the suffocating spread of mass culture. Relief demanded regulating births, returning to the land, and reining in excessive production with state capitalism. The capitalist nations faced a stark choice. They could either allow free market competition to "work itself into such a chaos that it collapsed." That would pull down also "the cultural achievements of centuries" and launch "a new Middle Age of bolshevism." Or, the Western nations could "separate politics from economics." That would enable "their intelligent classes" to put "business life on a socialist basis from above, without turning political power over to the proletariat."[49]

The elitist advocated a similar solution—economic direction by intelligent people such as himself—for Communism. "I believe in dictatorship, but not the dictatorship of the proletariat," he affirmed. "The proletariat, like a well-brought-up child, should be seen and not heard. It should be properly clothed and fed and sheltered, but not crowned with a moral halo, and above all not allowed to have anything to do with government."[50] Kennan, then, reacted to the crisis of the Great Depression and to the contest between communism and capitalism by advocating a rational and benign authoritarianism. He inclined toward eugenics though he did not specify how such control should be imposed. Some of Kennan's ideas veered dangerously close to fascism. Nevertheless, he also despised such core aspects of fascism as demagogy, militarism, and jingoistic nationalism.

Focusing narrowly on Kennan's views on human exploitation misses his more original and deeply Chekhovian critique of both communism and capitalism. A puzzle of Kennan's life is why he never wrote the lengthy analysis of Anton Chekhov that he said he was going to do. It was unlike him not to undertake or complete a task. And as for writing, he would complete twenty books, thousands of diary pages, tens of thousands of letters, and many, many lectures and reports. So why leave undone the study of his most beloved author? His sole extant writing on the topic is an eleven-page essay, "Anton Chekhov and the Bolsheviks," completed in 1932. He argued that Chekhov prepared the ground for the Bolshevik Revolution with vivid depictions of "the ridiculousness and the tragedy" of czarist Russia. No other force "did more to shake the composure of the Russian bourgeoisie and the Russian intelligentsia." Chekhov's "ideas rang with the spirit of bolshevism"; his words were "Bolshevik words." And yet this master of irony remained aloof from politics, never joining and barely mentioning the rising ferment. Two factors accounted for this abstention, Kennan explained. First, while Marxist-Leninism denied "the supremacy of art or science over political dogma," Chekhov treasured art and science and regarded them as inseparable. The second reason plumbed Kennan's deepest core values. Far more grievous than the upper classes' exploitation of the lower classes was the exploitation of both by the "terrible mistake" of the factory. Taking Chekhov to heart, Kennan affirmed that the very concept of machine production constituted a "misunderstanding," a tragic perversion of humanity's moral relation with the material and spiritual realms. As a doctor, Chekhov diagnosed the worst affliction as the "incurable disease of industrialism."[51]

Throughout his long life, Kennan would favor artisanal production while disdaining machines. The pioneering environmentalism of Kennan's later years traces back not only to his boyhood summers amid nature on Nagawicka Lake and his later years sailing, but also to his channeling Chekhov's view of industrialism as a terrible mistake. Though original, insightful, and well-researched, the article on Chekhov met rejection by both the *Yale Review* and *Scribner's Magazine* and was never published.[52] As for why Kennan did not submit the essay elsewhere and, apparently, wrote no further about an author whose work touched him more profoundly than that of anyone else, one can only surmise. Perhaps his feelings for Chekhov, who probed not only the suffering that people imposed on each other but also the misery imposed by machines, reached so deep that they became too personal to expose to possible rejection or misunderstanding.

Once in the Soviet Union, Kennan threw himself into meeting both ordinary Russians and Soviet officials and into figuring out how communism was remaking Russia. With the crisis of Western capitalism apparently terminal, Kennan looked to alternatives. He later attested that he and his colleagues in the embassy had read "our Marx and Lenin" and "thrilled to the exploits of John Reed, to the tales of the Revolution."[53] After attending a play, "I came out of the theater with my head swimming with this contagious excitement, feeling that for a brief hour I had shared the heady belief that all of mankind was being in some way redeemed in this great purifying revolutionary effort."[54]

Orientalist stereotypes inclined him toward Soviet communism for other reasons. His classes at Princeton and in Berlin and his experience in the Baltic region had led Kennan to conclude that, due to deficiencies of national character, most Slavic people, including Russians, suffered from "primitiveness and sloppiness."[55] Communism, then, offered "a cruel cure for a crueler disease.[56]

He remained "continually torn between sympathy for a nation which, within the limitations of its own character and imported dogma, is trying to reconstruct its life on a basis finer and sounder than that of any other country anywhere—and disgust with the bigotry and arrogance of its leaders, who not only refuse to recognize their own mistakes and limitations but pretend that they have found the solution of all the problems of the rest of the world in their crude interpretation of a worn-out doctrine." Because he did really want to understand Russia and its problems, he felt insulted by the self-satisfied propaganda. Wielding the jargon of the psychological theory that he was reading, Kennan diagnosed the "neurotics," the Western liberals who glorified the Soviet experiment as a way to treat "their own internal conflicts." They "sublimated their bitterness against themselves in the general Soviet bitterness against the rest of the world." As "good psychologists," the Bolsheviks were exploiting these gullible people preoccupied with their "subconscious minds."[57]

All this thinking, working, and partying took its toll on Kennan's always precarious health. "Woke up with a headache from a party at the

French Embassy," he wrote in his diary. Then, later, "had pains in my groin today so badly that I decided to stop drinking until summer."[58] But he did not relent on the day-and-night pace.

RUSSIA VERSUS NORWAY

Despite his criticism of the Soviet experiment, Kennan found much of it appealing. What he loved about Communist Russia reflected what he hated about bourgeois America. He applauded: "the seriousness and Spartan qualities of Russian life, newspapers without advertisements or sensationalism, movies without sexual romanticism, theatres without sentimentality, politics without pot-bellies and scheming matrons, justice without fear, and marriage without hypocrisy." The last spoke also to the perennial dilemmas of his personal life.[59]

Revolution he approved of—but with a Kennanish caveat. He agreed that it was "better to start with humanity in the rough" than to "fool with an older and more refined society which is far too selfish and cynical" to sacrifice enough for significant change. On this, the Communists' "point is well taken." The problem with Communist revolution, however, was that it lumped together "the remnants of decent humanity" with the "snobs and the grafters and the profiteers and the political vultures," and called for exterminating all. Kennan was never a fan of the proletariat. "I am interested in a revolution which would raise the best elements of society—and not the worst," he concluded. The stance was typical Kennan. He was at once attracted to the creative potential of revolution while also wanting to "preserve rather than sacrifice its most valuable portions"—thoughtful people such as himself.[60]

Kennan viewed Russia through the lens of his perennial conflict between order and creativity. A July 1934 vacation in Norway, so strikingly different in culture from Russia, highlighted the quandary. George and Annelise, now reunited with two-year-old Grace after six months apart, escaped gritty Moscow to an idyll that reminded him of Nagawicka. His in-laws had "an ideal place here," a summer home perched on a half-mile-long island a bit out to sea but protected by huge rocks. George had bought a used seagoing sailboat and was "enjoying myself to the

FIGURE 17. George playing cards with his Norwegian in-laws. Annelise
second from right. (Courtesy of Princeton University Library.)

limit." He appreciated the "paradise of cleanliness, order, and well-fed
respectability." In this sanctuary of convention, the disorder of Moscow
seemed almost unreal. Nevertheless, he would "be very glad to get
back," he confided to Bullitt. Genuinely fond of Kennan and worried
about his tendency toward overwork, the ambassador urged him to
"take care of yourself and not hurry back." He suggested that George
remain in Norway until September. Kennan, however, insisted on cutting the holiday short. "To stay longer would only mean to get rusty and
lazy from inactivity." Then he confessed what impelled him: "I am really
homesick for Moscow, and will be happy to be back."[61]

On August 1, the day after that last note to Bullitt, George revealed to
Jeanette the "bitterness and discouragement" that had darkened his
days while sailing around the beautiful waters of Kristiansand. Part of
the sadness arose from the churlish rejection by the widow of the elder
George Kennan. The younger had asked if he could use the papers of
her late husband to write his biography. She, however, looked down on
the Milwaukee Kennans as a "strange crowd of backwoodsmen,"

incapable of understanding such an accomplished figure. Apparently unhinged, the widow also rebuked George for having, as a boy, penned an inadequate thank-you note. Thirty-year-old George was crushed. Russians, such as President Kalinin, had often inquired about his famous relative. "It has been a little hard for me, bearing the same name and nationality and having so much the same interests, to explain that I know little more of him than the average reader of his works."[62]

But this bout of "the most miserable nervous depression, which almost made me physically ill"—this sadness while sailing and relaxing with his wife and bouncy daughter on a lovely island—stemmed from more than the crabby snobbery of an elderly widow. Two recurring problems, both stemming from his favoring duty over creativity, tormented him. First, his rising diplomatic career, for which he had worked so very hard, amounted to only "petty bureaucratic success." "I could take more pride in one page of decent writing than in being an Ambassador," he claimed. Second, was dread that marriage was squeezing him into a powerless, pathetic creature. He mocked himself "as a spineless, somewhat infantile, futile little man, passively growing older in the bonds of matrimony." Meanwhile, his aspirations grew "fainter and fainter, and farther and farther from realization as the years go by." Applying the psychological theory that he was reading, Kennan blamed his "over-obsequious subconscious" on the "strange, stiff motherless childhood" he and Jeanette had suffered and on the excessive "repression and sacrifice" they had inherited from their father.

Kennan resolved, at least for the moment, to tackle his dilemma by reaffirming order and obligation. That meant hunkering down in the box of marriage and career while resigning himself to a life with "no great elation, no blind eagerness, no fantastic vistas"—in sum, nothing "enchanting." He would abandon the quest for wonder that had impelled him ever since he had been a young boy looking for the fairies in Juneau Park. Now, as a middle-aged man, such renunciation was symbolized by the sane and sensible path of Norway. Whether George could ever totally give up on freedom and creativity remained a question, however. A few days after his pledge to stick with his wife and the pleasant vacations on the island, he penned a cryptic note to

Jeanette: he was "leaving Norway for what may well have been my last visit here."[63]

ALASKA, THE BASHKIR REPUBLIC, AND FASCISM IN AMERICA

Once back in Moscow, the breakneck pace of work and parties resumed. Over the summer, the members of Bullitt's mission finally moved into their new apartments and offices, and the ambassador was installed in a renovated Spaso House. Kennan could now focus on writing diplomatic reports. The pace, quality, and variety of his output impressed Bullitt as well as Robert F. Kelley and others back in Washington. Though he did not know it, he was educating himself for his broad responsibilities thirteen years later as director of the State Department's Policy Planning Staff. Considering that most of his reports were not solicited by the department in Washington and that Bullitt afforded him largely free rein, the topics reflected Kennan's personal interests.

The death of secret police (OGPU) chief V. R. Menzhinski and the expected reorganization of Soviet security forces spurred a despatch based on Kennan's reading of Soviet publications and on Moscow gossip. The significance of the report lay in what it assumed: the Soviet Union was evolving toward a rationalized state with less arbitrary police power. Such optimism would heighten Kennan's disappointment—and lasting resentment—at the onslaught of Stalin's purges a year later. "Observers in Moscow are generally agreed" that the hitherto largely autonomous OGPU would soon come under the wing of the central Soviet government, Kennan informed the State Department. That change would help confine the secret police to fixed channels and provide "a semblance of legal guarantees for individual rights in place of the unbridled and irresponsible authority" thus far exercised by the police.[64]

A despatch on the Bashkir Republic in Eastern European Russia revealed Kennan's interest in economic as well as administrative infrastructure. Bashkir boasted the huge steel complex under construction at Magnitogorsk. Mehnert, his German journalist friend, had spent several days at this supposed showcase of Stalin's rapid industrialization. While impressed with the scale of the project, Mehnert emphasized the hardships of the workers, the crudity of conditions, and the sloppiness of the construction. For a State Department file on "Living Conditions" in Russia, Kennan reported that fifty-eight families had to share one kitchen and were "forced to steal firewood for the lone stove." Only one outdoor spigot served several barracks of workers. Foreign engineers at the site did not expect the works to be completed until 1940, if not later. Food, however, appeared plentiful, especially in the collective farms of Bashkir. Peasants received "five kilograms of bread per workday." With the surplus, some villagers had bought bicycles, which "were proudly exhibited as signs of a new prosperity."[65] The implicit, orientalist message here, shared by Kennan, Mehnert, and many Westerners in Russia, was that only stolid Slavs could survive the hardships the Soviets imposed on their people.[66] Kennan concluded that Stalin's industrialization was making progress, however painful. Whether the Soviets could prepare in time to resist foreign threats remained, however, an open question.

Kennan monitored the tensions dividing Russia, Poland, the Baltic states, and Germany. He interpreted Soviet efforts to improve relations with these hostile neighbors as evidence of Moscow's "isolation in eastern Europe which has followed the break-down of Soviet-German friendship." Poland was leaning toward Germany. Germany was also benefiting from the growing appeal of fascism in the Baltic countries. Meanwhile, "Finland and Roumania are frankly hostile, Estonia cold and suspicious." Still fearing an attack from Japan, Russia was trying "with the greatest energy" to secure some "guarantee of the safety of its western frontiers." Despite his admiration for aspects of the Soviet experiment, his love for Russian culture, and his fondness for the Russian people, Kennan evidenced little sympathy, even within the constraints of Washington's official neutrality, for Russia's plight. Instead, he emphasized that all of Foreign Minister Litvinov's conciliatory efforts toward Russia's neighbors "have met with failure." Litvinov's only recourse had been "posing dexterously as the disappointed idealist whose peaceful proposals are rejected by scheming neighbors for ulterior motives."[67] Kennan also translated without comment a six-page TASS communique on the Soviets' sale of the Chinese Eastern Railroad to Japan, a step that eased tensions somewhat.[68]

Continuing the study of international communism that he had pursued in Berlin and in Riga, the diplomat analyzed the prospects for a deal between the Second International of democratic socialists and the Third International of the Communists. Since 1922, the two rivals for the loyalty of the international laboring class had worked at odds. Now, with the rise of fascism, the Soviets were seeking collective action regarding "the proletarian factions in Spain." Beyond noting the fascist domination of democratic socialist labor unions in such nations as Germany, Kennan, skeptical about labor unions in general, gave little indication that he felt much was at stake here for either Washington or himself. He also remained silent about whether he regarded the fascists as an international threat.[69]

Kennan worked hard on reporting Soviet impressions of the United States. In four despatches totaling twenty-eight pages written from late October to early December 1934, he translated articles dealing with the kidnapping of the Lindbergh baby, Soviet attitudes toward Alaska, the American elections, and "possibilities for the development of fascism in the United States." In the despatch about the kidnapping, the diplomat mocked the Soviets for simplistically assuming that the media frenzy stemmed largely from "a deliberate attempt by some mysterious omnipotent hand to distract public opinion from the 'crimes' of the police in the recent textile strikes."[70] The report on Alaska, taken from an authoritative article in *Pravda*, emphasized three points: the Soviets regretted that the czarist government had sold this vast chunk of strategic real estate, believed that only a socialist government could develop it adequately, and worried that Japan might seize it as a base for attacking the Soviet Union. While mildly skeptical about these concerns of the Soviets, Kennan was irked that they had thwarted his own ambition to analyze economic development on the Siberian side of the Bering Sea by refusing to release the data.[71] Kennan did not deign to comment on *Pravda*'s assertion that while Roosevelt's Democrats had won the recent congressional elections, only the Communist Party could really protect the working class of America.[72]

A long article on the prospects for fascism in the United States drew from a roundtable in the *Modern Monthly*. This liberal American magazine had polled the historian Charles A. Beard, author Theodore Dreiser, economist Stuart Chase, and other intellectuals. In a diary entry back in 1930, Kennan had regarded the rise of a fascist-like party in America as potentially positive but as nevertheless improbable. Now the diplomat translated without explicit comment Beard's acknowledgment that his earlier confidence in the long-term vitality of American democracy had evaporated. As to whether America would turn fascist, Beard offered: "I do not know; it may be very possible." Dreiser warned that fascism was not only possible but "that it is near." Chase predicted that fascism would attract many Americans, especially those in the vast hinterland, as a patriotic movement with marching bands and slogans. Bellicose enthusiasts would shout for "white hegemony" and "Down with the Negroes, Mexicans, Jews, Italians, Gypsies, and Chinese. Down with politicians, professors, the brain trust. Down with great capital, exchange sharks, and Morgan—back to the golden days of the old times, of small-scale trade in Main Street." The Soviet article concluded with a warning that militias were grouping under the slogan of "America First."[73] Kennan did not specify what he now thought about fascism possibly coming to America. Nevertheless, his private opinions remained clear. Though neither a jingoist nor a militarist, he did favor an ethnically homogeneous United States and an end to immigration. He despised both the politicians hustling for reelection and the market manipulators who had fleeced the inheritance from his mother. In 1938, he would write an essay (never published) calling for a far more authoritarian government in the United States. Now, in 1934, the question of fascism in America intrigued him enough that he chose this ten-page article to translate.

Despite his disdain for claims that communism could solve the problems of the outside world, Kennan respected, and at times enthused, about what practical-minded Communists were tackling inside Russia. He empathized with a number of Russian intellectuals and high civilian officials, and he counted some of them as personal friends. An elitist himself, he sympathized with their bid for "power and dignity" in carrying out their missions. He understood their rising impatience with "dictatorial interference and restraint from party functionaries" who were interested only in sustaining their "jealous discipline" and their "Byzantine scholasticism." Kennan appreciated above all that these practical-minded officials and thinkers "enjoyed association with foreigners, and travel abroad." His seeking closer contact with Russians fit neatly with the hopes of these Russians "to lean on the outside world and to learn from it." "It was among them" that Americans "had to look for cooperation" in building mutually beneficial Russian-American relations.[74] The decimation of these friends and budding allies in the purges of 1935–1938 would incite Kennan's lasting frustration and rage.

BREAKDOWN

As his time in Russia approached the twelve-month mark, Kennan was running low on steam. Packed days at work were usually followed by dinners or parties that dragged on until 3:30 A.M. or later. Caught up in the thrill, Annelise wrote Jeanette about how "we were all excited" to visit the Kremlin as guests of President Kalinin. The "huge ballroom in white marble was perfectly beautiful," while the buffet was served in an equally "perfect jewel" of a space.[75] The amount of alcohol drunk in a typical week was "depressing," George sighed, wondering "how long I can stand it."[76] Family life was also full. Grace, speaking her own mix of Norwegian and English, "tells me at once when I use the wrong washcloth . . . points out the spots on dressing-robe, and attends personally to the scrubbing of my back, whenever she is allowed to." "He is crazy about her," Annelise reported.[77]

When George took to bed with a cold in late November 1934, the momentary letup, plus the visit of Kent, George's twenty-one-year-old half-brother, brought past vexations to the surface. In Kent he saw "the shy, restless ghost" of his younger self. Both brothers were "terribly lacking in intelligent parental leadership and training." Both had inherited "Kennan sentimentality." Unfortunately for Kent, however, "he has not got the dark James fierceness to help him in his battle with Kennan timidity." George had also benefited, he believed, from "the physical rigors of St. John's and the moral rigors of Princeton." That strength was now melting away in the heated frenzy of Moscow. Moreover, restlessness with domesticity and duty was again gnawing at him. "Bad day," he confided in his diary. Echoing the phrasing of his August 1 letter, he continued, "Rainy day. Permeated by the suspicion that I am worn out and depleted by—oh, what the hell's the use?"[78]

In appraising Kent, he dredged up a memory that evidently still pained him. He saw Kent "as Mrs. Hard must have seen me in Washington, and I judged him harshly, as I myself was harshly judged."[79] Here was George, a married man and a father, a diplomat with a rising career and widespread respect, still holding up as arbiter Anne Hard, the mother of the fiancée who had dumped him and had failed to return his mother's ring. Kennan admired how Anne and William Hard had forged the conventional and unconventional elements of their lifestyles and politics into a balanced, coherent identity. His life, by contrast, was coming apart.

Kennan's physical and mental collapse, the most severe of his 101-year life, struck the evening of "December 12, a year to the day after my arrival in Moscow." Superstitious about dates, he was alert to the inherent drama of such anniversaries. On that Wednesday he was slogging through another exhausting, midweek workday. That evening, George went with Annelise and friends to a theater adaptation of Tolstoy's *Resurrection*. The melodrama portrays the seduction and disgrace of a servant girl by a young landowner. Inspired by the American single-tax reformer Henry George, the nobleman realizes the damage he has wrought and tries to make amends, not only to the aggrieved woman but also to the laborers on his estate. As the nobleman explains why he is turning his land over to the peasants, one of them exclaims, "Well, he had a head, that George!" While Kennan found all this absorbing, in the middle of the second act he abruptly stood up and rushed home.[80]

Agonizing stomach pains and nausea made up only part of his discomfort. As the customary after-theater party coalesced in their apartment, Kennan bravely staggered out of bed and tried to converse. "It was a normal Moscow night"—but not really. George realized, "with a sense of relief, that this was the end, that something had snapped, that my own responsibility was over for a long time to come." He was soon diagnosed with a gastric ulcer. But as the workaholic understood, the crumpling was in part self-willed. He welcomed the snapping of something, the sudden relief from his obligations.[81] Unable to slow down, he broke down.

Kennan lay in bed for eight weeks with a condition that, clearly going beyond ulcers, resembled depression. "Days and nights at first had no meaning for me." The bells of the "Kremlin gate rang out the hours . . . but what hours they were I didn't know—I didn't care." He and infant Grace, she singing her "bird-like, gay soliloquies, half in English, half in Norwegian," shared "our preoccupation with the present, our indifference to past and future." He felt detached when visiting friends sat on his bed to continue the discussions that had once fascinated him. He mustered some interest when a friend brought him volumes of nineteenth-century diplomatic despatches sent by American representatives from St. Petersburg. They reinforced his sense of eternal Russia: Russia had changed communism more than communism had changed that nation. He took comfort in the past wisdom. "There is no nation," an American had written of czarist Russia, "which has such a need of foreigners; and there is none which is so jealous of them."[82] He toyed with writing a historical analysis of "The Permanent Characteristics of Russia as a World Power."[83]

His gaunt appearance worried colleagues. An embassy official warned Bullitt, then vacationing in Florida, that Kennan was enduring "a most violent attack of stomach trouble; vomiting and pains." A doctor had diagnosed either a "very acute acid poisoning or caustic ulcers." In any case, "Kennan will not be able to remain long in Moscow." The official advised Bullitt to consult with Kelley in the Eastern European division about a possible successor.[84]

On December 31, nearly three weeks after his initial breakdown, Kennan pulled himself together enough to think about the future. "Personally, I am not unpleased at this turn of events," he confided to Jeanette. He was referring to the State Department's generous offer, finagled by Bullitt, to continue paying his salary while he recovered at a sanatorium in Central Europe for a period of up to six months. During this time,

Annelise and Grace would first remain in Moscow, and then "probably go to Italy . . . and stay there until I finish my cure." He welcomed this "peaceful and welcome change." For months he had been feeling miserable, only to have someone, probably Annelise, assure him "that it was all one's 'imagination,'" while others, likely friends, advise him to have another drink. He anticipated a break for up to a half-year from both work and wife.

George framed this change in his own life in a revealing way. He extrapolated from his domestic life to a generalized critique of bourgeois marriage, with its "personal sentimentality and cruelty, its economic selfishness, and its social blindness." Although unceasing labor had damaged his own health, he insisted that such work remained "the only solution for the stresses of matrimony." He mused that back on the farm homestead, women had spent their time helping to raise and prepare the family's food. But now middle-class women frittered away the day in "visits to the hairdressers," self-indulgent club activities, "tea-parties, and conversations about shopping." His sour, misogynistic comment caricatured an amalgam of women he had read about, his despised stepmother, and Annelise, who now enjoyed the help of two maids and a caregiver for Grace. "Few husbands," George warned, "are going to be interested" in such wifely activities. Instead, the typical man would develop a "real community of interests and mutual respect" with his "stenographer-secretary, who shares the trials and triumphs of his day." Hence the "iron logic" of the frequency with which "secretaries [but evidently not husbands] cause marital complications."

Kennan drew three conclusions from this analysis. First, "the character of marriage must be changed. Permanent and possessive intimacy must give away to something resembling—aside from sexual relationships—the attitude of college roommates to each other." George did not explain, nor did he seem worried about, how monogamy could survive such change. Second, the "family must disappear as an ideal of human happiness (for a very stuffy, selfish one it is)," even though it "endured as a housing arrangement." The setup paralleled what Kennan had prescribed after reading *Lady Chatterley's Lover* a few months earlier. Sex did not merit "introspection." Rather it "should be only incidental."

People should "spend as little time contemplating its pleasures as they do worrying about its results."[85] This vision of a more open marriage also reflected the ideas of George's hero at Princeton, the hobo poet Harry Kemp. His third conclusion was that "women must have their own work" outside the home, something that Annelise resisted. As to whether all this "sounds like a word from Moscow," George defiantly affirmed: "It is." So what if someone accused him of "having gone Bolshevist." The family, he emphasized, "is truly a relic of the patriarchal past." Not only did it create problems for individuals, but it also stood in the way of solving society's "fundamental problems."[86] As for his own family, George looked forward to having Annelise and Grace away for up to a half-year while he recovered.

Meanwhile, Annelise herself suffered health problems, probably aggravated by the strains of Russia and of living with George. "Something is the matter with my intestines," she complained to Jeanette, and "besides my kidneys are out of place."[87]

Although Kennan had managed to exchange convention for convalescence, he harbored no "boisterous hopes or enthusiasms," no unconventional ambitions, for the coming year. As a diplomat, he could aspire only to life as "a timid, minor official in a very muddled and depressing world." He referred cryptically to having "left too many problems unsolved before falling ill."[88] Those difficulties most likely related to personal relations. His work was so exemplary that it won unstinting compliments from both Bullitt and officials back in Washington.

"There is no one in the Embassy in Moscow in whom I have more confidence than in you or for whom I have more affection," Bullitt gushed. He added, "You have worked too hard, I know." He offered to reassign Kennan to Washington so that he could be treated by "the President's physician . . . a good friend of mine." Laying on the praise, Bullitt affirmed that in his long career he had met "few people in whose character one has absolute confidence. I have in yours and do not want to lose you."[89] Kennan soaked up the praise, acknowledging, "I react so strongly to the confidence or mistrust of others." He needed this boost to "my own self-respect."[90] The ambassador alerted the State Department, "I am so fond of that boy and have such confidence in him that I hate to see him leave Moscow." Nevertheless, ulcers could prove serious, and Kennan needed the rest. Despite its Depression-era pinched budget, the State Department generously granted him, in effect, several months off from work. Kennan was officially assigned as a consul in the legation in Vienna. That would enable him to recover at the Gutenbrunn Sanatorium outside the city and then, when he felt better, undertake some duties. The bottom line was that he would receive his paycheck and not even have to take sick leave.

Amid Kennan's physical ailments, his financial health had improved. A promotion and a raise had boosted his annual salary to $4,000 plus foreign exchange compensation of about $2,500. Their Moscow apartment was free. They could afford two Russian maids plus a Norwegian caretaker for Grace. George and Annelise were saving for a special purpose. The half-mile-long island where the Sorensens had rented their summer home was for sale for $5,000. Annelise's father had offered them a fifth of the island if they could come up with $1,000. "It's the most beautiful island around Kristiansand," George had written Jeanette before his collapse. It boasted "a magnificent view from the house over the sea." He dreamed of building a house that could "provide for little Grace—as Nagawicka did for us—the symbol of a home." While he could come up with two or three hundred dollars, if "Gene could help me out on that . . . I should be truly happy."[91] A few years earlier, Jeanette's husband, Gene Hotchkiss, a stockbroker, had exceeded instructions and had lost George's inheritance in stock market speculation.

THE CURE AT GUTENBRUNN

While Kennan in December 1933 had gone into Russia with intense excitement, he left thirteen months later with excruciating illness. That he endured the pain with emotions so under control that he could pen a running account of the ordeal testifies to his grit. He wrote as a way of managing and directing his turbulent feelings.

In mid-January 1935, Kennan received a telegram from the State Department ordering him to proceed to Vienna. At about the same time, he had his stomach x-rayed, which required drinking a lot of "x-ray porridge." That potion inflicted fever and diarrhea with pains worse even than his original attack a month earlier. His imminent departure necessitated "a lot of frantic packing" for the sanatorium and for his subsequent work at the legation. Too sick to do much himself, Kennan lay on a sofa in the apartment trying to entertain well-wishers while Annelise and an assistant packed. At the train station, Kennan, still suffering the diarrhea, stood for "interminable minutes" on the steps of the car while friends below wisecracked in the shivering cold.

Finally, the train departed—and only minutes later, George was horrified to see that the pile of baggage in his compartment "did not include my brief-case with my passport, visas, laissez-passers, etc." He suddenly recalled "that I had also taken pains to turn all my Russian money over to Annelise." She had forgotten to give it to him or to make sure that he had the precious briefcase. What could he do? Getting off at the next station meant "lying thru the night on the railway station floor with crowds of peasants and trying to handle my baggage, with frequent visits to a place where sanitary conditions would defy description." He decided to stay on the train. That night "fever pounded in my ears; my teeth kept chattering; the uneasy stomach gave me no rest." Eating was out of the question. Finally, a sympathetic porter rigged up a "primitive hot-water bottle," and he managed to fall asleep. At a train stop, George scraped together coins he had saved for tips and sent Annelise a telegram.

Finally, the train reached the border station that he and Bullitt thirteen months earlier had come through "amid so much excitement." Taking a room in the small hotel there, George awaited the arrival of his passport and documents on the next day's train. The pervasive smell was nothing to worry about, the manager assured him. It was just the fumigating against bedbugs.

Freed from the traces of work and wife, the achiever soon hitched his energies to more creative discipline. He feared that unbridled freedom could lead to "complete moral and mental decomposition." After years of talking about penning fiction, he was now, damn it, going to actually write it. He resolved to honor the "good literary habit of forcing myself to sit down and write for two or three hours every morning."[92] He started out with elaborate word-portraits, depicting physical locations, personalities, moods, atmosphere, and implicit as well as explicit meanings so finely wrought that they foreshadowed what scholars many decades later would term "thick description." In his first two days out of Moscow, he penned five pages of tightly packed script that he sent to Jeanette. He described, for instance, the playacting at the border rail station where he was waiting for his documents and money. Minutes before a train bearing Westerners came into at the station, "the place comes to life. Uniforms are donned over drab clothing. The orchestra assembles. The magazine stand is unlocked." When "the train arrives, the customs officials have only to button up their collars, the orchestra has only to strike up the 'Blue Danube,' and lo—Russia—Soviet Russia—is on parade, ready for inspection." This display of sophistication and material plenty, intended to impress Western travelers, convinced Kennan that "Russia, like Japan, faced the West with a sense of inferiority."[93]

Feeling inadequate was a Kennan family tradition, George reflected. They felt "condemned to loneliness and inconspicuousness." He may have had in mind the strange ineptitude of his father, a famed income tax expert. Despite his credentials, Kent Kennan had earned little money, had depended on the inherited income of his children and then on the rent of boarders, and had, only a year earlier, died nearly penniless. George resolved to free himself from such inherited inferiority. The Kennans were really second to none in "vision," "moral force," and "intellect," he insisted to Jeanette. Less than two months after his collapse from overexertion and ulcers, George was aiming toward "greatness, or what passes for greatness." In faulting the Kennans' "egotistical, cowardly self-deprecation" he was pinpointing his own personality. He resolved to write a major novel based on his life in Europe. Once he received from Jeanette all the letters and diaries he had sent her since 1927, "I am going to undertake something resembling fiction."[94] Despite this pledge, Kennan after two months and much procrastination, had "ground out [only] 8 pages of amateurish fiction." Just as he would never write the major study of Chekhov that he fantasized about, so, too, would he never write the fiction that he aspired to create. Perhaps both projects meant so much to him that he could not bear the imperfections of actuality.

Nevertheless, during his cure at the Gutenbrunn Sanatorium Kennan wrote many pages. Some of what he penned explored concepts of emotion, psychology, and politics that, a decade later, would undergird the long telegram of February 1946 and the "X" article of July 1947. Now, in February 1935, having little to do but stare at the bare walls, try to write, and talk with his doctor, George probed deeply into his past and his personality.

By reducing to words, and thereby ordering, the more inchoate feelings swirling through him, he strengthened the communication between his more emotional and more rational modes of cognition. His writing became more adept at discussing emotions and in mobilizing them to persuade others.

Kennan couched much of his introspection in the psychoanalytic theory he was reading at Gutenbrunn, not far from where the master, Sigmund Freud, lived and worked. His bent toward these ideas reflected his living at a time when Freudian ideas circulated throughout much of society in Europe and America. Kennan may also have been influenced by Bullitt, a friend and collaborator of Freud. Years later, in the post–World War II period, the widespread acceptance of Freudian theory would lend a scientific patina to Kennan's analysis of the Soviet Union in pop psychological terms. Also impelling Kennan to immerse himself in these ideas were confessional talks with his Freudian-minded physician, Dr. Frieda Por. Por, a Hungarian Jew, formed a deep bond with her patient that would endure throughout their lives. Kennan later helped her emigrate to the United States. She would remain the primary care doctor and confidant not only for George, but also for Annelise and their children.[95]

Another lasting outcome of these months stemmed from his reading clippings from U.S. newspapers. From them he honed a sharp critique of American society and politics. That criticism, along with his psychological discourse, would shape his subsequent writings, including the long telegram and the "X" article. Both those manifestos emphasized that in responding to the Soviet challenge, the United States had to reform its domestic institutions. To be sure, the mood and challenges of 1946–1947 remained a long way off as George sat propped up in his hospital bed outside Vienna in 1935.

Nevertheless, it was during those months of intense self-analysis that he developed some of the concepts, concerns, and patterns of thinking that he would stick with for the rest of his long life. Still missing, however, from what would impel the future Kennan were his trauma and fury when witnessing the gruesome purges of late 1935–1938, and then seeing the extension of that police brutality into Eastern and Central Europe in 1944–1945.

In this most introspective phase of a self-reflective life, Kennan in the first half of 1935 toyed with a variety of responses to his perennial dilemmas: obligation versus creativity, family versus sexual freedom, reality versus fantasy. He pondered whether aspiring to mental health was a trap and an illusion. As in years past, he searched for maternal succor and suffered the heavy hand of St. John's discipline.

Kennan remained unsure what to make of what he diagnosed as his "neurosis." Sometimes he mocked himself as "a scared young American who cracks up now and then with a loud thud against the realities of life."[96] Other times, he turned the problem upside down. Perhaps true health "in the physical and nervous sense" requiring taking "refuge successfully in unreality." Since dreams, as "Freud tells us, are designed to protect our sleep" from unresolved problems, was this "not equally true of our day dreams, our pet illusions?" Pushing the point further, he asked, "Cannot ill-health," the "nervous and physical dissolution" that he suffered, actually reflect "the only true health of the spirit?" Though cryptic in what he was getting at here, Kennan seems to have been pondering whether his penchant for being "distracted by dreams and illusions"—a release he had pursued since childhood—should be cultivated as the means for coping with the dilemmas of his life. Illusion might offer escape from that "ruinous, destructive thing called 'truth.'"[97]

In a remarkable dialogue penned on February 12, George in turn pleaded for the sympathetic, maternal understanding he had lacked as a boy, and then disciplined that yearning with the harsh voice of a masculine authority figure, someone like Headmaster Duke Smythe. Speaking of himself in the second person, he stressed "the need of unburdening your soul to the Frau Doktor. You are anxious to tell her that you are depressed." Then came the rebuke: No woman could help you, unless she were "beyond the last trace of femininity and treated you with the unsparing frankness and the contempt which you deserve." That description fit how he remembered his stepmother. George persisted: "Well, after all, she is in charge of my treatment. She is a doctor. Should she not know the state of mind of her patient?" Down came the cane: "Learn to take it, Kennan. Don't run away. It's your problem. It won't help you to enlighten the Frau Doktor. She doesn't care whether you face life successfully when you get out of here. No one does, and for that reason you cannot spite anyone but yourself by being unsuccessful. Cut it out!"[98]

He could not, however, cut out either that yearning for maternal succor or his equally problematic desire for sexual freedom. Again addressing himself in the second person, he wrestled with whether "you can beat down your own ego" enough to "save your family." Family demanded that he give up on creativity. "You will only grow older and cooler. Finally you will become impotent," he told himself. Another time, he approached the dilemma as a conflict between biology and sociology. "Men are unfortunately impelled by the instinct to reproduce his [sic] kind." Acting on those impulses, however, led to "complications." Therefore, "the man who lets himself get caught between the cogs of nature and those of society gets rubbed to pieces." A man could either "make himself an outcast" by pursuing sexual freedom or accept "death, a renunciation of one's own life."[99]

No matter how much he resolved to tamp down his desire, it flamed up. "Again a vista opens up," he recorded in his diary. "(How many more? How often?) This time it must not fade like the former ones. It must not!" Then came the equally impassioned rebuke: "You are beaten. Acknowledge it. You have no personal dignity any more. All that remains is your dignity as a husband, a father and an official. Say good-bye to this world. You have failed. Get that, god damn it,—you have failed."[100]

Meanwhile, Annelise, whom George had expected to stay in Italy throughout his months-long cure, came instead to Gutenbrunn in mid-February. She took a nearby apartment. Though glad to see wife and daughter, George groused to Jeanette that he had "written nothing here since Annelise & the baby arrived. They take too much time." He added, "Don't idealize our marriage. It's been near enough the rocks on more than one occasion."[101] On April 9, three days before he left Gutenbrunn for Vienna, Annelise and Grace left for a month in Norway. As their train was about to depart, Annelise could not reach down through the open window far enough to "kiss me, so she gave me her hand, and I kissed it. Then Grace took off her woolen glove and held her hand out, too, for the same purpose. That saved the moment—if not the day."[102]

While unsure how to navigate the Freudian dilemma of Eros versus Civilization, Kennan was firm in condemning what he saw as two malevolent forces, industrialization and American politics. He bemoaned the "universal sadness that covers human life wherever industrialization has forced its entrance." Whether combined with "poverty and dirt and disease" or with "the pomp of power," machines wreaked havoc. Industrialization bared "the nastiness and pettiness and ugliness of provincial towns, against the background of a violated countryside." The problem arose not from the "means of production," as the Marxists insisted, but rather from the more basic "damage which the machine has done to the human body and the human soul." Industrialization, beloved by both Communists in Russia and capitalists in America, ruined everything.[103]

CONTEMPT FOR WASHINGTON

Though he worked for the U.S. government, the diplomat despised how it operated. After reading the syndicated political columnists Frank Kent and Drew Pearson, Kennan on May 13 felt himself "falling, falling, falling into a bottomless abyss." In the columns leading up to that date, Kent and Pearson had served up their usual fare: the Washington intrigues and manipulations entailed in enacting and in carrying out Franklin D. Roosevelt's New Deal and his foreign policy.[104] Kennan peered at the proverbial sausage-making of legislation with the perspective of a vegetarian: "The whole thing is disgusting." He recoiled at the "cheap public curiosity" feeding off "the limited mental horizon and the limitless conceit" of the pundits. He despised the "vast, diffused machinery of government, divided within itself, trembling" before the voters and the demagogues. That this pathetic system was trying to deal with the challenges of the Great Depression he found "ludicrous, horrible and hopeless."[105]

At a time when fascist dictators had seized control in Italy and Germany, Stalin commanded Russia, and authoritarians were on the rise elsewhere, including Austria, Kennan lacked both understanding and appreciation of the U.S. system of checks and balances. Nor did he perceive the real progress achieved by Roosevelt's New Deal, however messy the hurly-burly process. Kennan favored instead "a strong government with dictatorial powers, manned by the best brains the country could muster." He would clearly include himself in that roster. Only such a "consistent and ruthless" dictatorship could tackle overproduction and other systemic problems. Acknowledging that this all sounded "un-American," Kennan embraced the label. He ranted: "I hate the rough and tumble of our political life; I hate the whole damned system; I hate democracy; I hate the press . . . I hate the 'peepul.'"[106]

Neither did he respect the State Department: "Our country has absolutely no European policy." As to what that policy should be, Kennan, characteristically, said nothing, even in this tell-all letter to Jeanette. He was writing from a suburb of Vienna, where the increasingly authoritarian government was trying to fend off the rival ambitions of Fascist Italy and Nazi Germany. He had to have had some opinions, for only weeks earlier Bullitt had written asking his "view of the possibility of Austria going Nazi this summer or autumn."[107] What Kennan replied has apparently not survived. A letter to Bullitt did opine that rising tensions in Europe might lead to "Moscow eating out of our hand" in the stalled war debt negotiations.[108]

Juxtaposed against Kennan's disdain for Washington's supposed ineptitude in making use of diplomatic reporting from Europe was his confidence that he could generate such intelligence. "I have more qualifications for reporting on conditions in northern and eastern Europe than any man I know. I know the languages as few do. I know the countries, and how to live in them. I know the people, and how to get along with them." Nevertheless, "all that means nothing to people like [Senate

Foreign Relations Committee chair William E.] Borah and [populist Louisiana senator] Huey Long." He feared that they might succeed in politicizing the Foreign Service and filling it "with salesmen and back-slappers." That would perpetuate "the traditional inefficacy of American foreign policy in Europe."[109]

THE FUTURE?

As for his own future, Kennan mused that he should leave the Foreign Service since its ineffectuality encouraged "too much estheticism," by which he meant frittering away energy in collecting "Persian carpets and old books." Wasting time on superficial beauty was far distant from working on great fiction, as George hoped to do. But standing in the way of a fresh start was his family. Annelise and little Grace "are both ladies, in the old-fashioned sense." For all his contempt for the U.S. government, Kennan appreciated that it paid enough for him to provide Annelise with "more dignity, comfort, and respect" than "she could have on $100,000 a year at home." If he lost his job, "God help us." "That's why," he added in a pointed comment to Jeanette, "I want the island." Jeanette had, in fact, started a kindergarten in her home, in part to earn money to pay back George for the inheritance that her husband had speculated away in 1931.[110]

Although George's rant about hating democracy stemmed in part from his ire at reading the columnists and, he admitted, from two painful carbuncles on his back, the underlying sentiment persisted. On April 12, having gained eighteen pounds and calmed his stomach, he had left Gutenbrunn Sanatorium and commenced working in the U.S. legation with his old boss from Berlin, George S. Messersmith, now the Minister to Austria.[111] Suffering a relapse in May, George returned to the sanatorium. He utilized the time to translate from the German the 200-page, highly technical social insurance law just adopted in Austria. From this weighty document, Kennan drew even weightier conclusions. The ironhanded Kurt Schuschnigg regime in Vienna had appointed a committee of experts to fix the social insurance program, which for years had run a deficit. The committee came up with a detailed plan, and the authoritarian government rammed it through the parliament. "There was no demagoguery, no public wrangling and debate by laymen, no appeal to the emotions and greed of the public."[112] In Kennan's view, those were precisely the sins disgustingly detailed in Kent's and Pearson's columns. Kennan embraced the wider implications. "If malicious despotism had greater possibilities for evil than democracy, benevolent despotism likewise had greater possibilities for good." Key was having "an intelligent, determined ruling minority" who felt responsible to the people at large rather than to politicians, lobbyists, or voters.

Amid this lauding of Austrian authoritarianism and lamenting about American democracy, Kennan, his health improving, was chafing to get back to Moscow. Worried that the State Department might not let him return, he wrote Bullitt, "I am very homesick for the Embassy," adding "I feel a little lonely and out of place still in this bourgeois environment." Bullitt reassured him, "I want you to come back here as soon as you can but there is no hurry." Moreover, "so far as the Department is concerned I think you can do what you please and get what you want," because "everyone there has the highest opinion of you." The challenge, Bullitt emphasized, was getting "well enough to stay well even in Moscow."[113] Annelise agreed, believing that it "would be silly of us" to rush back too soon because "George's stomach needs a longer holiday from the Russian food and the strain in there."[114]

Reassured that he could return to Russia, Kennan pondered how he might balance, finally, both creativity and obligation and thereby finesse his dilemma. He reflected that amid the excitement of 1934, he had been dangerously torn between his desire for Russia and the demands of his job. "I was too fascinated by Russia to take the restriction of a diplomatic status with equanimity," he acknowledged. "Moscow had me somewhat on the run." To Charlie Thayer he complained that "in a world as interesting as the U.S.S.R. we should have to reconcile ourselves to anything as boring and as out-of-date as life in the Moscow diplomatic corps." He reiterated his fear: the obligation "to political inactivity, self-restraint and objectivity" would "force a man to end up at an early age mentally, physically and emotionally sterile."

He had two ideas for avoiding such barrenness. First, he resolved to return to Moscow armed not just with physical health, but also with a "general mellowness which will permit me to witness with detachment the spectacle of a generation of young Russians engaged with the realities of life," while diplomats such as himself "entertain each other at dinner and collect carpets." Second, he would infuse the tedium of a diplomat's life with the creativity of writing. To Thayer, who was also a writer, Kennan proposed building up "within the framework of the foreign service" a corps "able to wield the pen as skillfully as the tea-cup." He envisioned a group talented enough to "develop a point of view much stronger and more effective than that of the Paris émigré crowd who made so much fuss about themselves."[115] Move over, Fitzgerald and Hemingway!

From April to November 1935, Kennan worked for Messersmith, first at the consulate and then at the legation. The minister grew concerned when Kennan suffered yet another digestive setback in June and "lost a few of the precious pounds he had gained." Messersmith assured Bullitt that though he had grown very fond of Kennan and would be "very glad to have him here" permanently, he recognized that George's heart remained in Moscow.[116] Also concerned about the convalescent's health, Bullitt asked Messersmith to "let me know frankly just what you think of Kennan coming back [soon] to Moscow." Given the limits on socializing being imposed by the secret police, Bullitt feared that "if Kennan should arrive in a nervous state . . . he might find the going difficult."[117] By late October, however, with Kennan increasingly impatient to return, the State Department assented. "I need not tell you," Messersmith wrote Bullitt, "with what regret I see Kennan go."[118]

Though his ten-month sojourn in Austria had calmed George's stomach, it had not cured his dilemma. He still fretted that "middle age and futility" would triumph. That meant "I won't alter the world, after all, before my imagination dies, or have another real love affair, on one of these summer nights, before my hair turns grey." When, he pointedly asked Jeanette, is someone of their family going to "actually do something?" For generations, the Kennans and Jameses had focused their energy into "breed[ing] an excellent stock." It was now time for "someone quite wonderful" to emerge.

FIGURE 18. George reveling in the Russian winter.
(Courtesy of Grace Kennan Warnecke.)

Could he rise to that exalted level? Kennan realized that any chance he had to "alter the world" depended on his expertise on Russia. Moreover, Austria seemed paralyzed and doomed. "No one here has any real hope for the future." And so, "I prefer Moscow." For all their arrogance and self-delusion, the Russians still believed they were making progress. Rather than dissipating their energies on their families, as he feared he had to do, Russians focused on a better society for all. "I am no Bolshevik," George assured Jeanette, but he admired some of what the Bolsheviks were doing, and he was "anxious to get back to Moscow."[119]

He had already stressed to Bullitt how "homesick" he was for the embassy in Moscow. Annelise affirmed, "We are both homesick for Russia."[120] Thayer used the same word. Realizing he had to take his Foreign Service examination in Washington, he "really hate[d] the idea of leaving Russia—I should die of homesickness in America."[121] Tragically, however, the Kennans and their friends would never return "home" to the excitement and the potential of Moscow in 1934.

That critical juncture passed in the months following Kennan's departure from Moscow in January 1935. No longer did a U.S.-Russian understanding directed against Japan beckon on the horizon. Seeking easier game, Tokyo's expansionists had shifted their gaze from Siberia to northern China. Moreover, Roosevelt, while prizing Russia as a check to Japan, had balked at committing the United States, especially with the ongoing Depression and a wary Congress. Interminable wrangling doomed Bullitt's dream of Monticello overlooking Moscow. Polo instruction had faltered after Thayer and Bullitt proved unable to stop Red Army cavalrymen from riding off with the ball. Even the effort to introduce baseball failed after an officer got beaned by a hardball. More seriously, negotiations over the World War I–era debt cratered after France pressured its Russian ally not to make a settlement that would pressure Paris to resume payment of its obligations to Washington. Even the radiance of Bullitt's personality had faded. When the boss visited Vienna, supposedly his second home and where he had worked with Freud, Kennan saw "with a rather horrible clarity" how flimsy the rich man's connections actually were. Ostensibly close friends "look suspiciously like acquaintances to me." Bullitt's exuberance and generosity only accentuated "a loneliness so profound that I dislike to contemplate it."[122]

Most grievous for the Americans in Moscow was the sea change wrought by Stalin's purges. Almost all of those "intelligent communist leaders" admired by Kennan suffered exile or death, or were so intimidated that they cut off contact with foreigners. Even more than Bohlen and Thayer, Kennan could never quite reconcile himself to the loss.

A few years later, Thayer offered a coda for their dream of finding in the soul of Soviet Russia answers for the imperfect West. "We came hoping to find something new—some sincere attempt to find a solution to many problems." Even after encountering the shortcomings of Moscow, "we still retained a hope that in time the mystic Russians somewhere—perhaps in the Caucasus or on the Volga or in Novgorod— could produce something if not revolutionary at least novel and interesting." Then "we lost even that hope."[123]

CHAPTER 4

STALIN'S TERROR AND KENNAN'S TRAUMA, 1935–1937

SEPTEMBER 11, 1935, his fourth wedding anniversary, found Kennan bored. "I look forward to returning to Russia," he wrote from Vienna. "God knows why, for I shall not be allowed to have much to do with the Russians." A chasm had opened between what he longed for in Russia and what "I can justify through any amount of rationalization." Friends in Moscow had warned that the secret police were cracking down on Russians who dared associate with foreigners. Yet he still ached "to rub elbows with them in the streets, to smell the earthy, almost touching smells which characterize them, to look into faces still so close to the stark realities of life and death."[1]

Upon returning to Moscow on November 14, Kennan found the situation even grimmer than he had feared. The Kremlin falsely accused top Communist Party and Red Army officials of treasonous contact with foreigners in cahoots with Stalin's exiled rival, Leon Trotsky. The Soviet propaganda machine whipped up a frenzied xenophobia. Most of the accused would suffer execution in 1937–1938. Kennan felt personally assaulted. He was outraged at *Pravda's* smearing foreign diplomats as representatives of the devil, as evil and dangerous.

The purges pummeled Kennan for reasons both personal and professional. Living in Russia grew so painful that by December 1936, a year after his return from Vienna and three years after his excited arrival in Moscow, he wanted out from the land he loved. Nonetheless, his duties for the State Department thrust him deeper into the horror. At the January 1937 trial of the brilliant Bolshevik publicist Karl Radek, a former guest at embassy parties, the overworked diplomat spent his days whispering a translation into the ear of the imperious new ambassador, Joseph E. Davies, and his nights writing reports for Washington.

THE LASTING PAIN

Suffering through the terror transformed Kennan in ways that would shape his political judgment for decades. The 1946 long telegram and 1947 "X" article, which provided a rationale and a doctrine for U.S. policy in the emerging Cold War, expressed emotions forged in Kennan's trauma during the purges. He would see post–World War II Soviet domination of Eastern and much of Central Europe as an expansion of Stalin's secret police–dominated, terror regime. Kennan's anger and disgust at the needless suffering inflicted on Russians he knew personally or by reputation rendered him a victim as well.

Amid the strain, he tried to control his fury. He knew that his breakdown in 1934–1935 and his reputation for emotional reactions rendered him vulnerable. Jealous detractors in the State Department envied his success. His credibility and continued rise in the bureaucracy demanded that he sustain a measured, rational tone in his despatches. He rarely permitted himself the dramatic flourishes that enlivened the reports of others in the embassy, such as Loy W. Henderson or Ambassador Davies.

Nevertheless, despite Kennan's effort to contain his explosive feelings, they often seeped into his conversations, despatches, diary, and letters. (It could not be otherwise given that the circuitry of the brain integrates more emotional and more rational thinking.) As a friend from Moscow, the British political philosopher Isaiah Berlin later testified, Kennan remained "terribly absorbed—personally involved somehow" in the horror inflicted by Stalin.[2] In his 1967 published memoir, Kennan acknowledged that the "heartrending" "hammer-blow impressions" of those "prolonged and incessant" attacks still tormented him. The pain "was never to leave me," and the "imprint on my political judgment" had persisted.[3]

Those blows rained down alongside other assaults inflicted by his own government, his associates, and his temperament. For at least ten reasons, Kennan suffered through much of 1935–1938. First, the forced isolation from Soviet intellectuals, artists, officials, and ordinary citizens contrasted painfully with the heady excitement of 1933–1934. Second, the purges snatched away many Russians that George and his colleagues knew or had admired from a distance. Especially shocking were the prosecutions of Radek, Nicolai Bukharin, and the Kremlin's liaison to the diplomatic community, Boris S. Steiger. Third, outrage within the Moscow diplomatic community circulated in a self-reinforcing loop. At the embassy and chancery, at dinner parties, and at their weekend dacha outside Moscow, American diplomats and journalists, together with their foreign friends (principally Germans, British, and Italians), fed each other's frustrations while trying to puzzle out Stalin's next steps and ultimate intentions. Fourth, the purges came in the context of an attack on the diplomats' personal finances. Kremlin regulations slashed the purchasing power of resident foreigners by drastically cutting the number of rubles they got in exchange for their dollars or other Western currencies.

Fifth, the terror reached into the Kennan household to endanger George and Annelise's daughter, Grace. As the four-year-old hovered near death from pneumonia, her father had to beg the Soviet foreign office to intervene so as to allow a doctor to treat her. Sixth, Ambassador Davies, who arrived in Moscow shortly before the Radek trial, assaulted Kennan in a different way. Ambassador Bullitt had respected Kennan's knowledge and hard work and had safeguarded the junior diplomat's career despite his breakdown in 1934–1935. Davies, by contrast, questioned not only Kennan's expertise, but also his psychological and physical suitability for duty in Moscow. Stalin delivered a seventh blow in March 1937 by ordering an even tighter crackdown on contact with foreigners. Kennan's work ethic, ambition, and determination to fathom the purges fueled an eighth factor. At the height of the terror in 1937 it was he who translated most of the trial transcripts, notices of officials shot, and *Izvestia* and *Pravda* stories sensationalizing the dastardliness of so-called foreign spies. In striving for an accurate translation, Kennan per force had to identify, at least heuristically, with the perspective of the persecutors. A residue of such identification, blended with anger and revulsion, no doubt complicated his emotional processing of the horror. A ninth element, what Kennan resented as the "purge" of the proudly independent State Department's Division of Eastern European Affairs, originated in Washington politics. So, too, did the tenth, the stifling of the scholarly approach to Russia championed by Kennan's mentor, Robert F. Kelley.[4]

Amid the pain, Kennan romanticized Russia as a tattered, soulful remnant of a preindustrial order foolishly forsaken by the West. In that mystical idyll he sought deeper meaning for his own life and for Western society. He treasured the Russians as warm, generous people, closer to the land than most Americans and relatively unspoiled by the machine. This was the focus, he liked to believe, of his agrarian forebears in Wisconsin and New England.

Along with his driving ambition, Kennan was also impelled, as he had been since his Princeton days, by dreams of escape, of "lighting out for the Territory," as Huck Finn had put it. He felt alienated from machine-dominated, urbanized, commercialized America. To his sister Jeanette he flatly asserted that he could no longer see himself living in the United States. Disgusted with America, he idealized Russia as a more plastic society in which creative young people such as himself were, despite Stalinist repression, forging a better order. Protesting that he was "no Bolshevik," he nonetheless praised "some of the visions of the more intelligent Communist leaders [as] the most impelling and inspiring human conceptions which it has been my lot to encounter."[5]

Russia shimmered in Kennan's orientalist imagination as a fount of both time-tested wisdom and futuristic social experiment. He fancied that the insights and esthetics of pre-1917 Russian culture could, if translated effectively into a U.S. idiom, inspire sensitive and discerning Americans to repudiate the crass materialism, tired cynicism, and unchecked individualism that marred domestic life. The unspoiled freshness of Russia could revitalize jaded America, while the enlightened efficiency of America could lift Russia out of its mud and Tartar past. The diplomat believed that his mastery of Russian language and culture, his family tie to the Russian expert George Kennan (1845–1924), and his rock-solid Yankee heritage qualified him to shepherd such healing contact. Throughout the half-century Cold War and the 101-year span of his own life, Kennan would cling to this dream of bringing together, somehow, the people of America and Russia.

BACK IN THE U.S.S.R.

Preparing for his return to Moscow after months of physical and psychological recovery in Vienna, Kennan felt "anxious to prove that . . . I could take it."[6] Upon arriving in Moscow on November 14, 1935, he felt that "life had begun once more."[7] Illness also resumed. Sick in bed when he had left Moscow back in January, he returned with a bad cold that kept him bedridden for three days.

Russia's chronic disorder appealed to his own need to balance against too much order. Half-humorously, he noted that when he, Annelise, and Grace first arrived back at their Moscow apartment "things seemed too quiet and well-organized. I felt better as soon as I discovered" that the busted chain on the toilet had been repaired with a paper clip. When he saw that the faucets leaked and that the water was "generously mixed with bad plaster . . . everything was all right. A couple of broken door knobs were just a needless luxury."[8]

In contrast to the eager anticipation of his first encounter with Russia two years earlier, he now felt gloomy apprehension. The Soviet government was recalculating the exchange rate of the ruble, imposing "an absolutely fantastic rise in the cost of living for the resident foreigners." This financial shock came on top of Kennan's earlier loss in the stock market of the money inherited from his mother and grandparents. Moreover, "the most attractive and amusing friends among the foreigners have left." Worse, "it is now practically impossible to have anything to do whatsoever with a Russian. They all disappear." He and other diplomats were cast as "enemy negotiators in a hostile camp in time of war." Indeed, actual "war seems unavoidable," though not with the United States. The only bright spot was that the conflict "might suddenly sweep" away the "stuffy" cult and repression of Stalin. Almost immediately after returning to Moscow, Kennan felt himself staggering under the "nervous strain."[9]

The suddenly frigid atmosphere of purge-era Moscow frightened and angered the foreign diplomatic community. Illustrating the freeze was the dramatic change since Bullitt's last embassy gala, held to welcome spring 1935. Undeterred by the seal fiasco at the Christmas 1934 party, Bullitt had assured Charlie Thayer and Irena Wiley that "the sky is the limit, just so long as it's good and different." To conjure an atmosphere of spring, Thayer and Wiley borrowed from the Moscow Zoo a half-dozen baby mountain goats and set them up in a small barnyard at one end of the ballroom. Plus, they had glass cages built and hung for crowing roosters and a huge fishnet gilded and attached to the ceiling to house a flock of finches. The party planners also arranged for a baby bear, who arrived with his nurse. As nothing was yet greening in the Moscow region, Thayer and Wiley had some birch trees uprooted and set in bathtubs. Heated with Bullitt's sun lamp, they leafed out just in time for the party. "It was perhaps the gayest party ever given in Moscow," Irena would remember proudly.[10]

The party, which boomed on until 10:00 the next morning, seemed gay at the time but gruesome in retrospect. The crisis stemmed not from Karl Radek's impishly replacing the milk in the bear's bottle with champagne, and the poor animal's throwing up on the resplendent uniform of General Alexander Yegorov when the officer tried to burp him. Nor was it that the finches escaped the netting and defecated all over the embassy's furniture. Rather, the crisis arose months later, when Radek and Yegorov were swept up in Stalin's purges. Radek would die in prison while Yegorov, along with General Mikhail Tukhachevsky who was dancing at the party with the ballet star Lolya Lepishinkaya, would be shot.

Horrified by the turn of events, Western diplomats in Moscow huddled together.[11] Particularly close with Kennan were Charlie Thayer, Chip Bohlen, Elbridge Durbrow, Norris Chipman, and their colleagues from the German embassy, Hans "Jonny" von Herwarth and Gustav Hilger. "We felt an unlimited need for discussion among ourselves," Kennan later explained.[12] The constant talk circulated and intensified the feelings of a group deprived of what Americans regarded as normal

FIGURE 19. Annelise and George in costume for a Moscow ball in 1937.
(Courtesy of Princeton University Library.)

contact. Fanny Chipman, Norris Chipman's wife, later recalled that "we knew our colleagues to an extent we never knew them at any other post." With the foreign colony shrinking, she and others tried to pump up the excitement: "I've never worn so many low-cut evening dresses as I did in Moscow, that's the truth!"[13]

Banding together at work and at dinner parties, they also gathered on weekends at a dacha outside Moscow. In April 1935, while Kennan was still in Vienna, Thayer, Bohlen, and Durbrow had leased what Thayer touted as a "country estate," complete with five bedrooms, hot and cold running water, "real bathrooms . . . rose garden, hotbeds and everything." Included was "the best in Moscow tennis court," a chicken run, and two fishponds, one with a fountain and one "for keeping eating fish—a catch 'em and cook 'em sort of thing." In winter they flooded the tennis court for ice skating. The house overlooked a pristine valley and rolling hills, perfect for horseback riding and skiing.[14] Fanny Chipman later remembered that "everybody came: the German ambassador [Friedrich-Werner Graf] von Schulenburg, the von Herwarths, [Italian ambassador Augosto] Rosso with his [American] wife, the Belgians, the French, the British." "It was a communistic organization," she remembered proudly. She recalled "von Herwarth bringing a whole case of vin du Rhin. Everybody sort of contributed a little."[15] The Germans and the British stabled their horses at the American dacha.

The Kennans became regulars. As he had in Berlin, George rode horseback as often as he could. At parties he strummed the guitar he had taught himself to play and sang mournful Russian folk songs. In contrast to the grimness of Moscow, "life there was very gay, and very informal; and very relaxing, which we all needed," Fanny Chipman remembered. "I don't think there were microphones there," she mused, but the Russians "must have heard plenty if there were."[16] The bugs would have picked up the anguish at the frightening purges.

Like Kennan, Thayer and Bohlen viewed Russia as at once progressive and primitive. They admired the innovative Soviet planners piloting Russia forward even as the capitalist West staggered in the Great Depression. In 1933-1934, when many in the embassy were socializing with Soviet artists, intellectuals, and officials, Kennan had longed to plunge even deeper into the excitement. As late as 1936, these young Americans nursed the hope that the Soviet government might evolve in a more liberal direction, a wish encouraged by the sweeping liberties and guarantees incorporated into the new constitution of that year but not subsequently honored. In viewing the gargantuan task of industrializing and modernizing the Soviet Union, the Americans, reflecting their orientalist views, tended to justify harsh disciplining of the supposedly inveterately lazy Russians.

Although Kennan and Bohlen would become America's twin Russian experts in the Cold War, it was Charlie Thayer in the 1930s who stood closer to George. Even after World War II, Thayer would visit the Kennans' weekend retreat in East Berlin, Pennsylvania, more frequently than would the Bohlens. Back in the glory days of 1933–1934, Kennan and Thayer, still in their twenties, had dashed around Moscow setting up the embassy. Both fancied themselves as writers. In May 1935, Kennan had confided to Thayer his dream of a corps of younger diplomat-writers, who might best the famous expatriates in Paris. Both had entered Russia, as Thayer explained, "hoping to find something new . . . some solution to many problems."[17] Both sought among "the mystic Russians somewhere—perhaps in the Caucasus or on the Volga or in Novgorod"—a source of innocence and creativity with which to revitalize their own lives and Western culture.[18] Like Kennan, Thayer self-identified as Russian as well as American. Catching himself as he used the word "we" to refer to Russia, he admitted that this sounded "as though I considered myself a Soviet citizen of good standing. Were I one, I feel sure I would support this regime."[19]

Like Kennan, Thayer and Bohlen remained "passionately convinced that the only sound approach to Russia was the scholarly one."[20] Immersion in the history and literature of pre-revolution Russia amid skepticism about political ties with the Soviet government summed up the creed of Robert F. Kelley, a graduate of Harvard and the Sorbonne and the first head of the State Department's Division of Eastern European Affairs. Kennan characterized Kelley as "an infinitely discreet bachelor" who resembled "a German university professor in his demand for accuracy, for documentation, and for detail. He believed in libraries and archives."[21] That commitment was bedrock for Kennan, who had idolized such professors in Berlin. This intellectual and emotional commitment to the scholarly approach would render especially bitter Kennan's pressured recantation during the State Department's 1937–1938 "purge" of its Russian experts.

Twelve years older than Kennan and skeptical of the younger man's Russophilia was Loy W. Henderson, manager of the Moscow embassy during the long periods when Ambassadors Bullitt and Davies were absent. Though Kennan and Henderson respected each other and did not openly clash, they differed in temperament, training, and ability. Henderson ranked as a perceptive observer and an austere, old-school diplomat. Kennan would later remember that while his superior worked hard, he "lack[ed] special training in the Russian field." In 1930, when Henderson had applied for such intensive study, the State Department, facing a crimped budget, had turned him down as too old.[22] In an interview years later, Henderson blurted out that Kennan "wasn't a man with much compassion." The younger star had "looked down in a patronizing way on people whom he didn't consider as intellectual." In describing Kennan, Henderson kept repeating the words "ambitious" and "emotional." About the latter trait, he explained that "George always had a romantic streak about Russia."[23]

IN SEARCH OF THE RUSSIAN SOUL

That streak impelled Kennan's quest for inspiration in the architecture and literature of old Russia. Speaking the language like a native and dressed in a Russian blouse, he traveled by train or river steamer and hiked overland to explore neglected churches and monasteries. One wintry day he skied far off into the countryside to an island in the River Nerl, where he beheld the exquisite little white Church of the Holy Shroud, erected when Moscow remained a primitive fortress. For a planned biography of Anton Chekhov, he determined to see all the places where he had lived and written. He found special meaning also in a pilgrimage to Yasnaya Polyana, the estate 130 miles south of Moscow where Leo Tolstoy had written *War and Peace* and was later buried. The weekend before Christmas in 1935, Kennan ventured into "the mysterious world of provincial Russia."[24]

The trip highlighted a persistent dilemma. On the one hand, Kennan's professional ambition, sense of duty, and scholarly curiosity impelled him to submit to the "cruel, always relentless intellectual discipline" entailed in analyzing "Soviet reality." Yet this implicitly masculine obligation also sparked his "powerful . . . yearning for escape" to a "refuge," which he imagined as feminine in ways both erotic and maternal. This swing between disciplined responsibility and self-indulgent flight echoed his boyhood behavior, his tortured soliloquy in the sanitarium in February 1935, and the Freudian predicament of Civilization versus Eros.

Kennan, then thirty-one, had planned the excursion with a "brilliant German journalist," the twenty-nine-year-old Klaus Mehnert, and his American-born wife, Enid Keyes, who was twenty-five. Twenty-seven-year-old Annelise Kennan, who was five months pregnant with their second child, would remain in Moscow. When Klaus dropped out, George and Enid, "to the edification of the foreign colony gossips," went on alone. Kennan, who mocked marital restrictions as outdated and unhealthy, relished that he and Enid, "a perfectly darling child," appeared to others as a romantic couple. He later reminisced, "Moscow, God bless it, was still broadminded enough not to care a damn who traveled with whom and why." Such maturity afforded freedom from "unnecessary" conventions. Both attired in skiing costumes, they shared a knapsack for their baggage. On the train they exchanged food and drink with a Russian engineer, who, Kennan recounted, sang "us a Russian 'romance.'" Whether George and Enid actually were lovers remains uncertain. At the hotel they took separate rooms. Working against sex was Kennan's sudden bout of dysentery, which forced him "to run to a place to which, as they used to say in Russia, even the Tsar went on foot." Then again, he did recover. Perhaps the bowel problem reflected Kennan's ambivalence about consummating the flirtation. Regardless of the degree of physical intimacy between George and Enid, an erotic frisson intensified the emotional valence of their pilgrimage to Yasnaya Polyana.[25]

Kennan imbued this shrine of Russian culture with a loving, maternal presence. Senses attuned, he discerned "something familiar in the atmosphere" as he stepped into Tolstoy's house. He flashed back to the Nagawicka Lake summer house of his Uncle Edward and Aunt Ida, "where I used to seek refuge as a little boy" from the hazing at St. John's.[26] Young

George probably knew that these close neighbors, as well as his mother's family, had objected to the decision of Kennan's father and stepmother to pack him off to a school that specialized in problem boys. To the adult George Kennan, memories of St. John's seem to have linked with an inner voice of masculine discipline, while the compound on Nagawicka Lake remained associated with feminine succor. Jeanette, in referring to their childhood memories of Nagawicka, explained, "I can't overstate what that house and place meant to us."[27] Now, two decades later in Russia, the smells of "apples and of wood-smoke" triggered an intense association and a painful ache. To Kennan, the Tolstoy house "had the air of having been tended for years by the hands of kind women—women who had intelligence and character, and had suffered"—women, in other words, like his lost, idealized mother, Florence James.[28]

After drawing that emotion-drenched connection, Kennan in the very next sentence wrote, "I searched in vain for some bond between the past and the present." That lonely quest for his lost mother, or some commensurate succor and solace, would occupy his long life. But his mother was gone, and so apparently was contemporary Russian appreciation for the values signified by Yasnaya Polyana.

But Kennan was not giving up. In a remarkable reverie of desire, intuition, and identification, he poured out his hopes. He longed for Russians to embrace the values of Tolstoy so deeply that he could also escape into that depth. Despite his lifelong pessimism and championing of "realism," Kennan indulged at times in a romantic optimism. He now implored: "Could one hope—that in young Russian hearts—beneath all the callousness bred by an unpitying environment—there still lived some dormant yearning for the simplicity, the culture, the profound ethical individualism of Yasnaya Polyana?" "I was not sure," came his careful answer. But then burst forth his longing: "If I could have believed" that yearning did persist, "no wars, no waste, no cruelties, would ever again have depressed me. I would, it seems to me, have dissolved in relief and happiness."[29]

In Russia, then, lay the potential solution—indeed dissolution—of the professional and personal problems afflicting Kennan. He imagined that immersion into traditional Russia could release him from the discipline imposed by masculine duty, rational skepticism, sexual restraint, Western modernism, and mass consumer-industrial society. This mystical quest would again and again impel him through the vicissitudes of World War II, the Cold War, and the collapse of the Soviet Union.

Senses aquiver, Kennan absorbed more than the smells of Yasnaya Polyana. He watched and listened as their guide, an old-fashioned "Russian gentleman with . . . the clear blue eyes of a child," recited passages from Tolstoy's work with "the most beautiful Russian diction . . . I have ever heard." Unspoiled by modern education, the man displayed a "charming lack of self-consciousness." Embracing Yasnaya Polyana as an engagement with traditional Russia, Kennan penned in the visitors' book that the tour had "revived for us with rare feeling and understanding what must unfortunately be considered as a bygone day."[30]

Ironically, the ubiquitous secret police, who in Moscow were exiling or executing Kennan's associates, extended here, far from the Kremlin, a "vigilant but benevolent hand." The "tactful solicitude" of the police rescued George and Enid from a raging blizzard, "got us rooms against the competition of a mob of howling Russians," secured a taxi to the estate, and tickets on the train back to Moscow.[31] Kennan was not the only American who at times benefited from these never-to-be-escaped, Kremlin-mandated monitors, who might guide a lost traveler, change a tire, or put through a phone call.

The weekend at Yasnaya Polyana illustrated that George and Annelise were not joined at the hip. The ethos of their marriage did not preclude separations. In January 1935, George had gone to Vienna to recuperate, expecting that Annelise would not follow for months. Another time, he noted that his wife was "leaving for western Europe tomorrow and will be gone some time."[32] In February 1936, Annelise, pregnant with their second child (Joan, who would be born in April), traveled with three-year-old Grace to the home of Jeanette and Eugene Hotchkiss in Highland Park, Illinois. She needed to give birth on American soil in order to guarantee the child U.S. citizenship. George would not arrive until mid-May.

REPORTING TO THE STATE DEPARTMENT

Work took up most of Kennan's time. Though concerned with the purges, George in his diligence also delved into other issues. From his return to Moscow in November 1935 to his transfer to Washington in August 1937, Kennan translated a stack of newspaper articles and official documents, wrote at least ninety-eight despatches and telegrams, and assisted Henderson, Bullitt, and Davies in preparing others. Among his reports to the State Department was a translation and comment on a Soviet story about the U.S. visit of Polina Zhemchuzhina, director of the Perfume and Cosmetics Trust and wife of Soviet president (and future foreign minister) Vyacheslav Molotov. In America, she toured factories, purchased "two Hartford glass-blowing machines and eight machines to mold soap," and met with the president and First Lady. "Mrs. Roosevelt impressed, Zhemchuzhina said, as being a highly cultured and energetic person" who was "very interested in the legal and economic position of women in the Soviet Union."[33]

Kennan reported also on press coverage of the pioneering transarctic flight from Los Angeles to Moscow of Soviet aviators Sigizmund Levanevsky and Victor Levchenko.[34] He predicted that Russia's ambitious plans for oceanographic research in the northern Pacific could prove "a great scientific event of world significance." The Soviets believed in the "great strategic importance" of the Aleutian Islands in driving the United States "close to the sphere of interests of the rival Japanese imperialism."[35] He penned a monthly report on the issues setting the Soviets against Japan in China and Outer Mongolia. The rising diplomat also mastered the intricacies of negotiations on past war debts and on future trade.[36] Responding to alarm in Washington that the Communist International (Comintern) might endorse FDR for reelection in 1936, Kennan telegraphed reassuring excerpts from a Soviet publication lambasting the New Deal as a fraud and Roosevelt as helpless against "the forces of reaction."[37]

During this twilight period between the world wars, Kennan familiarized himself with major global issues. He acquired a background in

European and Asian matters that would prepare him to direct, a decade later, the State Department's Policy Planning Staff.

Kennan also tackled two major questions debated by contemporaries and, later, by historians: First, was the Kremlin honestly seeking collective security through the League of Nations? Second, did Stalin place a higher priority on promoting Soviet national interests or on international Communist revolution? Kennan judged the Soviets as sincere though disappointed in their efforts to secure peace through an alliance with France and collective security through the League of Nations. He paraphrased Karl Radek's expressed "hope that some day the League [of Nations] will come to Russia's assistance against Germany or Japan."[38] He reported on "the energy with which [Soviet Foreign Minister Maxim] Litvinov promoted the collective security program and the sacrifices which the Kremlin" had made for that cooperative policy. Yet despite the Soviet effort, France had backtracked on imposing sanctions punishing Italy's attack on Ethiopia. With this weak precedent, "what assurances could Moscow have that France or other members of the League would support the Soviet Union in the face of a German attack?" Furthermore, "Moscow was disgusted with the instability of French politics," Kennan noted. While supporting collective security, the Soviets were also beefing up their own armed forces, the embassy was informed by its Kremlin liaison.[39] Eager for support, the Soviets were nervously "scrutinizing the development of American policy."[40]

As to whether the Kremlin gave priority to Russian national interests or to the international spread of communism, Kennan emphasized the former thesis. He saw this bias illustrated in the Spanish Civil War of 1936–1939, which pitted the Republican government of Spain, backed by Soviet Russia, against the Nationalist revolt of General Francisco Franco, supported by Nazi Germany and Fascist Italy. Many observers in Europe and America viewed the conflict as a precursor to a wider European war. The Soviets, frightened of an attack from Germany, sought the support of France and Britain. Hence, Moscow dared not scare off the Western democracies by encouraging or even allowing an overtly Communist government in Spain. He highlighted the Soviet press's labeling as "irresponsible acts" and "frivolous chatter" any steps by Spanish leftists toward overt social revolution.

Kennan underscored the broader historical significance: Here was "one of the first serious attempts to establish communism anywhere outside of the Soviet Union," and Moscow was "applying the brakes." The diplomat drew a broader conclusion: "The Comintern and the Communist parties subservient to it" operated as "an instrument of the Kremlin." They have "been wielded, and will continue to be wielded, in the interests of Soviet foreign policy" rather than on behalf of "the world proletariat."[41] This appraisal fit Kennan's usual emphasis not on Communist ideology but rather on Russian national interests and cultural predilections.

Another harbinger of future inclinations was Kennan's eagerness at researching a bit of diplomatic history. Responding to a request from the State Department, the scholarly minded diplomat asked the Soviet foreign ministry for copies of documents pertaining to the U.S. purchase of Alaska from Russia in 1867. His research proved both frustrating and satisfying. The Soviets, despite frequent reminders, sat on the request for more than a year and, worse, afforded Kennan "no opportunity at any time to talk with anyone" from the archives. "The whole matter was surrounded with the usual mystery" and behind the scenes action that in so many ways robbed Kennan of the interaction he longed for. Once he did receive the bundle of documents, it took him less than a week to translate, study, and comment extensively on them. His excitement at handling pages "bearing notations made by the Tsar in his own hand" and in exploring such tidbits as Russian concern about "the danger of the Mormons emigrating to Alaska" evidenced his love for archival research. That enthusiasm would carry through to later decades when he wrote Pulitzer Prize–winning books on the history of Russia's foreign relations. The State Department commended Kennan for "the competent and scholarly manner in which the material has been assembled and analyzed."[42]

In researching, translating documents, and commenting on these varied topics, Kennan grew confident in his intuitive grasp of things Russian. He observed himself forming "general impressions, which he

FIGURE 20. Annelise and George enjoying the Russian winter; Grace enduring it. (Courtesy of Princeton University Library.)

[knew] to be true on the basis of thousands of minor indications," even though he could not "demonstrate [them] by documentary evidence."[43] In 1946–1948, such intuition would enhance Kennan's reputation for having oracular knowledge about Soviet Russia; in subsequent years, it would hasten his fall from grace as a supposedly impractical visionary.[44]

As Henderson later recalled, Kennan preferred "research work in the archives . . . instead of doing the regular work of the embassy."[45] He spent much of winter 1936 delving into the history of Communist Party politics. Coming on top of his personal acquaintance with Soviet intellectuals and officials, this scholarly work enhanced his respect for many of the leaders who would soon perish in the purges. Throughout his life, Kennan's sympathy bent toward elites and the tradition, commitment, and seriousness he believed they usually embodied. That empathy heightened his horror at Stalin's destruction of the cream of the Communist Party and the Red Army, including many heroes of the Bolshevik Revolution.

THE SHOW TRIALS

The dictator's drive to eliminate any possible rivals would culminate in three show trials. Lev Kamenev and Grigory Zinoviev sat as chief defendants in the August 1936 trial, Karl Radek in the January 1937 affair, and Nicolai Bukharin in the March 1938 trial.

In a thoroughly researched and footnoted eighty-page report sent to the State Department in February 1936, Kennan explained that the opposition to Stalin stemmed from the disruptions caused by the dictator's insistence on hurried industrialization and forced collectivization of farmland. Many of the disgruntled had turned to the old-line Bolsheviks Kamenev and Zinoviev as well as to Trotsky, now in exile. Kennan characterized the dissident leaders as "intellectuals who occupied high positions in Moscow and who saw clearly the mistakes" of Stalin's rule. The dictator was hitting back by jailing opponents and by packing the Communist Party with naive industrial workers and younger people who fell for the "glory and infallibility of Stalin."

Though Kennan was trying to sustain the objective tone expected in an official report, he could not hide his dismay at this attack on the elite. Stalin was sacrificing quality for quantity, replacing "sincere and serious party members" with "passive, indifferent" neophytes. The struggle pitted "the older, genuine communists" against the "out-and-out careerists, adventurers and crooks," many of them "totally illiterate."[46] Stalin was destroying not only the "heroes of the early Bolshevist ideology" but also the creative solutions innovated by idealistic intellectuals. The diplomat regretted the dictator's quashing the Party's role as "a vital force" and as a "fountain of political feeling."[47]

Only five days after sending off that lengthy despatch, Kennan finished another report that criticized "the renewed baiting of [Nicolai] Bukharin." In the late 1920s, Bukharin had challenged Stalin's brutal approach to economic modernization. In keeping with the more humane philosophy of the early Karl Marx, Bukharin urged a slower pace for industrializing the Soviet Union and building communism. Bukharin, a darling of many contemporaries, would remain long after his 1938 execution an inspiration for those advocating socialism with a human face. Kennan admired the philosophy of Bukharin and the literary erudition with which he expressed it. He ranked as an "intelligent and cultured Communist" the "one man of sufficient stature" to challenge Stalin.

The empathy of the despatch blurred the division between Bukharin's writing and Kennan's commentary. Kennan wrote that on the anniversary of Lenin's death, Bukharin had published a "sincere tribute to [his] great and intimate friend." He praised Lenin for creating a world revolutionary force out of the "scarcely awakened masses of a . . . nation of Oblomovs." The American explained that Ilya Oblomov, the hero of Ivan Goncharov's novel, typified "the harmless, philosophic, ineffective and unutterably lazy Russian." Sharing Bukharin's orientalist perspective, Kennan endorsed his praise of Lenin for overcoming "this Russian muddleheadedness", "'This Asiaticness!', 'This 'oriental sloth'! 'This tangle, this mess, this lack of elementary order!'" Here was Kennan channeling Bukharin channeling Lenin as they all displayed a patronizing, Western perspective on a population that straddled East and West. While the two Russian revolutionaries hoped to propel Russian communism, the American romantic hoped to preserve Russian innocence. Kennan, who imagined the Russian soul as a feminine presence, could not resist including in his report to the stuffy State Department the poet Nikolay Nekrasov's famous couplet:

> You—the poverty-stricken, you—the bountiful.
> You—the mighty, you—the helpless.
> Mother Russia.

This literary exegesis-verging-on-identification flowed on for eight pages. Kennan endorsed the defense against the "pack which appears to be in full cry behind the lone figure of Bukharin."[48] The diplomat often regarded himself as a besieged lone figure. His cultural rapport with Bukharin fostered a dual outlook that recalled the frosty night in December 1933 when he had first crossed the border into Russia. Kennan's fond embrace of Russia's problems and potential helped him share the frustrated pride of Bukharin.

In March 1936, Kennan ventured into a still restive outpost of the Soviet empire, Stalin's home province of Georgia. He found the people "lazy, dirty, tricky, fiercely proud and recklessly brave." Allowing his biases full rein, he proclaimed that "Transcaucasian filth is the filth of the Orient. Compared to it, Russian filth seems earthy and wholesome." While appreciating the freer air of Georgia, Kennan, always the Russian nationalist, looked "forward with a certain satisfaction" to the Kremlin's "steam roller" crushing "Georgian arrogance, corruption and trickery"— while sparing the region's "pride, individualism and local color." Nevertheless, over the long run, he doubted the durability of Russia's domination. "It was difficult to believe that the crude stamp of Soviet Muscovy would leave a mark deeper than the mighty cultural influences of Greece and Rome." On his return home, "barbaric, battered Moscow appeared a haven of civilization, culture, and comfort."[49]

BULLITT EMBITTERED

Meanwhile, by April 1936 almost everything had gone wrong with Bullitt's mission to Moscow. His grandiose plans for a Monticello-inspired embassy overlooking the Soviet capital, his introduction of polo to the Soviet cavalry, and his hopes of playing the interlocutor between

Roosevelt and Stalin all had come to naught. Worse, political relations had soured over czarist-era debts, the welcoming of the American Communist Party to the 1935 Moscow congress of the Comintern, and Washington's reluctance to confront Japan. Hurt, disappointed, and resentful, Bullitt blamed it all on the Russians and their dangerous ideology. Eager to get home to campaign for FDR in the 1936 election, he wrapped up his Moscow job by asking Kennan to outline the "guiding principles of a far-sighted permanent policy" toward Russia.[50]

The wholesale changes that Bullitt made to Kennan's draft indicated that while the ambassador had already evolved into a proto–Cold Warrior riveted on Soviet ideology, the protégé retained a more benign focus on Russian culture. (In 1946–1947, Kennan's long telegram" and Mr. "X" manifestos would likewise spike political analysis with ideology to ferment a potent brew.) While Bullitt interpreted the challenge of Communist Russia as a problem of Communism, Kennan saw it as primarily the problem of Russia. The ambassador, whose influence with President Roosevelt rested on his financial donations and on his supposed expertise in European diplomacy, dismissed the notion of a German military threat to Russia. Japan did menace Russia, he acknowledged, but there the fault lay with Moscow. Bullitt's ideological thesis demonized Soviet-led communism as threatening "not only to destroy the institutions and liberties of our country, but also to kill millions of Americans." Kennan, in a calmer tone, focused instead on economics, culture, and politics. In the economic sphere, the Russians figured as not only a rival in agricultural exports, but also as a problem because of their propensity to be "so oriental in their business dealings." The ambassador deleted from the draft what his protégé regarded as basic: "the natural understanding and sympathy of the peoples of the two countries" and their "unquestionable potential value to each other."[51]

As Kennan saw it, the most serious difficulty between the two nations stemmed from the determination of Russian rulers "to keep their people in darkness rather to risk illumination by contact" with foreigners. His metaphor reflected the orientalist notion of a polarity between the enlightened West and the darkened rest. In keeping with beliefs about national character absorbed at Princeton and in Germany,

Kennan explained that Russia's harsh climate, lack of geographic barriers, and "contact with the Asiatic hordes" all spurred extreme behavior.[52]

Indeed, Russia as a nation suffered behavioral difficulties that hamstrung "normal administrative control" and "national self-confidence." Kennan depicted Russia as a psychological problem-state that had to be managed as a doctor treats a patient, "above all [with] an exceptional capacity for patience." Such psychological discourse, which reflected Kennan's absorption of Freudian theory, would figure also in his 1946–1947 diagnosis of the Soviet challenge. In 1936, as well as a decade later, the ambitious diplomat emphasized that relations with Russia had to be managed by experts with his qualifications: "understanding . . . self-effacement, a decent educational background," and "intellectual humility before the complexities of the Russian world."[53]

While George ventured to Georgia and drafted Bullitt's memorandum, Annelise journeyed over five thousand miles with three-year-old Grace to the home of Jeanette Hotchkiss in Highland Park, Illinois. Not until a week after Joan Elizabeth was born on April 24 did George leave for America, and then he took his time, arriving in mid-May. On the journey, he observed that outwardly at least, the capitalist West, "looked awfully good," even though it lacked the inner soul of Russia. Nazi Germany gleamed as "a garden country, green, fresh and well-ordered. Trains were incredibly fast . . . people incredibly neatly dressed." He found the theaters of London superior to those in Moscow, where "chauvinistic, dictatorship propaganda" had stifled creativity.[54]

Kennan experienced his weeks in the United States as a "bewildering interlude." He decided that it was "the home town" more than "the outside world which [had] become so unreal." Nevertheless, it was to that home that he intended to return if his diplomatic career collapsed. Bullitt helped Kennan secure an interview with Governor Philip La Follette. He came away reassured that "job-hunting in Wisconsin doesn't terrify me." Despite his rapid rise in the State Department, he feared that diplomacy remained "a precarious profession" in which someone with his personality could easily stumble. In an eerie premonition of the outburst that, sixteen years to the month later, would crash his career and get him expelled from the Soviet Union, he predicted: "Someday, sooner or later, I'll surely make some major slip" and "[speak] my mind on some ill-chosen subject."[55]

ALIENATED FROM AMERICA

The interlude in America coincided with the 1936 presidential election campaign. Kennan, who had returned to the Republican tradition of his family, was not impressed by the acceptance speech of that party's candidate, Alfred Landon. Nor did he sympathize with the complaints and forebodings "of my Milwaukee friends, who are all staunch Republicans." Nevertheless, even in the context of a long letter to Bullitt, who was home campaigning for FDR, Kennan ignored both President Roosevelt and the New Deal. Still hankering after a preindustrial idyll, Kennan failed to appreciate what President Roosevelt had achieved. (In World War II, Kennan would also fail to grasp the subtlety in FDR's plans for post–World War II collaboration with the Soviet Union.) Dismissing as irrelevant the reformism of the New Deal, Kennan advocated reining in the "destructive agencies of uncontrolled industrialism" with a "strong central power (far stronger than the present Constitution would allow)." He saw in America the problems that would worry him for the rest of his long life: "lack of proper public regulation, chaotic municipal growth, the despoilage of the countryside, etc." Making matters worse, Americans did not "want to be governed," preferring instead "a series of temporary compromises between warring interests." Rather than the American system of checks and balances, Kennan preferred the Austrian authoritarianism he had seen in Vienna.[56]

A few weeks after writing that letter to Bullitt, George, accompanied by Annelise, Grace, and baby Joan, departed for Europe during the worst East Coast heat wave in six decades. With them aboard the S.S. *Manhattan* was the U.S. Olympics team bound for Hitler's Berlin. The Kennans tried to stay out of the way of the "stalwart, gum-chewing" athletes practicing their fencing and sprinting on the deck. As the ship glided into Hamburg, the contenders "light-heartedly shouted their locker-room banter" at the uncomprehending Germans on shore. These quintessential Americans "failed to notice," Kennan sniffed, that here was a country "different—excitingly, provocatively different—from their own." He, by contrast, delighted in transatlantic crossings as "momentous, awe-compelling experiences." Reimmersion into European culture meant celebrating a "solemn rite" evoking "the mysteries of a deep, dramatic past."[57] Pre–World War II Hamburg claimed a special place in Kennan's heart; indeed, it was visiting the utterly destroyed city in 1948 that would convince him that no war, not even the one that had defeated Adolf Hitler, was worth the cost in human and material destruction.

The voyage from Hamburg to Leningrad demonstrated, first, the determination of George and Annelise not to let parental responsibility disrupt their other personal priorities and, second, the difficulties nevertheless in making such a trip with small children. Evidently proud of his and Annelise's practicality, George boasted in a letter to Jeanette, again in his unpublished memoir, and still again in his 1967 published memoir about their childcare solution for four-month-old Joan when the ship docked at Copenhagen and at Helsingfors. They went ashore "by the simple expedient of tying the baby-carriage—with baby inside—to a pipe on the top deck, and then leaving the whole outfit." Their casual approach sparked, Kennan observed with satisfaction, "the indignation of the other passengers." The Norwegian minister aboard "threatened to sic the G.P.U. [Soviet secret police] on us, upon arrival in Leningrad, for cruelty to children, but Joan didn't seem to mind."[58] Their missions ashore that justified leaving an infant unattended: while Annelise shopped for clothes and Georg Jensen silverware, George inspected a nineteenth-century sail-steam vessel, the onetime flagship of the U.S. Navy Pacific Fleet.

Steaming into Leningrad, Kennan, who found melancholy comforting, discerned "a great Russian sadness" in the shoreline. Transferring the family and their twenty-two pieces of baggage from the harbor to a Moscow-bound train proved an ordeal. With the luggage somehow missing, "Annelise stood hopelessly on the station platform . . . with one hand on the baby buggy and the other on Grace, while the Russians milled around by the thousands, trying to find places on the cars."

George frantically sought their possessions and accommodations on the train. Then—"as is the way of things in Russia"—it somehow worked out. He chanced upon the porter with the luggage, they boarded the train, and "someone"—probably a helpful hand from the secret police—"loaned us money and found us berths." Arriving in Moscow in late August amid a cloudburst, they reached the embassy "drenched, disorganized, and entirely happy to be again among people whose friendship and understanding still made Moscow the nearest thing in the world to home."[59] These friends, Kennan discovered soon enough, were aghast at the just-concluded inquisition of Zinoviev and Kamenev, the first of the three great purge trials of 1936–1938.

WHY DID THEY CONFESS?

Most baffling about the trials were the accusations and confessions of treason and terrorism by stalwart Communist Party and Red Army officials. Were these heroes of the 1917 revolution really scheming to wreck the Soviet economy, overthrow the government, assassinate leaders, abandon communism, and divide the Soviet Union among its foreign enemies? While most accounts written during the Cold War, including those by Kennan, summarily dismissed the charges as absurd and blamed the trials on Stalin's megalomania, recent scholarship suggests a more ambiguous picture. Stalin did mastermind the trials. He and his chief prosecutor, Andrei Vyshinsky, exaggerated offenses and used torture to elicit confessions. They crafted the trials as narratives scapegoating the accused for the economic shortages, poor planning, and foreign threats that plagued Soviet Russia. Stalin's personality also shaped the trials. He delighted in swinging the ax at all opponents, active and potential. As someone who had been battling real and supposed enemies for many decades, the *vozhd* felt comfortable with deadly struggle.[60]

Nevertheless, despite his responsibility for the show trials, Stalin was also responding to substantial resistance. Both elite and ordinary Russians had reason to oppose his regime. The forced collectivization and accelerated industrialization of the Five-Year Plans yielded not only growth but also economic dislocation, mass misery, crop failures, and a surge in industrial accidents, mine collapses, and train wrecks. Stalin's suspicions notwithstanding, economic disasters did not require intentional sabotage. The killing and dispossession of millions in the revolution, the civil war, the famine of the early 1930s, and in the unrelenting oppression of the Soviet secret police sparked broad resentment. Even the Stakhanovite worker-heroes, lauded for their superior productivity, ended up exploited by still higher work quotas and stagnant wages. Reports of widespread passive resistance and smoldering opposition flowed into the Kremlin. Stalin used the show trials to deflect such resentment away from himself and his inner circle and toward party veterans charged as double-dealing economic "wreckers" and treasonous collaborators with enemy nations and with the deposed Trotsky. A related dynamic was that the purges empowered younger officials to get rid of senior authorities blocking their advance.[61]

Domestic rivals and foreign enemies exploited these Soviet troubles. Trotsky, expelled from the Soviet Union in 1929, defiantly pledged cooperation with Stalin's opponents. The Western press, intrigued by the drama of a split among Lenin's heirs, played up the storyline that Trotsky could indeed overthrow Stalin, and that the new regime might improve ties with capitalist governments. Kamenev and Zinoviev, defendants in the trial that ended as Kennan returned to Moscow, had remained in contact with Trotsky while favoring the overthrow of Stalin.[62]

The extent of actual plotting, however, remains uncertain. Japan, Germany, Poland, and Finland sent saboteurs and spies into Russia and shared anti-Soviet intelligence. Hostile governments found it easy to recruit operatives within Soviet Russia and to slip others across the porous Soviet border. The Warsaw government cultivated spies among Polish Communists in Russia. Nazi Germany and Poland dispatched agents to assassinate Soviet officials and sabotage economic production. Stalin worried that the Soviets might even "lose Ukraine."[63] The Soviets were pursuing a massive espionage campaign against the capitalist nations in part because they perceived real perils. In sum, Stalin did not need to be paranoid to fear serious domestic and foreign opposition.

By no means, however, did the threats justify the grotesque response of the dictator and his inner circle. Determined to obliterate all opposition, they relied not on material evidence of plotting but rather on their "revolutionary instincts." Whim, revenge, and suspicion directed arrests. They intended the trials to persuade international and domestic observers that, first, the Soviet Union faced grave danger; second, Stalin was not responsible for the problems; and third, the dictator and his supporters were dealing forcefully with the crisis. Genuinely worried about an attack from Nazi Germany and Japan, Stalin resolved to root out any potential fifth column. He and his henchmen executed many innocents in order to eliminate a few enemies. As Stalin put it with regard to the purge of Red Army officers, "even if 5 percent of these denunciations are true, then it helps."[64] The regime convinced itself that its domestic and foreign enemies were conspiring in a monolithic Trotskyist-Zinovievite-German-Japanese plot. While these fears sound far-fetched, the Japanese were indeed seeking such broad collaboration.

In this didactic theater Stalin figured as the primary producer. He selected the actors, scheduled the performances, and fine-tuned the wording—and even the tone—of confessions tortured out of the accused. He directed that in the courtroom the defendants should be "admitting their mistakes and disgracing themselves politically, while simultaneously acknowledging the strength of the Soviet government and the correctness of [its] methods."[65] As choreographer he assigned an actual playwright, Lev Sheinin, who ranked as both a top NKVD official and the author of *Face to Face Confrontation*, a stage hit of 1937. Stalin, proud of his handiwork, avidly read the trial record, clippings from the overseas press, and foreign journalists' communications tapped by the secret police.[66] Despite the formative role of Stalin and his closest associates, the purges spun out of control. Ambitious Communist Party and Red Army officials seized the opportunity to accuse their personal enemies, rivals, and bosses of treason.

The trial of the "Trotskyite-Zinovievist Counter-revolutionary Bloc" in August 1936 riveted U.S. officials. Kamenev admitted to the court that he had assisted "counter-revolutionary plots to assassinate Stalin and other leaders." He acknowledged that "a death sentence for myself and for all of us sitting here is fully justified." Kamenev further confessed to plotting with "a foreign diplomatic representative," "foreign fascist organizations," and Trotsky. The cabal was scheming to "gain power through war. Terror was to help bring about the war." When Zinoviev admitted to collaborating in this treason, Andrei Vyshinsky pressed him further, asking: "And Kirov?" "Yes, I admit guilt of his death." Despite such abject compliance, Zinoviev also hinted at a defiant counternarrative. He reminded the court of Stalin's boast years earlier that the leaders of the 1917 revolution had been "forged by Lenin." "I also was forged by Lenin," Zinoviev asserted. The implication was plain: Stalin was cast of the same material as the veteran Bolsheviks he was now unfairly persecuting. Zinoviev's last words also suggested resistance: "When I die, I die as a man."[67] The execution of Zinoviev, along with Kamenev and other Bolshevik stalwarts, shattered the taboo against killing defeated opponents in the party. Following the drama closely, Thayer and Henderson concluded that while the accused had likely opposed Stalin, Vyshinsky had failed to prove any foreign involvement in their supposed crimes.

Henderson saw the trial as literally a drama. To the State Department he described the setting where "the trial was staged," the choreography, and the performances of the participants. Vyshinsky "conducted himself in a highly theatrical manner" reminiscent of Lionel Barrymore playing a criminal lawyer. Kamenev commanded "a magnificent, expressive voice." Though Zinoviev "talked in a high effeminate voice," he nevertheless proved an impressive orator. Zinoviev's last words moved "even the hostile Soviet audience," while "a number of foreigners, including the American Communist, [Joshua] Kunitz, were frankly weeping."[68]

Melodrama, with its conventions of evil plots, foul deeds, and villains masked as heroes, dominated not only the show trials but also, remarkably, contemporary Moscow theater.[69] The trials touched George so deeply perhaps also because melodrama resonated with him. He loved exploring inner meaning—to discover not evil plots, but rather the music or atmosphere of cities, landscapes, and old churches.

THE TRIAL OF RADEK

Kennan, who returned to Moscow in August 1936 after the Kamenev-Zinoviev trial and who left for Washington in August 1937, before the inquisition of Nicolai Bukharin in March 1938, had to witness only the January 1937 prosecution of Karl Radek. Nevertheless, he was battered by the constant "reports of disappearances, trials, executions and banishments."[70] His responsibilities included keeping tabs on the parade of henchmen heading up the interior ministry as Genrikh Yagoda was replaced by N. Ezhov and his followers. The newcomers included Matvei D. Berman, secret police boss of forced labor camps and G. E. Prokofev, expert on "the uncovering of sabotage and 'wrecking' plots."[71]

Though Kennan's official reporting on these upheavals remained coolly matter of fact, more emotional reasoning colored his odd judgment about the chief villain in these horrors. While powerless actually to remove the dictator, Kennan's wishful thinking led him to believe that Stalin was indeed on the way out. In Red Square in November 1936 for the anniversary of the revolution, Kennan perceived, as he would again in future years, Stalin's supposed decline. He "looked considerably thinner . . . and during the parade took the unprecedented step of . . . sitting down to rest . . . while the military parade was still in progress."[72] After the Kamenev-Zinoviev trial, Kennan suggested that the dictator was suffering some mental pathology, not because of the killing, but rather because of a supposed inability to control his emotions. This last imperative Kennan took seriously, in part because he struggled to contain his own feelings. He opined that "Stalin is almost abnormally sensitive about world reaction to the Zinoviev trial" which led one to "wonder whether the hand that guides Russia's affairs, usually so imperturbable, has not for once been a bit uncertain."[73] In subsequent decades, the Soviet expert would repeatedly assert that Stalin was losing physical or political strength. Though he did not subscribe to the Cold War era thesis that Stalin was paranoid or otherwise delusional, Kennan in the 1940s would describe the Soviet system itself as suffering a mental pathology.

By December 1936, Kennan felt life in purge-era Moscow "very much of a strain." Blared warnings against contact with conniving foreign agents made most Russians shrink from Kennan and his colleagues. "The isolation of foreigners has never been greater," he lamented. Despite all the years learning the language, culture, and history of Russia, he now wanted out—"I am ripe for a transfer," he wrote his sister. "The atmosphere of suspicion and fear weighs . . . particularly on those foreigners who have a real interest in Russia." Meanwhile, "the foreign colony gets smaller, more ingrown and more bored with one another all the time."[74] Others in that emotional community also felt the strain. Fanny Chipman would later recall that "there was this constant terror, you couldn't help but feel it. I felt it so strongly that I had to go away after a while."[75]

A medical crisis brought the purges home to the Kennans. Four-year-old Grace suffered a potentially fatal case of bronchial pneumonia. "For one whole day I literally didn't dare to hope that she would live," the father recounted. He could not get a nurse or doctor "because they are afraid to come to a foreign Embassy." They might not even "find a priest to bury the little girl." At the last minute, a top physician did save Grace, "but only, I suspect, after the Foreign Office" had intervened. (A few months later, Kennan would report on the trumped up, salacious charges against a well-respected doctor who had treated patients at the embassy.)[76]

The thirty-six-year-old diplomat, who for years had worried about aging prematurely, feared that he and his colleagues were slipping into "the psychology of old men." The tension aggravated his abdominal problems, sending him back to Vienna in late December 1936 for medical tests. The upshot was that "I am on a terrifically strict diet again." Meanwhile, infant Joanie was also ill, and "all in all, it's not a very happy family."[77]

Their unhappiness may have been the cause, or an effect, of the divergent schedules of father and mother. Annelise took advantage of George's absence in Vienna to go out almost every night. A dinner party the evening before New Year's Eve lasted till 4:00 A.M. Then "on New Year's Eve [she] was first at the Hendersons, afterwards at the Metropole [Hotel] and finally ended at Durbie's [Elbridge Durbrow's]." She commented, not unhappily, that "it always seems fatal when George is away about getting to bed at any reasonable hours."[78] In mid-February, he reported that she was "due back here some time during the next month." While noting that "Gracie is lonely," he himself had a different focus: "I'll be glad to leave this town."[79]

JOSEPH DAVIES AND DISCORD IN THE EMBASSY

Kennan grew even more stressed with the arrival in January 1937 of Joseph E. Davies, Bullitt's replacement as ambassador. Davies, a campaign donor and one of President Roosevelt's fix-it generalists, took pride in his lack of experience with either Russia or diplomacy. The ambassador and his wife, the cereal heiress Marjorie Post Davies, who had built the Mar-a-Lago estate in Florida, disembarked with a retinue of sixteen hangers-on and a host of demands for the embassy staff. Davies ordered diplomatic officers to obtain a private train for him even though the demand might threaten "a revolutionary disturbance in the Red Railway Administration." He "treated the [embassy] staff as hired help," Bohlen later groused.[80] Diplomatic officers were assigned to assist with the ambassador's art purchases, oversee the building of a garden and a skating rink, and—perhaps most humiliating—seal, stamp, and mail 3,000 appeal letters "for the Mount Vernon Girls' School at Washington, of which Mrs. Davies is a regent." At the end of Davies's first day, Kennan and his colleagues "assembled in Henderson's rooms and solemnly considered whether we should resign in a body from the [foreign] service." Decades later, the "dismay, bewilderment, and discouragement" still rankled.[81]

Alerted to the "astounding" problems in the Moscow outpost, the State Department sent out an inspector, J. K. Huddle. He found the embattled fortress in crisis. "Morale was almost at the breaking point," Huddle quickly saw. The entire embassy was "afflicted with a tenseness, a nervousness, an apprehension of the unseen—a victim as is everything and everyone else in Moscow—of the OGPU." Problems abounded. Henderson, "a man of very high-tension" appeared "very much disturbed" about his standing with Davies. Chipman was "not very happy at Moscow, nor is Mrs. Chipman." One of the clerks, involved with "a lady of the ballet," had made himself vulnerable to blackmail by the secret police. Huddle reported that the ambassador aggravated this "supercharged atmosphere" by venting his "irritable temper" and by acting "on the spur of a momentary impulse." Davies failed "to realize the nervous strain [all] were laboring under."

Bullitt, who admired Kennan, had ensured that the latter's breakdown in 1934–1935 did not wreck his career. Davies, by contrast, had "acquired a dislike for Secretaries Kennan and Durbrow"—in part, Huddle reported, because he "inwardly dislikes their superior knowledge of Russian affairs." Kennan, who struck Huddle as "very sensitive," complained that his new boss failed to appreciate his "vast knowledge about things Russian." Differences reached far deeper, however, than the ambassador's jealousy of Kennan or the latter's resentment of Davies's demands. At President Roosevelt's request, Davies was pursuing a global strategy: encouraging Russia to resist aggression by Germany and Japan. Kennan, having "become disgusted" with the Soviet Union, failed to appreciate Roosevelt's perspective.

Huddle concluded that living in Stalin's Russia had literally sickened Kennan. The young diplomat suffered not only "continued poor health" but also "moody spells" that jeopardized "his future peace of mind." He advised Kennan's removal from Russia, "at least until the spell cast by the semi-oriental, semi-savage atmosphere of Moscow has been completely cast off." Huddle's language reflected the belief pervasive in the State Department that Soviet Russia remained "half-Asiatic" and only half-civilized. In subsequent decades, Americans would use this notion to justify their own behavior in the Cold War.

Even before Huddle arrived in Moscow, Davies had moved to get rid of the star Bullitt had tried so hard to keep. The ambassador tried to maneuver around Robert F. Kelley, the director of the State Department's Eastern European Division, who had a voice in assigning personnel to Moscow and who respected Kennan. On February 10, 1937, Davies advised Kelley about a problem "that has aroused my personal interest to an exceptional degree." The letter came soon after the Radek trial, during which Davies and Kennan had spent long hours grating against each other. Aware that Kelley championed a research-oriented approach to the Soviet Union, Davies affirmed that "Kennan is of the scholarly type, most capable and thorough." Nevertheless, "Kennan is not at all strong and well now." Not only did he suffer from ulcers and shingles but also, psychologically, he was "of a rather high-gear, nervous type." Then Davies drove home his point: "Quite frankly, I think he has been here quite long enough—perhaps too long for his own good." In the remainder of this letter, Davies repeated three further times that Kennan "has been really ill ever since I got here."[82] Though Davies may have cared about Kennan's health, he was most likely stressing illness to blunt Kelley's resistance to transferring the young diplomat.

What Huddle labeled the "temperamental differences between [Kennan] and the Ambassador" were aggravated by cultural, political, and personal divergences. While the earnest diplomat valued intensive research and immersion into Russian culture, the easygoing generalist prided himself as a quick study. Kennan despised political appointees and amateur diplomats; Davies ranked as both. Regarding people as much the same throughout the world, Davies expected American-style tempo and efficiency to prevail against Soviet bureaucracy or diplomatic protocol. The well-traveled diplomat had no such faith. While Kennan despised consumerism, Davies and his millionaire wife stocked up on Russian art, sported a gigantic yacht, and stored a mountain of American frozen food in a battery of freezers they had shipped to Moscow. While the ambassador adored President Roosevelt and championed the New Deal, the diplomat was little impressed with either. Rather he resented the Roosevelt administration for cutting the salaries of Foreign Service officers in an economy drive in 1933. Decades later, still resenting Roosevelt's choice of Davies, Kennan recalled that "what mortified us most of all was . . . that the President himself knew nothing about, or cared nothing for, what we had accomplished in building up the embassy at Moscow." Identifying himself with that emotional community, Kennan felt Davies's presence as a personal insult. "If the President wished to slap us down and to mock us . . . he could not have done better than with this appointment."[83]

Despite his loyalty to the Moscow embassy and his passion for Russia, Kennan wanted to leave. "This has been for me the most unhappy winter on record, in every respect," he confided to his sister.[84] Unlike the ambassador and the inspector, however, he blamed not his physical or mental health, but rather the isolation imposed by Stalin and the incompetence imposed by Davies. He mused that even after escaping Moscow, "it will be some time before the moral effect of the impact of Joseph E. Davies and his retinue wears off, and I can take my profession seriously again." Even after putting "up with a lot in my 10 years" as a diplomat, he wrote on February 17, "what I have seen in the last few weeks has been a revelation."

Kennan had spent those weeks attending the Radek trial while tending to Davies. (He followed the proceedings so closely that he picked up on discrepancies between the Soviet stenographer and the published transcripts.) The trial of the "Anti-Soviet Trotskyist Center," held in the Supreme Court of the USSR, began on January 23, 1937, and ran for seven days, from noon until 4:00 P.M. and from 6:00 to 10:00 P.M. Though not sitting in the dock himself, Kennan felt assaulted and humiliated. Davies had assigned him the task of "hissing into his ear . . . a simultaneous translation of Vishinski's thundering brutalities, the cringing confessions" by the accused, "and the delicate innuendoes in the statements" of those hinting at resistance. "During the intermissions I was sent, regularly, to fetch the ambassador his sandwiches" while he discussed the proceedings with journalists.[85] The proud diplomat felt doubly insulted: not only did he have to "fetch" the ambassador's food, but he was also shut out of the substantive discussions. Excluded—even though "I understood more than almost any other foreigner present, and a great deal more than ever appeared in our press."[86] Kennan did not bother to conceal his resentment from Davies. The trial ended with guilty verdicts for Radek, three other principal defendants, and thirteen lesser offenders.

Davies and Kennan submitted separate, and revealing, reports to the State Department. The divergences reflected how each of them tried to manage their reactions to the disturbing spectacle, process those feelings, and craft a report that would win favor back in Washington.

Both despatches were eventually published—Davies's in his 1943 book, *Mission to Moscow*, and Kennan's in *Foreign Relations of the United States 1937*.

Davies acknowledged that the trial was "horrible in the impression it made upon my mind." Emphasizing the theatrical production of this "human drama," the ambassador detailed how Soviet authorities had staged the setting and the choreography. The star performer, Radek, appeared "short and stocky but with an aggressive and brilliant personality." As the trial wore on, most of the accused betrayed "despair . . . holding their heads in their hands." On the crucial question of whether the astounding charges of assassination plots and industrial "wrecking" were true, Davies concluded that "the State had established its case." Despite the "redundant embroidery in the testimony, the consistent vein of truth ran through the fabric, establishing a definite political conspiracy to overthrow the present Government." Going further, Davies asserted that "it would be difficult for me to conceive of any court, in any jurisdiction, doing other than adjudging the defendants guilty." Moreover, "all of the members of the Diplomacy Corps here, with possibly one exception" agreed with his assessment. As for a Trotskyite plot to commit treason by collaborating with Japan and Germany, Davies and his fellow ambassadors deemed the evidence insufficient. In sum, Davies's report acknowledged the mental toll of attending the trial, focused on the theatrics, and reached a clear-cut, positivist judgment: the suspects were indeed guilty of plotting to overthrow Stalin's government.[87]

MAKING SENSE OF THE TRIAL

While Kennan's letters, diary entries, and subsequent writings and behavior indicate that the trial sparked far greater—and more lasting—anguish in him, he, unlike the ambassador, tried to mask his own feelings in his report to the State Department. He cared too much to let it show. Moreover, given the hierarchical culture of the State Department, he probably hesitated to openly challenge his boss. Though Kennan referred to the "repressed excitement" in the verbal duel between Radek and Vyshinsky and sought evidence in "the bearing and the faces" of the prosecutor and the defendants, he nonetheless reined in expression of his own outrage. He offered instead an ostentatiously rational—indeed, semiotic and mathematical—understanding of the trial proceedings. Vyshinsky, Radek, and other defendants "were talking in symbols," he explained. Such expressions as "terrorism" were "algebraic equivalents, behind which the real values were concealed." Terrorism "was understood by all the participants in the spectacle to mean simply illegal opposition activity." Striving for a cool tone and an overtly rational analysis, Kennan argued that only in the light of symbolic representation "do the proceedings begin to make some sense."

Kennan appraised the accused as guilty to a significant degree. His conclusion here is important, because in subsequent decades he would deny both their guilt and any such judgment by himself. Kennan's nuanced view of the Radek trial accords with the interpretation of post–Cold War historians.[88] He reported to the State Department that of the "small fry among the defendants" who were accused of espionage and sabotage, some "were quite probably guilty of a great deal." Many had worked in German-built military industries, and "under these circumstances, espionage—in the Soviet sense [of discussing technical information]—is almost inevitable." Moreover, in the cases of others accused of "opposition activity," "it is highly probable" that they "were active in the maintenance of the skeleton of a Trotskyist organization in Russia." As for the four principal defendants, Radek in conjunction with the other three had gotten in touch with an agent "who appears to have been actually running the Trotskyist organization, [Ephim A.] Dreitser." That attempt to make contact led to Radek's arrest. Like Davies and the other ambassadors, Kennan concluded that the alleged plot "to sell out the Soviet Union to the Nazis [could] hardly be taken seriously."

As to why the defendants confessed to all charges, Kennan, in striking contrast to his later accounts of the purges, remained low key. They hoped "to save their own lives or at least the well-being of persons near to them." Kennan's reference to torture was conspicuous by its absence. He reaffirmed that while many of the prosecutor's accusations were clearly bogus, this should "not be interpreted as an attempt to give any of the defendants a clean moral bill of health." "From the point of view of the regime," he argued, "they have probably done plenty . . . to warrant their humiliation and punishment." That affirmation edged Kennan himself a bit toward the Kremlin's perspective.

After sustaining this coolly rational, positivist discussion with clear-cut categories of guilt and innocence for nearly all of his fourteen-page report, Kennan in the last two paragraphs allowed himself—or could not prevent himself—from shifting radically in tone and discourse. He drew on his own deeply held notions about Russia's character, culture, and differences from the West to offer a radically different explanation that stressed ambiguity and ambivalence. Rather than a clear-cut matter of right and wrong, the Radek trial "probably involved provocation and deceit on both sides." He surmised that "if it be true that some of the defendants had worked for Trotsky and foreign espionage services while pretending to be in the loyal service of the Soviet Government, it is equally possible that others had really worked for the Soviet Government while pretending to be loyal adherents of other masters." Holding out for the absolute truth was useless since all the facts would never become available. Moreover, the cultural and psychological chasm between Russia and the West rendered it "doubtful whether the western mind could ever fathom the questions of guilt and innocent, of truth and fiction." Much as he had in December 1933 when first entering Soviet Russia, Kennan positioned himself as straddling the East-West chasm and as having insight into both sides. He claimed that he "understood [the trial] more than almost any other foreigner." The despatch to the State Department ended with a Kennanish rumination: "The Russian mind, as [Fyodor] Dostoevski has shown, knows no moderation; and it sometimes carries both truth and falsehood to such infinite extremes that they eventually meet in space, like parallel lines, and it is no longer possible to distinguish between them."

In that last sentence Kennan abandoned a discourse of Western analytical positivism to elucidate a mystical Russian alternative. Since his days at Princeton, he had held to the orientalist notion that Russia, because of its climate, geography, and history under the Tartars, tended toward extremes. Dostoevsky, who celebrated extremes of personality in his novels, had in *The Brothers Karamazov* referred to non-Euclidian geometry, which asserted that parallel lines could indeed meet, in infinity. As Dostoevsky and Kennan both understood, if Euclidian geometry, a bulwark of mathematical order for millennia, could be refuted, supposedly bedrock ethical and philosophical principles might also prove shaky. If the separation between parallel lines could collapse, so too might the divergence between right and wrong, between truth and lies. Though Kennan had once criticized Dostoevsky for preferring the "abnormal," "feverish" life of the Moscow "bohème" to the Russian countryside, the diplomat seems to have shared, in his own conclusion about the trial, the novelist's skepticism that truth and falsehood stood dependably apart.[89]

Perhaps Kennan's cynicism was sharpened by the strain of tightly channeling his feelings. His February 18, 1937, report to the State Department figures as only one point on a spectrum of narratives, written over decades, that tried to make sense of this trauma. It is only by considering the array of Kennan's accounts of the purges, extending from the 1930s to the 1980s, that we get a full sense of how the horror affected his life. Before considering those other versions, however, we must first examine how Kennan in March–August 1937 experienced the disappearances, trials, and executions of other Soviet leaders he knew and/or respected.

On March 3, Stalin dragged Kennan and his colleagues further into the hell world of the purges. The *vozhd* admonished the Central Committee of the Communist Party not to forget that "capitalist encirclement" remained "very real and unpleasant." Not only overt enemies, such as Germany and Japan, but also ostensibly neutral nations, such as the United States, remained bent on "penetrating" the Soviet Union with "wreckers, spies, diversionists and murderers." The dictator conjured a monolithic threat from the "espionage-diversionist work of the Trotskiist agents of the Japanese-German secret police." Similarly melodramatic, the Soviet press depicted in "the gaudiest of colors," Kennan reported, "the sinister ways in which foreign espionage services weave their nets around the unsuspecting Soviet citizens." *Pravda* cautioned that foreigners would stop at nothing to put patriotic Soviet citizens "in a trance" and "completely in [their] power."[90] Kennan, who delighted in donning a Russian-style blouse and listening to ordinary Russians in the streets, was now cast as a "sinister and suspicious figure." His professional obligation to pursue "a normal and objective interest in Soviet conditions" was twisted by *Pravda* into a nefarious effort by "spies" to "collect the data they need by . . . riding around on the railways, visiting public places. They eavesdrop on other people." Russians were being indoctrinated, Kennan reported, that "practically every bourgeois foreigner is a spy" skilled at "diabolic methods of blackmail and intimidation." This all-out campaign to isolate Soviet citizens from such resident foreigners came in the context of the "veritable wave of arrests, personnel shifts, and public demotions—accompanied by endless denunciations, intrigue, muckraking and private snooping, which has taken place during the last few weeks." He added that in the Radek trial, "contacts with foreigners" had figured "as general incriminating evidence."[91]

THE PURGES REACH CLOSER

While the purges entailed over one million arrests and nearly 700,000 executions, most of them of ordinary people rather than the elite, Kennan and his colleagues were most disturbed by the persecution of persons they knew. These friends and acquaintances included their liaison to the Kremlin, Baron Boris I. Steiger, who was charged with homosexuality; Dmitri Pletnev, a doctor who had treated and socialized with embassy staff and was accused of sexual sadism; and top Red Army officers, who were denounced as traitorous collaborators with Nazi Germany and Japan.

Shaken by the disappearance of Steiger, Henderson commented that "no arrest in recent years, not even that of the highest Soviet officials, has made such an impression upon the Diplomatic Corps." Kennan affirmed the "deep effect" on him and on his colleagues. The Baron, forty-five years old in 1937, descended from a Swiss family that had long lived in Ukraine. Isolated Western diplomats liked Steiger because of his open manner and easy access to the Kremlin. Fond memories of what Davies called the "mystery man of Moscow" would endure for decades. Thayer later recalled "a cultured man with an excellent sense of humor and a fund of stories which he loved to tell in flawless French."[92] Bohlen, who had valued Steiger as a friend, remembered "a respectable bridge player" and "a good conversationalist, with a cynical turn of mind that always delighted members of the diplomatic corps." Henderson, who had lunched with Steiger twice a month, prized his wit and friendly manner. Steiger's disappearance wounded Western diplomats not only because he seemed cultural kin but also because he could convey messages back and forth between embassies "and the highest Soviet officials." Bohlen ranked him as "the most valuable official contact in Moscow."[93] As Fanny Chipman later explained, "when you wanted something to go back without all the official rigamarole, you asked Steiger to come in for lunch or dinner . . . served him the vodka he likes—the best, from Riga," and whatever the problem might be, he would "fix it."[94]

To Kennan, who hungered for satisfying contact with Russians, Steiger appeared unique. He stood out as "the sole Soviet citizen who had the courage and wit to discuss world affairs with foreign diplomats in a perfectly open and intelligent manner . . . without ever cluttering the discussion with useless repetitions of communist dogma, but also without . . . disloyalty to his own Government."[95]

The Baron had been briefing Americans on the thinking in the Kremlin ever since Bullitt had opened the embassy. At one such session on February 17, 1937, coincidentally the day before Kennan sent the State Department his report on the Radek trial, Steiger lunched with Davies, Henderson, and Kennan. He detailed the Kremlin's view of relations with Finland, Poland, Czechoslovakia, Germany, and Britain. With regard to Germany's attacking Russia, he asserted that "the German military machine was still not ready for major action." Germany had better chances for expansion into Austria, Hungary, and Yugoslavia, Steiger reasoned. As for U.S.-Soviet relations, he assured them "that if things were approached in a quiet, patient way, everything would be 'all right.'" After lunch, Davies took the go-between aside to ask if he was worried about getting purged himself. Steiger "shrugged his shoulders expressively and pointed his index finger to the back of his neck behind his ear"—the spot where the secret police customarily fired a bullet into their victims.[96]

Precisely two months later, on April 17, Steiger attended the opera along with Henderson and others. Fanny Chipman later recalled that one of her friends saw Steiger looking "as white as a piece of linen."[97] The Baron invited Davies's daughter and other young people for a post-opera bite to eat and dance at the night club at the Hotel Metropole. At the hotel, two men in civilian clothes tapped Steiger on the shoulder. Davies later recounted: "He left with them, excusing himself and saying he would be back shortly. He never returned." That December, Steiger was executed with a bullet to the back of his neck. The Kremlin insisted that Steiger had been arrested on charges of homosexuality. His admirers remained skeptical. Moscow diplomats were gossipy, Henderson explained, "and it would hardly seem possible that if Steiger was abnormal as charged, he could have successfully hidden his weakness." Most likely the Soviets wanted it to appear that Steiger had been arrested for nonpolitical reasons.[98]

Yet another of what Kennan suffered as "these depressing developments" destroyed Dmitri D. Pletnev, a famous and respected physician and a frequent visitor to the U.S. embassy. Pletnev, said to be Stalin's personal physician, had treated Davies and other Americans and had "also been a guest in their homes," Kennan reported to Washington. Davies affirmed, "I knew [him] quite well."[99] Pletnev may have been the physician who had saved four-year-old Grace Kennan, or perhaps he had referred the doctor who had treated her. Kennan valued Pletnev's sociability and expertise and did not blink at his prejudices. In praising the physician's "unusual courage," the diplomat cited the Russian's refusal to become a Communist or to "conceal his feelings toward the legion of younger and imperfectly trained" doctors, "mostly of Jewish extraction, who have invaded the Russian medical world since the revolution . . . despite their lack of good manners and professional ethics." Kennan's prejudice reflected anti-Semitic stereotypes, common in his time, of coarse, ambitious Jews pushing their way into elevated domains where they did not belong.

The American was dismayed when the police suddenly accused the doctor of a "horrible set of charges, involving perversion, sadism, violation of professional ethics, etc." A sensationalized article in *Pravda*, translated by Kennan himself, contains internally contradictory storylines that suggest a complex set of mishaps. Pletnev's troubles emerged from a murky mix of soured love, medical failure, psychological disturbance, anti-Semitism, and professional rivalry. The secret police knotted these strands together to pull down an independent-minded dissident. Pletnev had angered "high Party circles through [his] anti-Soviet and anti-Semitic remarks," Kennan explained. Soviet authorities worried that Pletnev might not return from an upcoming medical conference in Western Europe. The police exploited accusations by Dr. Broude, "a woman physician with whom Pletnev had intimate relations for a number of years until she developed definite symptoms of schizophrenia." In a long *Pravda* article entitled "Professor-Ravisher-Sadist," Broude told a different story. In July 1934, she had gone to Dr. Pletnev's house at midnight for treatment. Pletnev "began to bite her breast until it bled." The breast subsequently became infected, and the doctor failed to cure her. When she became an invalid, Pletnev tried to silence her with money. *Pravda* quoted her rant: "Curses upon you, you sadist who have practised your foul perversions upon me."

Much about this incident seems ambiguous. The supposed patient's presence in the doctor's home at midnight, the drastic shift in her symptoms, and Pletnev's repeated complaints to police and medical authorities that Broude was hounding him all blur the issues surrounding Pletnev's guilt. Unambiguous for Kennan, however, was that yet another Russian he knew and liked was suffering persecution. The diplomat admitted the uncertainty in the tangled case. Impelled by his feelings, Kennan argued that even if this "elderly and respected professor" had developed "perversive inclinations," he, not the "deranged woman," deserved sympathy and a chance to recover from "this pathological aberration from psychic health."[100] Though never a bigot, Kennan's lifelong prejudices short-circuited his empathy with Jews, women, and others different from him.

Kennan was horrified as the slaughter lopped off still more of the Soviet elite. Stalin, genuinely believing that such top generals as Marshal Mikhail Tukhachevsky were collaborating with Nazi Germany, launched a sudden purge. What the dictator initiated at the top would soon mushroom into a mass assault throughout the ranks.[101] The embassy noted that some of the arrested military officers were personally known to members of the staff.[102] In part to stanch his own anguish, Kennan worked furiously to discern some sense in this apparent madness.

Over a three-week period in May–June, he translated a ream of Soviet documents, composed eleven of his own despatches, and contributed to Henderson's reports. His calm exterior beginning to crack, Kennan found these latest arrests, including that of Moscow military chief Boris S. Gorbachev, all the more disturbing.[103] Poring over official Soviet documents, he detected significance in the poor drafting and the glaring grammatical errors of recent published regulations. Stalin was evidently replacing the better educated professionals, some of whom Kennan knew and admired, with loyal but unpolished neophytes.[104] When Ian B. Gemarnik, assistant commissar of the Red Army, committed suicide on May 31, Kennan, who may have personally known him, responded with empathy and a bit of eulogy. He wanted to "register the fact that one of the most prominent and capable—and also one of the most modest—of the Soviet military leaders has found it impossible to face the future."[105] Attuned to the geostrategic implications, Kennan warned Washington that the assault on Red Army officers was sparking "considerable anxiety by the Western European allies of the Soviet Union and is not being ignored by the Fascist countries."[106]

In June, Kennan reported that the police had executed all the accused military officers. "Everybody was so scared," Annelise later recalled. "At a big dinner party that Ambassador Davies gave that year, there were six people at the table who were later killed." Etched into her memory was a conversation with the head of the air force in Moscow. "We were talking, and two months later he was killed."[107] Similarly moved was Kennan's friend Thayer: "The terror here is pretty horrifying. I even dream of friends being arrested." Admitting that "the moral and mental strain is pretty severe," Thayer could not "help exploding from time to time in rage and disgust."[108]

Kennan fumed at *Pravda's* trumpeting the purges as advancing the "great proletarian revolution" destined to "conquer the whole world." He felt personally affronted by charges that foreigners were using "despicable methods . . . to entangle unsuspecting Soviet citizens in their meshes." All Soviet citizens, *Pravda* blared, should enlist as "voluntary workers for the People's Commissariat for Internal Affairs." Under severe strain himself, Kennan attributed the crimes of Soviet officials to their "lack of mental balance."[109] That foreshadowed his thesis in the early Cold War.

Kennan was slipping into melancholy. In March, he had explained to relatives back home that "I haven't written because it has continued to be a very depressing winter."[110] Spring brought little cheer, other than the departure of the Davies family on a visit to America. As if to taunt him about Stalin's omnipresence, Kennan, driving out to the dacha, encountered the *vozhd* himself, riding in an "enormous Cadillac limousine." Stalin "stared gloomily out of his window . . . and we stared back." Washington also aggravated him. He admitted "complete discouragement about the [foreign] service, both at the Moscow end and in Washington.[111] Even his diplomatic career seemed pointless since "no passionless democracy, like our own," the product "of millions of individual philistinisms, can have much in the way of a foreign policy."[112]

His marriage, too, frustrated him. During an intermission at the opera, a special someone "flitted past me, weaving like a wraith through the crowd, and was gone before I could do more than stare, and I had a feeling that she came because I was there." Although at pains to record such flirtations in his diary, he remained elusive about the details. He would later recall the "furtive, clandestine bonds of intimacy and affection" that, despite the secret police, had arisen between Americans and Russians. Kennan shrouded another hint in the passive voice: in Moscow's "strange environment . . . demoralization and tragedy [were] often inflicted on western lives and marriages." As to whose marriages, who were so inflicted, and how, he remained silent. One Sunday in May 1937,

> he arose in clouds of dark despair. Went alone out to the dacha, felt like a dried-up old governess. Whiled away the evening by lying on a sofa and doing nothing at all except reminisce."[113]

Was he reminiscing about Enid Keyes or some other woman? Dwelling on his marriage? Fantasizing about escaping, somehow, into the soulful Russia of pre-1917? Musing about a cultural mixing between Russia and America? Or had he sadly concluded that his dreams about Russia amounted to just fantasy?

Regardless of what Kennan was actually brooding about, his passion for Russia measurably declined from December 1935, when he had ventured with Keyes to Tolstoy's estate, to March 1937, when he journeyed alone to Chekhov's Yalta home. Kennan suffered much in those fifteen months. His cheery openness on the first pilgrimage, despite the hazards of dysentery and a blizzard, contrasted with his grumpy sourness on the second, despite his hagiographic view of Chekhov. His patience with the Soviet government and with the Russian people had drained. Fed up with the petty tyrannies of Davies and the totalitarian dictates of Stalin, he eagerly awaited an "end [to] my sojourn in Russia."[114]

KENNAN AND CHEKHOV

But before leaving, he had to see Chekhov's home in Yalta. The writer, whose short stories and plays sparkled with a sad though humorous irony, ranked as Kennan's favorite Russian author. The admiration created a writer's block in this most fluid of writers. In late March 1937, with his transfer imminent, he seized this last chance to see the home on the Black Sea coast, where Chekhov had retreated in hope that the mild climate would check his tuberculosis.

Though differing in grandeur and in location, the homes of Tolstoy and Chekhov appealed in parallel ways. What had enraptured Kennan about Yasnaya Polyana—the cozy smell, the feminine presence, the bucolic charm, and the personal possessions of a giant of pre-1917 Russian culture—permeated Chekhov's home as well. George and Enid had found Tolstoy's abode "surprising to us for its primitiveness and simplicity." He described Chekhov's dwelling as a similarly rustic, "attractive little bungalow . . . with a little garden and . . . a glimpse of the sea." While Tolstoy's home "had the air of . . . kind women," Chekhov's had the author's actual sister, who possessed "a kind and open face." Time stood still at both homes. In Tolstoy's, "everything has been left as it was. The same papers are on the desk, even his linen Russian smock is hanging by the wash-stand." In Chekhov's, everything was "just the way it was when he died. Even the unopened mail is lying on the desk." Also similar was Tolstoy's fleeing Yasnaya Polyana, intending never to return and the circumstance that "Chekhov hated Yalta."

Despite the similarities, Chekhov's home did not inspire the emotional reverie of Kennan's visit to Yasnaya Polyana. His overall mood and his attitude toward Russia had soured in the interim. Moreover, he had no attractive young woman with whom to share any rapture.

Another sign of embitterment was that his lifelong elitism trumped the sentimental longing he had expressed back in September 1935, "to rub elbows with [Russians] in the streets, to smell the earthy, almost touching smells."[115] Though Kennan always retained a fondness for country folk, he gravitated toward aristocrats of birth, culture, or intelligence. In Riga and Berlin, he had hobnobbed with Baltic and German lower nobility. He idealized the pre-1917 Russian gentry. What he objected to most in the Soviet system of the late 1930s was not the quashing of personal and economic freedoms, but rather the extremism of Stalin's cult and brutal dictatorship, the belief in the ends justifying the means, the enforced xenophobia, and the ascendancy, at least in theory, of the masses over the cultivated elites.

What before 1917 had glittered as a seaside resort for the upper classes now appeared "packed with proletarian vacationists," "shoddy and bewildered people," who had made "pig-sties of these hotels and villas."[116] Kennan hung history's ultimate judgment of the Bolshevik revolution, with all its sacrifices and bloodshed, on whether these proletarians would ultimately "learn something of the cultured relaxation and gaiety" of pre-1917 Russia. "If they do, then the revolution will probably not have been in vain." However, "if not, then the loss of the glamour of the Empire—the fine cafes, the uniforms, the private homes, the culture and the manners—will really have been an unredeemable tragedy." Kennan's final appraisal was that "socialism—whatever its virtues may be— seems to have a murderous effect on the joie de vivre." Though sour and snobbish, his evaluation did pick up on how drab and dreary was Soviet-style communism. A half-century later, that cultural failing would help bring down the Berlin Wall and the Soviet bloc.[117]

Soviet rule seemed not collapsing but rather coalescing around terror when Kennan returned to Moscow from Vienna in November 1935. In the subsequent two years, he himself suffered as Stalin's purges arrested, tortured, tried, and then executed millions of victims. As the killings reached a "savage and dramatic" crescendo, the embassy assigned Kennan to cover the gruesome story. Three decades later, his published memoir evidenced the strain of that work. "To be forced to follow [the purges'] course, day by day, and to write analytical dispatches" had educated him in the horrors of Stalinism.[118] The quotation pointed up his dual challenge: enduring the emotionally wrenching purges while yet producing coolly analytic reports about them.

KENNAN AND THE TRAUMA

Kennan coped admirably. His reports to the State Department integrated his more emotional and more rational thinking into explanations that at the time stood out for their balance and intelligence—and that still shine in light of recent history written with the benefit of Russian archives.[119] But writing those despatches was only one step in Kennan's decades-long processing of the pain of the purges.

An unpublished memoir from 1939–1940 hints at the complex evolution of George's constructed memory of the trauma. He recounted that in 1938, when he "had to spend a hot summer in Washington and had little else to do," he pored over the trial testimony and the records of opposition activities in Russia and then used "card indexes and chronologies to sort out this material systematically." Using this explicitly logical methodology, he sought a rational explanation that would make "more sense than the monstrous accusations and the absurd confessions" of the melodramatic show trials.

With his emotional impulses channeled into this overtly rational effort, Kennan began a dispassionate, third-person analysis of the trials. As he had in his February 1937 despatch (and in contrast to his Cold War era accounts), he argued that the charges against the accused "were not all false. There was usually a thread of truth in them," albeit a truth that "was generally distorted and exaggerated." He repeated his analogy of "algebraic substitution" by which the court substituted "terrorism" for "party opposition." Kennan now allowed himself to use the language of theatrics also employed by Davies and Henderson. The "stage-director" had ensured that courtroom performances were "as carefully rehearsed" as those "on the stage of the Moscow Art Theatre."[120]

Then Kennan tackled the key puzzle: why had victims confessed to fiendish crimes they had not committed? He implored the reader to "picture to himself the loneliness, the terror and the hopelessness" of a prisoner tortured into making a false confession. With this request, the tone and language of Kennan's narrative abruptly shifted. In attempting to write coolly about the horror, he again succumbed to it. He crowded into a single page one emotional phrase after another: "cruelest and most horrible"; "no compassion, no restraint, no mercy"; "indefinite pain, loneliness, strain and uncertainty"; "unnerved . . . bewildered . . . exhausted . . . shocked and discouraged . . . intimidated . . . forsaken." As this litany of suffering peaked, Kennan's story suddenly changed voice from third to first person. Empathizing and identifying with the prisoner prostrate before the torturers demanding a confession, Kennan as victim and as narrator expostulated: "For God's sake, do what you want with me! I am yours to command."[121] It was always a struggle for Kennan to contain his emotional impulses. Even though he had started out with a coolly rational analysis, he had still ended up with an on-the-page scream.

Nevertheless, his mix of more emotional and more rational thinking about the purges did fuse into two solid conclusions. The first was a set of principles about the essential nature of communism that he would adhere to for the rest of his long life. He decided that communism was doomed because of its basic errors: belief that the end justifies the means, and that there is "no such thing as abstract truth or abstract justice, that all truth is relative and subjective." While accepting positivism as simple fact, he also argued that "the end cannot justify the means because it is itself the product of the means." Kennan was enunciating ideas that he would later flesh out into a philosophy of principled conservatism. He argued that "form is more important in government than direction. This is why kings and courts, whose actions must at least *appear* gracious and dignified" can succeed beyond regimes with "lofty ideologies."[122]

What Kennan pinpointed as the fatal errors of communism drove him to a second gloomy conclusion. That one, however, he could not accept permanently. The Russophile had long dreamed of fulfilling his "professional aspirations" as well as his personal aims by shepherding a history-making cultural exchange between Russia and America. Even in discouragement he found himself breathing life, even if only for a moment, into his

> hope that somewhere in that Russian world—in the freshness and spontaneity of its human relationships, in its childishly blunt reaction to the problems of civilization, in the unfathomable warmth and beauty of its language—things could be found which would help us in solving the problems of our own culture.[123]

Tapping the primal genius of Russia to revitalize America is what Kennan and Thayer longed to do. And while Kennan in the aftermath of the purges declared this dream dead, his passion for Russia resisted that doleful conclusion. For much of the subsequent six decades he would soldier on—trying to act on, tamp down, or otherwise cope with the frustration of his desire to enhance ties with the people, culture, and land of Russia. This most fervent wish would temper his pursuit of the Cold War. But even before he had to deal with that conflict with Russia, Kennan had to endure what he called the "purge" in Washington, an attack that he faced while sitting on the Russia desk in the State Department.

CHAPTER 5

KENNAN AND THE DESCENT
INTO WAR, 1937–1939

WORN DOWN by the isolation in Moscow, Stalin's terror, and the State Department's own "purge" of its Eastern European Division in June 1937, Kennan was fed up with Russian affairs. He welcomed a cable promising a transfer to Jerusalem, then part of the British Mandate of Palestine. "George has already gotten . . . . a grammar of the Yiddish language!" Annelise reported.[1] The Kennans left Moscow on August 11, deposited five-year-old Grace and sixteen-month-old Joan with their grandparents in Norway, and then ventured to the French Riviera. They intended, George later explained with a touch of sarcasm, to blow their meager funds on six weeks of "sybaritic, plutocratic luxury, sunshine, rest, and exercise."[2] As it would turn out, however, the Kennans got neither to relax on the Mediterranean nor to relocate to Jerusalem.

A "palace revolution in the State Dept." has catapulted "some of my best friends, especially Mr. [George S.] Messersmith, very decidedly on top," Kennan was excited to discover in September 1937.[3] Messersmith, who had overseen Kennan's Russian studies in Berlin in 1929–1931 and had then worked with him in Vienna in 1935, had teamed up with William C. Bullitt, Kennan's former mentor in Moscow, to get their protégé a plum job. George was promoted to chief of the Russian desk in the Department of State's just reorganized Division of European Affairs. Still only thirty-three years old, Kennan now commanded a voice in shaping relations with the Kremlin bosses who had so frustrated him. He approached the work in Washington with feelings that had festered in Moscow. On a gut level, he interpreted the Kremlin's cruel isolation of diplomats and journalists as a bellwether for overall U.S.-Soviet relations.

Kennan's attitude put him at odds with President Franklin D. Roosevelt, who viewed the Kremlin, despite its cruelties to domestic opponents and to foreign diplomats, as a potential partner against aggressive Germany and Japan. Kennan also remained blinkered about the progress of Roosevelt's New Deal. Although the diplomat would meet twice with the president in the White House, he never fell for FDR's charm. Kennan neither admired Roosevelt as a person, respected his political skills, or grasped his foreign policy vision. Temperamental opposites and separated by rank and experience, each of them remained, unfortunately, clueless about the other's talents.

Kennan's time in the United States from October 1937 to September 1938, his longest stay during the entire 1926 to 1946 period, would shape his conceptions about twentieth-century America. Conditioning those judgments were his idealizing of the preindustrial era, his ideas from interwar Germany and the Baltic nations, and his intense experience in Soviet Russia. While Russia had frustrated Kennan's longing for transcendence, America would frustrate his longing for a homecoming.

Kennan linked domestic and foreign matters. The United States could pursue "a truly beneficial and constructive" foreign policy only if its domestic society mobilized "enthusiasm and self-sacrifice . . . to solve its own problems."[4] He would apply that lesson from the late 1930s to the argument in his 1946 long telegram and in his 1947 "X" article. In both documents he followed up warnings of an existential threat from the Soviets with recommendations for down-to-earth reforms at home. Foreign and domestic matters intertwined also because of Kennan's emotional identification with both Russia and America and his desire to shepherd, somehow, a coming together of the two nations.

BACK IN THE USA

Leaving behind the "magic and unreality of Russia," the Kennans in the summer of 1937 plunged into the materialist reality of the West. He felt out of place in Paris, "crowded with flat-voiced, flat-chested [American] women" and husbands who, like characters out of a Sinclair Lewis novel, sat in "hotel lobbies wistfully reading the comic strips" while abusing the staff in loud tones in order "to keep these French from putting something over on [them]." Seeing "so many things we couldn't buy depressed" the couple. Still more irritating was the Riviera, hot, "grotesque and deserted." They ate at "gloomy little restaurants because [they] did not have much money." Across the bay a beacon advertised "the Riviera's most spectacular brothel." Indeed, the entire coastline had apparently degenerated into a "great brothel, selling pleasures more hollow than those of the purchased flesh." Kennan, steeped in Oswald Spengler's warning about the decline of Western culture, interpreted this "sterility" as "the breakdown of European society and the approach of a new debacle." The anticipated "sybaritic" vacation collapsed in anxiety as George and Annelise succumbed to "a sudden panicky impulse to get back to the children. Frantically, as though their lives depended on it," they rushed "to the familiar refuge of southern Norway." Having left the community of foreign diplomats in Moscow, they found the outside world "too big, too bewildering for us."[5]

Nor would the Kennans fit in easily during their eleven months in Washington. Problems abounded, particularly with family finances and the recent changes at the State Department. With no rental allowance (because he was not stationed abroad), a salary of $365 a month, and Washington area apartments going for $120, "financially it's going to be definitely hard," Kennan worried. Moreover, "Annelise isn't used to American house-keeping," and so they needed to stretch the family budget to pay for a servant.[6] A bit later, George reported to Jeanette that "Annelise is filled with admiration at . . . your getting along without a maid, and has been exclaiming about it all day."[7] Although the husband was pointing up his wife's European ways, he himself had hired domestic help when he was single and after they were married. He had grown up in a household with two servants plus a cook and other hired hands. Indeed, for the rest of his life, George would regard domestic help, including caregivers for the children, as the norm for professionals, and as necessary for achieving anything creative. After a few months in Washington, George confided to Jeanette, "We're living over our income and see few prospects of retrenching. In other words, everything is normal."[8]

At the office, Kennan fumed over the reorganizing in the State Department and the banishment to Istanbul of another of his mentors, Robert F. Kelley. He opposed White House efforts at encouraging the Soviet Union to resist Germany and Japan. Finally, this bookish diplomat, bowing to pressure from superiors in the department, had to criticize the scholarly approach to diplomatic reporting that he had learned from Kelley and found personally satisfying.

"We have been already liquidated, both physically and legally," Kelley wailed. In charge of the Eastern European Division since 1926, he had indoctrinated specialists with his affinity for pre-1917 Russia and his antagonism toward the Soviet regime. Slamming them just as Stalin was shutting down all opposition, the axing of the division was labeled by Kelley and his supporters as yet another "purge." On paper, the State Department was also eliminating the Western European group and creating a unified Division of European Affairs. But in terms of bureaucratic clout, "Western Europe has been enlarged by taking in Eastern Europe," a veteran affirmed.[9] Heading the new division was J. Pierrepont Moffat, who had little interest in Russia. Kennan and his colleagues blamed Eleanor Roosevelt and other leftists for supposedly pressuring FDR into making the change. Decades later, Kennan could still sniff in this change, "the smell of Soviet influence, or strongly pro-Soviet influence."[10]

At stake were not only bureaucratic and political independence but also cherished cultural values. "So strong did emotions run" among Kelley's foes that they tried to junk his precious library of Russian books. Files painstakingly assembled over the years also were to be destroyed, Kennan, still fuming, recalled much later. As if in a dictatorship, Chip Bohlen secretly wrapped valuable reference books in brown paper and hid them. When Kennan arrived, he rescued the trove.[11]

Though the First Lady may have played a minor role, it was President Roosevelt, working through his friend, Under Secretary of State Sumner Welles, who folded the divisions. FDR faulted Kelley and his acolytes for fixating on Soviet sins while ignoring the possibility of Russian cooperation against the Axis of Nazi Germany and imperial Japan. Moreover, what Kelley had nurtured as his fraternity, Moffat and others deplored as "clannishness." Diplomats stationed in Moscow or Riga had confided more to Kelley than to the secretary of state. The Eastern European Division had insulated itself "very much as an *imperium in imperio*," Moffat and others groused. The new team also welcomed what Kelley's disciples mourned: "less detail, less compilation of material."[12]

After the frenetic pace of the Moscow embassy, the Russian desk "could not have been more quiet," Kennan found.[13] During the sweltering summer of 1938, with official Washington emptied out and Annelise and the girls vacationing in Wisconsin, Kennan put pen to paper in a search for rational understanding. He assembled index cards and chronologies in hopes of coming up with a logical explanation of the seemingly irrational and emotionally disturbing purge trials. A second project was beginning what would become a 109-page memoir of the emotional, cultural, and political storms wrenching his personal life as well as Russia and America. (Although Kennan submitted the manuscript to Little, Brown, hoping to make some money, the publisher turned it down. Ironically, the same company would decades later publish his best seller, *Memoirs 1925–1950*.) Third was another book fragment, "The Prerequisites." Here he argued for transforming the United States into a frankly authoritarian state run by selfless young patriots such as himself. He believed that only through such an upheaval could Americans roll back the modernizing forces, especially urbanization and industrialization, undermining what he idealized as traditional U.S. society.

Even as he pushed for cool understanding, Kennan was pulled by desires and distastes. "I felt a powerful longing to identify myself more closely with everything America had once been; and a decided reluctance to identify myself with what it seemed to be becoming."[14] Two decades as an expatriate had attuned him, like a "musical instrument . . . to the most minute phenomena" of America.[15] Much of what he saw and heard offended him. American radio, movies, and magazines offered only shallow content, tawdry sensationalism, and bait-and-switch advertising. From such a hollow culture, sensitive young adults such as himself could imbibe only a "puzzled sense of frustration, disappointment and bitterness." To contain this "stifling, demoralizing flood of commercialized mush" would require either self-restraint by business, which seemed unlikely, or order imposed by government, which he favored. Freedom did not mean license, he insisted.[16]

A proto-environmentalist, Kennan was disgusted by the degradation surrounding him. The riverfront of Alexandria, Virginia, a block from his rented house, exposed "ruin and neglect worse than anything I had ever seen in Europe: sunken boats, silted slips, rotting rat-infested wharves."[17] Even a pleasant country walk was marred by "the roar of the Sunday traffic." "Man is a skin-disease of the earth," he concluded bitterly.[18] The bus ride from the office carried him "past the junk heaps and the automobile graveyards, past the sign boards, the n-shacks." (He had found congenial the racism of the city's "old Southern society" stalwarts, whom he "rather liked.")[19] He wondered whether there still existed, "somewhere in America . . . a valley full of quiet farms and woodlands [and] a house where . . . human warmth and simplicity and graciousness defied the encroachments of a diseased world and of people drugged and debilitated by automobiles and advertisements and radios and moving pictures."[20] Such longing reflected George's loneliness, disgust, and, most important, his bedrock objection to "the unhappy partnership of man and the machine."[21]

Trying to revisit his own bucolic past, Kennan in June 1938 bicycled 100 miles past farms and through small towns on Wisconsin Route 50 to his paternal grandfather's homestead. An overnight stay yielded rare contentment. Lying awake "listening to the chirping of crickets, the croaking of bull-frogs, and all the familiar sounds of the Wisconsin summer night" made him "happier than I had been for years. . . . I had at last come home."[22] The homecoming was brief.

He remained lonely. Highways struck him as "the most deserted places I had ever encountered." As the cars whizzed by, his only companions were the roadkill, "and here the turtles, whose corpses strewed the pavement for miles," had suffered the worst. The automobile-dominated road symbolized "the sad climax of individualism"; Americans "had forgotten how to think or live collectively." Such isolation seemed pathological, for a rich "association of human beings is a prerequisite for a healthy social and political life." Far different had been "the vigorous life of the English highway of Chaucer's day." Longing for contact, Kennan complained that even the villages lacked any "place where strangers would come together freely, as in a Bavarian beer hall or a Russian amusement park, for the mere purpose of being together."[23]

Mourning this "sad breakdown of human association in urban America" sparked in Kennan a strange, disturbing response. He would "welcome almost any social cataclysm—a flood, a hurricane, or a war—however painful and however costly," that would stifle "this stuffy individualism" and compel Americans "to seek their happiness and their salvation in their relationship to society as a whole." Indeed, he was looking forward to such a healing disaster, much as his favorite Russian writer, Anton Chekhov, had in the 1890s anticipated "that cruel and mighty storm which will blow all the laziness, the indifference . . . and the rotten boredom out of society."[24]

Less than a decade later, Kennan would exaggerate the challenge of the Soviet Union into a "cataclysm" that impelled Americans to cooperate in a vigorous program of containment. His 1946 long telegram admonished Americans that every effort to "improve [the] self-confidence, discipline, morale, and community spirit of our own people is a diplomatic victory over Moscow worth a thousand diplomatic notes."[25] Similarly, he concluded his 1947 "X" article with gratitude that the "implacable challenge" of the Kremlin had made Americans' "entire security as a nation dependent on their pulling themselves together."[26] With doleful consequence, then, Kennan in 1946–1947 would see in foreign threats a welcome stimulus for mobilizing Americans to tackle domestic reforms long on his agenda.

While claiming that his years abroad had attuned him to American phenomena, Kennan remained tone-deaf to the reforms of President Roosevelt. Though he admired his "friends among the young New-Dealers" for their sincerity, he dismissed their efforts as futile because of the political "compromises necessary to achieve them."[27] Nor did he sympathize with those further on the left. He judged John Steinbeck's populist novel The Grapes of Wrath "damned good literature and damned poor sociology."[28] He found more congenial "friends among the younger business group" in Milwaukee, a group including Eugene

Hotchkiss, a stockbroker and the husband of George's sister Jeanette. His Uncle Alfred Farragut, now the James family patriarch, despised Roosevelt as a spendthrift. In explaining to fellow New Deal skeptics the underlying reason for "the unpleasant phenomena . . . of Roosevelt, [Wisconsin governor Philip] La Follette and the CIO [Congress of Industrial Organizations]," Kennan likely expounded on his favorite thesis: industrial capitalism not only led to overproduction and depression but also degraded human beings and nature.[29]

Unsympathetic with the liberal and working-class influences reforming America in the 1930s, Kennan urged instead the radical change he sketched in "The Prerequisites." During the months when Kennan was writing this book fragment, Messersmith, now assistant secretary of state, was warning Roosevelt and Secretary of State Cordell Hull that the European dictators presented threats with their ideology as well as their military might. Kennan, by contrast, disparaged both "the fetish of democracy and the specter of dictatorship." This supposed polarity represented not clashing values and ideologies, but rather two "vague cliché[s]" that people had seized upon "for emotional reasons." He disparaged Roosevelt's New Deal as the "degeneration of American political life." Meanwhile, "hasty and uncontrolled industrialization," aggravated by extreme individualism, had spawned problems beyond the reach of any such reform.[30] He saw the federal government as "bound to flounder hopelessly . . . and to break down completely." Eventually, "in the throes of suffering and perhaps of bloodshed," there would emerge "a new national government."[31] Kennan welcomed a revolution to restore effective governance, raise living standards, and rope individuals into a "common program" so that "their efforts are not purely individualistic and selfish."

Who might spearhead such a movement? Kennan asserted that minorities ran all governments, including democracies. While the Republicans trusted in business elites, Roosevelt's party, the Democrats, "have no clear idea." That left power in the hands of party bosses and of "bewildered" voters incapable of choosing wisely. He ridiculed the claim by Marxists and union leaders that workers should run affairs.

He vouched instead for a coterie of talented young men, whose "fitness must be determined by character, education and inclination." This elite "must be selected, organized and trained." That Kennan in these last quotations had to resort to the passive voice underscored that he had no idea who or what could actually choose and train these rulers. Nevertheless, his description of this meritocratic elite as disciplined, devoted, and displaying decency and responsibility underscored both the high bar he set and the assumption that he could meet it. Like the guardians of Plato's Republic, these "untrammeled young people" would "abandon the philistine attractions of private life" and "the prospect of making money" while subjecting "themselves to discipline as . . . if they entered a religious order." Such single-minded self-sacrifice appealed to him, as did the prospect of true comradeship.[32] Again and again, Kennan would champion collective values, group welfare, and coercion over the individualism and free choice that characterized American ideology.

Although the twenty-page "The Prerequisites" did not get far in outlining a new government, the manuscript did argue, to Kennan's embarrassment decades later, for taking away the right to vote of naturalized citizens, nonprofessional women, and "the negroes." (This would disqualify his wife, Annelise, on two grounds.) He advanced the specious argument that "bewildered, semi-digested new arrivals," suffering exploitation by political bosses, would "be happier as passive citizens of a government they can respect."

With regard to gender, "this country is already a matriarchy," Kennan groused. Women supposedly dominated the family and the nation's purse. They shaped the culture by purchasing the popular media that he despised. "They have their lobbies in Washington, and the politicians tremble at their approach." According to this misogynistic screed, domineering women were harming themselves as well as the nation. His caricature of the American woman recalled his detested stepmother, Louise Wheeler Kennan, who had devoted herself to women's clubs. Annelise also pursued a social life with women's groups. The "club-life" of women—a longtime target of Kennan's ire—symbolized the "futility and inanity" of do-goodism outside the home. He fumed that American women, evidently through some sociological-physiological-psychological devolution, had "become, in comparison with the women of other countries, delicate, high-strung, unsatisfied, flat-chested and flat-voiced." George, whose life was wrenched by sexual fantasies, flirtations, and flings, regarded such "ruin" as a betrayal. Women, to safeguard their health and their attractiveness, should limit themselves to nonpolitical "family picnics, children's parties, and the church social."

The amateur social theorist also assailed people of color. He claimed that "urgent measures are required to stop the economic decline and the physical and nervous disintegration" of "negroes." Here his specious argument was that forbidding African Americans to vote would spur whites' sense of responsibility for their wards. "The Prerequisites" petered out with a call for disbanding Congress, which suffered terminal dysfunction and partisanship. The Founders, he claimed, would also deplore how their constitutional republic had degenerated "into a boss-ridden democracy."[33]

Xenophobic, misogynistic, and racist—not to mention naively unrealistic and nearly fascist—Kennan's vision reflected his exposure not only to German and Eastern European hatreds but also to solidly American prejudices. With the spigot on immigration from Southern and Eastern Europe shut only fourteen years previously, the United States was struggling to integrate millions of newcomers. In the 1920s, the anti-immigrant Ku Klux Klan had spread throughout northern states. And with the looming threat of the Axis, Kennan was not the only American worried about the loyalties of German Americans and Italian Americans. His misogyny was more sui generis, reflecting painful experiences in his childhood, his subsequent sexual proclivities, and prevailing American attitudes about women and the home. White racism was as American as apple pie.

Kennan's bleak appraisal of the U.S. government had greater justification. His months in Washington coincided with the third sharpest economic recession in U.S. history and the political nadir of Roosevelt's presidency. From the fall of 1937 to the summer of 1938, real gross domestic product shriveled by 11 percent, industrial production plummeted

32 percent, and unemployment jumped from 14 to 19 percent.[34] FDR's New Deal had no new rabbits to pull from the hat. These months witnessed also the failure of the president's attempted "purge" of conservative Southern Democrats in primary elections. With Roosevelt apparently a helpless lame duck, far more sanguine observers shared Kennan's worry that Washington might "flounder hopelessly."[35] In actuality, however, Roosevelt, remained his ebullient self.

What Kennan found appalling about America, FDR found appealing. Roosevelt sought to combat such negativism as Kennan's. About the time when the diplomat was penning "The Prerequisites," FDR, referring to the Foreign Service, warned Messersmith that "too many of the men did not know enough about their own country." He proposed rotating diplomats so that they would regularly "spend a year . . . in various parts of the country learning something about our people and our problems."[36] Roosevelt assumed that such contact would rekindle even an expatriate's love of country. While Kennan did long for nurturing connections, it was not with the commercialized and industrialized powerhouse of his day, but rather with the imagined America of his grandfather's time or the imagined idyll of pre-1917 Russia.

As someone whose ambition extended to transforming the U.S. government, Kennan was easily frustrated by ordinary life. Moreover, just as he remembered his years at Princeton as more humiliating than they probably were, so too would he later recall his time on the Russian desk as more humiliating than the archival evidence indicates. Decades afterward, he still fumed that Hull and Moffat had consulted with him, "the 'expert' on the Russian desk" only four times. His quotation marks around "expert" underscored how unappreciated he felt. Loy Henderson, however, remembered Kennan as playing a "fairly important" role at the Russian desk. The rising star remained a favorite of Messersmith, whose influence reached into the White House and the State Department.[37]

Kennan's greatest impact was in pushing Messersmith, Hull, and, eventually, Roosevelt into realizing that the anger of U.S. diplomats in Moscow could doom efforts to enlist Russia against the Axis. In debating how to approach Russia, the Roosevelt administration focused on a central question: What purpose did the embassy in Moscow serve? Was that outpost primarily the seat of FDR's representative charged with seeking an understanding with Stalin, or was it a research bureau staffed by such scholar-diplomats as Kennan? Bullitt—now ambassador to France, still influential with Roosevelt, and lastingly bitter about his failed mission to Moscow—asserted that the Soviets' isolation of diplomats and intransigence on war debts made it really not worthwhile to maintain any embassy. Roosevelt disagreed. Foreshadowing his strategy in World War II, the president, supported by Davies and Messersmith, wanted to foster Russian resistance to German and Japanese aggression.

But how could the Roosevelt administration pursue such contact? Soviet foreign ministry officials were so terrorized by the purges that they shrank from even talking with foreigners. Also crippled by xenophobia was the capacity of U.S. diplomats to gather information. Although Kennan hated the restrictions on contact, he and other acolytes of Kelley had grown adept at viewing Russia through a peephole, as they had done from Riga before 1933. The Kelley-ites possessed the language skills and the perseverance to page through obscure reports and newspapers to piece together significant evidence.

As Roosevelt, Davies, and Messersmith saw it, however, such monastic production remained irrelevant to geostrategy. Plus it was expensive. Pressed by congressional penny-pinching amid the 1937–1938 recession, the State Department and Roosevelt concluded that embassies were overstaffed. An obvious target for cutting was Moscow, where the secret police hobbled reporting and the Kremlin's manipulation of the ruble drove up costs.

Assistant Secretary of State Messersmith, who managed the department's finances, proposed slashing Moscow's budget in half. To Henderson, in command at Moscow while Ambassador Davies sailed his yacht, he pressed the "brutal" fact that the large staff was "indefensible" because, "through no fault of your own," the embassy was "ineffectual."[38] Messersmith insisted that much of the in-depth reporting and translation, the activities that Kennan had enjoyed pursuing, could be discontinued. Once back in Moscow, Davies sided against his underlings by affirming that "a great deal of unnecessary work is being done, and that the staff can be materially reduced."[39]

Here, then, lay further reason for Kennan's unhappiness in Washington. His conception of the Moscow embassy and relations with Russia conflicted with those of Roosevelt and top State Department officials. The Moscow outpost had nurtured him over four formative years. He remained emotionally attached to the community there and to the scholarly approach that he had learned from Kelley and found personally rewarding. Kennan, still fuming at Davies, argued that if cuts were needed, why not eliminate the ambassador? Davies was transferring from Moscow to Brussels. (Part of the impetus for moving on was that he and his go-go wife had purchased all the icons they desired; they hated Russia's climate; and they preferred warmer waters for the yacht.) Kennan urged holding off on replacing the ambassador until Stalin's government ended its noxious behavior. As Kennan saw it, while an ambassador in Moscow had little to negotiate, embassy staff there did crucial investigative work. Indeed, what the Kremlin preferred was an ambassador whose presence "would contribute to Soviet prestige," but who, "deprived of adequate assistance," would remain deaf and blind to developments. Not replacing the ambassador would inflict "a loss which would be definitely felt in Soviet circles."[40] Kennan's argument for lowering the profile of the American mission foreshadowed his advocacy of containment a decade later. In retaliation for the Soviets' isolating foreign diplomats, Washington should isolate Moscow. Missing in Kennan's "vehement remonstrations" against a new ambassador was any consideration that having a U.S. representative in Moscow might encourage Russia to stand up to Nazi Germany and imperial Japan.

That geostrategic perspective was absent also in a private rant. Kennan fumed at rumors that the president would replace Davies with "a liberal newspaper editor," "an elderly liberal philanthropist," "an ambitious businessman," or, the putative front runner, the former "wife of a congressman." The phraseology underscored Kennan's conviction that Roosevelt had a weakness for liberals, women, and generalists— and that such associated types had common faults. According to the president's own files, however, no woman was actually under consideration.[41]

Nevertheless, as someone who held Eleanor Roosevelt and her liberal friends responsible for purging his beloved Eastern European Division, Kennan feared further meddling. None of the supposed candidates met his criteria for an ambassador: "modesty, patience, experience with . . . foreign service work, and a good disillusioned understanding of Russia"—qualities that just happened to match Kennan's view of himself. He groused that an inexperienced new ambassador would burden the "long-suffering, hard-working" career officials. Yet again, they would have to play "nurse-maid" and "high-paid flunkey" for the neophyte. All this so that some political creditor of the administration could bask in the glamour of an ambassadorship.[42]

Messersmith, backed by Hull and Roosevelt, viewed all this differently. He insisted that "Russia is too great a country and is going to play too great a part in the world for us to cut ourselves off from that people regardless of the difficulties." Despite the purge of the Red Army, Russia remained "stronger than some have believed." Indeed, Russia seemed "prepared to take action in Europe" if Germany attacked Czechoslovakia.[43]

If Kennan was to continue his rocket-ascent and keep Messersmith as his patron, he could not openly disagree on such strategic issues. Not for the last time, he kept to himself the differences with his superiors. Unlike them, however, he could not overlook the horrors and the slights he had encountered in Moscow. Nor did he share the hatred and fear of Nazi Germany that impelled the Roosevelt administration. He neither wrote about a possible strategic alignment with Moscow nor had a voice on such a key matter. But on the pregnant issue of whether to trim the work of the Moscow embassy, Kennan did have some authority. That made it more humiliating when he had to recant core beliefs.

Responding to Messersmith's query, J. J. Murphy, a State Department official not engaged in Russian affairs, disparaged the mission's scholarly approach as self-indulgent, "excessive documentation and research." He ridiculed a forty-two-page report that "could have been covered in one brief despatch." Murphy also belittled the value of Kennan's speciality, detailed translation of Soviet documents.[44] Messersmith passed the critique to the Russian desk. On May 4, 1938, Kennan, citing Huddle's positive inspection report of the Moscow embassy in early 1937, insisted that the "room for improvement . . . is not great." George proposed only minor changes.[45] He then suffered through an evidently harrowing meeting. The very next day, a chastened Kennan re-submitted drastically different recommendations that emphasized "restriction of bulk, avoidance of long translations."[46]

The proud Russia hand had been forced to recant. The Roosevelt administration's purge of Kelley, the Eastern European Division, and the scholarly approach was far milder than the horrors in Moscow. As Kennan acknowledged, in Washington no heads rolled. But the ambitious thirty-four-year-old had to renounce an approach that he valued intellectually, found emotionally satisfying, and, decades later, would return to in his prize-winning diplomatic histories.

Kennan's greatest impact in 1937–1938 was in getting higher-ups to understand that the contact issue was serious. How the Kremlin treated Americans influenced what they felt and reported from Moscow. With Secretary Hull slated to meet Soviet ambassador Alexander A. Troyanovsky, Kennan stressed the toll of forced isolation. One cost was mental problems. The anti-foreign campaign operated in such an "insulting and humiliating" way that it imposed "constant strain—of a nature difficult to describe—on the self-respect and peace of mind of our people."[47] Hull, bolstered by a further memorandum from Kennan the day of the meeting, talked frankly with Troyanovsky. Since arriving in 1934, the Russian emissary had befriended Americans and had sent his son to Swarthmore College.

Hull recalled that in 1933 Washington had set up the Moscow embassy intending to join with Russia, Britain, and France in "developing their combined moral influence for peace." If these nations had stuck with that goal, he claimed, the aggression in "both the Far East and in Europe would have been reduced at least 50%." To be sure, the Russians' "uninviting hospitality" toward U.S. diplomats seemed like only "small pinpricks" when measured against the global crisis. Nevertheless, these offenses "are seriously handicapping supremely important efforts."

When Troyanovsky denied the truth of these "small objections," Hull stressed the salience of emotional perceptions: "They might just as well be true because our people feel that way and feel the atmosphere which they believe they create." In a follow-up with Moffat, Troyanovsky again tried to pooh-pooh these "small administrative difficulties . . . preoccupying the members of the American embassy." Moffat reiterated Hull's insight that mood and feelings shaped perceived reality. While the Russians might dismiss these "trivialities . . . their cumulative effect was creating an exceedingly difficult atmosphere." In the context of the Americans stressing emotional atmosphere, Troyanovsky dared bring up his own plight. Twice he referred, plaintively, to "the state of tension in Moscow"—a euphemism for the bloody purges decimating thousands, including his colleagues in the foreign ministry. (Six months later in Moscow, Troyanovsky, who had disappeared into a "sanitarium" after pulling his son out of Swarthmore and returning to Russia, attended a dinner at the embassy. The diplomat Alexander Kirk observed that "something had happened to him. He was thinner, very much preoccupied and apparently under some physical disability." An American doctor at the dinner diagnosed "a form of hysteria based on shock.")[48]

By December 1939, with relations soured by Russia's attack on Finland, Roosevelt himself broached the contact issue. The president angrily condemned the "downright rudeness" of Soviet officials, from customs agents on up to Stalin. FDR decided to "match every Soviet annoyance by a similar annoyance here against them." He threatened the ambassador that Moscow's "complete disregard for the ordinary politeness and amenities between civilized governments" raised the issue of whether it wanted "to continue diplomatic relations" with Washington.[49]

Though both Americans and Russians grasped that emotions were integral to thought and behavior, they differed in their cultural expectations and expressions. Americans generally placed a higher value on the right of individuals to associate freely. To Russians such as Troyanovsky, it must have seemed trivial indeed for Americans to complain about isolation from Russians, when Russians had to fear a bullet in the back of the neck for doing their job.

Messersmith, trying to align Russia and America against the Axis threat, fretted that "the two governments cannot really talk with each other." The Soviet foreign ministry itself seemed isolated from the Kremlin. How to vault the "stone wall" between power brokers in Washington and Moscow? One possibility was easing the isolation and hence resentment of U.S. representatives. Another was sending a special envoy from Roosevelt to Stalin. This tactic seemed crafted with Kennan in mind, and indeed he may have planted the idea with Messersmith. In 1948, Kennan would nominate himself for a similar mission to Stalin. In January 1938, Messersmith proposed to Hull that "someone should go for us to Russia, quietly and unostentatiously, who would under very specific instructions from the President and the Secretary get in touch with Stalin." They needed to send a diplomat who spoke Russian for such talks to work.[50] With Bohlen at the embassy in Moscow, Kennan remained the sole Foreign Service officer totally fluent in Russian and available for instructions directly from Roosevelt and Hull. Back in 1931 in Berlin, Messersmith had trusted Kennan with a delicate, secret job because he respected his intelligence and facility in German. This time, however, Hull or Roosevelt judged the mission too risky; in any case nothing came of it.

The third option for contact with Soviet power brokers did come to pass, and that was initiated by Stalin himself. On June 5, 1938, as Davies was making his goodbyes to Molotov and other Soviet leaders, Stalin walked into the room. This was the ambassador's first meeting with the dictator. Stalin, claiming that he wanted to improve relations with the United States, asked why the U.S. Navy was holding up Russia's purchase of a new warship for the Soviet fleet. He offered to settle the vexatious Kerensky-era debt issue if the United States would extend a new credit for Russian purchases in America. While these proposals excited Davies, they eventually faltered. With the shocking purges of Nicolai Bukharin and of many Red Army and Navy officers splashed across the headlines, Roosevelt remained unwilling to push for the Russian warship or loan.[51]

Two weeks before the surprise Davies-Stalin meeting, Kennan lectured to Foreign Service recruits. His ideas reflected long-term influences. As a protégé of Kelley, he saw the Soviet Union through the prism of pre-1917 Russian history and literature. He had absorbed from

Freud the notion that "nations, like individuals, are largely the products of their environment," and "their fears and neuroses . . . are conditioned by . . . their early childhood." Twice he quoted the epigram of a former minister to Russia: "No nation has more need of foreigners, and none is so jealous of them." His explanation of Russia mirrored what he had learned in college about climate and geography and in Berlin about Asia. He attributed Russian patience to the long winters, "spurts of intense activity . . . in 'Five-Year-Plans'" to the short summers, and inclination toward extremes to the "vast plains." Expanding on orientalist notions picked up in Germany, Latvia, and America, Kennan argued that from "oriental Byzantium" Russia had inherited "its intriguing and despotic political system, its dark cruelty . . . and its utter lack of the chivalrous spirit which characterized medieval Christianity in the West." Further baleful influence stemmed from the Mongols. From these barbarians the Russians had learned "to think of the foreigner as an enemy rather than a friend." Juxtaposed against a sense of inferiority toward the more advanced West was the Russians' "strange superstition that they are destined to conquer the world." It was these feelings of inadequacy— and not Japanese and German designs—that fed Russia's "hysterical suspicion of other nations" and fear of foreign invasion.[52]

Here, then, lay the germ of the historical/psychological interpretation of Russia's supposedly neurotic foreign policy that would become Kennan's core thesis during his rise to prominence in 1946–1947. He used the supposed science of Freudianism to diagnose the "very definite personality" of the Soviet Union. He had mastered Russian history and literature. He could reference seemingly irrefutable facts of climate and geography as well as prevailing notions of "Asiatic" behavior.

In 1938, when Eastern Europe seemed remote to U.S. interests, he found it "almost impossible to conceive of our being Russia's enemy." Nor did he expect the Soviets to become America's friend. Significant trade also seemed unlikely. For Kennan, the exciting promise lay with personal and cultural ties.

One wonders how fledgling Foreign Service officers reacted as Kennan listed the traits that supposedly united Americans and Russians: "the same sense of humor, the same openness of character, the same generosity of thought, the same disrespect for . . . the narrowness and formalities of Western European thought." There seemed "no limit to the extent to which the youth of the two countries could mingle." While Americans could teach Russians about industrial efficiency, practical training, and individual rights, Russians could show Americans how to feel. "We need their imagination" and to learn from "the spontaneous, unrestrained fashion in which the Russian expresses his emotions." Such mixing meant so much to Kennan. Cruelly thwarting it was the Kremlin's "Asiatic" "fear of foreign influence on the popular mind."[53] Therein lay the wellspring of his personal sorrow—and his political resentment of the Kremlin.

PRAGUE

For Kennan as well as for the United States, relations with Russia were complicated by Germany. By immersing himself in Russia's language and history while in Berlin, the young Foreign Service officer had also steeped himself in Germany's perspective on its eastern frontier. His familiarity with both Russia and Germany made him a natural for posting to Prague in September 1938. Hitler was demanding that Czechoslovakia cede its German-speaking Sudeten border territory. With Stalin's secret police making it difficult to report from Moscow, the State Department valued the Czech capital as another Riga, as a window onto Soviet Russia. As Moffat explained, the "Czechs' judgment of Russian developments" was revealing, for "they are Slavs, close neighbors, and it is a matter of life and death to them."[54]

George was anxious to go abroad, for, as Moffat acknowledged, "Kennan unfortunately cannot stand the financial strain of being in Washington."[55] The previous Christmas, George and Annelise had splurged their "last farthings on a grand big tree and things for the kids' stockings, a vase of flowers . . . charged a turkey and a plum pudding at the corner grocer's, and had a real celebration."[56] Moreover, despite his heading the Russian desk, the ambitious diplomat chafed at the limits of his influence. He felt ignored by Hull and Moffat and unmoved by Messersmith's fervor for an anti-Nazi coalition. Henderson, slated to

FIGURE 21. Kennan aboard the S.S. *Washington* en route to
Europe amid the crisis of September 1938. (Courtesy
of Getty Images.)

rotate back into the department, believed that Kennan preferred leaving the Russian desk rather than sharing authority with him. Perhaps
another factor was nostalgia for Europe's nonchalance regarding extramarital affairs. After attending a diplomatic reception in Washington,
Kennan penned a cryptic diary entry in Russian: "In Europe, it is possible; here it is difficult."[57] In July, he asked Ambassador Bullitt for a
position in the Paris embassy. "I should love to have you personally,"
the latter replied, but there were so many senior officers in Paris that
you would be stuck "in a cubbyhole preparing data on motion picture
quotas. You are much too useful to the U.S. Government to be wasted
on that sort of work."[58]

The ship bearing the Kennans steamed into the storm of the century, the deadly 1938 hurricane barreling up the coast toward New England. Then, with Europe teetering on war, the voyage was aborted and the passengers dumped in England. As Kennan later recalled, "There was a frenzied interval while the family threw things into trunks and suitcases."[59] They managed to get to Paris. From there, "at 6 A.M. on September 29, the day of the Munich conference," he left the sleeping family and snared a seat on the last flight to Prague.[60] Annelise and the girls would not follow until November.

Although political crisis overhung Prague, Kennan's mood lifted immediately. "I am quite happy and feel much more in my element than I did in Washington," he reported. "The work—after all the headaches of Moscow and the Department's Russian desk—seems like child's play." Prague offered a "very full" life, with "Czech lessons, official calls, tennis lessons, and riding lessons twice a week." On Sundays he walked "cross-country, all decked out in my Abercrombie & Fitch outfit, which made the natives' eyes stick out." He had a "really interesting . . . visit at the country estate of some Czech fascist acquaintances."[61]

Those fascists welcomed the news of Hitler's triumph at the Munich conference, blaring on loudspeakers as Kennan landed in Prague. Britain and France accepted Hitler's demand for the mountainous, German-populated Sudeten areas, critical to Czech defenses. Walking around the city that night, "there was real sorrow and bitterness in the faces of the passers-by, and it was no night to be heard talking French or English in the streets."[62] The plight of the Czechs soon worsened. Kennan witnessed the grim scene on March 15, 1939, when German troops, barreling through a blinding snowstorm, occupied the rest of the rump nation. He remained in Prague to report on political and economic conditions until war broke out in September 1939.

The State Department then transferred Kennan to Berlin, where he served as number two in the overworked mission until Germany declared war on the United States on December 11, 1941. Finally, Kennan, along with 130 American diplomats and journalists, were interned by the Germans at Bad Neuheim until May 1942. For three and a half years, then, Kennan saw the seemingly unbeatable Nazi machine close up.

This experience followed his education studying Russian in Berlin and, as an eight-year-old, German in Cassel. George had grown up in Milwaukee, that most German of American cities. Wanting to expose his children to European culture, George's father, Kent Kennan, had chosen to bring them to Germany.

Though familiar with Germany, Kennan never loved it as he did Russia. He later reflected that Germany "was a country with which I was never able to identify extensively in a personal sense." While he knew the language intimately, he felt that he "was never in character when speaking it." The observation of a Russian friend stuck in his mind: "'When you speak Russian, you are yourself; when you speak German, you are nothing at all.'" Nevertheless, "intellectually and aesthetically, Germany had made a deep impression on me."[63] He loved pre–World War II Hamburg, delighting in "its multi-sonic buzzing song. I simply avow myself to this city as to a goddess and am exuberant that the city exists."[64] Such exuberance was rare.

Respecting German order and efficiency, Kennan at first hoped that Hitler's conquests would produce greater stability. He had never liked the "unsatisfactory status quo" set up by the Versailles treaty in 1919 and in particular he "deplored the breakup of the Austro-Hungarian Empire."[65] Though appalled at Nazi brutality, Kennan saw promise in Berlin's domination of Czechoslovakia. Germany might unify Central Europe and, ironically, Czech society. His essay "The Prerequisites," penned only few months earlier, had disparaged the divided politics and shallow culture of the United States. Now in Prague he criticized "the many squabbling political parties, petty bourgeois timidity, and the shallow materialism" of Czechoslovakia.[66] The catastrophe that he had wished for in the United States was now squeezing this Central European nation. In both cases, disaster had a potential upside. The crisis could quash excessive "individualism and sectionalism" while bolstering "unity and discipline" among the people and greater "personal responsibility" and "spiritual authority" among their leaders.[67] This perspective led to his initial belief that Czechoslovakia had to "adjust" to the "dominant force" of Germany.

Kennan was disappointed, however, as he witnessed clumsy bullying by the Germans undermine their potential as consolidators. Only if the victorious Reich developed "greater spiritual power and greater political maturity" could it perform the organizational role fulfilled in past centuries by the Catholic Church and the Hapsburg Empire.[68] This naive, almost sunny view of German rule darkened as he witnessed the reality of Nazi brutality.

As general war approached, Kennan psychologized the crisis in terms of out-of-control feelings. Those backing the Nazis seemed "emotional rather than reasonable." A "vengeful, emotional, and unrealistic spirit" also distorted French foreign policy. Not only Hitler but the very unification of Germany had sparked "the jealousy, the uncertainty, the feeling of inferiority, the consequent lust to dominate Europe" that were now inciting war. He saw Europe as a whole "seething with fear and hatred and excitement."[69]

Decades later, Kennan would face sharp criticism for not "seething with fear and hatred" as he reported from Prague on the persecution of the Jews. To be sure, he neither witnessed nor knew about Hitler's extermination campaign, which accelerated with the invasion of Russia in June 1941 and the "final solution" adopted that December. What Kennan did observe, and describe in a cold, analytical tone, was the relentless pressure inflicted on Jews in Czechoslovakia. This anti-Semitism, though spurred by the Germans, was also supported by much of the population, especially in Slovakia. It is important to remember the context for Kennan's prejudice: the prevailing anti-Semitism in the United States during his childhood, and the more virulent hatred of Jews in the Baltic nations and Germany where he had spent his early adulthood. Though deplorable, Kennan's prejudice did not prevent him from aiding and befriending individual Jews.

Nevertheless, in Kennan's view, "Jews" constituted a distinct racial group, and "the Jewish problem" demanded attention. Though he criticized the cruelty and violence of the Nazis and their supporters, he believed they were addressing a serious concern. In rural Slovakia, he reported, Jews exercised a dominant economic role as merchants, saloon keepers, druggists, doctors, and lawyers. They had achieved this status "partly through their superior intelligence" and "partly—the Slovaks feel—through their trickiness and unscrupulousness, through . . . their evasion of any and all inconvenient restrictions, and through an incurable clannishness and nepotism."[70]

Without detailed instructions from the State Department, Kennan could choose what topics to analyze. In February 1939, he sent the State Department a lengthy study of "The Jewish Problem in the New Czechoslovakia." He accepted without question the racist categories of "full-blooded Jews," "Aryans," and "non-Aryans," and their relevance to "the Jewish question." He explained that in Czech-populated Bohemia, the government had bowed to German pressure by barring Jews from governmental service. The harm was not serious, he claimed, because it "applied only in the case of full-blooded Jews," affected only one thousand civil servants, and those dismissed would receive a small pension. While Jewish physicians faced ejection from public clinics, "most of these doctors have private practices as well." Failing to empathize with innocent victims under assault, Kennan concluded that "very little has happened in Prague thus far to justify the panicky atmosphere . . . in Jewish circles."[71] Kennan acknowledged that Jews fared worse in Slovakia, especially in the villages. He reported without comment his talk with president Dr. Jozef Tiso, a priest. Backed by the Roman Catholic Church, Tiso intended to repress Jews more harshly. Kennan did commiserate with the "real suffering" of two hundred Jews stuck homeless and stateless on a spit of land between Slovakia and Hungary. With regard to Ruthenia, the poorest, most rural part of rump Czechoslovakia, he referred to governmental claims that while Jews made up only 12 percent of the population, they were "officially stated to control 95 percent of the economic life."[72] Kennan's reporting came close to endorsing the anti-Semitic arguments percolating through Central Europe.

After German troops occupied the Czech capital on March 15, 1939, the danger to Jews and other victims intensified. In notes on the crisis that were personal—that is, not meant for the State Department—Kennan clinically described the "disheveled men, ashy pale with fear," and two other German fugitives "almost dazed with terror" who begged for asylum at the U.S. legation office. Kennan told them he could do nothing for them. "Their faces were twitching and their lips trembling when I sent them away." He was carrying out official U.S. policy: weeks later, the *St, Louis*, a ship filled with Jewish refugees from Germany, was denied asylum in the United States by President Roosevelt. Many of those who returned to Europe would perish in the Holocaust.

The calamity reached into Kennan's home but not, apparently, deep into his heart. In the same flat, cool tone, he described how "a Jewish acquaintance who had worked many years for American interests" had come to the house. "I told him that I could not give him asylum, but that as long as he was not demanded by the authorities he was welcome to stay." For a day and a night, "he haunted the house, a pitiful figure of horror and despair . . . smoking one cigarette after another, too unstrung to eat or think of anything but his plight." When he said he might commit suicide, George and Annelise pleaded with him not to do so, "partly on general Anglo-Saxon principles and partly to preserve our home from this sort of unpleasantness."[73] Annelise explained to Jeanette that "the Jews are panic-stricken. Our Consulate is swarmed with them. We have heard about many suicides already. I feel sorry for them, but not half as sorry as for the Czechs."[74]

Even more egregious was George's extending such anti-Semitism to the United States. In July 1943, after a visit home, Kennan would claim that the most "dangerous prejudice" lay in ignoring the "Jewish problem in our country." He claimed expertise because "I have seen a great deal of this question in central and eastern Europe." He dismissed tolerance as the "smugness which laughs off twenty centuries of experience of other peoples in their relations with the Jews." Since 1939, he had shifted from a biological to a cultural and psychological explanation. He now believed that through the "stubborn transmission from father to son" of aggressive behaviors—which amounted to "a mass neurosis"—the Jews had rendered themselves "an indigestible element for Western countries." A telltale sign that a situation affected George deeply was that he described it with words that resonated with him throughout his life. Two such habitual expressions were "bewildered" and "penetration." He employed both to assert: "Wherever society finds itself bewildered with Jewish penetration, resentful of Jewish methods of competition and incapable of coping with Jewish pressure . . . feelings are aroused which are primitive and exceedingly unlovely." The only way to head off the "degrading ugliness" of pogroms or Nazi-like persecution was for the U.S. government to limit the extent of "Jewish penetration" in the professions, business, and the arts.[75] Until the very end of the war, Kennan remained unaware of the full horror of the Holocaust. Nevertheless, he did witness how the German occupation of Czechoslovakia intensified the persecution of the Jews. He reacted to this suffering with anti-Semitic prejudice.

———

As the war that would permanently entangle America in European affairs loomed in 1937–1939, George F. Kennan seemed ill suited to become, as he would a decade later, the planner of that U.S. engagement. Since graduating from college, he had spent most of his time away from the United States. The anti-Semitism and other prejudices he had imbibed in Milwaukee and at Princeton had condensed in the cauldron of Eastern and Central Europe. His preoccupation with Stalin's purges and with the painful isolation of foreign diplomats in Moscow seemed provincial and almost irrelevant to Roosevelt, Messersmith, and others hoping to deploy Soviet Russia as a buttress against German and Japanese aggression. The eleven months that George spent working in Washington and bicycling through Wisconsin had yielded neither sympathy nor understanding for the domestic reforms sweeping America. Hoping to make both sense of his experiences and some money, George had written an autobiographical fragment that revealed his inner thoughts, but failed to snag a publisher. He also crafted "The Prerequisites," a tract so racist, misogynistic, and antidemocratic that, in later decades, he would disavow it as an immature rambling.

Nevertheless, Kennan in 1937–1939 also honed his expertise in foreign affairs, his experience in diplomacy, and his skill in bureaucratic infighting. He continued to advance within the State Department and he remained the protégé of powerful benefactors. It would take the upheaval of a global war and its glaring juxtaposition of Nazi ineptitude with U.S. ingenuity to re-Americanize Kennan. He would never, however, totally outgrow his prejudices and his impatience with democracy.

He would also continue believing that America suffered from excessive individualism, commercialization, and reliance on machines. He would persist in looking for some means to promote collective over individual priorities. In 1946–1947, this search for a usable crisis, even a catastrophe, that could mobilize America's too diffuse energies would become one of his motivations for depicting the Soviet Union as an existential threat.

CHAPTER 6

KENNAN AND A WORLD
AT WAR, 1939–1944

ONCE WAR ERUPTED in September 1939, the State Department assigned Kennan to the capital of the Nazi empire. Despite the shortages and the sporadic bombing, he felt "at home in Berlin."[1] This metropolis, where he had studied a decade earlier and where he would spend two and a half years witnessing the widening war, proved "formative for my own education and thinking," he reflected years later. Indeed, it was from a focus on Germany's relations with its neighbors that Kennan would view the conclusion of World War II, the course of the Cold War, and the possibilities for the post–Cold War era.

From the early 1940s onward, Kennan, though often at odds with official U.S. policy and seemingly bent on some quixotic mission, was actually tacking toward geostrategic goals he had developed in 1938–1939. He was influenced by a French thinker, Jacques Bainville, who castigated the victor powers at Versailles for not only breaking up the Austro-Hungarian empire, which had provided a home for disparate nationalities, but also for leaving Germany intact as a behemoth surrounded by weak states. Kennan saw two possible solutions to the resulting instability. First was dividing Germany into two or three states that would be integrated into a confederation extending from Western Europe to Eastern Europe west of Russia. Second was setting up a united but neutralized and largely disarmed Germany "capable of serving as the balancing fulcrum for all of central and eastern

Europe." Despite his love for Russia, it was to Germany that Kennan looked to bring order and stability to this borderland. He dismissed French and British fears of a too-powerful Germany, claiming that such apprehension, "never fully justified, ought to have no place in any new postwar settlement."[2]

These foundational ideas would underlie Kennan's policy preferences during World War II and beyond. Not only did the professional orientation of Kennan the diplomat and strategist pivot on Germany, but also the personal obligations of George the husband and father became entangled with his work there.

For much of George's stay in Germany between September 1939 and May 1942, Annelise was not with him, and for nearly all that time young Grace and Joanie were not either. Over the course of Kennan's thirty-two months in Hitler's Reich, his wife was away in Norway or in America for seventeen months, and the children for thirty-one months.[3] Most of this absence was mandated by safety considerations during an ever more frightening world war. By the summer of 1940, the British were bombing the German capital in retaliation for the air attacks on London. Wartime Berlin was no place for children, and Annelise had either to care for them herself or find someone who would do so. From the attack on Pearl Harbor and Germany's declaration of war on the United States in December 1941 to his repatriation in May 1942, George, along with some 130 other Americans, was interned by the Germans. They were held in genteel but frustrating captivity in a hotel near Frankfurt.

Not only external constraints but also internal fissures shaped the family's wartime experience. Overworked, under pressure, and away from his wife for many months, George sought comfort in the arms of other women. He had engaged in, or fantasized about, extramarital affairs almost from the start of his marriage. Meanwhile, Annelise, with no source of income after the U.S. government terminated the salary of her husband during his internment (officially, he was not working), had to somehow pay the rent and feed her two daughters. She had never worked at a job and did not take one now. Annelise also perceived the dangers to their marriage of leaving George alone in Berlin.

FIGURE 22. George taking a break from his duties at the U.S. embassy in Berlin in 1940 or 1941. (Courtesy of Princeton University Library.)

Though frenetic, Kennan's life in Berlin did have benefits. He rented a house eight miles from the center near the Grunewald Forest, which most days enabled "a good walk or an hour on horseback before breakfast." On Sundays, he sailed his boat on a nearby lake, perhaps the Wannsee. He liked his duties. And he expected that he would be rewarded with a rise in rank and salary. In happy contrast to Washington where money was tight, in Prague and Berlin he managed to save $2,000. George asked Jeanette to look for "a farm suitable for the retirement of a diplomatist," perhaps his grandfather's old place in Packwaukee.[4]

Moved by the misery of German acquaintances and friends displaced by the war, he tried to make their house a temporary refuge "where there is real food and a normal atmosphere and where you can trust your host and his servants not to repeat what you say."[5] Although Annelise would soon condemn the Germans for invading Norway in April 1940, she at first admired their pluck: "If the British think they can wear these people out easily, they are wrong. They can take it on the chin every day and I swear they can go on for a good long time."[6]

In the furnace of wartime Berlin, Kennan bonded with two idiosyncratic mentors, the American diplomat Alexander C. Kirk and the German count Helmuth von Moltke. Kirk, whose father had built up America's biggest soap manufacturing company, flamboyantly displayed his wealth, eccentricity, and sexual orientation. Living alone with his mother in a huge Berlin mansion staffed with Italian servants, Kirk filled his "inner emptiness" with work. Here was another older mentor with a fluid sexual identity, like Bullitt or the teacher at St. John's, who admired tall, slender, blue-eyed George. (Even Henderson would remark on how very handsome Kennan was.) Decades later, Kennan, still fond of his former boss, detailed how Kirk, "as a gesture of defiance and self-protection, and in the indulgence of a fine sense of the theatrical," had played, indeed camped, the stereotypical diplomat: "elegant, overrefined, haughty, and remote." On some level Kennan probably also admired Kirk for his ability to negotiate, or at least blur, the conflicting demands of Eros and Civilization.

Kennan reflected that he had "learned much from Kirk—more, perhaps, than from any other chief." The teaching extended to "personal, and even political philosophy"—and, significantly, to a reliance on intuition.[7] After World War II, Kennan ranked as a seer or prophet about Soviet Russia because so many accepted without questioning his intuition—that is, his educated hunches. Kirk encouraged such out-of-the box thinking, and displayed, despite his foppish pose, "great intuitive shrewdness." The younger man admired Kirk for demonstrating the greater "importance of the means as compared with the ends. The only thing worth living for, he once told me, was good form." The priority of the means and of good form fit Kennan's conservative bent. As for the

Nazis, then astride much of Europe, Kirk foresaw: "They have undertaken something they cannot finish. They will find no stopping point. That is the cardinal sin: to start something you cannot finish."[8] Loyalty to Kirk and obligation to the embassy trumped other priorities. Although George had not seen his daughters, parked with Jeanette, for months, he chose not to accompany Annelise on a visit to the States. "I simply cannot leave my chief here at this time."[9]

While Kennan appreciated Kirk as a wise, European-oriented eccentric ill suited to Roosevelt's America, he admired von Moltke as a wise, democratically inclined aristocrat out of place in Hitler's Germany. When Kirk left Berlin, Kennan took over his informal contacts with von Moltke and other potential leaders of a post-Nazi government. Feeling his way through the blacked-out city to von Moltke's hideaway apartment, Kennan was moved to find this "tall, handsome, sophisticated aristocrat. . . . immersed in a study of the *Federalist Papers*," researching models for a future German republic. Indeed that discovery, coupled with the horrific example of Hitler's rule, impelled Kennan to rethink his blithe assertion in "The Prerequisites" that dictatorship was intrinsically no better or worse than democracy. He would later judge von Moltke as "the greatest person morally" and the "most enlightened that I met on either side of the battle lines in the Second World War." Even at the moment of Hitler's triumph, von Moltke saw Germany's defeat as not only inevitable but also as desirable. Disaster-as-opportunity, what Kennan anticipated for complacent America and saw as a possibility for German-dominated Czechoslovakia, was what von Moltke viewed as unavoidable for Germany. The aristocrat anticipated the ultimate catastrophe and "the necessity of starting all over again, albeit in in defeat and humiliation, to erect a new national edifice on a new and better moral foundation."[10]

Kennan was so taken with von Moltke and the prospect of a reborn Germany led by thoughtful, moral conservatives that he vowed to midwife the process. He confided to the count that he was going to "quit the [foreign] service at Christmas, go home, and devote himself to this task." The "task" was probably drumming up support for ending the war on the basis of entrusting post-Hitler Germany to republican-minded aristocrats. Von Moltke reported that Kennan "is a good and a nice man and I hope that he really will prove to be an asset for us." He also quoted in English George's explanation for this momentous shift in his life's work:

> You know, my personal affairs are all in a muddle just now, and I did not know how to get out of it, but this work will put me right again and I hope by that way to be able to repay my debt of gratitude to Europe for the most important 15 years of my life.[11]

Although fate prevented Kennan from immediately carrying out his pledge to von Moltke, he would for decades nurture the count's dream. George would not leave the Foreign Service at Christmas, not least because Pearl Harbor intervened, and Germany declared war on the United States. Kennan was interned for months, and, after returning to America, he was given a series of important jobs in the Foreign Service. Opposing Roosevelt's policy of unconditional surrender, Kennan urged instead negotiations with such upright, untainted aristocrats as von Moltke. When the war ended, George inquired about his friend, only to learn that the count had been executed in the wave of killings in reprisal for the attempted assassination of Adolf Hitler in August 1944. Throughout the four decades after 1948, when most U.S. and Allied leaders remained quite content with Germany's remaining divided, Kennan pushed for negotiations to reunify Germany as a neutral, largely unarmed nation, the vision also held by von Moltke.

At this juncture—mid-September 1941, in Berlin—Kennan's personal and professional lives tangled in a knot. What he described to von Moltke as his personal muddle likely entailed his shaky marriage. The problem probably seemed especially messy in the context of both his tenth wedding anniversary, only two days earlier, and the imminent departure for the United States of Annelise, feeling "very unhappy and sorely tried," as George later recalled. Annelise was then in Berlin because in April she had decided to accompany George to the German capital after his brief visit home. She was making the move in order "to save the marriage."[12] She had discovered that George was carrying on an affair. In order to return to Europe with her husband,

FIGURE 23. Kennan in Berlin with Under Secretary of State Sumner Welles in February 1940. Welles, a trusted adviser to President Roosevelt, was exploring the possibility of ending the war in Europe. (Courtesy of Getty Images.)

Annelise had to leave young Grace and Joanie with George's sister Jeanette Hotchkiss.

Both George and Annelise leaned heavily on Jeanette. The confidant and correspondent of her brother since childhood, Jeanette shared his aspirations as a writer. She penned poems and stories and would later put together unpublished family histories. Friendly, generous, and open-hearted—"the cheeriest and sunniest of human beings," Grace would remember—Jeanette was devoted to George, Annelise, and the two girls.[13] She was married to a stockbroker, Gene Hotchkiss, who appreciated cocktails more than books. Back in the Depression, he lost the money that Kennan had inherited from his mother and grandparents by violating George's instructions and speculating heavily in risky stocks. Though Gene appears to have paid back a small portion of what he had lost, and George generously forgave any further financial obligation, a moral debt remained.

Regardless of whether the Hotchkisses and the Kennans explicitly discussed the terms, the former in effect repaid the latter with extended childcare. Grace sensed the dynamics. "Maybe Uncle Gene's role in the loss of my father's inheritance explained why my parents felt comfortable dumping two little girls, aged four and eight, on a family living in a crowded house with three adolescent boys."[14] George also dropped off with Jeanette and Gene his dog, Kimmy. That proved a "catastrophe," a Hotchkiss son later remembered, because he repeatedly had to use scarce rationed gas looking for the dog.[15] Space was even tighter in this Ravinia, Illinois, home because Jeanette was running a nursing school to make ends meet. During the summer of 1940, Annelise herself moved in with the Hotchkisses at their little house on Pine Lake outside of Milwaukee. More puzzled than penitent, George later commented, "How they all squeezed into the cottage—Gene and Jeanette and their three sons, plus Annelise, the children, and a maid—is still a mystery to me."[16] Though cramped, it felt cozy to Grace. "When I was with my parents, we had a succession of nannies and nurses tend to us, but in Ravinia I felt part of a family."[17]

George, while understanding that he and Annelise were imposing on Jeanette and her family, nevertheless prioritized his professional duties, the most important he had ever undertaken. He was number two at the U.S. embassy in Berlin, the chief administrative officer of a beehive of 150 employees busy not just with America's relations with Germany but also those of a dozen other nations no longer represented in the Nazi capital. Work ended only after dark. With the blackout, he often had to finger the cobblestones to find his way home.

"Life is just more work and responsibility," he moaned to Jeanette. "Your brother is buried under mountains of red tape—German and American."[18] Relieving her was "just simply devilishly complicated," George, clearly frayed, wrote his sister in July 1941. "Perhaps Gracie— poor child—could go back to the yearned for MDS [Milwaukee Downer Seminary, an exclusive boarding school, financed by friends of the family], after all, and surely you will have no great difficulty shopping little Joanie around." As the last phrase underscored, concerns about the children remained secondary. "Life here weighs heavily at the moment," he emphasized.[19]

While sympathizing with her brother, Jeanette resented her sister-in-law. Annelise "will let other people work for her," she blurted out years later. "She imposed on me. She left the children with me, and went back to Germany to be with George, a maid, and with help, and was living comfortably."[20] Now, in September 1941, Annelise had to remove the girls from Jeanette's over-bursting household. The poor woman was in a bind: returning to her daughters would enable her husband to cheat on her again.

George, however, categorized his dalliances as related more to art than to adultery. His obligation to spend long hours dealing with war-time bureaucratic hassles was pushing the balance toward Civilization and away from Eros. "We *are* artists," he reaffirmed to Jeanette, and to himself. That meant creativity was impeded by "our consciences, which have kept us from violating the responsibilities we have assumed, and from indulging in the necessary amount of Bohemianism." Artistic expression and a vibrant life "almost invariably involve a certain amount of carelessness and irresponsibility toward other persons."[21] Those impacted "other persons" would, on occasion, include Annelise, his daughters, and Jeanette.

Rafting the turbulence of the war and his personal life, Kennan weighed his options. He felt himself still "gathering rather than losing strength"—"only I don't know what to use my strength on, when this is all over." While getting a top diplomatic job appealed, he doubted that narrow-minded interest groups and congressional politics would permit Washington to pursue a serious foreign policy. Fitting in back home seemed a problem, since "I am Europeanized."[22] Nevertheless, he was "thinking seriously of leaving" the Foreign Service. He probably had in mind helping von Moltke. He again asked Jeanette to inquire about "Grandpa Kennan's old farm." Perhaps he could combine farming with teaching at the University of Wisconsin–Madison, an hour away. Lacking a permanent home since childhood, he longed for roots. Years of depression and war had convinced him, moreover, that "every form of existence except that of the small land-holder has been pretty thoroughly shattered."[23]

Despite his larger salary, money continued as a worry, particularly because of the aspiration to buy a farm. He wondered how "is someone like myself going to earn regularly upwards of $8,000 a year at home"?[24]

News that Annelise, then staying with Jeanette, was buying an expensive "radio-phonograph saddens me," he confided. The purchase would take "a chunk out of savings." "But let her have it," he conceded. He alluded to tensions over finances that traced back to his boyhood in Milwaukee: "I *am* so poor" at managing "the family purse strings, as poor as Father was."[25]

All these private musings bent before the storm of war. The German invasion of Norway and Denmark in April 1940 and France in May had turned Kennan sharply against the Nazi regime. Hitler's Germany no longer seemed a potentially beneficent agency for organizing Slavs in Czechoslovakia and farther east, but rather an "overpowering force of nastiness and perversion and brutality" attacking the decency and lives of Western Europeans.[26] He was aghast at the bombing of Kristiansand, where, only days earlier, his daughters had been living with their grandparents.[27] Though already overworked, Kennan took up what he termed a hobby—figuring out "the mechanics of German exploitation of the conquered countries."

The resulting study, plus his reading Gibbon's *Fall of the Roman Empire* on long transatlantic flights, cemented his belief that any imperial power—be it ancient Rome, Nazi Germany, Soviet Russia, or Cold War America—was bound to fail in holding on to conquered territories over the long term. By late 1941, he concluded that Nazi Germany was "actually consuming the goose that lays the golden egg." The Germans were exploiting occupied Europe so relentlessly that they were sparking resistance and stifling economic production.

Germany was squandering its opportunity to "restore order and peace and hope" by efficiently unifying Europe's economy. Only six years later, such unification would figure as the centerpiece of Kennan's conception of the Marshall Plan. Now, however, German oppression was making workers "sullen and bitter and feel[ing] that they have nothing to work for." Nazi governance seemed chaotic. Insiders' fighting coupled with Hitler's remoteness had spawned a "sordid free-for-all of lawlessness, corruption, favoritism and mutual destruction." Despite its conquests, Nazi Germany suffered from a fragile emotional disposition. With demoralization already rampant, even minor military setbacks would spark major "psychological repercussions."[28] That fragility did not, however, stop Hitler from widening his circle of enemies to include the Soviet Union and then the United States.

From Berlin, Kennan responded to the German invasion of Russia on June 22, 1941 with a perspective reflecting his repugnance of Stalin's repression. He worried that Roosevelt would follow Churchill in embracing Stalin as an ally against Hitler. In a letter to Loy Henderson, who had taken his former job at the Russian desk, Kennan reiterated the Soviets' abominable record. In 1939–1941, they had destroyed the Baltic states, seized half of Poland, and snatched territory from Romania and Finland. The domestic policy of the Kremlin, which had crushed religion and inflicted terror on millions, made Russia "widely feared and detested"; indeed, "Russia is generally more feared than Germany."[29] That ranking reflected Kennan's own feelings. Although he deplored Hitler's regime, the loathing did not reach to the core as did his animus against Stalin's rule. In the purges of 1935–1938, George—personally, grievously, and inconsolably—had lost friends, acquaintances, people he respected and admired, and the chance to fulfill his profoundest longings. Kennan liked, respected, and felt comfortable with the Germans. His feelings toward the Russians packed greater passion: he loved the people while hating their government. He would sustain that differential in emotional intensity even through his five-month internment by the Germans.

INTERNMENT

Upon learning of the Japanese attack on Pearl Harbor on December 7, 1941, Kennan first called Leland Morris, the chargé in the embassy and then emptied "his desk and started burning everything that could conceivably have been of any interest to the German authorities." On December 9, two days before Germany declared war on the United States, a triple priority cable from the State Department ordered Kennan to neutral Sweden. The Germans, however, blocked all such travel and cut off communications with the outside world. No one at the embassy knew when, or even if, they would make it home. The Nazis might

"storm into our offices ... seize our archives, and throw us into prison."
After a week of uncertainty, the Germans informed Morris and Kennan
that they would intern embassy officials, their families, and American
journalists in Jeschke's Grand Hotel at Bad Nauheim, a resort near
Frankfurt. Ironically, President Franklin D. Roosevelt as a boy had vacationed at Bad Nauheim. A special train transported the 130 Americans
with their 900 pieces of baggage.

Kennan, to whom Morris turned over the day-to-day leadership, believed that warding off harsh discipline from the SS guards required
"insert[ing] ourselves between the German authorities and the members of our group"—that is, assuming as many administrative functions
as possible. He had to maneuver between the limits imposed by the
Germans and the laments voiced by homesick Americans. Food remained meager, and the hotel rooms frigid.

In this nerve-wracking situation, Kennan tried to tamp down the
emotional outbursts of both sides. Cooped up for months, the internees
grew "unhappy and touchy, and little things began to look very big to
them." He allocated the scarce hotel rooms while keenly aware that
"there is no more sensitive or irrational side of human nature than that
which has to do with the living quarters of the individual." Of utmost
importance was preserving "dignity and 'face' in the eyes of the Germans." To minimize the sway of the guards, Kennan inserted an insulat-
ing element of ambiguity. For instance, he pleaded with the internees
not to walk to the very end of the allowed path when exercising, for to
do so "gave the guards the chance to demonstrate authority by turning
them back." The status of the internees should remain a gray area. If the
guards never had a chance to boss the Americans, Kennan reasoned,
they would remain uncertain as how far they might go. But once the
guards cracked down and found nothing to stop them, "then we could
rapidly lose prestige and begin to have hard sledding."[30]

Safeguarding that prestige remained his priority in dealing with those
few internees conniving with the Germans for special privileges. With
his customary diligence, Kennan investigated and then wrote a fourteen-
page report on an American who had sneakily arranged with the Germans to have his wife visit. He typed a twenty-eight page, almost

hour-by-hour account of a journalist whose "moral and nervous dissolution" had rendered him susceptible to German blandishments.[31]

The pressure wore heavily on George. "Worst of all," he later recalled, "was the mental strain arising from the sheer fact of confinement" and from not knowing when and how it would end. Assorted worries taunted him. Would Washington in fighting Hitler forget about the sins of Stalin? Would he ever make it home? Could he buy a farm? How could he help von Moltke? Was Annelise's family in occupied Norway suffering? What was Annelise doing? How were Grace and Joan? The Germans did not permit any direct communication with America, and the Swiss, who handled U.S. interests, allowed only minimal exchanges.

The internees invented ways to pass the time. They organized a baseball series. Bats they made with sticks, baseballs with "old golf balls, twine, rags, and the leather from a diplomatic despatch bag," sewn together with surgical thread. Evenings rang with singing, drama, and lectures at "Badheim University," which boasted fourteen courses and instant traditions.

Kennan offered the most popular course, on Russian history. With few books at hand, he composed lectures based on his memory and imagination. In explaining Russia, he was also explaining himself. His talks developed into a wishful, wistful narrative that reflected his longing for roots, whether in Russia, Wisconsin, or in his imagined eighteenth century. Reflecting his devotion to the great man's theories, Kennan explained the "parallel between the childhood psychology of peoples and of individuals . . . developed by Freud." He explained that Russia during its "adolescence" in the seventeenth century had faced a crisis of identity. Should it opt for a Slavophile, anti-Western orientation, as Ivan the Terrible had insisted, or copy the West, as Peter the Great had attempted? Perhaps thinking of his own crisis in early 1935, Kennan mused that "there are moments in the lives of peoples, as there are in the lives of individuals, when no one can help them . . . when they must find in themselves the strength to grow up to their troubles."[32]

For years, he had linked himself to Russia, in a variety of ways, starting with his mystical and familial links to the elder George Kennan. He had mastered the language, culture, and history. His living in Russia also had an influence. "I am a great believer in the power of the soil over the human beings who live above it," he explained. Soil, climate, and geography shaped culture. "People who stay for an entire generation in China begin to become Chinese," he asserted. So, too, had Euro-Americans become "similar in many respects to the American Indians."

He identified in particular with the typical young aristocrat of late eighteenth-century Russia, "a character for whom I personally have great liking and sympathy." Kennan liked to claim that he really was a person of the eighteenth century. He reckoned that his tradition-minded father, born in 1851, figured as a relic of the previous century. Slipping the bounds of a grim present, George fantasized about a happier past when American and Russian gentry had shared a common culture. Since Americans and Russians had inherited similar elements from the past, they could come together again in the future.

Kennan portrayed the young Russian aristocrats with colors from his own palette. Disillusioned with Western European culture, these Russians, many with intellectual or artistic aspirations, felt torn between foreign influences and homeland traditions. Dissatisfied with the formalism of the traditional church, they had discovered "a new outlet for religious feeling in romanticism and mysticism." They felt disappointed and adrift, much as Kennan himself did. He called up his own esthetic ideals as he celebrated the cultural efflorescence of the young aristocrats as "something very fresh and very tragic: a deep naivety, a deep sincerity, a deep intellectual honesty." This Russian creativity was to "run wild in the XIX century," inspiring the "half-hopeful and half-desperate" music of Tchaikovsky and the "tremendous analytical literature of Dostoyevsky, Tolstoy, and Chekhov." Such intensity also inspired, tragically, the radicals who instigated the Russian Revolution.

Kennan polished this picture by reaching beyond tangible reality, as he often did on matters dear to him. Claiming to see deeply into the Russian soul, he discerned a mystical tie to Americans. The creativity of the nineteenth century not only remained "latent today in a myriad of Russian hearts," but that sensibility also rendered the Russian people "and its sufferings so appealing to the American mind."[33] This imagined affinity certainly appealed to George's mind.

While the internment afforded Kennan a chance to hone his ideas about Russia, the strain also exhausted him. He later acknowledged that "I had moments of real neurosis."

A soured affair pushed him close to the edge. "I am shocked, discouraged, and humiliated," he confided in his diary. "What I have been guilty of was in my eyes a folly, to be sure, but a minor one, and there were plenty of ameliorating circumstances. That it should have been punished in so grotesque and humiliating a manner is what sets me back." Contempt for many of his fellow internees heightened the embarrassment. "I cannot face these people now. I am burning inside with rage and humiliation. To think that I, George Kennan, should be in the position of having to conceal anything."[34] Kennan's dalliance was not unusual. Wartime affairs, even war "marriages" were commonplace. Home was far away, and no one knew when the war would end or whether they would survive. Romance and gossip about it wafted through the rooms of Jeschke's Grand Hotel.

Getting jilted prompted a basic assessment. "What do I actually want in life?" he asked himself. He listed, first, "a happy, balanced personal life" and, second, "work which I considered positive." By "balanced" he evidently meant a solid marriage that allowed for affairs. The "tragedy" of his botched affair, however, made such "balance" seem unlikely. "Women," he admonished himself, "you can't have." Instead, at age thirty-eight, he had to force himself "to feel old," because being young with his desires required someone "very tough of heart, very gay, very well-balanced in human relationships, and relatively irresponsible." Successfully balancing Eros and Civilization demanded a temperament more in tune with his sometime muse, the vagabond poet Harry Kemp. Lacking this Bohemian sensibility, George could not "be young successfully."

As for rewarding work, prospects looked dim. While unhappiness had swept over him in Washington in 1937–1938, what he termed depression was engulfing him at Bad Nauheim. He told himself that such sadness brought him closer to reality than the "irrational hopefulness" prevailing at other times. With this dour perspective, he decided that the "biologically undermined and demoralized" American people had no happy future "regardless of the outcome of the war." No longer confident that a cadre of talented young idealists could radically remake the U.S. government, as he had sketched in "The Prerequisites" in 1938, he now feared that trying to "overthrow the system" would "merely open the floodgates to evils worse than anything." Kennan's personal out seemed to lie in "gentleman farming . . . the only form of playing with toys which is not ridiculous in elderly men." Farming also appealed to this proto-environmentalist as a "chance to acquit our responsibilities toward at least a small section" of the "misused and disfigured" earth. Unfortunately, however, farming would not yield enough income for his family. Hence, he would try to both farm and keep his job, even though "the Foreign Service is pure drudgery. Its sole merit is that it pays a cash income. Otherwise it has no significance."[35]

After Germany declared war on the United States, Annelise knew only that her husband had been interned. Her own family was suffering in occupied Norway. Although George managed to cable his bank in Wisconsin to allow his wife to draw from his account, he did not have much money there. Nor, as he later angrily recounted, were he and his colleagues paid during the internment because, according to the U.S. government, "we had not, you see, been working."[36] No one in the Kennan family had much money, and there is no evidence of assistance from the James family.

Annelise, largely on her own, had to cope. Though she had no job, she had to support her daughters and a live-in housekeeper named Betty, who helped care for the children. As Grace later recalled, "Mother soon made friends and went out a lot." She moved into an attractive house in upscale Bronxville, New York, "where she had an admirer, a bachelor named Carl [Siegesmund], who came to call and of whom I was very jealous."[37] Resentful of Siegesmund's intrusion, Grace tried to run away. Of the only two cables to Annelise that Kennan managed to send out through the Swiss, one addressed to her in Bronxville read: "Please try to find other place in East when lease expires. Deepest love. George"[38] Shortly before he returned home, she wrote him: "As for you and me, Sweetheart, I am not bitter and haven't been really for a long time. All that I went through last year has been healed, and I hope I am a better person for it."[39] Decades later, when Grace, facing marital problems, was considering divorce, her mother advised: "You can have affairs, and everyone will be satisfied. It hasn't been easy living with your father, but we stayed married."[40]

Finally, on May 12, 1942, the Germans let the detainees leave on a train for Lisbon. There they boarded the S.S. *Drottningholm*, which had a big "diplomat" painted on the hull to ward off attacks, for the voyage home. Upon his arrival in the United States, Kennan updated his reports on the disloyal Americans, debriefed officials at the State Department, and moved the family out of the Bronxville house in pursuit of his pastoral dream.

THE FARM

Packed into a Ford convertible, George, Annelise, and the girls looked for a farm within driving distance of Washington. They found what would become the anchor of their family life. The property featured 252 acres of fields and woodland, a residence for the hired farmer, barns, and a run-down, once ornate twenty-two-room country house stuffed with treasures and junk. The Kennans bought it all for $14,200, using his back pay as a down payment and taking out a mortgage for the remaining half. It seemed meant to be: an opportunity to put down roots in the land and a home designed by a Russian Jewish immigrant inspired by country estates in his native Odessa. Since the nearest town was East Berlin, Pennsylvania, they could use their old stationery from the German capital by inking in "East."

Ecstatic, George informed Jeanette: "We have just spent the first night in our 'Cherry Orchard'; it looked something like the 7 dwarves' hut in Disney's *Snow White*: cobwebs everywhere, and I had no idea what sort of beasts or ghosts would emerge during the night."[41] The Kennans adored the place. Annelise appreciated having George to herself and away from possible admirers. "My father loved organizing projects," Grace later recalled. "We planted 500 trees. My father also built a tool shed, with all his work tools carefully arranged and displayed. Just sitting around was impossible. He had to be constantly busy." If he wasn't reading or writing, he was "building, chopping wood, laying paths, or cleaning out his workroom." For Grace, who loved helping out, "my family life was transformed from black and white to color." She and Joanie now "had our father to ourselves." Always a storyteller, he beguiled them with tales of animals who had voices and personalities.[42]

LISBON

Though Kennan was considering resigning from the State Department, the agency needed him. At a meeting in Washington on August 11, 1942, barely three months after his return from internment, top officials urged him to accept the number two post at Lisbon, as counselor of the legation. With most of Europe occupied by the Germans, neutral Portugal remained fully accessible to the Axis, the Allies, and all their spies. Moreover, Portugal produced wolfram, a mineral essential for hardening steel, and it owned the strategic Azores islands. All this made Lisbon "the most important post which they had to fill in the entire world," Kennan was told. He stood out as "the only person who had earned [their] approval," and "they meant this assignment as a special honor." To Annelise, dismayed at the prospect of again going abroad, George explained that the job was "clearly of Class I caliber" in the Foreign Service even though he had only recently advanced to Class III. He would also rank as the youngest counselor in the service.[43] On the Friday before Labor Day, a call from Washington, made through the village bank as the farm house had no telephone, ordered him to proceed that very weekend to Lisbon.[44] While officially serving in the Foreign Service, "my real mission," he later revealed, was to "straighten out the dreadful confusion" among the Military Intelligence Division, Office of Naval Intelligence, Office of Strategic Services, Federal Bureau of Investigation, and their British counterparts—all the while thwarting Axis agents and protecting the turf of the State Department.[45] Since much of the work would be done at diplomatic parties and dinners, George needed Annelise as hostess. She had two weeks to close the house at the farm, place Grace in a Washington boarding school, and get herself and Joanie to Lisbon. "I am sick about it," Annelise wailed. "It leaves my stomach empty."[46]

The Lisbon post advanced Kennan's career in three ways while affording a glimpse into a fourth. First, he grew accustomed to covert operations and secret intelligence, aspects of policy that he would advance in the early Cold War. Second, he honed his skills at diplomatic analysis and negotiation. Third, he caught the attention of the White House by audaciously challenging the Pentagon, refusing a direct order from the State Department, and requesting a meeting with the president.

As a result of this one-on-one meeting with Roosevelt and a second encounter in 1944, Kennan, never lacking in ambition, probably fantasized about becoming an adviser to the president, like his former Moscow chum, Chip Bohlen. Kennan's intelligence and earnestness impressed White House Chief of Staff Admiral William D. Leahy and FDR's fix-it man, Harry L. Hopkins. Roosevelt also valued Kennan's advice. After a briefing by him on the best tactic for getting air and naval basing rights in the Azores, the president overrode his Pentagon advisers. With a different shake of the dice, the White House might have tapped Kennan, with his flawless command of the language, to serve as the president's interpreter and Russian expert at the Tehran summit with Churchill and Stalin, just a month later. When necessary, Kennan could trim his advice to suit powerful patrons, as he did with Messersmith in 1935 and Moffat in 1938 and would do again with James V. Forrestal in 1946–1947. Kennan might even have adopted some of Roosevelt's more optimistic view of postwar cooperation with Stalin if he, rather than Bohlen, were serving as liaison between the White House and State Department in 1944–1945. Kennan might have developed into the more appropriate adviser to Roosevelt as the Big Three wrestled with how to divide Europe. Bearing such burdens would probably have taken a toll on his health.

As it was, the workload in Lisbon drained George's nervous and physical energy, Annelise observed. He suffered colds and stomach upsets. "George works like a slave," she reported. Plus, he did not like Lisbon, "so you know what his frame of mind is." As for herself, while appreciating the many "domestic servants, I would go home to the farm or to Bronxville like a shot, if given the chance." Although Annelise was working in the local Office of War Information bureau—the only paid employment she ever took—money remained tight because of Grace's boarding school, wartime taxes, and the entertainment mandated by George's job. "We almost turn hand springs to save 15 dollars a month," she groaned.[47] Farm expenses also drained. "I never realized it would take so long for the corn money to come in," Kennan worried. "I hope the people in East Berlin won't get too excited about our arrears."[48]

Kennan plunged into the "seething cauldron of espionage and counter espionage" of Lisbon, where "the main warring countries spied on each other and on the Portuguese, and often—by mistake—on themselves. Sometimes all this was exciting and tragic; more often it was funny."[49] The "Germans financed their own espionage organization in Lisbon by getting their agents hired by the British and Americans," and having those spies dribble out just enough information to remain on the British and American payrolls.[50]

Loyal to the State Department, Kennan defied the Pentagon's demand that he "not disclose his intelligence activities in Lisbon to anyone except the armed services and the OSS."[51] He helped "perfect a set of American controls on all persons" moving between Lisbon and the Western Hemisphere. He imposed U.S. intelligence control over Latin American diplomats in Lisbon.[52] Much of this work was under cover. He transmitted from "the Professor" a coded message that "Father and mother have approved who will attend the family meeting. Do not let Countess Erika de Hojon learn of any of the plans since she was and may still be an enemy agent."[53] The Kennans hosted the chief of staff of Supreme Allied Commander General Dwight D. Eisenhower and his British counterpart, who "arrived in Lisbon by plane, traveling incognito." During an all-night session at the villa north of the city, U.S., British, and Italian generals dickered over the terms for an armistice and Italy's switch to the Allies. Kennan, in taking the minutes and in drafting the final document smoothed the accord.[54]

Just as espionage and intrigue centered in Lisbon, so too did vital sea and air routes converge on the Portuguese Azores. At a time when even a transatlantic flight via North Africa–West Africa–South America–Bermuda took five grueling days, the U.S. Air Command enthused at the prospect that planes refueled in the Azores "could be flown from Washington or New York to Northwest Africa in less than 24 hours."[55] Also impelling was the threat that Hitler could grab the Azores and then bomb the United States. With that nightmare in mind, Roosevelt in the spring of 1941 had prepared an expeditionary force to seize the islands. (At the last minute he sent the troops to Iceland instead.)[56] Florida senator Claude Pepper, a friend of both the president and Bert Fish, the minister to Portugal, urged occupying the Azores. "The people who own those territories know that our purpose is not aggression," Pepper insisted, and besides, it was better "to lose a few lives now" than to suffer a Nazi attack later.[57] Roosevelt redrew the map by declaring the Azores to lie in the Western Hemisphere. Unimpressed, the Portuguese government threatened war against any invader. Adding to the tension, the OSS was "busy planning a minor revolution in the Azores," Kennan worried.[58]

Meanwhile, on November 8, 1942, U.S. troops landed in North Africa. While the United States had succeeded in moving thousands of troops and many tons of equipment across the Atlantic, invading German-held Italy and France would require vastly more transportation. And that mandated U.S. bases in the Azores. On arriving in Lisbon in September 1942, Kennan had found British diplomats already negotiating for air and naval rights. Although the crafty dictator of Portugal, António de Oliveira Salazar, was insisting on neutrality so as not to provoke a German invasion, he also agreed to a limited British presence in the Azores to honor Portugal's 1373 treaty with England.

In the Azores as elsewhere, the United States and Britain both cooperated and competed. London officials worried that "the Americans [were] out to supplant us." Foreign Secretary Anthony Eden alerted Churchill that the Americans had to understand that Portugal "is not a second Guatemala, from whom anything which the Americans desire can be obtained simply by threats or bribes. We know Salazar and the Americans do not."[59] As Kennan saw it, dealing with the British loomed as "the essential problem of this Mission."[60]

The challenge reached into the Kennans' home. In the spring of 1943, George and Annelise accepted the invitation of Ralph Jarvis, the British counterintelligence chief in Lisbon, and his wife, Coney, to join in renting an ancient villa in the mountains north of the city. Imprinted in the memory of nine-year-old Grace would be the perfume of orange, magnolia, and gardenia blossoms in this earthly paradise and the ancient Roman basin that served as the swimming pool. Joined by the Jarvises' two children and supervised by a stern English governess, Grace and Joanie, along with two maids and a cook, spent weekdays at the villa. Though no doubt busy, the Kennans were again farming out childcare. On weekends the parents would arrive with friends for lively parties. It was at the villa that the Allied and Italian generals negotiated armistice terms for Italy. Annelise and Coney began a lifelong friendship. Coney was also "having a big affair" with George's colleague and Princeton classmate, R. Walton Butterworth.[61]

Relations between George and Annelise had their own complexities. "There are always little clues that children pick up," Joan later recalled. "One day my mother threw something at my father, either a vase or a lamp."[62] With George and Ralph enmeshed in intelligence and diplomacy, with their respective nations rivals as well as allies, and with their wives, children, friends, and living arrangements intertwined, personal and political borders must have blurred. Indeed, the initiative to have Jarvis's American counterpart share the villa may have come from London officials anxious to surveil the Americans and tap their rising power. This was the kind of "mixing up" of U.S.-British interests that Churchill was pushing—to the extent that he turned a blind eye to his daughter-in-law's affair with Roosevelt's personal representative W. Averell Harriman, who a year later would become Kennan's boss in Moscow.[63]

Kennan found it humiliating living in a country, and in a household, dominated by the British while working for a department ignored by the president. He ranked as only an accidental head of mission and as a minister rather than an ambassador. How could he, with only a small staff, "hold up [his] end against a British Embassy staffed by several hundreds of people and headed" by a prestigious ambassador? Neglect by Washington aggravated his frustration. He protested to Dunn, the

State Department's political adviser, that while U.K. officials were accelerating their "penetration" of the Azores, he could do little. It demeaned the Americans in the eyes of the Portuguese and the British "to have it demonstrated that our Government did not consider it worth while to inform or instruct us." Silence from Washington condemned the Americans to political inactivity. An embarrassed Dunn confessed that since the Azores remained the domain of the White House, State had "no clearer picture than you of the general plan." He added, in a reprimanding tone, that "it is not clear to me just what type of political activity . . . you would suggest."[64]

Kennan knew precisely what political activity he would initiate. To the challenge of negotiating base rights in the Azores he brought values and experience honed at Bad Nauheim, Berlin, Prague, Moscow, and Riga. For all his complaints about the life of a diplomat, he remained a firm advocate of diplomacy. He believed that patient talk could yield breakthrough agreements. He aimed for negotiations both respectful and persistent, flexible yet focused. Rather than demand drastic change and total capitulation, he preferred amelioration of problems and, if necessary, obfuscation of differences. He compared conditioning the behavior of other nations to training plants. He contrasted his eagerness to negotiate with Salazar with the reluctance of his predecessor. Fish had told him: "Kennan, I ain't goin' down there and get my backsides kicked aroun.'"[65]

Kennan remained stymied, however. No lowly State Department official was invited to the high stakes poker played by Roosevelt and Churchill. By the spring of 1943, George felt torn: proud at having mastered a "strenuous . . . job of real responsibility," yet also resentful that his achievements promised "no triumphs, no glory, no recognition." He was "shamed and discouraged" by the White House's seeming indifference to his efforts.[66]

MEETING WITH ROOSEVELT AND SALAZAR

It was not surprising, then, that Kennan bet all his chips when finally allowed into the game. In October 1943, he received a proposal, drafted by the Joint Chiefs of Staff and approved by the president, demanding base rights in the Azores vastly exceeding those granted to Britain. He flatly refused to transmit the order to Salazar. He also broke protocol by saying he would take full personal responsibility for his defiance and by requesting a meeting with President Roosevelt himself.[67] The junior diplomat was challenging the judgment and authority of the president and the Pentagon. Roosevelt replied through the State Department that while there seemed no reasons for Kennan to return to the United States, he should cable his arguments.[68]

The audacious diplomat then laid out his thesis: "The Portuguese are allergic to theory but relatively impervious to practice." Rather than insist on sweeping privileges that would violate Lisbon's neutrality and invite a German attack, Washington should accustom the Portuguese to seeing U.S. planes and ships using British facilities obtained under the ancient treaty. Once "we have thus gotten our foot in the door," we could press the Portuguese for greater rights."[69] He warned against push- ing too hard, for Salazar "fears association with us only slightly less than with the Russians." Furthermore at this stage of the war, the no-nonsense dictator remained skeptical that the Anglo-Americans would actually triumph. Roosevelt, now agreeing with Kennan, told him to negotiate with Salazar.

Emboldened, Kennan then risked telling Salazar's aide "a big lie." He went out on a limb by promising that Washington would guarantee Por- tugal's empire after the war. Kennan knew that Salazar would never agree to base rights without such a pledge. The pledge also reflected the fact that Kennan, unlike Roosevelt, valued the Portuguese empire as a venerable and viable institution. (Even in 1947, when colonial empires in India and elsewhere were collapsing, Kennan would still argue that "the stability of the Portuguese homeland really rested on the stability of the Portuguese Empire.")[70] Suddenly, just as Kennan was about to meet with Salazar, a miscommunication resulted in his being recalled to Washington. After an exhausting five-day air trip, George arrived "un- nerved, overtired, jittery, not myself."[71]

Things only got worse. Kennan was hauled into the Pentagon, where Army Chief of Staff General George C. Marshall, Secretary of the Navy Frank Knox, and a bevy of generals and admirals fumed about the inex- cusable delay in getting base rights. "Who is this guy Salazar, and what does he think he is anyway?" someone snarled. They ignored Kennan until Secretary of War Henry L. Stimson barked: "Who is this young man?" Informed that this was the chargé in Lisbon, the seventy-five-year-old exploded: "Obviously, it is time we sent a real ambassador to Portugal." Kennan was summarily dismissed.[72]

Humiliated, he "slunk away," taxiing to a favorite diner near the State Department. But then, "the more I thought about it the madder I got and I decided I wasn't going to let it go without a fight." So he contacted Admiral William D. Leahy, the president's chief of staff, whom he had gotten to know on the voyage home after internment. He warned that if America pressed Salazar too harshly, Portugal would appeal to its ancient ally, Britain. That would certainly complicate the Grand Alliance. Leahy listened sympathetically and sent him to Hopkins, who "paced up and down" and "asked some very penetrating questions. Finally, Hopkins said: 'Well, I am really not sure that we don't want to sock the Portuguese but you have pretty good reasons why we shouldn't, and you had better see the president.'"

In the Oval Office, FDR, already briefed by Hopkins, "waved me jovially to a seat at the other side of his great desk." Roosevelt promised to assure the Portuguese that after the war Washington would return all base facilities. "I'll give you a personal letter" for Dr. Salazar, "and then you just go ahead and do the best you can." Regarding the agitation in the Pentagon, Roosevelt, "with a debonair wave of his cigarette holder, said 'Oh, don't worry about all those *people* over there.'" In his memoir, Kennan recounted that with the president's letter in hand, "my position was now impregnable."[73]

Less sanguine at the time, he did all he could to buttress his position. Before leaving Washington, he urged the State Department to delay sending a new minister to Lisbon until he, Kennan, had struck a deal with Salazar. Nevertheless, Roosevelt, despite his joviality with Kennan, did appoint a new ambassador.[74]

Kennan's actions highlighted patterns in his beliefs and behavior. Confidence in his judgment rendered him brave, even brazen, in challenging the Pentagon and the president. Though envious colleagues might marvel at how this junior diplomat had wrangled a meeting with

Roosevelt, Kennan came away unimpressed. He would continue to confront superiors for the rest of his life. In a 1947 lecture at the National War College, he would hold up as the moral of this tale "that small fry in the presence of their superiors . . . ought to find the courage to speak up and speak their minds, and not to be so damn bashful as I was about it."[75] That Kennan remembered himself as "bashful" was telling. For a junior diplomat to challenge the State Department and appeal to the president of the United States was, as a British diplomat understated it, "very unusual."[76]

How did Roosevelt and Kennan assess each other? It irked the diplomat that the president did not override the Pentagon's demand for a new ambassador. Already skeptical of FDR's domestic agenda, Kennan criticized what he perceived, incorrectly, as a naive foreign policy. Roosevelt, a world-class judge of personality who kept his own emotions under a tight lid, probably sensed the anguish in Kennan, who was overwrought even before his ordeal at the Pentagon. In any case, Roosevelt, who days later would leave for his Tehran summit with Stalin and Churchill, did not tap the diplomat as his interpreter/adviser. It was probably also telling that Kennan found greater satisfaction in dealing with the Portuguese dictator than with the American president.

But here, too, hurt feelings and confusion threatened to derail Kennan's agenda. Upon returning to Lisbon and discovering that the State Department had, after all, appointed a new ambassador, Henry R. Norweb, Kennan, stung, requested a transfer.[77] Norweb, however, admired Kennan and insisted on him remaining. The ambassador protested to the State Department that removing Kennan would be a great loss and all the more disturbing since he, Norweb, had been assured in Washington "that there would be no change of personnel during the negotiations."[78]

In the end, Kennan conducted the crucial negotiations with Salazar. The seminary-educated former finance professor, fifteen years Kennan's senior, had ruled Portugal since 1932. His corporatist, antimaterialist, pro-Catholic, and pro-family "New State" regime had violently quashed dissent in an effort to stabilize his poverty-stricken nation. In their many hours in conversation, the diplomat and the dictator found they agreed on much. Kennan shared Salazar's worry that an American victory would mean "the triumph of Wall Street materialism and Hollywood immorality." Himself a skeptic of industrial modernism, Kennan would have smiled at the strongman's aphorism that Americans were "a barbaric people illuminated not by God but by electric light."[79]

He admired Salazar as "one of the most able men in Europe and a man of high moral principles." The praise recalled another of his conservative heroes, von Moltke. Kennan told his friend Isaiah Berlin that of all the leaders he had ever met, Salazar was his favorite statesman. Berlin discerned that Kennan identified himself with Salazar. In Salazar's Portugal Kennan saw the virtues vanishing from Roosevelt's America. He affirmed the dictator's rise as a natural reaction to "unbridled demagoguery" and the "weariness of modern democratic experiments." Himself appalled at consumerism and industrialization, Kennan faulted imported "materialistic doctrines" for rendering the Portuguese "bewildered and demoralized." He sympathized with efforts to once again make authority respectable. Reflecting his own priorities, Kennan valued Salazar's favoring "the power and prosperity of the community, rather than that of the individual." He lauded the dictator's astute, firm, and balanced foreign policy. Kennan seems to have imagined himself, or someone like him, exercising analogous authority in America.

Kennan had to square his admiration for Salazar with the latter's affinity for fascism, the ideology of the wartime enemy. Like the fascists, Salazar opposed liberalism, democracy, and communism while favoring authoritarian, hierarchical, and at times violently repressive policies. He supported the Spanish fascist dictator Francisco Franco, who in turn remained close to Hitler and Mussolini. Salazar remained neutral in the war and sold tungsten and other vital materials to Nazi Germany. Yet he also differed from the Axis dictators in ways that Kennan appreciated. The Portuguese strongman deplored Nazism and Italian Fascism as pagan and as lacking in moral or legal limits.[80]

The author of "The Prerequisites" appreciated a prudent dictator who would rein in labor, business, and the media; check individualism, commercialization, and change; abide by limits, procedure, and good form; favor elites, tradition, and high culture; and promote religion, collective action, and an astute foreign policy. Salazar appeared to promise all this without embracing the gaudiness, vulgarity, and conspicuous brutality of the outright fascists. He differed from the "flashy dictators, like Mussolini and horrible people like that."[81] Pessimism about democracy in America helped the diplomat appreciate the dictator of Portugal.

Driven by ambition and duty, Kennan habitually worked himself to the verge of collapse. He had never totally recovered from the internment in Germany, and "in Portugal I have literally done three men's work."[82] Particularly tough was February 22, 1943. Pan American Airways' *Yankee Clipper* luxury boat plane, en route from New York, crashed into the Tagus River in trying to land near Lisbon. Of the thirty-nine passengers and crew members aboard, only fifteen survived. "A rather gruesome night," Kennan wrote Jeanette. "I had to leave directly from a Washington's Birthday reception where we were entertaining a mere 450 people and go right to the airport." He was the first from the legation to arrive, "and they were just bringing in what could be rescued from the black, rain-swept reaches of the river." Among the lucky few were his Princeton classmate and fellow Foreign Service officer W. Walton Butterworth, who managed to swim ashore with a satchel of classified documents. Helping Butterworth get to a hotel and pin the documents on a clothesline was only part of the weeks of heavy work following the crash.[83]

In April 1943, x-rays revealed that Kennan suffered a duodenal ulcer, like the one that had forced—or enabled—his breakdown in December 1934. "Actually, I do not feel anything like as badly as I did some eight years ago, when I fell ill in Moscow," he wrote Jeanette. "But an ulcer is an inexorable sort of thing. You just have to let down and treat it with respect. It can't be by-passed."[84] He had to buckle down in order to relax. Illness offered license: "I must obviously have a prolonged relief from this sort of life." With Annelise staying in Lisbon, he used sick leave and vacation time to secure a few months relaxing on the farm in East Berlin.

Work on the land gratified his need to build and to belong. He relished the challenge of making the 252-acre place pay for itself, yield some income, and benefit nature. The incessant demands of the house and barns that needed fixing and of the crops and animals that needed tending absorbed his energy in emotionally satisfying ways. He taught himself plumbing, carpentry, and roofing. Months later, facing a return to duty, he wrote, "I simply love the place; and it remains for me something deeply satisfying and refreshing." Nevertheless, "what the future will bring, I just don't know." He hoped to quit the Foreign Service after the war and have the farm "become the haven of permanency and solidity which our family so sadly lacks."[85]

But it all hinged on finances. "I am doing all I can," he wrote Jeanette. "I have paid off $1,800 on the mortgage," and it soon would be down to $5,300.[86] But even so, how could they "ever make the $2,500 per year which would be necessary to enable us to live on it?"[87] He and Annelise expected a lifestyle that included domestic help, which the Foreign Service made possible. Despite his feeling underappreciated, Kennan was earning rapid promotions and hefty pay increases. He rose from a Class IV Foreign Service officer in 1940 with an annual salary of $6,000, to Class III in 1942 at $7,000, to Class II in 1944 at $8,000, to Class I in 1945 at $9,000.[88] Plus he received significant foreign post allowances. (By comparison, in 1943 the average annual salary for executive positions in war agencies reached only $2,328.[89])

Even though working on the farm gave him a lift, he remained "simply too depressed" to write, he confided to Jeanette in July 1943. Part of the problem was his ulcers, which "drag a person down." Traveling to Washington to consult with the department meant that, "except for one night at Cousin Grace's, I have not been in a single house this time where they had servants and three meals a day at home. The result has been: either restaurants or pick-up suppers. And neither is just the thing."

REMAKING AMERICA

Also weighing him down was a far larger complaint. "I have been really appalled and alarmed by what I have seen of Washington, and of this country in general."[90] On July 21, 1943, he departed for Portugal with Grace, whose boarding school in Washington was draining the family finances. Aboard ship Grace basked in the attention of her father as he read aloud Shakespeare's plays, *Treasure Island*, and *Jane Eyre*, "acting out the parts of the characters in the novels, dialects and all."[91] Despite this loving attention to his daughter, Kennan remained mired in what he acknowledged as depression.

The mood soured George's view of the challenges supposedly facing America.[92] It would be a mistake to attribute this July 1943 jeremiad to a momentary funk. After rereading the letter, apologizing to Jeanette for its dire tone, and acknowledging all the "decency and humor and good-nature still present in the American character," Kennan nonetheless reiterated his argument for radical change. "New forms [of government], new ideas must gain currency, new associations of collective effort must come into being," he insisted, or else frustration would triumph. He repeated much the same assertions in a talk to Foreign Service officers in Lisbon in June 1944.[93] He had made a similar, though more extreme, argument in his 1938 book fragment, "The Prerequisites." All three manifestos depicted America in crisis and urged a restructuring of society and government, particularly by favoring collective over individual action. In formulating these statements, George fused his feelings and ideas into solid convictions that, with some modifications, would persist for the rest of his long life. Striking in these pre–Cold War declarations is the deep concern with domestic problems that would anchor Kennan's foreign policy analysis in his long telegram of 1946 and in his "X" article of 1947.

Again channeling the Russian playwright and short-story writer Anton Chekhov, Kennan emphasized the human and natural devastation arising from "hasty and uncontrolled industrialization" and from its destructive twin, urbanization. City living fostered emotional problems: "the violent separation of life and work, the nervous tension . . . the vicarious quality of all emotional experience, the passive spectator psychology, the decay of communal activity." Citizenship then faltered because "these are not influences which make people happy" or "defendants of the rights of man." The frenzy of wartime industry had aggravated the crisis. Thus the retreats in America's civilian life moved in lockstep with America's military advance. Visits home left him depressed and "in a state of helplessness," he confided to Jeanette, because few of the values and lessons of their childhood retained a grip on U.S.

society. To the Foreign Service officers in Lisbon, he admitted, "No one has been more depressed than I" about the changes wrenching the "country that we were brought up in."

To his sister, Kennan openly complained about the alleged problems of America's class structure, its Jewish and African American populations, and its labor unions. "Our republic was founded on the existence and influence of an upper class," he asserted. By upper class he meant not necessarily the rich, but rather people who could afford servants and therefore time for reflection. Only an "enlightened and responsible dominant minority" could stem the otherwise inevitable slide from democracy, to "demagoguery, to dictatorship." In his reading of history, "it is always the few, never the many, who are the real obstacles in the path of the dictator." Egalitarian principles had "produced Napoleon as inevitably as they produced Hitler and Stalin." He revisited the alleged "Jewish problem" he had described in Prague in 1938–1939. The migration of African Americans to jobs in urban war factories constituted another alleged calamity because of their supposed "inability to bear the strains of big-city life." Unions enjoyed too much clout. "I know too well the smell of fascism to mistake it," Kennan claimed, "and the associations of American labor fairly reek with that familiar stench." On and on he ranted.

To the Foreign Service officers, he warned that "it would be a miracle if we could survive these crises without violence and disorder." Industrial mobilization had produced mountains of war matériel at the cost of neglecting "internal discipline." "Masses of war workers" had been "corrupted and spoiled" by easy jobs, easy living, and high wages. He worried particularly about women in the workforce who had "neglected their homes and children. Family life has suffered. Juvenile delinquency has grown enormously." Kennan was mouthing here a critique of working women that would resonate widely among more conservative Americans in the postwar era. Anxiety about excessive "momism" and about the supposed wave of juvenile delinquency would peak in the 1950s.

Although Kennan blamed the war for aggravating these problems, his concerns bracketed the conflict. Whether it was in 1938, 1943, 1944, or in 1946–1947, he looked forward to a crisis that could mandate

sweeping changes. His goals remained consistent. He wanted to see excessive individualism, commercialization, and environmental degradation replaced by collective welfare, esthetic values, and stewardship of
nature. He wanted to encourage manual over industrial production. He
wanted the president and the Congress to cede to the State Department
most of foreign policy. He wanted male workers to demand less and
female workers to return to the home. He wanted Blacks to retreat to
rural areas and Jews to rein in their competitiveness. He wanted to halt
if not reverse urbanization and industrialization. He wanted roads populated with pedestrians and cyclists rather than emptied of all but whiz-
zing cars and roadkill.

How to bring about such a remaking of America? In the summer of
1938, Kennan had suggested domestic upheaval, including bloodshed if
necessary, to achieve an authoritarian state run by self-sacrificing, smart
young men such as himself. By July 1943, he envisioned international
disaster as the impetus. America could "readily become the greatest of
the fascist nations" and embark on disastrous wars. "Eventually, the terrible punishment of national defeat and foreign domination might bring
us to start all over again, in shame and humility, at the bottom of the
ladder" to relearn the "great principles." What were those precepts, sacred enough to justify such painful sacrifice? His answer: "The great
principles of collective living." This remained throughout his life an unshakeable goal, an ideal that alienated him from the individualism of
modern America while aligning him with the communalism of traditional Russia.

Speaking to the embassy staff in Lisbon in June 1944, Kennan suggested a version of the "The Prerequisites" solution, a cadre of determined patriots. Foreign Service officers held "a peculiar position: somewhere between the armed services and the public at large." While the
duties of soldiers would cease with the peace, those of diplomats were
just beginning. Diplomats had seen the world, they understood America, and therefore they had an obligation to help remake the nation
while advancing its global interests. Building the Foreign Service into a
dedicated elite was not a sudden notion. At Bad Nauheim, Kennan had
drawn up "a plan for a Foreign Service Academy along the lines of West

Point or the Naval Academy," and he had later promoted the project to journalists and State Department officials. That Princeton and Dartmouth were considering such schools seemed insufficient. Kennan envisioned a more rigorous academy in which the students, employees of the U.S. government, "would be under very special obligations of honor and discipline. I doubt that any private institution could serve the purpose I have in mind."[94] With "honor and discipline" Kennan had steeled himself against the cruelties at St. John's. He believed that America needed such masculine-inflected toughness to combat the weakening effects of wartime prosperity.

Shortly before leaving for Lisbon, Kennan had warned against softness in what he called an "allegorical story" about some walnut saplings planted on the farm.[95] This morality tale, with lessons for both persons and polities, reflected his belief in the value of struggle and suffering. Not to be admired but rather pitied were the "extroverts" among the saplings, "thrusting themselves up with the most uninhibited abandon" in the full sun. He predicted that these "children of fortune will be relatively easy meat for the pests" and their fruit "big and lush and relatively tasteless." By contrast, those less favored by the sun "will suffer, and many will not last at all." The weak would perish. "But to them that last shall be given gifts that no extrovert can boast of: inner strength, and the fortitude born of suffering and great persistence. And their fruit, fine-flavored and delicate, will be the prize of the epicures."[96] The story encapsulated Kennan's anxieties and ambitions regarding himself as well as America.

At Lisbon, Kennan urged his fellow diplomats to tackle not only foreign relations but also "some of the really crucial internal problems." The draft of this speech reveals how George, already a masterful prose stylist, was fine-tuning his language so as to infuse the issue of domestic reform with a martial imperative that packed emotional force. In a key sentence he first penciled the verb *develop*, then crossed it out and replaced it with *define*, then crossed that out and settled on *defend* as his action verb. With this metaphor for combat in place, he exhorted: "If we are going to defend successfully . . . the things most of us were taught to feel as children: things like independence of speech and thought, honesty and courage of public life, dignity and quiet and serenity of the home and of the family we had better start arming ourselves right now intellectually and morally for what is coming: for some pretty unpleasant and tough fighting." One wonders how the Foreign Service officers conceptualized this intellectual and moral combat. When Kennan used such military metaphors in 1946–1947 in warning about the Soviet Union, Americans, to his consternation, came to think in terms of armies and weapons. It bears noting that the values George wanted to defend not only derived from an idealized childhood, but also implicitly balanced Eros and Civilization. Along with the independence, honesty, and courage necessary for creativity were the dignity, quiet, and serenity yielded by honoring obligation.[97]

Kennan's foreign policy prescriptions in 1943–1944 flowed from his assessment of world affairs, his sense of the needs and limits of America, and the imperatives of his own emotions and aspirations. He began with the premise that victory would bring "enormous potential power." While in the past, "we have had to take the world pretty much as we found it," in the future America would have far more sway. Nevertheless, dangers abounded. In July 1943, well before the expansion of the Soviet Union set off alarm bells in Washington, Kennan was formulating concepts and language that would emerge in the early Cold War. Most of mankind, especially the "rising masses" of Asia, remained "cruel, bigoted and primitive"—in other words, irrational. He cautioned against frittering away U.S. might on "a vague Sunday-school responsibility to humanity at large." Rather, America should, in a more masculinist manner, promote its own interests with a "firm, consistent and unceasing application of sheer power." This phraseology would come to describe the containment policy.

Danger threatened also because the American public was bamboozled by the "exhibitionism" and "improvisation" of Roosevelt's summit meetings with Winston S. Churchill and by the "missions-to-Moscow" of Kennan's nemesis, Joseph Davies, who, unlike the diplomat, had put behind him the horrors of Stalin's purges. In their "naivety and bewilderment," ordinary Americans appeared, like the sun-blessed walnut saplings, "easy prey" for adversaries who sought "the disruption of our national life." Freedom and individualism could imperil the nation, for they made it easy for foreign governments to infiltrate alien ideas and values. That vulnerability "plays in directly with the purely domestic dangers," he wrote in reference to the supposed perils posed by Jews, African Americans, and labor unions. Only three years later, Kennan's long telegram would emphasize that naive or weak elements of the population opened the nation to "penetration" by Soviet "habits of thought and feeling." Domestic and foreign matters intertwined also in how he would defend against this attack. Washington needed to transfer foreign policy making from "the sphere of internal political intrigue," the realm to which Kennan mistakenly relegated Roosevelt, to the "old high-backed armchairs of the State Department." Only the "skeptical," "unhurried," and "unhysterical" State Department—described with language suggesting calm, rationality, and masculinity—could quiet the "competitive screaming" of politicians and business.[98]

Between the July 1943 letter to Jeanette and the June 1944 speech in Lisbon, the still junior diplomat initiated another immediately successful yet ultimately frustrating encounter with President Roosevelt. After completing the initial negotiations on the Azores bases, Kennan in January 1944 was transferred to London, where he assisted Ambassador John Winant on planning for postwar Germany. Determined to keep such vital matters under White House control, Roosevelt, backed by the Pentagon, refused to send Winant any meaningful instructions. Still fuming two decades later, Kennan recalled that they had "to stumble along in total darkness."[99]

For all his success in ascending the ranks, Kennan's audacity in the Azores matter had provoked some jealousy and disapproval in the State Department. It was easy to resent George for being smarter than most and acting like it. No longer could Bullitt and Messersmith protect his flank. The former had gotten into a bitter fight with the president, and the latter had gone off to Mexico City as ambassador. As Kennan left for London, he was warned "to bear constantly in mind that in wartime" the State Department remained subordinate to the Pentagon as well as the president.[100] Ignoring this directive, Kennan "objected strenuously" to an ill-conceived instruction from the department regarding the future zonal borders of Germany. On almost all matters concerning Germany, Kennan disputed most other U.S. officials. "I was substantially alone in my views," he admitted.[101]

KENNAN AND ROOSEVELT

Ironically, Kennan was not so alone, because Roosevelt shared some of those views. Nevertheless, the two came at German policy from different directions and they never understood each other's viewpoint. Both the diplomat and the president insisted on realistic negotiations with Moscow and London based not on popular sentiments but rather on power realities. While Roosevelt intended to conduct those discussions himself or with a few aides, Kennan believed in reserving diplomacy for diplomats such as himself. Though both Roosevelt and Kennan favored dividing defeated Germany, the president favored a harsh peace and the diplomat greater leniency. FDR envisioned a strict denazification and a partial deindustrialization of Germany, while Kennan opposed such measures as unrealistic and as threatening "the collapse of the unity and the significance of Western European civilization." Rebuilding at least the western portion of Germany was vital to rehabilitating Europe, and "a vigorous and hopeful Europe [was] necessary to the prosperity, if not the survival of the Anglo-Saxon world." He argued that it was foolish to indulge in the "emotional satisfaction . . . from the continued gratuitous infliction of suffering" on Germany.[102] While Roosevelt insisted on unconditional surrender, Kennan favored a negotiated peace that would force Nazi leaders, rather than such figures as von Moltke, to bear the onus of the lost war. Treating postwar Germany too harshly would foster a regime of suffering and struggle, thereby hastening the rebirth of a vigorous, resentful adversary.

While Roosevelt put a premium on postwar cooperation with Stalin, Kennan remained skeptical of such collaboration. Kennan's personal and political perspectives were shaped by his love for the Russian people and his horror at Stalin's purges; Roosevelt was not wracked by such passions. Nevertheless, both men inclined toward well-demarcated though unofficial spheres of influence as the means to head off conflict between the Soviets and the West. While Roosevelt was prescient in imagining the postwar world as dominated by the United States and the Soviet Union, Kennan realized the necessity of integrating western Germany into "some framework of European federation" that could defuse ancient rivalries.[103] Resenting the president for ignoring and humiliating the State Department, the diplomat never, even in subsequent decades, understood FDR's postwar aims. Despite Kennan's belief that Roosevelt was naively trusting in the one-nation, one-vote UN General Assembly, the latter was cynically planning on using the UN Security Council to cement collaboration among the big powers.

Temperament also made it difficult for the two men to appreciate each other. In March 1944, Washington sent garbled instructions regarding zonal boundaries for Germany. Kennan again saw "no choice but to go to the president and try to explain." After a harrowing transatlantic flight in which the plane skidded on a runway "like a toboggan" stopping only ten feet from the open sea, he arrived in Washington "rather dazed and unnerved." The trip recalled his flight from Lisbon in 1943. He had again worn himself out: "I was at this point physically exhausted; a rest had become necessary." Even the State Department "urged me to make the vacation a good long one." Roosevelt, with his acute emotional intelligence, no doubt picked up on the younger man's mood and exhaustion. And so, rather than drawing on Kennan's expertise regarding Germany, Russia, and other vital issues, the president kept their encounter superficial. "He laughed gaily" and advised Kennan to "relax—he would see to it that the mix-up was straightened out."[104]

It was unfortunate for both men that more did not result from this meeting. Roosevelt needed more assistance. He had just been diagnosed with a severe heart condition requiring him to cut back on work. His right-hand man, Harry Hopkins, was also succumbing to illness and, moreover, had developed personal differences with FDR. Secretary of State Hull had been replaced with Edward S. Stettinius, who had limited capabilities. Although FDR had Bohlen as a personal adviser, he would in his remaining year of life have benefited from Kennan's perspective, especially at Yalta. Despite their significant differences, the two men agreed on the fundamental issue of working out with the Soviets separate spheres of influence in Europe. Moreover, the diplomat could, as he had in the past and would do in the future, bend his recommendations to suit a powerful benefactor. But it was not to be. Kennan instead went away to the farm for a blissful five weeks of planting trees—the walnut saplings.

———

Kennan's experiences in 1939–1944 set him up for the influence he would wield after the war. Service in Prague, Berlin, Lisbon, and London honed his skills as a diplomat and his reputation in the State Department and the White House. He became known as a brilliant if sometimes quirky analyst supremely confident of his ideas and ready to buck the chain of command. Despite his swift rise in the Foreign Service, he remained on the margin. He repeatedly considered resigning. He challenged superiors. This insider-outsider status would also mark his future career in Washington.

Purchasing a farm within driving distance of Washington would enhance Kennan's ability to work effectively in the U.S. capital. At the farm he could vent his physical energies and connect with nature. The never-ending projects gave George and Annelise, whose marriage had frayed during wartime separations, something to work on together. Friday and Saturday evenings they were in East Berlin, often with weekend guests, rather than at Georgetown parties where the tall, handsome star could turn heads. Toward the end of his Bad Nauheim ordeal in 1942, with his ulcer in spring 1943, and again with his exhaustion in spring 1944, Kennan realized that he had to ease the pace. The farm provided that needed break.

In terms of policy, Kennan's work at the Russian desk had educated top State Department and White House officials to the seriousness of the contact issue. The Kremlin's insistence on isolating foreign diplomats and journalists in Moscow became a major thorn in U.S.-Soviet relations. Although the alliance in World War II would subsume that issue, Kennan, in Moscow from 1944–1946 and back in Washington afterward, would revive it. He had no choice, because isolation from the

Russian people pained him so deeply. Nor could he forget or forgive the horror of the purges. Indeed, abhorrence of Stalin's regime meant that Kennan never really embraced the wartime tie with the Kremlin as an alliance. While he despised the Nazis, he seems to have retained a shadow of neutrality about the Russo-German war. Opposed to unconditional surrender as a policy, in mid-1944 he recommended retaining lower-level Nazi officials so that they, and not such principled Germans as von Moltke, would shoulder the defeat.

Kennan's experiences in Prague and in Lisbon also helped orient his later work. In Prague, he witnessed the failed promise of German organizational talents in bringing order and unity to central Europe. He concluded that while conquest almost always backfired, countering centrifugal forces remained important. By 1944, he envisioned a postwar European federation, with at least the western part of Germany at its core, as the vehicle for instituting order and common purpose. Salazar's effort to favor collective over individual purposes in Portugal helped Kennan overlook the dictator's commonalities with less savory dictators. Kennan's admiration for Salazar foreshadowed the postwar orientation of U.S. policy that welcomed in the Free World an array of anti-Communist dictatorships. He would draw on his Lisbon experience with covert intrigue in assigning the newly formed CIA missions in Eastern Europe.

Kennan developed these strategic ideas while writing entries in his diary, letters to Jeanette and others, and lectures at Bad Nauheim. He considered retiring from the Foreign Service and becoming a professor as well as a farmer. He honed the skills that after 1945 would make him an effective lecturer at the National War College and elsewhere. The breadth of knowledge and the aptitude for policy analysis that he advanced in Riga, Moscow, Prague, Berlin, and Lisbon would enable him to write highly influential papers as director of the Policy Planning Staff in 1947–1949.

Kennan could not have operated successfully in these highly visible positions after the war if he had continued to express the anti-Semitic, racist, and anti-union sentiments he expounded in 1937–1944. America, as he must have realized, was progressing in a different direction. His ideas would moderate as he put behind him the impressions gathered in Germany, Latvia, and Czechoslovakia. Nevertheless, he would retain remnants of those prejudices for the rest of his life. Moreover, Kennan continued to believe that America suffered from excessive individualism, commercialization, and reliance on machines. He would persist in looking for some means to promote collective over individual priorities. In 1946–1947, this search for a usable crisis, even a catastrophe, that could mobilize America's too diffuse energies would become one of his motivations for depicting the Soviet Union as an existential threat.

CHAPTER 7

COLD WAR FOUNDER AND
SKEPTIC, 1944–1950

"I REACT INTENSELY to everything I see and hear," Kennan marveled after returning to Russia in July 1944. The "pulsating warmth and vitality" of the Russian people jolted him with "an indescribable sensation." Living as "part of them," even in frigid Siberia, appealed more than luxuriating on "Park Avenue among our own stuffy folk." By immersing himself "deeper into Russia" he could come "face to face with that indefinable something, so full of promise and meaning, that I always have felt to be just around the corner."

George had been seeking wonder and mystery ever since his boyhood ventures into Juneau Park looking for fairies. This quest for something beyond the ordinary stemmed, or so he thought, from the everyday loneliness of growing up without a loving mother. As in 1933–1934, Kennan sought succor in the nurturing warmth and wisdom of traditional Russia. He also hoped to find there insights on how to balance what he characterized, in Freudian terms, as the conflict between Eros and Civilization. Despite such pining for transcendence, Stalin pinned Kennan to cruel reality. The wartime alliance had eased but not erased purge-era restrictions on contact between foreigners and Soviet citizens. He found the ostracism "harder than ever to swallow."[1] Years later, he reflected that only during his heartbreak months as ambassador to Moscow in 1952 did the isolation "weigh more heavily on me, or more deeply affect my thinking, than in these first weeks following the return to Russia."[2]

Examining precisely how love for the Russian people and hatred for their government affected Kennan's thinking is key to understanding his shifting stance toward the Cold War. As World War II ended and relations with the USSR soured, he at first pushed for confrontation—and then just as firmly pushed away from it. To both acts of this drama he brought urgency and personal engagement. He conceptualized the containment of Soviet expansion as a nimble policy akin to fencing. If the Soviets, parried by America's pushback, seemed open to negotiation, Washington should pursue such talks.

Kennan's pivots in policy remained grounded in consistent emotional beliefs and attitudes. His fierce ambition, yearning for transcendence, and preconceptions changed little even as his career rocketed upward. He loved the farm and other contact with nature. To his family he remained devoted—though his eye still strayed. This believer in Freud regarded foreign policy as a matter of managing emotions. With his formative experiences in the Baltic nations and in the pre-Nazi Germany of 1927–1932, he regarded the international framework of those years as still normative: Germany unified; Eastern Europe independent; Russia hemmed-in; Asia, Africa, and Latin America quiescent; and America above the fray.

A gifted communicator, Kennan moved others with his emotional language, striking analysis, and authoritative tone. He often failed, as in his long-shot effort to sway the 1945 Yalta Conference. Yet he packed lecture halls at the National War College and around the country. His most consequential pronouncements, the long telegram of February 1946 and the "X" article in *Foreign Affairs* of July 1947, crackled with emotion even as they claimed the authority of cool reason and "realism." The tragic irony—for both Kennan and U.S. foreign policy—is that by using explosive language to puff up an existential "Soviet threat," these two manifestos seemed to justify militarizing the Cold War. That dangerous development would appall Kennan and alienate him from the Washington policy brokers he aimed to advise.

DOMESTIC PROBLEMS AND THE COLD WAR

Though lauded by the American establishment, Kennan remained an America-skeptic. In earlier years, he had lashed out at the nation's government, commerce, and culture. In 1944–1945, some of that disdain was tempered as he admired GIs liberating and then administering parts of Europe. Moreover, the high-profile, plum positions his manifestoes initially brought him—as deputy commandant at the National War College from September 1946 to May 1947 and then as founding director of the State Department's Policy Planning Staff from May 1947 through 1949—demanded toning down the criticism. Nonetheless, Kennan remained Kennan: impatient with the influence of Congress and the public on foreign policy; unsympathetic toward immigrants, labor unions, African Americans, and women's groups; and fearful that industrialization, urbanization, technology, overpopulation, consumerism, and environmental depredation were destroying the country of his youth.

These feelings about American society predisposed the rising star to see foreign policy dangers as inseparable from—indeed, as a spur to solving—domestic problems. He pressed for rebuilding the economic and psychological strength of Western Europe not only to stem Soviet expansion, but also to buttress U.S. culture with companionate societies. The threat of "penetration" of the West by Soviet-inspired political agitation presented the catalytic catastrophe, the impetus for mobilizing a domestic collectivized effort, that Kennan had been urging since the 1930s. "The issue of Soviet-American relations is in essence," he asserted in his famous "X" article, a test of whether the United States could prove itself worthy. Though dangerous, the Soviet threat merited not complaint or panic but rather "gratitude to a Providence which, by providing the American people with this implacable challenge, has made their entire security as a nation dependent on their pulling themselves together."[3] In an astounding burst of candor, Kennan told military officers that if Communism "had never existed, we would have had to invent it to create the sense of urgency we need to bring us to the point of decisive action."[4] As America's foremost Cold War strategist, he laid out both the rationale and the direction for that action.

Kennan postulated an interlocking set of ideas that shaped Cold War discourse. The first tenet championed containment as the alternative to appeasing or attacking the Soviets. The strategist envisioned that policy not as a global or military initiative, but rather as a focused deployment of political and economic measures to stave off Soviet influence in the industrialized, prize areas of Western Europe and Japan. He saw U.S. military might as remaining in the background as a deterrent.

A second principle emphasized psychology, which meant focusing on appearances and containing excessive emotions, whether by Russians, Western Europeans, or Americans. "It is the shadows rather than the substances of things," he instructed, "which move the hearts and sway the deeds of statesmen."[5] In arguing for "all measures short of war" to block Soviet influence in the West and undermine their control of Eastern Europe, Kennan offered concrete, proactive solutions to officials and the wider public looking for answers. To his later embarrassment, such measures included covert actions that spun out of control.[6]

A defining irony of these years is that while pressing for coolly rational realism in others, Kennan himself engaged in highly emotional thinking, particularly in matters of great importance to him, such as responding to the Kremlin or seeking union with the Russian people. Nonetheless, Kennan's thinking, like that of all of us, integrated more emotional and more rational thoughts. Even his most emotional impulses followed their own logic and hence are analyzable by historians.

Some of Kennan's basic ideas diverged from the consensus among U.S. officials. Although his period of greatest influence, the late 1940s, coincided with Washington's building the "Free World," he had little interest in such informal empire. He preferred the United States to remain flexible, nimble, and unencumbered in its exercise of power. He focused on strategically important areas rather than the whole globe. He trusted more in political and economic measures than in military might. Skeptical of the efficacy of U.S. institutions even at home, he doubted that Americans had the temperament, the duty, or the wherewithal to fulfill *Life* magazine editor Henry Luce's ambition for an "American Century."

Largely because of these divergences, the strategist managed little more than a year of unalloyed success after becoming Policy Planning Staff director in May 1947. He masterminded the overall strategy of rebuilding the economy of Western Europe through the Marshall Plan. With only a tiny staff, he churned out myriad policy statements, most of which became official policy. His July 1947 article in *Foreign Affairs* widened his fame, especially after the journalist Arthur Krock identified "X." Soon, however, Kennan grew discomfited by the Cold-War fervor that his long telegram and "X" article had helped fuel. As early as February 1948, he was anticipating talks with the Russians—ideally conducted by himself. He envisioned a settlement enabling Germany to reunify, Allied military forces to pull back to garrisons on the German frontier, and Russia to allow some independence in Eastern Europe. He regarded covert operations and black propaganda as fair game in pressuring the Soviets into accepting such a deal. After Dean Acheson became secretary of state in January 1949, however, the Policy Planning Staff lost much of the clout it had wielded under Secretary George C. Marshall. Even as the containment doctrine became the lodestar of U.S. policy, its author sank in influence. Kennan's mood tracked this power trajectory of frustration-satisfaction-frustration. By 1949, he was once again planning to resign.

ANGER AT MOSCOW AND WASHINGTON

Personal as well as political factors spurred Kennan's fury at the Kremlin in October 1944. He concluded, bitterly, that the secret police would not allow him to connect with the Russian people. Also maddening was the cruel ending of the Warsaw uprising as the Germans killed or captured the last of the brave street fighters staving off Nazi tanks. The Red Army, camped just across the Vistula River, had refused to aid these resisters, who had hoped to expel the Germans before the Russians could impose their own domination. Nor did Stalin permit U.S. and British planes dropping supplies to the Warsaw fighters to refuel at the U.S. airbase in Ukraine, inaugurated with fanfare by Ambassador W. Averell Harriman only months earlier. Kennan later pinpointed these developments as justifying a "political showdown with the Soviet leaders."[7] Harriman, "shattered" by the evidence of Soviet designs on Poland, heeded his aide's increasingly hardline advice.[8]

Kennan's narrow focus on the Kremlin's brutality came at a particular moment in the war. He was in Germany and in Portugal in 1941–1942 when German invaders slaughtered, pillaged, and raped Soviet citizens. The atrocities he heard about instead were those perpetrated by the avenging Red Army as it smashed its way to Berlin in 1944–1945. Stalin made no effort to rein in the vilest impulses of his troops.[9] Although Kennan claimed that few Americans "had more intimate knowledge than I of German atrocities," he in actuality had witnessed only the relatively benign German occupations of Czechoslovakia, France, and Holland. He had also heard family stories from occupied Norway. He had not witnessed the Germans' killing of Jews and other civilians on the Eastern front. He argued that by making the Russians allies, the United States had tacitly accepted the brutalities that had prevailed "in Eastern Europe and Asia for centuries in the past." Atrocities, he insisted, were "not the peculiar property of the Germans."[10]

Firsthand stories of outrages by Red Army soldiers circulated in the Moscow embassy as U.S. POWs liberated from German camps in Poland and bailed-out bomber pilots straggled in with tales of horror. Harriman's secretary concluded that "the Soviet troops are behaving like animals or worse." Especially egregious were the mass rapes: "Cases of thirty or forty Soviet soldiers raping one woman and then killing her are common."[11] While Polish villagers, desperate for U.S. support against the Russians, went all-out for American ex-POWs and downed flyers, many Red Army soldiers robbed the Americans' watches and left them to live off the land. Such stories, recounted on frigid evenings around the kerosene stove in the drafty Moscow embassy, had a dramatic impact on Kennan and others. These accounts served to personalize, Americanize, and further emotionalize Russia's seizure of Poland.[12]

Kennan's revulsion at Soviet domination was intensified still further because he viewed it as an extension of the late-1930s purges that had nauseated him: this was yet more cruelty and violence imposed by Stalin's police. Before leaving Washington, he had met with Jan Wszelaki of the Polish embassy. From him Kennan got "the strong feeling" that Stalin's "acute embarrassment" over the Katyn forest massacre and other horrors inflicted on occupied Poland in 1939–1940 had spawned a problem "far uglier and more recalcitrant" than Western governments realized. Regardless of any deal with Roosevelt and Churchill, Stalin simply could not permit Poland to have a government independent enough to protest past Soviet atrocities.[13]

Harriman initially assigned Kennan not to reporting on such political matters but rather to administering the embassy, as he had done in Berlin in 1940–1941. But the younger man's expertise on Russia, proclivity for research, strong beliefs, fierce ambition, and flair for writing propelled him into policy. Harriman later recalled that while his aide was informed on Russian history, he "had very little knowledge of the United States and didn't realize that some of the things that he proposed would be quite shocking." As a consequence, "Kennan was a little upset, I think, that I used to change some of his telegrams."[14] A telling sign that Kennan got more than a little upset was how easily he lost patience as Harriman fiddled with the embassy stove. That would "drive George absolutely up a tree!" a friend later recounted. He would mutter, "'That man doesn't know how to build a fire!,' and it would make him so nervous. His eyes, you know those large eyes, practically popping out of his head."[15] Kennan later disparaged Harriman as "an operator" who assumed his "direct line to Stalin . . . was the only important thing."[16] Yet despite the tension, the two respected each other. After September 1944, Harriman shifted focus from Roosevelt's commitment to postwar collaboration with Stalin to Kennan's more combative stance.

"George has his ups and downs," Annelise reported from Moscow. "There was a great deal of work and things which will upset a nervous tummy."[17] Dorothy Hessman, his secretary, would remember that he had often had to drink milk during the day to soothe his gnawing ulcer.[18] With telling language that linked his body and the body of his deceased mother with the body politic of Russia, Kennan referred to his "time of troubles." The phrase, which famously referred to Russia's near demise prior to the Romanovs' seizure of power, seemed to him an apt description of his health problems, which usually "climax toward the end of

March, and April brings the solution." The implication was that a dark force was condemning him to reenact the illness of his mother during those months long ago. George would indeed die in the month of March, in 2005.[19]

Now, at the embassy, he was pushing himself so hard that "neither Sundays or night mean very much."[20] When he fretted to seven-year-old Joanie that he wasn't "gay enough to make a really good Daddy," she replied: "'Oh, Daddy, that's all right. With a little forcing, it would do. And if you wouldn't work in that office all the time."[21] Despite his strenuous efforts, Moscow remained "full of pitfalls." "A single wrong word—a single mistake" could jinx relations with the "hyper-sensitive" Russians.[22] (A devastatingly "wrong word" would indeed sink Kennan's ambassadorship in 1952.)

As in the 1930s, the isolated diplomatic community turned inward. "It was a tremendously incestuous kind of relationship," Kennan's friend and China expert John Paton Davies, Jr., and his wife, Patricia Davies, recalled. While John compared the atmosphere to "a rather macabre cruise ship," Patricia thought "it was more like a concentration camp." Parties featured dancing to the beat of the "Kremlin Krows" with Kennan on the guitar. (When the Kremlin protested the name, the Americans shot back with a new moniker, the "Purged Pigeons.") The journalist John Hersey, who would win fame for his graphic depiction of the Hiroshima bombing, enjoyed Christmas 1944 with the Kennans. He described George as "bald, very bright indeed" and "generally nice." Annelise appeared "pretty, not as bright as George but lots of fun." A daughter later wondered whether her mother and Hersey were more than just friends. Patricia Davies remembered Annelise as not tremendously popular but rather as respected and liked.[23]

The ample living allowance in Moscow enabled the Kennans to pay down the mortgage on the farm. George looked forward to retiring soon with a pension of about $5,000 supplemented by income from crops plus teaching and writing. But for now he had to survive Moscow.

Years later, John Paton Davies recalled that "Kennan at that time seemed to me to be under a good deal of strain. Certainly I don't think he was happy with Roosevelt's policy."[24] That unhappiness peaked during FDR's last wartime summit, the Yalta Conference of February 1945.

Kennan wanted so badly to take part that he would literally paint himself into the scene. Touring Yalta in the 1970s, he glanced up at the huge tableau of the gathering. He imagined that the depiction of Roosevelt's interpreter, George's friend Chip Bohlen, "looked more like me; I wondered whether they had confused us." Back in the real world of 1945, however, Kennan remained parked in Moscow while "nothing was further from the thoughts of the President and his entourage than to consult me about anything at all."[25] Although the diplomat had demonstrated his expertise to the president during their meetings in 1943 and 1944, Roosevelt had not asked Harriman to bring him to Yalta. Indeed, the ambassador himself was kept on the sidelines. Unlike the British ambassador, Harriman garnered no seat at the conference table, most likely because Roosevelt disagreed with his increasingly anti-Soviet, Kennan-influenced stance.[26]

Kennan resisted the exclusion. Upon arriving at Yalta, Bohlen found an eight-page letter from George astoundingly audacious in thesis and tone. The forty-one-year-old, midlevel diplomat was challenging the four-time elected president. Though protesting that he "neither expected nor hoped" to "have any influence on the thinking" at the conference, that was precisely Kennan's apparent ambition. Some of the letter read like the policy memoranda that he would churn out as director of the Policy Planning Staff. The missive juxtaposed careful analysis with emotional rant.

Kennan was banking on his ties with Bohlen, of whom he later recalled, "I loved him like a brother, without knowing him very intimately, and this is why we argued so." One night they quarreled "into the wee hours of the morning. I went home through the streets just weeping with the anguish of this debate."[27] Despite their differences, these two protégés of Bullitt had bonded over the excitement of Moscow in 1933–1934 and its terror in 1937–1938. Kennan's long-shot hope was that if the summit hit an impasse, Bohlen would circulate his recommendations to Roosevelt's inner circle. That scenario was not totally far-fetched. In the 1943 controversy over the Azores bases, Kennan had impressed both

Harry Hopkins, the president's close adviser, and Admiral William D. Leahy, his chief of staff. Moreover, Bohlen had drawn close to Hopkins.[28] What Kennan evidently did not know, however, was that Roosevelt and Hopkins had grown apart since early 1944. Part of the problem for FDR was that Hopkins was influenced by Bohlen, who opposed collaboration with Stalin if that required sacrificing Eastern Europe. Both Bohlen and Kennan remained close with Bullitt, who was publicly slamming Roosevelt for "appeasing" Stalin.

In the deepest of ironies, Kennan's disdain for Roosevelt as a glib politician and amateur diplomat blinded him from seeing that, despite coming from different directions, they both agreed on how to respond to the thorny issue of Soviet domination of Eastern Europe. When Stalin in December 1941 had proposed to British foreign secretary Anthony Eden a division of influence in postwar Europe, Roosevelt had vetoed the scheme. The president feared that a naked sphere-of-influence deal would alienate the American public. But after the Soviet victory at Stalingrad in early 1943 and the Tehran summit later that year, Roosevelt realized that ceding to Stalin at least temporary domination over Eastern Europe was requisite to postwar collaboration. Moreover, the Red Army was seizing de facto control as it rolled back the Germans. FDR shifted focus to a deal with Stalin and fig-leaf gestures, like the Declaration on Liberated Europe approved at Yalta, to disguise the extent of Soviet dominance.[29] About this cynical though practical approach, Kennan, like others in the State Department, knew little. His experience with Roosevelt's breezy manner still rankled, as did the 1937 purge of the Eastern European Division. Kennan would have agreed with Durbrow's mockingly misogynist assessment of Roosevelt's "Grand Design" as promising that "we're all going to be girls together."[30]

Like the long telegram and the "X" article, the letter to Yalta grabbed attention with scary language and sweeping claims. Lest he be dismissed as just another anti-Soviet State Department bureaucrat, Kennan started off: "Please do not get me wrong. I do not mean to say that the Russians have any sinister aims." He then depicted those aims as indeed sinister. He portrayed the Soviet Union not as an ally and potential postwar collaborator, as Roosevelt believed, but rather as an alien, heartless menace. The Kremlin cared nothing for "Western values, either spiritual or material." Worse, it would spare "no evil" in trying to wreck Europe's cohesion, balance, and moral integrity. Left unmentioned was the Nazis' devastation of the Soviet Union and Stalin's determination to use Eastern Europe as a barrier against yet another invasion from the West.

Kennan ignored such defensive imperatives to represent Russia as the inveterate aggressor. It loomed as a "jealous Eurasian land power always seeking to expand westward," threatening the "stable, self-respecting," commerce-oriented states on the Atlantic rim. The language evoked frightening stereotypes: emotional, barbaric "Eurasia" imperiled the rational, civilized West. Kennan was conjuring a Russian menace both mechanistic and excitable. Negotiations with the Russians were supposedly fruitless since their harsh climate, limitless plains, and Mongol heritage rendered them extremists contemptuous of compromise. Such dire determinism echoed Kennan's lectures at Bad Nauheim and to the Foreign Service recruits in 1938.

Missing was any mention of U.S. and British predominance in the richest nations of liberated Europe: France, Italy, Belgium, and the Netherlands. Moreover, Allied military might was rising as General Dwight D. Eisenhower advanced, despite the Germans' last gasp defense at Ardennes, into the industrial heartland of the Reich.

Instead, Kennan, echoing Bullitt, assailed Roosevelt's "weak," "ineffective," and "unsound" policies. Charging, mistakenly, that FDR and his advisers were wandering about with their "heads in the clouds of Wilsonian idealism," he failed to see that the president was trying to avoid Wilson's errors. He dismissed as bumbling what was actually Machiavellian. Roosevelt, while selling the American people on the idealistic, one-nation, one-vote UN General Assembly, was himself focused on the more cynical, big-power arena of the UN Security Council. Foreshadowing the long telegram, Kennan repeatedly used the evocative word "penetration" to describe the Russians forcing themselves on other nations. His Eurocentric focus ignored the life-and-death importance of enlisting the Red Army in the bloody invasion of Japan. (At this point even the Manhattan Project scientists remained unsure whether they would produce a usable atomic bomb.) He charged Washington with cravenly abandoning Eastern Europe even though it had little leverage there. The vehemence of Kennan's criticism indicates the depth of his frustration and resentment. Surely Bohlen could not show these particular passages to the president or his circle.

After slamming Roosevelt for "wishful thinking" about collaborating with Stalin, Kennan pushed for a policy that, paradoxically, matched that of the president: dividing "Europe frankly into spheres of influence—keep ourselves out of the Russian sphere and keep the Russians out of ours." While the diplomat advocated making that deal explicit, the politician understood that such cynical understandings had to be tacit, lest the American people reject the peace settlement, as they had done in 1919.[31] Although neither Kennan nor Roosevelt understood or appreciated the other, by 1945 they had converged on the primary postwar challenge of U.S. foreign policy. Kennan's long-shot hope was that in a deadlocked conference, Bohlen might urge on Roosevelt Kennan's proposal to formally divide Europe. Roosevelt, however, never heard about Kennan's idea. Nor would he have risked repeating Wilson's mistake of reaching a peace that the American people would reject. Rather, the old fox preferred ambiguity and deception.

A month after Roosevelt died, on April 12, 1945, Kennan immersed himself in that "pulsating warmth and vitality" of the Russian people—but only for a brief, tantalizing day. May 9, Victory in Europe Day in Russia, found Harriman away in Washington and Kennan in charge. A massive crowd of cheering Muscovites gathered around Spaso House, the residence of the U.S. ambassador. Kennan ordered a huge Soviet flag to be hung next to the American banner. "This produced new roars of approval and enthusiasm," he later recalled. Then the lanky diplomat clambered out a first-floor window and onto the pedestal of one of the great columns that lined the front of the building. He addressed the crowd in Russian: "Congratulations on the day of victory. All honor to the Soviet allies!"[32] With that, all barriers seemed to fall. An embassy official weighing some 240 pounds was hoisted off his feet by cheering Russians and passed atop the sea of shoulders all the way across Red Square, and then back again, without his feet touching ground. Another colleague of Kennan's would never forget the euphoria and rapport, "the

Russian people being absolutely uninhibited about the contacts" with Americans as they surged through the embassy. Well into the evening one could find "Americans and Russians together in virtually every, every apartment."[33]

On the next day, however, the secret police resumed their vigilance, and such contact ceased. Also brought back to grim reality, Kennan penned two essays that he deemed so significant that decades later he would include them in his published memoir.

ANALYZING RUSSIA

"Russia's International Position at the Close of the War with Germany" (May 1945) reiterated Kennan's view of Russia as both expansionist and susceptible to U.S. pressure. He repeated his warning that Russian psychology drove the Soviet Union toward seeking "complete mastery of the shores of the Atlantic and the Pacific." What the Soviets already controlled burdened them with what Edward Gibbon had termed "the unnatural task of holding in submission distant peoples." Adding to the problem was that Soviet leaders had forfeited their "moral dominion over the masses." The people's "most intimate hopes, the finest ideals" were "no longer the Kremlin's to command."[34]

The diplomat claimed that he could look not only into the Russian soul, but also into the minds of Stalin and his henchmen. Eight times in a single paragraph he repeated the phrase "the Kremlin knows." The Kremlin "knew" that Roosevelt had bamboozled American opinion into expecting either war or "intimate collaboration" with Russia. Stalin would lever these expectations into economic aid and moral support. American aid was helping in "the establishment of Russian power in Eastern and Central Europe."[35] What frustrated Kennan was that while so much stood at stake in terms of Washington's policy, he remained stranded and voiceless in far-off Moscow.[36]

While this May 1945 essay laid out Kennan's need to reconnect with Americans, his June memorandum, "Trip to Novosibirsk and Stalinisk," illustrated how he engaged with Russians. He had long dreamed of retracing the Siberian journeys of the first George Kennan, a father figure.

In the vast hinterland, Kennan could mix with Russians relatively free of official duties or the secret police. Indeed, the police seemed more help than hindrance, as on his pilgrimage to Tolstoy's estate in 1935. In mingling with ordinary Russians, George attired himself like a pre-1917 squire. He enjoyed a plane ride with "a little old working woman" who displayed the "pungency and charm" of those "who had never known the printed word." During a layover, they sat on the grass as he shared his picnic lunch and read to her from Tolstoy's *Peter the Great*. Soon he had half the passengers gathered around. "I felt immensely at home among them," he sighed.[37] As a secretary later recalled, Kennan "liked to have disciples—people who would sit at his feet."[38] He found it "pleasant and homelike, if slightly vulgar" to saunter with a group of Russians through town "spitting the husks of your sunflower seeds philosophically before you as you walked." I could "almost forget that I was a foreigner in a country governed by people suspicious and resentful of all foreigners."[39]

Kennan empathized with peasants and workers. He was pained by the deprivation of "the widows and war-cripples, the crowded homes, the empty cupboards, the thread-bare clothes," the suffering and death stemming not just from the German invasion but also from the purges, famine, and civil war before that. He admired these downtrodden people for their "wistfulness, hope, and irrepressible faith in the future."

Nevertheless, despite his sympathy for ordinary Russians and his identification with nineteenth-century gentry, Kennan could also fit into the Soviet elite. He admired how the Party apparatchik, Borodulin, brandished his authority "in wangling a room with four beds for the two of us" while expelling needy others. A secret police woman, "associated herself with Borodulin and me as the most privileged and influential element among the passengers." During a layover, she rustled up a scarce car and a driver to show them around. On a boisterous night out on the town, Borodulin and Kennan barged through the side doors of several theaters, commandeered the government box, and then routed out of bed "a very mussed and sleepy station master" for a tour of the rail station. Kennan's recounting of this experience spoke volumes: "For one lovely evening I was, to all intents and purposes, a member of the Soviet governing elite."[40]

Returning to Moscow in a Lend-Lease cargo plane, the diplomat, sitting on his suitcase, tried to discern "some sort of pattern" out of his jumbled, deeply felt impressions. It was like the summer of 1938 in Washington, when he had struggled to impose orderly calculation on the trauma of the purges. No matter how much Kennan tried to segregate his yearning, elation, and frustration from his notions of rational foreign policy, emotional responses would suffuse his overall conclusions.

Kennan's Siberia report revealed the apparent pathways of his thinking. He admired the Russians, not least for the healthy dose of Eros that fueled their creativity. This "gifted, appealing people" had proven themselves through suffering. Their hardships had purified them "of so much that is vulgar and inane in the softer civilizations." Russians displayed the sexual vitality of "a virile, fertile people." While mourning the idealistic Bolsheviks slaughtered by Stalin, he admired those Russians still intent on building "a decent, rational society." Such people, "capable of absorbing and enriching all forms of human experience," figured as natural partners to Americans such as himself, yearning for contact and the opportunity "to feel themselves helpful to others."

Then, abruptly, this indulgent longing, like his February 1935 cry in the hospital, was reined in by the internalized taskmaster. "But the fact is: there is no way of helping the Russian people.[41] With this re-imposition of determinedly rational constraints, with Civilization disciplining Kennan's own Eros, his conclusion jerked from soulful perception to state policy. Stalin and Molotov were just then appealing to the new Truman administration for a huge economic reconstruction loan to be repaid with raw materials, a deal that Roosevelt, his Treasury Department, and a number of corporate titans had favored. The exchange would link the postwar U.S. and Soviet economies. Kennan, however, was encouraging Harriman to overload the loan by demanding that in return, the Soviets pull back from Eastern Europe. When the representative of a major U.S. manufacturer of ball bearings came to Moscow to scout out postwar sales, Kennan challenged him on "whether it was wise to make all the latest American inventions available to the Russians."[42]

It was in this context, absolutely crucial for future U.S.-Soviet relations, that Kennan arrived at his reasoning for why the welfare of the long-suffering Russian people should figure neither in his conclusions nor in those of Washington. "The benevolent foreigner cannot help the Russian people; he can only help the Kremlin." Moreover, "he cannot harm the Kremlin; he can only harm the Russian people." Stalin's regime would use any economic aid for its own purposes while deflecting onto the people any imposed sanctions. "With the sights and sounds of Siberia still vivid" in his imagination, Kennan vowed to resolve the dilemma of yearning/frustration by imposing on himself a rational analysis entailing distance and isolation. He would leave Russia and ratchet down the emotions. He recommended much the same for U.S. policy. America should "leave the Russian people—unencumbered by foreign sentimentality as by foreign antagonism—to work out their own destiny in their own peculiar way."[43]

Kennan shared his Siberia report with his British friend and colleague, Frank K. Roberts. Roberts agreed that U.S. economic assistance should now flow to Western Europe rather than to the Soviet Union. "The U.S. Santa Claus could sit back" and wait for the Russians to come, hat in hand, to him. Roberts endorsed Kennan's notion of economic exchanges with the Soviet Union on the basis of "tough and hard-boiled bargaining" rather than on "one-sided help from sentimental or frightened" allies.[44] Over the seven months from the Siberia report to the long telegram, Kennan's low-key distancing would ratchet into high-pitched containment.

Two days after her husband finished his homage to Siberia, Annelise, visiting her family in Norway, cautioned him that "going with a longing in you for another country makes it impossible to be happy anywhere else." While referring to her own preference for America over Norway, she may also have been thinking about George's passion for Russia. Probably remembering her husband's affairs in Berlin, she fretted about his being "all alone" in Moscow. (A lesser problem was that color-blind George wore "the darnedest getups." Embassy colleagues noticed "weird shirts going with the ties and the socks."[45]) Annelise cautioned George to "have a good time, but not so good that you forget all about your 3 girls who love and miss you so much." She could not help but ask: "What do you do with yourself?" George had pushed her buttons by suggesting that she stay in Norway for a while; then, months later, the whole family would return to America. "It seems unwise to go in for another long separation when it isn't necessary," she countered.[46] Annelise insisted on returning to Moscow. There she was further peeved when Supreme Allied Commander General Dwight D. Eisenhower, on visiting the Soviet capital, requested that she arrange a dinner party for Kay Summersby, his intimate companion.[47]

In August 1945, Kennan, frustrated by his isolation from both the ordinary people in Moscow and the policy makers in Washington, sent the State Department a letter of resignation. He confided to Matthews the "impelling personal considerations" as well as his "deep sense of frustration" about both the fecklessness of U.S. policy and the "helplessness" of career diplomats.[48] To Jeanette, he affirmed: "We all dream of the day when we can get away from here and back to the farm."[49] He was reading the East Berlin, Pennsylvania, newspaper cover to cover and devouring the back-to-the-land primer *The Egg and I*. Planning to live off of his pension, farming, and teaching, Kennan was pleased that Bullitt was arranging a job for him at the University of Pennsylvania.[50] Teaching and writing would enable him to influence public opinion, he hoped. In the end, however, he did not resign.

The State Department, aghast at losing Kennan's expertise as Washington and Moscow butted heads over Eastern Europe, Germany, and China, dangled yet another promotion while appealing to his sense of duty. The assistant secretary in charge of administration penciled on an internal memorandum, "I want to do everything for George Kennan that we can possibly do."[51] Kennan would remain in Moscow until April 1946.

The rising star was developing into America's preeminent Russian strategist. Having already offered to resign, he felt freer to say and write as he pleased. With some Americans talking about a war with Russia, Kennan felt impelled to speak out. Since Harriman was away at conferences, he could cable Washington on his own. He could advance from the day-to-day running of the embassy, as he had done since July 1944 and as he had done for Kirk in Berlin in 1940–1941, to proposing policy to Washington. No other foreign diplomat in Moscow could match

Kennan's experience, knowledge, and passion. He towered as "a giant among the dwarves."[52]

He attracted a coterie of fans. William A. Crawford, a young Foreign Service officer, still "very wet behind the ears" admired Kennan as not only modest but also "very charming, sensitive, intellectual." George held "informal little confabs" to guide the newcomers' thinking. He advised them to undertake their own specialized research projects, much as he had done in the 1930s. "We got a lot of personal, personal attention, and you felt a very close relationship to him," Crawford would fondly remember.[53] The British political philosopher Isaiah Berlin, then a young diplomat, met Kennan in late 1945. He was astonished that his new friend seemed so much "more thoughtful, more austere, and in a way more melancholy" than other Americans. Berlin pegged George as a "monarchist" with a "rather White Russian point of view."[54]

As tensions between Washington and Moscow mounted, the approach to Eastern Europe that Kennan had advocated in his January 1945 letter to Bohlen—in effect, why don't we just turn over the whole damn thing and wash our hands of Eastern Europe?—and his advice to indulge in neither sentimentality nor antagonism toward the Russians were growing irrelevant.[55] Kennan, irritated with both Washington and Moscow and anxious to make his voice heard, was also adopting a harder line. By the time Truman sent Harry Hopkins and Bohlen to Moscow in May 1945, Hopkins had dropped FDR's policy of downplaying the explosive issue of Poland. In talks with Stalin, Hopkins, backed by Bohlen, Harriman, and Kennan, hinged U.S.-Soviet relations precisely on Russia's making concessions regarding its control over Poland, Germany's invasion route into Russia.[56]

Frustrated with the Kremlin's rigidity, Kennan likened dealing with the Russians to playing a slot machine. As he explained to a British diplomat, "We put our penny in the slot by asking for what we want, the wheels go round, and then we either get our bar of chocolate or draw a blank." Too often we get no answer at all. He was coming to the conclusion that we needed "to bang the sides of the machine so as to shake down one's chocolate."[57]

No matter how much Kennan hardened toward the Kremlin, he could not prevent Russia from melting his heart. A visit to Leningrad in September 1945 felt "like coming home." The hardship suffered by this great city, like that endured by his shaded walnut saplings planted in 1944, yielded value and meaning suffused with wonder. Leningrad packed the allure of a place "where the spark of human genius has always had to penetrate the darkness, the dampness, and the cold." Yet for that very reason, the city had acquired a strange and intense beauty.[58]

As the scope of U.S.-Soviet relations withered, Kennan's focus on contact—which touched on core American values about the free association of goods, ideas, and people as well as the traditional Open Door foreign policy—moved to the center. In the context of policy debates going back to the late 1930s, this development marked the triumph of the Kennan-Bohlen-Henderson perspective, which emphasized how the Kremlin treated Americans residing in Russia, over the Roosevelt-Davies-Messersmith thesis, which focused on the geostrategic considerations making Russia a natural ally of America. That Germany and Japan no longer figured as dangerous foes of the United States allowed this personal aspect of the Open Door to come to the fore.

Kennan's frank dinner conversation with a Soviet official in November 1945 underscored how, in his view, the entire U.S.-Soviet relationship hinged on the contact issue. Surely, he argued, it was in Moscow's interest to ensure that those "foreigners who were honest and well meaning were treated as they would be anywhere in the world." Washington's relations with London were smoothed by the frank talk among diplomats and by the thousands of marriages between GIs and British women. These couples constituted a formidable lobby for good relations. In contrast, only about a dozen American service men had married Russian women, and several of these wives had been forbidden permission to leave with their husbands. U.S.-Russian relations also suffered from the absence of tourism and from the restrictions on the casual mingling that Kennan had so enjoyed in Siberia. Unmoved, the otherwise friendly official insisted that Soviet citizens needed to approach contacts with foreigners with "the greatest caution," adding that while good diplomatic ties seemed difficult, they were by no means impossible. Kennan came away convinced that the impasse over contact made friendly relations indeed impossible. That conviction had been burned into him by the purges. As long as the secret police dominated "the personal life of Russian citizens" and remained "hostile to the outside world . . . I do not see how any real stability can ever be introduced into our relations."[59]

Soviet-American squabbling at postwar conferences held in San Francisco, Potsdam, and London boosted his authority. "Whatever Kennan says carries great weight in the State Department," affirmed Secretary James F. Byrnes. Roberts, number two in the British embassy, remembered that "George was the great expert" on Russia, "and I benefitted enormously from this."[60] Isaiah Berlin admired the focus on "attitudes, ideas, traditions"—in sum, on "mentalities."[61] Kennan's informal seminars widened his influence while enabling his "blowing off steam."[62] Not everyone, however, bought into his teaching. The Canadian ambassador observed that Kennan "suffers from having been here in the pre-war days when foreign representatives became indoctrinated with anti-Soviet ideas as a result of the purges and subtle German propaganda."[63]

In December 1945, Kennan helped kill the last gasp of Rooseveltian diplomacy, Secretary Byrnes's compromise deal at the Moscow foreign ministers conference. Kennan feared a portent in Byrnes's arrival in Russia. Lost in a blizzard, the plane skimmed treetops searching for familiar farmhouses and then landed at the wrong airport. The South Carolinian emerged wearing a light coat and no overshoes. Standing in deep snow, he made an opening statement swallowed up by the howling wind. Awaiting the arrival of Byrnes, Bohlen, and State Department official H. Freeman Matthews, Kennan grew "thoroughly enraged." He was steaming at Moscow's "insulting, total isolation" of diplomats as well as Washington's seeming indifference to such indignities. He despised Byrnes as a naïf seeking "*an* agreement" to curry favor from what Kennan mistakenly believed was a still pro-Soviet American public. By contrast, Molotov, "eyes flashing," a cigarette dangling from his mouth, bet like the "passionate poker player who knows he has a royal flush."[64]

Kennan undermined what he despised as Byrnes's feckless diplomacy. "Matthews looked so crestfallen at the things that he had heard from Roberts and myself I felt sorry for him," Kennan recorded. He was frank about the shock strategy that would prove so effective in the long telegram. In introducing "newcomers to the realities of the Soviet Union there are always two processes; the first, which is to reveal what these realities are and the second, which is to help the newcomer to adjust himself to the shock."[65] From such adjustment arose much of Kennan's influence.

Although Byrnes secured significant agreements in Moscow, he was soon repudiated by Truman. The president was irked at his secretary of state for grabbing the spotlight and keeping him in the dark. Congressional opinion was also turning against the Soviets. On January 5, 1946, Truman bluntly announced that policy was changing. "I'm tired of babying [the] Soviets."[66]

THE LONG TELEGRAM

Unaware how rapidly U.S. opinion and policy were souring on Russia, Kennan in January 1946 decided that he should return to the United States and dedicate his "authority, objectivity and courage" to enlightening the American people about the dangers posed by the Soviet Union. In December, Bohlen and Matthews had urged their friend not to do anything foolish.[67] They advised him to ask for a paid home leave, relax at the farm, and then talk things over at the department. Implied was the prospect of a position with greater authority.

Frustration with both Moscow and Washington probably aggravated Kennan's health problems. To soothe the burning pain of his ulcers he was injecting himself with vitamin C as well as with larostidine, shipped from New Jersey.[68] He sipped milk throughout the day. In February, he came down with the grippe, which in the "sunless and vitamin-less environment" of Moscow was hard to get over, "especially when demands of work leave no time for leisure or relaxation." A junior colleague observed "George feeling very, very low."[69]

In response to this intertwined political, psychic, and physical crisis, Kennan reverted, it appears, to a long-standing behavioral pattern. When as a boy George was forbidden to play outside in the afternoon, he would revenge himself by staying inside all morning as well. Similarly, if vacations from military school were not warmed by "understanding and sympathy," especially from some pretty girl, he would refuse to socialize at all. If denied succor and inclusion, he would, he later recalled, deepen the deprivation and thereby exact "retribution." Let those responsible "feel his bitterness." "He had his pride. They could bend it but they could not break it. And let them pay for their folly in bending it. A martyr he was, and a martyr he should remain, to the end of his days."[70] As a middle-aged man, he reaffirmed: "If I cannot have all, or the greater part, of what I want most desperately, no one is going to deprive me of the glorious martyrdom of having none of it at all." Rather proud of what he termed this "neurosis," he noted that "my father was much the same way."[71]

It was, then, not just his strategic and emotional concerns about the expansion of Stalin's police state but also his practice of seeking "retribution" and "martyrdom" by widening the breach and deepening the pain that impelled Kennan to urge containment of Soviet Russia. Containment meant many things. Among them was his saying, in effect: let those in the Kremlin who kept him from the people and culture he loved "feel his bitterness" and "pay for their folly." If Kennan could not engage freely with Russians, he (and by extension the United States) would almost totally disengage from them. If Soviet authorities wanted to cut him off, he would push for an isolation more extreme than anyone imagined. Kennan wanted Washington to contain the Kremlin, which had so cruelly contained him. His long telegram would single out as the "most disquieting feature of diplomacy in Moscow" the foreigner's isolation from ordinary Russians and from Soviet policy makers, whom one cannot "see and cannot influence."[72]

In actuality, however, Kennan's argument about the Soviets being impervious to influence ignored recent experience. Roosevelt, Churchill, and Harriman had met with Stalin, who, especially in his "Uncle Joe" persona, had indeed been influenced to make significant agreements.

Moreover, even amidst deteriorating relations from 1945 to 1949, Stalin repeatedly signaled that his aims remained limited and that he was open to compromise. Rather than having a master plan for domination, the dictator often seemed unsure how to proceed. Stalin preferred post-war collaboration with Washington and London, especially to head off renewed aggression by Germany or Japan. He withdrew Soviet forces occupying the strategic Danish island of Bornholm. He initially permitted free elections in Hungary and in Czechoslovakia. He refused to aid the leftist partisans in Greece and discouraged the large Communist parties in France and Italy from seizing control. The dictator permitted Finland to retain a significant degree of independence. Stalin did insist on Soviet control of Poland, the corridor for yet another German invasion. And he kept a tight rein on East Germany. But he allowed four-power control to operate in Austria. Stalin would back down after the Berlin blockade to permit renewed access to West Berlin.[73]

Although by 1948 Kennan would propose serious negotiations with the Soviets, in 1945–1946 he firmly opposed such talks. He believed the Russians, overconfident after their victorious march into Eastern and Central Europe, first had to be deflated and disciplined by isolating them and containing any further attempts at expansion.

In urging the containment doctrine, Kennan fused personal and political preferences. He accorded to old habit by sharpening a painful situation. His emotion-infused reasoning jumped from accepting (or, more precisely, resolving to accept) that personal contact with the Russian people was cut off to deciding that political contact with Soviet leaders would be, and should be, also cut off. America's strategist was in effect embracing and extending the Kremlin's regime of isolation. Containment offered a rationale and a strategy for Washington to shift from trying to compromise with identifiable Kremlin leaders to blocking every move of an implacable and impersonal nationalist/ideological force.

"He wasn't feeling well at the time. . . . he was having problems with his ulcer . . . he always was drinking milk . . . and so he just closeted himself off for a couple of days in his apartment in bed"—so Crawford would remember the origins of the long telegram.[74] On Washington's birthday, February 22, 1946, Kennan's aggravation, ailments, and aspirations—his personal and political imperatives—came together in cable number 511. At 5,540 words, it remains the longest telegram ever sent to the State Department and the most consequential document of George's career. As it was the Friday of a holiday weekend, Kennan's secretary "wasn't all that thrilled" at being summoned to his apartment. She found him lying prone but eager to dictate. He thought better in a horizontal position, he explained. Hours later, Kennan ordered the clerk in the code room: "This has to go out tonight." "Why tonight? I've got a date," she protested. He insisted.[75]

The cable had been instigated by hardline colleagues in the State Department, principally Matthews and Durbrow. They knew that their proud friend, furious at both the Soviet and U.S. governments, was "boiling with moral indignation," as Berlin later put it.[76] Meanwhile, on February 9, 1946, Stalin had given a major address lauding Marxist ideology while glossing over U.S. and British assistance in the war. The State Department, in prodding Kennan for his analysis of the speech, anticipated "a real deep one, one of his better efforts."[77] An aide later explained that "Washington wanted George to assemble his concepts in some kind of a 'think piece' that could be used in promoting [a] stronger line toward the Soviets."[78]

He did not disappoint. The long telegram invoked, in the name of realism, a fantastic scenario in which the Soviet Union loomed as an inhuman force, without morality, unable to appreciate objective fact or truth, and pathologically compelled to destroy almost every decent aspect of life in the West. Russia was again, as in the sixteenth century, under the thumb of "Asiatic" tyrants. After inflating this existential threat, Kennan in his conclusion tried to reassure. He emphasized that the Soviet Union did not want war, differed from Nazi Germany, remained weaker than America, and could be contained without war if the United States and Western Europe instituted reforms. Indeed, heading off talk of an inevitable war was part of the motivation for advocating containment. Yet it was not the late-coming assurances, but the scary depiction of the Soviet threat and Kennan's militarized language that resonated in Washington. The Kremlin was "impervious to logic of reason and . . . highly sensitive to logic of force," Kennan insisted.[79] Not surprisingly, U.S. officials concluded that containment mandated a military buildup.[80]

In his July 1947 "X" article, Kennan again depicted the Kremlin as unapproachable—indeed, as an insensate piece of metal: "a persistent toy automobile wound up and headed in a given direction, stopping only when it meets with some unanswerable force." Containment was necessary because the Soviet-other was not only unfeeling but also, contradictorily, prone to hyperemotion. His doctrine would checkmate dangerous Soviet emotions and the aggression they provoked. While painting this somber picture, Kennan held out the possibility of a brighter future—and of renewed contact with the Russians. Containment would "promote tendencies which must eventually find their outlet in either the break-up or the gradual mellowing of Soviet power."[81]

In keeping with his decade-long critique of U.S. society, Kennan concluded both the long telegram and the "X" article with calls for domestic reform. "To avoid destruction" by Russia, "the United States need only measure up to its own best traditions." Echoing comments going back to the 1930s about the utility of catastrophe, he affirmed that Americans should welcome the Soviet challenge as a prod for "pulling themselves together."[82] He countered the Communists' thesis with the premise of his favorite Russian writer, Anton Chekhov. The basic problem was not that capitalism inevitably exploited workers, but rather that the "advanced urbanism and industrialism" of both capitalism and communism exploited nature as well as human beings.[83] In sum, Kennan's urging of containment reflected not only pushback against Soviet expansion, but also long-standing impulses and concerns: his passion for the Russian people, resentment of Soviet repression, propensity for self-punishment, professional ambition, environmental concern, aspiration to reform U.S. society, and faith that U.S. interaction with Russia, whether hostile or friendly, could spur needed change in America.

For the rest of his long life, Kennan would combat the widespread conclusion that containment necessarily entailed a military buildup and possibly a military confrontation. He would protest that he had intended containment as a primarily political policy to be applied by adroit diplomats. Nevertheless, despite his caveats in the long telegram and in the "X" article that the Soviets lacked a fixed timetable and did not intend military aggression, most observers concluded otherwise.

Within a year of the greatest war in history, Kennan presented the Soviet Union as another existential threat. Not surprisingly, most Americans assumed a military response was again necessary.[84]

IMPACT OF THE LONG TELEGRAM

Bohlen underscored the immediate impact of the long telegram by shutting down debate within the State Department. Gone was the "need to go into any long analysis of the motives or the reasons for present Soviet policy." Instead, "we can take as accepted the principle" that the United States faced "an expanding totalitarian state" convinced that "the world is divided into two irreconcilably hostile camps." Bohlen depicted the Soviet offensive as two-pronged: first, the "use or threat of Soviet armed force" and, second, the deployment of "political psychology." Therefore the United States had to build up its military and reach out to Western Europe.[85] Thus from the start and even with Kennan's closest associates, the long telegram helped militarize the Cold War.

The Truman administration broadcast the manifesto as the rationale for its ongoing policy of countering and isolating Russia. The document circulated throughout the War and Navy Departments as well as to diplomatic posts across the globe. The Kremlin obtained a copy through its spy network. Henry Norweb, Kennan's former boss in Lisbon and now the ambassador to Cuba, celebrated the best political reporting he had ever seen, this "masterpiece" of "realism devoid of hysteria." "Astonishing!" embassy staff gushed. "This is an answer to prayer."[86]

The triumph changed Kennan's life. "My voice now carried," he exulted. "My reputation was made."[87] Two decades earlier, George, pushed by his then-fiancée, Eleanor Hard, had aspired to becoming "both respected and powerful," to "make the very pillars of the State Department tremble, as I walked through the ringing corridors."[88] Now those corridors did reverberate with his words. While the astounding success of the long telegram assured Kennan a place in history, it also added another layer of tragedy to that story.

Kennan had overreached. He mobilized his talent for emotion-evoking prose, his expertise on Russia, and his ease with pop psychological discourse to fashion a narrative so persuasive that it would dominate U.S. foreign policy for the rest of the Cold War and beyond. For the rest of his life, Kennan would chip away in vain at the edifice he had hardened. In the long telegram and in his "X" article, Kennan simplified to the point of distortion the challenges presented by the Soviet Union. The Russians, in their own brutal way, were asserting victor's rights after their grueling slog to Hitler's Berlin. Though the Soviet Union had extended its reach into Central Europe, it remained only a regional power that had suffered terrible wartime devastation. While Communist ideology was attractive to many in restive Western Europe, the decision to abandon capitalism for socialism would be made, if at all, by the people of France or Italy, rather than by a Soviet invasion. Kennan realized that the Kremlin represented a political and ideological rather than a military challenge to Western Europe and hence to the United States. Nevertheless, he allowed his frustration and ambition to conjure up a Soviet menace so existentially frightening that his manifestos would assume a life of their own. The long telegram, along with the "X" article the following year, helped create the monster of a militarized Cold War. Though Kennan would combat this beast for decades, not until nearly the end of his life did he acknowledge his responsibility for having helped create it.

With Kennan's voice now echoing throughout official Washington, his private voice went silent. No longer did he write wrenching, revealing letters to Jeanette. The Department of State supplanted the devoted sister. Nor did Kennan keep up the diary begun as a young boy. Entries for 1946 included mostly reading or lecture notes, while that for 1947 consisted of only a single page of verse on human mortality. Serious diary-keeping would commence again only in 1949, when Kennan once more met frustration in influencing policy. And what of his hitherto persistent dilemma pitting Eros against Civilization? Absent letters to Jeanette or diary pages with confessional fantasizing or guilt, it is difficult to determine whether that battle abated. While George agonized about an affair in 1942 and another in 1951, he remained silent about such dalliances in the decade in between. Mandatory family weekends at the farm precluded some opportunities. Kennan also worked long hours during the week. Nevertheless, George, still in his early forties, remained a good-looking man with star appeal, Washington was filled with adoring women, and foreign travel afforded other possible occasions. Grace would muse that her parents decided to have another child, after a lapse of thirteen years, probably in order to shore up their marriage. Christopher James Kennan would arrive on Thanksgiving Day in 1949.

RETURN TO THE UNITED STATES

"I am really tired," Kennan confessed shortly before returning to the United States in May 1946.[89] He nevertheless then pursued a hectic schedule. Top officials, including Admiral Chester W. Nimitz and General Carl Spaatz invited him to lunch to tap his expertise on Russia. He was called in to consult with the forerunner of the CIA. Top universities and the Council on Foreign Relations clamored for lectures. He pushed himself, excited about the opportunity to reach "large numbers of influential people."[90]

Most influential was secretary of the navy and soon-to-be secretary of defense, James V. Forrestal. In this self-assured, ultimately self-destructive man, Kennan found another powerful mentor who, like George C. Messersmith in Berlin, William C. Bullitt in Moscow, and Alexander Kirk in Berlin, utilized the younger man's talents for their own agendas while also boosting his career.[91] Forrestal, a former Wall Street banker, feared Roosevelt's efforts to get along with Stalin were naively opening the door to global Communism. He embraced Kennan's long telegram and made it required reading for top officers in the armed services. Forrestal shepherded Kennan's recall from Moscow and appointment at the new National War College, which he had helped birth. He also instigated Kennan's subsequent appointment by Secretary of State Marshall to head the Policy Planning Staff. Kennan later testified that the first draft of his "X" article was written not for publication but "merely for the private edification" of his booster. Moreover, the scope of the final essay reflected in part "what I felt to be Mr. Forrestal's needs at the time when I prepared the original paper for him."[92]

Though proud of his independent judgment, from 1946 to 1949 Kennan also bent to the prevailing winds to advance his career. He endorsed more militant actions against the Communists than he later wanted to admit. If America's premier expert on Russia wanted his voice to carry in the atmosphere of a worsening Cold War, he could not speak directly into the storm. He probably convinced himself that he was doing the right thing. After all, the sooner containment brought the Russians to heel, the sooner Washington might move on to negotiations with Moscow. Cruising on the Potomac aboard Secretary Forrestal's luxurious yacht no doubt helped put such priorities into perspective.[93]

THE NATIONAL WAR COLLEGE AND THE POLICY PLANNING STAFF

In late July 1946, the State Department dispatched its rising star on a speaking tour across the western United States. That September, Kennan, appointed as deputy commandant at the National War College in Washington, began lecturing there. In May 1947, Secretary of State George C. Marshall named Kennan the founding director of the Policy Planning Staff. The last was George's dream job: overseeing the entirety of U.S. foreign policy. His reputation continued to climb. When Dean Acheson, who would later replace Marshall as secretary of state, informed a colleague that Kennan had just become the Policy Planning Staff director, the official commented that "a man like Kennan would be excellent for that job." Acheson snapped back: "A man like Kennan? There's nobody like Kennan."[94] George loved the prestige. For the rest of his life he would remember how at the War College military heroes of the recent war and cabinet officials, including Forrestal, "used to come and listen to me."[95]

The praise could not, however, totally eliminate the self-doubt. "What eats on me particularly," he confided, was that "what I now know is . . . a chance aggregate of odds and ends, gathered without system."[96]

By reading extensively, writing lectures, and talking with colleagues at the War College—as well as drawing on his own long-held beliefs—Kennan organized those odds and ends into a comprehensive explanation of the Russian problem. He offered cogent answers at a scary time when Americans sought explanations, reassurance, and a path forward. He insisted that the United States could build up the "Free World," ignore the Kremlin's complaints, and still avoid war. In Kennan's system the Russian people figured as attractive but unreachable, the Soviet government as aggressive but anxious, the American public as good-hearted but naive, and the U.S. government as powerful but poorly organized. He warned against the dangerous legacy of President Franklin D. Roosevelt's policy of cooperating with the Soviets. He expected the international crisis would force Americans to address their internal problems. He even hoped that the Russian people would end up benefiting from the contest. These interlocking emotional and rational arguments, packaged with characteristic rhetorical flourish, helped construct the ideology of the Cold War.

Kennan's first principle held that war, especially in the atomic age, had grown too dangerous. His lectures at the War College explained how "measures short of war," such as psychological and political pressure, could contain the Soviet Union. To back up such ventures, the United States needed to sustain military predominance. While some later scholars labeled these principles "Grand Strategy," Kennan himself urged coherence in strategy while advising, "drop the word 'grand.'"[97]

A second tenet was tamping down emotion on all sides while trusting in psychology. By 1945, psychiatry had soared in prestige in the United States, particularly in treating soldiers suffering battle fatigue and in explaining the supposed neuroses of many women. Kennan had read Freud in Vienna in 1935 and remained close with his Freudian-minded medical physician, Frieda Por. (He had also helped her emigrate to America, where she would become the family doctor.) He had befriended the master's daughter, Anna Freud, while in London in 1944. There was even a remote family tie: Annelise's sister's husband's mother had lived with Anna Freud as a couple.[98] While faulting psychoanalysis for excusing personal failings, Kennan nonetheless clung to Freudian tenets as a scientific explanation of human behavior, including his own.

He applied pop psychology to the postwar mess. Western Europe suffered problems more psychological than economic, namely "maladjustment, bewilderment, bitterness and disillusionment." Modern war, Kennan explained, amounted to "an emotional debauch always followed by terrible hangover." The French, by voting in large numbers for the Communist Party, were displaying a neurotic "flight from freedom," even "nostalgia for the German occupation."[99] He depicted the "heart and soul of our policy" as restoring not a balance of power, but rather a "balance of vitality, hope, confidence."[100]

He warned Americans against pining for collaboration with Russia or despairing about inevitable war. "There must be no threats and no waving of clubs" by Washington. Instead U.S. leaders had to act "quietly and flexibly, with subtlety and sophistication." Though wrenched by his own feelings and dangerously adept at arousing the emotions of others, Kennan argued for calm in confronting the Kremlin.

He went further by claiming that he could diagnose the supposed mental problems of the Soviet Union. Depicting Soviet mentality as "frightfully complicated," the would-be analyst asserted that "Russia is at least a dual personality and sometimes I think quadruple or more."[101] Psychological discourse removed relations with Moscow from the realm of popular judgment—where some Americans favored cooperation and others believed a war necessary—and placed it in hands of such presumed experts as Kennan. Like a psychiatrist, U.S. policy makers had to exercise "understanding, firmness, and patience" in leading their patient toward objective "realizations and recognitions." He positioned himself as the doctor prescribing for a difficult patient: "I do not want him to be pampered. I do not want his worst traits pandered to." Having thus psychologized and personalized the Soviet challenge, Kennan admitted: "It is complicated for me by the fact that I like the Russian."[102]

His thinking also reflected the concept of an inveterate struggle between Eros and Civilization. Whenever U.S. society failed to uphold the order and discipline of civilization, that is, when Americans suffered "indecision, disunity and internal disintegration" that weakness sparked an "exhilarating effect on the whole Communist movement." America's crumbling energized the Communists' creativity. Kennan warned that with every evidence of U.S. problems "a thrill of hope and excitement goes through the Communist world; a new jauntiness can be noted in the Moscow tread . . . and Russian pressure increases all along the line in international affairs."[103]

Policy boiled down to psychology. Containment meant reining in the emotions of "fanatics . . . not amenable to reasonable argument." While the Russians complained about atomic-armed America, it was really "themselves and their own backwardness that [they] fear." Soviet leaders, perversely rejecting the friendship of America, cast Washington as an enemy in order to justify domestic repression. Such neurosis could not be relieved by U.S. concessions. Indeed, generosity would only strengthen "the most arrogant and impossible elements in Russian psychology." Yet the foe was perversely also hyperrational. "The Russian is by nature a master psychologist, calculating and cynical in his judgment of others." While Roosevelt had struck deals with flesh and blood leaders, Kennan shifted the arena to dealing successfully with a difficult psychological pattern.

LECTURE TOUR IN THE WEST

Intent on the "creation of an informed public opinion" regarding deteriorating relations with Moscow, the State Department sent its star Russian expert on a lecture tour of western states. Kennan saw his mission as getting ordinary Americans to adopt "a calmer, more realistic, less extreme and less alarmist view of the tensions." Having lived most of his adult life in Europe, Kennan now crossed the Mississippi River for the first time.

His subsequent report to the department revealed as much about Kennan as it did about his audiences of businessmen, women's clubs, academics, and foreign affairs associations. Reflecting his underlying notions about the natural feelings and thoughts of men and women, Kennan categorized those responses along a male-female axis. He assumed that masculine men tended toward rational thinking, while women, feminized men, "do-gooder" groups, and children inclined toward emotional thinking. These assumptions reflected his upbringing in the largely patriarchal culture of early twentieth century America as well as his impatience with amateur foreign policy strategists. He reiterated his old complaints about the dangerous influence of unde-serving women. His most successful talks were given to "stag gatherings of businessmen," who were consistently "friendly, curious, and anxious to be enlightened." He linked masculinity with rational thinking. The businessmen displayed "clarity of thought," "realism in judgment," and understanding about political conflict. In contrast, women's clubs and foreign affairs associations viewed international issues as "a form of es-cape from the boredom, frustration, and faintly guilty conscience" that afflicted those with too much time on their hands. To such people Rus-sia looked "mysterious and inviting, with just enough of wickedness and brutality to complete the allure." Focus on Russia enabled them to avoid such pressing domestic difficulties as "race problems, labor problems, or slum control." Finally, high government officials—Kennan tiptoed around a direct attack on the hallowed deceased president—had as-sured them that collaboration with Russia was key to world peace.

Far from offering an escape, dealing with Russia demanded a masculine-inflected approach of "setting will against will, force against force, idea against idea." Kennan illustrated the gendered polarity of his thinking by contrasting the *Milwaukee Journal*'s "hard-headed and grate-ful" male staff with the League of Women Voters, who represented "nei-ther the brains nor the power" of the city.

San Francisco offered a distasteful mix of woman-like frailties, small-minded cowardice, and outright disloyalty. He complained that a cen-tral organization sheltered "under its maternal wing" groups that "cramped my style" with their "wary, pussy-footing" responses. Stanford and Berkeley professors displayed the "jealousies and inhibitions, and the cautious herd-instinct" that typified college faculties. Even worse were signs of "direct Soviet interest and of real Communist activity." The professors appeared "easy meat for Soviet agents," while atomic scien-tists from the Livermore laboratory worried about atomic war seemed as politically "innocent as six-year-old maidens."

The lecture tour ended on a masculine high note. In Los Angeles, he encountered "a rough-and-ready lot, mostly oil men, retired army offi-cers, etc., untouched by liberalism." They "expected a real speech. So I shed my coat and let them have it, and they seemed pleased." He enjoyed upending the image of State Department officials as "spats-wearing and tea-drinking persons out of touch with the real problems of the world."[104]

Kennan's lectures helped form the Cold War consensus. That ideological project required delegitimizing President Roosevelt's policy of seeking collaboration with Russia. The smearing of former Vice President Henry A. Wallace as pro-Communist greased the way for this attack. Wallace, a left-leaning Roosevelt loyalist, was openly challenging both Truman and the emerging Cold War. Using Wallace as the whipping boy, Kennan distorted FDR's legacy. In actuality, Roosevelt had operated as a cynical practitioner of *realpolitik*, a juggler who kept multiple policies in play, and a tough global strategist. Kennan, however, recast Roosevelt as a weak, emotional, feminized naïf controlled by public opinion and fearful of the Russians. The wordsmith understood that slogans shaped perceptions and hence policy. The "Solidarity of the Big Three" boosted by Roosevelt was rejected by Kennan as a "Russian propaganda line." He charged that vanity had driven Roosevelt to expect "the golden touch of his particular personality" to charm the "firm," "stern" ideologues in the Kremlin. Although FDR had shown Stalin personal respect and had offered him a hardheaded deal, Kennan dismissed the late president's efforts as humiliating "gestures of sheer appeasement."[105]

Even as Kennan insisted on a cool, calculated policy toward the Kremlin, he indulged his own passion in astonishing ways.[106] On December 10, 1946, he was asked at the last minute to speak informally to spouses and other guests at the War College. In this cozy atmosphere, Kennan not only bared his innermost longings, but claimed they were shared by the foe. The nation's foremost Russian strategist assumed a Russian persona.

He discerned "a national loneliness," a yearning by the Russians to connect with the outside world (matching his yearning to mix with them). Gratitude for wartime help from the West had "sunk deeply into Russian minds" along with "a dim thrill of hope and excitement about more contact." The Kremlin's crackdown on such association had poisoned its relations with the Soviet people. He used a favorite metaphor: "It was like a woman who had been romantically in love with her husband," but had grown disillusioned. Though they did not divorce, "the honeymoon was definitely over." The Russian people yearned for a meaningful exchange with America. Though he did not explicitly say it, he longed to consummate such interaction.

Positioning himself and the Russians in a *mise en abyme*, a double-mirrored communication, Kennan assumed the perspective of the Russians while having them voice his concerns. "The Russian people are powerfully inclined to admire us," he claimed. To the probably astonished guests, he asserted that the Russians "wish in their heart of hearts that they could be proved wrong in their skepticism about us," that we would "have the answers which they so desperately need."[107]

Kennan then reiterated his core conviction: the showdown with the Soviets would actually be waged in the American homeland. "The Russians, I can assure you, have never been a menace to us except as we have been a menace to ourselves." Seeing America "through Russian eyes" had convinced him "that we cannot escape" dealing with "these failings which the Russians have detected in our society." He explained that "the real threat to our society, the threat which has lain behind the Soviet armies . . . will not be overcome until we . . . purge ourselves of some of our prejudices, our hypocrisies, and our lack of civic discipline."[108] He had railed about such failings in the 1930s, and he would continue to do so in the future.

Kennan may have revealed himself so openly because he was, uncharacteristically, content. "You'd be amazed, what seems to be coming my way," he boasted to Jeanette shortly after the informal talk. "Very flattering and unsolicited personal letters" arrived from top universities. As an undergraduate, he had agonized over whether he fit in at Princeton. Now, decades later, came fulsome approbation from the university president: "I can't tell you how happy we should all be to have a Princeton man spearheading our work here in Russian studies."[109] Not to be outdone, the State Department offered another promotion and a hefty raise to $15,000. The director of the forerunner of the CIA appointed him "Special Consultant for Intelligence." Kennan felt he had hit the jackpot as a Russian expert.

Yet not everything or everyone pleased him. Liberal intellectuals he dismissed as having sunk "below criticism." America's emotional strength could buckle in a crisis, for the nation was weakened by "so much immaturity," so many "artificialities in manner of living," and such "lack of humility and discipline." He hoped the challenge of containing the Soviet Union would compel Americans to deal with those failings.

Moreover, his ulcers were gnawing at him, and he wondered "how long I can keep this ball rolling." Nevertheless he "loved the game."[110] Intellectual stimulation at the War College tasted "like manna" after the bland "philistinism" of foreign posts. Fitting in with the combat-hardened army and navy officers in this first class exhilarated him. "These people respected me," he later remembered. "They were very responsive to the lectures. They loved them. I loved them." He appreciated that his students "are all going out into policy making jobs . . . their influence will be tremendous." He also enjoyed the support of Jim Forrestal, the soon-to-be-named secretary of defense who had commissioned the "X" essay. Decades later, Kennan's biographer would observe of 1946–1947 that "he always smiles when he mentions that year."[111]

Family and farm life also gratified. Courtesy of the War College, the Kennans lived in a 200-year-old redbrick, white-columned house on "General's Row" with top brass as neighbors. "My mother liked it as it came complete with army household help," Grace would later recount. George appreciated that the military commissary served to "considerably reduce the cost of living." Weekends they spent in nearby Pennsylvania. To fourteen-year-old Grace, "the farm was simply work, work, and more work." Weekend guests were not exempt. She recalled her mother's saying brightly, "'Today I thought we would paint the garden furniture' . . . and sophisticated Washingtonians would pick up paintbrushes and develop major sunburns." George, believing physical labor a key to health, threw himself into gardening, construction, and overseeing farm operations. Annelise appreciated that she had her husband to herself—and away from the adoring women haunting weekend parties in Washington.[112]

Physically exhausting but satisfying work projects were transforming a rundown Pennsylvania farm into the Kennan homestead. The Kennans'

FIGURE 24. Kennan balanced his heavy workload in the State Department with strenuous labor on the farm in East Berlin, Pennsylvania. (Courtesy of Princeton University Library.)

own Cherry Orchard afforded not only exercise, escape from Washington, and encounters with nature but also connection with Russia. The very first line of their Farm Diary, dated May 21, 1946, set the context: "Arrived from Moscow." Such Moscow veterans as Elbridge Durbrow, Charlie Thayer, Tommy Thompson, and the British diplomat John "Jock" Balfour, along with their families, visited on weekends. No doubt they talked about Russia around the fire, as they had in the Moscow embassy. For what Kennan called Operation Workshop, he dug the foundation and then enlisted the former *New York Times* bureau chief in Moscow to help build the walls. The weekend before a major speech at Yale, he wrote the talk, shooed wayward cows out of the vegetable garden, and planted strawberries. The farm was rejuvenating but not isolating. East Berlin was close enough to Washington that Kennan could drive in for lunch with General Dwight D. Eisenhower or an overnight with General Alfred Gruenther, the War College's commander. The Gruenthers weekended at the farm before returning to Washington with Kennan for the opening of the college.[113]

"X" AND THE POLICY PLANNING STAFF

Kennan's ascent into the foreign policy elite took off with his January 1947 talk to the prestigious Council on Foreign Relations in New York City. He laid out his stock analysis. Marxist ideology was crucial in justifying the Kremlin's cruelty, belief in the ends justifying the means, and lack of restraint. Also formative were Russia's extreme climate, limitless plains, the past rule of the Mongols, and the messianic belief in Moscow as the "third Rome." The government's xenophobia frustrated the people's desire for outside contact. As a consequence, "the Kremlin had lost control of the soul of the Russian people." While Soviet leaders were "fanatical," there was "no cause for despair," for time was not on the Soviet side. As for remedies, he cautioned against both a "get-tough policy" and the "glad hand and winning smile" approach of Wallace, standing in for Roosevelt. He urged instead a "dignified and self-assured position." If contained, the Soviets would mellow over time. When that happy day arrived, "no one will be more grateful than the Russians themselves."[114]

Listening to the animated speaker were major titans of finance, the law, and journalism. The bankers Frank Altschul and R. Gordon Wasson would support Kennan's future career as a scholar. It was to Wasson that he would dedicate his first scholarly book. Also impressed was Arthur H. Dean, a leading corporate lawyer who would later negotiate the Korean War armistice. Hanson W. Baldwin, chief military reporter for the *New*

York Times, and Joseph Barnes, foreign affairs editor of the *New York Herald Tribune*, would relay Kennan's ideas to millions of readers. Also present were Harold Sprout and Grayson Kirk, prominent in foreign and military affairs. Michael T. Florinsky and Geroid T. Robinson wrote on Russia. Though he impressed this sophisticated group, Kennan also met pushback. (He could not blame women since the council's audience included none.) An expert on the Russians challenged the assertion that they were disillusioned with their leaders. Another questioned the extent of antiforeign sentiment. A State Department official pointed to the Soviets' eagerness to improve relations with the Western democracies in the lead-up to the war.[115]

Overall, though, Kennan held his own. Even as critics disputed this or that point, no one proffered an alternate thesis. The self-reinforcing loop of Kennan's ideas, expertise, and appealing personal manner constructed a convincing discourse. With tensions between Washington and Moscow worsening, the Soviet Union appeared more the dangerous adversary than the difficult ally. Better to be safe than sorry. Finally, Kennan's promise of an eventual happy solution, even for the chastened Russians, enhanced the appeal of his containment thesis.

The greatest boost to Kennan's influence came from Hamilton Fish Armstrong, the exquisitely connected editor of *Foreign Affairs.* He invited Kennan to write an article for his prestigious journal. The State Department gave its okay as long as the author would be listed as anonymous "X." Busy writing lectures at the NWC, Kennan submitted a version of the piece he had done for Forrestal. Hamilton praised the essay for marrying "objectivity with eloquence." Here emerged the fruition of Kennan's decades-long ambition to instruct "an informed public" on the complexities of foreign and domestic problems.[116]

"X" cast his iconic article as a "psychological analysis" of the "political personality of Soviet power." Shaping this collective psyche were the Marxist-Leninist ideology, the compulsive cruelty of an insecure dictatorship, the need for a foreign enemy, and the legacy of Russian extremism. Kennan mocked as dangerously irrational and naive those Americans who, like the unmentioned Roosevelt, would "leap forward with gleeful announcements" that the Russians had changed and that we could get along with them. He made such deal-making seem utterly unrealistic by depicting Soviet leaders as inanimate forces impervious to persuasion or compromise.

Success depended on reining in the feelings of both America and Russia. Washington needed to remain "cool and collected" as it enforced a "long-term, patient but firm and vigilant containment" of Soviet expansion. Americans had to refrain from "outward histrionics" and "threats or blustering."

Here at long last, and with the perverse spur of hostility rather than amity, was the beneficent Russian-American exchange Kennan had dreamed of. Ten or fifteen years of this stern, masculine-coded regimen would "force upon the Kremlin a far greater degree of moderation," thereby promoting "either the break-up or the gradual mellowing of Soviet power."[117] Calibrated discipline from Washington would liberate Russia while tightening up America.

After becoming the founding director of the State Department's Policy Planning Staff in May 1947, Kennan kept the unit small and the discussion under his control. Robert Tufts, the economic specialist, later recalled that "Kennan was a very dominating personality, and he certainly led these seminars. The rest of us kept our remarks much briefer." Ware Adams, an expert on Europe, described how "we'd all gather around the table, and George would start talking. And often none of us would say a word. And he, by watching us, seemed to know just what we were thinking." Looking for nods or frowns, "George would understand immediately, just by the appearance." Whether it was around a conference table in the State Department or on a streetcar in Moscow, Kennan trusted his ability to discern feelings. After such meetings, the director would "decide that the time had come to write the great paper," Paul M. Nitze, a personal friend and later a policy rival, would remember. Kennan would disappear into the Library of Congress with his secretary, Dorothy Hessman, and dictate the document. A week or so later, he would come back with the finished paper. "He'd let us read it, but certainly wouldn't listen to any criticism of any kind." This was "his creation. He'd done his work, and he wasn't going to change it, no matter what anybody thought about it."[118]

FIGURE 25. Kennan, relaxed and clearly in charge of his Policy Planning Staff.
From left, Bernard Gufler, George Butler, Kennan, Carlton Savage, Harry Villard,
and Ware Adams. (Courtesy of Princeton University Library.)

During the glory years of 1947–1949, Kennan crafted a remarkably influential series of papers that outlined policies for the United States across the globe.[119] The most consequential initiative fed into Secretary of State George C. Marshall's famous speech at Harvard on June 5, 1947, which pledged U.S. aid to jumpstart economic recovery in Europe.

The very next weekend, George's longtime friend the British chargé John "Jock" Balfour visited the farm. As they installed a new trough in the pigsty of the barn and uprooted docks near the farmhouse, Kennan explained the projected Marshall Plan to Balfour. The American stressed that the specific details had to come from the Europeans, who should meet and then outline their joint requirements. This was necessary to blunt Communist propaganda that the Europeans "were allowing themselves to become the tools of American imperialists."

FIGURE 26. Kennan in 1947 as America's top expert on Russia.
(Courtesy of *U.S. News & World Report.*)

At this pivotal juncture in early June 1947, Kennan himself seemed poised between the containment that he, as "X" in *Foreign Affairs*, would urge only weeks later, and the engagement alternative that he would entertain in 1948 and embrace for the remainder of the Cold War. On Saturday evening, Kennan assured Balfour that the State Department favored Britain's "promoting commercial relations with Poland and other Eastern European countries, including the Soviet Union itself." Indeed, anything "to break down the barriers of trade between the East and the West was entirely welcome" to Washington. By the next morning, however, Kennan had reconsidered such immediate engagement with the Communist nations. As the two friends were digging in the garden, Kennan, "apropos of nothing," Balfour later reported, suddenly charged the British with being "unduly hopeful of improving relations with the Russians." When Jock protested, George repeated his criticism of "your tendency to a mistaken approach."[120]

Though not always consistent, Kennan prided himself that his ideas reflected a no-nonsense realism. In his short book *American Diplomacy*, published a few years later, he would contrast that realism with senti-mental, legalistic moralism, which, he charged, had hobbled earlier U.S. policy.[121]

Nevertheless, feelings figured prominently in Kennan's work as Pol-icy Planning Staff director. He "was never able to detach himself emo-tionally from the issues we had to consider," recalled Dorothy Fosdick, the only woman on the staff. She added that he "was the prince, and we were the advisers to him." George "could go into a bad slump when he thought he was not being listened to."[122]

President Truman listened to neither Kennan nor the rest of the state department when he recognized the independence of Israel in May 1948. In Policy Planning Staff papers, Kennan had warned that supporting the partition of Palestine and encouraging the migration of Jews into a por-tion of that territory would result in "deep-seated antagonism for the U.S. in many sections of the Moslem world over a period of many years." Further, conflict between Jews and Arabs in Palestine might provide an opening for Russia to send peace-keeping troops. Such Soviet forces threatened "an outflanking of our positions in Greece, Turkey and Iran."[123] For Kennan, these geo-strategic concerns were not balanced by sympathy with the project of creating a homeland for people so re-cently victims of the Holocaust. A residue of the anti-Semitism that he had earlier imbibed in Milwaukee, Princeton, Riga, and Berlin would persist throughout his life.

Kennan owed his perch atop the State Department bureaucracy to support from both Forrestal and Secretary of State George C. Marshall. That prop cracked when Dean Acheson replaced Marshall in Janu-ary 1949 and Forrestal resigned as defense secretary two months later. Along with others in the Truman administration, Acheson increasingly appreciated that with the Soviet Union as a permanent menace, West-ern Europe, especially West Germany, had little choice but to huddle under the U.S. umbrella. Through the Marshall Plan, the North Atlantic

Treaty Organization, and the never-ending planning sessions, conferences, and exercises these institutions entailed, the United States was
acculturating its allies and shepherding them into an informal empire.
Washington was also covertly funding anti-Communist parties and
labor organizations in France and Italy. Thus were the "Free World" and
the Soviet bloc coalescing into two imperial regimes that, despite their
mutual hostility, contained the rivalries that had sparked two world
wars. Although Kennan was instrumental in setting up the Marshall
Plan and initially active in planning covert activities, he, unlike Acheson
and most other U.S. officials, also worried that Western Europe was
becoming dangerously dependent on the United States and divided
from Eastern Europe.

THE CIA

The most controversial and ultimately embarrassing aspect of Kennan's
career as a Cold Warrior was his push for covert actions to undermine
Moscow's control of Eastern Europe. He intended to carefully ratchet
up the pressure so that the Soviets would accept a negotiated pullback
from their overextended empire. In September 1947, as a secret consultant to the CIA, he urged setting up, with airtight deniability, a covert
"guerrilla warfare corps" to operate in the Soviet satellites. In a May 1948
Policy Planning Staff paper, the strategist proposed a comprehensive
program of political warfare that included "liberation committees" to
focus "national hope and revive a sense of purpose among political refugees from the Soviet World." Other initiatives included clandestine
radio stations for "penetrating the iron curtain," heading off sabotage in
friendly nations, and, more audaciously, launching covert actions in the
Soviet bloc. Afraid that such operations conducted by the covert Office
of Policy Coordination (OPC) could get out of hand, Kennan insisted
that one person "must be boss," answerable to the secretary of state.[124]
Clearly he had in mind either himself or someone close to him. Although Kennan later downplayed his association with the controversial
OPC boss, Frank Wisner, the two men and their families remained
close. Indeed in 1958, when the Kennans' daughter Grace decided on a

FIGURE 27. Kennan in his State Department office. (Courtesy of Princeton University Library.)

large wedding even though her parents remained in Oxford, the Wisners graciously hosted the affair at their home in Washington. Kennan at times was guilty of faulty judgment, as when he supported Operation Fiend, a harebrained scheme in 1949 to air drop anti-Communist nationals into Albania. Betrayed by Soviet agents, the anti-Communist Albanians were executed as soon as they landed.[125]

Years later, Kennan would rue his role in promoting covert activities as "probably the worst mistake I ever made in government."[126] But in 1947–1948, with U.S. power and his influence at their peak, Kennan got swept up in the Cold War fervor. Overconfident that he knew what the Soviets would likely do, and what the Truman administration should do, he pushed almost any measure short of war. He succumbed to the romance of cloak-and-dagger, the opportunity to indulge in the secret dealing that he had enjoyed in Lisbon in 1942–1943 and had gotten a taste for while working for Messersmith in Berlin in 1931. The sad irony was that while seeking to pressure Moscow into negotiating a mutual pullback from Europe, he succeeded only in escalating tensions.

MOVING PAST CONTAINMENT?

Kennan's eagerness for talks was underscored in a major foreign policy review delivered to Secretary Marshall on February 24, 1948. The timing was significant. Only six months had elapsed since the "X" article. A prevaricating Congress had not yet passed the Marshall Plan bill, and it would not do so until April. The Communists still hoped to win the pivotal April 18 Italian elections (a contest that they would ultimately lose, in part because of Kennan's role in directing covert intervention). Nonetheless, in February the strategist was already anticipating a chance to negotiate a tacit deal with Stalin. Irrepressible desire to reconnect with the Russians, even the hated leaders in the Kremlin, was, it seems, conditioning his policy recommendations. He predicted that after aid started flowing, the Communists lost the Italian election, and confidence in Western Europe rebounded, "the Russians will be prepared . . . to do business seriously with us about Germany and about Europe in general." As Kennan knew, the Soviets worried about U.S. and British plans to combine the three zones of western Germany into an economic powerhouse. Moscow feared that a reborn Germany might tap America's nuclear power in seeking revenge. Although Kennan in 1945 had favored the division of Germany, by 1948 he worried that establishing West Germany would permanently split Europe. That would postpone indefinitely the withdrawal of Moscow's troops, the liberation of the Soviet satellites, and the easing of the Cold War.

Relying on his intuition, Kennan affirmed that the Russians "are conscious of [the potential for serious negotiations] and are making allowances for this possibility in their plans." Though the United States could not accept a formal sphere-of-influence deal, Kennan believed Washington could convince the Soviets that it was in their own interest to "reduce communist pressures elsewhere in Europe and the Middle East." We would then "withdraw all our armed forces from the continent and the Mediterranean."[127] While it remains unknowable whether Stalin would have accepted such a deal, the dictator was signaling that he wanted to head off the rise of a U.S.-supported, revenge-minded West Germany.[128]

Kennan argued that such a momentous deal demanded "secret and delicate" talks with Stalin. (Although he did not draw the analogy, this approach, greased with Rooseveltian charm, had been FDR's tactic with the dictator.) In effect nominating himself for this breakthrough diplomacy, he stressed that the negotiator needed to be someone who knew Russian and was familiar with Soviet philosophy and strategy.[129] Dealing one-on-one with the Kremlin boss was what he had been preparing himself for since the 1920s. Whatever understanding the negotiators reached could not be written down, he believed, nor could it include China, engulfed in civil war. But in terms of easing tensions in the hot spots of Europe and the Mediterranean, the proposed deal was breathtaking in its audacity.

Misjudgments and bad faith doomed the initiative. In May 1948, Stalin infuriated Kennan by not only publicizing the scheme but also offering to negotiate in the open with Henry A. Wallace, the left-wing Progressive Party candidate for president. The Kremlin chief was calling for talks, but not confidentially and not with Kennan. A stickler for traditional secrecy and protocol, the strategist concluded that by going public, Stalin was displaying contempt for the possibility of diplomacy. Decades later, he still recalled being "very much upset that the Russians responded as they did."[130]

Kennan's back-and-forth turmoil over the East-West conflict surfaced in a rambling letter to Walter Lippmann, the respected columnist who had sharply criticized him. His official position and his outrage at the Kremlin positioned him as a Cold Warrior. "Remember, these people are our enemies," he reaffirmed. This was the conventional, tough point of view that he advanced out loud and in public. And yet George fervently hoped for an accord. The "Russians will want to talk to us, sooner than many of us suspect," he wanted to believe. This was the quieter, more private stance. He reconciled these conflicting viewpoints with the notion that hounding the Kremlin with all "measures short of war" could spur them to negotiate. But as Kennan himself liked to say, the means shaped the ends: Cold War pressures prolonged the Cold War.

Nonetheless, he fantasized how he, personally, would settle the conflict. "I would be willing to let bygones be bygones," he declared. With further "I" statements, he elaborated: "I would be willing" to extend economic aid if Moscow ceased threatening America. And "I would be prepared for . . . a permanent stabilization" between "Soviet totalitarianism and Western liberalism." Then, following a lifelong habit, he harshly disciplined his fantasy: Any such deal was doomed, because the Soviets aimed to destroy "the soul of the Western world." The fantasy, however, defied repression. He could not help but add that just in case the Russians, bending to pressure, *did* pull back from Eastern Europe, "I would make their retirement as easy as possible for them."[131]

In contrast to Acheson, Nitze, and others who regarded the Cold War as dangerous but useful and stabilizing, Kennan saw the conflict as dangerous, unnatural, and inherently unstable. While they viewed relations with Moscow as largely frozen, he regarded them as always malleable. In September 1948 in the midst of the Berlin crisis, Secretary Marshall invited a wholesale review of U.S. policy. Kennan informed the panel that with regard to the moderation or demise of Soviet power that he had predicted in the "X" article, the possibility now seemed more real than it had in 1947.[132]

GERMANY

Seeking to ease rather than exploit the division of Europe, Kennan disputed the drive for a separate West Germany. He worried that "the danger of continuing Germany divided is that it formalizes the German split and the split formalizes the east-west break." That meant that Poland and other satellites would have to escape from the Soviet system not only economically, "which in certain contingencies they might be able to do, but escape wholly and enter into the Western security system." Only a total collapse of Soviet power or a war, he warned, could force such a humiliating defeat. Hamilton Fish Armstrong, a member of the review panel, expressed the doubt held by many: "Would the united

Germany which would result from a negotiation with Russia be one which we really preferred to a split Germany?" Kennan, with a world view still influenced by the pre-Nazi era, did prefer a reunited, independent Germany.[133]

Indeed, Germany remained a touchstone for him. George spoke and at times dreamed and thought in German, which he had learned as an eight-year-old boy in Kassel. That was two decades before he studied Russian in Berlin. Kennan's clandestine meetings in 1940–1941 with the aristocratic Nazi resister Helmuth von Moltke had profoundly moved him. The day after the Nazi surrender, he nominated his friend as a possible leader of postwar Germany. But von Moltke had been hanged by the Nazis after a failed assassination attempt on Hitler. Kennan then turned to rescuing the Russian-born German diplomat Gustav Hilger, a frequent guest at the American dacha outside Moscow in the 1930s and an interpreter at the negotiation of the Nazi-Soviet pact in August 1939. The CIA valued Hilger as "a living encyclopedia on Russia and Russians." Stalin vouched that "German heads of State and German ambassadors to Moscow came and went—but Hilger remained."[134] Although it remains unclear how much Kennan knew about his friend's activities in the war, Hilger was complicit in German war crimes on the Russian front and had aided in the internment of Italian Jews. In 1948, Kennan vouched for Hilger's expertise and urged that the CIA bring him and his family to the United States. He then hosted his old friend at the farm.[135]

Kennan believed world dominance pivoted on which side controlled German industry and organization. "In combination with Germany, Russia is the greatest of world powers," he warned. But "without Germany she is seriously outclassed by the Western world." By contrast, Asia, the focus of U.S. agitation in the wake of Mao Zedong's October 1949 victory in the Chinese civil war, meant little to Kennan. Even if Russia conquered all of the largest continent except for Japan, it would "still only be a giant with feet in the mud."[136]

In the long run, Kennan calculated, neither America nor Russia could stop the dynamo that had nearly won two world wars. "We are trying to contain both the Germans and the Russians, and I don't think . . . we are strong enough to do it." The Germans needed a wide outlet for their energies. Reunification seemed desirable and probably inevitable. Kennan did hope to stave off a separate German army. That would lead "right back to about 1933." The Germans would "start chiseling, and what they openly have will serve as cover for what they secretly have." The economic and political resurgence of Germany, however, he saw as a solution rather than a threat. When some in the State Department questioned the wisdom of "making it easier for the Germans to dominate" Europe again, Kennan rejoined that no other Europeans had "enough energy and gumption" to take the lead.

"It often seemed to me, during the war living over there, that what was wrong with Hitler's new order was that it was Hitler's." Amid the Allied bombing and blockade, the Germans had "kept production up very well, and they managed to get food distributed pretty well." If not militarily defeated, "they would have made a go of it." At a time when Washington officials debated how to deal with the "dollar gap" that is, Western Europe's inability to earn enough dollars to pay for its imports from the United States, Kennan again pointed to the wartime achievements of Hitler's planners. They had "come very close to making Europe self-supporting." He thought it worthwhile "studying the German experiments." As for the future reintegration of central Europe, "the Germans know more about how to handle such problems—in Czechoslovakia, Yugoslavia and Poland—than we do."

Kennan envisioned an independent Germany that would "gather around [it] the sort of in-between countries of Europe." The Germans would reestablish a balance by building "something antagonistic to the Russians and ourselves perhaps."[137] That would restore Europe's independence from both Moscow and Washington.

Kennan differed from Acheson and the many others who embraced the opportunity afforded by the Cold War to enfold Western Europe and other regions into the "Free World." He doubted that the United States possessed either the temperament or the wisdom to foster democracy in western Germany. America's "vision was clouded by our habits, our comforts, our false and corrupting position as conquerors and occupiers."[138] Empires inevitably unraveled, he believed, regardless of whether they were held together by tanks or dollars, led by Moscow or Washington. While realizing that an economically and politically powerful Germany might build an army, he accepted the risk.

What Kennan envisioned, then, was a return to the international regime prevailing during his years in the Baltics and in Berlin. In the late Weimar era, Germany under Gustav Stresemann was expanding its economic influence in central Europe while using diplomacy to dismantle the Treaty of Versailles. In the post–World War II era, Kennan would never accept the Cold War order as permanent. Ironically, his nostalgia for a bygone era gave him the independence of mind to posit an alternative to the dangerous status quo of the Cold War.

Reconnecting with his prewar roots in Germany also inspired Kennan's lifelong disgust with war. Visiting Berlin in 1949 overwhelmed him with "the immensity of its ruin."[139] Still more disturbing was the destruction of his beloved Hamburg, where over 75,000 civilians had perished in the Allied firebombing of 1943. There welled up "an unshakeable conviction that no momentary military advantage, even if such could have been calculated to exist, could have justified this stupendous, careless destruction of civilian life and of material values."[140] He resolved to oppose any mass bombing, whether with conventional or atomic weapons.

Kennan reached this conclusion about the bomb only months before the Truman administration, shaken by the Russians' explosion of an atomic device in August 1949, decided to build "the Super," a hydrogen bomb far more powerful than the Hiroshima weapon. That decision was not the only one alienating Kennan from Acheson and most others in the administration.

EASING THE COLD WAR

In contrast to 1946–1947 when he had depicted the Kremlin as an inexorable danger, Kennan now argued that the Soviets were "'grinding themselves into the ground' even without pressure from outside."[141] Gibbon was proving right. Empires, whether centered in Rome or Moscow, overextended themselves and then frayed. "Every day that goes by,"

Kennan assured planners at the Pentagon, "the people in Eastern Europe hate the Communists worse."[142] Danger threatened not from the calculated aggression of Kremlin leaders against Western Europe but rather from their emotional overreaction to trouble in Eastern Europe. The open defiance of Yugoslav Communist leader Tito "has really aroused the emotions of the men in the Kremlin in the most extraordinary way, and anything might happen."[143] Washington needed to calibrate containment so as to ease the Russians out of Eastern Europe without a panicky reaction. Finally, while "the Russians conceivably could drop atomic bombs on this country," such an attack ran counter to their interest. Americans and Europeans had to focus on their adversary's intentions rather than capabilities.[144]

Even Communist ideology presented only a limited threat, Kennan now insisted. Marxist-Leninism attracted mostly "intelligentsia" on the "margin of human psychology" with personalities warped by "jealousy, sense of inadequacy and inferiority." The allure was "emotional rather than economic." Kennan exposed his prejudices in his characterization of Communism's appeal as concentrated in "maladjusted groups: in our country—Jews, Negroes, immigrants."[145] With Communist ideology fading even in Russia and with the Kremlin anxious to avoid war, containment seemed nearly achieved. All the more troubling, then, was the Truman administration's globalizing and militarizing what Kennan had envisioned as a limited, political effort.

Also diminishing the relative danger from the Soviet Union was the rising threat from what a later generation would term the Global South. Kennan lasered in on economic inequality as "the most important single fact in our entire foreign policy." Americans had "fifty percent of the world's wealth and six percent of its population." "How long are we going to be able to defend a position that favored?" Desperate Asian nations with exploding populations posed a modern-day Yellow Peril. With "teeth and nails," they were scratching for "the increasingly scarce fertility of the world."[146]

America stood vulnerable because key pillars of society, the family and the local community, were falling. Throughout his adult life Kennan had mourned the loss of his childhood, perhaps because it had not been happy enough for him to let it go. Now, before a War College audience of military officers roughly his age, he opened up by referring to that loss and linking it to societal decline. They stood "only a generation away from the simplicity, the security, the total unawareness of the turn of the century." Modernity had shredded "the Booth Tarkington innocence of the American middle class in the days before World War I," what he romanticized as "the shady streets and the wooden houses and the backyards in which the kids played at cowboys and Indians." He extrapolated from his own past to depict America as a boy who had "suddenly lost his parents." Orphaned, isolated Americans huddled "bewildered and anxious because they are trying to solve as individuals problems which they could solve only by a collective approach." Faith in group rather than individual solutions inclined Kennan toward Russian culture rather than American ways.

Another bedrock belief was in Chekhov's notion that industrialization amounted to a mistake, a misunderstanding that tragically distorted relations among people and with nature. Kennan admired Henry Adams, his turn-of-the-century precursor, who had also faulted the machine, the "dynamo," for destroying the unifying bonds of religion and tradition. The only hope was to regain "social mastery over the run-away horse of technology" by "confining and bending to our will those forces which Adams said are now flinging us about." Out-of-control modernity reared as "the real problem of Western democracy," Kennan now affirmed. Communism figured as "only a complication to the disease," he told the probably startled military officers. Then, to maintain his Cold War bona fides, the strategist quickly added that Communism could become "more immediately dangerous."

Despite this last caveat, Kennan by 1949 was feeling his way toward a radical attack on the Cold War edifice that he had helped lock into place in 1946–1947. In the conclusions to the long telegram and the "X" article, he had linked addressing internal problems to meeting the Soviet challenge. Now he went further by insisting on the primacy of the domestic sphere. "Our real victories" over the Soviet foe, "the ones that really count, and the ones that are going to be decisive, will have to be registered in this struggle within ourselves in our own Western world."[147] America's domestic failings meant that "we are not yet really ready to lead the world to salvation. We have got to save ourselves first." That sober reality should "jolt" those "who talk about this being the American century."[148]

While publicly challenging the American Century—that is, the notion that the United States should dominate and police the world—Kennan privately went further by questioning American democracy. "We are a society which has no control over the direction in which it is moving, socially and technologically," he fretted to Policy Planning Staff colleagues. Imposing such control required "a firm, strong government capable of exerting extensive disciplinary power." Gadgets, machines, and the obsession with "higher wages and more leisure" had "already produced illnesses which can only be cured by a high degree of paternalism. Only some form of a benevolent authoritarianism"—he did not shrink from that phrase—could "restore a framework for healthy and vigorous citizenship." Although Kennan usually prevailed in staff meetings, with this astounding argument "the others largely disagreed."[149]

In other ways, too, Kennan found himself sliding back toward the outsider position that had so frustrated him before 1946. Though his reputation would endure, and he would, to his annoyance, forever be linked with containment, he had become a misfit in the Truman administration. With Acheson at the top, the Policy Planning Staff lost most of its clout over the rest of the State Department. The unit "has simply been a failure," the founding director confided in his diary. He was once again filling that journal, especially with thoughts at odds with prevailing opinion. Reading John Quincy Adams as he surveyed the messiness of managing the "Free World," Kennan longed for "a return to the historic policy of neutrality and isolation." If Washington insisted on playing a global role, officials had to be "thoroughly and severely indoctrinated" in a "firm theoretical groundwork." But since "our present governmental system lacks the disciplinary authority for such indoctrination, it can come really only through an intensive educational effort" directed toward public opinion and the universities. That reasoning spurred his decision to leave the State Department.[150] In September 1949, Kennan asked to step down from the Policy Planning Staff. He planned a study leave for 1950 at the Institute for Advanced Study in Princeton.

Frustration also beset his personal life. In verse he memorialized what was either a fling or a fantasy with a passenger during an overnight stopover in Bermuda. He implored her to share with him "this magic isle." Though the magic was real, it was too fleeting, the woman replied. Each of them had to be "impelled upon his way, aware of loss, but saying 'I must not care.'" Such was "the sadness of a bitter time."[151]

Amid mounting East-West tensions, Kennan clung to his dream of bringing Americans and Russians together. In May 1950, he bared his deepest longings, as he had in his December 1946 speech to guests at the War College and in his October 1944 letter to Jeanette. Refusing to accept the ossifying Cold War as permanent, Kennan asserted that cultural currents could erode even the hardest political structure. He held up the classics of nineteenth-century Russian literature, music, and ballet as "phenomena in Russian life which speak with tremendous power and meaning to the American perception." They spark "wonder and excitement at their scope and boldness and emotional intensity." Through the medium of emotion, the "experiences of the Russian people" could speak to what Americans "are now experiencing, and are yet to experience." Despite his fervor, Kennan was wrong about Americans absorbing Russian culture.

With respect to Russia itself, however, he demonstrated astounding prescience. Traditional Russian culture would indeed undermine Soviet control. Despite czarist and communist repression, pre-1917 individual ethics had survived, George claimed. "All you have to do is listen to the stream of casual conversation among Russian people . . . on the streets, in the parks, in the public conveyances"—a listening-in that Kennan loved to do—to confirm that "an impressive number still believe profoundly in certain abstractions such as decency, honesty, kindliness and loyalty." Pre-Bolshevik art and literature remained popular even among hard-boiled Communists. A shared love for this heritage bonded he himself with the Russians.

He told about a fairy tale that, decades later, would actually come true.

> And when you go today to the ballet at the Bolshoi Theater in Moscow . . . you find intact and living before your eyes . . . all that is colorful and stirring and dramatic in life, the fairy-tale world of the age of chivalry. And the story ends with the king and queen sitting serenely on their throne, in gorgeous, regal robes. . . . [amid the] elation and gratitude which connote the happy ending, the victory of that which was kindly and gentle and compassionate over the evil spirit.

Even the most callous Party member "follows with avid interest this struggle of conflicting moral forces . . . identifies himself with the power of good and approves the outcome."

"You cannot tell me," Kennan insisted, "that in these Russian minds the lessons of the nineteenth century have been lost." Despite the repressive might of the state, "in the realm of the spirit there is a moral life being led under the noses of the regime." This "organic development of moral feeling . . . must some day take its place in the creation of new political forms."[152] Persistent religious faith was likewise "a fact of immense underlying importance" in the "spiritual breach between the rulers and the ruled."[153]

In the grim context of the early 1950s, Kennan's scenario seemed totally fanciful. Nevertheless, he had identified the emotional forces of Russian cultural pride, romantic nationalism, religious faith, moral idealism, and nostalgia for the czars that—along with rising consumerism and shifting technology—would undermine Soviet ideology and power and help end the Cold War.

Kennan reached this profound insight by integrating his various faculties for knowing. George read and pondered the nineteenth-century classics. He listened and watched the people on the streets and in the theaters. He experienced Russian life as much as restrictions would permit. He extrapolated from these observations with intuition. And in identifying himself with the Russian people, he grasped the emotional and moral force of the fairy tale. In celebrating their shared passion for the great artists, Kennan was in effect affirming that he and the Russian people remained, despite all the barriers, faithful to each other; they still remembered "their song."

———

In terms of Kennan's relations with America, what was the ultimate impact of his authoring the documents that would forever be linked with his name, the long telegram and the "X" article? If Eleanor Hard had defied her parents in 1928 and had married George, and if he had then resigned from the State Department in order to make money, as he had said he would do, the Cold War would still have occurred. Kennan might have become a lawyer, a prospect he had considered while at Princeton, or he might have followed the Hard family into journalism. As a columnist covering world affairs, Kennan would surely have bumped up against Walter Lippmann. As an attorney, perhaps specializing in international law, George could have matched wits with Dean Acheson, a corporate lawyer with Covington and Burling in Washington, or with John Foster Dulles at Sullivan and Cromwell in New York City. With this heavy dose of Civilization in his life, George probably would have sought balance by writing fiction or pursuing affairs. Then again, marrying someone more his intellectual equal might have assuaged George's lifelong loneliness. That happy development would have required George and Eleanor to work out the differences in personality that both of them in later years would emphasize with a vehemence that may have masked some regret. One can imagine in this alternate scenario Kennan's endorsing the ascension of Dulles as secretary of state in 1953 instead of enduring, as he did in actual life, a humiliating rejection.

While such a turn of events would not have prevented the Cold War, it probably would have affected how rapidly and totally the U.S. government shifted to and embraced a Cold War stance. Kennan's 1946–1947 manifestos were so persuasive and so consequential because they appeared at a pivotal time when Americans were puzzled about the breakdown of the wartime alliance. The pronouncements avoided the unpleasant alternatives of war and appeasement; they advanced a way forward with a distant happy ending, and they portrayed the Soviet Union as both frightening and manageable. They achieved these aims with language that evoked emotion while claiming hardheaded realism. Moreover, the statements bore the imprimatur of America's leading expert on Russian affairs. Kennan offered the right words at the right time. The long telegram made it easy, as Bohlen confirmed, for the State Department to stop worrying about the recent ally's legitimate national interests and to focus instead on restraining a dangerous foe's illegitimate expansion. Forrestal and other ideologues now could claim intellectual justification for the hard-line policies they were already pushing. The "X" article and its popularization by the press offered reductive clarification for the public. Incipient allies in Europe noted Kennan's arguments as did the irritated dictator in the Kremlin. In snaring the imagination of Washington and of the public, the two documents trapped Kennan as well. While he loved the acclaim and influence, and he endorsed more militantly anti-Soviet policies than he later liked to admit, he also chafed at the constraints imposed by his own doctrine. He grew increasingly unhappy as the militarization of the Cold War took on a momentum of its own.

That American leaders and the public so readily adopted a militant stance toward the Soviet Union and would so reluctantly budge from that Cold War position testified to the force of two factors. First, in the context of 1946–1947, Kennan's long telegram and "X" article were enormously persuasive. Second, the American tradition of mobilizing against demonic foes, and of defining the nation in that struggle, is a constant that traces back to warring against indigenous peoples in colonial days.

By the spring of 1950, Kennan had returned nearly full circle to his fall of 1944 position as an outsider. Though his voice still had listeners, he again felt marginalized and unable to stop U.S. policy from careening down a dangerous path. Even as Washington and Moscow were swerving from allies to adversaries, he had tried to separate his wistful love for the Russian people from his withering scorn for their government. In actuality, however, Kennan's dichotomy, like the polarity between emotion and reason, collapsed. Whether enraptured at the Bolshoi or reckoning in the Kremlin, Soviet leaders, including the Russified Georgian dictator, remained Russians. In discerning the problems of Soviet leaders, Kennan could not help but develop some empathy for their predicament in the Cold War. Therefore he, unlike most U.S. officials, could perceive areas of possible compromise. Containment meant for its author a dynamic policy that allowed, indeed demanded, flexibility, moderation, and a readiness to move on to diplomacy. As ambassador to Moscow in 1952, Kennan's eagerness to negotiate would set him up for the biggest heartbreak of his career and his 101-year life. He never fully recovered.

CHAPTER 8

"CHOSEN INSTRUMENT"

Kennan's Tragedy in Moscow, 1951–1952

WHY DID HE DO IT? Why did George F. Kennan sabotage the crowning mission of his diplomatic career, his ambassadorship to Moscow in 1952? And why was this most Russophile of U.S. officials declared persona non grata by the Soviet government, the only American ambassador expelled in the entirety of U.S.-Russian relations? Kennan's outburst—publicly comparing the Soviet Union to Nazi Germany, an insult hurled while he was in the former Nazi capital—astounded U.S. officials as much as it angered the Soviets. How could an experienced diplomat, especially someone so sensitive to criticism, damage his career so badly that it would never recover?

The answers to these questions go to the heart of Kennan's personality. The story of his four months as ambassador to Moscow entails hubris and therefore tragedy. While Kennan probably knew more about Russia than any other American, he did not know as much as he thought he did. He over-relied on what he called his "antennae," his supposed ability to discern the thoughts and feelings of the Soviet people as well as their leaders in the Kremlin. He also over-estimated his ability to bend U.S. policy toward compromise with the Soviet Union. He sought fervently to ease Cold War tensions and head off what he feared was imminent war. He was so determined to broker peace between Washington and Moscow that he ended up infuriating officials in both capitals. If Kennan can be excused for failing to influence powerful leaders over whom he had little or no control, he nonetheless remains responsible for failing to control himself. He allowed his passion for Russian culture and for the Russian people to distort his analysis of their leaders. He focused so intently on himself and on his dignity that he made himself a laughingstock to the many colleagues anxious to knock him down a peg. Although diplomacy requires flexibility, he proved brittle. While his persuasiveness in writing had fueled his rise to the top, his prolixity undercut his credibility.

And yet, despite these and other failings, Kennan stood alone among top U.S. officials in caring enough about the horror of nuclear war to put himself on the line in trying to prevent it. No one else shared his prescience in predicting that the Soviet government would soon seek to ease the Cold War. The changes in the Kremlin he foresaw did occur, less than a year after he arrived in Moscow. By then, however, Kennan was already gone. That proved the final element of the tragedy.

Kennan entered Russia in May 1952 on "a sentimental journey" with "a mystical sense of purpose," a close friend observed.[1] He aimed to halt the slide toward all-out war while gratifying his passion for the people and culture of Russia. His ambitions were matched only by his angst. He steeled himself into accepting, indeed almost welcoming, disappointment; nevertheless, he also resisted it. He toggled between, and at times blended, yearning and foreboding. He remained conflicted also about Kremlin leaders. Should he consider them as rational interlocutors open to diplomacy or as a fanatical criminal gang? Though officially Kennan represented President Harry S. Truman and Secretary of State Dean Acheson, personally he objected to their principal foreign policy objective: integrating a rearmed West Germany into the U.S. camp. He hoped to leverage his expertise, intuition about Russia, and authority among other diplomats in Moscow into influence on Washington's policy, especially after a new administration took office in January 1953. Sadly for Kennan—and for the chance of peace—all these ambitions would come crashing down after only five months in Russia.

After spending decades studying Russia, George might have celebrated becoming Ambassador Kennan. Instead, he foresaw "my real trial in life." Do not be surprised if my mission ends badly, he warned Frieda

Por, who had nursed him back to health after his physical and psychological breakdown in Moscow in December 1934. The Freudian-minded physician, whom he had helped bring to the United States in 1938, had remained his confidant and family doctor. The expected ordeal in Russia "is something I deserve" because life had been "too easy and successful." He anticipated abuse and injustice from the Soviets and misunderstanding and ingratitude from the Americans. Against such emotional onslaught, he resolved to steel himself with qualities of character modeled by his father and his Uncle Alfred Farragut and honed at St. John's: "manliness and balance and good grace."[2]

In Russia, Kennan faced high-decibel assault from all sides. The Soviet press greeted his nomination by denouncing him as a spy. His arrival in Moscow was welcomed with macabre propaganda billboards depicting alleged American germ warfare in Korea. Sensationalized leaks to the press by someone in the State Department undercut the ambassador's effort to tone down the invective on both sides. The secret police tried to entrap him in a bizarre plot to assassinate Soviet leaders. His careful efforts to pry open a channel to the Kremlin came to naught. Failing to find an interlocutor in the Kremlin, Kennan vented in rambling communications to the State Department. To puzzled officials back in Washington he spun scenarios detailing the supposed impact of his presence in Moscow on purported divisions within Stalin's circle. The wunderkind Russian expert of 1946–1947 now undermined his own credibility. He further antagonized Acheson and others with skepticism toward their aim of rearming West Germany and integrating it into NATO. Meanwhile, George's personal life careened from an intoxicating flirtation with a Russian woman to the tedium of dealing with Annelise and their newborn daughter. For many reasons, Kennan's frustration mounted during his summer in the Soviet capital.

BEFORE MOSCOW, 1950–1952

Kennan's troubles in Moscow came on the heels of other strains. Feeling increasingly out of place in the State Department, he took leave in 1950–1951 to pursue a research project at the Institute for Advanced Study in

Princeton. He confided in his diary three pressing concerns: his differences with Acheson and others in the State Department, his dread of imminent war, and his agonizing over a sexual affair and continued attraction to other women. Adding to the unhappiness was pain from a dislocated collarbone suffered while riding his old-fashioned bicycle.

His feeling of estrangement seemed especially humiliating after his success at diplomacy. In June 1951, Kennan, at Acheson's request, initiated talks with Yakov Malik, the Soviet Ambassador to the United Nations, to lay the groundwork for a cease-fire in the Korean War. Fearful that the fighting could escalate into another world war, Kennan warned the Department that "we are moving much closer to the edge of the precipice than most of us are aware." Weeks of patient diplomacy with Malik in New York paid off with the rough outline of a settlement. Trying to play the Russians off against the Chinese, Kennan told Malik that while the Soviet Union "was run by people who took a serious and responsible attitude," the Chinese Communists, by contrast, were "excited, irresponsible people."[3] Here was Kennan, revisiting the implicitly racist, rational-emotional dichotomy that underlay the long telegram and the "X" article, but with the Russians now slotted into the normative position of rational actors. While Kennan yearned to conduct this kind of diplomacy with the Russians to settle the larger issues of the Cold War, he could not. Acheson and Truman preferred instead utilizing the heat of East-West tensions to forge a tight Western alliance that included a rearmed West Germany.

He felt like an "intellectual gadfly," Kennan admitted to Acheson in September 1951.[4] Though tolerated, he no longer ranked as the influential seer of the State Department. Indeed, on issue after issue, he thought otherwise. He advocated downplaying the United Nations, especially the General Assembly. He wanted the United States to end its strategic dependence on the atomic bomb and "renounce any intent to use it" except in retaliation for an atomic attack. His vision recalled, though Kennan would have choked at the idea, the power-sharing principle of Franklin D. Roosevelt's Four Policemen. Kennan would have a chastened Germany and Japan organize their respective spheres while the United States pulled back from global predominance. He favored grouping continental Europe around a Franco-German core that would "stand on its own feet and constitute an effective third force." He believed that "our best chance of avoiding war with the Soviet Union lay in the opening up of a wide area in central Europe which was neither 'ours' nor 'theirs.'" Such a grouping, which would invariably result in leadership by Germany, might eventually take in the Soviet satellites. NATO had little place in this setup. He dismissed the Middle East and Southeast Asia as regions benighted by "immature and impetuous policies" and "the less we have to do with them the better."

With regard to Japan as well, Kennan wanted to reverse the unconditional surrender that he had opposed during the war. Most of the problems in the Far East stemmed from "our insistence on the elimination of Japanese power from areas for which no other satisfactory political arrangement" appeared possible. He favored an agreement with Moscow for neutralizing Japan, thus ending America's extensive military presence there. He also urged a return to the pre-1950 status quo in Korea. Condemning both the Chiang Kai-shek government on Taiwan and the People's Republic in Beijing, Kennan concluded that "the less we Americans have to do with China, the better." He blindly insisted that "China is *not* the great power of the Orient." As for the McCarthyites and others who blamed U.S. diplomats for "our loss of China," Kennan countered that "we never 'had' China," and hence it was not ours to lose. He would also cut back ties with Latin America and aim to have those nations respect rather than like us.[5]

Exercising hegemony nowhere, the United States would pursue diplomacy everywhere. This worldview recalled historian Charles A. Beard's *The Open Door at Home*, which he had read in 1934. Kennan also shared Beard's preference for ending immigration. Believing that only the industrial powerhouses of the world—the United States, the Soviet Union, Great Britain, Germany and France, and Japan—really counted, the diplomat would ignore large swaths of the globe. If the Soviets gained control over, say, Southeast Asia, that would be their problem. Kennan's thinking was overtly racist. Moreover, he ignored the economic ties that made the industrialized areas dependent on trade and investment in the supposedly unimportant nations. Nevertheless, he would persist in favoring only a limited U.S. global presence for the rest of his long life.

Kennan did not, however, expect to live that long, especially if a major war erupted. In 1951, with Korea in flames and Truman facing condemnation for firing General Douglas MacArthur, Kennan depicted the world scene as "a crowd of drunken men on a raft, squabbling and gabbing while we drifted down to the brink of the falls." The worst welled up not from Moscow, but from within America, where "McCarthyism has already won, in the sense of making impossible the conduct of an intelligent foreign policy. War will break out within two years." Such fear was not far-fetched. Prominent generals were calling for a preemptive attack on the Soviet Union, and *Collier's* cover story fantasized about conquering Russia. Kennan resolved to seek a commission in the armed services, commenting darkly that were it not for his young son, Christopher, he should "get myself killed."[6]

If he failed to die, he had to at least grow "much older in a short space of time." How else to blinker his wandering eye? Tortured over an affair, he concluded that "in one tremendous field of life, the one in which failure was personally most horrible and painful, I have failed." Though ever elusive as to details, his diary suggested remorse over more than just another infidelity. Appalled by "the damage I have done," he condemned himself as "half a murderer." He felt a "horror of myself."[7] Nonetheless, he could not stop "staring after women." Walking along Fifth Avenue in Manhattan, he tried to convince himself that "I do not really want them." Sexual desire he disparaged as just "an echo of youth." To harden this renunciation, he stepped into St. Patrick's Cathedral to pray. "And then I walked again down the Avenue, and before me and around me was the parade of women going to work." Resigned to his impulses, he resolved to "teach myself to have nothing to conceal but that which is really worth concealing."[8]

Desire for other women figured as the sexual side of his broader needs. Leaving for Chicago in April 1951 to deliver the Walgreen lectures (which would become the basis for his widely read *American Diplomacy*), George foresaw the usual temptations. "Here will be all the things that are difficult for me: a strange city, a hotel, solitude, boredom, strange women." He would, he knew, react with a "sense of time fleeting, of time being wasted, of a life pulsating around me—a life unknown, untested, full of mystery, and yet not touched by myself." He wanted to touch, to respond to that pulsating. But no! In keeping with his decades-old pattern, he resolved to discipline himself with rational "deliberateness, thoughtfulness, awareness of all that is involved."[9]

Parallel with this sexual desire was Kennan's yearning for the people and culture of Russia. Here, too, he felt an urge to seize the moment, plumb the mystery, and immerse himself in pulsating life.

Kennan attached such weight to his mission to Moscow that he looked to God for help. Foreshadowing the increasing role of religion in his later life, he formally joined the First Presbyterian Church in Princeton in January 1952. To the pastor he explained that the "responsibilities that are now being placed upon me [are] so unusual and so vast in their implications" that he could cope with them only with "dedication to purposes higher than myself and greater than myself." His success depended on an "inner posture of humility, conviction and self-renunciation."[10] Given George's other impulses, however, such self-abnegation would prove difficult.

As he prepared to leave for Moscow in the spring of 1952, Kennan needed to know what the administration wanted him, and would permit him, to say to the Russians. At a meeting on April 1 with Truman, the president could spare the ambassador to America's arch foe only fifteen minutes, half what he gave a delegation of rail workers that same day.[11] To Kennan's dismay, Truman offered "no instructions of any kind." At a private luncheon the next day, Acheson, remaining "very reserved," also said nothing about "the basic line of policy I was to follow."[12] Truman and Acheson aimed not to ease tensions with Moscow, but rather to mobilize them in securing the integration into the Atlantic community of a rearmed West Germany.

Just as Kennan was failing to wring from Truman and Acheson even a scrap of a concession to use for negotiations, Josef Stalin offered a plateful. In March, the Soviet leader sent the three Western powers a formal note proposing elections to reunify Germany as a neutral state. Though probably a ploy to disrupt the creation of a separate West

Germany, the sincerity of Stalin's offer was never tested.[13] With the threat of war looming, Kennan thought it foolish to dismiss the chance that diplomacy might yield a deal that neither party had originally expected. Then, in an April interview, the dictator reassuringly declared that despite the conflict in Korea and America's massive rearmament, chances for major war had not increased. The grizzled veteran of Tehran and Yalta agreed that another such summit could prove beneficial. Asked whether he believed the time ripe to unify Germany, he affirmed: "Yes, I do." He added that "the peaceful co-existence of capitalism and communism is fully possible."[14]

In confidential testimony before the Senate Foreign Relations Committee regarding his appointment, Kennan referred to his potential interlocutors in the Kremlin not as fanatical foes but rather as tough but worthy opponents. "They are gangsters but they are extremely intelligent men, and look rather impressive." He portrayed them as "rascals," lacking morality but extremely able and shrewd. Revealing a hint of fondness, he affirmed that "you cannot help but respect them for their ability. They are no slouches." As for himself, the Russians "consider me a serious person, and that is all I want from them. I want their respect. I do not want their liking."[15] Serious diplomacy depended on such mutual respect.

At a lengthy press conference, Kennan again came across as a semi-independent actor with his own outlook and agenda. Since 1948, he had believed that the American public needed to understand that productive negotiations with the Russians were indeed possible. Now he spent an hour educating those who might influence the public. With Washington abuzz about Stalin's pronouncements, Kennan paid lip service to the administration's line that the dictator's assurances remained too "cryptic" to follow up with negotiations. He also disparaged the idea of a summit meeting, just as he had criticized FDR's wartime summits as amateurish stunts that complicated the work of real diplomats. (Another problem, of course, was that Roosevelt had failed to include him in his entourage.) In response to Stalin's concurrence that a summit might prove beneficial, Kennan snapped: "Beneficial from whose standpoint? Beneficial for what purposes?"

He turned more optimistic when discussing his own possible dealings in Russia. Now he invoked Stalin's statement as added evidence
that "Soviet leaders would prefer a less tense atmosphere." Deprived by
Truman and Acheson of anything substantive to offer the Kremlin, Kennan seized on style. He hoped that "old fashioned . . . diplomatic amenities" free of emotions could pry open the door to informal talks. He
resolved to bend the curve with dealings that were respectful in manner,
less confrontational in tone, and transparent in terms of process.

Kennan's approach, a reporter observed, seemed rooted in the
1930s, "to which you look back with such nostalgia." The forty-eight-
year-old did indeed regard relations in the pre-purge 1930s as "normal," a word he used repeatedly. He wanted to make it again ordinary
"to have a meal with a Soviet diplomat or somebody to talk to so and
so." Of utmost personal importance was easing the Soviets' "pathological fear of the individual foreigner." While political differences
remained crucial, "there are other things in life besides politics," like
music and art. He recalled that back in the thirties, so many Americans
went to Moscow. "They went to the theater and went around. There
were Soviet people in this country." He would revive this "great cultural exchange. It did exist in the old days." This mixing between
Americans and Russians—so dear to Kennan's heart—had gone on
without "much of a hullabaloo"—meaning without repression from
either the McCarthyites or Moscow.

In longing for that lost world, Kennan made a leap of faith, and tragically set himself up for a fall. He told himself that Kremlin leaders also
"think that the state of isolation of the Soviet Union from the West has
gone to abnormal lengths." They also sought "a little more coming and
going between the worlds."

With the two camps sliding toward war, Kennan tried to debunk
some Cold War shibboleths that his long telegram and "X" article had
set in stone. No longer did he represent Soviet Communism as an existential threat. Now he now stressed that Soviet leaders, despite their
ambitions, remained highly rational and hence cautious. "The men in
the Kremlin think things over very carefully." Moreover, "I have not
thought at any time that the Soviet leaders have wanted a third world

war." They could, however, be pushed into a war by U.S. belligerence or by miscalculation. As for the canard that the Kremlin was determined to conquer the world, Kennan, imbuing the Russians with the wisdom that he himself had imbibed from Edward Gibbon, asserted: "They do not want unlimited power, if unlimited power means unlimited responsibility. AND I think those things are very carefully calculated." Here, then, was Kennan painting, for himself as well as for the American people, a portrait of Soviet leaders as rational practitioners of realpolitik receptive to freer, more normal relations. He was conjuring fit interlocutors for a savvy diplomat such as himself.

Regarding the fierce anti-American propaganda in Russia, some of it aimed directly at him, Kennan—while still in Washington—remained nonchalant. "Propaganda is propaganda, and business is business," he asserted, "and I don't think that the two really meet." He recalled that in August 1939 when Stalin had met with the Nazi foreign minister Joachim von Ribbentrop, the dictator had dismissed the fierce Nazi-Soviet propaganda war as a "grand joke." More telling than the nasty talk was "whether you are respected," whether someone was deemed "a serious person who it's worth talking to or not." Kennan had no doubt that he passed this test. The slander might even signal a compliment. "The fact that you have been the butt of their propaganda does not necessarily mean that you're not respected. It may mean almost the contrary." Unhappily for Kennan, however, he could not remain so coolheaded after reaching Moscow.

Asked by reporters what more normal relations might achieve, Kennan stressed the imminent danger of another world war. Fear of such a catastrophe had impelled him since visiting firebombed Hamburg in 1949. Not only would an atomic war kill millions, but "values will be destroyed, the absence of which will be terribly, terribly missed." If, in ten or fifteen years, "it's still possible for our kids to go out and play baseball . . . a great deal will have been achieved." Though careful not to openly defy Acheson on the policy of integrating a rearmed West Germany into the U.S. fold, Kennan came close. Geopolitical more than ideological differences were driving the Cold War, he argued. The basic problem stemmed from Franklin D. Roosevelt's disastrous policy of unconditional surrender. The Americans and the Soviets "were both lured . . . with our own military forces into this explosive territory of Germany right in the heart of Europe." This occupation of the former foe by rival armies jostling each other sparked "situations of really tremendous delicacy and dangerousness." Though he refrained from saying it within the bowels of Acheson's State Department, Kennan believed that the United States and the Soviet Union should both withdraw their armies and political control and create a neutral, lightly armed Germany. That formula, as he knew, was close to what Stalin was calling for and what his own government opposed.[16]

In contrast to the silent treatment he got from Truman and Acheson, Kennan met "genuine cordiality" at a luncheon at the Soviet embassy. "In a serious tone," the ambassador assured him that Stalin's conciliatory statements ranked as "most authoritative." Another Russian broke in to say that "there were not any questions which the Soviet Government was not willing to discuss with us." Moscow "was willing at any time to enter upon" serious talks.

Regardless of how sincere Stalin and his representatives were about talking with the Americans, such affirmations could, as Kennan appreciated, open the door to negotiations. What might then develop from diplomacy and compromise by both sides no one could say. The key differences between Kennan and almost every other leader in Washington was that he sought to negotiate an easing or end to the Cold War, and they did not.

Like Kennan, Soviet diplomats in Washington had suffered personally from the rift. Stereotypes of evil Bolsheviks held such sway that some Americans had refused to believe the embassy officials were actually Russian. "Impossible, where is your beard?" they would ask or, strangely, "Why aren't you black?" Even educated Americans despised them as "barbarians."[17] That Kennan quoted these personal laments in his official report on the luncheon evidenced his empathy.

Sympathy for the Russians aggravated Kennan's sourness toward the U.S. government. He believed it crucial to respond to "Soviet willingness to enter on some new phase of discussion and negotiation with the Western powers."

Kennan was also incensed that Acheson was caving in to FBI-assisted McCarthyite attacks on his friend, the China expert John Paton Davies, and others accused of insufficient loyalty—a charge to which he, Kennan, actually stood vulnerable. Kennan himself never had any trouble from the FBI, perhaps because he made it a point to cultivate its touchy director. In 1947, Kennan had reached out to the FBI to advise on how best to obtain information from Russian émigrés in the United States without raising their hackles. He volunteered an explanation of why he subscribed to Soviet newspapers. Far worse, he had reported on the supposed Communist sympathies of some "minor employees" of the State Department. In 1963, he would send a handwritten apology to FBI director J. Edgar Hoover for allowing some mild criticism to slip into a published interview. "I am heartily sorry" for not editing out these "misimpressions" of the Bureau, "for which I have always had the greatest respect." He hoped that Hoover would "continue to think of me as a friend of the Bureau and an admirer of its work . . . and call on me in instances where I can be of some small help." Untouched by Kennan's fawning, Hoover commented to an aide, "I am *not* impressed by his explanation."[18]

Now, in 1952, as Kennan was preparing to leave for Moscow, he implored Chip Bohlen to set up another meeting with the secretary of state. Shaken by Kennan's warnings, Bohlen cautioned Acheson that "if Stalin was convinced that the route of negotiation with the West was definitely closed," he might start preparing for war. While not halting the rush to lock in West Germany, perhaps Kennan might be instructed to "seek an interview with Stalin."[19] Unmoved, a stony-faced Acheson again denied Kennan any guidance as to what and how he might negotiate in Moscow. He wanted the ambassador not to talk with the Russians but just report on what they were doing.

Kennan exploded. On the hot issues of German reunification, disarmament, and the war in Korea (where he thought the Russians should be brought in "as a responsible partner" to guarantee the peace), "our Government could not be more on the wrong tack," he protested. Acheson was expecting to prevail "without making any concessions whatsoever to the views and interests of our adversaries." Like that of Roosevelt, the current administration demanded unconditional surrender, this time from the Russians. That was arrogant, unrealistic, and danger-ous. Far better to seek "accommodation with our adversaries than [risk] complete defiance of them." Kennan remained too good a diplomat, too wedded to a balance of power, and too attuned to Russian sensibilities to ignore the Kremlin's point of view.[20] He later complained to an aide that he had been "railroaded" out of Washington so that he would not complicate the negotiations about integrating West German into NATO. "Dean Acheson had it in for him personally."[21]

After this latest disastrous meeting, a depressed Kennan concluded that there was no one left in Washington with understanding for his views—not even Bohlen, his comrade from the glory days of 1933–1934. A stormy visit at the farm exposed their differences. Kennan lamented that Bohlen's defense of administration policy, especially its reliance on nuclear weapons, "shocked me deeply, for he and I have been closer than any other people in Washington." Now dead was "any further intellec-tual intimacy."[22] Bohlen, meanwhile, was astounded by the vehemence of his friend's deep dissent. "How fundamentally stronger your bitter-ness against the Govt in general and the State Dept (& the Sec) is get-ting," he charged in a letter. "You seem to get really angry when I make *any* defense of our policies—past or present."[23]

Despite feeling abused and abandoned, Kennan remained unbowed. He was no stranger to the satisfaction of sacrifice. Isaiah Berlin, a British intellectual and diplomat who knew him well, observed that with George, "the great thing is to be tormented by your unavoidable task."[24] "Though empty handed, uninstructed, and uncertain," he was entrusted by fate with "the most important and delicate" diplomacy in the world. In terms of personal as well as official support, the gladiator was ventur-ing out alone. Annelise was remaining in West Germany to await the birth of their fourth child. Kennan left for Russia "feeling extremely lonely."[25]

MOSCOW: THE INITIAL EXCITEMENT

All the more delightful, then, was a connection with new friends. Shortly after arriving in Moscow, Kennan strode "with a loose-jointed boyish pace" up to a suburban cottage and inquired of Harrison E.

Salisbury, the *New York Times* correspondent, "Do you have a spare room to let upstairs?" Speaking in Russian, Kennan repeated the precise words he had used in 1933–1934 when wandering about Russia. He was trying to rekindle some of the magic of those years. Back then, he had thrown himself into late-night parties filled with impassioned talk and Russian music. Now, in a reprise, he bonded instantly with Harrison, journalist and former embassy official Tom Whitney, and Yulya "Juli" Zapolskaya, Whitney's Russian wife. They all shared a dacha in Salty-chikhi outside Moscow. The foursome enjoyed "rattling away in Russian" or singing Russian folk songs, with Kennan on the guitar. Salisbury observed George "at once nostalgic, a little lonely, romantic, and at ease, at least for a moment, deep in that Russia to which he had long ago lost his heart."[26] Kennan easily got enmeshed in the web of feelings centered on Juli. Harrison described her as not only smart, sophisticated, and socially conscious, but also as an embodiment of Mother Russia.[27] It was obvious even to Kennan's daughter, Grace, who visited later that summer, that "Juli was so attractive a woman that all the men were captivated by her."[28]

"Flirtation . . . was dear to Juli," Salisbury later recounted. Night after night, with her husband in the next room, Juli would keep Harrison up until early morning "talking, talking, talking, 'clarifying our relations,' as she said." It was "talk from the soul—laying bare the deepest of feelings." She engaged Harrison in a sensual ritual: a feathery pressing together of the fingertips while shutting out all other stimuli. The lighter the contact, the more intense the feeling. The ultimate sensation required the most intense concentration. Juli and Harrison would gaze intently at each other, "drawing in the essence of the other with each breath until the *feeling* became as powerful as, more powerful than, any physical contact or sexual response."[29] Emotions entangled. Even as Harrison and Tom remained friends, and Juli and Tom remained married, Harrison and Juli fell in love. Harrison Salisbury's papers at Columbia University include a small envelope with a lock of Juli's hair and, in imperfect English, her pledge: "I promist marry Harrison any time when he wants to, after Tom will divorce me."[30]

Into this scene sauntered George, lonely and looking to connect with Russia. Harrison, who admired Kennan, observed that Juli greeted their new friend "with the adoration of a Juliet. No one who saw Juli's face light up and her eyes glow in George's presence could mistake the feeling." She loved that he stood between America and Russia. He possessed a "philosophy and emotion close to the Russian heart. He was Russian but not Russian, American but a special kind of American." They talked "all day and night, no bounds to the talk." George felt "much the same" and seemed "strongly . . . drawn to this most Russian of relationships." Perhaps they also touched fingertips and gazed into each other's eyes. But they went no further, Salisbury asserted years later, because Kennan remained "an extraordinarily happily married man" and worried about the danger to his official position.[31] Harrison apparently knew nothing of George's affair the previous year nor of his weakness for beguiling women. Neither Harrison and Tom, nor the secret police, could know for sure what George and Juli did or did not do. The key point, however, is that regardless of the degree of physical intimacy between them, an emotional intimacy evidently developed, and that, as Harrison testified, could prove more powerful than sexual contact.

Kennan prized the dacha as an idyll for the senses, a refuge where he could engage with this most Russian of women while also hearing the "sound of hammers, dogs barking, chickens, children's cries, and distant trains."[32] There was "something old-Russian" in the village, "an atmosphere of health and simplicity and subdued hope which I drank in." He prized the preindustrial, pre-1917, Chekhovian feel of a place where "people were doing things with their hands, with animals and with Nature, a life little touched by any form of modernization." How much richer and more satisfying, he sighed, was human life without machines. In the countryside, he could feel, as he had in the 1930s, "the sense of Russia all about me" and could entertain, "momentarily, the illusion that I was part of it."

On evening walks in summertime Moscow, the ambassador, though flanked by his four guards, could see, hear, and smell ordinary Russians. "Never did I long more for the privilege of being, if only for a time, a part of these people, of talking with them, of sharing their life." Russia was "in my blood. There was some mysterious affinity which I could not explain even to myself; and nothing could have given me deeper satisfaction than to indulge it."[33]

Saltychikhi was only part of George's reimmersion in Russia. On a nostalgic visit to Yasnaya Polyana, Tolstoy's estate, where he had ventured with Enid Meinert back in 1935, he encountered the same guide— Tolstoy's private secretary, Valentin Fedorovich Bulgakov. To Kennan's delight, they talked about nineteenth-century Russian literature, with Bulgakov speaking in the authentic accent of the educated circles of the time, "rich, polished, elegant, and musical." This was a world to which "I could really have belonged . . . much more naturally and wholeheartedly" than to the sphere of a twentieth-century American diplomat.[34]

Exhilarated by the challenging and stimulating atmosphere of Russia, he felt empowered to find "within myself the ability to feel my way into its mysteries and nuances."[35] That confidence would prove dangerous. Kennan trusted in his antennae for insights into the sensibilities of the people and officials of Russia. Ever since 1946, this intuitive understanding of the Russians had bolstered Kennan's authority within the U.S. government, among diplomats of other nations, and with the educated public. Now, however, that authority hit two snags, only one of which he recognized.

He knew that his policy ideas diverged from those of the Truman administration, especially with regard to negotiating a deal on Germany and an easing of the Cold War. In his heady first weeks in Moscow, he found respect for his views among other Western diplomats and from a few in the State Department. After the humiliating frustration in Washington, he again commanded "a certain amount of influence and power." If only he could pry open "any sort of quiet communication" with Soviet leaders, he might then wield "sufficient authority and self-confidence to challenge our existing lines of policy," especially with the new administration in January 1953.[36]

The enormity of Kennan's ambition was matched only by the gravity of the danger he aimed to address. He feared that the United State and the Soviet Union were allowing themselves to be swept toward the precipice of nuclear war. By deploying his expertise, intuition, and prestige, Kennan, though almost alone, might begin to turn around the enormous lumbering vessel that was the Cold War. He might then get to shepherd negotiations to ease the most explosive issues between the United States and the Soviet Union. The moral imperative of that fervent ambition blinded him to the second challenge. His antennae could pick up false or ambiguous signals, a situation worsened by his tendency, especially in times of stress, to interpret them in light of what was going on within himself rather than within the Kremlin.

For Kennan, blocking the Soviets in the short run had always presumed diplomacy in the long run. He regarded containment as an if-then proposition. If the United States restrained Moscow's expansion, then eventually Kremlin leaders would accept that reality, change course, and negotiate a settlement that eased tensions. Containment would compel a return to diplomacy. For Truman, Acheson, and their successors, however, containment remained an axiom. Walling in a hostile Soviet Union became an end unto itself. The never-ending "Soviet threat" justified and facilitated the expansion of U.S. influence into a global Free World held together by American economic, military, and cultural predominance. Fear of the Soviets buttressed this informal empire, especially in America's prizes from World War II, West Germany and Japan. Though Kennan remained fierce, and old-fashioned, about access to vital raw materials—for instance, he advocated seizing and holding oil fields in Iran and elsewhere in the Middle East by force if necessary—he had no interest in empire as such. He doubted that Americans had the temperament to sustain such an enterprise, and he never forgot Gibbons's warning that overextension abroad corrupted institutions at home. Here, too, Kennan's views harked back to the geopolitics of the early 1930s.

A marker of Kennan's intimacy with his dacha friends was his divulging to them the outlines of the analysis that he detailed to the State Department. Sitting in a canvas chair under the pines at Saltychikhi, Kennan told Salisbury that Stalin and his cohort, despite their hostility, remained "pragmatic, shrewd men." Once they realized that containment had walled them in, they "would change instantly from total antagonism to a willingness to meet and resolve mutual problems." The danger came from Washington, where blinkered officials like Acheson might not discern the improvement in Moscow. It became vital, therefore, "that someone like himself be on hand to catch the first hint" and to assist. "Like a good obstetrician coping with a difficult birth," Kennan might have to "use the forceps a bit."[37]

Impelled by his "mystical optimism," Kennan hoped that Saltychikhi might lead to wider contacts. He played his guitar not just to relax with friends but also to inch closer to his goal. "Somehow he saw himself playing his Russian songs as a way to winning someone's confidence— finding a totally irregular and undiplomatic route that would put him in touch with the men of the Kremlin." He fantasized that Juli, Harrison, or Tom might offer a link to some influential Russian, and thus the dacha "would be the first step."[38]

Another slender arrow in his quiver lay in the hope that Ralph Parker, a British expatriate now living in Moscow, might arrange for an inter-mediary to the Kremlin. After the Germans marched into Prague in March 1939, most journalists and foreign diplomats, aside from Kennan and Parker, left. The two grew close. Parker had come to the former Czech capital to report for both the *New York Times* and the London *Times*.[39] When Britain declared war on Germany, Parker had to flee suddenly. He left a treasured painting with Kennan for safekeeping. Parker's troubles had only begun. His wife was killed by a German bomb. A few years later, the London *Times* sent him into Russia via a perilous convoy to Murmansk. Reporting from Moscow, he moved sharply to the left. No longer a widely respected journalist reporting for the most prestigious newspapers in America and Britain, Parker became a hack writing anti-American and anti-British slanderer for Communist publications. The shift was probably not voluntary. His new wife, Val-entina Bobren, worked for the secret police. (Bobren was also the for-mer wife of Henry Scott, an African American tap dancer who had won wide acclaim in Russia.) Salisbury later explained that "Parker was a complicated man who was having his nuts squeezed all the time."[40]

In 1949, Parker tried to ingratiate himself with Soviet authorities by attacking Kennan. In his book *Conspiracy Against Peace*, Parker recalled visiting Kennan on V-E Day, May 9, 1945, when a huge crowd had gath-ered at Spaso House to cheer the U.S. ally. He claimed, falsely, that Ken-nan, amid this joy, had perversely predicted war between America and

Russia. By 1952, Parker, having cast his lot with the Kremlin, had cut all ties with his former friend. All the better, calculated George, who had taken the trouble to lug Parker's painting to Moscow. He hoped that Parker's anti-Americanism had earned the journalist some credibility in the Kremlin. Kennan hoped further that Parker, grateful for the return of his painting, would introduce George to someone in the Soviet leadership. Just as Baron Steiger in the 1930s had served as a link to those close to Stalin, so too might Parker or someone he knew discreetly intervene, and "words would begin to flow up and down the chain."[41]

Adding to Kennan's daily frustration was that while the Kremlin seemed beyond his grasp, it hovered in sight. Though the ambassador's office was neither large nor luxuriously decorated, the view was magnificent. He could look out a broad picture window across a large square and over the thirty-foot wall of faded rose brick "right into that storybook mélange of four centuries of Russian architectural tastes—the Kremlin." No other foreigner in Moscow had that view. Furthermore, as Salisbury noted, "no foreigner in all Russia is closer, physically, to the Kremlin than the American Ambassador in the Embassy building on Mokhovaya Street." Yet the proximity was irksome because in terms of contact, Kennan remained afar. Back in 1934, he himself had conducted much of the negotiations that secured this prized location for the embassy. In July 1952, by contrast, Kennan as ambassador had to deal with the Soviet Foreign Ministry's request that the embassy move from the Mokhovaya building, which it did the following year.[42]

As Kennan sought a channel into the Kremlin, he resolved, repeatedly, to remain calm. He just as consistently lost his cool. A letter written before his arrival in Moscow illustrated the pattern. He started off stressing his determination to reside in the Soviet capital patiently, cheerfully, and with dignity. Then, as he focused on the "hostility and insults" as well as the "lies and distortions" awaiting him, he pecked out an agitated, nearly page-long sentence demonstrating his difficulty in remaining patient and cheerful.[43] On landing in Moscow, he affirmed that "diplomatic negotiations and relations between states should not be influenced by emotional considerations" but rather based on rational national interests.[44]

FIGURE 28. As ambassador to Moscow in 1952, Kennan from his office could
see the walls of the Kremlin, but not reach the Soviet leaders inside.
(Courtesy of Princeton University Library.)

Despite his determination to remain unemotional, Kennan immediately became offended by the grotesque anti-American propaganda visible in the newspapers and on the streets of Moscow. British ambassador Joseph Gascoigne reported that the slander "came as quite a shock"
to his American colleague, a "disappointed man."[45] Kennan regarded
the propaganda as a personal insult. Returning from a walk, he told his
aide, Hugh S. Cumming, Jr., "I am shocked to discover how the Soviets
regard me as such a dangerous person." "Why George, those damn
[posters] have been there for months! I honestly don't think they have
anything personally to do with you." But the sting could not be salved.
He got "that rather distant, misty look in his eyes, which showed that
he wasn't really listening to me," Cumming later recalled. The ambassador "lay down on the sofa to dictate, almost like a patient in a psycho-
analyst's office."[46]

A long cable to the State Department expressed his hurt and fury at
the "viciousness, shamelessness, mendacity, and intensity" of the campaign. It outdid the worst Nazi propaganda that he had witnessed in

FIGURE 29. Kennan in Moscow grew distraught at the vicious anti-American propaganda splayed on billboards and in newspapers. This poster amplified Soviet charges that Nazi-inspired U.S. military forces in Korea were waging bacteriological warfare. (Courtesy of Krokodil.)

wartime Berlin. He quoted *Izvestia*'s front-page editorial accusing the U.S. military in Korea of "mass destruction of innocent women, old people and children" and of "torturing prisoners of war with red hot irons, hanging them upside down, pouring water into their noses." He could not help but hark back to the 1930s and 1940s. Back then, as he now remembered it, the Soviets had displayed a "relatively good-humored attitude of ideological and political competition." Recent events, however, had sparked a "deep and burning embitterment" directed at Americans. Kennan feared that "we have succeeded in touching deep sources of genuine fury and resentment," which could prove dangerous in people with "pathological habits of mind . . . too quick to suspicion and false conclusions of every kind." The ambassador urged the Truman administration to rein in talk about preemptive war and about new biological and chemical weapons.

While stressing that the U.S. government had "to remain utterly calm," he himself had problems containing "the personal feelings with which no American can fail to be affected" while viewing "this incredible torrent of abuse and falsehood." He emphasized the "question of dignity." Especially "in this semi-oriental country," Americans had to ensure that calm indifference was not interpreted as "our weakness, our lack of pride and dignity, and our helplessness in the face of insult."[47]

George was also upset by the unpleasant situation at Spaso House, especially before Annelise's July 1 arrival with baby Wendy, three-year-old Christopher, twenty-year-old Grace, and two live-in Danish servants. "It's not what it used to be," he warned his wife.[48] Cowed by the secret police, the padded staff of Russian workers—consisting of twenty-two cleaners, furnace men, handy men, and others with indeterminate responsibility—remained "tight-lipped ghosts" who stubbornly did as little work as possible. What most bothered Kennan was that the staff could not "permit themselves to enjoy, or feel a part of, the family" of Spaso House.[49] At night, alone in the huge house, as he wandered about "like a ghost, and looking out of the dark windows," he saw the guards "peering up to try to follow my movements." Soviet police stationed at the front door decided who was permitted to enter. Recalling his internment in wartime Berlin, he found the atmosphere more like "a prison-hotel than like a home."[50] Publicly drawing that comparison of Soviet to Nazi rule would, only a few months later, destroy his mission.

Even the dinners hosted by Western diplomats seemed empty and pathetic. The British embassy appeared "the most depressing place," "absolutely morbid with gloom."[51] Kennan had problems fighting the gloom. One day the usually dutiful ambassador simply canceled all engagements and stayed home.[52] After less than three weeks in Moscow, he felt like telling the U.S. government that the Soviets had made it "impossible for a foreign envoy to live in their city in comfort and dignity."[53] Not all the fault, however, lay with the secret police.

Kennan was infuriated also by the disastrous indiscretion of Lydia Chapin Kirk, the wife of his predecessor, Ambassador Alan C. Kirk, who had just published tell-all magazine articles. "The reason the Spaso staff are terrorized, avoid conversation with me, and melt away like ghosts is that Mrs. K was so unwise" as to expose their personal secrets, such as how a particular woman had managed to communicate with her husband in a concentration camp. "Her articles have left a legacy of bitterness, alarm, and tightening up." Lydia's snide remarks about the wives of Soviet officials, including Foreign Minister Andrei Vyshinski, meant that Annelise could not "possibly ask to call on these ladies after the damage that has been done."[54] Another concern was that if war erupted, Annelise and the children might get stuck in Moscow.[55] Life in Russia imposed not only ugliness, sadness, and danger, but also strain on the family budget.

Concerned about his finances ever since he had lost his inheritance in the Great Depression and mindful of his not-far-off retirement, George toted up what the ambassadorship was costing him. The Soviets extorted such an exorbitant rate for rubles that the dollar bought little in Moscow. Two pounds of summer strawberries cost five dollars. Hence diplomats had to stock up in Germany and elsewhere and fly in their groceries. He warned Annelise that the aide purchasing these supplies "will require lots of money for this, once more—a thousand dollars or so." Annelise later complained that it was "like running a grocery store," with $1,500 spent on canned goods and another $700 on frozen meat. Plus "the investment on whiskeys and wines is no small item." She added, sadly it would turn out, that "in order to come even we have to be here a while."[56] On top of it all, they had to personally pay for the servants brought in from Denmark.[57]

Kennan bore these burdens out of commitment to his mission. Of utmost importance was, first, prying open a channel to the Kremlin and, second, bolstering his standing with other diplomats in Moscow, the shadowy men in the Kremlin, and already skeptical associates back in Washington.

PROLIX SPECULATIONS

Even before he first got to Russia in 1933, Kennan had impressed State Department leaders with extensively researched, detailed despatches. Such reports had fueled his rapid rise in prestige, promotions, and pay. Now, however, Kennan, spinning his wheels as he awaited some opening from the Kremlin, sent missives to the State Department that undercut his credibility there. With little to go on other than his memories and his hunches, Kennan laid out the supposed inner history of Soviet Bolshevism. His account reached back to before the 1917 revolution, touched nostalgically on the early 1930s, and reached its denouement with his appointment as ambassador.

The way that Kennan told this story was almost as telling as the narrative itself. For decades he had written vivid descriptions of characters, their thoughts and emotions, and their settings. Although he wrote mostly prose, he had long aspired to pen fiction. He had acquired a knack for writing plays. He now crafted a drama pitting the villainous "criminal-defiant" wing of the Bolshevik leadership against the "cosmopolitan-intellectuals" he and other Americans had befriended back in the 1930s.[58] While Kennan formerly had confined such speculation to his diary, he now staked his reputation on it. He laid out his thesis in official despatches and letters to Washington that he shared with British, Canadian, and perhaps other diplomatic colleagues in Moscow. He told a similar story to his Saltychikhi dacha friends.

The gifted prose stylist had mastered the art of inoculating fantastical arguments against criticism. He often started off by laying out the counterargument in such a way that he could diminish or demolish it. He would also deflect skepticism by first acknowledging that something "may sound a bit far-fetched," then adding that, nevertheless, "it is not impossible" nor "it is not out of the question." While acknowledging that a scenario was "only a hypothesis . . . for which proof is lacking," he would nevertheless affirm that "my intuition tells me . . . the 'truth' will be similar." "You know," he affirmed to Bohlen, "how much has to be done in this city by sheer intuition."[59]

Ever since his long telegram of 1946, Kennan's arguments about the Soviet Union had encountered little pushback because few dared challenge his claim to knowing the psychology of the Russian people and their Kremlin leaders. Much of that knowledge rested, by necessity, on conjecture. From observing the villagers of Saltychikhi, people on the street in Moscow, and the inhabitants of the few places he visited, he could extrapolate, he believed, leanings and attitudes across the vast Soviet Union. He peered through the microscope as if it were a telescope. For six years, Kennan's hunches and surmises, what he picked up with his antennae, had won wide acceptance because he undeniably did know a great deal about Russia, his prose packed a persuasive punch, and he advocated what most Americans, especially leaders, wanted to believe. The United States could avoid both all-out war and capitulation to Russia, and need focus only on building up the Western alliance. The strategist's repeated protests that his containment policy envisioned not military but rather political pressure on the Soviets could be, and largely was, ignored.

THE JUNE 6 LETTER

Writing to top State Department officials about the Soviet propaganda campaign on June 6, Kennan acknowledged that it was not easy for him to put his "revulsion and indignation far enough aside" to undertake "a calm and dispassionate analysis." What he claimed as detached judgment reached a self-important conclusion that sustained his fondest hopes. He proposed that the propaganda campaign "might have something to do with my own appointment and arrival" and with the possibility that the Soviets wanted "confidential talks looking toward the amicable adjustment of certain of the more dangerous of the issues" of the Cold War. Anticipating raised eyebrows, Kennan assured that while it was all too easy to overrate one's own importance, "I am experienced enough not to fall into this error." He laid out four possible reasons for the anti-American propaganda: first, to spur the flagging ideological zeal of the Russian people; second, to prepare for a planned hot war; third, a fight within the Kremlin; and, finally, the thesis that revolved around him and the diplomacy that he so longed to pursue. He then dismissed the first possibility as insufficient, the second as unlikely, and the third as lacking in evidence.[60]

Then he got to the nub, why his presence in Moscow carried such weight. "My name and personality are known" to many "prominent Soviet intellectuals and artists" who appreciated that here was an American who valued "Russian cultural values" and "the Russian spirit." Furthermore, Stalin and others would logically assume that Washington's appointment of a diplomat with his expertise might mean that the Americans sought "real discussions." Indeed, Kennan himself fervently wished for such logic to prevail with Truman and Acheson. Spinning the scenario further, he suggested that Soviet leaders might also decide "to move, or appear to move," toward talks.[61] Certainly Stalin as well as the Soviet embassy in Washington had called for diplomacy.

But why would the Soviets prepare for possible talks by slandering America? As Kennan pointed out, Stalin's practice was to destroy the proponents of a policy before he himself moved in that direction. To the "Soviet intelligentsia" the Kremlin chief might be warning: "You hate America. *We*, not you will be the moderate ones." As for Kennan, who symbolized those in the West still hoping for better relations, Stalin might be using the propaganda campaign to send a personal message.

There followed in this June 6 letter an astounding passage. The determined diplomat, who had failed to wring from Washington anything to offer the Russians and who had thus far elicited from the Kremlin only nasty noise, fantasized that the Soviet leadership did appreciate his background and aims. He ventriloquized a gruff Stalin wagging his finger while saying,

> You come here to us making reasonable and disarming noises and letting on as though you thought that some day we might be able to talk to one another. Very well. We are not saying that we would totally exclude the possibility. But don't think that just because you speak Russian and have had a few friends here and are known as a person interested in Russian culture that you are going to be able to play on the cosmopolitan weaknesses of our artists and writers. [If you are] going to talk with anyone around here, it is going to be to Papa and not to these neurotic intellectuals still longing for the fleshpots and the sterile estheticism of Paris. Whoever wants to talk business talks with us, and leaves our subordinates alone.[62]

In channeling "Papa," Kennan revealed his longing for Moscow-in-1934. Back then, his mastery of the language and culture and his status as the namesake of the elder George Kennan (1845–1924) had won respect from Soviet officials and a welcome from influential artists and writers. At parties they had indeed debated "the sterile estheticism of Paris" while indulging in their own "fleshpots." Having returned as ambassador, he did yearn to talk with those cultural subordinates as well as the political bosses. By sending this free-flowing fantasy to Acheson and other caustics in the State Department, Kennan exposed his mix of self-confidence and desperation. He granted that the whole scenario "may sound a bit far-fetched. How much of this is real, I cannot vouchsafe." Then, characteristically, he doubled down: "I dare say a good deal of it is."[63]

In disputing the assertion by Cumming and others that the propaganda campaign amounted to nothing new, Kennan again exposed his nostalgia. "I can say on the basis of personal experience that in the thirties and again during the war" Soviet leaders had remained cautious about their relations with the capitalist West. They had valued, as still did he, "the intactness and good repair of the normal and polite channel." Then, revealing himself still more, Kennan alluded to his longtime aspiration not just to ease differences between America and Russia but also to foster beneficial exchange. The Kremlin was shortsightedly forgetting "that there might be times when this channel would prove useful and necessary to them—indeed perhaps the only thing they might have to fall back upon."[64]

Peering beyond the wall of the Kremlin, Kennan saw what was inside his head. Drawing on his intuition—or as he put it, drinking in "those ineluctable touches of atmosphere in which the moods and influences [of Soviet leaders] are so marvelously reflected on the Moscow scene"— this lover of Anton Chekhov recalled the climactic scene of *The Cherry Orchard*. He was "again witnessing the swaggering arrogance of the drunken peasant-speculator Lopakhin," who, having bought the gentry's estate "now loses control of himself in his excitement and elation." "Impervious to the presence of the weeping family," the arrogant Lopakhin was "confident that never again will he need their respect, their help, or their solicitude." Kennan, who adored Chekhov and who had dressed like gentry while riding horseback in the Russian countryside in the 1930s, had named his own country estate the Cherry Orchard. Nothing would have pleased him more than to have Russians need his respect, his help, and his solicitude. In concluding this distinctly Kennanish despatch, he justified its length much as he had the long telegram. "When you are dealing with matters so strange and intricate as the psychology of the Bolshevik regime," the danger lay in saying too little.[65]

While Kennan's long telegram had crashed the barriers of official indifference, his June 6 letter helped crash his reputation among top officials. He had self-importantly specified a wide distribution to leaders in the State Department. Bohlen offered little more than a perfunctory response. Acheson did not reply. Matthews, speaking for the department, acknowledged "your extremely interesting letter" while ignoring its substance.[66]

The June missive and similar emotional expressions also undercut Kennan's standing among foreign diplomats. British ambassador Gascoigne edged into sarcasm by noting that his American colleague liked to "pose as *the* expert on the Soviet Union."[67] While affirming that Kennan was "regarded by all of us as being the No. 1 specialist on this country as regards Soviet psychology, ideology and policy," the expert's letter was "rather prolix" and made "too much of a mystery" of the propaganda campaign. Back in London, Foreign Office officials offered less deference. "Eminent though he is in his sphere, he has become . . . overelaborate in analysis and unable to see the wood for the trees." They dismissed the claim that the propaganda stemmed from his arrival in Moscow. The Soviets were simply trying to whip up apathetic public opinion. The American's "abstruse speculation" seemed "over-subtle" and "unconvincing." The mockery deepened as Gascoigne, in reply, referred to "George Kennan's magnum opus. I am so glad that you feel this is 'over-subtle'; I certainly do."[68]

Kennan's standing sank further when the ambassador, piqued by the propaganda campaign, banned the Soviets from the Fourth of July celebration at Spaso House. The Foreign Office concluded that "Kennan is behaving foolishly" and seems to "have lost almost all sense of proportion." Other Western diplomats criticized the ban "openly to me," Gascoigne reported. In reducing contact, the American was ironically "playing the Russians' game."[69]

In punishing the Russians by restricting contact with them, Kennan was indeed practicing what he detested the Kremlin for doing on a far grander scale. Pressuring the Russians in this way undercut what he himself so deeply desired. Such self-punishing behavior was, unfortunately, not alien to Kennan. He protested the gruesome propaganda by "refraining from asking for interviews with the Soviet Ministry for Foreign Affairs." He also broached to Gascoigne the possibility of having NATO representatives in Moscow discuss whether, with regard to the Soviet Union, "it was dignified and right to continue to . . . deal with it through Ambassadors." In considering removing these representatives from Moscow, Kennan "has the question of his own dignity very much in mind," Gascoigne observed.[70] Alarmed that such a pullback would feed Soviet fears that Washington was "entering upon a more hostile phase," William Strang, permanent under secretary of state for foreign affairs, implored Gascoigne to "continued to urge patience upon Kennan."[71]

Kennan's premise here—that his dignity and the conditions Western diplomats encountered in Moscow ranked as a major issue—harked back to battles he had fought since first going to Moscow in 1933. In the lead-up to World War II, while such practitioners of realpolitik as George Messersmith, Joseph E. Davies, and Franklin D. Roosevelt had focused on the strategic advantages of a tie with Russia, Kennan, Bullitt, and others burnt by their personal suffering in Moscow had questioned such links.

Kennan's prestige suffered another hit. Gascoigne began "wondering how much 'ice' Kennan cuts in Washington." From the British embassy in Washington came word that "Acheson did not regard Kennan as an oracle on general policy but he might regard him as an oracle on the Soviet Union."[72] The word "might" and the ambiguity inherent in advice from oracles signaled Kennan's decline as America's foremost Soviet expert. Given the Soviet spies that riddled the British Foreign Office, Stalin may well have reached a similar conclusion.

Kennan, however, still viewed himself as destiny's "chosen instrument" to ease the Cold War.[73] He proposed psychological, though not military, pressure to push the Russians into negotiating mode. He reasoned that the more the Soviets realized that their Marxist and geostrategic aspirations amounted to mere fantasy, the more readily they would compromise. Containment presumed first pressure, then diplomacy. Claiming that he discerned among Soviet leaders "extreme nervousness" about their "Commie algebra" calculating that the capitalist West faced inevitable collapse, Kennan urged Washington to launch "a psychological attack direct at the Kremlin itself, designed to shake its confidence." U.S. authorities should pursue the line that he himself was taking in Moscow, namely, "You people are continuing to live on the basis of a dream. . . . indulging yourself in an error of cosmic proportions." Absent a major war, both socialism and capitalism were not going away. Rather than pursue "escapist alternatives," Kremlin leaders should seek "decent and respectful negotiations."[74] He, of course, stood ready to conduct such talks.

Soon after making the above recommendation, Kennan urged Washington to curb provocative spying in Moscow. He complained about needless snooping "of a childish and 'Boy Scout' nature." This reduced Soviet respect for the embassy. The espionage undermined Kennan's two aspirations. First, it tightened the "drastic and total isolation" of officials such as himself from contact with the Soviet people. Consequently, life was becoming "practically impossible for foreigners in this country." And second, running spies out of the embassy jeopardized the already precarious chances of opening a channel of communication with the Soviet government. On this complaint, Kennan got at least lip service agreement in Washington from military and even intelligence chiefs.[75]

Kennan also took heart from a serious conversation with Soviet Foreign Minister Andrey Vyshinsky on June 19, their first since his arrival six weeks earlier. The two men had a history, since Vyshinsky had prosecuted the 1938 purge trials that had torn Kennan apart. Assuming that the Soviets were indeed picking up on his signals, Kennan congratulated himself that "my long silence and restraint" had yielded "a certain concern for my opinion." In complaining about the propaganda campaign, Kennan "emphasized how painful this had been to me," especially since he was doing "all in my power to bring about an improvement in the atmosphere." Manner and tone remained key for Kennan, and he appreciated that Vyshinsky "spoke quietly and reasonably with no trace of vehemence or unfriendliness." The Russian did protest the fierceness of anti-Soviet propaganda in America, a problem that Kennan promised to tackle. Not much concrete progress, the ambassador concluded, but satisfying atmospherics, especially when Vyshinsky on parting assured him that "the Soviet Government had high regard for my person."[76]

To Kennan's dismay, the tentative progress then reversed. To mark the second anniversary of the Korean War on June 25, Moscow newspapers launched an all-out assault against America's supposedly instigating West Germany to unleash "fascist aggression in Europe" and Japan to attack the "peoples of Asia." The United States was following "the path of Hitlerite tyranny and bloody banditry" by slaughtering "hundreds of thousands of civilians" in Korea.[77]

Intent nevertheless on opening some channel to the Kremlin, Kennan moved beyond the fantasies of charming Russians with folk songs on his guitar or leveraging the return of Ralph Parker's painting. The ambassador cross-examined his top staff as to who might have a contact with the Soviets.[78] He then asked Cumming to inform Boris Podtserob, a top official in the Foreign Ministry whom Kennan had known in the 1930s, that the ambassador hoped to talk informally with an "ostensibly private Soviet citizen," as had formerly been done with Baron Steiger and others.[79] What then ensued, however, horrified him.

THE INTRUDER

On July 5, a nervous looking, disheveled Russian dressed in a Western-style suit entered the embassy and, while refusing to give his name, insisted that "I must see Ambassador Kennan" about "a very personal matter." Kennan's thoughts immediately turned to his recent outreach to Podtserob. Hoping the young man "might have some personal message for me from some member of the Ministry, I agreed to see him." The visitor blurted out that "he needed money and arms and he was in a position to supply information." He implied that the arms could be used for assassination or other violence. Kennan flatly turned down the outlandish proposal. Yet he did not immediately dismiss the young man. Instead he kept him for ten to fifteen minutes, probably to ascertain what, if anything, might link this visit to the bid to Podtserob. Upon being ordered to leave, the visitor, growing more agitated, begged for help in exiting the building undetected. Was there not a secret tunnel? Could he not be smuggled out in an American car? Otherwise he faced certain persecution and death from the secret police. Unmoved, Kennan told him that he must have known about this danger before entering the building. The intruder wailed that this was "very cruel" . . . "I replied that there was no other position I could take."[80] Upon leaving the embassy, the man was seized by the police and shoved into a car with the curtains down. Kennan soon discovered from photographs that the visitor was a former interpreter for the Foreign Ministry, who it later developed, was indeed an agent provocateur, probably sent by the secret police.

The most telling aspect of this bizarre incident was how Kennan interpreted it as part of an elaborate drama about seismic rifts within the Soviet leadership, his impact on the Kremlin, and the prospect of easing the Cold War. In an "eyes only" cable to Acheson, he asserted that because the intrusion was "directed personally to myself," the extraordinary episode packed considerable significance. He advanced four explanations, all revolving around himself. First, the Kremlin had sent an "insulting answer" to his bid to Podtserob. In effect, the Soviets were accusing him of reaching out only because he sought "diversion and espionage." The second possibility reflected his own yearning: the Soviets aimed to "test me before following up the suggestion made to Podtserob." If he "showed no interest in any improper activities," they might open the channel of communication. Third, strongly anti-U.S. circles had grown alarmed about an "independent channel of access" to top officials in the Kremlin. This move to block accurate information reflected bitter differences within Stalin's circle. Fourth, the incident signaled an effort to discredit the embassy and Kennan himself.

Kennan judged the third, most intricate explanation as the most "close to truth." He posited that the Soviets had been "much agitated and torn as to how to treat my mission here, and this may have led to bitter internal differences" regarding relations with the United States. "My own connection with the matter is explosive in the extreme," he warned, because the Soviets might falsely accuse him of encouraging the espionage and violence. He asked for permission to confront Vyshinsky about the incident.[81]

Concluding that Kennan himself was "much agitated," the State Department tried to calm things down. It remains uncertain whether Acheson ever read the cable addressed to his eyes only. The reply was sent by Matthews, who tersely allowed that "one or more interpretations you mention may have validity." Formerly he had deferred to Kennan on most Russian matters. Now Matthews instructed him not to mention the incident to Vyshinsky. Kennan vented instead by sending to Bohlen on July 16 an even more elaborate version of the scenario sketched in his June 13 cable.

THE JULY 16 LETTER

Kennan crafted a drama pitting outright villains against near-heroes in a fight over him. Relying once again on his intuition and "strong instinctive feeling," he claimed to have "stumbled into something which is not only both dangerous to myself and the mission, but may be extremely revealing" about the basic nature of the Soviet Union. For years he had swung back and forth, sometimes in the same document, as to whether Kremlin leaders were primarily rational potential interlocutors or hyperemotional, dangerous criminals. He now argued that the two impulses had competed since before 1917. The Bolshevik Party had arisen from two conflicting though overlapping groups, the cosmopolitan-intellectual and the criminal-defiant. The former included sophisticated, sincere Marxists, many of whom had been influenced by their experiences in the West before the revolution. The latter had pushed the purges and included Stalin, though he also kept a toehold in the other camp.

This bifurcation was "extremely important for foreign relations." While the cosmopolitan-intellectuals, like Kennan himself, regarded the Soviet Union as "as an integral part of its world environment" concerned to some degree with "real respect and understanding" by the outside world, the criminal-defiants had "no sense of dependence upon the outside world and no feeling of the necessity for any genuine sort of adjustment to it." Kennan included Foreign Minister Maxim Litvinov as a part of the cosmopolitan-intellectual group in the 1930s, along with "other people we knew." Though decimated by the purges and the 1939–1941 alliance with Nazi Germany, this more responsive group had revived during the war. Afterward, Stalin, who as a criminal Bolshevik had perversely colluded with the czarist police, instigated the Cold War. "This was the sense of Stalin's remark to Averell Harriman that from now on they would go their own way."[82] From 1946 to Kennan's arrival, the Kremlin had remained "almost completely dominated" by the criminal-defiant perspective, personified by Stalin's henchmen, Georgy Malenkov, and secret police chief Lavrenty Beria. When wartime foreign minister Vyacheslav Molotov had balked at totally abandoning "respectable" ties to the West, Stalin had replaced him with Vyshinsky, symbolic of the purges in the late 1930s.

By 1952, Kennan continued, the Soviets faced the challenge of surging U.S. military and political might, especially in Korea and Germany. That spurred thinking that the Kremlin should "re-don its sheep's clothing and seek something like real contacts and possibly agreements" with

Washington. "My own appointment as Ambassador here served to bring this tension to a new pitch. In the minds of people here I was associated with the Harriman era . . . when Molotov was predominant, when the Soviet Government profited . . . from an outwardly decent diplomatic relationship with the United States." At this point Kennan brought on stage his cultural companions, the remnants of his Russian friends from the 1930s. The yearning for a more open political and cultural order, an alternative brightened by Kennan's arrival "reached deeply and dangerously into Soviet intellectual and cultural circles where the cosmopolitan tendencies had never been overcome." Desperate, the criminal-defiant forces launched an "an extreme and violent anti-American campaign" of propaganda. (The narrative here ignored what Cumming had told Kennan, that this nastiness predated his arrival.)

Cumming's reaching out to Podtserob about an informal channel set off "a minor bombshell" within the Kremlin. The criminal-defiants feared that the ambassador might open a link to Stalin himself. That would break the monopoly on incoming information held by the hard-liners ever since they had poisoned relations between Roosevelt and Stalin near the end of the war. "If real information and ideas" were now to filter up to the top leaders, "the consequences could be terrific." This game changer had to be spiked at any cost. Hence, the provocateur was sent to the embassy with the offer to assassinate Soviet leaders. If the ambassador had taken the bait, the hard-liners would have triumphed. Sending the agent, Kennan warned, "was a risky and extreme thing do—the work of worried, violent men, with a pronounced criminal psychology," characters who, still worse, had "very little understanding for diplomatic niceties." The takeaway from all this drama was that the split in Moscow offered Washington opportunity as well as peril.

How did Kennan's scenario fit with actuality? Was the Kremlin really divided into two factions, one opposed to and another in favor of better relations with the West? Kennan argued his case with a characteristic strategy. He headed off criticism by allowing that his hypothesis undoubtedly contained serious inaccuracies. Then he doubled down: "But I would not dismiss it completely. The invisible antennae which years of life here have forced me to acquire tell me that in this instance—*shto-to-est*"—which meant "there is something."[83] But what was there?

While Bohlen thanked his friend for these insights, neither he nor anyone else in the State Department seemed intrigued by the ambassador's thesis. Indeed, the apparent flights of fancy further dimmed Kennan's authority. Under Secretary of State David K. Bruce criticized the onetime sage as "far too emotional and egocentric." He "simply could not read Kennan's reports and telegrams because they were so long-winded and so blatantly seeking to be literary rather than provide information."[84] Kennan was getting undermined also by someone leaking distorted versions of his cables that were then criticized in the press. These reports depicted Kennan not as seeking to improve relations, but rather as sounding the alarm about Russian intentions.[85]

Within the Kremlin during this last year of Stalin's reign, the leadership was indeed fractured and fearful, but not in the way that Kennan conjured. Stalin's suspicion of almost everyone and everything including, he once admitted, himself, hatched the bizarre "doctors' plot." Scores of physicians, especially Jews, were arrested on charges of treasonous contacts with foreigners. The dictator's lieutenants feared that the boss might turn against any one or all of them. They also worried that Lavrenty Beria, who ran the secret police, might attempt the same.

What united this cohort was anxiety about the United States. Future premier Nikita S. Khrushchev later recalled that "in the days leading up to Stalin's death we believed that America would invade the Soviet Union and we would go to war."[86] After Stalin died, on March 5, 1953, Beria and Khrushchev, along with Georgy Malenkov, Nikolai Bulganin, and Vyacheslav Molotov, jostled for power. Yet they agreed on the need to ease the foreign danger. Like Kennan, Beria envisioned negotiations leading to reunifying a neutral, largely disarmed Germany. When Molotov questioned giving up on communism in East Germany, Beria reportedly replied, "All we need is a peaceful Germany; whether it is socialist or not isn't important to us."[87] While Beria was soon deposed and executed by rivals worried about his control of the secret police, the post-Stalin leaders still sought a relaxation of tensions with Washington. If Kennan had remained in Moscow into 1953, as he expected, he would have been on hand to shepherd any diplomacy between these Soviet leaders and the new U.S. president.

Nevertheless, the strain was getting to him. After three months in Moscow, Kennan in August 1952 found it impossible to adjust to the "volume and hatefulness of lies" in the anti-American propaganda. To Jeanette, for decades his closest confidant, he complained about being "detached . . . to so fantastic a degree" that he felt literally invisible. He could "haunt the streets and public places like a ghost," but could not speak with anyone. "I have eyes and ears but no voice." Adding to the sense of unreality was that he was permitted to view only the "carefully prepared puppet show" staged by the Soviet government. His detached life in Moscow could not "end well or happily, and may well end in catastrophe."

And yet the bubble had its attractions. With a mix of sarcasm, self-mockery, and self-revelation, he confirmed that within the embassy, "I am king. I have all the attributes of royalty: servants, marble halls, outward respect." In view of the hit to the family budget of ambassadorial expenses, he appreciated that, "like royalty, I don't carry money; and if I go broke I do so in the quiet, painless regal manner." More importantly, he felt "protected from much." He found in Russia the "peace of mind I could never find in Princeton." He had *"no* plans for coming home," nor did he desire to "do anything, if I ever do come home, except to farm."[88]

Kennan assumed that any chance of easing the Cold War depended on his remaining as ambassador for a while. Before leaving the United States, he had affirmed to both the Senate committee confirming his appointment and the political scientist Hans Morgenthau that he expected his tenure to last two or three years.[89] That meant serving as ambassador well into the term of whoever became president on January 20, 1953. Kennan's confidence that his standing as a Russian expert made him indispensable was reflected also in his cautioning Acheson about the "nightmarish" McCarthyite investigations into the loyalty and possible perjury of Kennan's friend and former subordinate John Paton Davies. If Davies were convicted, Kennan warned, he, Kennan, might resign and refuse any further "major responsibility in Government." He suggested that Acheson "might wish to tell the President about this."[90]

Salisbury reported that Kennan was "quite ready to sit here and wait" until the pressures on Russia produced "a desire on the part of the Kremlin for a change in policy. He thinks another seven or eight months will be required for this"—that is, until March or April 1953.[91] That prediction of a change in the Kremlin proved eerily, and for Kennan tragically, accurate.

That Kennan was patiently waiting until the Russians realized their "policy is running up a blind alley" and signaled a greater willingness to compromise did not mean that he had ceased trying to hurry the process along. He wanted America to maintain its pressure on the Soviets while minimizing its provocations.

On August 11, he sent Truman a plain vanilla version of the dramas portrayed in his June 13 and July 16 messages. What "strikes me hardest here" was the absence of a "real channel for any exchange of views." In a thinly veiled complaint about his brush-off in Washington back in April, he noted that he "had not yet had a single bit of business to take up with the Soviet Government." He was careful to fix most of the blame on the Kremlin's "mood of arrogance and over-confidence." Now, however, with containment largely a success, "people here are beginning to have serious doubts as to whether it would not have been better" to have maintained "polite and decent relations" with the West. But, he cautioned Truman, "these feelings are still only in the stage of uneasy doubts"—or as he had put it to Bohlen, the influence of the cosmopolitan-intellectuals remained shaky. If the United States stood firm but also receptive to diplomacy, the Soviets would likely arrive at "a desire to treat us decently and talk to us respectfully." For Kennan, the form, tone, and process of diplomacy all amounted to substance, and all were requisite to political compromise.

While holding out to the president the prospect of serious negotiations with the Russians, the ambassador was anxious to head off any repeat of FDR's summit diplomacy, which had sidelined professionals such as himself. Kennan instructed Truman that when the Soviets signaled that they wanted to talk, "I would force them to deal with us decently at *all* levels," including relations between the embassy and the Foreign Office. Kennan wanted not "rare and intermittent conversations with Stalin" followed by long periods of no contact, but rather orders from Stalin to his officials to treat all U.S. representatives "with greater politeness and circumspection and respect."

In going forward, Kennan would set two prerequisites for the Soviets before any negotiations: a cease-fire in Korea and ending "the violent and dirty anti-American propaganda put out daily here in Moscow." Then, to the discomfort of State Department officials who previewed this letter before relaying it to Truman, Kennan added a prerequisite on the U.S. side. The American press should halt "the more extreme types of attack against the Kremlin." He wished "our press could be induced" to "lay off the subject of war" and stop indicating that "we regard a third world war as inevitable." How the press could be so induced Kennan did not say, nor probably did he care. Such war talk only played into the hands of Soviet "peace" propaganda, "frightens our friends"—and frightened Kennan still more.

Truman responded to the letter with a bare "thanks very much," as empty of content as were the replies to Kennan's request for instructions back in April and the reactions to his long letters in June and July.[92] Despite all his efforts, he had won little appreciation and no satisfaction.

Disappointment darkened even a glimmer of hope. Kennan had known the Italian ambassador, Mario di Stefano, since the old days when both had served as junior diplomats in Moscow. In late July, di Stefano confided to Kennan, and to him alone, the substance of an interview between Stalin and Pietro Nenni, leader of the Italian Socialist Party. After talking with Stalin, Nenni queried di Stefano whether Kennan "really entertained friendly feelings toward Russia." Di Stefano replied that his American friend "had come here in hopes of bettering the situation."[93] The Italian ambassador believed it likely that Stalin had prompted Nenni to ask about Kennan. The Russophile was justified, then, in thinking that maybe the old fox did intend to engage him. Because di Stefano had relayed this story only to Kennan, the latter in his report to the State Department stressed the utmost importance of preventing any leaks.

Nevertheless, someone in the department leaked the story to the Alsop brothers, who published the cable almost verbatim in their widely syndicated column. Kennan was betrayed by people high up in the department to which he had devoted his entire working life. Moreover, this was the fourth damaging leak. So much for the ambassador's hope of gathering around him in Moscow a cluster of Western representatives who confided in him, looked to him for advice, and constituted a coordinated influence in relations with the Soviet Union.

CRASH AND BURN

Kennan's frustration and anger were justified. He was singlehandedly trying to head off an atomic holocaust while his government remained indifferent when not hostile. It was a far cry from the glory days of 1946 to 1948, when his influence had appeared nearly boundless.

The suffering mounted. He grasped at the slenderest straw. During a theater performance of Tolstoy's *Resurrection*, he was "electrified" to hear the leading man say, as he seemed to look down on Kennan: "'There is an American by the name of George, and with him we are all in agreement.' I could not believe my ears. Was this a message of sympathy . . . a disguised demonstration?" After the play he and a friend rushed home to see whether the line was in the script—and to their great disappointment found the reference to Henry George, the American reformer.[94] Startling evidence that he was indeed being listened to led to stress of another kind. Suspecting the Russians were bugging Spaso House, technicians zeroed in on a beautiful inlaid-wood Great Seal of the United States given by the Soviets to Ambassador Averell Harriman. Smashing it apart, they found a powerful listening device that could be activated remotely. Suddenly thwarted, the secret police took revenge by making Kennan feel even more unwelcome in his own home—or so he perceived. The morning after the discovery, "the faces of the guards at the gate were frozen into a new grimness. So dense was the atmosphere of anger and hostility that one could cut it with a knife."[95]

Back in the spring, he could flee the gloom by venturing out to Salty-chikhi, where he could imagine himself back in old Russia and relax with Juli, Harrison, and Tom. Now, however, with Annelise, infant Wendy, and two-year old Christopher ever present, visits to that refuge became problematic. Evidence suggests that Annelise may have suspected that something had gone on at the dacha before her arrival in Moscow. Back in 1941, she had hurried to Berlin, dumping her two daughters on Jeanette, whose house was already crowded, because she did not trust her husband when alone. In a 1983 interview, Annelise displayed strong feelings herself as she recollected George's anguish in 1952. She stressed how "very much" she believed that "it was tremendously bad that he came" to Moscow two months before her and had "spent this time alone." "I think things might have worked out differently if he had come in with the family," she reiterated.[96]

A sign of Kennan's unhappiness was that he asked the CIA for cyanide poison capsules. He later explained that if war had broken out, he might have been tortured by the Soviets for information.[97] Years later, Paul Nitze, his successor on the Policy Planning Staff, arrived at a different theory after investigation. According to a memo that Nitze kept in his files, Kennan wanted the cyanide because he "got in trouble with some 'dame' and thought the Russians might in some way publicize it." Another account claimed that Acheson became upset because "Kennan had had an affair abroad that could get him in political trouble."[98] Such gossip would have inflamed the guilt Kennan had felt the year before. Despite the flings with Eros, he remained a family man in the embrace of Civilization.

On September 9, ten days before his fatal outburst, Kennan groused that his professional life was "studded with danger and pitfalls and invitations to catastrophe." He added that "while the peacemaker may be blessed in the eyes of the Lord," he faced likely damnation in the eyes of the people. As for his personal life, it was bizarre and disorienting. Four months in Moscow had not yielded a single conversation with an ordinary Russian. If he or a member of his staff entered a crowded train, the compartment or even the entire car was promptly emptied of passengers by the secret police. "It is as though we had some sort of plague." Kennan increasingly doubted whether his remaining as ambassador was either necessary or desirable. He was giving up on his mission of peace. Ironically, attacks on him back in the United States might offer a way out of this hell. John Foster Dulles, the likely secretary of state if the

Republican Dwight D. Eisenhower won the November 1952 election, was loudly insisting that "containment is not enough." While the containment policy certainly had problems in Kennan's view, it remained associated with his name. Hence, a Republican victory would "achieve my return to the United States."[99]

A small but wrenching incident proved the final straw. Back when he had first arrived, George wrote Annelise that the park just outside the high iron-spike Spaso House fence was full of children, and he hoped that their son would be able to play there normally.[100] Even that innocent wish was thwarted by Soviet-imposed isolation. Christopher had to remain inside the gate. A day or so before he departed for a meeting of U.S. diplomats in London, George watched as the young boy walked over to the fence and began playing through the bars with some Russian children. Though seemingly trivial, this American-Russian interaction assumed for Kennan enormous symbolic significance. "Soon, to much mutual pleasure, a game was in progress." But then the Soviet guards at the gate "rushed up and shooed the Soviet children sternly away." This incident "came at the end of a difficult and nerve-wracking summer." He had his fill of this "vicious, timid, mediaeval regime of isolation." Kennan understood that the perfect ambassador would not have lost his patience. But he was too worked up to let go of this latest outrage.[101]

Salisbury, who was at the airport to see Kennan off on September 19, noticed his friend's "silent, withdrawn mood." Further stress came from Annelise, who resented being left behind to care for Christopher and Wendy while her husband got to escape to London. "I am already beginning to be sorry for myself," she confided to Jeanette.[102]

A sure sign that Kennan was torn up about something important to him was that he would try to calm those feelings by encapsulating the problem in a coolly rational written analysis. He sensed that if he was rigorous enough in choosing his words and in constructing his sentences, the language could rein in the emotions. He had tried this tactic in describing the frightful purges in 1938 and when writing to Cummings about his foreboding in December 1951. Such efforts at containment usually failed, however. His feelings broke through the language, and he ended up communicating something quite emotional. As Cumming observed, Kennan operated with the "strange combination of a well-drilled mind," a "fine command of the English language," and a pattern of "emotional response to external stimuli, which somehow or another his well-drilled mind doesn't seem to be able to control."[103]

In preparing for the flight to London, he tried so hard to repress an outburst that he ended up wrecking his career. The day before leaving, he invited in Salisbury, Whitney, and other friendly journalists. For more than an hour he rehearsed with them the questions he should expect from reporters in the West and the "answers that would not offend the Russians." Such focus on reining in chance and feeling struck Salisbury as "a bit eerie."[104] The ambassador boarded the plane with a little notebook in which he had neatly inked several of these questions and for each an innocuous answer. On the bumpy flight he wrote in a shaky hand: "Don't be a boy and don't feed the little ego. Be deliberate. Learn not to mind pauses and silences."[105]

During the stopover at Tempelhof airport in West Berlin on September 19, reporters posed the expected questions. Then someone asked if Americans in Moscow had much social contact with Russians. That query was not in the little notebook. But constant frustration had burned it into Kennan's psyche. "The question itself annoyed me," Kennan later recalled. "'Don't you know how foreign diplomats live in Moscow?'" Then he cracked. "There welled up in me the whole dismal experience of the past four months, ending with the experience of seeing my little boy's playmates chased away from him." As Jack Raymond reported to the New York Times, Kennan blurted out that "Western diplomats resided in Moscow in an 'icy-cold' atmosphere of isolation so complete" that it "is worse than he experienced as an interned U.S. diplomat in Germany after Pearl Harbor." It was impossible to engage Russians in ordinary conversation. He added that the anti-American propaganda campaign had not diminished despite his formal protest.

Even more startling than what Kennan said was how he said it. He did not caution reporters that his complaint about the isolation in Moscow was off the record. This lapse was strange, Raymond commented to Salisbury, because "Kennan had frequently discussed this subject in the past but had always put such remarks off the record." This time "Kennan was very tired," Raymond explained charitably.[106]

Also startled was Cumming. He later recalled how Kennan had "drilled in on all" of the staff "never, never, never, never compare the totalitarian structure of the Soviet Union with that of Nazi Germany."[107] Whatever the actual parallel in the regimes, Soviet citizens from Stalin to the street sweeper treasured their victory over Nazi Germany. Now, however, the diplomat blatantly violated his own dictum. He not only compared the isolation in Moscow to that in wartime Berlin, but he flung this insult while in Hitler's former capital.[108]

Flying on to London, Kennan met further trouble when his comprehensive analysis of relations between Russia and NATO, which he had expected would be a focus of his fellow diplomats' discussion, was almost totally repudiated. The United States and its allies would not negotiate with Moscow to neutralize Germany, but rather rearm West Germany and integrate it into NATO.

Kennan realized that his views on NATO and on Germany brought him closer in some respects to Russia than to America. If someone in the Kremlin were to ask him, "'What is it you want of us with respect to Germany?' My only answer would have to be: 'the collapse of your power.'" Seeking Moscow's unconditional surrender struck him as unrealistic and dangerous. Washington's uncompromising position made war "inevitable, or very nearly so." He dreaded returning to Moscow where he would face not only "foul, malicious, and insulting propaganda" charging America with warmongering but, worse, the realization that "we *were* actually following" a path toward war.[109]

On September 26, an editorial in *Pravda* charged that Kennan in Berlin had "lied ecstatically." He was castigated as an enemy of the Soviet Union.[110] He reflected bitterly that "what the United States Government started on one day, the Soviet Government finished on the next." On October 3, the Kremlin formally declared this lifelong Russophile persona non grata. Stalin's associates later explained why they had so dramatically punished Kennan. In 1955, Anastas Mikoyan and Lazar Kaganovich confided to Chip Bohlen, now ambassador to Moscow, that precisely because they had regarded Kennan as serious and intelligent they had regretted his insult. They still did not understand "how Kennan could have departed from the accepted tenets of diplomacy." In defending his friend, Bohlen did not contest the seriousness of Kennan's remarks, but rather stressed how easy it was to slip in the "informal give and take" with the press. Mikoyan then explained, "In Berlin it was too much. That we should be insulted precisely from Berlin was intolerable." The two left Bohlen "with the impression that it was Stalin himself who had ordered George's expulsion."[111]

Meanwhile, Kennan, with the storm swirling around him, was ordered by Truman and Acheson to hunker down until after the November 1952 elections. Annelise, stranded at Spaso House with two young children, then had to pack up their belongings and fly to Bonn, West Germany, where her husband was ensconced in embassy guest quarters in nearby Bad Godesberg.

Kennan had crashed not only his ambassadorship in Moscow but also his standing as the U.S. government's most respected expert on Russia. Although he would remain concerned with Russia for the second half-century of his life, he would do so largely as an outside critic.

———

"It is a real shock to lose him," mourned Salisbury. He already missed the "special pleasure of having him use the dacha" as his private retreat and of listening "by the hour as he sprawled in front of the fireplace arguing about Chekhov" or Soviet politics. Puzzling why Kennan had permitted himself such indiscretion, the friend concluded that "when a man feels something as deeply as George Kennan did, sometimes those feelings come to the surface regardless of whether he is a diplomat or an ambassador."[112]

Tellingly, in the week between his denunciation by *Pravda* and his being declared persona non grata, Kennan in effect expelled himself from Moscow. For months he had subsisted on the slender hope that "if my own Government were ever to provide me with something to say, it might just be that someday there would be someone in Moscow to say it to." But that proved just a dream. Still trusting in his intuition, he mourned that it could not blast through the recalcitrance of the two governments. What he had detected were signs "too subtle and too delicate, too deeply founded in the peculiarities of Soviet reality" for anyone else to discern. And now, he himself had lost credibility in both Moscow and Washington. He was giving up and he wanted out. As with his previous tours in Russia, it had all become too much to sustain. As Isaiah Berlin observed, "[Kennan] doesn't bend. He breaks."[113] Assuming that the State Department expected him to return to Moscow, he appealed to Bohlen that "if there must be an Ambassador, I do not favor its being me."[114] He also anticipated pressure from Annelise, who would insist on remaining.

Among the feelings that impelled Kennan's outburst at Tempelhof was a buildup of frustration and resentment. He hated living in Russia as a ghost, as someone forbidden to mingle with the Russian people, soak in their culture, and feel the sense of Russia all about him. The deprivation seems to have triggered an ancient behavioral pattern. He had entered adulthood, he later recalled, "full of pride, self-pity, defiance, and determination to revenge myself, by various means of self-affliction, for the indifference in my environment."[115] Though he was referring to the coldness of his childhood, the extreme frigidity he encountered in Moscow seems to have goaded him into further self-affliction, the worst of his life.

While Kennan knew what Washington and Moscow needed to do to ease tensions, he could not get either government to allow him to conduct the necessary diplomacy. He had reached a dead end. As a colleague who had observed him for decades commented: "George was too damn smart and too seasoned and experienced to make that statement not realizing it might just get him out."[116]

In getting himself out, he had also invited widespread ridicule. Comments in the State Department about "Kennan's silly press comment" ranged from "he has seriously compromised his usefulness" to "doubtful—I never did think there was any to compromise."[117] British Foreign Office officials wondered whether "the Sage of Princeton" "was angling for his own removal. If not, his lack of self-control is extraordinary."[118] Louis Joxe, the French ambassador in Moscow, concluded

FIGURE 30. Looking emotionally stricken, Kennan gazes out
the porthole of the ship carrying him and his family back to
America after he was declared persona non grata by the Soviet
government. (Courtesy of Getty Images.)

that "Kennan had been a damn fool to make the Tempelhof statement."[119] A humiliated Kennan suffered "a loneliness greater than any
I had ever conceived." Nowhere could he find understanding and support. He was caught between America and Russia, "tossed into this
impossible position between two worlds."[120]

In retrospect, he framed the drama as a tragic love story. While
depicting the Russian people as an "attractive lady," he characterized
the Kremlin as a "very rough, cruel, and dominating gent who has her,
and doesn't intend to let anyone else have anything to do with her."[121]
In 1933–1934, 1935–1937, 1944–1946, and again in 1952, Kennan tried to
romance the "lady." His "real love for the Russian people pops out all
the time," a colleague observed.[122] That passion was nevertheless
thwarted by the Kremlin, by Washington, and—not least—by his own
temperament. Kennan's struggle to contain his emotions was overwhelmed by his desire for Russia and dread of nuclear war. Impru-
dence, impatience, and self-punishment widened his separation from

the beloved. He concluded, sadly, "You can't rescue this damsel, you can't help her."[123]

———

The final act in the tragedy of Kennan as ambassador opened in early 1953, with the inauguration of President Dwight D. Eisenhower on January 20 and the death of Stalin on March 5. Kennan had expected to remain as ambassador into the new administration. Back in June 1952, he had commented that with the aging of Stalin and other longtime leaders, "it is time nature began to play her usual tricks."[124] While Secretary of State John Foster Dulles blustered about the "rollback" of Soviet influence, his bark was worse than his bite. Moreover, Eisenhower himself was open to easing tensions, starting with ending the Korean War. In Moscow, Beria, Malenkov, and Khrushchev also hoped to tone down the Cold War.[125] If Kennan were in Moscow, he might have been able to conduct the diplomacy for which he had prepared himself since the late 1920s. He might have fanned the flickering light of wistful thinking into a flame that warmed relations. Then the subsequent four decades might have developed more safely and without the perilous crises over Berlin and Cuba. Kennan's place in history would also have been far different. None of that happened, of course. The curtain came down with Washington and Moscow fumbling while Kennan, back in Princeton, fumed.

CHAPTER 9

CONTESTING THE COLD WAR, 1953–1966

"AN UNUSUAL HUSH fell over the pre-lunch drinkers at the Metropolitan Club here today," the *New York Times* reported on February 10, 1966. "Government officials, bankers, lawyers and journalists grouped, glasses in hand, around a television set. Their silence was a tribute to George Frost Kennan," who was testifying on the war in Vietnam. "Speaking softly, choosing each word with care, and peering owlishly over his old-fashioned 'half-glasses,' Mr. Kennan held not only the attention but the respect of those committee members, like Senator Stuart Symington, Democrat of Missouri, who plainly disagreed with his proposals" arguing for diplomacy rather than escalation of the war.[1] Kennan's testimony pre-empted *I Love Lucy* and other popular daytime shows as millions of viewers tuned in to the author of the containment doctrine explaining why that was the wrong policy in Southeast Asia. One viewer focused so intently on Kennan's words that she burned the shirt she had been ironing.

Thirteen years after his humiliation by the Soviet and U.S. governments, Kennan commanded a respectful, nationwide audience that included ordinary women and men as well as hawkish opponents like Senator Symington. A friend observed that George "can't help being a leader," someone who approached problems from a broad perspective and offered solutions.[2] Dressed in a three-piece gray suit with a heavy gold chain affixed to his pocket watch, Kennan was making it respectable to dissent from the Vietnam War. Containment did not apply to the civil war in Vietnam, Kennan explained. Moreover, the spectacle of Americans attacking "a poor and helpless people, and particularly people of a different race and color," wreaked "psychological damage" to America's global image.[3]

He urged the United States to switch from fighting over unimportant territory in Southeast Asia to negotiating with the Soviet Union over the pressing problems of nuclear weapons and divided Germany. "Very patient diplomacy" with Moscow could yield an easing or even a disengagement from the Cold War.[4] The iconoclast opened a crack—a narrow one—in the establishment. While Dean Acheson and the other so-called Wise Men would in 1968 tell Johnson that he had to shift course in Vietnam, they, unlike Kennan, remained comfortable with the division of Europe and the nuclear arms race.

By the time of the Vietnam hearings in 1966, Kennan had won acclaim as a scholar by publishing a Pulitzer Prize–winning two-volume history of U.S.-Soviet relations in 1917–1920. In 1955, he snared, despite some skepticism from professional historians, a coveted lifetime professorship at the Institute for Advanced Study in Princeton. That perch guaranteed a sizable income, staff support, and a congenial environment. He served as U.S. ambassador to Yugoslavia from 1961 to 1963. Despite these and other achievements, Kennan nonetheless suffered bouts of what he termed depression. Even when his mood lifted, he felt weighed down by what amounted to five dilemmas.

FIVE DILEMMAS

First, Kennan, despite his esteem as a private citizen, longed to return to power in government. He believed he merited a high position because of his insights and his prescience. As he saw it, he had been right about how to deal with Soviet expansion in 1946–1948, and since then he had foreseen the dangers of not moving on from containing the Soviets to negotiating with them. Frustration about his ouster from power was aggravated by fear that Washington and Moscow were sliding toward nuclear war. He wrestled with how he might leverage his personal influence into political power. He hoped, in vain, that the Eisenhower administration would appoint him to some high position. He made the most of his being called in as an expert consultant. He gave hundreds of lectures to various quasi-governmental, business, public affairs, and academic audiences. He created not waves but a tsunami of controversy with his 1957 radio broadcasts over the British Broadcasting Company. He felt exhilaration, for him an unusual reaction, about the prospect of running for Congress in 1954 and for the U.S. Senate in 1960, and was dissuaded only for personal financial reasons. He briefed presidential candidate John F. Kennedy, only to agonize as others snared the plum appointments.

Even Kennan's successes aggravated his frustrations. No matter how much he tried to tamp down his ambitions, Kennan could not stop hoping, and half-expecting, that he might once again wield influence within the government. Elated when John F. Kennedy appointed him ambassador to Yugoslavia in 1961, Kennan then tried to parlay that modest position into a major role as interlocutor between the president and Soviet Premier Nikita S. Khrushchev.

Second, Kennan fretted over all the time and energy eaten up by his responding to hundreds of lecture requests. Moreover, public engagement conflicted with the scholarship that he had committed to when taking his position at the Institute for Advanced Study. He feared that the self-promotion required to remain in the public eye, no matter how modestly veiled, cheapened him. He had sunk down to a showman. But what else could he do? Though he resolved time and again to pull back from public life, he could not stop aspiring to leadership.

Third was the contradiction between feeling estranged from American society—expressed in private rants against cars and California, self-dial telephones and television—and his remaining in the country that he supposedly despised. While he fantasized about pursuing the life of an esthete on the west coast of Scotland, Annelise remained unwilling to give up her comforts and friends in Princeton. Nor would he give up the two cars in his garage. Moreover, he needed the salary from the Institute and the solace he got from the farm in Pennsylvania. Though fired by the U.S. government, he continued, despite his fuming, to love (and live in) the United States. Similarly, though expelled by the Soviet government, he continued to love, and at times even identify with, the culture and people of America's atomic rival. As a neighbor observed, it was not easy being George F. Kennan.

Fourth, he continued to suffer the agonies of lost intimacy that had plagued him since infancy. What he called his wandering eye continued to roam, notwithstanding his half-hoping that old age would cure him. He deployed psychology and theology in theorizing extramarital sex. Kennan regarded as scientific fact Freud's theory of an inherent conflict between sexual expression and creativity, on the one hand, and societal restraint and order on the other. Male privilege and normativity were also a given. He doubted, therefore, "that human beings are destined to rot in hell because their efforts to combine an animalistic nature with the discipline of civilization are not always successful." Even the Biblical prohibition against adultery "envisaged marriage as a polygamous affair and women as a slave; it was easier to observe when you had 35 of them."[5] The intellectual work that now filled much of his time justified, he told himself, sensual diversion. He detailed in his diary dreams of sexual desire, often with women of color and usually with Annelise helpfully gone, either through divorce or death. While remaining elusive as to details, he alluded to discreet affairs. More poignant than his philandering, however, were his fantasies of breathing into life the nurturing parents he never had. In dreams, in waking hours, and in between states, Kennan conjured visits of comforting intimacy with the mother who had died shortly after his birth and with the father whose shyness had kept him distant from his son.

Finally, other personal trials: Though he would live another half-century, Kennan suffered painful ailments, including recurring shingles, a burning kidney stone, duodenal ulcers, and repeated influenza. He endured quarrels with Annelise and tension with his older children (Grace, twenty-two, and Joan, eighteen, in 1954) who, he lamented, "do not love me."[6] Such stress foreshadowed his public and private confrontation in 1968 with countercultural opponents of the Vietnam War.

Although he had repeatedly predicted the end of his career in government, Kennan was shocked at being fired in April 1953. The separation pained even more because it came after six months of waiting for a new job after being declared persona non grata by the Soviets. Under State Department regulations, an officer who failed to secure a new position was terminated. That was Kennan's humiliating fate despite his decades of service. Neither the outgoing Truman administration nor the incoming Eisenhower team offered Kennan a post-Moscow job. "My father was very, very upset," Grace later recalled. "He suffered almost a year's depression after that."[7] Despite brief interludes of government service, Kennan over the next half-century would have a say in public affairs only as an outside critic. He never ceased, however, in aiming for influence within the U.S. government.

Even though Kennan had wanted to get out of Moscow, he was shocked at being declared persona non grata. He felt further offended when Acheson and Truman ordered him and the family to remain near Bonn until after the U.S. elections in November. Then, when he did return, they showed no interest in hearing what he had to say about the Soviet Union. After the election, neither President-elect Dwight D. Eisenhower nor John Foster Dulles, his designated secretary of state, both of whom Kennan knew personally, reached out to him. A chasm opened in Kennan's sense of duty and self-worth. It seemed unbearable to him to have his judgments about the Soviet Union unexpressed and "of no use to anyone anywhere."[8] Impelled by frustration and resentment, he accepted an invitation to speak in Scranton to the Pennsylvania Bar Association. He gave the talk on January 16, 1953, four days before Eisenhower's inauguration, and only a day after Dulles promised the Senate Foreign Relations Committee he would move beyond containment and "roll back" Soviet control of Eastern Europe.

KENNAN VERSUS DULLES

A showdown between Kennan and Dulles over containment versus rollback had been brewing for years. While the author of the long telegram had moved on from emotional alarms about the Soviet threat, Dulles declared during the Korean War that America had to "paralyze the slimy, octopus-like tentacles that reach out from Moscow to suck our blood." In May 1952, when Kennan arrived in Moscow hoping for informal talks with the Soviets to ease the Cold War, Dulles, coincidentally, flew to Paris to confer with Eisenhower, still the commander of NATO, on an electoral promise to ramp up that conflict. Dulles urged "A Policy of Boldness," as he titled an article for *Life* magazine. Though cautioning that any rollback of the Soviet empire had to be peaceful, Eisenhower appreciated Dulles's approach as a winning issue.[9] Dulles's dislike for the doctrine associated with Kennan's name went beyond the election campaign, however. As Robert Bowie, director of the Policy Planning Staff under Dulles, later explained, his boss "simply did not like the overtones of containment . . . as settling for the status quo."[10]

Ironically, Kennan shared Dulles's discontent with the status quo as well as his aim to get the Soviets out of Eastern Europe. While Dulles would pressure the Soviets to withdraw unilaterally, Kennan would offer them a mutual pullback. That would ease the threat of war, free both halves of Europe from foreign military occupation, and allow a re-knitting of sundered economic ties. Kennan's policy of disengagement amounted to rollback through diplomacy.

At Scranton, Kennan lashed out at "emotionalism" in foreign policy. Rollback amounted to a demagogic "striking of heroic attitudes" and an "irresponsible experiment."[11] Such a direct assault on Russia's vital interests could lead to war, he warned. Already deemed damaged goods after his indiscretion at Tempelhof airport, Kennan could ill afford to antagonize the incoming secretary of state. He evidently believed that his stature and duty obligated him to resist escalation of the Cold War. Adding to the acrimony was that Dulles, who in the 1930s had offered legal advice to businesses in Nazi Germany, had issued a moralistic critique of Kennan's call for realpolitik in *American Diplomacy*.[12]

Kennan waited at the farm for the call from Washington. Speculation in the press about his becoming ambassador to Japan, Switzerland, or Israel brought flurries of excitement to the Kennan household—and then disappointment, Grace would later recall.[13] The day before the inauguration, Annelise confided to Jeanette that "we still don't know any more about what we are going to do. With each appointment it becomes clear that they are not going to use the top Foreign Service people."[14] With still no word a month later, she reported that "it has been a very hard time for him."[15] It could also prove hard financially, since her husband would have to retire if he did not receive another post. A White House aide observed that Dulles was using "the crude— and silent—expedient of simply failing to offer him a diplomatic post." It amounted to a "studied insult."[16]

It was the torturer in the Kremlin who broke the torment. When Stalin died on March 5, Kennan "naturally wondered whether in this crisis I would be called to Washington for consultation." He impatiently noted that while the news came on Wednesday, it was not until Friday morning that Bohlen called and asked him to come to the State Department. In Washington, Bohlen reported that he had still heard nothing about Kennan's future. Kennan returned to the farm, only to trek again to Washington at the request of C. D. Jackson, Eisenhower's appointee for psychological warfare, who was sure there was some misunderstanding. Unable to believe that the president had meant to ignore Kennan, Jackson promised to clarify the issue with Dulles. In Washington yet again at Jackson's request, Kennan on March 13 learned from a front-page *New York Times* story that high administration sources had announced his retirement from the Foreign Service.

Later that same day, Dulles brutally informed Kennan, the star diplomat of his generation, that there was "no niche" for him. The secretary claimed that he would have trouble getting the Senate's approval for a high-level position. A shaken Kennan retorted that he "would not be able to conceal from my friends or the public the fact that no position had been offered to me." Then, "pulling myself together as best I could," he engaged Dulles in a discussion of Russia. The secretary of state responded, "You interest me when you talk about these matters. Very few other people do." He looked forward to similar such discussions. As George later put it to Annelise, Dulles was in effect saying: "You know, I'm divorcing you as of today. But I love the way you cook scrambled eggs, and I wonder if you'd mind fixing me up a batch of them right now, before you go."[17] Eisenhower, supportive of his secretary of state and probably appalled by the gaffe at Tempelhof, still valued Kennan. "I respect the man's mind as well as his integrity and knowledge," he had affirmed in 1950.[18]

FIGURE 31. After being told by Secretary of State John Foster
Dulles in 1953 that there was no niche for him in the State
Department, a humiliated Kennan found some solace in
working on the farm. Here, he is shingling a roof.
(Courtesy of Princeton University Library.)

In the summer of 1953, the president enlisted the fired diplomat in
the "Solarium" exercise to defuse Dulles's incendiary rhetoric of rollback. Working sixteen hours a day, Kennan and twenty other foreign
policy and military experts reviewed past Cold War policies and
drafted suggestions for the new administration. "It was all highly secret. I was not permitted—nobody was permitted—to say anything
about it," Kennan later recalled.[19] Meeting at the National War College, where Kennan in 1946–1947 had honed his ideas about strategy,

FIGURE 32. Kennan at the farm operating his road grader, a device that had to be towed by a tractor. The big wheels, one on each side, were turned by hand to raise or lower the blade as it moved along the dirt road. "It was a great, primitive but magnificent thing," recalled Christopher Kennan, "and I sense that our father reveled in feeling it was something he could operate." (Courtesy of Joan E. Kennan and Christopher Kennan.)

groups A, B, and C were charged with making the case, respectively, for containment, threatening Moscow with nuclear war, and rollback. In arguing for the last, Dulles explained to the group that "what we are hoping for is a time when the Russians turn their ponies back to the east, as Genghis Khan had done so many centuries before."[20] Kennan chaired "Task Force A," which carried the day with its superior logic and plain common sense. After five weeks, they were exhausted, remembered General Andrew Goodpaster, a participant and one of Eisenhower's aides.[21]

On July 26, in the White House basement before an audience of top foreign policy and military officials, Kennan exacted his revenge on Dulles. Years later, he still recalled with pleasure his exhilaration in presenting the conclusions of Task Force A—which Eisenhower would ultimately endorse. As Kennan lectured, "Foster Dulles sat at my feet and was thus instructed on what the policy ought to be toward the Soviet Union. I could talk, and he had to listen." The deposed diplomat succeeded even in "getting into the report some of my own thoughts about Germany."[22] Task Force A envisioned "the removal of all foreign occupation forces," the reunification of Germany, and German rearmament outside of NATO so as not to prejudice negotiations for reunification.[23] Kennan's success regarding Germany would prove fleeting, however, as the Western European Division of the State Department, which called the shots on German policy, pushed back. More lasting was Task Force A's reinscription of the policy of containment augmented by intensified psychological warfare in Eastern Europe. An administration insider noted that Eisenhower used the Solarium exercise to bury the rollback idea.[24] Even Dulles, whose own bark was worse than his bite, appreciated the outcome as a means to muzzle dangerous war talk coming out of the Pentagon.

Although Kennan helped set the Eisenhower administration on the trajectory of continued containment, he would have no share in implementing that policy. Even more frustrating, he could not advance U.S. policy from containment to negotiation on such issues as disengagement and German reunification. His exclusion during the pivotal months of Eisenhower's inauguration in January, Stalin's death in March, and the East Germans' uprising in June 1953 proved unfortunate. Kennan had intended to remain in Moscow beyond the transition to a new administration. He had expected to guide the new administration toward possible negotiations with the Soviets. Given Eisenhower's respect for Kennan, the latter's presence in Moscow just might have made a difference. As Goodpaster later recalled, "The administration did a great deal of floundering around trying to see what the significance of [Stalin's death and the German uprising] might be in terms of U.S. interests and U.S. actions."[25]

REFUGE AT THE INSTITUTE FOR ADVANCED STUDY

Expelled first by Stalin and then by Dulles, Kennan looked for a soft landing at the Institute for Advanced Study in Princeton. "I didn't have anything else to do," he later recalled. "I was unemployed."[26] He had enjoyed his time at the Institute during his leave from the State Department in 1950–1951. The ex-diplomat appreciated Oppenheimer's offer of a temporary $15,000/year salary paid by the Rockefeller Foundation and a $5,000 subsidy for secretarial and other expenses drawn from his director's fund.

As for the longer term, Kennan remained wide open. "I have a grant for one year," he wrote his former Moscow buddy, Charlie Thayer, who also had been fired by the U.S. government.[27] "After that, I don't know. It will depend on what I have been able to accomplish during this academic year." To remain at the Institute, Kennan would have to retool himself as a historian. He was not sure he could, or wanted, to do that. He worried about having enough money. His pension from the State Department amounted to a little over $5,000 per year, plus he could earn some from writing. Already gagging on a "steady diet of American suburban living," he asked Charlie, "Is there any place in Europe where a family can live comfortably on six or seven thousand per annum?" While becoming an intellectual eccentric living in Europe appealed to him, there was "always the drawback that children insist on having some sort of a nationality." Still another option was that "I run for various public offices," as some were suggesting. He might go into politics if Adlai Stevenson, the Democratic presidential candidate and an acquaintance, urged him to take the plunge.[28]

In the end, Kennan stayed at the Institute. Part of the attraction was his tie with Oppenheimer. The two men liked each other and shared some similarities in temperament and perspective. Both had opposed Acheson and Truman's proposal to escalate the arms race by building the "Super," a hydrogen bomb in response to the Soviets' explosion of their first atomic weapon. In April 1954, Kennan, testifying before the Atomic Energy Commission, refuted accusations that Oppenheimer's leftist sympathies had made him anything less than loyal to the United States. The strategist also warned about the dangers of the atomic arms race. With "we building all we can build, they building all they can build," there loomed the threat of mutual destruction. The peril could lead to pressure for preemptive war. "The public mind will not entertain the dilemma, and people will take refuge in irrational and unsuitable ideas as to what to do."[29]

While the author of containment had lost his top perch as policy adviser, the father of the atomic bomb had, despite the testimony from Kennan and other supporters, lost his security clearance. Both Kennan and Oppenheimer deplored the witch-hunting influence of Senator Joseph McCarthy, the Republican from Wisconsin. The two intellectuals respected the humanities as well as the sciences. They valued careful thought expressed with elegant style. They both tended toward a melancholy view of life and often gave way to emotion. Each bore some responsibility—Kennan with the long telegram and "X" article, Oppenheimer with his direction of the atomic bomb project—for the darkening of the Cold War. Both deplored this trend and were frustrated in trying to check it. Their shared abhorrence of the atomic arms race was reflected in Oppenheimer's satirical response when Kennan sent him a State Department suggestion to develop solar energy for "peaceful as well as warlike purposes." Oppenheimer sketched out a crash program: (a) classify the sun as Top Secret, (b) establish a showcase commission to manage it for the benefit of all mankind, (c) focus on developing a super weapon based on the sun, (d) announce that we intended to use the sun not for war but to better mankind.[30]

Although the Institute had granted Kennan a safe haven after expulsion from the government, it declined to finance his return as a congressman. In March 1954, Kennan seriously considered entering the race for representative from Pennsylvania's nineteenth congressional district, which included the south-central region of the state and the farm in East Berlin. The proud elitist as a glad-handing, baby-kissing politician? "I was horrified" at the idea, recalled his otherwise staunch supporter, Jeanette. "That's the last thing in the world he could have done."[31] Another fan, the political scientist Hans J. Morgenthau, worried that while Kennan in Congress would enhance "the intellectual and moral stature of that body," Kennan himself and the nation as a whole would suffer from his becoming political.[32] One wonders about the reaction of the voting public to what Kennan later confided to his diary was "the depth of my estrangement, the depth of my repudiation of the things [American society] lives by."[33]

CONGRESSMAN KENNAN?

That so unlikely a politician grew so excited about the prospect was telling. In both his memoir published in 1973 and in his interview with Gaddis in 1983, Kennan recounted ostensibly verbatim conversations from 1954. Regardless of the extent to which these remembered words matched what was actually said decades earlier, this was the narrative that resonated with him and that he had committed to memory. The import was that he, George F. Kennan, former diplomat and farm owner in East Berlin, was, after all his humiliation, now being chosen by the ordinary folk of rural Pennsylvania. A young farmer and his wife drove 150 miles to Princeton with a request. Some fellows had got together, did not like the proposed candidate for Congress, and "we were wondering if you would run." Kennan was very much moved by this. He later explained that "if your fellow citizens want you to represent them, you don't turn it down." The prospective candidate met with local Democrats in Pennsylvania, who assured him that, aside from the machine politicians in the only city in the district, all the locals, including the many Republicans in the East Berlin area, enthusiastically supported him. In recounting the discussion many years later, Kennan underscored how much the simple, honest, plainspokenness of it all "positively delighted my heart."[34]

"I've never forgotten the things they said: 'Why, he ain't even registered as a Democrat. Yeah, but his wife is. Why, hell, we could run him for the Senate.'" In recounting this experience nearly three decades afterward, Kennan's voice broke into a happy chuckle and then a laugh. With delight, he explained: "I just loved this, because there was something sort of wonderful about it that I had never come into contact with before. These were such absolutely genuine people." He enunciated "I just loved this" with particular joy and with stress on each word. He had felt much the same way about contact with down-to-earth Russians. He recounted how, driving with the Democratic county chairman along a deserted country road, he dutifully came to a full stop at a corner, remarking that now he had to be on his best behavior. At that point in his narrative, Kennan, usually a stickler for elegant grammar not only in

English but also in German and Russian, slipped into a patois that betrayed a patrician idealization of unadorned honesty. The politician leaned over, put his hand on Kennan's knee, and said, "'Listen. I want to tell you something. If you're a drinkin' man, keep on drinkin'. If you're chasin' women, keep on chasin' women. They're goin' to know it anyway.'" After telling this story, Kennan repeated, again with emphasis: "I loved these people." He burbled on, "I think I would have been elected. And I think I would have enjoyed it. I might have gone on to a senatorial position."[35]

Even decades later, he still felt exhilarated remembering how, for a few giddy days in March 1954, respect from the sturdy people of rural Pennsylvania had offset rejection from the governments of the Soviet Union and the United States. In later years he would often talk about that fleeting venture into politics, a neighbor would observe.[36]

Kennan's enthusiasm rested on some key premises. The other Democratic candidates pledged to drop out if he ran. He believed he could easily beat his Republican opponent. As for fundraising, that "was exactly what I didn't want to do." He aimed to graciously accept the office without the hurly-burly of grubbing for it. Kennan envisioned himself as American gentry of sorts, a farm-owning, organic leader endowed with foresight, looking out for the ordinary people of his district and positioned to influence the nation. As previously mentioned, back in 1930s Russia, he had dressed like a member of the pre-Revolution gentry when riding horseback in the countryside outside Moscow. Whether it was in Russia or in America, this would-be leader "believed in wise, selfless, noble elites," recalled his friend Isaiah Berlin.[37]

Financial concerns, always a priority for Kennan, destroyed his brief foray into politics. He soon realized that he would indeed have to raise money for his campaign. He hated the prospect of groveling for cash. Further, the Rockefeller Foundation and the Institute warned that they would have to immediately cut off his salary. "I had two children in school or college at that time. It's an expensive business." The financial constraints amounted to an ordinary enough problem. What was extraordinary, however, was the intensity of his desire and his sense of responsibility. Perhaps running for Congress satisfied, as few things did,

George's need for both Eros and Civilization in his life. As he remembered it, "I was full of agony over this. I felt I'd let down the people in the country."[38]

COMMUNING WITH MOTHER AND FATHER

Agonizing also were the never-healed wounds of his childhood. He comforted himself by conjuring up his lost mother. On April 19, 1955, the anniversary of her death, he tried to imagine her "near me and to live through the day as I think she might have wished me to live through it: unhurriedly, with grace and dignity, secure and relaxed in the consciousness of her love and her forgiveness, not pecking at myself for past faults."[39] A few months later, he and Jeanette visited their parents' graves in Forest Home Cemetery in Milwaukee.

He sorted his swirl of emotions through a succession of personas: first, the forever-lost child, then the adult eulogist, the devoted son, the objective biographer, and finally the self-critical memoirist. "I got out of the car, and walked, dazed and excited among the headstones, a little panicky like a lost child (Father, Father, where are you?) and it was as though, if I did not find the grave, we would be forever lost and separated." Upon seeing his mother's grave, he started off with a formal eulogy only to melt upon juxtaposing his birth and her death: "First—my mother, Florence James Kennan, whom I never knew, struck down by death only a month after the birth of her fourth child. (Here, buried and helpless, all the love that could not be expended, all the tenderness that could not be bestowed.)" He could never get over losing all that love and all that tenderness. Nevertheless, he tried as a grown-up to empathize with her own suffering. He switched from third to second person as he affirmed her children's love: "Dear Mother, it must have been hard and bitter to leave your little children. We have all held you in a sort of awed adoration." Death had sanctified "our ever-young dear mother, beautiful, unworldly, full only of love and grace for us, like a saint." The good son assured her that "in imagination, we have received all you would have given us." Yearning to support her much as he had longed for her to support him, he wished that "we with our youth could not have borne some of your frailty, could not have breathed back into you some of the strength you gave us." Then, a farewell: "May our love, somehow or other, reach you."

Moving on to his father, George first settled old scores, then delivered a warm but calculated assessment far different from the emotional reverie inspired by his mother. "God be praised that they lie side by side," he observed with relief. In 1933, with George in distant Moscow and his sisters scattered as far as Alaska, Kossuth Kent Kennan's burial next to the wife who had died three decades earlier was not a given. No doubt present at the interment was his current spouse, Louise Wheeler Kennan, the stepmother despised by the Kennan children. Florence's and Kent's side-by-side graves meant that George did have a family, even if a deceased one. "It was a real marriage," he celebrated, beset by "family differences, differing social origins, and what not—but full of real love and a total mutual commitment."

He then delivered a third-person, dry-eyed appraisal of his father. In contrast to the jerky shifts in tone, voice, and grammar betraying Kennan's struggle to reduce to writing the flood of feelings aroused by his mother, the description of his father evidenced easily mustered rationality. Memory of his father, at least on this occasion, inspired no heart-rending conversations and interactions, but rather a long, elegantly constructed single sentence stuffed with adjectives rather than verbs: "My father: awkward, shy almost to the point of cowardice, often putting his foot in it, unable to explain himself, oversensitive, proud, slightly boyish to the end of his days; always in some ways a yokel, in others a man of noble intellect; capable of being utterly broken up and disinterested by too much beauty, a sentimentalist like the rest of us; a man from whose taut, severe, lawyer-like face the love of someone else could suddenly shine forth with great warmth and intensity; a man of much loneliness and much suffering; gaunt, tough, abstemious; scarcely knowing illness after his youth, he lived life to the very end: to a dark and tortured and lonely old age."

George identified with much of this portrait. He remembered himself as "a moody, self-centered, neurotic boy, as shy as he, and confiding in no one. I must have given him little solace in his old age, but I loved him as I have loved no other man but my son. We never grated on each other; I appreciated his silence and his forbearance. And I understood, perhaps better than anyone in the family, his loneliness, his unhappiness, his despair, and his faith." Though his mother remained first in his heart, he bore mostly the influence of his father.[40]

While admiring his father's character, Kennan did not share the older man's indifference to money. Most of the gap in family and in social origin that had complicated his parents' marriage stemmed from the huge difference between the wealth of his mother's family and the modest income of his father. While he kept servants and vacationed on occasion, Kossuth Kent Kennan also had to tap his children's inheritance income to make ends meet. At the time of his death, he owned almost no property and had borrowed half the value of his $2,500 life insurance policy. He distinguished himself, first, by helping introduce the income tax to the United States and then, second, by not utilizing his expertise to become a wealthy tax lawyer.[41]

In January 1955, as George mulled over his future, he griped that while he would prefer a simple life on the west coast of Scotland, he faced college expenses for Joan, the raising of two young children, Annelise's spending for the family and on herself, and the maintenance of the house on Hodge Road in Princeton and the farm. He needed $30,000 a year. "On less than that," he said sourly, "one cannot live. As to what one *does* do to earn $30,000 a year, I am wholly ignorant, but the problem is 7 months away."[42] Though he received a salary from the Institute for Advance Study, his position there remained temporary. Harvard, Yale, and Princeton had tried to lure Kennan ever since the publication of his "X" article. But the Institute held special attractions. Arguably more prestigious than the top Ivy League schools, this scholarly idyll boasted Oppenheimer, the nation's foremost atomic physicist, as its director, and such faculty as Albert Einstein (who died in 1955) and John von Neumann, one of the conceptual inventors of the computer, who built such a machine in an Institute garage. At the Institute, Kennan would have no obligation to teach and few if any administrative or service responsibilities He had bought the nearby Hodge Road house, and Annelise liked living in Princeton. To snare a permanent professorship, however, he would have to publish much more than *American Diplomacy*, the slender volume based on his 1951 lectures in Chicago, and collections of his speeches. As the unofficial motto of the Institute warned, "In paradise there are no excuses."

THE HISTORIAN

Kennan's diligence in researching and writing *Russia Leaves the War: Soviet-American Relations, 1917–1920*, the first volume of his densely detailed *Soviet-American Relations*, paid off with a lengthy manuscript that circulated among Institute faculty in 1955 after the School of Historical Studies on March 8 voted unanimously to offer him a professorship. Oppenheimer also favored the move. The prestigious School of Mathematics, however, vehemently opposed on the grounds that "Mr. Kennan's published books are directed to the general public and are largely propagandistic."[43] A battle of letters ensued.

The controversy offers a snapshot of Kennan's standing among scholars in the mid-1950s. At that point, his diplomatic career lay largely behind him; he had written a number of speeches and articles on Soviet-American relations, and *Russia Leaves the War* was completed but not yet published. Gordon A. Craig, a renowned historian of Germany then at Princeton University, praised the manuscript of *Russia Leaves the War* as "fascinating," "beautifully written," and extensively researched. Nevertheless, its author "had a long way to go before" becoming a distinguished historian. Like the mathematicians at the Institute, Craig faulted the former diplomat because he tended to "stop being the objective historian and to slip into the role of the polemicist, arguing the case of 1950 from the circumstances of 1917."[44] Rather than disputing Kennan's presentism and public focus, those arguing for him cast these passions in a positive light. Theodore E. Mommsen of Cornell asserted that "what really impressed me most deeply . . . was the personality of the man himself." Not many contemporaries ranked "as profoundly humane" as Kennan or matched his profound "moral and civic responsibility." On vacation in Europe, the art historian Ernst "Eka" Kantorowicz reported to Oppenheimer, "I have been asked, time and again, by

European historians about George Kennan." They held a very high opinion of this international figure.[45]

From Oxford, the philosopher and historian Isaiah Berlin, who had known Kennan since Moscow in 1945, acclaimed his friend's "extraordinary sympathy" with anything and everything to do with Russia. Almost no one commanded a "wider knowledge or more original ideas about the history of Russia" than the former diplomat. A gifted wordsmith himself, Berlin praised Kennan's flights of fancy in support of fixed opinions as admirable and as evidence of "rather mysterious intellectual processes." Moreover, he had "that rarest of all possessions—something to say."[46] In late November 1955, the Institute Board of Trustees appointed Kennan as a professor—but of international relations rather than history and with a salary of $19,000 rather than $30,000.[47]

He would move into Fuld Hall 208, a stunningly beautiful office, twenty by twenty-four feet with a fourteen-foot ceiling. Four huge windows looked out onto the Institute Woods, the 589-acre preserve of towering trees and paths where Kennan loved to walk, think, and at times cut firewood.

Getting onto the faculty of the Institute did not boost his spirits for long. Three weeks into his professorship "with what amounts to security for life," he felt more "deeply and consistently depressed" than in years. He alluded to problems at home. "Scholarship would be a pleasure if personal life were serene," and if he did not face incessant lecture requests.[48] Moreover, notwithstanding the appeal of scholarship, it did not match government service. When Oppenheimer enlisted him to help with damage control on a publicity problem, Kennan flung himself into "a good deal of phoning around and manipulation," which "reminded me so much of the immeasurable minor crises of diplomatic life, particularly in Russia, that I suddenly realized how long it was since I had 'operated'—how passive and placid and pointless and eventless, in other words, is the life of a scholar."[49]

Kennan's standing as a diplomatic historian now advocating diplomacy with the Russians sounded in the applause at the American Historical Association meeting of December 1955. He deplored "the bombast, the demagogue, the jingo, the poseur" among leaders who for political reasons risked war. Even if conflict did not erupt, diplomats had to step in to tidy "up the messes other people have made." And if war did break out, it would benefit only the Communists. While Kennan complained that the story in the *New York Times* made him seem "strange, bitter, desperate," Oppenheimer received from a friend a different account: "It was really a most magnificent speech and more than a thousand professional historians in attendance gave him a rousing, standing ovation after he had finished."[50]

The criticism by Gordon Craig and others became irrelevant after Kennan published *Russia Leaves the War* in 1956. The most consequential critique bore gold-plated credentials. In the *American Historical Review,* the nation's foremost historical journal, Dexter Perkins, president of the American Historical Association and diplomatic historian at Cornell, extended the imprimatur of the profession: "This book has a substantial and a lasting value." Perkins perceived that the author, intent on qualifying as a scholar, had gotten "unduly involved in the minutiae of the period." Kennan must have been pleased by the homage to him as "one whose insights into the Russian scene are unrivaled."[51] The book swept the field, garnering the Pulitzer Prize, the National Book Award, the Bancroft Prize, and the Francis Parkman Prize for literary distinction in history.

"I don't know what to make of this flood of honors," Kennan tried to fret. "I can't believe that the book was that good." He resolved to leverage this standing, deserved or not, into influence regarding national issues. "I now have the ability to be widely heard on my own merits and not just by virtue of a governmental office." Although the triumph of Eisenhower, and Nixon, (and thus Dulles) in the November 1956 election ensured that he would not soon be returning to government, the respect from wide swaths of the public promised "a rare possibility of usefulness." By late 1957, Kennan concluded that most useful would be halting the final division of Germany and Europe into two nuclear-armed camps. Though he would ultimately fail, he succeeded, as did very few others, in rattling the Cold War establishment in the United States and in Europe.

For Kennan it was always about Germany as well as Russia. He grew up in the German-American city of Milwaukee. Brought by his father to Germany when he was eight, he picked up lasting impressions as well as the language. The summer after graduating from Princeton he wandered about the Weimar republic, reading Goethe and Spengler in the original, and speaking not a word of English. In university lectures and seminars in 1929–1931, he absorbed much of the distinctly German perspective on the giant to the east. He came to know and admire such German aristocrats as von Bredow and von Moltke. Many of his romantic adventures took place in Germany, and that is where he met and wooed Annelise. The young couple lived at first in Riga and Tallinn, Baltic cities that still bore the cultural imprint of the Teutonic Knights who had pushed into this German frontier. In 1930s Moscow, Kennan shared good times and gripes with his German friends, and he ranked as the only top postwar U.S. official to have spent part of the war in Germany, where he was interned.

While appalled by the Nazis' brutality in occupied Europe, he appreciated their success in knitting together a European economy. This model would inspire his commitment to European integration as part of the Marshall Plan. Though at first, he favored dividing Germany, he switched by 1948 into advocating Plan A, the reuniting of eastern and western Germany and the pullback of Soviet and Western occupation troops from most of Europe. That scenario would doom Acheson and Dulles's fondest hope: integrating a prosperous, rearmed West Germany into the Western alliance. With German troops under the command of the U.S. Supreme Allied Commander of NATO and with the Bonn government locked into the Cold War, Washington would consolidate its hold on the biggest prize of World War II. Though handcuffed by Truman and Acheson, Kennan in Moscow in 1952 had hoped to open the door to preliminary talks with the Soviets about something akin to Plan A. After getting kicked out of Moscow and then the State Department, the persistent ex-diplomat continued speaking out against U.S. policy on Germany. Opposed by Acheson, Dulles, and nearly all their advisers on Germany, Kennan fumed, "I knew more about Germany than any of these people. What the hell do these people know about that country?"[52]

When the Red Army temporarily evacuated Budapest during the Hungarian revolt of November 1956, Kennan's hasty conclusion revealed his own yearnings. He surmised that with the Red Army gone from Hungary, pressure would build for a similar pullback of U.S., British, and French forces from West Germany. If the Russians then withdrew from Poland and East Germany, "the East German regime won't last three days." With time, the rest of Eastern Europe could gain greater freedom. "I have always said [the Russians'] rule might come to an end if it could be done gradually and without loss of prestige."[53]

Then came the hammer blows. Soviet tanks blasted their way back into Budapest and brutally put down the revolt. In the Middle East, newly reelected President Eisenhower, to Kennan's dismay, pressured the British, French, and Israelis to back down from their military bid to retake the Suez Canal from Egypt's Nasser. "The events of these recent days have been so shattering" that he interpreted them as yet another personal repudiation. "I must regard my role in the public life of this country as played out. My future is purely private life." Nevertheless, no matter how dour his outlook or how doleful his self-estimation, Kennan could not stick to that renunciation. The raft of honors in early 1957 from *Russia Leaves the War* renewed his ambition to bend events away from Cold War confrontation.

DISENGAGEMENT

His big opportunity came with the invitation to deliver six radio addresses over the British Broadcasting Company in December 1957. Without backing from government or any other powerful institution, Kennan shook the very foundations of Cold War regime in Britain, West Germany, and the United States.

This achievement was arguably more impressive than his more famous intervention in 1946–1947 with the long telegram and the "X" article. Back then, he had friends in the State Department who had prompted him to draft the telegram, and advocates, such as Secretary of the Navy James V. Forrestal, who disseminated it throughout the Truman administration. His rise also benefited from power brokers who made sure that this promising publicist and Russian expert got access to such vehicles of influence as the Council on Foreign Relations, *Foreign Affairs*, and popular newspapers and magazines. With this help and with his undeniable talent, Kennan had reason to celebrate that his voice now carried. Now in 1957–1958, despite a brutal public assault by Dean Acheson and opposition from the governments of Britain, West Germany and the United States, that voice again carried. In 1946–1947, Kennan's task was easier. He had to convince leaders and a public already soured on cooperation with Russia and yet fearful of war that containment promised an effective, safe alternative. Back then he had pushed an open door.

Now, however, the door seemed bolted shut by Cold War orthodoxy. Both elites and ordinary folk assumed that the Red Army was panting to lunge toward the English Channel. Supposedly only America's nuclear arsenal held back the Russian hordes. Common-sense wisdom also asserted that while the division of Germany had problems, it remained the safest choice. Having two Germanys kept the Germans contained, and it safeguarded from Russia the richest portion of the former enemy. NATO orthodoxy also promised that the United States would maintain its nuclear guarantee and troops in Europe indefinitely. Finally, the best way to enhance security was to deploy still more nuclear weapons, particularly smaller, so-called tactical ones, in the heart of Europe, including on the German-German frontier. That this massive concentration of deadly weaponry would be on trigger alert and could—by accident, miscalculation, or intent—incinerate central Europe should not be a concern, most leaders insisted. In his six radio addresses over the BBC, Kennan ripped holes in all these assumptions.

In July 1957, Kennan fretted about his "utter lack of enthusiasm for the [BBC] Reith Lectures." When his son Christopher asked what interested him, he replied, glumly, boats—and "growing things, if life permitted." As for international affairs, repeated frustrations and disillusionment had taken their toll. Nevertheless, he never totally gave up his concerns and aspirations. As to what he might actually say in the lectures, he mused that if he were fully honest, he should point up the sterility of America's society, the inadequacy of its institutions, and then criticize the "overpopulation, the nastiness, the recklessness of the outside world." He imagined redrawing the map by dividing the United States into separate nations. The South, Texas, and California would form one unit and the Northwest another. The East and the Middle West would link up with Canada and Britain, establishing a new capital near Ottawa. Kennan, who liked to say that he would rather have lived in the eighteenth century, imagined re-creating a pre-1776 British empire centered in North America. "As for alliances, Scandinavia & the Siberian Peninsula to be neutralized, continental Europe on its own." The Atlantic nation would then pursue "rigorous population reduction," "autarchy," and a weaning away from the motor car. "How would all this sound over the BBC?"

He realized that "none of this is going to happen."[54] What did happen is that Kennan broadcast over the BBC not a cranky fantasy about remaking the world, but rather an audacious, wildly popular proposal to save it from nuclear war.

The opportunity to give the Eastman lectures at Oxford came as a signal honor but at a significant cost to Kennan and his family. The invitation, promoted by his friend Isaiah Berlin, arrived in 1955 just as Kennan's appointment to the Institute hung in the balance. Whether a coincidence or engineered, the award bolstered his status as a distinguished scholar. Nevertheless, fulfilling this honor proved demanding. Kennan had to write and deliver eighteen historical lectures at Oxford plus six talks on current events over the BBC. He later calculated that, counting all the revisions, he had to compose nearly forty thousand words each week. Plus he had to research the historical lectures in the scattered library system of Oxford. He gave the talks in The Schools, a "marvelous great old building," with attendees dressed in university gowns. "I loved it, the atmosphere of it," Kennan would recall of Oxford. Nevertheless, he never penetrated beyond the surface of that atmosphere. "What a tight, tough community this is, underneath," he wrote Oppenheimer, and how closed it remained to even a distinguished visitor.[55]

Day-to-day living in this splendid setting also proved not so marvelous. Already by September, their apartment, with its massive stone walls, was proving hard to heat. Annelise related that "with no little black slaves to keep the fireplaces going," George had to carry the coal up and the ashes down two flights of stairs. Those totaled fifty-seven steps, a number etched into his memory by innumerable trips. Since they could not drive to a food shop, Annelise often made two treks a day. "You'd be surprised how heavy 1 doz. oranges get," she grumbled. Only one room was fitted with a coal stove while the others had less efficient fireplaces. A feeble electric heater for their bedroom made sleeping bearable. The incessant cold took its toll. "We all became sick with the Asian flu—all four of us," Kennan later recalled. The parents "had to put the children on mattresses on the floor between our beds so we could watch them."

Far from Princeton, where his spacious office overlooked the Institute Woods and where their large house enabled him to spread his writing out into four rooms, George had to compose the lectures in the room where they also ate. English secretaries, hired at his own expense, typed away in that cramped space as Kennan dictated, interrupting himself to tend the coal fires or rush down the hall to answer the telephone. While appreciating the majesty of the ancient colleges of Oxford, the city itself appalled him with its traffic-choked streets, shoddy merchandise in the stores, and bleak, deserted parks. The only escape he could imagine was "becoming young again and falling wildly in love."[56] Absent such a miracle, he faced tensions at home. Christopher, eight years old at the time, would remember Oxford as marked by "horrible fights between my parents."[57] Referring to Oxford, Annelise confided to Jeanette: "Between you and me we just loathe it."[58] George would conclude that life in Oxford "was beyond my strength."[59] Ironically, the stress of writing the lectures in this environment may have generated the emotional force that made them so effective.

"The terrible thing was that the lectures in The Schools were tremendously successful," Kennan later explained. His talks on Russian history preceded those of Isaiah Berlin, and so the hall filled with listeners eager to see both luminaries. A student recalled that even after the lectures were moved to the largest available room, the space was "overflowing all the time, with dons hanging from the chandeliers and sitting on the radiators. The sense of occasion was just overwhelming."[60] "Here was something extraordinary a remarkable individual," another would remember. However extraordinary and remarkable he seemed to others, Kennan remained isolated. He could not "recall having anything in the nature of a real discussion since I've been here," he complained to Oppenheimer, "except with Isaiah Berlin—where you can't help having it."[61]

The six Sunday evening Reith Lectures, broadcast from November 10 to December 15, 1957, broke almost all records for audience and subsequent impact. Two factors combined to produce Kennan's riveting impact on these listeners. First, he spoke with a voice animated by the force of his frustrations. Second, his analytical mind disciplined that energy into persuasive arguments that addressed the unease with the Cold War that most other leaders preferred to ignore. To Kennan's delight, "half of England was listening to these things on Sunday night." It had exhilarated him when the locals in Pennsylvania had asked him to run for Congress. Now he felt moved by "the little people in England," like the greasy-handed auto mechanic who interjected when Kennan asked about his car: "Where did I hear that voice before?"[62] The voice carried far beyond the local garage. The broadcasts were replayed in Canada and in the United States, and, in translation, in West Germany. Newspapers and magazines featured transcripts.

As a BBC postmortem noted, Kennan's message had "echoed around the world." Soviet Premier Nikita S. Khrushchev praised Kennan's proposals. At the NATO summit meeting that, by coincidence, began the morning after the final lecture, nineteen hundred assembled journalists reportedly devoted more attention to Kennan's lectures than to the speeches of the delegates. A West German magazine noted that two absent people—Kennan and Soviet Premier Nikolai Bulganin, who had just called for a nuclear-free Central Europe—had "influenced the Paris NATO Conference more than all the assembled statesmen and politicians." Kennan, who collected clippings of such accolades, must have smiled at being paired with a Soviet leader who, in a happier world, might have sat across from him at the negotiating table. Kennan's arguments were referenced by a majority of participants in a key Parliamentary debate. While the ruling Conservative Party denounced the proposals, the opposing Labourites defended them. Though highly critical, both the London *Times* and the *Daily Telegraph* reviewed the lectures in lengthy editorials. The philosopher Bertrand Russell, who had recently exchanged letters with Khrushchev on disarmament, praised Kennan's powerful advocacy.[63]

This torrent of interest flowed from the content, context, and cadence of the talks. Most observers focused on the third lecture, on Germany and Central Europe, and on the fourth, on the hydrogen bomb. Kennan stressed that he was "trying to tell governments what they ought to think about, not what they ought to do."[64] In the lecture on Europe, he disputed a central precept of the Cold War catechism: that a divided Germany and Europe offered the most stable solution. He proposed instead that the United States, Britain, France, and the Soviet Union— the major victor powers of World War II—pull their military forces out of Germany. Such a negotiated military disengagement from Germany could, Kennan argued, be linked to the Soviets withdrawing their troops from their Eastern European empire. He surmised that the Russians were weary of garrisoning rebellious Poles and Hungarians. If the Russians no longer faced Western forces across the Elbe River, they might well agree to withdraw to their own borders. As part of this disengagement from confrontation, the Americans and the Soviets would encourage East and West Germany to negotiate reunifying on the basis of a neutral, lightly armed state. Here Kennan was conjuring the international position of the Weimar republic, absent resentment over the Versailles treaty. If Germany reunited, so would Berlin, thereby eliminating a tinderbox that had set off dangerous crises in 1958–1959 and would do so again in 1961–1962. Although such a Germany would likely develop extensive economic and cultural ties with the West, it would not remain in NATO. Kennan's proposals roughly paralleled the deal proposed by Stalin in 1952 and by his successors at various times since then.

With regard to military issues, Kennan flatly disputed a second tenet of the catechism: that the Soviet Union was hell-bent on conquering

Western Europe (and then the world) and was held back only by the threat of U.S. nuclear retaliation. With regard to nuclear weapons, he proposed temporarily keeping a modest number for deterrence against the remote chance of a Soviet attack but moving away from reliance on these terrible devices. He warned that the deployment of so-called tactical nuclear weapons on the continent of Europe including West Germany, as Washington was planning, would prove disastrous. Such weapons would cement the division of Germany and Europe and magnify the risk of nuclear war through brinkmanship or miscalculation. In what Kennan later termed "the greatest mistake of the entire lecture series," he ended the talk with a hasty proposal that Western Europe could effectively deter Soviet aggression by focusing not on massive armies on the scale of World War II but rather on paramilitary forces, "of a territorial-militia type, somewhat on the Swiss example." Such lightly armed forces could combat any internal, Soviet-inspired subversion while also, in the unlikely event of a Soviet invasion, provide overt resistance and help train a civil resistance movement.[65] That would render a Soviet occupation costly and doomed to eventual failure. He ended the lecture with words that again and again would be thrown in his face: "I think I can give personal assurance that any country which" set up such low-level but effective resistance "will have little need of foreign garrisons to assure its immunity from Soviet attack."[66]

Kennan's proposals stirred such intense debate in part because the issues of nuclear weapons and of Germany already stirred passions. The Soviets had been warning against rearming West Germany and stationing nuclear weapons there. Divided Berlin remained a flashpoint, especially since East Germany was bleeding citizens through this escape hatch. The British Labour leader Hugh Gaitskell had called for something similar to disengagement. At the United Nations on October 2, Polish Foreign Minister Adam Rapacki proposed a nuclear-free zone to include East Germany, West Germany, Poland, and Czechoslovakia. Five days later, the Soviets shocked the world by launching Sputnik, an artificial satellite. The implications were obvious. If Soviet rockets packed the power to hurl a satellite into space, they could also lob nuclear weapons onto New York and Washington. No one was safe, and adversaries had to share the same planet. Moreover, atmospheric testing of ever larger and dirtier hydrogen bombs literally brought home the dangers of the arms race. Despite these bids for change, the U.S., British, and West German governments remained committed to the Cold War status quo. Leaders continued to intone such shibboleths as peace through strength, no Munich-style appeasement, and maintaining resolve.

Along with content and context, the third reason for Kennan's impact flowed from the cadence and tone of his delivery. The impact of what he said was conditioned by what was going on inside him as he spoke. Kennan sat in front of the BBC microphone as someone both adept at influencing audiences and assailed by pressures. He was overworked. He was exasperated by having to compose in a cramped space, lug coal and ashes, deal with sick kids and his own illness, argue with Annelise, and cope with torrents of publicity. He felt compelled to keep up with Isaiah Berlin in the Oxford lectures to the elite while not disappointing the multitudes now tuning in on the radio. Aside from these personal concerns, he was disturbed by the lemming-like determination of governments to pile on still more too-dangerous-to-use weapons while failing to defuse the ticking bomb of a divided Germany and Europe.

Although pressed for time, Kennan had to drive into London on Saturday for a rehearsal and revision of his weekly lecture. On Sunday, he would drive in again. Then, "frantically scratching corrections and insertions on my text to the very last moment," he would be ushered into the studio. Kennan's description of the countdown to his performance suggested that he felt the very core of his being was at stake. The context and the repetition in his narrative indicate that he was not joking. As the deadline of 9:15 P.M. approached, the clock's "movement took on a dread inexorability," as if it were marking "my own execution." The announcer's curt introduction concluded with the "final terrifying and merciless: 'Mr. Kennan.'" Then flowing through him were feelings that, it seems, revisited his earliest anxieties as a child. For twenty-eight and a half minutes, "I would be left alone—alone as I had never been before—alone as I had never hoped to be—alone to acquit or disgrace myself . . . alone beyond the power of any other human being to help me."[67] Repeating "alone" five times signaled something basic.

Wound tight by problems both trivial and earthshaking, talking about matters that he knew intimately, and arguing theses that he had honed for years, Kennan performed brilliantly. He spoke in a voice modulated by leashed outrage—at the needless rush toward nuclear war, at the senseless push to build and deploy yet more deadly weapons, at the determined closure of options for reuniting Germany, and at the failure to explore Moscow's bid to initiate talks. He likely also felt outrage on some level for his humiliation by the U.S. government, to which he had devoted decades of service, and by the Soviet government, whose behavior he had tried so hard to understand and at times to excuse. Finally, in emphasizing to such a degree his feelings of being "alone" in the studio, he seems to have been tapping into the primal agony of abandonment. Ever since early childhood, that fear had both terrorized him and inspired the self-discipline enabling his rise to the person now on the world stage.

What gave such emotional force to Kennan's lectures was not just what he said but how he said it. He was addressing the most pressing issues at a fraught time. He spoke with a staccato of clipped yet precisely enunciated words studded with points of emphasis that conveyed controlled emotion. Kennan probably realized that while short bursts of anger-tinged irony and provocative language could enhance the credibility of his argument, unleashed anger would destroy it. He was, after all, calling for self-restraint, empathy, and negotiation with the adversary, not a traditionally "tough," "realistic," and masculine stance. Hence, he had to maximize the rationalist feel of his talk. The Reith Lectures displayed Kennan at his most effective: point-by-point, relentless analysis expressed with elegance and conviction, that rationality reinforced by momentary shifts in loudness and pitch that invited listeners to share his leashed outrage. With carefully controlled language and voice, he simultaneously parsed and integrated reason and emotion. The whole was greater than the sum of the parts of this magnificent performance.[68]

An example: With evocative words and palpable exasperation, Kennan laid out the consequences of the runaway nuclear arms race. "Are we to flee like haunted creatures from one defensive device to another, each more costly and humiliating than the one before, cowering underground one day, breaking up our cities the next ... all the while sacrificing all the values for which it might be worthwhile to live at all? ... Let us at least walk like men, with our heads up, so long as we are permitted to walk at all."[69]

Such talk seemed dangerous because it appealed to ordinary people. While rulers in Washington, London, Paris, and Bonn insisted that the Cold War, despite its dangers and its devouring of resources, offered the only avenue for security, stability, and survival, Kennan lighted a path toward less stress and more safety. This heretic posed an even greater threat because he had authored the containment doctrine that supposedly justified the Cold War.

The fiercest opponents of disengagement included Chancellor Konrad Adenauer, who since 1949 had ruled both the Christian Democratic Party and the government of West Germany. American leaders such as Acheson and Dulles prized Adenauer because he had largely followed their lead with rearmament, nonrecognition of East Germany, and fervent anti-communism. Nevertheless, fears that the Bonn government might reach out to Moscow or elsewhere haunted Washington and London. Indeed, later in 1958, Adenauer would sidestep the Americans and British to strike up a special relationship with Charles de Gaulle, the ambitious new president of France. Now, in January, the chancellor complained angrily to Eisenhower that the "lectures by George Kennan unfortunately had made quite an impression." The president tried to reassure him by disparaging the troublemaker as just "a headline-seeker." Nonetheless, Adenauer retorted, "The opposition papers are quick to pick up this kind of thing."[70]

"This kind of thing" created an emotional storm in Britain. The U.S. embassy explained the tempest in terms of the "depressed and uncertain recent mood of informed Britons." They feared obliteration in "the event of a Third World War, no matter what the outcome"; moreover, such a catastrophe could be ignited by a simple mistake or "a fit of nervousness." Dependence on America's nuclear weapons imposed "a national humiliation." Kennan appealed because he pointed "toward a possible way out of the present impasse." Not surprisingly, then, "most of his listeners emotionally hoped with yearning that Kennan was right in his analyses and recommendations." Heightening the tremendous impact was his status as a highly responsible, nonpartisan, and informed expert, a respected scholar, and a statesman who had helped devise the Marshall Plan as well as containment. "Kennan's lectures were all the more effective . . . because of the character and personality of the lecturer." By speaking out, the iconoclast demonstrated that "a whole body of opinion in America was also at odds with official American foreign policy." Some wondered whether Kennan might become secretary of state in the next Democratic administration.[71] That possibility frightened and infuriated Kennan's former boss.

KENNAN VERSUS ACHESON

Acheson, who would title his memoir *Present at the Creation* [of the Cold War], regarded the tenets of that conflict as nearly sacred. He interpreted enthusiasm for Kennan's lectures as dangerous rebellion against the burdens of the struggle. That the arms race and the doctrine of mutual assured destruction did in fact violate commonsensical notions of survival made adhering to orthodoxy all the more crucial. In looking for the big picture, Acheson turned to pop Freudian theory, then popular among many Americans, including Kennan. Freud had posited the notion of a primal, inescapable struggle pitting the freedom and creativity of Eros against the order and organization of Civilization. To Hamilton Fish Armstrong, the editor of *Foreign Affairs*, the austere elder statesman complained that "Kennan has released the libido and all the inhibitions which made a non-communist world organization possible." To quash this threat, Acheson mobilized "responsible" opinion to reimpose societal inhibitions, notably acquiescence to policies that risked nuclear war. Acquiescence made politically possible the organization of the Free World with a mindset that did not challenge rearming West Germany and deploying nuclear weapons on its soil.[72]

Soon after the Reith Lectures, Christopher Emmet, vice president of the American Council for Germany, an influential pro-West Germany lobby, alerted Acheson to the "cumulative, snowballing hysteria in Britain as well as Germany over the Kennan views." The word "hysteria" suggested public sentiment out of control and unnatural, as did Emmet's characterization of Kennan's "grotesque" "bewitchment of German and British liberals." The Bonn government worked through Emmet to make sure Acheson would respond to Kennan.[73] Paul M. Nitze, Kennan's hawkish successor on the Policy Planning Staff, also weighed in with the former secretary of state. Acheson needed no such prompting to draft a searing assault. Soon Emmet had a schedule for action: publicize Acheson's statement in the major newspapers of America and Europe on Sunday, January 12; line up statements of support from prominent Democrats starting with Truman; and then on the following Sunday follow up with another broadside against Kennan signed "by a pretty formidable group of authorities on Germany." The foreign policy establishment was mobilizing for the Cold War catechism and against Kennan.

Though Acheson had admired Kennan, he had also judged him, even back in the Policy Planning Staff days, as someone who "lived part of the time in a world of fantasy," recalled an associate of both men. He added that while Kennan was very sensitive, Acheson "was very insensitive."[74] Acheson's daughter, Mary A. Bundy, would later recall that her father was appalled by disengagement. "It seemed to work against everything that they had built up." Consequently, Acheson "lost his confidence in the stability of this man's thinking." More generally, "my father was very unhappy about the way the world was going at that time in 1957, and was inclined to hit hard."[75] Acheson probably also hit hard because he was exasperated by suffering with a painful bone fracture that required him to sleep sitting up.

Acheson launched his January 12 public statement by attacking Kennan's standing and expertise. He denied that the former diplomat spoke for the Democratic Party. He recalled that when Kennan had proposed disengagement in 1949, it had been roundly rejected by the State Department. Acheson next sought to shrink the scope of his opponent's authority. This assault required a rewriting of history. Back in 1947–1948, when Kennan ranked as director of the Policy Planning Staff with an office next door to Secretary of State George C. Marshall, he had written influential policy papers on virtually every aspect of U.S. foreign policy. On a visit to Japan he had instigated a reversal of the harsh occupation policy. Compared to Assistant Secretary of State Acheson, Kennan at the time commanded equal if not superior prestige and influence. Now, however, on the front page of the *New York Times* and elsewhere, Acheson reduced Kennan's expertise to "Russian history and culture and Soviet ideology." Nothing about Germany, even though Kennan, unlike Acheson, had lived there for years and was fluent enough to give academic lectures in German.

Hitting harder, Acheson assailed his opponent's credibility as a sound, rational thinker—and not just with regard to their current dispute: "Mr. Kennan has never, in my judgment, grasped the realities of power relationships, but takes a rather mystical attitude toward them." He bore in where Kennan had made himself most vulnerable, the assertion that European nations could guard against invasion by building up local militia forces. Though easy to ridicule, such a strategy had, as Kennan would subsequently point out, proven effective. Mao Zedong's Communists had used decentralized resistance against Japanese occupiers in China, and Ho Chi Minh had done much the same against the French in the 1946–1954 war in Vietnam. Years later, Ukraine's decentralized military resistance would thwart Russia's expectation of a quick takeover of its neighbor. Acheson, however, zeroed in on Kennan's unwise "personal assurance" that such a strategy could ensure immunity from Soviet attack. He mocked the former diplomat for speaking on the basis of "divine revelation."

Acheson's visible fury enhanced the force of his argument, many believed. From his perch as a top Washington journalist, James Reston celebrated Acheson's overt anger as a "public service," for "next to the Lincoln Memorial in moonlight, the sight of Mr. Dean Acheson blowing his top is without doubt the most impressive sight in the capital."[76] For his part, Kennan seems to have understood that challenging Cold War orthodoxy demanded leashing his expressed feelings. Given prevailing assumptions about foreign policy, gender, and thought, advocating compromise or peace could easily be delegitimated as unrealistic, soft, and emotional. By contrast, pushing for weaponry and rigidity in negotiations had the presumptive claim to masculinist realism, strength, and reason. Acheson and his supporters instinctively grasped that for them as powerful men, a tough stance freed them to let loose, to express their anger, and to lash out with little risk of being criticized as emotional. Acheson instead won praise, even from his own harshest critics, like Vice President Richard M. Nixon and Secretary of State Dulles. "I was very glad [to see your statement]," Dulles wrote Acheson, adding that Kennan's lectures "were doing considerable harm abroad" to policies promoted by both the present and preceding administrations.[77]

Acheson escalated still further. He advanced from attacking Kennan's proposals and expertise to disparaging his thinking as evidence of, literally, evolutionary throwback. The first issue of *Foreign Affairs* subsequent to the Reith Lectures featured a lead essay, "The Illusion of Disengagement," invited by Armstrong and written by Acheson. Acheson had the audacity to attack Kennan's proposals in the context of a quotation from a book on simians. Those "frowzy, unlovely hordes of apes and monkeys" from mankind's evolutionary past, those "flighty" creatures with "so much love for absurd and idle chatter" remained "a terrible obstacle to all high advancement." Such traits persist, he warned. Rather than penciling out the words associating Kennan's thinking with the chatter of chimpanzees, Armstrong, himself a champion of the Cold War, praised the essay as beautifully written.[78]

In challenging the Cold War, Kennan made himself a target. William Hard, an editor at *Reader's Digest*, asked Acheson to "send me George Kennan's skin to hang up as a trophy on my office wall. You took it off him completely." Three decades earlier, Hard nearly became George's father-in-law. Anne Hard, who had sabotaged her daughter Eleanor's engagement because she had believed Kennan would never amount to much, now condescended toward "poor dear George." While granting his "integrity, and sweetness and kindness," she also remembered his "pedantic mind." Not tough enough to be a leader, George was "one of those personally lovable people who," when he sees something ugly, "turns and flees or reaches for his kid gloves." Continuing to mix the metaphors, she saw him as "a fish in water too deep for him." Equally dismissive, Acheson explained that while Kennan had done some good work in the 1940s, he "was very erratic. It finally became quite impossible, after his performance in Berlin while Ambassador to the Soviet Union." He quite understood Dulles's subsequent decision to fire Kennan.[79] Acheson's caustic opinion of Kennan probably came into play when he was advising President-elect John F. Kennedy on appointments to high-level positions.

Lauris Norstad, Supreme Allied Commander of NATO, jabbed that Kennan's giving his personal assurance regarding the Russians amounted to "the height of egotism." "What authority does he speak with? Is he speaking of the divisions of the Princeton School of International Studies?" NATO Secretary General Paul-Henri Spaak also attacked disengagement.[80] While failing to sway these heavyweights, the iconoclast had inspired huge numbers of citizens to question Cold War orthodoxy. As Frank K. Roberts, a stalwart of conventional thinking in the British Foreign Office, warned, "Public opinion will not allow us to continue simply to turn down proposals such as this without suggesting any alternative."[81]

Meanwhile, Kennan, exhausted by all the work and stress, had fled Oxford with the family for a skiing vacation near Zurich. While the Reith Lectures had made a great splash with the public, they had not swayed those who mattered most to him. "The governments certainly could not have been less impressed."[82] Then on Sunday, January 12, he glanced at a favorite newspaper, the *Neue Zürcher Zeitung*, and saw, "wholly unexpectedly," the entire front page devoted to the full text of Acheson's assault. He "wandered around half the day, in the snow, trying to adjust to the blow." He also winced at Truman's jibe that Kennan could do good work only when instructed by Acheson.[83] He despaired that no one else in public life remained "interested in a political settlement with the Russians." The United States was determined to "plunge blindly, recklessly ahead with the weapons race." These people "will have their war, on which they all seem so intent." He was now "in the truest sense a voice crying in the wilderness; and never, I think, have I felt a greater sense of loneliness."[84] That loneliness persisted even at home. Though overwhelmed by misery, George apparently did not feel comfortable confiding in Annelise. In a four-page, newsy letter to Jeanette written the very next day, Annelise did not mention Acheson's attack. Knowing that George's devoted sister closely followed her brother's career, Annelise usually filled her in on what was happening.

Annelise did note that "George has felt absolutely rotten." He suffered "intellectual brokenheartedness."[85] The vacation had only worsened his cold and sinus condition; the infection invaded his chest and stomach. The ulcers flared up again. As at other times of overwork and stress, such as in December 1934, Kennan crashed. Annelise observed "days when he could not even read." On Tuesday, January 14, Kennan entered a Zurich hospital for a thorough examination.[86]

By early February 1958, the Kennans had settled back in Oxford, despite their loathing for the place. He could not warm to an environment "as forbidding, as unassailable, as cold, and as unimaginative as the stone of the walls."[87] Friends observed that he "looked very wan after his go of ulcers and nervous depression in Switzerland."[88] The whole family was "having a hard time, this winter," Kennan confided to Oppenheimer. Though the family problems were not new, "Oxford has a way of concentrating them."[89]

Then twenty-five-year-old Grace Kennan decided to marry her fiancé, the newspaper heir Charles "C.K." McClatchy, while her family was in Britain. While happy for her daughter, Annelise wrote Jeanette, "[Gracie has] certainly thrown everybody into turmoil." Flying over for the wedding "would cost a lot of money which we could ill spare." Moreover, she had no one "to look after George and the children. George is not very well." While Annelise had been "harping on a small wedding reception," she feared that "Gracie and C.K. will easily be carried away and think that every last Tom, Dick, and Harry they know should be invited." Nevertheless, "we are of course insisting on paying for everything."[90] Jeanette once again stepped up to play substitute mother to the Kennan children. (A few years earlier, Annelise had appealed to Jeanette to take care of six-week-old Christopher while she went skiing. "There were a couple of weddings I wanted to go to, and there were things that I really wanted to do," Jeanette would later recall, "but I up and went to Washington." In the 1950s, Jeanette on several occasions assumed care of Christopher and Wendy, as she had done in the 1940s with Grace and Joanie.[91]) Oppenheimer also tried to help. He "was foolish enough to try to talk Grace out of having so ceremonial a wedding in your absence," he wrote George, "but that was not to be done."[92] In Washington, Frank and Polly Wisner, family friends since George and Frank had plotted together in the Office of Policy Coordination in the late 1940s, hosted the large gathering, which included Supreme Court Chief Justice Earl Warren.[93]

Amid this personal and public drama, Kennan resumed lecturing on history and dazzling admirers. His aura from the BBC broadcasts still glowed. As a student remembered, "all my liberal friends, and the journals—the *Manchester Guardian*—I would say the whole country, almost, was eating out his hand, with the exception of the *Daily Telegraph.*" She viewed the Reith lectures as "secular sermons." And "George Kennan was the best sermonizer I've heard, anywhere." He was so effective because he believed so fervently in what he preached. "The hardest part of this, for me is that I am quite confident that in most respects I am right," he told himself. "What does one do with such a burden?"[94]

Again and again over the years, Kennan would grow frustrated with the limits of his influence. He repeatedly renounced any further effort to influence national and international affairs. But such renunciation never lasted because he cared, and believed in himself, too much. Though routinely discouraged, he never remained daunted.

SENATOR KENNAN?

Musing about his post-Oxford return to the Institute, Kennan regarded himself as trustee of a voice that was "listened to by millions of people with interest and respect." Moreover, he reminded Oppenheimer "there are not so many voices of this sort in our Western world today." He proposed shifting his activities at the Institute "from diplomatic history to what is now called Sovietology—Soviet studies."[95] While warm in his personal response, the IAS director confessed to doubts and questions about this change.[96] Back in Princeton, Kennan continued to juggle. He completed one book, wrote another, and delivered some

forty academic lectures, all the while commenting on public affairs—
and declining over 460 requests for further such commitments.[97]

The issue of his future came to a head in December 1959. Princeton
University president Robert F. Goheen told Kennan of a move to nominate him as the Democratic candidate for the U.S. Senate from the state
of New Jersey. Kennan grasped at this chance for the prestige and forum
of a senator. He asked Oppenheimer if the Institute could continue his
salary during an election campaign. The reply "was very discouraging."
The would-be senator penned a six-page letter to Oppenheimer detailing why the refusal "makes me very unhappy." Kennan, tellingly, thought
that he could win the election and that he owed it to his supporters to
run. "There are thousands of people, not just in this country but in Europe and Asia as well, who have given me a measure of personal and
intellectual confidence." They "look to me" for "answers to problems
and dilemmas we all have on our minds. Many of these are young
people." He found it increasingly difficult to speak on public affairs without edging toward "precisely that participation in public life which is
involved in Mr. Goheen's inquiry." Finally, Kennan warned the director,
he was growing restless with the isolation of the Institute and was looking forward to again participating in public affairs. Here was George F.
Kennan at age fifty-five: excited by his influence with the public, willing
to throw over his scholarship, and dazzled by the prospect of returning
to Washington as Senator Kennan. Despite Kennan's shimmering vision, not many of his far-flung admirers were eligible to vote in New
Jersey elections. What brought George back to earth was money. He
could not support his family without a regular salary.[98] "Trapped in this
manner," his elation deflated, he concluded that "my usefulness as a
commentator on political affairs, and in fact my usefulness to this country, has really come to an end." Again.

And again, he could not actually abandon such hope for influence
and service. No matter how much he bristled at the vanities and inani-
ties of American society, and regardless of how he raged at the repression and cruelty of Russian society, this sentimental, self-proclaimed
realist remained wedded to both. Hearing the voice of an American
woman, Kennan, then in Oxford, suddenly realized how much he loved

"my own people" who, he lamented, are "destined within my children's time to know unprecedented horrors and miseries." Nevertheless, they "have certain qualities of modesty and candor and helpfulness" that the postapocalyptic world would miss. Only three months later, seeing *The Cherry Orchard* stirred up his "Russian self, which is entirely a Chekhovian sense and much more genuine than the American one."[99] His feelings for both America and Russia made it especially painful watching them career toward nuclear conflict—over the issues of Berlin and Germany that he had tackled with his disengagement proposals.

CRISIS OVER BERLIN

In a BBC radio symposium after the Reith Lectures, Kennan had pointed to divided Berlin as the most dangerous flashpoint. The vulnerability of West Berlin, situated deep within East Germany, might force the West to take military action that could escalate. Having lived there for years, he had special feelings for the former German capital. In a reunited Germany, "the city would immediately be restored" to its rightful place.[100]

By the late 1950s, East Germany—officially the German Democratic Republic—was hemorrhaging people. Its citizens, especially technicians trained at government expense, were fleeing through the Berlin escape hatch to the freedom and higher wages of West Germany. As the saying had it, the former Soviet zone was neither German, nor democratic, nor a republic. Now it was collapsing. That outcome would humiliate Moscow while bolstering what the Soviets most feared: a powerful, revenge-seeking West Germany backed by U.S. nuclear weapons. In November 1958, Khrushchev intervened. He demanded that the Western allies withdraw their troops from West Berlin and negotiate with East Germany for access into the divided city. Eisenhower and Dulles refused. A series of crises over Berlin brought the world to the brink of nuclear war. Fear for West Berlin would also escalate the stakes in the 1962 Cuban missile crisis.

Kennan reflected bitterly that he had seen this coming. He had long warned that the continued division of Germany and Berlin was dangerous. In the Reith Lectures he had pointed the way to a negotiated solution. Moreover, Kennan had, as even his opponent in the BBC symposium, Royal Air Force Marshal John Slessor, acknowledged, done much to create a climate of opinion favoring talks toward disengagement. In Washington, the prospect of such talks had run into a stone wall. In Moscow, however, Khrushchev, in talking with Averell Harriman, "said he found many of Mr. George Kennan's ideas expressed in the Reith Lectures coincided with his own. He liked particularly the idea of a gradual withdrawal in Central Europe." Harriman, still proud of his service as FDR's wartime emissary to Stalin, had disparaged disengagement as just another of his former assistant's "strange ideas."[101] Now he listened as the current Soviet leader proposed Kennan as the go-between, at least in terms of ideas: "Many of Mr. Kennan's ideas would be acceptable to us and should be to the advantage of the United States as well."[102]

A visit by Khrushchev to the United States in September 1959, a summit planned for Paris in May 1960, and a projected visit by Eisenhower to the Soviet Union the following month sparked hopes for a breakthrough. Then CIA chiefs brazenly sent another high-flying U-2 spy plane over the Soviet Union. The Soviets shot down the plane and displayed the captured pilot, all to the embarrassment of Eisenhower, who had initially denied any spying. Khrushchev arrived in Paris only to lambaste Eisenhower and cancel the invitation to Moscow. Tensions spiked once more.

Though no fan of summit diplomacy, Kennan was dismayed at the rupture. His thoughts turned, again, to how the crisis could have been averted if Washington had listened to him. He characterized the difficulties between America and Russia as stemming more from problematic personalities than from power politics. While granting the difficult side of the Soviet personality, he faulted also "the American official mind" that preferred to dwell on "its own familiar images" of the Soviets as Hitler rather than "try to understand what a fellow like Kennan had to say about Russia." There was no need, he insisted, to send spy planes over Russia to make sure the Soviets were not planning a surprise attack. "I could have told our people this—did, in fact." He hastened to add, "so could anyone else who knew anything about Russia."[103] Although Kennan never fully forgave Acheson for his brutal attack over disengagement, he and Annelise became close friends with Dean and Alice Acheson's daughter, Mary, who lived in Princeton with her husband, William P. "Bill" Bundy, a top State Department official and later professor at Princeton and editor of *Foreign Affairs*. A perceptive observer, Mary saw in Kennan a deep sadness. Kennan believed that his tendency toward melancholy stemmed from the death of his mother when he was a two-month-old infant.

He coped with that loss by making it so tangible that he could steer it. As he had in the visit to his parents' graves, he fantasized into near reality connections that never were. He breathed into life the intimacy and love that he missed so much. In a dream, he recorded in 1959, "I encountered my own mother. I recognized her instantly. There was in the face something so infinitely close and familiar." She appeared not only maternal, but also sensuous and very much alive. "The eyes struck me with the intensity of the life that shone through them, and in the mouth, sensitive, sometimes slightly pouting . . . I was startled to become aware of a real human being . . . not the angel I had always pictured." A touch of reserve made her even more alluring. "She accepted with politeness and with an enigmatic smile my own instantaneous gesture of recognition and joy and tenderness. She was, for the moment, the main thing in my existence; I was not the main thing in hers." The distance in her attitude toward him corresponded to the distance of this dream from the waking world, and this concurrence may have enhanced the perceived reality of it all. The next day, writing in the Firestone Library at Princeton, Kennan had "no doubt that I saw her as she really was."[104]

KENNAN AND KENNEDY

However much fantasizing soothed his loneliness, such imagining could not quench his desire for influence in foreign policy. If Kennan could not afford to run for political office, his only other recourse was appointment by the president to some high position. Dulles barred the door for most of the Eisenhower years, and Acheson aimed to shut Kennan out of the next Democratic administration. Kennan, however, had his own access—to the ambitious senator from Massachusetts, John F. Kennedy. Back in 1938 in Prague, Kennan had assisted this scion of Joseph P. Kennedy, ambassador to Great Britain. Meeting Senator Kennedy in the early 1950s, "I was impressed with his youthfulness—he looked like a sort of overgrown student in those days," Kennan later recalled. He was also "impressed with Mrs. Kennedy's beauty."

Kennedy, planning to run for president in 1960, needed some stick with which to attack the peace and prosperity of the Eisenhower years. Open to fresh ideas, Kennedy admired Kennan as someone who thought outside the box. After Acheson's slashing attack on the Reith broadcasts, the senator commended Kennan on the "brilliance" of the lectures and "the service you have performed by delivering them." Implicitly siding against Acheson, Kennedy found nothing in Kennan's talks or career "which justifies the personal criticisms that have been made." That was welcome balm. Nevertheless, Kennedy did not explicitly endorse disengagement.

Moreover, JFK's concern with the threatened "sweep south of the Chinese with their endless armies" foreshadowed military entanglements by him and by his successor that would later torment Kennan.[105] Kennedy found intriguing the so-called Rockefeller Brothers report, which urged deploying more long-range nuclear missiles to check the Chinese and Russians and building up counterguerrilla, Green Beret forces to fight Chinese and Soviet-inspired insurrection, especially in Southeast Asia and Latin America. In 1966, Kennan would speak out against the escalation of the Vietnam War that President Johnson had inherited from President Kennedy. And in the late 1970s and 1980s, he would rail against the nuclear arms race stepped up by Kennedy despite his partial nuclear test ban.

While Kennedy respected Kennan, he did not embrace him. Two weeks before the November 1960 election, JFK volunteered that he intended to "urge Chip Bohlen not to retire." When then asked about Kennan, he confided that "since George is involved with things like disengagement, he wouldn't want to mention his name at this time."[106] Nor would he for a while.

On January 2, 1961, Kennan despaired that future possibilities looked all too familiar. It was "now nearly two months since the election, and I have had literally nothing from anyone in Washington." He feared a repetition of the torture after Eisenhower's election, when he had waited by the telephone in vain. Most of Kennedy's foreign affairs appointments had been made, "and to a large extent to people whom I thought of as friends." Even worse, "concerning myself, the press has not printed a single world." He berated himself for a "double failure." He had failed as a government official. Not only had Dulles rejected him, but now even his friends did not want him. "I have also failed as a publicist." His reasoning here revealed the underlying motive in all the effort put into his myriad public lectures and articles. He had hoped to create a groundswell of public support that would compel the next president to appoint him to high office. While Kennan could blame Acheson for poisoning the well with the new administration, "this cannot explain the indifference of the press. For this, I can have only myself to blame."[107]

The next day, however, Kennedy invited Kennan to lunch on January 10. In responding to JFK's queries, Kennan reiterated the arguments he had been making for a decade. He asserted that "there were two camps in the Kremlin," one that "did not care about relations with this country," and one that "was reluctant to burn all the bridges." Regarding the Soviets' eagerness for a summit conference, Kennan voiced the skepticism about such meetings he had held ever since Yalta. The Soviets should explain "why these questions should not better be treated at lower and more normal levels"—with diplomats such as himself. Moreover he wondered, in an echo from his trauma in 1952, how "an American president could conceivably meet" with Soviet officials responsible for anti-American propaganda. Kennan displayed enthusiasm, however, for Kennedy's proposal to set up in the White House a "small staff of people who worked just for him" on foreign policy. No doubt tantalized by the possibility of serving in such an inner sanctum, Kennan described in detail General Marshall's reliance on the advice of the Policy Planning Staff, of which he was the founding director. While Kennedy did not appoint Kennan to his National Security Council, a week later he offered him the ambassadorship to either Poland or Yugoslavia. Kennan eagerly accepted the latter post.

Kennedy became Kennan's favorite president. Indeed, after the death of JFK, Kennan ranked him as an American statesman second to none in the twentieth century—that is, more accomplished than Theodore Roosevelt, Woodrow Wilson, or Franklin D. Roosevelt.[108] Having never understood FDR, Kennan disdained him as a lightweight meddler in diplomacy. He appraised Truman as a good enough politician but no statesman. He judged Eisenhower as charming, disarming, and yet distant. Kennedy was different. Kennedy listened carefully to what Kennan had to say.

Kennan imputed to the young president many of his own beliefs. He wrote after Kennedy's death, "I think it likely that he saw military policy . . . in relation to NATO and Western Europe as embracing certain unnecessary rigidities." Similarly, "I suspect that his attitude" toward nuclear deterrence "was a skeptical one." Most importantly, Kennedy considered "his greatest responsibility as President of the United States was to avoid the catastrophe of a nuclear war."[109] For his part, "Kennedy always went out of his way to show great respect for Kennan," the historian and presidential adviser Arthur M. Schlesinger Jr. observed.[110] National Security Adviser McGeorge Bundy later reflected that Kennedy prized "the kind of unusual, sensitive, independent intelligence that George Kennan has."[111] While flattering to Kennan, the personal chemistry with Kennedy dangerously inflated the ambassador's expectations of what he could accomplish in Belgrade.

"George Kennan looks 20 years younger and is *so* full of smiles and cheer and *dying* to get started," Avis Bohlen wrote Charlie Thayer, her brother and the sidekick of George and her husband, Chip Bohlen, back in the glory days of 1933–1934. "Poor Annelise is facing the domestic problems *less* joyfully but still pleased." Avis's chatty February 1961 letter revealed something else: the power dynamic within the Kennedy administration that would frustrate and ultimately crash Kennan's ambitions. Kennedy had assigned George to manage relations with a second-tier, bristly nation in Eastern Europe whose Communist government had antagonized vocal émigrés influential in the U.S. Congress. The president did not include Kennan in a group of heavyweights—ambassador to Moscow Llewellyn "Tommy" Thompson, special assistant for Soviet Affairs (and later ambassador to Paris) Chip Bohlen, Secretary of State Dean Rusk, and Ambassador at Large Averell Harriman—that met with Kennedy "for a total of about 7 hours—background-filling-in, discussing the USSR." It was "all very satisfactory, and Tommy and Chip are delighted—natch!" Avis enthused.[112]

Kennan, being Kennan, nevertheless tried to insinuate himself into the inner circle. Also characteristic was how he threw himself so totally into his new job that he set himself up for disappointment. Back in 1948, Kennan had welcomed Marshal Tito's escape from Stalin's grip as the first step in the devolution of the Soviet empire. He now aimed to nudge Belgrade further away from Moscow while also increasing trade and other ties with the United States.

He sought to leverage his stationing in far-off Belgrade into a central role in U.S.-Soviet relations. Kennan urged the president and Rusk to authorize him as a back channel to Khrushchev through "my Soviet colleague in Belgrade, Aleksei Yepishev." The two ambassadors could speak in Russian without any interpreter and without detection, since Belgrade had few Western reporters. "It was perfectly easy for me to walk right over from my home to the Soviet Ambassador's home and sit down with him in his own living room," Kennan later explained. After getting the go-ahead, he and Yepishev, a rising star in the Soviet government, discussed how to downplay the conflict in Laos. They also talked about the issue threatening to explode into nuclear war: Berlin. Kennan enthused that Yepishev's remarks seemed to be coming directly from Moscow. He would have grown even more excited if he had known that Khrushchev had proposed to Kennedy that the two emissaries move from just "sniffing each other" to serious diplomacy.

On September 29, 1961, the Soviet leader wrote to the president: "I never met Mr. Kennan, but, so far as I can judge by the press, he is, to my mind, a man with whom preparatory work could be done, and we would accordingly authorize our Ambassador." But, he gently admonished Kennedy, "our Ambassadors would have to be given firm instructions to start talks on concrete questions without needless procrastination and not merely indulge in tea-drinking, not walk round and about mooing at each other when they should talk on the substance."[113] Strategic circumstances, fluency in Russian, and his own emotional and intellectual stance had once more positioned George between America and Russia. Both Kennan and the Kremlin chief sought substantive talks that could ease the Berlin crisis.

By the time Khrushchev's letter reached the White House, however, Rusk, evidently with Kennedy's permission, had shuttered the back channel. More than rivalry with Rusk was entailed, Kennan later concluded. The State Department "didn't really want any agreement about Berlin." Instead, Rusk and other hard-liners, influenced by Acheson, "wanted the Russians to simply desist and capitulate, but they didn't want to discuss it with them."[114]

Kennan still would not give up. As tensions over Berlin tightened, he sent to Ambassador to Moscow Thompson, Secretary of State Rusk, and National Security Adviser McGeorge Bundy a four-page, single-spaced letter that ripped apart the administration's policy on negotiations with the Russians. The letter no doubt appeared to its recipients as audacious and transgressive. Here was a mid-level official daring to challenge the long-standing U.S. policy of refusing to grant legitimacy to the rump state of East Germany. All Kennan was saying, however, was give diplomacy a chance. In 1943 and in 1944, he had appealed directly to President Roosevelt. Sure of himself, Kennan again reached high in an effort to bend U.S. policy.

The persistent diplomat was contesting the bedrock premises of the Cold War. Rather than "shillyshallying" around, Washington should accept Moscow's request, made repeatedly since 1958, for serious talks on the future of Berlin and Germany. The two superpowers should negotiate directly, in secret, and without the complicating presence of European allies. "I fail to understand how we could ever have gotten ourselves in a position where it takes a series of summit meetings with our allies to make it possible for us to conduct perfectly normal" diplomacy with the Soviets, he chided. Successful negotiations required concessions from both sides. He suggested that Washington agree to establish diplomatic relations with East Germany as Moscow had done with West

Germany years earlier, and accept the Oder-Neisse line, the de facto border between East Germany and Poland since 1945. Kennan confessed "bewilderment" at the administration's pretending that the "Soviet asking-price" for a deal equaled "what Moscow would likely agree to" after successful negotiations. While radical in the context of the Cold War, these proposals offered a reasonable off ramp from confrontation.

Kennan pushed further by highlighting his vantage point between America and Russia. He had received from the Russians "many assurances that Khrushchev had a high opinion of me personally." In recent years, Soviet officials had pressed him, "'Why don't you come to Moscow?'" Kennan told Thompson, Rusk, and Bundy that, if they approved, he was "thinking of paying a visit to Moscow at some time in the next two or three months." He wanted to "get a smell of the atmosphere of Moscow in the 1960s." He aimed to assess the prospect for diplomacy and perhaps nudge it along. Kennan being Kennan, deep down he probably also hoped that conditions might break so as to enable him to promote or even broker a deal between Washington and Moscow, as he had aspired to do in 1938, 1948, and 1952. With regard to the fiasco of that last effort, the Soviets seemed to be assuring that the "unpleasantness of 1952 was purely Stalin's doing."[115]

Rusk pushed back hard. He rejected Kennan's suggestion of bilateral U.S.-Soviet talks, reiterated stock charges of Russian aggressiveness on Berlin, and refused to let Kennan visit Moscow "until after Tommy [Thompson] has had this series of talks. Let's take it up a bit later." That "later" would never arrive.

In looking back on his experience as ambassador, Kennan complained that "Kennedy had promised him that he'd have access to the President," but he had grown "quite disillusioned." His effort "was just wasted. I couldn't do anything."[116]

Kennedy may have cooled toward Kennan for reasons of tone as well as substance. The president and his chief advisers prided themselves on their cool rationality. They liked to think of themselves as so self-possessed that they could remain calm and calculating as they skirted close to nuclear war. Far different was Kennan, not at all cool that "the chances of war were fifty-fifty."[117] Kennan spoke with great earnestness about the imminent threat of nuclear war, Schlesinger observed. Even though the problem of Berlin amounted to only a transient situation, there were "those who would blow up the world" over it. With palpable emotion Kennan twice repeated: "The only thing I have left in life is to do everything I can to stop the war."[118]

Other situations also sparked strong feelings. As Avis Bohlen had observed, Kennan invested heart and soul in the success of his mission to Belgrade. Bill Bundy noticed that an element of vanity colored the emissary's dedication. He thought the Yugoslavs should appreciate the great honor shown them by sending "somebody of George's stature as ambassador." Such pride complicated diplomatic issues. In September 1961, Tito sided openly with Khrushchev after the latter broke the tacit nuclear test moratorium by exploding a huge hydrogen bomb. Bill Bundy, then in the Pentagon, later remembered that "George absolutely hit the ceiling." He cabled, "This is an outrageous thing; we must punish them" by cutting Belgrade's already meager military aid.[119] The British ambassador reported that "my American colleague is becoming increasingly bitter and irritated" toward the Yugoslavs."[120]

Kennan also grew upset at his failure to get Congress to drop its annual "Captive Nations" resolution, a Cold War relic that called for overthrowing the governments of the Soviet Union and Yugoslavia while also restoring such national entities as "Ude-Ural" and "Cossackia"—which had existed only through the conjuring of Nazi occupiers of Russia and Ukraine. Though Kennedy had promised his support, he succumbed to political pressure and did not protest the resolution. While JFK dismissed the resolution as small ball, Kennan, insulted, did not.

A more serious problem emerged when Congress, swayed by what Kennan called "organized McCarthyite Catholics," proposed eliminating the most-favored-nation tariff status of Yugoslav exports, which would cripple sales to the United States.[121] Anxious to protect his Yugoslavs and furious at the ignorant meddling of Congress, Kennan went all-out to save the day. He telephoned Kennedy on an open line, knowing that the Yugoslav government would tap the call and realize that he was fighting for them. Not willing to risk his own political capital, Kennedy sent Kennan out to "lobby for all I was worth." And so Kennan in the summer of 1962 spent day after frustrating day tramping from one legislator's office to another. In pouring rain, he "traveled all the way to Gettysburg, where I called on General Eisenhower," who agreed to telephone a pivotal congressman.[122] It all came to naught, however, as Congress passed the offending legislation. Kennedy, facing more serious problems, refused to block it. Crushed, Kennan resolved to resign immediately. He was persuaded by Annelise to wait a decent interval so as not to advertise his frustration with the president. Instead, he "went off for a long walk, totally discouraged—feeling defeated as I have not felt since 1953."[123]

Days later the Cuban missile crisis erupted. This proved the most dangerous collision with the Soviet Union in the entire Cold War. Neither Kennedy nor anyone else in Washington sought the advice of the man once held up as America's foremost expect on Russia. Kennedy handled the crisis largely as Kennan would have advocated, however. He pulled back from military confrontation and pursued instead secret diplomacy. The resulting deal traded the withdrawal of U.S. missiles from Turkey and a pledge not to invade Cuba for Khrushchev's removal of the nuclear-armed missiles from Cuba.

On a personal level, Kennan found Belgrade far more pleasant than Moscow with its imposed isolation. Often superstitious, he worried about his departure date for Yugoslavia, April 29, the same day that he had left for Russia in 1952. Nevertheless, George and Annelise were "very happy in Belgrade," their daughter later recalled. "They had a fabulous house, swimming pool, and garden." They loved exploring the mountains and villages in their beat-up old car. Her father "liked heading his own operation."[124] Conscious of his elder-statesman image among the younger staff, Kennan dutifully sought to mentor his flock. He failed to perceive, however, how his shyness and sense of propriety came across to others. He assumed that his status as ambassador erected "a curtain of deference" that unavoidably "separated him from his subordinates."[125]

Some of those subordinates, however, saw something different. "There was not much personal warmth" in the new ambassador's greeting, Owen T. Jones, an economic adviser, noted in his diary. Jones picked up on what had impressed audiences at Oxford and elsewhere: "Kennan has the touch of greatness about him," which "had an immediate effect on me."[126] As Jones got to know "the great man," awe dimmed into ambivalence. "I am attracted to Kennan's essential kindness and decency, his brilliance," and the "long-term soundness of his judgments," he wrote a year later. "I am repelled by his self-centered egoism," "his mercurial moods, his intellectual arrogance, his arm's length treatment of myself as virtually a rival," and, in general, "the unevenness of his performance." Kennan's was a mind "brilliant but not flexible." Finally, the ambassador's "lode-star is his own personal position and the mark he wants to have on diplomatic history."[127] Jones had penned a sharp but fair appraisal.

Effective as of July 28, 1963, Kennan resigned from what he judged a disastrous tour of duty in Belgrade. It had not been that bad. But he interpreted his mission as a failure because he had gone into it expecting so much. Most ambassadors met frustration. As Bill Bundy put it, diplomats often faced a situation where "the government you are accredited to are behaving like sons-of-bitches, and there isn't a hell of a lot you can do about it. . . . [But] George found it hard to accept."[128] Kennan also hated to accept that despite Kennedy's respect for him, he had not become an insider in the making of U.S. foreign policy.

Just as Kennan tried to satisfy his itch for a leadership position, so too did he struggle with his sexual desires. Allusions to affairs, flirtations, and fantasy, some written in Russian, run as a red thread through his diary. He tried to balance his desires and obligations—Eros and Civilization, as Kennan read in Freud—by remaining discreet about his dalliances. He even left posthumous instructions for his son on the theory and practice of extramarital affairs. Even the most successful marriages, he wrote, did not always satisfy instinctual sexual desires. Hence the need for affairs, which created their own problems.[129]

Erotic images filled dreams he judged important enough to record in his dream diary. In these visions Annelise was usually dead or otherwise absent. One dream suggested still smoldering feelings for a long-ago fiancée. He encountered Eleanor Hard, "looking very young and beautiful." Redoing the past, they decided to marry. There followed "various adventures," as he discreetly phrased it.[130]

COMMUNING WITH FATHER

More striking than Kennan's fantasizing about sexual intimacy was his conjuring of familial intimacy. Flooded with literally hundreds of lecture invitations each year, he chose to talk in February 1965 at Ripon College in Wisconsin, his father's alma mater.

He was assigned, perhaps by request, to the apartment where his father had lived as a student. After the lecture and reception, he retreated to the apartment and sat in the dark gazing out the window at the blowing, "blessed snow, covering everything mercifully and impartially." The white blanket seemed to erase differences and distances. Relaxed, he opened himself to sensibility and imagining. "I was suddenly struck with a surge of feeling for my long-dead, honored father." He embraced that surge by recounting the personality traits of Kossuth Kent Kennan, many of which he shared. Here was "this shy and lonely man," "this misplaced esthete," someone "whom almost no one [especially not George's stepmother!] understood." The dutiful son regretted having hurt him "in my boyhood by inattention, by callousness"; he deplored "our respective lonelinesses"; and he sensed again our "fumbling, helpless affection for each other."

The cascade of warm, fuzzy, emotion-evoking words transported George beyond "time and death" to his father. "I wondered suddenly whether we were not, at that moment, very close." Given the fantastical logic of that snowy night, it seemed reasonable. Kent must also have looked out this window on snowy nights and must also have seen what George was seeing. Kent's "wonder of what lay further afield" paralleled the son's own questioning. With his imagination now fully engaged, Kennan, longing for intimacy, pushed further. "Were these chasms of time and death real ones?" Or were they the actual illusion? Was there not under the blanket of snow "a unity and a fellowship in the sensing, the living of this moment?" Could wanting something hard enough make it so?

Pivoting now between "the dust and rubbish" of ordinary life and fantasy, he tendered a "silly dialogue." The child, beseeching affection and approval: "Father, father. Have I done right to come all this way to make myself close to you through the scenes of your youth?" The adult: "Or was this an act of maudlin sentimentality?" The loving son: "There is so much I could have given you, and didn't. Does this help?" These words of filial devotion lifted him up, finally, beyond the quotidian and into the enveloping, validating intimacy that he craved.

"Soft, soft, my son." (This from the father who had sent him off to military school to harden up.) "The moment is indeed the same as you suspect. This is the same snowfall. The ninety intervening summers are as nothing." The warm, now expressive father blessed the son's yearnings: "Do what your deeper nature tells you to do. Take comfort in the beauty of the storm and the night; see the strength and indifference of the snow for all it falls upon, sense its lesson." "If you feel nearness, then know that it is true."[131] Feeling and filial devotion had trumped reason and reality. If you felt and wanted something strongly enough, it could happen. Kossuth Kent Kennan, a sentimentalist who had died while George was in far-off Moscow, might himself have fantasized about such an encounter with his son.

Kennan *needed* such succor, whether from a desirable woman or a loving parent. A few months later, after another guest lecture, "I lay on my bed in blackest depression." He went out "for a long, lonely walk in the rain, through the darkened, dripping parks, in utmost agony & helplessness of spirit."[132]

Kennan confided to the diary his agony about so many things: his lost mother, distant father, and sexual dilemma; his difficulty at times with his wife and older children; his shoddy treatment from the Soviet and U.S. governments; his ability to discern but not to alleviate international problems; the looming prospect of nuclear war; the dim prospects of American society; and, not least, his failed efforts at disengaging America and Russia from the Cold War—whether as ambassador in Moscow in 1952, over the BBC in 1957, as ambassador again in Belgrade in 1961, before televised Senate hearings on Vietnam in 1966, or in the eloquent passages of his many lectures and articles.

Missing from this catalog of sorrow and regret was his own responsibility for having helped ignite the Cold War with his incendiary rhetoric in the long telegram and in the Mr. "X" article. Determined to gain a hearing and to advance his career, he had exaggerated the threat posed by the Soviet Union as a geopolitical and ideological rival. Though he knew that Russia, devastated by the war, remained cautious, he deployed his rhetorical brilliance to cast the Kremlin as an aggressive, existential threat to America, Western Europe, and everything decent. Kennan had specified that he favored containing the Soviet Union primarily through political, economic, and psychological measures rather than military ones. Nevertheless, the force of Kennan's rhetoric, the tendency of leaders to "play it safe," and the fact that the United States had just deployed massive military force to win a smashing victory in a total war all led political and military chiefs to turn to weapons of force, especially the atomic bomb, to deter a Soviet military attack that Kennan thought highly unlikely.

Appalled by the military interpretation of containment, Kennan as early as 1948 began pushing for talks with the Soviets. He had always intended containment as a two-step process, first revive and stabilize such key areas as Western Europe and Japan, then follow up with the long, patient process of diplomacy to ease tensions. He envisioned a grand settlement that would restore something like the world order of the early 1930s absent the dictators. Hence his repeated efforts to bring about a disengagement from, or at least easing of, the Cold War.

A GUILTY DREAM?

Even as he worked hard to bring about a reversal of the Cold War policies that he had helped launch, Kennan until his last decade apparently did not reflect on his own role in helping to instigate the conflict. For someone so given to self-criticism, so attentive to feelings, and so gifted in seeing the big picture, it seems remarkable that he never articulated remorse for what he had done. While blaming others for misinterpreting him, he resisted blaming himself for making misinterpretation so easy. Such regret or guilt, conspicuous by its absence, may have been too painful to acknowledge, even to himself.

Interpreting dreams is a risky business, certainly for historians. Nevertheless, it seems that Kennan's suppressed guilt, or some such feeling, flickered into a dream so graphic that he would recall it in detail. Two months after the February 1966 televised hearings in which he criticized a war pursued in the name of containment, Kennan dreamt that once again he occupied an office in a "building like the War College, in Washington," just as he had in 1946–1947, when he was winning acclaim for the long telegram and lectures on Cold War strategy. Upon learning of a murder, he failed to say or do anything to stop it. Then he was trapped. People would ask "why I had said nothing sooner. I was the prisoner of my own guilty knowledge, the implications of which I had not previously pondered—nay, worse than that, I, by my silence, was an accomplice to the crime."[133] Whether Kennan in this dream was acknowledging his guilt as an "accomplice to the crime" of the Cold War is unknowable. He did not admit to such a painful connection.

More important, however, than the question of guilt for the past were his unceasing, brave, and selfless efforts in the present to disengage America and Russia from the Cold War and a potential nuclear showdown. Unlike virtually every other leader present and active in the creation of the Cold War, Kennan worked hard to reverse course. While he had spent the four years from 1944 to 1948 promoting the Cold War, he devoted the subsequent forty to undoing what he and others had wrought. That's not a bad record.

CHAPTER 10

KENNAN EMBATTLED, 1967–1982

KENNAN EXPECTED TO DIE on May 9, 1983. That departure would afford him a life span precisely that of the elder George Kennan (1845–1924).Their lives had paralleled in so many other ways. Both were born on February 16, loved Russia and suffered expulsion from it, and played the guitar and sailed. "There is really something of the older Kennan in myself," he believed.[1] This sense of mortality spurred Kennan to redouble his battle against environmental depredation and the nuclear arms race. He saw the two threats as linked, not just in terms of their horrific consequences, but also in their origins in misguided reliance on the machine. Industrialism and the concomitant huddling in cities had distorted humans' relations with each other and with nature. Kennan fantasized about reversing Genesis, about some catastrophe, perhaps a plague, that would give the earth "a chance to breathe, to recover, to cause these atrocities of man's handiwork to decay into the ruins they deserve to become, and to restore to the trees, the natural shrubs, the streams and wetlands, and the self-accommodating, non-destructive animals, the dominion over God's great and beautiful creation which they deserve to have."[2] This thread of radical environmentalism ran through much of what Kennan said and wrote, even his critique of student protestors of the Vietnam War.

Fearing his influence in the present was slipping, Kennan compensated by trying to both shape the story of his past and safeguard his legacy in the future. He wrote a best-selling, prize-winning memoir. He pushed hard against the "revisionist" historians who criticized the U.S.

policy of the late 1940s, his glory days in the State Department. Kennan was aided in this struggle over the past by the historian John Lewis Gaddis, who would later become his authorized biographer. George tried to avenge the past by demonstrating a fatherly concern for Svetlana Alliluyeva, the daughter neglected by his nemesis, Joseph Stalin.

BATTLING THE ANTIWAR PROTESTERS

Decorum and dignity mattered to Kennan. In his televised testimony on the Vietnam War before the Senate Foreign Relations Committee in February 1966, he had come across as a coolly rational expert impeccably dressed and quoting John Quincy Adams. He had shown and received respect as he explained why the conflict was harming not only the United States, but also the people and environment of Vietnam.

Kennan lost that cool, however, in responding to radical student protesters against the war. As usual, the personal and political intertwined. A secretary observed how her boss recoiled at "this great unwashed youth running around [Princeton University's] Firestone Library in bare feet and with long unwashed hair." His own family agitated Kennan still more. Mary Acheson Bundy later recalled that "the way he talked about his children just about killed me." He complained that "the younger kids were into drugs and long hair and revolting, and all that. The two older girls were getting divorced for the second time, or whatever. . . . [He] didn't want to see them; he didn't want to have anything to do with them." "It was not just the world" that was infuriating George, she confirmed, "it was also his own children, and he was disgusted."[3] An otherwise admiring neighbor, J. Richardson Dilworth, would remember that "George was somewhat shrill, at least we thought so, and our children thought so."[4]

He was certainly shrill when speaking at Swarthmore College on December 9, 1967. Coming from Princeton, where the former university president, Woodrow Wilson, had venerated colleges as idylls of ascetic, calm reflection, the sixty-three-year-old lambasted the young people in his audience: "embattled students" swept by "transports of passion." His vehemence recalled that of 1946–1947, when he had exaggerated and pathologized the threat from the Soviet Union. He again used pop psychology to diagnose behaviors as abnormal and neurotic. Clearly wrought up himself, he criticized student protesters as hyperemotional, even unhinged. He charged them with "screaming tantrums and brawling in the streets"; "throwing stones, breaking windows, overturning cars"; being driven by "angry militancy," "hatred and intolerance," and "prepared to embrace violence"; all the while brandishing "a selfishness, a hardheartedness, a callousness, an irresponsibility, and an indifference to the feelings of others"—especially the feelings of parents. In "their defiant rags and hairdos" there glowered "a perverted and willful and stony-hearted youth."[5]

Even the Swarthmore president was embarrassed by this tirade from an honored guest. As Kennan left the auditorium, he met "a group of angry young men, mostly bearded, who hissed their disagreement . . . like a flock of truculent village geese."

Kennan's rant went national. Exploiting the sensation, the *New York Times Magazine* published the diatribe on January 21, 1968, the first day of the Battle of Khe Sanh in South Vietnam and nine days before the onset of the Communists' Tet Offensive that would temporarily overrun Saigon. In this tense atmosphere, students and their supporters responded with over two hundred letters to Kennan and to the *Times*. Some of the missives openly mocked him, including one that taunted: "Oh Dad, poor Dad, we'll be around long after you are dead and gone."[6] Nevertheless, many letter writers retained respect, and some even remained fans. "I am currently a senior at Columbia University who has long been one of your admirers," began a typical letter.[7] Kennan read all the messages and answered many of them. He then seized the opportunity to secure a wider audience for his views while also making some money. He cobbled together his Swarthmore address, selected letters, and a lengthy (104-page!) reply for a mass-market book. While *Democracy and the Student Left* now conceded that the draft remained unfair since young men could be drafted at age eighteen but could not vote until twenty-one, Kennan otherwise stood his ground.

Indeed, he compared the antiwar students to the most dangerous youth of the twentieth century. He likened them to the naive anti-czarist youth of pre-1917 Russia, many of whom later supported the Bolsheviks. He also cited the students of Weimar Germany who had fallen for the Nazis. Current protesters were playing "into the hands of [Communist] propagandists."[8] He dismissed as "hysteria and exaggeration" anxiety over the war's rising death toll. After all, the death rate for young adults from traffic accidents reached twice as high. These radicals failed even at having real fun. Instead, they pursued "frantic, compulsive" "indulgence in sex and narcotics."[9] Back in his day, college campuses as well as the "bohemian-intellectual colonies in the great cities" had shrugged off the dangers of dying from Spanish influenza or the scarlet fever that had nearly killed him. They had enjoyed "a great deal of gaiety, good spirit, confidence and love of life."[10] Despite the sexagenarian's rosy memories, the rule-breaking muse of his Princeton years, the "hobo poet" Harry Kemp, had long since departed. Kennan now stressed the "the good order of society. There is little that can be done about men's motives; but if men can be restrained in their behavior, something is accomplished."[11]

Even more revealing, and appalling, than this petulance was Kennan's projecting onto the students blame for damage to the environment and the industrialism sparking it. The radical student is "a distinctly urban creature," he assumed out of thin air. Also presuming that any such student was male, Kennan faulted "his estrangement from nature, his intimacy with the machine, his familiarity with the world of gadgetry, and his total lack of understanding for the slow, powerful processes of organic growth."[12] Tilting against this imagined enemy, Kennan self-righteously asserted that "not only do my apprehensions out class" those of the students, but "[my solutions] are far more radical than theirs."

Far worse than the tragedy of Vietnam, he contended, were the "apocalyptic danger" of nuclear weapons and the "blind destructiveness" attacking the environment. How long, he asked, "can man go on overpopulating this planet, destroying its topsoils, slashing off its forests, exhausting its fresh water . . . making sewers of its rivers and seas," polluting "its atmosphere, its streams, and its oceans"—in sum, "disregarding and destroying the ecology" of the earth?[13] Climate change was foreshadowed in his concern that a wild proliferation of machines was altering the atmosphere. How could Washington squander such vast sums on the military, especially in Vietnam, when the United States ranked as the world's "most wasteful and industrially dirty society?"[14] Ironically, Kennan's overreaction to the long hair and bare feet, and to his own rebellious children, blinded him to the concern for the environment and the "back to the land" movement embraced by many of the students he was condemning.

The diatribe against the protesters was in press as Kennan on February 29, 1968, introduced Senator Eugene McCarthy to a cheering crowd of 1,600 in Newark, New Jersey. The senior senator from Minnesota had come out as the antiwar challenger to President Lyndon B. Johnson for the Democratic nomination for president. The *New York Times* observed that while the diplomat-turned-historian had in 1966 "delivered a scholarly critique" of the war, he now displayed a "hostile and bitter" tone. In this, Kennan's deepest foray into a presidential election, he deplored the damage done by the Vietnam War to U.S. power and prestige in the world, to relations with Russia and China, to civilians in South Vietnam, and to America's ability to deal with domestic problems that demanded "concentrated, first-priority attention." The war was "filling many of our young people with bitterness and bewilderment and poisoning their relationship" to American society. Any hope of saving the nation depended on the "faith and enthusiasm" of "our student youth," and the war was destroying that. Kennan especially admired the "Clean for Gene" movement that encouraged college men to cut their hair and shave their beards before going out to campaign for McCarthy.[15]

At a gathering of intellectual luminaries in Princeton in December 1968, Kennan again warned that much of the nation's student youth was "floundering around . . . in its own terrifying wilderness of drugs, pornography and political hysteria." As for America's image before the world, "we cannot hide this country, unfortunately." The jeremiad prompted an old friend, the playwright Lillian Hellman, to deplore Kennan's sourness toward youth while also praising him for doing "a very brave thing; he refused to be a swinger."[16]

Resolutely not a swinger, Kennan did not allow his disagreement with U.S. policy in Vietnam to soften his opposition to drugs, civil disobedience, beards, and long hair. Even as he attacked the students for their emotional excesses, he indulged his own rage. Inextricable from Kennan's discussion of domestic and international politics was his visceral concern for the environment and for himself.

BATTLING THE REVISIONISTS

With the Cold War, too, Kennan navigated between the shoals of orthodoxy and opposition. In the late 1960s and early 1970s, he tried to get Washington to move from strict containment to serious negotiations with the Soviet Union. He upheld fiercely, however, the traditional narrative of the origins of the Cold War. According to this interpretation, the United States in 1946–1948 had reluctantly accepted the burden of leading the Free World in order to contain Communist expansion. Some versions of this story had Moscow bent on marching the Red Army to the English Channel. Kennan, however, had stressed instead the danger of the Soviets using propaganda, intrigue, and the large Communist parties of France and Italy to "penetrate" a devastated and demoralized Western Europe. In 1946–1947, Kennan famously argued that to meet this immediate crisis, Washington had to contain Soviet ambitions through adroit diplomacy, economic aid, encouraging Western European integration, and reforming American society. He always insisted that he had neither intended, nor had ever approved, using military force to rein in Moscow's ambitions.

Present at the creation of formal U.S.-Soviet ties back in December 1933, Kennan took pride in his unique status. Only he ranked as witness, practitioner, theorist, and historian of relations with the Soviet Union. And as chronicler, he wanted to make sure the story was correct—and stayed that way. Concern with setting the record straight with regard to containment helped spur Kennan to pen his *Memoirs, 1925–1950* (1967).

Kennan reacted with dismay when "revisionist" scholars in the late 1960s, outraged by containment's legacy in the Vietnam War and inspired by William Appleman Williams's *The Tragedy of American Diplomacy* (1959), began telling a different story. Williams, a democratic socialist teaching at the University of Wisconsin, argued that since the 1890s, U.S. foreign policy had determinedly pursued an Open Door policy focused on exporting America's products and institutions. Influenced by Williams during their graduate school days, Walter LaFeber and Lloyd Gardner emphasized the economic imperatives that impelled U.S. political and business leaders to view with alarm the spread of Soviet-style, state-dominated economies. LaFeber and Gardner, respectively professors at Cornell and at Rutgers, insisted that these economic considerations, and the democratic ideology that sugarcoated them, were the real reason why Washington objected to Moscow's control of Eastern Europe and parts of Central Europe. These historians depicted the Soviet Union as a war-torn, largely defensive nation that, despite its ideological pretensions, ranked only as a regional power. Kennan regarded such arguments as an insult to U.S. government officials.

The diplomat-turned-historian nursed an earlier, more personal grievance against Williams, whom he disparaged as a parvenu. For his first book, *American-Russian Relations, 1781–1947* (1952), Williams had obtained the papers of Raymond Robins, the Red Cross officer in Russia during the revolution who had tried to broker a deal between U.S. authorities and the Bolsheviks. Williams still had Robins's papers, which Kennan needed for his own book, *Russia Leaves the War* (1956). Kennan's prestige ensured respectful treatment as he combed through U.S. and European archives. By contrast, he suffered "through many vicissitudes in the effort to get access" to Robins's papers, which the elderly man had "foolishly handed over in toto to an ambitious and half-baked young scholar at the University of Wisconsin."[17]

Another offending historian in Kennan's eyes was Gar Alperovitz, who presented an explosive argument in *Atomic Diplomacy* (1965). He charged that in August 1945, the United States, despite knowing that Japan was likely to surrender, had dropped atomic bombs on Hiroshima and Nagasaki nonetheless, in order to intimidate Russia. Equally sacrilegious to Kennan was a trickle of historical articles by C. Ben Wright and others, citing instances in which "X" himself had in the late 1940s favored military responses that went beyond the politics-only interpretation of containment that he claimed as his unwavering position.

FIGURE 33. Kennan at Princeton in the 1980s. Photograph
by his friend Allen H. Kassof. (Courtesy of Allen H. Kassof
and his estate.)

Sensitive to criticism and defensively proud of his efforts at the onset of
the Cold War, Kennan pushed back hard against the revisionists,
through both public and private channels.

Sandwiched between the publication of Kennan's Swarthmore
speech and his public endorsement of McCarthy, the Institute for Advanced Study, Kennan's home base, hosted a seminar on revisionist history and the Cold War. Discussion revolved around an October 1967
article in *Foreign Affairs* by Arthur M. Schlesinger, Jr., the historian and
former adviser to President John F. Kennedy. Schlesinger claimed that
the Cold War had been inevitable because the Soviet Union was an
ideological state bent on world conquest, and because Stalin suffered
acute paranoia. This was a curious thesis inasmuch as Schlesinger's

research depended heavily on his June 1967 interview with wartime ambassador to the Soviet Union W. Averell Harriman. Fending off Schlesinger's repeated queries as to precisely when Stalin had "gone mad," Harriman insisted that the dictator had remained rational until shortly before his death in 1953. Harriman maintained, moreover, that while ideology was important to Stalin, the Kremlin boss had focused above all on the national interests of the Soviet Union.[18] Now, on February 15, 1968, an array of intellectual heavyweights from the Institute and from Princeton University gathered around a table as LaFeber and Gardner, both trained at the University of Wisconsin, challenged the thesis of Schlesinger, who was also present.[19]

In preparing for the seminar, Kennan, lumping the revisionists together, focused not on the recent book by LaFeber on the origins of the Cold War nor on the volume by Gardner on the diplomacy of Roosevelt's New Deal, but instead on Alperovitz.[20] Footnote by footnote, Kennan paged through *Atomic Diplomacy*, detailing what he claimed was the author's "careless and inaccurate," indeed "unscrupulous use of reference material" in a book "so slippery & dishonest that its very publication is a disgrace."[21]

As LaFeber and Gardner countered Schlesinger's thesis with document-based analysis, Kennan sat sideways in his chair, looking away from the two heretics. At one point he swiveled suddenly toward LaFeber, asking him to repeat a sentence about Woodrow Wilson's "great distaste for Bolshevism," the topic of Kennan's prize-winning volumes. Then he turned to look away again. The disdain was so palpable, Gardner later recalled, that he and LaFeber felt they were standing on trial.[22] Kennan's studied indifference harked back to a put-down technique he had proudly mastered at Princeton decades earlier. In the discussion that ensued, Kennan did not engage with the arguments made by the two revisionists. Nor had he done the homework of looking at what LaFeber and Gardner had written. Such uncharacteristic laxity constituted in itself a statement.

Instead, Kennan offered his own meandering narrative. First he defended U.S. actions with regard to Russia's failed attempt to obtain a U.S. loan in 1945–1946. Then he indicted the Soviets for the "unmitigated catastrophe" following their annexation of the Baltic states and takeover of Eastern Europe. The audio record of the Institute seminar underscores the emotional force in Kennan's empathy with the victims and his fury at their tormenters. Moscow had demanded "Communist governments penetrated and dominated through the Soviet Secret Police. If they were not able to penetrate them, they became enemies, as happened with Tito" of Yugoslavia.[23] While certainly deplorable, the Soviets' sins in Eastern Europe had not led directly to the formation of the Cold War, as Kennan himself understood.

While Schlesinger tried to rebut the arguments of LaFeber and Gardner, the other worthies sitting around the table went off, for the most part, on their own tangents. None of them knew the history as well as the visitors did. So ended an effort to quash revisionism.[24]

An undaunted Kennan in ensuing months waged a private campaign against the heresy. Again lumping together the offending "revisionists," he advised the State Department's institute for training Foreign Service officers that "the works of this entire school of writers deserve proper evaluation and rebuttal." The books ranked "shockingly low in scholarly quality," some of them bordered on dishonest, "and yet they have been reviewed, and peddled to students, as though they were serious contributions."[25]

When Theodore Sands, a former State Department official teaching at a small Midwestern college, sent him a book manuscript with a revisionist perspective, Kennan, who commanded prestige in both academic and governmental circles, pounced. Without making any explicit threat, he warned Sands in a single-spaced, seven-page letter of his "unhappiness." "I deplore the practice . . . of W. A. Williams, G. Alperovitz, and others of weaving quoted fragments of other people's language into one's own prose." That style invested the writing with "a specious air of authority." Far better to follow his practice of quoting entire sentences and paragraphs. Kennan faulted revisionism as neither scholarly nor patriotic, and as derogatory toward him. This view of the past "impugns the good-will and good judgment of such men as President Truman, Henry Stimson, Joseph Grew and Averell Harriman" by charging them with responsibility for the Cold War. Revisionism ignored "the unanimous opinion of myself and others who had lived for many years in Russia" and who ranked as "experts on that country." Finally, he saw a dangerous convergence between radical students protesting the Vietnam War and radical professors revising the history of the Cold War. Such views eroded "the confidence of the present student generation . . . in the integrity of American statesmanship generally."[26] Hit with this onslaught, Sands, evidence suggests, abandoned his book project.[27]

Kennan widened his campaign by circulating his scathing critiques of Alperovitz and of Sands (while omitting Sands's name). The writer Elie Abel, who was collaborating with Averell Harriman on the latter's memoir *Special Envoy to Churchill and Stalin* (1975), appreciated the warning about Alperovitz. "I had no idea," Abel replied, "that the fellow was capable of such sharp practice."[28] Chip Bohlen, also writing his memoir, agreed "100 per cent with everything you say and think there should be more of this refutation of some downright dishonest history."[29]

Amid the general challenge to authority in the 1960s and early 1970s, there arose a contest between aging policy makers from the 1940s and younger historians questioning the judgment of these elders. The revisionists doubted that U.S. foreign policy in the late 1940s, the period of Kennan's heyday, had been as innocent or as wise as Americans liked to think. In this dustup, Kennan had to balance his authorship of the containment doctrine, his challenge to contemporary policy based on containment, and his defense of the prudence with which he had pursued this design in the late 1940s.

Such juggling grew more difficult in the late 1960s and early 1970s as the State Department published the *Foreign Relations of the United States* (*FRUS*) volumes for 1945–1949, the official documentary history of the early Cold War. Kennan added to the flood of documentation by making available at the Princeton University Library some of his papers, including his lectures at the National War College in 1946–1947. Kennan so embodied the containment doctrine, both as its original author and as its later critic, that he presented an irresistible target for historians investigating his consistency. In his *Memoirs 1925–1950* and elsewhere, the Cold War strategist claimed that he had always tried to limit

containment to political rather than military means. But did that assertion match the newly available archival record?

Decidedly not, young historians charged in articles published in 1976
and again in 1978. In *Slavic Review,* C. Ben Wright, a scholar trained at the
University of Wisconsin, cited documents proving, he claimed, that Kennan considered preventive war against Russia in 1947, the military occupation of Italy to head off a victory at the polls by the Communist
Party in 1948, and taking over Taiwan to forestall an invasion by Mao's
Communists in 1949. As an outraged Kennan saw it, Wright, speaking
for a cabal of upstart scholars, was pasting together "scraps of language
from my writings" to charge "the wily Kennan," along with other militarists, with trying "to force an innocent Russia to her knees" by military
blackmail, and thereby provoke the Cold War. Kennan's sarcastic response was so petulant that it should have embarrassed him. "I stand, as
I see, exposed," Kennan fumed. Wright "has stripped me of my own pretense and has revealed me as the disguised militarist." The septuagenar-
ian resented this criticism as not only unfair, but also as generationally
inspired. He was battling young radicals smashing windows in the name
of protest and smashing reputations in the name of revisionism.

The breach with younger people, aggravated by his own aging, ate at
him. At a dinner party with Chip Bohlen, Paul Nitze, and their wives,
Kennan found talk about "the youth . . . depressing, so much so that I
had a feeling the ground was shaking under us." The earthquake was
widening the chasm. "The youth detest what [America] was to us; we
detest what the youth are making of it." Meanwhile, his own youth was
long gone. Around a swimming pool, he could only watch "young
women in bikinis being courted by other men."[30]

With regard to the issue of Kennan's militance as a policy maker,
most of the disputed quotations originated in the context of fuzzy discussions with hazy conclusions or hasty judgments quickly reconsidered. Nevertheless, the larger context here—transcending what Kennan
had or had not said or meant in 1947–1949 with regard to military action
in Italy and Taiwan and against Russia—was that while he had preferred
keeping containment political, U.S. policy was moving toward greater
militarization. If Kennan wanted to retain his credibility as the seer on

Russia at the National War College and in the State Department, he had
to go along to some extent. Moreover, he had never ruled out the use of
military force, especially where the United States had victor rights or
treaty obligations, as in Italy and Taiwan. He had always regarded America's preponderant military power as a useful shadow that enhanced its
political and economic influence. Underlying the diplomacy of the
United States was the credibility of its military machine. Finally, Kennan
had, to his later regret, endorsed quasi-military actions to undermine
Soviet influence in Eastern Europe.

As for the key issue of preventive war, Kennan's drawn-out, conflicted
response at the Air War College in April 1947 afforded, decades later,
grounds for both the self-righteous indignation of Kennan and sharp
attacks of critics. Queried about a preemptive attack on Russia, the strategist had responded: "If we see the total war-making potential of Russia
developing at a rate considerably faster than that of ourselves, I think we
would be justified in considering a preventive war." An explosive assertion! But then he pulled back by emphasizing that such a power imbal-
ance did not exist and remained highly unlikely. Moreover, his strategy
promised a way out of the dilemma. "If we can contain Russia for a
while," that would lead to a "mellowing of Russian policy." He twice
repeated, "I really don't want to go into a war unnecessarily with Russia."
Finally, perhaps thinking that he owed these air force officers some military plan, he opined that if a conflict were necessary, the United States
had "to smash the war-making potential of Russia to hell." That would
give American bombers plenty to do. He concluded, however, by reit-
erating that we should "try for a peaceful solution."[31]

Kennan's 1976 appraisal of relations with the Kremlin since the revolution revealed as much about himself as it did about the Russians. He
now unambiguously denounced preemptive war as a crazy idea spawned
by the "exaggerated military apprehensions and phantasmagoria" of a
bygone era. He could not resist honoring the memory of the "magical
afterglow of the hope and idealism" that in 1934 had so excited him. All
such wonder had been snuffed out by the purges. Kennan now asserted
that Stalin, despite his killings and cruelties, had remained "entirely rational in his external policies." If Kennan had voiced that judgment

during the Institute for Advanced Study seminar in 1968, it would have blown to bits Schlesinger's argument that the dictator's paranoia had made the Cold War inevitable.

Though jaundiced against the revisionists, Kennan shared more of their viewpoint than he wished to admit. Nevertheless, he kept his distance. In the 1970s, Kennan befriended a student who had studied with LaFeber at Cornell and then had come to Princeton. The student later reflected that not only did Kennan dispute the revisionists' emphasis on economic causation but "there was also an emotional component." Kennan "felt there was considerable '20/20' hindsight in the revisionist second guessing of his original containment arguments. You would have had to be around Berlin in 1947 with the Red Army in the center of Europe to appreciate where he was coming from."[32]

Now, in 1976, Kennan tried, astoundingly, to erase his role in demonizing the Kremlin in the long telegram and in the "X" article. Back in 1946–1947, these influential manifestos had depicted the Soviet Union as "inaccessible to considerations of reality" and as "committed fanatically" to disrupting "the internal harmony of our society," "our traditional way of life," and "the international authority of our state." Now, in 1976, without mentioning his own jeremiads, he deplored the emergence, somehow, of the apparition of a Soviet "monster devoid of all humanity and of all rationality of motive, at once the embodiment and the caricature of evil."[33] Despite his verbal agility, Kennan on his own could not sustain such fencing with written history without exhausting his energy, his equilibrium, and his credibility.

All the more welcome, then, was the eager help from John Lewis Gaddis, a historian who had written a prize-winning book on containment.[34] Both sons of the heartland, Gaddis, thirty-six years old in 1977, and Kennan, seventy-three, developed a rapport. Each admired the intellectual achievements of the other. Both somewhat shy, culturally conservative, and concerned about their reputations, they made common cause. On the one side a talented, educable, respectful young historian; on the other an aging star frantic not only about losing his bid to shape the present but also about losing his purchase on the future in terms of the written history.

Gaddis volunteered as a lieutenant in battling the revisionists. For the professor at Ohio University, close ties with the famous diplomat-strategist-historian offered a boost to his career. To mark the thirtieth anniversary of the "X" article, *Foreign Affairs* in 1977 published Gaddis's glowing reappraisal. While gently faulting the haziness of the essay with regard to the role of military force in containing the Soviets, Gaddis praised Kennan's arguments as still salient, especially when supplemented by the strategist's other writings. He likened him to the famed theorist of war and peace, Carl von Clausewitz. Moreover, "there is in Kennan's writings a degree of foresight and a consistency of strategic vision for which it would be difficult to find a contemporary parallel."[35] He courteously sent a draft of the article to Kennan, who, delighted, pronounced it among the best essays ever written on containment. Encouraged by this praise, coming on top of an interview and lunch with the great man, Gaddis replied that Kennan's views "influenced my own to a very considerable extent." The mentor, in turn, singled out this protégé as "the best of the younger historians" of recent U.S. foreign policy.[36]

In 1978, two young historians, Michael Hunt of Yale and Robert W. Coogan of the University of North Carolina, challenged Gaddis's interpretation of Kennan. They charged in a newsletter that the "X" article was not "consistent and foresighted" as Gaddis had claimed in *Foreign Affairs*, but rather "often vague and sometimes contradictory." Gaddis brought the offending essay to Kennan's attention. What followed was a replay of the 1976 dispute in *Slavic Review*, but with a significant twist. Again, the junior historians cited the miliary actions that Kennan had, at least briefly, advocated in Italy and in Taiwan. Again, Kennan, stung, replied at length—but this time in a private letter to Gaddis. He detailed the narrow circumstances in which the use of military force was justified and then sent this ammunition to his advocate. He deeply appreciated Gaddis's efforts to ensure that his views got "a fair historical appraisal." And so it was Gaddis, not Kennan, who published a sarcastic put-down of the upstarts. He mocked the critics for combing through Kennan's vast writings to find the occasional "inconsistencies, anomalies, even curiosities, wonders, and prodigies." The progression in this sentence made light of historically significant "inconsistencies" by associating them with antiquarian "curiosities."[37]

BATTLING THE MACHINE

To anyone, revisionists or supporters, who ventured to understand his thinking, Kennan warned that some of his attitudes were contradictory, and others had changed over time.[38] On one matter, however, Kennan remained consistent to his last days. He never wavered in his love for nature, concern for the environment, discomfort with cities, and hatred for the hegemony of the machine.

In a thirty-three-page interview published in *Encounter*, a magazine covertly subsidized by the CIA, Kennan put front and center his contention that "the Industrial Revolution itself was the source of most of the bewilderments and failures of the modern age."[39] He wanted the West to switch emphasis from containing the machinations of the Soviets to containing actual machines. Modern society had mistakenly allowed technological change to run rampant. Governments had ignored how this or that invention would alter society. Uncontrolled change had spawned ugly urbanization, alienated labor, and widespread misery. As he had in his 1932 essay on Anton Chekhov, Kennan cited the Russian writer's insight that industrialization figured as "a great misunderstanding." Ordering human beings into factories to mass produce goods misconstrued how people should interact with each other and with the world around them. This grievous mistake, perpetrated by both the Communists in Russia and the capitalists in the West, overshadowed what divided the Cold War antagonists. In his "X" essay in 1947, Kennan had argued that Soviet society harbored within itself the seeds of its own destruction. Now he warned that industrial society "bears the seeds of its own horrors—unbreathable air, undrinkable water, starvation."[40] The environmental crisis dwarfed ideological and political differences.

Consciously grounding himself in the preindustrial eighteenth century, Kennan was also prescient in reaching out to the postindustrial twenty-first century. He urged a smaller population and organic ties with agrarian life and nature. While Kennan's critique, like many of his pronouncements, had whiffs of self-indulgent idiosyncrasy, it also offered responsible elucidation of an emerging crisis.

In April 1970, Kennan published in *Foreign Affairs* a pioneering manifesto about a transnational crisis: "To Prevent a World Wasteland: A Proposal." The historian and farmer argued that "the entire ecology of the planet" transcended national borders, and hence saving the environment was inescapably an international challenge. He saw the big picture: "the massive spillage of oil into the high seas," "the plundering of the seabed," the danger of oil rigs to "the purity and ecological balance of the sea," the depletion of fisheries, the "noxious effluence emerging from the River Rhine," the transoceanic jets emitting their "own particular brand of poisons," the uncertain "disposal of radioactive wastes," and the challenge of safeguarding the polar regions as well as outer space. Only concerted international action could avert irreparable damage to the environment.[41]

With Kennanish logic, he laid out the case for an international watchdog agency to protect the environment from damaging economic development. Only an international group with "great authority, great prestige, and active support" from the most powerful nations could wield the necessary clout. Always distrustful of politicians and private interests, he would vest authority in scientists and other experts who might evolve into "environmental statesmen and diplomats . . . true international servants." While initially advisory, this group could develop into an International Environmental Authority with real teeth.[42]

Protecting the ecology of the earth dovetailed with Kennan's other pressing concerns: mobilizing the energy of aimless youth and moving past the Cold War. He hoped that a robust environmental movement would offer disillusioned young people "a new opening of hope and creativity." To people on both sides of the Iron Curtain, caring for the earth promised an alternative to the "sterile, morbid and immensely dangerous preoccupations" of the Cold War. Implicitly referring back to 1946–1947 when he had pushed confrontation with the Kremlin as a spur for needed domestic reform, he now pinpointed the environment as "a new and more promising focus of attention."[43] While clear-eyed in discerning threats to animal and plant life and to the atmosphere, Kennan remained too blinkered by his prejudices to appreciate how his concerns dovetailed with the enormous, youth-oriented Earth Day celebration in April 1970, coincidentally the very month his *Foreign Affairs* article appeared.

STALIN'S DAUGHTER

In transcending the Cold War, Kennan focused on rescuing not only the imperiled environment, but also the imperiled daughter of Stalin. The dictator and his legacy cast a dark shadow over Kennan's life. All the more meaningful, then, was the opportunity to best his old enemy in an intensely personal way and in doing so, to shepherd a coming together of Russia and America. Kennan became the key person in bringing Stalin's only living heir to the United States. Indeed, at his invitation she spent a summer with his daughters at the farm in Pennsylvania and then became a neighbor in Princeton.

In March 1967, Kennan's secretary, Constance Goodman, received a call in the middle of the night from a CIA agent who worked in counterintelligence. "I've been trying to get in touch with Mr. Kennan, can you tell me where he is?"[44] She told him that Kennan was at the farm. What then ensued Kennan dubbed "Hell Day—phone ringing before I even finished breakfast, & then phone calls back and forth all day." He might soon "be receiving a very well-known & radio-active guest here at the farm."[45] As the CIA agent put it, "We have a tremendous defection here." Forty-one-year-old Svetlana Alliluyeva, Stalin's daughter, had walked into the U.S. embassy in New Delhi, India, and requested asylum. Leaving her two children behind in Moscow, she had gone to India for the funeral of her husband. She had also written a book manuscript, *Twenty Letters to a Friend*, about her suffocating existence in the Soviet Union. The defection seemed especially embarrassing to the Kremlin since it came only months before the fiftieth anniversary of the Bolshevik Revolution. Before the Soviets could snatch her back, U.S. officials smuggled Alliluyeva out of India to Italy and then to Switzerland. The CIA had borrowed her manuscript and needed an expert to evaluate its intelligence information and commercial value. To Kennan's gratification, the U.S. government appealed to him for advice. An agent drove the manuscript up to the farm, where George, though "ill with the grippe and in bed," stayed up all night leafing through it. He pronounced the work "highly revealing, interesting, and probably worth hundreds of thousands of dollars published."[46] The State Department then asked Kennan to journey quietly to Switzerland and meet with Stalin's heir.

As Joan Kennan later recalled, her father grew "really excited about the defection and about contact with Svetlana." He eagerly assumed "responsibility for Stalin's daughter, as he would want his daughter looked after in a parallel situation."[47] More cynical about Alliluyeva, Grace Kennan Warnecke would remember how her father had "succumbed to Svetlana's helpless-and-alone-in-the-world facade."[48] In playing a paternal role with the daughter of the deceased dictator, Kennan was symbolically securing the link that had eluded him in actuality. As father to father, Kennan could empathize with Stalin's getting angry at young Svetlana when she fell in love with an opportunistic movie director: "Quite correctly, the old rascal, had slapped her face, saying, 'You little goose! What do you think he has in mind marrying you?'"[49] Yet Kennan was also besting the tyrant who had tormented not only his daughter, but also Kennan's friends and millions of other Soviet citizens. The challenge presented by Alliluyeva gratified the former diplomat in yet another way. "I need, more than anything else," Kennan understood, "a task."[50] The challenge offered a rare opportunity to flash his talents as an operator.

In preparing to meet Alliluyeva, Kennan called on his Princeton neighbor, Edward Greenbaum. Greenbaum headed what Kennan unself-consciously termed a "good, smart New York Jewish firm" whose clients included the *New York Times*. He asked the lawyer to arrange a tentative sale of the manuscript to a publisher. Kennan calculated that the Greenbaum connection would guarantee the newcomer "decent treatment in the *New York Times*," which in turn would boost sales of the book. With a book contract lined up, Alliluyeva could "arrive here with money in her pocket, and not as a ward of the United States Government."[51] Kennan, though still suffering from his cold, departed for

Europe. Secrecy remained crucial because the Swiss, fearful of the Kremlin's wrath, would permit Alliluyeva only covert contact with her rescuers.

The future American eagerly awaited the famed Russian expert. Kennan appealed to Alliluyeva at first sight: "tall, thin, blue-eyed, elegant; his elegance struck one from the very start." She was relieved to find him "amiable, agreeable, and well-disposed toward me."[52] Svetlana also appreciated Kennan's familiarity with Russian customs. She soon looked up to him "like a God." Likewise impressed, Kennan reported to the State Department that Alliluyeva "has iron in her soul."[53] He enjoyed playing the cultural go-between by explaining to this scion of the Kremlin such alien concepts as personal lawyers, book contracts, and private publishers. Astonished at the $1.5 million advance cobbled together by Greenbaum from Harper & Row, which would publish the book, and from *Life* magazine and the *New York Times*, which would serialize it, this daughter of the Bolshevik Revolution pledged to give away most of it. Harper & Row stock jumped on news of the deal.

On April 21, 1967, Svetlana Alliluyeva arrived to a tumultuous welcome at Kennedy Airport. Blue-eyed, red-haired, she "had a girlish, ingenue-like quality that endeared her to many, especially to men," observed Grace.[54] Worried that Kremlin agents might try to abduct this prize, Greenbaum's firm had hired six bodyguards. Sharpshooters manned the tops of neighboring buildings. The law firm's pull probably also helped inspire the lavish coverage in the *New York Times*. Such glowing stories as "A Stalin Says, 'Hello America'" fed the excitement. At a press conference a few days later, Alliluyeva was asked if she would seek U.S. citizenship. She charmingly replied, "Love must come before marriage." Then, laughing, she added, "If I will love this country and this country will love me, then the marriage will be settled."[55] To the gnashing of teeth in the Kremlin, she lauded the freedom and other wonders of her new home.

Kennan publicly framed the spectacle in terms of his larger strategy. Americans should welcome Stalin's daughter by rising "above the outworn reflexes and concepts of the 'cold war.'" He was trying to sweep that conflict into the dustbin of history by rendering the name in lowercase letters and placing it in quotation marks. "A new era is dawning," Kennan stressed, and Americans should welcome Alliluyeva as a talented but otherwise ordinary contributor to this emerging post–cold war world.[56] Concerned that the newcomer might find aspects of American life offensive, Kennan offered fatherly assurances. Many Americans were "struggling, as best we can, against all this ugliness and errors." With regard to Russians, Americans "are in a sense your brothers and sisters—and you must look at us as such."[57]

While the excitement of Alliluyeva's arrival would ebb, Kennan's exertions on her behalf did not. His laboring one New Year's morning until "4:00 A.M. digging out of the snow Svetlana's car," stuck in their Princeton driveway, underscored the range of his efforts.[58] He invited her to hide away for the summer at the Kennan farm, where she could escape the glare of attention. While George and Annelise would be in Africa and then Norway, their daughter, Joan, her husband Larry Griggs, and their two young boys welcomed the émigré to East Berlin.

Attuned to scenes and personalities, Svetlana marveled at how the farmstead, long ago named the Cherry Orchard, appeared so very Russian. The large house had been rebuilt by a Jewish merchant from Russia. The Kennans prized as good luck charms the mezuzahs still affixed to every entrance. The house was stuffed with "old engravings, pictures, porcelain and small Fedoskino lacquered tables" carried from Russia. Every room contained some beloved memento, whether it was a samovar or a nest of painted wooden dolls. A large photograph of the Kremlin Embankment prompted the former denizen to shudder, "Not again those Kremlin walls!" Svetlana picked for her room George's large third-floor study, flooded with sunshine, with a huge wooden table and bookshelves filled with books, newspapers, and journals, most of them in Russian. His old-fashioned typewriter perched on a support made of plain boards that he had nailed together.[59] Joan later recalled that Svetlana also prized the third-floor room because it had a door that she could lock during visits from her lover, Max Hayward, Oxford professor and translator of *Doctor Zhivago*.

Svetlana's presence at the farm had to be kept secret lest the Soviets, still furious about her defection, harm or abduct her. George reminded Joan and Grace that the Soviets had assassinated Leon Trotsky in Mexico after he had fled Russia. Russian propaganda, reviving old rumors that Stalin had stashed $300 million in gold in Swiss banks when Germans armies had advanced to the outskirts of Moscow, charged that Alliluyeva had stopped in Switzerland to recover her father's loot. The Soviet press slammed the defector as a money-grubbing nymphomaniac who had betrayed her country, abandoned her children, and dishonored her father's memory. Soviet Premier Alexei Kosygin weighed in that "Alliluyeva is a morally unstable person. She is a sick person."[60] Assailed by such attacks, Svetlana enjoyed her seven-week retreat at the farm.

She was doted on, first, by Joan and then by Grace. Also on hand were Grace's boys, Christopher, and an au pair, Simki Mattern. The sisters had to prepare not only the vegetarian curries that Alliluyeva preferred, but also the meat dishes expected by their families. "I desperately worked my way through *Joy of Cooking* to stay ahead of the game," Grace later explained. She and Joan did the laundry, including that of Svetlana's lover, Hayward, by lugging it to a nearby town. Alliluyeva grew especially close with Joan, who later recalled how Svetlana would sit in a chair and talk to her as she worked in the garden. Less charitable about the "Kremlin Princess," as the press had dubbed her, Grace noted that Svetlana "had done little housework and was not starting to learn on my watch."[61]

One day the "royal" guest announced to Grace that a sudden breathing problem could be cured only with pear brandy "with a pear in the middle of the bottle." After trying in vain to find this elixir in rural southeast Pennsylvania, Grace called friends in Washington, "pleading, 'Please, please, this is a crisis—I absolutely must have a bottle of pear brandy.'" She could not, of course, explain why she needed the brandy or who was demanding it. A friend dropped what he was doing and drove up to the farm with "a forty-dollar bottle of the lifesaving liquid." Svetlana thereafter sipped some every evening. Perhaps lubricated by the brandy, stories of her life poured forth. She blamed the purges and other horrors of her father's rule on the evil influence of Lavrenty Beria, boss of the secret police. In her telling, Stalin appeared as "more of a hapless bystander." She also told her side of the confrontation with her father after he learned about her movie director. The dictator had "slapped her so hard that she fainted."[62]

On August 8, Svetlana suddenly summoned Christopher and Simki to the barbeque grill.[63] Svetlana squirted lighter fluid on the fire, then solemnly announced: "Christopher! I am burning my Soviet passport in answer to lies and calumny." The teenagers watched in silence as she tossed the document into the grill, and it flared up brightly. Then she blew the ashes into the wind.[64] "It was a magnificent and symbolic event—at least for Svetlana," Christopher recorded in the Farm Diary. "She feels happy!"[65] Once George and Annelise returned from Norway, they spent some quiet days at the farm with their guest. Simki would remember the adults sipping pear brandy before dinner. The Kennans then helped Alliluyeva find a rental house only a five-minute walk from their own home on Hodge Road in Princeton.

Despite extraordinary efforts on her behalf by the entire Kennan family, Alliluyeva eventually broke with all of them, even, at the end, with Joan. The émigré's guilt at leaving her children, feelings fanned by relentless Soviet propaganda, plus a never-ending series of spats with the translator of her book, her lawyers, her lovers, and her husband for a while, the architect Wesley Peters, took their toll on her mental equilibrium.[66] In advising the defector on how to navigate these minefields, George offered paternal guidance. That stance appears to have reanimated some of the resentment that had poisoned relations with her biological father. In a letter to Joan, Svetlana underlined that while she appreciated George's advice, they were "the words of (it is very difficult for me to say that!) the *father*."[67]

In later years as Svetlana's bitterness at George deepened, the would-be good father interpreted the nastiness in terms of her "bad inheritance" from the actual father. Little wonder that the scion of a dictator flaunted the "mannerisms of a princess." Her intelligence and intuition also recalled Stalin's personality. Finally, there was "no doubt about it:

Svetlana has inherited" a poisonous trait. Like Stalin during the bloody purges, she eventually attacked everybody who had supported her. "I had a certain affection for her," Kennan later acknowledged. "But she's a dangerous woman; dangerous in the sense that she is highly emotional. I wouldn't want to have any further involvement with her." Years afterward, Kennan did quietly involve himself further when Alliluyeva, by now nearly penniless, seemed likely to go on welfare, even become homeless. That would embarrass the United States and buttress Moscow's propaganda. And so Kennan helped arrange for a small subsidy to keep Stalin's daughter afloat.[68]

GETTING OLDER

While Stalin had died only a few years after turning seventy, Kennan upon reaching that milestone on February 16, 1974, still had nearly a third of a century left. He did not expect such longevity. Ill health had plagued him since his near death from scarlet fever back in 1921. His stomach had never totally recovered from the dysentery contracted in Italy in 1924. In the 1960s, Kennan got hepatitis, which, a secretary later recalled, "left him quite depressed, and, I think, perhaps affected him psychically." At the age of sixty-one, he underwent major surgery to remove his prostate gland through the abdomen. The recovery took nearly two months. In the 1970s and 1980s, a kidney stone inflicted "persistent, gnawing" torment. Often it got so bad that "he would just have to get horizontal to relieve the pain."[69] He filled decades of diary entries with complaints of aches and pains both physical and mental. "Still in ill-health & dreadfully depressed" ran a typical entry; "laid up with stiffness, dampness & internal cramps," he bemoaned in another.[70] In Paris to do research, he "had great difficulty with [my] eyes, and had finally to give it up." A few days earlier, he "was suddenly overtaken by a strange sense of weakness, bewilderment, and momentary loss of the power of concentration." Though the sensation passed, he could "think of no explanation other than a slight stroke."[71]

With such intimations of mortality, Kennan upon reaching the biblical three score and ten mark, took stock by composing a witty and telling lyric. Of the forty-four lines, the first twelve emphasized death; they included

> On the highway of life there trudges behind you, and glowers morosely, [a] bearded old man with a curious knife.

There followed eight lines disparaging his supposed successes as really "stupidities spawned by your madness" and "injustices done in your name." He remained coy as to whether he was writing out of modesty, or rather rebuking himself for excesses justified by containment. He then devoted thirteen lines, the plurality of the lyric, to what he had earlier acknowledged as his "uncontrollable wandering eye."[72] While admitting to "the sins you've committed" in terms of the "fingers that roamed and the tongues that betrayed," you "grieve even more for the ones you omitted: the nectar untasted, the record unplayed." In his seventies he could no longer win the "heavenly creature," the "voluptuous female" who aroused him to "conjure up dreams too delightful to mention."[73] Kennan's dilemma between Eros and Civilization had not lost its bite.

As he entered what he believed were his last years, Kennan's lifelong struggle with sex eased but did not disappear. On the anniversary of his mother's death, he reflected that his "relations with women were unfortunately affected by the bewildering succession of female figures" who had cared for him as a young child. He still found allure in a nurse's white uniform. "I wish they wouldn't let female dental assistants wear such seductive clothes, he grumbled."[74] A visit to Prague sparked guilt at his "personal failings" when he had served in the Czech capital in 1938. He now wondered "what had become of those, other than my wife, who were in one way or another (not always innocently) the victims" of his desire.[75] Musing about the Biblical verse, "'Thou shalt not covet thy neighbor's wife,' he exclaimed: My God, I've coveted ten thousand of them in the course of my life, and will continue to do so."[76]

Intending to write his son a letter, to be opened after his death, about the perils of the sex drive, Kennan ended up with a five-page autobiographical plaint. The missive was laden with sexist assumptions and couched in the Freudian theory he had absorbed decades earlier. "The sexual instinct," he affirmed, "simply does not fit with civilization." This impulse throbbed with such fierceness that men were "assailed with it, tortured with it, whipsawed by it." Women, by contrast, did not so suffer. Partly because of that difference, marriage was "too narrow to encompass more than the smaller part" of this urge. For "well-meaning, sensitive and responsible" men such as himself, repressing this instinct came "at the cost of their completeness as people." This was the price that George, since the very beginning of his marriage in 1931, could not bring himself to pay.

Wherein lay the solution? The easiest answer, a sexually satisfying marriage, was "not easy to find." Moreover, "not every man who finds it succeeds in keeping it." While a purely physical relationship outside of marriage might work for a while, one should "never underestimate the difficulties." If the woman were not married, "you may be fairly sure she wants to be," to safeguard herself against the "the ultimate loneliness and barrenness of the unmarried state." As for an affair with a married woman, that entailed "all the humiliations of concealment and deceit." Clearly speaking from experience, Kennan warned that "for the sensitive person," clandestine sex was "demeaning" and "in the long run an intolerable form of servitude, incompatible with any peace of mind, the source of endless gnawing shame and apprehension." Akin, ironically, to sexual repression, affairs did not allow a man "to unfold his full powers." A married mistress could prove dangerous if she aspired to changing spouses. Moreover, "to be intimate with a married woman" could entail "a sudden and unwanted intimacy with her husband." He remained unsure "which is worse: the friendship of an unsuspecting husband, or the resentment of a discerning one." In rounding out this dissertation on the dilemmas of sexuality, Kennan touched on what he termed "the perversions." Homosexuality, too, he framed in terms of seeking artistry amid the conflicting pulls of Eros and Civilization. "The unnatural sexual bond" simply could not engender the ease and strength necessary for "creative pursuits."[77]

In reflecting on the tribulations of life, Kennan could not help but notice that even though the "bearded old man with a curious knife" was

FIGURE 34. Though often dour, Kennan could also flash a sense of humor and a lively sensibility. (Courtesy of Joan E. Kennan.)

for the moment sparing him, the specter was snatching contemporaries. Charlie Thayer, Kennan's friend and colleague from their boon days in Moscow in 1934 and a frequent visitor to the farm in postwar years, died in 1969 during a heart operation. In 1973, another close companion from that time, Chip Bohlen, formerly so smooth and affable, now suffered from pancreatic cancer. Bohlen, who would die on New Year's Day in 1974, appeared "very grey but in some way ennobled by his long and horrible ordeal."[78]

CARTER AND *THE CLOUD OF DANGER*

Even though he appraised his own life as nearly over, Kennan could not give up trying to influence policy. With the inauguration of the inexperienced former governor of Georgia Jimmy Carter as president in January 1977, Kennan's ambition flared anew. He cobbled his suggestions for dealing with problems into a would-be manual, *The Cloud of Danger: Current Realities of American Foreign Policy*.[79] Kennan and his secretary, Constance Goodman, threw the book "together very quickly. We just sort of pounded it out on the typewriter, the two of us," she later recalled. The rushed writing lacked Kennan's trademark elegance. More important than style, he believed, was laying out the substance of what might be accomplished "in approximately three or four years' time." He explained: "I have tried, in this book, to place myself in the position of the U.S. government," to consider problems from that perspective, and to lay out priorities for the president and Congress.[80] This latest effort to mobilize opinion flopped. The book "didn't attract much attention," Goodman later recalled, and "that was a big disappointment to him. He expected that it would attract attention."[81]

Kennan's standard for appropriate notice underscored how very ambitious he was. *Cloud of Danger* did merit notice in the three publications he cared about most. Yet the review in the *New York Times* sandwiched Kennan's book with two others, noted that it was "hastily written," and contrasted his "soft, weary tones" with the "hard, vigorous voices" of his hawkish opponents. The assessment in the *New York Review of Books* by Ronald Steel, the biographer of Lippmann, who had praised Kennan's *Memoirs 1925–1950*, pinned the former diplomat to the wall. "Behind the Princeton recluse, obsessed with Russia . . . there stands the diplomat counselor, yearning to advise presidents, never quite understanding why lesser men are in such powerful positions." While praising Kennan's advocacy of détente toward the Soviet Union, Steel criticized his disparagement of the Third World.[82]

Kennan may have been most offended by the implicit slight from *Foreign Affairs* editor William P. Bundy, his Princeton neighbor and the son-in-law of Dean Acheson. The July 1977 issue of this establishment journal marked the thirtieth anniversary of the "X" article by allotting the once-feted "X" only a paragraph-long, thumbnail sketch for his would-be policy manual, while devoting thirty pages to Gaddis's historical assessment of the 1947 article. Though welcoming this buttressing of his 1940s legacy, Kennan probably viewed the contrast as yet another instance of his failure to leap from past glory to present-day influence. Gaddis, then spending a year at the Naval War College, praised Kennan's new book. "I'm confident it will be on the required reading list here, and at other comparable institutions for some time to come."[83] Disappointingly, however, Kennan's *Cloud* never hung over the White House or influenced decisions within it.

Though the book failed in terms of Kennan's purpose, it crystallized his agenda. Arguing that domestic crises militated against an ambitious U.S. foreign policy, he urged a general pullback of commitments overseas. He would have the United States pledge to defend only Western Europe and Japan, the industrialized core of the Free World. Israel he would support, but not to the extent of sending U.S. troops. He would attenuate ties with South Korea and pull back even more from Africa and Latin America. Lessening dependence on the oil-rich Middle East dovetailed with his aim of reducing the "addiction to the automobile." He would tread warily with regard to China while edging away from the defense of Taiwan.

With regard to the Soviet Union, Kennan's book pushed back against the hawkish stridency coming from Paul M. Nitze and other leaders of the Committee on the Present Danger, a legacy from the 1950s reconstituted after Carter's victory in November 1976. Kennan disputed their claims that Moscow presented an existential military threat. He pointed instead to the cautious old age of Soviet leaders, their preference for stability, and their domestic problems with sagging ideological fervor and lagging technology. The Soviet Union faced, moreover, increasingly restive nationalities, especially in the formerly independent Baltic nations and in the predominantly Muslim areas of central Eurasia. Kennan criticized the "dehumanization of the opponent—the insistence on seeing him as the embodiment of all evil, unaffected by motives other than the desire to wreak injury upon others." The hawks were caricaturing themselves with the "most extreme, most pessimistic, least sophisticated, and most improbable assumptions they could make."[84] The erstwhile Cold Warrior did not mention that he himself had rung such alarms in 1946–1947.

Though maintaining his usual skepticism of summit diplomacy, Kennan applauded the agreements reached between Richard M. Nixon and Leonid Brezhnev. The former diplomat proved astoundingly short-sighted, however, in pooh-poohing the 1975 Helsinki talks, in which Moscow had won final acceptance of Europe's post-1945 borders in return for making a commitment to human rights. Kennan viewed those broad declarations as hopelessly vague and as inevitably inconsequential. By 1989, however, the Helsinki agreements would prove the thin wedge that helped pry open the Soviet satellites.

Taking on the complex issues of the nuclear arms race, the strategist underscored the illogic of the dire warnings. Claims that Soviet spending had exceeded that of the United States relied on calculating the costs of Soviet weapons as if they had been produced in America, with its higher prices for labor and materials. Alarm about force levels failed to account for the strength of America's allies. The Russians, unable to forget the devastation wrought by Germany only a generation earlier, faced a Germany nearly as large and now allied with, rather than pitted against, Britain, France, and the United States. Most importantly, Kennan insisted, the Soviets' defensive intentions counted far more than their military capabilities. The existential threat lay not in the remote chance of a Soviet attack, but rather in the real danger that the nuclear arms race "will become wholly uncontrollable," and then, through intent or accident "carry us all to destruction."[85] He called for a policy that would gain traction in the subsequent decade: the United States should follow the Soviet example and pledge no first use of these terrible weapons.

He touched, only lightly, on Moscow's stifling of dissent. While some exiled Soviet dissidents and their American supporters were whipping up animus against the coercive Soviet regime, Kennan took a different tack. He edged toward sympathy for the repression—to be sure, far milder—that he had so fiercely condemned in the 1930s and 1940s. He disapproved of the crackdown on the dissidents. And yet "I almost feel sorry for a regime whose sense of weakness is so great that it cannot find better ways than this to cope with differences of opinion between itself and a relatively small band of intellectuals."[86]

Frustrated at not getting official support for his foreign policy views, especially regarding the nuclear arms race, Kennan was also disheartened that none of the major reviews took seriously his perspective on domestic problems. *Cloud of Danger* warned of the nation's voracious military-industrial complex, its dependence on foreign oil, the decay and crime of its cities, rising inflation and unemployment, inadequate public transportation and its twin the "addiction to the private automobile," ubiquitous and duplicitous advertising, and his personal bugaboo "pornography," by which he meant overt displays of sexuality in the media as well as in porn shops.[87]

One further challenge, however, "probably exceeds all these others" in its peril: "environmental degradation." He applauded the progress in establishing the Environmental Protection Agency and increasing public concern. Nevertheless, deterioration was still accelerating in terms of topsoil lost to development and erosion, wetlands bulldozed, national parks degraded by mining and excessive grazing, forests cut down, and water tables overdrawn. Pesticides and nuclear waste threatened pollution. Kennan's answer to the crisis harked back to the Chekhovian perspective he had outlined in 1932.

He condemned not just the abuses of industrialization and urbanization but also "those very phenomena themselves." A healthy environment required rolling back the concentration of production in factories and people in cities. Kennan wanted to restore "the proper relationship between Man and Nature," which meant challenging "the very heart of the American idea of progress."[88] Though his vision appeared so far-fetched at the time that reviewers ignored it, Kennan was foreshadowing trends that would emerge in postindustrial, even postpandemic America. He urged increased use of hand labor, shifting from full-time employment in factories and officers to part time, and to creative work at home with handicrafts and backyard gardening. Touting what decades later would be called green energy from "Nature's free offerings," he pointed to "windmills and dams, and sun reflectors" as alternatives to fossil fuels.[89]

The visionary concluded this manifesto with a creative linking of his two fundamental concerns. He urged shifting America's focus from the "fixations of military rivalry to more constructive and hopeful tasks—notably, the restoring of a healthy balance between modern industrial civilization and the natural environment."[90]

Though admirable in his work for peace and for the environment, Kennan was nevertheless incorrigible in his ugly notions of racial purity. A conservative in many ways, Kennan remained molded by his early experiences in predominantly white Milwaukee, at elitist Princeton, and among racist circles in Germany and Latvia. Not all his friends among prewar German aristocrats had the democratic sensibilities of Count Helmuth James von Moltke. In some ways foreshadowing twenty-first century replacement theory, he mourned the decline of the once ascendant Anglo-Saxon majority in the United States into "not only a dwindling but a disintegrating minority." America's mixing pot he deplored as "a sea of helpless, colorless humanity, as barren of originality as it is of nationality, as uninteresting as it is unoriginal—one huge pool of indistinguishable mediocrity and drabness." He mused that perhaps only the Jews, Chinese, and "Negroes" would retain their ethnic distinctiveness—and hence wield the power to "subjugate and dominate" the rest of society.[91] Kennan was aware enough to confine such racist drivel to his diary and to the dinner table, where his adult children squirmed.

LESSONS FROM THE PAST

His public writings throughout the 1970s and into the early 1980s focused on the twinned concerns of throttling down the arms race while stepping up protection of the environment. He dealt with the specter of unchecked rivalry cascading into nuclear holocaust by diving into the long-term origins of the First World War, "*the* great seminal catastrophe of this century."[92] He produced two densely detailed volumes, *The Decline of Bismarck's European Order* on 1875 to 1890 (1979) and *The Fatal Alliance: France, Russia, and the Coming of the First World War* (1984).

FIGURE 35. The widely respected scholar. (Courtesy of
Grace Kennan Warnecke.)

Seeking lessons from the past, he combed the archives of Britain,
France, Germany, Belgium, Denmark, and, not least, Russia. He filled
thousands of note cards with his archival findings as well as his jottings
on published documents, memoirs, and secondary sources.

A quarter century after their humiliating expulsion from the Soviet
Union, George and Annelise were gratified by an invitation from the

USA and Canada Institute to do research in Moscow. Trying to make amends, the institute addressed the letter to "Ambassador G. Kennan," offered to pay all their expenses in Russia, and stood ready to facilitate meetings with Russian historians. Kennan was thrilled.[93]

He wanted his books on the pre-1914 period to expose the "massive misunderstandings" that had impelled millions to welcome with euphoria an ultimately disastrous war. "Where was it that all these people went wrong?" A major factor was the alliance between France and Russia, which enmeshed Western Europe in the intrigues of the Balkans as well as in the insecurities and ambitions of Russia, Austria-Hungary, and Germany. Worse, participants had failed to understand how "apocalyptically destructive" modern war had become. "If we could see *how* they went wrong," in their era, Kennan hoped, we "might see where the dangers lay for ourselves."[94]

"It was a huge amount of work," Goodman confirmed. The diplomats, politicians, and journalists Kennan researched "become very real to him, his characters." To track them all, he kept color-coded note cards, pink for the French, blue for the Russians. Being color-blind, however, produced some amusing mix ups. Researching and writing this history "he enjoyed so much more than any other work," she later testified.[95] Kennan being Kennan, he was also responding to duty. He regarded the book as a "final payment of my own great debt to the scholars—[J. Robert] Oppenheimer, [Erwin] Panovsky, [Ernst H.] Kantorowicz, and others—who welcomed me and taught me and gave me an alternative when I left government in 1953."[96]

Growing concerns about the environment made Kennan appreciate the Institute for Advanced Study even more. The wall of windows in his office opened onto the ancient trees and gravel paths of the Institute Woods, where he loved to stroll and think. The farm in Pennsylvania he prized as a delicate ecosystem. The pollution of the seas infuriated the heart of this avid sailor. One year he took the bus from Princeton to New York City each week for lessons in celestial navigation. In preparation for a sail, he and Annelise "studied into the depths of the night the charts of the English Channel & North Sea that had arrived during the day."[97] He detested petroleum not only because it fouled the environment but also because it fueled the addictive automobile. He hated seeing huge oil rigs mar the beauty of the Norwegian coastline. Saudi Arabia's decision during the 1973 Yom Kippur war to punish America by cutting off oil shipments he celebrated as "the best thing that could have happened to us."[98] Reliance on the internal combustion engine had led to shortsighted neglect of pre-industrial farming and fishing.

The hegemony of the machine that Chekhov criticized as a foolish misunderstanding Kennan now condemned as a violent, implicitly gendered desecration. "Modern-industrial man is given to the raping of anything and everything natural on which he can fasten his talons. He rapes the sea; he rapes the soil, he rapes the natural resources of the earth. He rapes the atmosphere." Further, "he goes on destroying his own environment, like a vast horde of locusts."[99] With uncontrolled Eros violating the natural world, it was all the more important to mobilize the restraining elements of Civilization.

Kennan feared that he would die before fulfilling his obligation to the environment and his "duty to ponder the national interest and the general interest of mankind." He believed he knew what needed to be done in the future because he had been prophetic in the past. He recalled his prescience with regard to Franklin D. Roosevelt's supposed mistakes in 1944–1945 and the need to contain the Soviets in 1946–1947. He listed his insights into the atomic bomb's perilous transformation of military strategy, the ineffectiveness of foreign economic aid, democracy's limitations on foreign policy, the futility of a quantitative approach to nuclear arms limitation, the need for a no-first-use policy with regard to nuclear weapons, and the urgency of developing alternative sources of energy. He believed that he had performed this public service well, "even better, perhaps, or at least more deeply and farsightedly, than any American of my generation, except Reinhold Niebuhr." And yet, infuriatingly, with the exception of his "least profound" public statements— namely, the "X" article and his dashed-off 1951 lectures in Chicago— "almost nothing you said was appreciated, very little of it noticed at all, and almost none of it understood."[100]

JOHN LEWIS GADDIS

Having failed thus far in his obligation to the nation and to humanity, Kennan deemed it all the more crucial to extend the potential for his influence beyond his own lifetime. He mused about publishing his collected works—the many thousands of letters, lectures, and diary pages he had written over the years. Unfortunately, however, he lacked the time and energy to do the editing or otherwise make his case. "Who else is to do it?"[101] Into the breach stepped Gaddis, eager to set right a crucial part of the story: how Kennan had conceptualized containment in 1946–1947 and how that policy was then implemented by various policy makers. In 1980, Gaddis sent Kennan a draft of his book, *Strategies of Containment.*

While praising the manuscript, Kennan highlighted the insufficient "emphasis to the fact that I always regarded containment—successful containment—not as an end in itself but as the prerequisite" for negotiations with Moscow to bring about a mutual military withdrawal from the heart of Europe. Instead, the United States had held out for the Soviets' "unconditional capitulation," and the Western Europeans had remained too timid to push for reunifying their continent. "The basic flaw in the position taken by Acheson and Dulles and Adenauer in 1958 was, as I said in the 1957 Reith lectures, that it made no realistic provision for a relaxation of the Soviet hold on Eastern and Central Europe."[102] While Kennan in the 1970s and 1980s saw the Cold War as a dangerous rivalry that could explode into a nuclear holocaust, Gaddis increasingly regarded the conflict as a stable, "long peace." Gaddis's appraisal of the Cold War ironically aligned his historical interpretation more in line with Acheson and Dulles than with Kennan. He was skeptical of many of the post-1950 peacemaking efforts that Kennan regarded as key to his life's work and to the survival of humanity.

This divergence on a basic issue persisted even as their friendship flowered. Gaddis spent the 1980–1981 academic year as a Fulbright fellow in Helsinki. Learning that George and Annelise were passing through the Finnish capital on their way home from the Soviet Union, he arranged to meet them at the train station and take them to their hotel. George appreciated not only Gaddis's courtesy but also his accomplishments as "the best of the American (and Americanist) diplomatic historians of this generation." The following day, Gaddis and his wife treated the Kennans to lunch at an upscale restaurant overlooking the harbor. "I felt ashamed for letting them do it," the older man penned in his diary, "for they are young and Helsinki is an expensive town, but remonstrations were useless."[103]

In November 1981, Kennan returned to Gaddis his comments on the final draft of *Strategies of Containment*.[104] The pattern of the previous year repeated itself. Kennan fulsomely praised Gaddis's effort to "understand my own views on 'containment.'" Nevertheless, he protested, politely, the manuscript's "neglect of the 1957 Reith lectures as well as the Congressional (& televised) testimony about Vietnam before the Senate Foreign Relations Committee."[105] The published book, which soon became a staple in college courses, made no mention of the Reith Lectures or of Kennan's proposed disengagement from the armed standoff in central Europe. Nevertheless, neither the historian nor the strategist wanted to jeopardize their ties over this difference.

Instead, Gaddis immediately followed up Kennan's letter with a bold proposal. Had the older man arranged for a biographer? If not, he would love the challenge of writing an authorized, posthumous biography with full access to Kennan's papers. He envisioned a major project that would be "fair-minded but not hagiographic." He modestly added that Kennan had given him reason to believe that he "had not been completely wrong" in writing about the former diplomat's career.[106] Kennan quickly accepted. In ensuing decades, however, their relations would develop in directions that neither had envisaged.

Kennan at the time was agitated by the situation with his personal papers. After publishing his memoirs in 1967, he had deposited a portion of his papers at Princeton's Seeley G. Mudd Library on the condition that the archive set up a review committee composed of a secretary from the Institute, his friend Frank Taplin, and a Princeton archivist. Scholars had to petition the committee, explaining "what they wanted to see, and why, and what the purpose was," Kennan's secretary, Constance Goodman, later explained. Confronted with "this very cumbersome process," most historians just backed off. Aside from Kennan, "everybody hated it," and so the effort at control was abandoned in the late 1970s.[107] Now, Kennan fretted, the story and lessons of his life could be misinterpreted by "practically anyone who comes along."[108]

He worried about what critical scholars "burrowing in my papers at the Mudd Library" might unearth. One such historian, David A. Mayers, uncovered "The Prerequisites," Kennan's 1938 call for an openly authoritarian U.S. government.[109] However much the elderly man dismissed the document as "quite immature," it figured as a more extreme forerunner of his later criticisms of American society. Kennan feared that an article based on this embarrassment would "lend welcome fuel to the fires of my various critics and opponents." In a letter that began "Dear John (if I may call you that)," Kennan asked his biographer for advice. He explained: "Mr. Mayers has been clamoring for some time to see me," and had petitioned to have a multitude of documents copied from the library. Kennan had turned down both requests.[110] Gaddis replied, graciously, that while pleased to be so carefully informed about competing historians, he did "not want the work that other people are doing to stop just because I'm doing this book."[111] The efforts by Mayers and by other scholars, such as Walter Hixson, to pry open space for their own contributions would lead to future contestation. In the meantime, Kennan removed "The Prerequisites" from the open portion of his papers—too late, however, because copies were already circulating among historians.

THE NUCLEAR DANGER

In the late 1970s and early 1980s, Kennan whipsawed between elation about his visibility as a critic of the nuclear arms race, and despair that this attention was failing to make an actual difference. He castigated the foreign policy of the Carter administration as unequaled in "dilettantism, amateurism and sheer bungling."[112] That was before the Carter team overreacted, in Kennan's view, to the Soviet invasion of Afghanistan in December 1979.

Though President Ronald Reagan talked about eventually eliminating nuclear weapons, he assumed office in 1981 determined to ramp up the U.S. nuclear arsenal. As a key adviser on nuclear issues, Reagan picked Kennan's personal friend and frequent nemesis, Paul M. Nitze. Nitze had succeeded him as director of the Policy Planning Staff, and in that position he had pushed for further militarizing the Cold War through the policy document NSC-68 and through building the "Super" or hydrogen bomb. Kennan, backed by his friend and later boss J. Robert Oppenheimer, had viewed all this as madness.[113] In 1976, Nitze had been instrumental in reviving the Committee on the Present Danger to push for increasing military spending, especially on nuclear weapons. The committee's skilled publicity efforts helped polarize the national debate, ramping up emotions among both those favoring a tougher stance against Moscow and those fearful of such steps. Nitze approached the nuclear competition with Moscow as a matter of numbers: How many ICBMs could the Soviets deploy versus how many did the Americans have, and how did the missiles on each side compare in throw weight, accuracy, and in their chances of surviving the enemy's first strike?

Kennan disparaged Nitze as a former banker who saw only numbers. He suffered from the blinkered, "characteristic view of the military planner," who simply assumed that the enemy "wishes us everything evil," that realism demanded positing the worst-case scenario, and that the key issue was not the intentions of the enemy but rather the capabilities. Finally, Kennan asserted, his rival was deluded by his figuring in terms of "a fictitious and inhuman Soviet elite, whereas I am dealing with . . . the real one." That self-congratulatory comparison, made in 1982, glossed over Kennan's own creation of a "fictitious and inhuman Soviet elite" in the long telegram and in the "X" article. Nitze, meanwhile, disparaged Kennan as a dreamer, "whose chosen profession should have been that of a poet." To Soviet ambassador Anatoly Dobrynin, Nitze opined that Kennan was "an historian and a poet" rather than a strategist. Missing the point about how rivals could slide into unintended though catastrophic war, Dobrynin commented, according to Nitze, that "he could not understand Kennan's interest in the Franco-Russian negotiations of 1895; they had no visible bearing on today's issues."[114]

Reading in a magazine of Kennan's warning that environmental and social destruction threatened more than anything the Soviets were likely to attempt, Nitze angrily scrawled in the margin: "He's on their side."[115] He, by contrast, stood on Reagan's side.

Amid the tension heightened by Reagan's inauguration in January 1981, the attempted assassination of the president that March, and the worsening conflict between the Solidarity workers in Poland and the Soviet-supported Warsaw government, Kennan, now seventy-seven, pushed for de-escalation. At a dinner meeting of six former ambassadors to Moscow, including Averell Harriman and current Under Secretary of State Walter J. Stoessel Jr., Kennan argued that the Reagan administration was "overdoing the rhetoric concerning the Soviet threat." He stressed the Soviets' vulnerabilities and their recent setbacks in Africa and elsewhere. Above all, Washington had to "seek a meaningful dialogue with the Soviet leadership." Stoessel reported that "Kennan spoke with some emotion about his concern" regarding the accelerating nuclear arms race.[116]

At a ceremony in Washington a week later, Kennan became the first recipient of the $50,000 Albert Einstein Peace Prize. He warned of a "collision course" with the Soviets, especially because rational communication had broken down. "Discouragement, resignation, perhaps even despair" were overwhelming many. Piling weapon upon weapon, people on both sides seemed like the "victims of some sort of hypnotism, like men in a dream, like lemmings heading for the sea." The blind obsession ominously recalled the lead-up to the catastrophic First World War. Kennan broke fresh ground by calling for surgically slicing through the tangled, "sophisticated mathematics of destruction" championed by Nitze and others. Washington should propose to Moscow a bold, clear-cut reduction of nuclear arsenals by 50 percent.[117] A similar speech made in Norway at the end of the summer appeared in publications ranging from *Die Zeit* in West Germany to the *New Yorker* on the other side of the Atlantic. Encouraged, Kennan resolved to set aside his writing of history and focus on the current crisis. After all, "unless another great war can be prevented, there may be no more history to write about, and even if there were, no one who could write it, or read it."[118]

Also gratifying was the respect Kennan encountered while on a research trip to Moscow. As always, Russia affected him intensely. The

FIGURE 36. The family in Norway. Front row: George, Christopher's son Oliver, Annelise. Back row from left: Grace Kennan Warnecke, Wendy's son George Pfaeffli, Wendy Kennan, and Christopher Kennan. Like George Kennan (1845–1924) and George F. Kennan, George Pfaeffli was born on February 16. (Courtesy of Grace Kennan Warnecke.)

FIGURE 37. A reunion of George and his siblings in 1982. From left, Kent, Constance, George, Frances, Jeanette. (Courtesy of Princeton University Library.)

sensations moved him so deeply that he could only allude to "the wisps of memory, the impulses of sympathy and pity, clashing with those of revulsion, the everlasting battle of contradictions." At the embassy, chargé d'affaires Jack Matlock toasted Kennan with "the kindest and nicest things I have ever heard from the lips of anyone in this government." The compliments almost allowed him to forgive "all the slights and rebuffs I have had from the U.S. government from John Foster Dulles on down." Two days later, Georgy Arkadyevich Arbatov, founding director of the Soviet Academy of Science's Institute of United States and Canada, offered similarly "warm and moving things from the Soviet side," which also had not offered "posies and compliments in earlier years."[119]

The former Cold Warrior was rising high enough that the current warriors tried cutting him down. One such attack came from Eugene Victor Debs Rostow, Nitze's comrade in the Committee on the Present Danger. Rostow, though named for the socialist who had gone to jail for speaking out against World War I, and though serving as director of the U.S. Arms Control and Disarmament Agency, wanted Washington to press the Soviets hard, even if meant nuclear war. After all, Rostow explained, Japan had "not only survived but flourished after the nuclear attack." He disparaged Kennan as "an impressionist, a poet, not an earthling."[120]

By January 1982, Kennan had fallen back to earth. He now concluded that the "eager responses on the part of thousands of people" had misled him into thinking that his words carried serious weight. He had dutifully penned columns for the New York Times and other publications and had even let himself "be wheedled into appearing" on Meet the Press. But "this rather pathetic effort to affect governmental policy" had ended in failure. As for the Reagan administration, his efforts amounted to a "slightly annoying mosquito bite, the bite of an insect to be absentmindedly brushed off and at once forgotten." He reluctantly accepted, for the moment, his failure. Kennan believed that his role "was that of a prophet. It was for this that I was born." His tragic destiny, he feared, was that the world would ignore the truth in his prophecies until it was too late.[121]

And that end seemed near. Always prone to drama, Kennan now felt himself "a witness at the final, apocalyptic self-destruction of this marvelous Western civilization, with all its immense monuments of architecture, music, art, and literature"—a civilization that seemed incapable of saving itself.[122] Increasingly interested in Christianity, the one-time agnostic linked the political crisis to nature and to God. "This habitat, the natural world around us, is the house the Lord gave us to live in." It "was not given to us to destroy or to exploit," but to pass on "with all its beauty and fertility and marvelousness to our children and to future generations." Now, however, all this is "placed in jeopardy by the very existence of nuclear weapons."[123]

His own end-time also seemed at hand, especially if he continued to retrace the pattern set by the elder George Kennan. On February 16, 1982, his seventy-eighth birthday, Kennan stressed his longing to leave behind Princeton and his other obligations and move to "an abandoned farm in the northern-most regions of Vermont or New Hampshire." There he could settle down to "a life of doing the small chores: cutting the firewood, feeding the chickens, baking bread, and carrying water to the horse. Nothing, to me, could sound more inviting." To Annelise, however, such isolation sounded totally uninviting.[124]

Despite these premonitions of mortality, Kennan, civilization, and their respective dilemmas persisted. In April 1982, he joined with former national security adviser McGeorge Bundy, former secretary of defense Robert McNamara, and former arms control negotiator Gerard Smith to issue a statement in *Foreign Affairs*, written by Bundy, urging Washington to pledge, as the Soviet Union had done, not to be the first to use nuclear weapons. That assurance could reduce the chance of nuclear war starting through preemption or miscalculation. If this effort succeeded, the former Cold Warrior wrote in his diary, "I would regard it as the most important thing I had ever had a part in accomplishing."[125] Like its predecessors, however, the Reagan administration refused to make such a no-first-use pledge.

"I thought thoughts," Kennan recorded on Christmas Eve 1982. The thinking illustrated his flaw as a visionary: at once the insightful prophet with advice for the twentieth and twenty-first centuries, and the blinkered relic mired in prejudices from the early 1900s. Both the United States and Western civilization lay "doomed, in the first instance, by the nuclear weapon—this viper which we have seized to our breast." Doomed also by "overpopulation and environmental destruction." He discerned the real perils of nuclear weapons and rampant pollution. But Kennan could also slip into a rant that harked back to the racist eugenics of pre–World War II Germany and America. His concern with over-population reflected anxiety that the United States was filled with too many people not like him. He believed that only those "heirs to the traditions and habits, the capacities for self-restraint and self-discipline and tolerance" of the worthies living on the shores of the North Sea could really appreciate and practice effective self-government. A "great American delusion" was "that these values are readily communicable to others who did not inherit them—that all you had to do was to bring these others to our shores, plunge them into the midst of our civiliza-tion, and they would instantly be penetrated by this political ethos."[126] As his children and other admirers readily acknowledged, it was difficult listening to such prejudice. The only thing easier than condemning the man was admiring him.

Kennan ranked as a pioneering environmentalist, a prescient critic of outmoded Cold War policies, and an eloquent opponent of the nu-clear arms race. He tried, as he always had, to bring America and Russia together, whether with his paternal interest in Stalin's daughter, his ad-vocacy of negotiations with Moscow, or his scholarship on the lessons of the First World War. He would enter his final decades of life still in command of his awesome abilities, still in thrall to his undying ambi-tion, and still intent on advising the nation and the world, both during his lifetime and beyond it. It bears repeating: It was not easy being George F. Kennan.

CHAPTER 11

ALMOST UNSTOPPABLE,
1983–2005

PROBABLY THE MOST gratifying moment in Kennan's eight decades of engagement with Russia took place at the Soviet embassy in Washington on December 9, 1987. At a reception for Mikhail Gorbachev, the embattled Soviet reformer spied Kennan in the crowd. He threw out his arms and embraced the startled eighty-three-year-old.

Gorbachev delighted Kennan still more by holding on to his elbows, looking him in the eye, and affirming: "Mr. Kennan. We in our country believe that a man may be the friend of another country and remain, at the same time, a loyal and devoted citizen of his own, and that is the way we view you." Here was empathy with Kennan's deepest feelings, easing of the hurt from his expulsion in 1952, and endorsement of his efforts to bring America and Russia together. Though affirmed by Moscow, Kennan felt rebuffed by Washington. He remarked sourly that "if you cannot have this sort of recognition from your own government . . . it is nice to have it at least from the one-time adversary."[1]

Frustrated with the unsteady progress of Washington's reconciliation with Moscow, Kennan made a separate peace with the Soviet Union. Then, after pushing for an end to the Cold War, he threw himself into heading off renewed conflict with Russia. He pressed forward, fearing his time was short. Again and again in the quarter-century before his death in 2005, he announced an imminent end. Typical was, "I shall soon be 80 years old. I am not in good health. My days are narrowly numbered."[2]

Assuming death was near, Kennan doubled down on ensuring that future generations would have the true story of his life and work. That meant, he believed, encouraging his authorized biographer, John L. Gaddis, while discouraging supposedly less talented competitors. Kennan was pleased to see efforts by the public and by the Environmental Protection Agency to restrict pollution. Nevertheless, he continued to worry about the evil effects of industrialism on nature and on people. His focus proved prophetic. In pointing up the perils of relying on machine mass production, the iconoclast was also feeling his way toward the postindustrial, more localized world of the late twentieth and early twenty-first centuries. Cantankerous, cranky, and outrageously prejudiced, Kennan remained unstoppable in his efforts to rescue humanity and nature. He even, on occasion, allowed himself to have a good time.

———

The self-taught musician enjoyed playing for himself and others. "George loves to sit down at the piano," Frank Taplin, a Princeton neighbor, observed. "He loves jazz, he loves classical, he's just very relaxed, in a social sense." Delighting in doggerel, he would, while sailing aboard his beloved *Nagawicka* or *Northwind*, burst out such gems as "Oh mistress Mary, we do believe, that without sin thou didst conceive; oh mistress Mary still believing, teach us to sin without conceiving." While all in good fun, the verse also reflected his longtime struggle to balance the sexual freedom of Eros with the constraints of Civilization.

Reaching his eighties and then nineties, Kennan just kept going. Taplin marveled that his friend "rides his bike over there" to the Institute, "and he's producing, and he's thinking, and he's working all the time." Such labor did not necessarily yield satisfaction. Appraising the 40,000 letters written from the late 1960s to the late 1980s, the two books of diplomatic history published, and the Kennan Institute for Russian Affairs (named for both the elder George Kennan and himself and housed at the Smithsonian Institution) he had breathed into life, this self-critic bemoaned "how little I accomplished" and "how little I grew, intellectually and in understanding."[3] What frustrated Kennan most of all, however, was his difficulty in bending U.S. official policy away from confrontation with Russia.

ENDING THE COLD WAR

In 1983, with President Ronald Reagan seemingly still referring to the Soviet Union as an evil empire, Kennan cozied up to the supposed devil. He accepted an invitation from Soviet ambassador Anatoly Dobrynin. "I marched bravely into the old embassy building on 16th Street, under the amazed eyes and furiously clicking cameras of God knows how many agents of the FBI and others of the intelligence fraternity, was kindly and jovially received by my ambassadorial host, lunched and talked pleasantly with him for an hour or so, well aware that the recording devices of both governments" were whirring away.

On research trips to the Soviet Union in the 1980s, Kennan was greeted warmly by both the Russians and his friends at Spaso House. Gone was the tension and fear sparked by the secret police. Now cramping his ability to mix freely with Russians in Moscow was not the regime but the arthritis in his knees. As he walked, more slowly now, along the street so beloved a half-century earlier, "the ghosts of memory arose to surround me and accompany me." Nearly all the people and many of the places he had known had perished in the purges or the war or with the passage of time. A day in Riga proved "highly traumatic." He had lived there as "a bewildered, foolish, but sensitive young man." Back then, the landscape had imparted to him a "mysterious meaning, not to be put into words. How much of this lay in what I was seeing and how much in myself, God alone knows."[4]

The nature lover still communicated with his environment. He evidenced empathy and anger in seeing from the summer home in Randesund, Norway, "the sea—the abused, raped sea, deprived of its dignity and mystery by the ubiquitous oil rigs, the monstrous thundering automobile ferries, the airplanes overhead, the pipelines underneath. No wonder that it rises up sometimes in winter and strikes out in its fury against everything that men have been trying to do it. My heart is with it in these frantic, angry outbursts."[5]

Rage against the machines that would shackle the sea and the rest of God's creation spurred Kennan to imagine His perspective. "How sad the real God must be," he mused, "to see these hundreds of millions of tiny bipeds . . . for whom he provided this uniquely rich and beautiful planet as a habitat, destroying the planet and the future of their civilization for the childish pleasure of chugging around in their little motorized buggies."[6] Like Anton Chekhov, his most beloved Russian writer, Kennan disparaged machine production as a tragic misunderstanding of the relations that should prevail among people and with nature. The "romantic nationalism" that, foolishly, had welcomed the catastrophic first world arose from a "fever that occurred primarily in people who had been displaced by the Industrial Revolution."[7] He longed to seclude himself in northern New England with plants and animals. "Here in Princeton, what remains of Nature does its slow suburban death."[8]

In his radical critique of late twentieth-century American life, Kennan not only offered perceptive insights but also offended normative standards, especially with regard to ethnic stereotyping. A visit to Italy prompted him to observe, "When I see the mess the modern Italians make of their own country, I am less surprised by what the Italian contractors do in New Jersey."[9]

More egregious was prejudice about Jews that traced back to the Riga and Berlin of the 1920s. Some of Kennan's closest friends, such as J. Robert Oppenheimer, and his literary agent, Harriet Wasserman, were Jewish. Nevertheless, he continued to believe that most Jews, because of inheritance and culture, rigidly fit the negative stereotype. Kennan also resented the criticism made by some readers of his *Memoirs 1925–1950* (1967). While at the embassy in Berlin in 1940–1941, he had failed to report to Washington on Nazi persecution of the Jews. In 1987, he submitted a selection of diary excerpts for publication by what he called "the very Jewish firm of Straus & Farrar" [Farrar, Straus and Giroux]. The manuscript was rejected on the grounds of "Kennan's 'German problem.'" Stung, he fumed that while "I have never been anti-Semitic . . . this episode brought me as close as I have ever been to becoming one." Of course, he had not reported to Washington about the Jews, he exclaimed. His duties had remained largely administrative.

Moreover, "to whom should I have addressed such outpourings?" His superiors in the embassy or in Washington "would have thought I was mad." They already knew about the iniquity of the Nazis. "And what good would it have done?"[10] It took little reading between the lines to see Kennan's defensiveness about this chapter in his career. His concern for European Jewry had indeed remained minimal. That appalling letter to his sister in 1943 highlighted an anti-Semitism that would recede but never totally evaporate. To the extent that it was known, such lingering, distinctly out-of-fashion prejudice may have undermined Kennan's influence in his last decades.

That lack of sway bothered him. "What I find hard to adjust to is the acceptance of my own failure: of the failure, that is, to exert any useful influence on the dominant trends of official American thought and policy," he lamented.[11] Throughout the 1980s, Kennan tortured himself that he had influence "almost everywhere but where it counts."[12] He remained convinced that the nation and indeed the world would benefit from heeding his ideas. Democracy held out little hope, for "the 'people' haven't the faintest idea of what is good for them." He did know. Left to themselves, the people "would (and will) simply stampede into a final, utterly disastrous, and totally unnecessary nuclear war," he feared in 1984. And if they managed to avoid that fate, they would complete their devastation of the environment, "as they are now enthusiastically doing."[13]

Kennan had grounds for believing that most policy makers remained bound to the past and beholden to public sentiment. He, by contrast, aimed to "lead that opinion and mold it."[14] The former policy maker disputed the comforting argument advanced by many, including Gaddis, that the nuclear stalemate had yielded a relatively safe long peace.[15] Kennan feared that Reagan's Star Wars project could overturn the precarious nuclear balance. Moreover, nuclear conflict could ignite through inadvertence: "by human error, by confusion, by misread signals, by computer failure, by nuclear terrorist attack," or from a regional dispute.[16] Kennan's ingrained pessimism, especially when putting pen to paper in his diary, also shadowed his private life. He foresaw "nothing but grievous problems and dangers on every hand, in the progressive physical and emotional degeneration of old age for myself and Annelise, in the failures and tragedies of our children.[17]

Amid this doom and gloom, George failed to foresee two developments: the Cold War would soon end, but he would endure into the
new era. "I distrust all efforts to produce abrupt changes in the life of a
society," he asserted in 1986. Changes should be "gradual, organic
ones."[18] This ingrained conservatism and preference for controlled
change achieved through diplomacy would inspire Kennan's skeptical
response to the revolutionary, people-led changes of 1989–1991 that
transformed Russia, Germany, and much of the rest of Europe. Although he had predicted such shifts, and while he now gained plaudits
for his foresight, the unplanned nature of the upheaval and the threat of
unmoored nuclear weapons worried Kennan. Moreover, his decades of
admiring the culture of pre-1917 Russia had inspired a measure of sympathy with Moscow's traditional empire.

All this still remained in the future, however, when Kennan turned
eighty-five on February 16, 1989. After celebrating with a lunch in New
York City with Arthur M. Schlesinger, Jr., he returned to Princeton feeling "utterly drained, good for nothing." He wondered, for the first time
in his life, "What if I simply can't, anymore? What if the battery had finally run out? What if this is 'it'?"[19] That battery would stay charged,
however, for another sixteen years. Though running low at times, it
would be continually energized by Kennan's undying sense of obligation toward great problems, especially relations with Russia.

Eager to help unspool the tangle of U.S.-Russian hostility, Kennan
viewed the shift from the Reagan administration to that of George H. W.
Bush as a chance to influence the newcomers. And so "I tried to put my
word in where I could."[20] He gave two interviews on the *MacNeil-
Lehrer Report* television program, penned an article for the *New York
Times Magazine* and another for a German publication, and accepted
an invitation for a solo appearance before the Senate Foreign Relations
Committee.

His April 4 testimony triumphed in terms of both style and substance. A *Washington Post* column by Mary McGrory, headlined
"Kennan—A Prophet Honored," celebrated the grandeur he brought
to Capitol Hill. The octogenarian's straight back, chiseled jaw, and serious
tone all conveyed gravitas. His "lucidity, learning, and large-mindedness"
entranced the audience. Communism had failed in Russia for many

reasons, Kennan explained, not least because "it has no answer to death." Chairman Claiborne Pell (Democrat of Rhode Island), who, like the other senators, "seemed transformed into an eager schoolboy by Kennan's presence," pressed him for what countries did have an answer to death. Kennan did not know. But he affirmed that people had "to live by some form of faith. They have to feel that when they to do the decent and right things, that it is for values that exceed the period of their own lifetimes."[21]

Kennan seized this flash of authority to press seven arguments. First, Washington should pay fuller attention to Gorbachev's overtures to reduce nuclear armaments. Second, U.S. authorities habitually exaggerated Soviet superiority in conventional weapons. Third, both sides deployed "vastly redundant" numbers of dangerous though "essentially useless" nuclear weapons. Fourth, Washington and Moscow should join in not only reducing their own nuclear weapons but also in attacking "the whole problem of proliferation." Fifth, Kennan disputed the claim that Gorbachev's initiatives would likely be overturned by his successors. Sixth, the Soviet Union should be considered not as a likely military opponent, but rather as a fellow great power and diplomatic partner. Kennan's final lesson harked back to his decades-long aspiration. Relations with Russia should pivot to developing the significant "positive possibilities" of the relationship.[22] He rendered the committee an emotional thanks for honoring him with the opportunity to speak. While some of his testimony was "not as wise as it could be," it remained "the best I have to offer."[23]

Kennan's stature, wisdom, and grace sparked an electrifying response.[24] All the senators, staff members, nearly the entire audience, and even the Senate stenographer erupted in a spontaneous standing ovation. A clerk noted that the last time anything like this had happened was "in 1966 in a hearing on the Vietnam War—and that the witness was George Kennan."[25]

The attention rippled. Not only did the *Washington Post*, the *New York Times*, and *Newsweek* report on the hearings, "quite handsomely," Kennan noted, but General John Galvin, Supreme Commander of NATO, invited him to address a gathering of experts. Coincidentally, the *Atlantic* published excerpts from *Sketches from a Life* (1989), a collection of diary entries that included an account of Kennan's embrace by Gorbachev. At a White House ceremony in July, President George H. W. Bush awarded Kennan the Presidential Medal of Freedom, the nation's highest civilian honor. Though the president did not broach policy issues, the inveterate activist hoped that he had jolted the "complacency of the new administration" with regard to Gorbachev's outreach.[26] Kennan credited the celebrity to his advanced age. "I am living amid a generation of people who knew very little about me." Their ignorance "explains the primitive naivety of their enthusiasm. Also, there is not much competition." In the end, however, despite all the hoopla, the golden ring of securing an "effect on governmental policy" still eluded his grasp.[27]

Then, on November 9, 1989, history raced past the frustrated strategist. Jubilant East Germans surged through the Berlin Wall, opened suddenly and mistakenly by the demoralized East German government. As symbol and substance, the breach rent the Iron Curtain and portended the collapse of the Cold War.[28] Kennan felt overwhelmed, primarily not by joy but rather by the pressure of responding to the flood of requests for comments. While unwilling to give up his stature with the public, he longed to focus on his historical scholarship. He talked about doing a third volume of his history of the pre–World War I Franco-Russian alliance. A week after the fall of the Wall, the White House invited him, along with other former ambassadors to Moscow, to meet with President Bush, Secretary of State George Shultz, and other top officials. At the gathering, Kennan urged caution and not taking advantage of the Soviets' embarrassment. He came away, however, disappointed that the consultation had amounted to only a "useless and trivial" charade. The president's subsequent statements demonstrated that nothing Kennan said to him had "made the faintest impression on his mind."[29]

Even as the media demanded his wisdom on these epochal events, Kennan worried that he had less of himself to give. On Thanksgiving Day, he was jolted by the apparent onset of dementia: "not only physical weakness, jitteriness, unsteadiness, etc., but also emotional reactions— lack of buoyancy, moments of impatience and irritation . . . dark apprehension of I know not what, and a sense of being not fully in control of my own reactions and behavior."[30] Juxtaposed with Kennan's fear of his own collapse were his mixed feelings about the fall of the Cold War order.

Uncharacteristically self-indulgent, Kennan stayed tuned all weekend to "Messrs. [Boris] Becker, [Stefan] Edberg, and [John] McEnroe playing tennis—while the Communist domination of Eastern and parts of Central Europe was going up in flames, and Messrs. Gorbachev and Bush were meeting in the middle of a Mediterranean near-hurricane, at Malta."[31] Thereafter he buckled down to writing remarks for an address at the Council on Foreign Relations on December 20 and for testimony before the Senate Foreign Relations Committee on January 17, 1990.

As he gathered his thoughts, the stirring changes famously predicted in the 1947 "X" article were crystalizing. "[The] revolution in the Communist world fails, for some reason, to excite me very greatly," Kennan confessed in his diary. The suddenness and spontaneity of the upheaval made him uneasy. The Russophile had his own priorities: the people who had grown accustomed to Communism, the national interests of Russia, and the precarious position of Gorbachev. He worried that "these excited peoples," the non-Russians of the disintegrating Soviet bloc, not only lacked experience with self-government, but they also had failed to learn "from the sensible Finns that the only way to establish their true independence is to show a decent respect for Soviet security interests." If the Poles, Czechs, and the others dared "challenge Soviet security, they will simply destroy Gorbachev."[32]

While Kennan as a young man had oscillated between Eros and Civilization, that is, between creativity and duty, as an octogenarian he pivoted between weariness and duty. In addition to his spacious office at the Institute, Kennan maintained in the Hodge Road house four places to write: Wendy's former room for paying bills, a desk in the living room for writing in the diary, a place in the television room for penning letters, and, his favorite, the tower on the fourth floor. For serious writing such as these talks, he preferred the tower, if his arthritic knees could manage the stairs.[33] Up there he crafted a talk to the annual Christmastime sons-and-daughters gathering at the Council on Foreign Relations. Since news of his scheduled address had gone around, he anticipated "a great crush. And people expect great things of me." His topic was Europe, "in the throes of the greatest upheaval since World War II," and he had fifteen minutes of supposedly extemporaneous remarks in which to explain it all. Kennan enjoyed giving such talks. And yet he also longed to break free from "this futile and exhausting bondage." He grumbled that unless he freed himself, death would do it for him.

To the crowd gathered at the elegant council building on New York's Upper East Side, the eighty-five-year-old still had his moxie. "It was better than I could have imagined—he's unbelievably with it," enthused a twenty-nine-year-old artist and daughter of a power broker.[34] So many people showed up that the council had to move the event to the theater of nearby Hunter College. In terms of the larger influence he coveted, however, Kennan, was dismayed at the press coverage, which relegated the speech to the local news section and ignored his political analysis.[35]

Nevertheless, this December 1989 lecture shines as one of Kennan's most insightful and prescient statements. He viewed the end of the Cold War in terms of the intrinsic nature of the conflict. He condemned the political division of Europe and the standoff between the NATO and Warsaw pacts, for which his containment doctrine bore some responsibility, as "the greatest of artificialities." While the Cold War had kept the lid on smaller rivalries within Europe, it proved a "cumbersome and undesirable" way of maintaining stability. And now "this status quo has broken down—broken down on its own unnaturalness, its own artificiality." Americans and Western Europeans stood "poorly prepared" to deal with swiftly changing events because they had been "concentrated, too closely and for too long, on the sterile and hopeless mathematics of a military rivalry"—a competition spiked by "our own feverish imagination."[36]

After faulting the Cold War for current problems, Kennan cautioned, prophetically, against naive optimism about the long-term outcome of popular uprisings. While Americans tended to assume that democracy remained the natural order of things, and that the newly liberated people would easily adopt this best-of-all systems, he warned otherwise. The people of Eastern and Central Europe were poorly prepared for political freedom. Many of the former Soviet satellites had suffered under authoritarian government long before Moscow had seized control.

At this point, Kennan invoked a favorite premise about democracy. That maxim failed to appreciate how the acculturation of immigrants continually revitalized democracy in the United States. Unfortunately, however, Kennan's belief did apply to many other nations. "The aptitude for democracy is not something just born into people," he insisted. It came slowly and "has to attain the quality of a habit." Freedom "is not achieved, and certainly not preserved, by a series of emotional street demonstrations." In later decades, authoritarian tendencies would indeed plague such nations as Poland and Hungary. Intimately familiar with the descent into the First World War, Kennan warned that "the removal of the Russian hand" from the Balkans, "that great breeding ground of wars and troubles," would release not only the thirst for freedom but also the region's "romantic and intolerant and dangerous nationalism." This prediction would prove tragically true in the Balkan wars only a few years later.[37]

Fortunately for the peace of the world, Kennan proved unduly pessimistic about the consequences of reunifying Germany. In pointing to the so-called German question, he wondered whether an independent Germany, outranking all its neighbors in population, economic strength, and underlying military power, could peaceably integrate into Europe.

While that danger did not materialize, another problem he foresaw did spur renewed tension with Russia and, three decades later, a tragic war in Ukraine. Not a fan of NATO at its creation in 1949, fervently opposed to arming it with nuclear weapons in the 1950s, and appalled at the prospect of deploying more such weaponry in the 1980s, Kennan now argued that events had rendered the Atlantic alliance, just like its Soviet-dominated analog, the Warsaw Pact, an anachronism. No alliance "predicated on an assumed mutual hostility" of East and West could suit the Europe of the future. Instead, "a new all-European security structure—a structure resembling nothing that has ever existed in the past, will have to be created." While Americans could participate in forming this new arrangement, they should also abandon their reliance on massive nuclear forces. Moreover, it would be Europeans, including Russians, who would pioneer this new pact, while "we Americans, poorly prepared as we are," played a secondary role.[38]

Kennan decided that the dawn of the 1990s and the sunset of the Cold War marked a fitting end to his forty-four years of public life. And so he diligently prepared for his January 17 testimony before the Senate Foreign Relations Committee with the intention of making it the book-end to his career. In contrast to the previous April, however, only a single senator, Joe Biden, Jr. (Democrat of Delaware), the future U.S. president, was present. Undeterred, Kennan presented his case for slow-ing down the cascade of changes. The United States should promote an international moratorium of at least three years with regard to altera-tions in NATO, the Warsaw Pact, and the division of Germany. The time would allow for "careful and deliberate" talks for rationally planning a new European security structure.[39] Kennan's proposal would prove a nonstarter, however, as leaders in Washington and in Bonn, spurred by the enthusiasm of most Germans, would speed ahead toward reunifica-tion and what would become NATO's triumph over the Warsaw Pact. In part because of Russia's fury at NATO's expansion, Kennan's resolve to retire from public life also proved futile.

Kennan kept being Kennan. Even in his nineties, he remained "too much the servant of our government" to give up trying to influence Washington, especially with regard to Russia and Germany.[40] Though suffering increasing physical impairment and intermittent intellectual problems, he still spoke out in letters, articles, and lectures. He outlined his personal and political philosophies in a best-selling book, *Around the Cragged Hill* (1993). Remaining in the public eye as he outlived most of his contemporaries, Kennan assumed the status of a sage. "I am prob-ably the most widely honored person, outside the entertainment indus-try and the political establishment, in this country."[41] Fame was his, but also frustration: he wanted to be heeded as well as honored. Having become an institution, he aspired instead to institute policy. His ambi-tion was to return to that political establishment.

Though many of his ideas would prove prescient in the future, they rubbed against the contemporary grain. He warned that uncontrolled, popular-driven change was rushing Germany toward unification and the Soviet Union toward dissolution. He distrusted political agitation in the streets, whether it was shaking up Berlin and Moscow in 1989–1991, or Washington and Princeton in 1967–1968. Kennan believed that change should come about only through the kind of careful, ostensibly rational policy making that he had promoted as Policy Planning Staff director back in the late 1940s. Ever the Russophile, he echoed Russian nationalists in regretting the dissolution of the Soviet Union. He seriously underestimated Ukrainians' determination to become and remain independent. Kennan's long-held disdain for so-called Third World nations persisted as he found no reason for the U.S. ventures in Iraq in 1990–1991 and in Somalia in 1992–1993, nor grounds to celebrate the end of apartheid in South Africa after 1990. Amid his intellectual activity, Kennan continually forecast his imminent demise.

Though Kennan's fame had originated in his urging containment of the Soviet Union until that nation mellowed or broke apart, when that objective came into view four and a half decades later, he found it worrisome. He feared "strange and dark things happening: Russia disintegrating, drifting into the collapse of the traditional Russian Empire, experiencing the failure of perestroika and the ruin of Gorbachev, moving into a new Time of Troubles."[42] He faulted the "foolish Lithuanians" for pushing their independence so hard that they weakened Gorbachev. He feared Washington would back independence for Lithuania and the other Baltic states, and thereby spur "the break-up of the traditional Russian Empire, with all the chaos, bloodshed, and horror that is going to mean."[43]

Amid the tumult of 1990–1992, Kennan sustained a wide range of concerns. He wondered whether Princeton's spate of summer weather in March evidenced the "menacing warming of the planet."[44] He worried that the NATO allies were excluding Russia from their reorganization. It peeved him that despite "their great military effort in World War II," the Russians would now be confronted "with a Europe dominated militarily by Germany" made even stronger by its ties with Moscow's wartime allies. "I thought it always a mistake," Kennan said wisely, "to take advantage of the momentarily weakened position of another great power." Such grasping for short-term gain "always revenged itself at a later date."[45]

While holding Russia at arm's length in NATO, President Bush invited Gorbachev to a state dinner at the White House. Kennan attended with Annelise, who looked "very beautiful in her multi-colored chiffon dress." Again he was embraced by Gorbachev, who praised Kennan's recent essay urging greater outreach to Moscow by the Western allies.[46]

The honor did not prevent him from feeling that he was, "with increasing acceleration, dying." Pondering whether there was life after death, Kennan took to heart Swiss psychologist C. G. Jung's theory of the collective unconscious uniting humans past and present. He appreciated Jung's advice to parse dreams for such communication as well as evidence of life after death. The immortal soul was "not identical with the body," Kennan concluded, and would persist after the body became "only a rotting substance."[47]

Both body and soul would in fact stay together an additional fifteen years, and for most of them Kennan remained active. En route to Norway, he admonished himself that in "some way or other, the time has to be spent, not wasted." And so he began writing what he would publish as *Around the Cragged Hill*. He tackled first an issue that had tormented him nearly all his life, sexual desire. He started with the premise of original sin: "man even the best of him is an imperfect creature, a cracked vessel." [48] Even the few capable of creativity or virtue remained susceptible to corruption by self-interest and by the sexual urge. Still expressing the Freudian theory absorbed in Vienna six decades earlier, Kennan regarded sexuality as conflicting "with civilization, with order, with reason, even with human dignity." This urge wreaked consequences "so silly," "so destructive and so self-defeating" that they undermined "orderly, responsible life." He warned about confusing lust with love. "The two do indeed sometimes meet, though seldom for very long," he confirmed. Evidencing remorse for the sexual adventures of his earlier years, Kennan ranked himself as also an injured party. He, too, had suffered from this "chaotic, anarchic force," this "beastly, demeaning" drive that mocked "the dignity of its helpless victims" and left "a trail of shame and frustration in its path."[49]

Kennan was probably thinking in part of Charlotte Böhm and other young women he had dated in Germany, the scene of many of his formative experiences. As a schoolboy in Wilhelmine, Germany, he had watched military cadets marching through the streets. As a diplomat in Weimar, Germany, he had viewed socialists and fascists demonstrating in the boulevards. He had fallen in love with Hamburg and Berlin, immersed himself in German culture, taken up with Junkers and liberal aristocrats, soaked up German notions of Russia in university seminars, befriended German diplomats in Riga and in Moscow, toured through German-occupied Europe, administered the embassy in Berlin in 1940–1941, and had negotiated with German authorities during the internment of the embassy staff in 1942. After the war, he had reknit ties with German friends, questioned the allied occupation, pushed so hard for German reunification that he undermined his standing in the State Department, again called for unification in his Reith Lectures, and participated in the exclusive Order Pour le Mérite for Sciences and Arts. In firebombed Hamburg, he had experienced the epiphany that would turn him forever against war. Kennan knew the language so intimately that upon reading a clumsy translation of one of his books, he exclaimed: "Oh dear, oh dear! What has happened to the ability of Germans in this age to write their own language?"[50]

All the more poignant, then, was Kennan's sour response when ordinary Germans seized the initiative to reunify their nation on October 3, 1990. Having gone to Berlin for the occasion, George and Annelise joined the tens of thousands of Germans shuffling in both directions across the now-erased dividing line. "We joined the west-going stream, and continued with it for one or two miles (we had no choice, in fact, for we could, over all this distance, find no other means of transportation other than our own legs, of which my right one complained rather emphatically)."[51] Far more than the sore leg pained Kennan. He believed in principle that change should attune "with the slow rhythm of social life."[52] By contrast, the Cold War order was collapsing rapidly because of "outbreaks of impulse on the part of poorly informed and unreflective people." Thousand of East Germans were seizing the opportunity "of getting better jobs, making more money, and bathing in the fleshpots of the West."[53]

Kennan saw this spontaneous assertiveness as violating the residual authority of Washington and its wartime allies. Popular action had rendered the German situation "from the standpoint of American policy, essentially out of control." Although he had for decades criticized the 1945 Yalta Conference, which had affirmed the victors' dominion over Germany, he now invoked its jurisdiction. He complained that the Germans were unifying on their own rather than according to "an agreed policy on the part of the powers that were allied in the Second World War." Looking past the immediate jubilation, Kennan asked, "Was this what we really wanted?—the establishment of a united and armed Germany as incomparably the great economic and potentially the greatest military power in Europe?"[54] As this strategic-minded historian understood, it was Russia and the satellites slipping from its grasp that had the most to fear from any rekindled German ambition.

On October 4, the day after their walk through reunified Berlin, the Kennans flew to Moscow, "where we were met at the airport by representatives of the Central Committee (of the Party) and of [Georgi I.] Arbatov's Institute [for U.S.A. and Canada Studies]."[55] As Kennan's friend Robert C. Tucker observed, the former ambassador, who had been "traumatically affected" by being declared persona non grata, was now celebrated as "persona grata." At U.S.-Soviet colloquia in Moscow, Tucker marveled at the Russians' "almost iconographic attitude toward George Kennan." They treasured him as the most "forthright voice of the Establishment" favoring improved U.S.-Soviet relations. "Therefore he's recognized as a very important man, and a very valuable man." Kennan's "special relationship" yielded invitations to "come as the official guest of the Arbatov Institute" and "special access to the archives on 19th century diplomacy—how could all these things not affect somebody?" Tucker asked. He suspected this favoring by official sources helped account for Kennan's indifference to the plight of dissidents opposed to Soviet authorities.[56]

Kennan's star status rose even higher under Gorbachev. During his October 1990 visit to Moscow, he was driven to the Kremlin for a three-hour conversation, mostly in Russian, with Alexander Yakovlev, a historian, reform-minded Soviet vice president, and close adviser of Gorbachev. Change was in the air as glasnost and perestroika pivoted between triumph and disaster. Kennan began with a quotation from Fyodor Tutchev, a nineteenth-century romantic poet and diplomat: "Blessed is he who visited this world in its fateful minutes." Heaping the praise, Yakovlev gushed, "You, Mr. Kennan, are history personified" in terms of U.S. relations with Russia. He conveyed Gorbachev's best wishes. When Yakovlev brought up the "X" article, Kennan, a bit embarrassed, responded with a nervous "Ha-ha." "I would not have written such an article today," he assured Yakovlev, "but it was forty years ago." It was the end of the essay, the section emphasizing the need for domestic American reform and aid to Western Europe, that packed "lots of truth." In effect apologizing for his long ago militance, Kennan explained, "I was here during the purges of the 1930s, and then again during the war, and we felt a certain frustration and desperation regarding Soviet-American relations. You understand, we had very little hope." At one point, the eighty-six-year-old confessed that while he enjoyed speaking in Russian, "My language got a little rusty. I have not spoken Russian for forty years."

Kennan explained the Cold War as resulting, on the U.S. side, from "a full misunderstanding of Soviet attentions." Americans had suffered "Cold War hysteria, an exorbitant exaggeration of Soviet might." Many had confused the Soviet Union with Nazi Germany. Moreover, for Pentagon planners, hostility toward Moscow had become "not just their habit, but also their means for existence. It is their life." He assured Yakovlev that never did he himself, even when writing the "X" article, believe that Moscow would attack the West. He had asked his fellow Americans, why would the Russians invade Western Europe? How could they control all of Germany or Western Europe? Why would they want to repeat on a larger scale their difficulties in Eastern Europe? "But they refused to think as politicians." Americans and many Western Europeans had persisted in believing that if you have big military potential, you must be planning to use it. He cited the maxim he had derived from his story of the origins of the First World War: assuming war was inevitable helped make it so.

As Yakovlev detailed Gorbachev's gargantuan challenge in reforming the ossified Communist system, an empathetic Kennan offered suggestions mirroring his personal experience as well as his professional expertise. He pointed up the societal damage wrought by decades of hardship under Communism and war. With regard to his own life, the absence of a mother, the coldness of his stepmother, and the distance of his father had all warped him, he confided. He affirmed that "the sense of personal security should originate from the family first of all." Children needed "families—real families—fathers, mothers, so that there will be love." Perhaps the most serious wound inflicted by decades of dictatorship was the suppression of individual initiative and spontaneous expression. Kennan, who situated his own life within the competing pulls of freedom and restraint, saw the present historical juncture as demanding that Russians tilt toward greater freedom in their personal lives, while Germans exercised greater restraint in their national affairs. Russia's dedicated teachers had to nurture the moral sense of the new generation. He cited his beloved Chekhov, who understood questions of morality better than any other Russian writer. Individual responsibility also was key to reforming the inefficient Soviet agricultural system. Remarking that "I myself have a farm in the United States," Kennan urged dividing the collective and state farms into individual family plots. With such a setup, "if a cow gets sick in the middle of the night, the farmer gets up and calls the vet because it is his business."

As context for the crisis in the Soviet Union, Kennan stressed America's own difficulties. Indeed, the perils facing America were "more serious than your problems," he told a probably astounded Yakovlev. "We have great problems with poverty in inner cities, with drugs, with dropping educational standards, the financial system." Russians visiting America needed to think critically about what to borrow and what to reject. Reviving a wish that traced back to the magic of 1934, Kennan hoped that "maybe some day [Russians] will be able to help us, too."[57]

After this frank conversation, Kennan reflected privately on "the progressive disintegration of the Soviet Union itself." He worried that Gorbachev "is going to wake up one of these mornings" and discover that while he had put in place a more democratic governance, "there is no such thing as a Soviet Union left to govern." Though not surprised that the three Baltic nations and the traditionally restive Caucasus republics were breaking away, Kennan feared that "much trouble lies ahead in connection with the Ukraine." He had long regarded Ukraine as an intrinsic part of Russia. To be sure, Russia itself, under the nationalist leader Boris Yeltsin, was also going its own way. Sympathetic toward the Russian empire and worried about the dispersal of Moscow's nuclear arsenal, Kennan did not want to see the actual breakup of the Soviet Union he had predicted nearly a half-century earlier. Indeed, that dissolution threatened "great dangers for everyone involved, including ourselves." If the union did break up, he hoped that Gorbachev would somehow remain as leader. "Russia, whether united or not, needs him."[58]

In late January 1991, sandwiched between the coming together of Germany and the falling apart of the Soviet Union, and just as a war with Iraq loomed in the Middle East, Kennan and Gaddis met for what both assumed would prove their last interview. Their discussion offers a snapshot of how Kennan at this pivotal time appraised issues of the past, present, and future. "I'm sorry that I continue to linger so long!" the almost eighty-seven-year-old apologized to his posthumous biographer. He assured Gaddis that the end was near. The heart palpitations had intensified, and he experienced a "strange psychic state": vague apprehension, emotional brittleness, and "regrets for the callousness I showed toward others when I was young." Affirming that death was "normal and natural and not tragic," he regretted only leaving Annelise to survive him. As someone who for decades had tried to discipline his life, Kennan now aimed to regulate its end. "My contribution was roughly coterminous with the forty-year period of the Cold War. I don't feel like taking on another period."[59] Sidestepping this confession of impending demise, Gaddis focused instead on the Cold War: How and why had it ended so abruptly?

Kennan's response resonated with memory from both his late 1940s experience with the Cold War and his subsequent efforts to ease that conflict. His narrative reflected ingrained beliefs as much as it did international behaviors. The strategist-turned-historian refused to credit Reagan, whom he had never liked. Rather, on the American side, "the hard-line Cold War impulses" had faded even before Reagan took office. While paying the major tribute to Gorbachev, Kennan also emphasized the ideological decay that traced back to Stalin's cruelty immediately after the Great Patriotic War. Despite the magnificent sacrifices and ultimate victory of the Soviet people, the dictator, according to Kennan, bluntly told them there would be no "relaxation, not even relaxation on the economic front." The Kremlin chief had insisted on rearmament rather than "any better treatment of living standards." The resulting disenchantment sealed "the end of communism as an inspiring force in the minds of the people."[60]

In this recollection of Stalin's famous "election speech" on February 9, 1946, Kennan was simply wrong. Moreover, this memory reflected the priorities and the state of mind that had impelled him to dictate the long telegram from his sickbed. Stalin had, in fact, called for economic relief to the Soviet people. While proposing a massive upsurge in the postwar economy to prepare for "any eventuality," the Kremlin chief had also promised that "special attention will be focused on expanding the production of goods for mass consumption, on raising the standard of life of the working people." Many Western observers, including Frank K. Roberts and Isaiah Berlin, Kennan's British friends from Moscow, had flagged this "special attention to consumer goods and improving the standard of living." With Ambassador Averell Harriman absent in early 1946, Kennan, as the ranking U.S. official at the embassy must have read the speech closely. Nevertheless, he had ignored the inconvenient evidence of Stalin's balanced agenda in order to assemble the indictment his hard-line State Department friends were expecting.[61] The distortion had apparently lodged in Kennan's mind and had remained there ever since. This memory of Stalin's callous disregard for his long-suffering dependents also fit Kennan's emotional disposition. Whether the victim was the tyrannized daughter, Svetlana Alliluyeva, or the entire Russian nation, Kennan judged Stalin as the unworthy master and himself as the caring though thwarted benefactor.

In continuing his explanation of how the Cold War had ended, Kennan highlighted Nikita S. Khrushchev's secret speech in 1956 detailing Stalin's crimes, the crackdown on Czechoslovakia in 1968, and the advent of a new generation in the Communist Party. Also influential were the progeny of such Soviet leaders as Khrushchev and Antastas Mikoyan. "These kids seemed to have sort of gotten together." While respecting their fathers, they also sought new answers. Kennan lamented that East-West tensions had persisted far longer than he had expected.

He blamed the Western allies, who "steadily and stubbornly declined for over forty years ever to discuss with the Russians . . . the possibilities for a disengagement" in Europe. He had urged such talks in his Reith Lectures of 1957, Kennan recalled. Gaddis responded with skepticism about the Soviets' good faith.

On this fundamental issue the biographer and his subject would always disagree. With a professional's faith in diplomacy, Kennan believed that negotiations always had potential for progress. "For goodness sake, talk with them, and see." Gaddis doubted "there would have been a corresponding response from the Soviet side." The West had needed to wait for a Gorbachev. To which Kennan replied that earlier Soviet leaders might have responded to Western offers to negotiate. Tapping into a vein of memories separate from those of 1946, the former Cold Warrior affirmed that even "Stalin was interested" in talks. So was the seemingly likely heir, Lavrenty Beria, especially in 1952 over Germany. Unfortunately, Kennan emphasized, "we never tested those things." He decided that he himself had "underestimated the cautiousness and flexibility of Stalin." Despite all the anti-American propaganda, "Stalin wasn't burning his bridges."[62]

Kennan offered yet another argument for disengagement, one that would resonate well into the twenty-first century. From the 1950s onward, he had predicted that "someday this Russian hegemony in Eastern and Central Europe is going to break down." Into what would these nations then be fitted? While integrating Poland and other former satellites into a European economic bloc was something the Russians might accept, fitting them into "a Western military alliance" like NATO, "is something that the Russians will not be able to accommodate themselves to."[63]

Though Kennan in the early 1930s had viewed Russia's future from a German viewpoint, he now considered the hasty coming together of Germany from a Russian perspective. "What you've got is the unification of a very heavily armed Germany—actually the strongest power in Europe—with its treaty relationships in a state of great confusion." Rather than a Germany in NATO, he had long pushed for a neutral, disarmed, reunified state. Just as the manner and style of student anti-Vietnam War protesters had irritated him in 1968, so, too, was he now jaundiced at the apparently unthinking, selfish behavior of "these young people who fled from Eastern Germany." In satisfying their personal desires, they had pushed "everybody over the cliff." He angrily asserted, "I'll tell you this: I don't think these young people had any realistic answer to the question as to how the future of European security should be held." Skeptical of popular movements, Kennan fretted that in both Russia and Germany, "events are taking charge. They're under nobody's control. That has bothered me a little bit, because I was used to thinking in a world where people did have control."[64] Always partial to organic change, Kennan perceived the tumultuous changes of 1989–1991 as unbalanced: too much creativity, not enough order and obligation.

Although his body tired easily, Kennan had not exhausted his desire to influence public issues. After waiting so long for the Cold War to end, he hated to see the United States get militarily involved in Iraq. The war would thwart efforts to restore "our shattered finances and endangered economy."[65] For decades he had publicly deplored America's dependence on oil from the Middle East, the commitment to Israel, and the notion that war could solve complex problems. His urging had fallen on deaf ears. Was it not a "grotesque anomaly" that he, at age eighty-seven "the most extravagantly honored private individual in this country," could make "no perceptible impact at all on our official thinking, or even on public opinion"? He wondered what he possibly could have done to secure for "my thoughts a public attention commensurate with the

FIGURE 38. George at age eighty-nine, beaming during
the celebration of a grandson's wedding. (Courtesy of
Grace Kennan Warnecke.)

respect paid to my person."[66] The only belief of Kennan matching the
conviction that he was right was the certitude that others should accept
those views.

Frustrated that leadership was ignoring him, he looked to other ave-
nues of influence. He published a column in the *Washington Post* that
urged independence for the Baltic republics, greater autonomy for other
restless republics, and sustained ties with Moscow. "I wrote it, really, to
be read by Mr. Gorbachev (as I rather expect it will be)." At times,

though, he felt overwhelmed by his responsibility to the many who did look to him for answers: "When I am asked, 'What do I think of the situation in Russia?' my reaction is: 'How lovely it would be to live somewhere deep in the country.'"[67] Such retreat was ruled out, however, not only by Annelise's refusal to leave Princeton but also by George's own stubborn spirit. Thwarted at influencing the present, Kennan increasingly focused on swaying the future.

He rushed to finish *Around the Cragged Hill: A Personal and Political Philosophy*, which stressed the inherent limits of the human experience: Individuals were flawed. Democratic governments needed to restrict their ambitions in foreign policy. Environmental pollution threatened disaster. Finally, the shortsightedness of Congress and the presidency required setting up a "Council of State," a permanent group of wise and respected citizens who would advise government and help shape public opinion. He hoped the volume would not only move contemporary opinion but also that people "will pick the book up and read it fifty to a hundred years hence."[68]

KENNAN AND GADDIS

Putting such weight on "the chance of being re-discovered after my death" made it all the more important to have the right story available in that future.[69] Kennan regarded his biography as a precious opportunity to extend his influence. Yet that chance was also precarious, because some unauthorized, inept biographer might scoop Gaddis and blur Kennan's legacy. While focused on the record of his professional life, he hoped that readers would also appreciate his personal dilemmas and emotions and the literary effort he had devoted to recording them. That was why he had recorded his anguish in his diary, which he expected to be read by others. Kennan wanted the biography to buttress his claim of having conceptualized containment as primarily political and not military. The narrative also needed to document his efforts in the 1957 Reith Lectures and in other venues to spur negotiations that would ease the Cold War. Readers should appreciate how he had pushed for disengagement from the military confrontation in Europe and for caution in intervention in the Third World. He hoped also for an appreciation of his ideas about the evils of advertising, automobiles, and industrial automation, and about the necessity to save nature from environmental depredation.

In August 1982, Kennan had granted his authorized biographer, John Lewis Gaddis, exclusive access to all his papers and full freedom to write the posthumous biography as he wished. He had closed his most revealing papers to other scholars for the rest of his life. He further restricted the record by removing some documents from the Kennan papers available at Princeton. While granting Gaddis multiple, free-ranging interviews, he denied others such access to his memories. Kennan's imprimatur opened the door for Gaddis to interview more than thirty of George's associates and family members. Finally, historians other than Gaddis were not permitted to photocopy the available Kennan papers, but instead had to take notes.

Fears of having his reputation sullied and his message lost to future generations, bound Kennan to Gaddis. Ironically, however, the authorized biographer, while burnishing the record on containment, would disparage Kennan's far longer campaign to move past that Cold War shibboleth. The divergence between them would become clear only with time, as Gaddis grew more orthodox in his views of the Cold War.

What initially gave Kennan pause was something else, however: whether this able though conventional political historian could handle the personal side of his subject's life. In his case, Kennan opined, the personal aspects would be "particularly difficult, because my life, while not lacking ironies, has not been a dramatic one." He had long agonized over his dilemmas, and he wanted that story told, with details discreetly blurred. He candidly questioned Gaddis whether "you could do it. I simply don't know."[70] The historian forthrightly acknowledged that he viewed the biography as "primarily political-intellectual." While agreeing that life and character were important, he quickly circled back to keeping "his eye on the main task at hand" and not getting "diverted into either irrelevant gossip on the one hand, or irresponsible psychohistorical analysis on the other."[71] He confessed his "trepidation" over "whether I could handle the personal side of things." While the biographer's hesitation about wading into then-fashionable, rigidly Freudian "psycho-history" was understandable, it also conflicted with how the subject thought his life should be analyzed. To Gaddis, Kennan bluntly "stressed the importance of the psychological dimension." He recommended as a model Leon Edel's "psycho-biographical" study of Henry James.[72]

In ensuing years, Gaddis would heed Annelise's urging to include the personal side of George's life. The net result was twofold. The biographer did cite long quotations, often from the diaries, that expressed his subject's inner agonies, affairs, and other dilemmas. But he largely abstained from explicating this evidence. While he wisely avoided the rigidly Freudian "psycho-history" that Kennan had recommended, he also shied away from the empathetic, common-sense analysis that could illuminate what George was feeling, and how those feelings changed or stayed constant over time. Gaddis did include much of the personal story, but he presented it with a formal tone that preserved his distance from the messy inner life of George F. Kennan. In trying to game how history would treat him, Kennan ceded control over how the authorized history of his life actually would treat him.

Over the course of Kennan's more than two decades of collaboration with Gaddis, three interlocking developments sparked his consternation. First, other historians, "inadequate pens" in Kennan's view, started writing books about him. Second, Gaddis achieved such outstanding success in his career that, the older man feared, he might lose interest in the biography or fail to find the time to write it. Third were recurring doubts that even Gaddis would validate the struggles of his personal life or value his efforts to push for negotiations to ease the Cold War. Kennan fretted that his legacy and potential future influence might still, despite all his efforts, end up on the ash heap of history.

In 1984, Kennan confided to Gaddis his uneasiness about the efforts of David A. Mayers, a young historian and political scientist then at the University of California at Santa Cruz, who had sent him drafts of chapters. The project was "developing into a biography of sorts—albeit a weak and superficial one." The study suffered such a "deficiency of background knowledge" that he appraised it as unlikely to "have any major impact." Nevertheless, "I would have preferred that it not be written." In detailing his objections, Kennan revealed what he considered proper and improper history, at least of himself. He faulted Mayers for basing his book more on the early, unpublished papers in Mudd Library than on the "more mature," "authoritative" material in Kennan's published works. In other words, Mayers was interpreting Kennan for himself and arriving at conclusions not always matching those of the strategist turned historian. The danger was that such errant interpretation "may give rise to a misimpression" and thus undercut Kennan's future influence. In a gentle hint to Gaddis, Kennan affirmed that he would "rely on your own work to place things, eventually, in proper perspective."[73]

The following year found Kennan piqued at having to order from a bookseller Barton Gellman's *Contending with Kennan*. The volume, with his name and face on the cover, had appeared "without a single word of prior notification or warning from the author or the publisher," and "without anyone's having had the courtesy even of sending me a copy."[74] Gellman had published his Princeton University senior thesis, which organized Kennan's lifelong ideas on strategy, democratic decision making, and the wielding of power into a rough-hewn structure. While admiring the achievement, Kennan judged its "greatest deficiency" as having "utterly ignored chronology." Beliefs stated in the 1940s "were cheerfully mingled with things said 25–35 years later," as though neither he nor the world had changed in the interim. Kennan once again delicately offered Gaddis a suggestion: he should "look at my statements as part of a dynamic and not a static process."[75] Kennan mustered far more enthusiasm for another compiler of his ideas, the young Swedish historian Anders Stephanson. He had written "an enormous and very impressive" dissertation at Columbia "on my thoughts (not at all my person)— the weaknesses and inconsistencies as well as the occasional merits."[76] The octogenarian welcomed the efforts by Stephanson and Gellman to systematize and critique his thinking because they stimulated his own thinking. Indeed, with regard to writing *Around the Cragged Hill*, he affirmed that he "was goaded into this" by these two books.[77]

He bristled, by contrast, at the biographies by Mayers (1989) and by Walter Hixson (1991). "I'm not too happy about them," he confided to

Gaddis. "I feel a little sorry for [Mayers]. I think it was a mistake for him to try to write this book." Kennan, despite his decades as a prize-winning historian, still thought like a State Department official when it came to his own history. "With all these chaps I really rather resent their taking stuff that was put into the unclassified portion of the papers by mistake by the Mudd Library." He was referring to such material as "The Prerequisites," his 1938 screed criticizing American democracy, which he had removed from his available papers, but only after it had been quoted by C. Ben Wright and others in the late 1970s.[78]

What Kennan could not accept was that such papers, whether available or not, remained archival documents, the raw stuff of written history. He fumed that it was improper for historians to write his biography from documents "that I'd never offered for publication." That last phrase implied that the only legitimate sources for a biography by anyone other than Gaddis were documents that Kennan himself had selected for dissemination. Some of the sources used by Mayers and Hixson amounted to "only scraps of diary material," he groused. The next day he might have "written the contrary to that." The nub here was that unauthorized historians had mined these early documents "as evidence of my mature thinking"—and it was only that mature thinking that Kennan wanted disseminated. He saw a further offense. While Kennan had repeatedly alluded to sexual indiscretions in his diary, he remained a highly private person. He appreciated that unlike other writers, Stephanson remained "very impersonal—Stephanson didn't look for lurid things."[79]

Lurid in a different way, but equally infuriating to Kennan, were charges that he had helped redeem "Uncle Sam's Nazis" by heading up an illegal program to whisk suspected German war criminals into the United States.[80] Legal investigator John Loftus in 1983 and popular author Christopher Simpson in 1987 each completed manuscripts that fingered Kennan for rescuing officials involved in the Nazis' brutal wartime occupation of Soviet territory. Back in Moscow in the 1930s, Kennan, along with Chip Bohlen and Charlie Thayer, had knit close ties within the isolated foreign diplomatic community. Among the regulars at the Americans' weekend dacha parties were Gustav Hilger and Hans-Heinrich "Jonny" Herwarth von Bittenfeld from the German embassy.

Hilger would leak to Bohlen initial reports of the Nazi-Soviet pact of August 1939. Though neither Herwarth von Bittenfeld nor Hilger joined the Nazi party, both Soviet experts had dirtied their hands in working for German victory. After May 1945, they contacted U.S. authorities, stressed their need to escape Soviet revenge, and promised to reveal what they knew about the Russians.

Though later denying that he was "some sort of central grey eminence" in these rescue efforts, Kennan certainly sympathized. In October 1948, he applauded as "humane and decent" the work of Frank Wisner at the CIA in bringing Hilger and his family to the United States. Kennan regarded his German friend as an honorable man who had merely done his duty. He asked Wisner to share with the State Department anything valuable obtained from the informant.[81] Hilger would visit Kennan at the farm in Pennsylvania. As for "poor old Jonny," who was part Jewish, "here the charges and insinuations are even more bizarre," Kennan fumed. He admired Herwarth von Bittenfeld as a great friend of Claus von Stauffenberg who had barely escaped the latter's terrible fate when the 1944 attempt to assassinate Hitler failed.

Hurt and outraged—"I never knew I had such enemies"—Kennan did more than just condemn the studies by Loftus and by Simpson as "scurrilous and wholly disreputable." On the stationery of Stroock & Stroock & Lavan, Loftus received a sharp letter from Walter Pozen, an intellectual property attorney (and the husband of Joan Kennan). Pozen informed Loftus that "Professor Kennan enjoys a world-wide reputation as a distinguished, brilliantly insightful diplomat and historian, earning him honors and distinctions of the highest order." Hence "unfounded, untrue, and perhaps actionable" public statements by Loftus could warrant a costly libel suit.[82] Kennan later confided to Gaddis that "the letter seems to have served its purpose." Loftus pulled his punches in the published book.

To deal with Simpson, Kennan turned to his authorized biographer. The day after receiving from Kennan six single-spaced pages detailing the sagas of Hilger and Herwarth von Bittenfeld and of Loftus and Simpson, Gaddis wrote the publisher of Simpson's book, who had asked him for a blurb. While denying that it was his role as Kennan's biographer to "serve as the guardian of his reputation," he nonetheless served guard duty. He disparaged Simpson's manuscript as marred by such "sloppiness—I strain to put this as charitably as possible—" that it failed to qualify as "a work of serious historical scholarship." Atop a copy of this letter was penciled "Noted G.K."[83]

While sensationalist or pedestrian historians might bungle his legacy, Gaddis would burnish it, Kennan was sure. His initial confidence that he had chosen well with this authorized biographer slid into concern that he had chosen too well. In the years after signing the contract with Kennan, Gaddis published three influential books on the Cold War. He was honored by the prestigious Harmsworth Visiting Professorship at Oxford. At Ohio University, he built his Contemporary History Institute into a major center, where he hosted a conference of Soviet and American historians. Gaddis had the university plane fly the Kennans to that conclave, where George warned about "Nuclear Weaponry" and "Worldwide Environmental Deterioration."[84] In June 1987, he attended a conference of Cold War historians in Moscow that Gaddis had helped organize. As the scholar's career soared to the height where the *New York Times* christened him the dean of diplomatic historians, Kennan feared that the star might never get around to actually writing his biography. Compounding that anxiety was growing respect for Gaddis, who, "with his intelligence, his strength, his decency, and his relative youth," gleamed as "the hope of the country for the understanding of the past and the future."[85] Such fulsome praise underscored how the dynamics between them had reversed.

Though Gaddis had played the suitor in the late 1970s and early 1980s, Kennan did so afterward. In response to Gaddis's essay "Fault Lines, Forecasting, and the Post–Cold War World: An Experiment in Geopolitical Tectonics," which explored how historians might forecast such seismic events as the collapse of the Cold War, Kennan simply gushed. "I was overwhelmed by this paper," he confessed. "I find myself standing in the presence of one of the really great American thinkers of this age." By comparison, his own *Around the Cragged Hill* seemed "very small potatoes indeed." Then, the anxiety: "What the hell [are you] doing fooling around with a subject so insignificant as the life and work of a single man of limited distinction?" Perhaps the still-hoped-for biographer "might find it restful," after pondering weightier issues, to "slide back into the comfortable myopias of a single individual and his curious mini-accomplishments." If Gaddis decided not to take this intellectual respite, would he, Kennan implored, help him find a replacement? While he could not expect another Gaddis, he hoped for someone "better than any of those" who had already written about his life.[86]

He treasured Gaddis for still another reason. As the historian had risen in stature, he had also moved to the right in terms of his interpretation of the origins of the Cold War. He increasingly assailed the Soviet Union while absolving the United States for the tensions after 1945. He blamed much of the Cold War on the supposed paranoia of Stalin. At the 1968 seminar at the Institute for Advanced Study and on other occasions, Kennan had defended this "orthodox" interpretation of the Cold War's origins against the challenge of such "revisionists" as Walter LaFeber and Gabriel Kolko, who emphasized instead America's push for economic open doors and an informal global empire. Now Gaddis explicitly took up the cudgels. In 1983, he urged historians to move beyond revisionism to a "post-revisionist synthesis." While Gaddis's interpretation was disparaged by critics as orthodoxy with archives, it fit with Kennan's own thinking. He was so taken with this essay that he sent it to a colleague at the Institute for Advanced Study recommending his biographer for a permanent faculty appointment. That effort at the Institute went nowhere.[87] Gaddis, however, went further in assailing the revisionists. He entitled his 1992 presidential address before the Society for Historians of American Foreign Relations (SHAFR) "The Tragedy of Diplomatic History." He was mounting a broadside against the revisionist bible, William A. Williams's *The Tragedy of American Diplomacy.*

On at least three occasions from 1992 to 1997, Kennan confided to Gaddis his worry that the latter would end up not writing the biography. Another gnawing concern was that the biographer simply did not appreciate or agree with his struggle to ease the Cold War. Kennan entered his nineties fearing that, despite all his efforts, memory of his life and his lessons might be muddled.

"I think you should not unduly postpone the completion" of the biography, Kennan urged in April 1992. Confidence that Gaddis would give the public a "fair and discerning appraisal" of his life and work "has been a major source of reassurance to me." At age eighty-eight, he could not live much longer, and the book should appear not long after his death. The study's "impact (not to mention its sales) will be greatest when the public memory of me is fairly fresh." Of the five books already published about him, "three of those were written by persons quite inadequate to the task," and the other two focused on only a slice of his life. "You may be sure," he warned Gaddis, "that if nothing is done to preempt them, there will be in the immediate aftermath of my death" more aspirants "who will try their hand at the task despite their lack of qualifications for performing it." These inferior books would imperil Kennan's legacy by "weaken[ing] the impact of what you may later write." Moreover, Gaddis's exclusive access to the bulk of his papers would be difficult to sustain if, after Kennan's death, no evidence of the biography had appeared.[88]

"I hear what you're saying," Gaddis quickly responded. He reminded Kennan that in 1990, they had revised the 1982 agreement to extend his exclusive access to 2000. He would be willing to share that access if Kennan wished. He then laid out a timeline with publication set for 1998.[89]

In 1995, Kennan again affirmed both his hope that the biography would cement his ideas in the public mind and his fear that Gaddis's other opportunities would preempt the project. When the historian in November sent him a book manuscript that would be published in 1997 as *We Now Know: Rethinking Cold War History*, Kennan responded with an astounding plea: "I think it important that anything you have in mind to write about myself be completed before your book appears." Otherwise, the "volume and violence" of attention devoted to the new book would suck up all of Gaddis's time and energy. The nonagenarian had grown so anxious about the biography that he proposed reducing it to a quick study that Gaddis could sandwich in before publishing *We Now Know*.[90] As for the posthumous requirement, that might be moot in view of the recent deterioration of his heart condition, "kept in tenuous abeyance" only with a pacemaker and medications.[91]

Though his heart kept ticking, Kennan was rattled by a series of events in 1997. He marveled how Gaddis, about to assume the Robert A. Lovett Professorship of History at Yale, had advanced from being "a relatively modest scholar at a minor Ohio place of learning" to snaring a major position at a distinguished university.[92] "I fear for the effects of this change on what you call the biography," Kennan confided. Again he urged publishing without delay, even if he, Kennan, remained alive. "Do write *something*, even it is only a long essay." Only Gaddis could "bring some balance, good sense, and authority into the now rather abundant literature" pouring forth. Kennan assailed another book he totted on the negative side of the ledger, John Lamberton Harper's *American Visions of Europe* (1994), which compared the perspectives of Franklin D. Roosevelt, Dean Acheson, and Kennan. In nearly three tightly filled pages, Kennan detailed why he was "not much impressed" with this "strange," "rather curious," and "confusing" volume that evidenced little recognition of "my tragedy as a senior Washington policy-maker." The tragic element lay in his tendency to conceptualize policy "much further ahead in time, usually several years," while his colleagues and superiors suffered short-sighted vision. He added, pointedly, that Harper's omissions and distortions remained matters that you "will have to face if and when you come to grips with the causality of my life."[93]

I was partly responsible when Kennan's anxiety crescendoed in May 1997. I had published in the *Journal of American History* an article that used the techniques of literary criticism to analyze how and why Kennan's rhetoric in the long telegram and in the "X" article had packed such a punch. Through close reading of Kennan's language, I showed how he had heightened alarm over the threat from Moscow by implicitly depicting the Soviet Union and international Communism as figurative rapists, forcing their way into the vulnerable institutions of the West. Quoting a phrase from the long telegram, the essay was provocatively entitled "Unceasing Pressure for Penetration." Applying this innovative methodology to the iconic figure of Kennan in the age of the Internet provoked a storm on H-Diplo, a listserv for those interested in diplomatic history. On May 17, Gaddis sent Kennan the article and a sheaf of printouts from the listserv.

Kennan, who evidently only skimmed the essay, drew from it a distorted and unwarrantedly hurtful conclusion. Whereas I had argued that Kennan's language had depicted Soviet Communism as a rapist, he read the essay as charging his own words, and him as a person, "with concealed desires to violate, to rape, and thus to dominate." Perhaps he felt vulnerable to such an accusation because he was, as his diary made clear, suffering bouts of guilt about his behavior with women as a younger man. Clearly stung, he linked my supposed perspective with that of "Messrs. Mayer and Hikson [*sic*]. Had these critics not, after all, already demolished me—exposing me to the unpitying scrutiny of their wiser and more perceptive minds? Why did he have to re-do their work?" Gaddis, while thanking Kennan for "your crisp reaction to the soggy pontifications of Professor Costigliola," did not correct the ninety-three-year-old's misperception.[94]

The controversy rubbed Kennan's apprehensions raw. He saw a crisis looming. Gaddis was going to Yale, where demands could render it impossible to write the biography. Worse, the outpouring of wrongheaded history by the likes of Harper and Costigliola foreshadowed the flood that would follow his death. On May 22, he wrote Gaddis that the absence of the definitive biography "would invite hasty efforts on the part of various assistant professors, thirsty for tenure at God knows what places, to fill it quickly with whatever scraps of information (and the more lurid, the better) the Internet could provide." As a result the "cream . . . will then be skimmed off," leaving only "the less interesting debris to be scraped together, however authoritatively, by yourself." Rather than have his legacy reduced to tatters, Kennan would prefer a few "authoritative essays from your pen" collected in a brief book, if necessary without footnotes, but published soon. He dreaded the prospect that "something immature and superficial [would] come up first from other people's inadequate pens."[95]

While fuming at the supposed spoilers of his legacy, Kennan also disputed its presumed protector. The agreement was that Gaddis would write the biography as he saw fit without interference from his subject. Nevertheless, one issue loomed so large in Kennan's appraisal of his life's work that he could not resist some instruction. A "weak spot" in

Gaddis's otherwise excellent scholarship on the Cold War was his slighting the possibilities "for a limited military disengagement in the center of Europe, particularly in the years 1956–1957." Kremlin officials, embarrassed by the Hungarian revolt and the unrest in Poland, might have accepted a mutual U.S.-Soviet withdrawal from their "unnatural, exposed, and dangerous military confrontation in the center of Europe." The occupation armies facing each other along the tense German-German border would have gone home as Germany reunified into a neutral, disarmed nation. Such diplomacy, which Kennan had tried to nudge forward, most famously with his 1957 Reith Lectures, could have eased or ended the Cold War thirty years earlier. That happier scenario could have spared the world the risk of nuclear war over Berlin in 1958–1961 and over Cuba in 1962.[96]

During the summer of 1997, Gaddis was busy moving to New Haven, buying a house, and settling in with his new wife. Knowing Kennan as well as he did, he must have realized that the elderly man, so sensitive to criticism and so anxious to have his legacy safeguarded by an authoritative biography, remained on tenterhooks about whether the book would appear, and whether it would appreciate his efforts for disengagement. Gaddis finally replied on August 10, nearly three months after Kennan's anguished letter. He assured Kennan that he intended to write the biography, that Yale actually provided a more suitable venue and more generous leave time, and that the book would appear after Kennan's death unless he himself got "wiped out by an incautiously driven beer truck while crossing Whitney Avenue." Regarding disengagement, he soothed that he was making "just that argument" in a course lecture, and that he hoped to direct a graduate student to explore the topic.[97]

"I was much relieved by your recent letter," Kennan quickly answered. Moreover, "there is no one whom I would prefer to have as a biographer." If Gaddis were to "disappear under the wheels of the fanciful beer truck," Kennan could not imagine collaborating with anyone else. "I shudder to think to what wild and irresponsible winds my poor posthumous image would then be subjected."[98]

By 1999, the disagreement between Kennan and Gaddis over disengagement in the 1950s had widened into a polite though portentous difference over the basic rights and wrongs of the East-West conflict. Gaddis informed Kennan that "the whole question of 'missed opportunities'" was "heating up now, although the weight of the evidence seems to be tilting toward the view that there weren't very many of them," even in the 1950s. He recommended a paper done by Ruud van Dijk, his graduate student, on the Stalin Note in March 1952 proposing negotiations over the future of Germany. The dictator's apparent openness to diplomacy had figured hugely in Kennan's initial hopes and ultimate frustration as ambassador to Moscow.[99]

Kennan, now approaching ninety-five, shot back with an incisive critique of basic U.S. assumptions in the Cold War, premises that for Gaddis remained unquestioned. To van Dijk's charge that the Soviets had sought to thwart the Western program for integrating West Germany into "an essentially anti-Soviet military alliance," Kennan rejoined: "Why, of course. Why should they not have had this purpose?" What Gaddis's student had ignored were the positive possibilities in the Stalin Note, "namely *negotiation*, and especially *real* negotiation, in distinction from public posturing." That Kennan felt so deeply about the potential in such talks was expressed in his stress on those words. The Stalin Note had signaled merely the Russians' "asking price" for a deal over Germany. What the Soviets—horrified by the prospect of a revenge-minded West Germany, militarily resurgent and allied with nuclear-armed America—might have conceded during serious negotiations, no one would ever know. Van Dijk's paper contained not "the faintest evidence of any point" where Washington and its allies would consider "departing one jot from their own established positions, no matter what the Russians might have offered." The U.S. position remained the one "so beloved of American governments ever since the Civil War: unconditional surrender." Kennan admonished his biographer: "I cannot too strongly urge that you and Mr. van Dijk read . . . my Reith lectures of 1957."

Kennan was not done. Pricked by this indifference to Russian anxiety over Germany—the very concern that underlay much of Moscow's behavior throughout the Cold War—he recounted some basic history. In doing so, Kennan implicitly recanted the alarmism of the long telegram and the "X" article. A half-century earlier, he had castigated the Soviets as an "other" lacking any legitimate self-interests. Now, however, he appraised the Russian challenge after 1945 with a hardheaded empathy that, if infused into policy, might have obviated the worst of the Cold War. "Stalin and the men around him were a nasty, dangerous, and prickly bunch to deal with," he affirmed, "and no one, I believe, ever said this more emphatically and authoritatively than I did." Nevertheless, "the USSR put forward 80–90% of the ground force effort it took to defeat Hitler in Europe. This being the case, it was demanding a lot of the Soviet leaders to ask them to accept . . . their total exclusion from even the slightest voice in the future of the greater part of Germany." Since the Western powers had needed the Russians to beat the Nazis, "they had to expect to pay some price" for that aid.[100] As Kennan saw it, the price was granting the Soviets some voice in the future of Germany. He believed that what Stalin had offered in 1952 had stood within negotiating distance from what Kennan had proposed in Plan A in 1948–1949 and had continued to push for in the 1950s. In this view, much of the Cold War figured as a tragic, dangerous, and unnecessary waste. Moreover, Kennan probably thought, he and Stalin together might have settled the conflict.

Despite this basic difference, Kennan never regretted choosing the author of *Strategies of Containment* to write his authorized biography. Deep down, he had never totally left the State Department. It made sense, then, to prioritize in his biography the story of how he as a State Department official had conceptualized containment. Moreover, he believed that the success of containment would make disengagement possible. Finally, he liked Gaddis and judged him "a thoroughly honorable person." He was not so sure, however, whether the historian would do justice to his postgovernmental efforts, to his personal life, and to his philosophy.[101]

Although Kennan would never read the biography, which would appear six years after his death, a foretaste of Gaddis's account inflicted some "extremely painful [days] for me." In May 2000, happening upon his biographer's interview with J. Richardson Dilworth, a neighbor and friend, Kennan realized that Gaddis "had no idea of what was really at stake" in the "lone battle I was waging [in 1948–1958] against the almost total militarization of Western policy towards Russia." This struggle to "bring about a reasonable settlement of European problems of the immediate postwar period" ranked in Kennan's mind as "the most significant of the efforts of the first half of my career." Tilting against the Cold War, not for it, was what the former strategist accorded first importance in the story of his life. That "this battle should not be apparent even to the most serious of my postmortem biographers" meant that the efforts that had been most meaningful to him "will never find their historian or their understanding. And this is hard."[102] The historian John Lukacs, a friend, would remember that Kennan "was not very happy with his relations with Gaddis."[103]

Kennan had committed to Gaddis, believing him the sole chance for ensuring that in the future people could read an accurate, sympathetic account of his life story, career, and the lessons they embodied. He appreciated that the historian understood his conception of containment as a limited and largely political policy that could avoid both appeasement of the Russians or going to war with them. He had hitched himself to the rising star not knowing how long he himself would live nor how high Gaddis would ascend. While the biographer would fulfill Kennan's expectations with regard to the history of the early Cold War, he did not sympathize, as Kennan realized too late, with his fervent efforts to ease that conflict before it blew up into a nuclear holocaust. Indeed, Gaddis regarded the nuclear-armed standoff of the superpowers not as a recipe for disaster, but rather as a beneficent "long peace."[104] Despite all his prescience and persistence, Kennan proved unable to control the future of his past.

COPING IN THE POST–COLD WAR ERA

The drama between the biographer and the subject played out amid the surprising and sudden demise of the Cold War and the unsurprising and extended decline of Kennan. "He's always felt unwell," observed Dilworth about Kennan, though, ironically, the latter would end up living two decades longer than his neighbor.[105]

"Annelise complains, even to others, that I complain too much about my health," he complained to his diary.[106] He articulated these gripes with such precision, however, that the resulting narrative transcends the personal to become a moving story of the fate that awaits us all. He felt he was aging unevenly. The various aspects of his being—"the physical, the mental, the emotional-sexual, the imaginative, the control over the nervous structure, etc." were advancing or regressing at their own pace.[107] At other times, the collapse seemed frighteningly coordinated. "My own condition—physical, mental, and emotional—is now deteriorating rapidly, and has progressed to a point where, in addition to being physically crippled, I can no longer trust either my memory or my mental coherence."[108] "Normally, the kidney stone merely gnaws and hurts," he noted.[109] Other days it tortured him so badly that he had to inject himself with a painkiller.[110] When he finally had lithotripsy to pulverize the offender, the procedure inflicted him with uremic poisoning. In 1992, atrial fibrillation required the insertion of a pacemaker.

The surgery underscored the public notoriety that Kennan regarded as both a burden and a boon. The doctor, who had read one of his books, "bombarded the helpless me with questions about Russia. I replied as best as I could in muffled tones from underneath the blankets that had been placed over my face."[111]

Even after suffering a mild stroke he remained sharp enough to ponder such complexities as the thought processes of Jesus Christ, policy toward China, and his proposed Council of State. Increasingly focused on Christian theology, he tried to think through how Christ had mediated between God and man. "The vision Jesus had of God was one not only of imagination but of intuition and of super-conscious conviction, and it was a vision of such power and magnificence that he could see only some deeper meaning in his very awareness of it—that it must have had some ultimate reality, and that he was in some way selected as the conveyor of it to the life of his time."[112]

The longtime strategist outlined a determinedly "isolationist" foreign policy for the United States in the post–Cold War era. He would uphold the alliances with NATO and with Japan, while dealing with Latin America, Africa, the Middle East, and southern Asia only as U.S. national interests dictated. He deplored as a "dreadful error of American policy" the humanitarian mission in Somalia launched by President George H. W. Bush. Kennan pinpointed the logistical difficulties that would soon degrade an obligation to feed starving people into a rout of U.S. military forces. Such interventions "the founding fathers of this country never envisaged or would ever have approved."[113] Toward China, he advised a policy coupling respect for its impressive culture with caution regarding a population "extremely ruthless when crossed, and essentially xenophobic." While treating the Chinese with "impeccable courtesy," he would have "as little as possible to do with them." Americans "should guard against allowing our business world to develop any extensive dependence on China in commercial matters," and resist corporations seeking the "great Chinese market." Nor would he have Washington "press the Chinese government now or in the future, in matters of human rights. That is their concern, not ours."[114] Such was Kennan's feelings about human rights in other nations as well. Though he did not mention the potentially explosive issue of Taiwan, he probably would have recommended allowing the mainland to retake the island.

While buoyed by the commercial success of *Around the Cragged Hill*, a *New York Times* best seller, he also bore familiar frustrations. "Neither the Clinton administration nor the media have shown the faintest interest" in the substance of his recommendations, not even in the suggestion for a Council of State. "A strange fate, mine: to move so many compatriots, but never those in power." Though relishing the veneration "as some sort of a sage," he remained "totally without influence where it counts."[115]

Such powerlessness, coupled with weakness so extreme that some days he could not do "any normal mental work" fed his urge to escape. While in his youth he had fantasized about hiding out in some bohemian enclave where he could write his great novel, now he longed, persistently, for a small place in the country, where he could "live alone, keep a dog, feed some chickens, and stumble about among the remains of what was once a garden."[116] The idyll remained only a dream, however, since his wife refused to leave Princeton while his ambition refused to leave him.

FIGURE 39. George with grandchildren at Christmas. (Courtesy of
Grace Kennan Warnecke.)

Despite his grousing, Kennan did have friends in the Bill Clinton
administration. Watching the peaceful transfer of power at Clinton's
inauguration in January 1993 had moved him to tears. He experienced
"a moment of pride and affection for my country such as I am not often
permitted to enjoy." While appreciating President Clinton's public lauding of post–World War II "visionaries like Truman, Marshall, and Kennan," he noted that "'visionaries' was not exactly what we three gentle-
men were."[117] When the Council on Foreign Relations marked Kennan's
ninetieth birthday with a dinner for a hundred of his friends and family,
Clinton sent as his representative ambassador to the UN Madeleine
Albright, who read aloud a greeting drafted by the president. Soon after
the inauguration, Frank G. Wisner, a top official at the Defense Department and the son of Kennan's 1940s CIA associate, and Strobe Talbott,
deputy secretary of state in charge of relations with Russia, invited him
to Washington to air his views on post-Communist Russia. Though
"both men were extremely kind to me," Kennan came away "chastened
and saddened," since it was clear that his "observations were not to be

taken seriously when it came to public policy."[118] The nub was whether to expand NATO to take in Poland, Hungary, and other onetime Soviet satellites and even such former Soviet republics as Lithuania, Latvia, and Estonia.

As the issue of NATO expansion heated up in the 1990s, Talbott, who had long revered Kennan, repeatedly invited his mentor to Washington to meet with the Russia policy team. Talbott had been the future president's housemate at Oxford when both were Rhodes scholars. As a young man, he had translated *Khrushchev Remembers*, and he had later written books on the nuclear arms race in the 1980s. He treasured the memory of his first meeting with Kennan in 1969, at a dinner hosted by his Oxford tutor, Max Hayward, the famed translator of Russian literature and, coincidentally, the visitor of Svetlana Alliluyeva when she had spent the summer of 1967 secluded at the Kennan farm.

At a State Department dinner honoring Kennan, Talbott and Secretary of State Warren Christopher relayed the president's request for a one-word slogan with which to characterize U.S. foreign policy. With passion, Kennan, who had long regarded containment as an albatross around his neck, cautioned against repeating his mistake of employing a bumper sticker that would encourage "great and misleading oversimplification of analysis and policy." Far better, he urged, was to explain the policy with a thoughtful paragraph or more. On hearing this exchange, Clinton remarked with a laugh, "Well, that's why Kennan's a great diplomat and scholar and not a politician."[119] Never easy on himself, the honored guest spent much of his evening at the State Department ruminating how, decades ago, John F. Dulles had casually fired him, and how "there was no one in the building whom I knew well enough to say good-bye to except the charming 5th floor receptionist."[120]

An elephantine memory for ancient slights spurred Kennan's initial enthusiasm for Clinton's invitation to accompany him to Moscow to celebrate the fiftieth anniversary of V-E Day. He longed to go. "I was, after all, the senior American official present in Moscow on that memorable day." And it "would give me much satisfaction to be there as an honored and friendly guest of the government in the Kremlin in place of the dangerous enemy that I was always supposed to be," not only when he was expelled in 1952, but also when he had thwarted the police and had "addressed the cheering Soviet crowd" in May 1945. That magical moment, when he had felt such respect and affection from ordinary Russians, would forever remain a highlight of his life. Now, a half-century later, Annelise, his children, and his doctor—who pronounced him healthy despite "the failing heart and the arthritic knees"—all urged the ninety-one-year-old to go with Clinton. Yet upon waking every morning, "I find myself in such a condition that I say to myself: 'Never, never. Under no circumstances should I ever attempt anything like that.'"[121]

While Kennan appreciated the kindness of Talbott and Clinton, he would have preferred influencing their decisions. By January 1997, with plans to expand NATO advancing, the veteran strategist warned Talbott that he was going public with his opposition. The many people who looked to him for guidance and the fateful importance of the issue impelled him to speak out. He warned, presciently, that in pushing "NATO's borders smack up to those of Russia we are making the greatest mistake of the entire post-Cold-War era." The provocation would inflame the nationalistic, anti-Western, and militaristic tendencies within Russia, hobble the fragile democracy, and set back further nuclear arms reductions. It would sour Russian policy toward the West. Having spent nearly a half-century trying to ease tensions with Russia, Kennan was aghast at a policy that would "restore the atmosphere of the Cold War."

Endowing his personhood as a kind of statehood, he affirmed that just as Clinton officials, "without consulting me, have nailed their flag to their mast, so must I nail my flag to mine. Let them see how they can extract themselves from the mess they themselves have created." His op-ed piece in the *New York Times*, entitled "A Fateful Error," galvanized attention. Commentators in Germany and in Russia took notice. The same day, perhaps by coincidence, the French prime minister called for a NATO summit to discuss these issues. Kennan congratulated himself that even if "I did not change American policy by this intervention, I at least set the policy makers . . . back on their heels."

Kennan caught Clinton's attention. A copy of the op-ed essay lay on the president's desk as he pressed Talbott: "Why isn't Kennan right?" Clinton often probed his advisers sharply to find the holes in measures to which he was already committed. "But in this case," Talbott recalled, "there was a hint of doubt about the policy itself—not the desirability of enlarging NATO, but the feasibility of reconciling it with the integration of Russia." A savvy politician, Clinton worried about this "forecast of a train wreck from a revered figure with a reputation for being prophetic about Russia." Unfortunately for the future of U.S.-Russian relations, however, Talbott convinced his boss that on this issue, his former mentor was wrong. The Russians would adjust to an expanded NATO, he over-optimistically assured the president.[122]

Although Kennan's skirmish had put NATO expansion temporarily on the defensive, he lost the battle. He predicted "a new Cold War, probably ending in a hot one, and the end of the effort to achieve a workable democracy in Russia."[123] Despite his prescience, most others, including Annelise and Marion Dönhoff, editor of *Die Zeit* and a close personal friend, did not share it.[124] He felt alone and defeated. In this needless provocation of Russia, there loomed "the final failure of the efforts to which I have given so large a portion of my life: the effort to find a reasonable area of understanding and sympathy between the great Russian people and our own. But how old I am! How weak! How helpless!"[125]

With the regime that had perpetrated the purges no longer running the Kremlin, Kennan inclined more than ever toward Russia. In a 1999 interview with his friend, the Princeton historian Richard Ullman, Kennan, now ninety-five, repeatedly referred to the Russians as in many ways a great people. By contrast, "we are not, really, all that great." He empathized with the suffering and death inflicted on the Russians by a century of violence and repression. Kennan opposed not only the expansion of NATO into former Soviet domains, but also the premise that these reborn nations should be protected by the West. Instead, the former U.S. policy planner viewed geostrategy also from the perspective of Moscow. "These are sensitive borders," Kennan emphasized in reference to the lines once again separating Latvia, Lithuania, and Estonia from Russia. These nations "were included in the Russian empire for nearly two hundred years" prior to their independence after the First World War. And then "it took Hitler to virtually compel the Russian government to take them over in 1939." Moreover, the Russians reoccupied the Baltic nations in 1944–1945 "in the process of pushing the German army out of that region—a process which had our most compete and enthusiastic approval." While he had supported the independence of these small nations, he predicted that integrating them into "an anti-Russian military alliance" would prove dangerously shortsighted. Opining on another issue that would inflame relations with Russia in the twenty-first century, Kennan deplored the "thoughtless tossing" into Ukraine "the totally un-Ukrainian Crimean peninsula, together with one of the three greatest Russian naval bases."[126]

While sweet on Russia, Kennan had soured on America. As a friend once remarked, Kennan in his reactions to the United States seemed the spurned lover. He mocked U.S. expectations of bringing Western ways to the Chinese. "They are not going to love us, no matter what we do. They are not going to become like us," he warned presciently. Exasperated with America's sense of mission, he exclaimed: "For goodness' sake, can't we get away from that sort of nonsense? Let people be what they are." Kennan disputed policy makers and pundits who celebrated America's military supremacy in a so-called unipolar global system: "This planet is never going to be ruled from any political center, whatever the military power." No fan of American soft power either, he mocked the export of the "cheapest, silliest, and most disreputable manifestations of our 'culture.'" He told Ullman that the United States ranked "as the world's intellectual and spiritual dunce."[127]

PERSISTENCE

Though aging, Kennan seemed never at a loss for projects. As workers installed a seat lift to spare his arthritic knees from climbing the stairs, he faithfully recorded their progress and the costs of the construction in a special journal, "Diary of the Princeton House & Property."[128] In addition to keeping his principal diary from the age of eleven to 100, Kennan reported in a Farm Diary on the weather, crops and animals, and family and visitors to the farm in Pennsylvania. On occasion he jotted down more personal observations in this journal as well as in the one maintained at the summer house near Kristiansand, Norway. He kept a separate diary of his dreams.

One year, he packed for the annual vacation on the Norwegian coast a massive volume of Shakespeare's collected works. He dutifully ploughed through it play by play. Another year, "I brought along the *Confessions of St. Augustine*, and I am, at this moment, deeply into them." Not for the first time, he empathized with an overworked, long-suffering God. The "extremely personal nature of St. Augustine's relationship to God" struck him as unfairly trying to monopolize "the concerns and attentions of the Deity." After all, many others had also needed His succor. Addressing St. Augustine in his diary, Kennan admonished: Although you were a great man, "it was not for you" to claim so "high a place in the measure of God's values." He recalled a religious placard somewhere in England that read "Jesus saves," to which some irreverent—or really reverent?—person had added: "Jesus is tired. Save yourself."[129]

George himself seemed tireless in researching his final book, on the genealogy of the Kennan family.[130] From Scotland to Connecticut, to Massachusetts, to New York, he poked around local historical societies tracing the wanderings of his forebears. In a letter to a grandson, to be opened in the future when the boy reached twenty, Kennan explained his "strong feelings about the importance, for anyone, of a sense of family continuity—the feeling that one is not alone, either upwards or downwards."[131] He intended the letter, like so many of his efforts, to reach into the future, to project his voice beyond his death.

Convinced of the lasting grip of heredity, Kennan also reached back to the past, searching for the origin of his own bent toward scholarship. That surely did not stem from the practical-minded Jameses of his mother's family, he believed. He concluded rather that the love for books prominent among the Kennans traced back to his great-great-great-grandmother, Abigail Sherman, born in 1747 in Woodbury, Connecticut, who married a George Kennan born in 1752. From his research Kennan surmised that Abigail was actually an illegitimate child. Perhaps, he suggested to a cousin, "the real father was none other than Ezra

Stiles, good friend of Ben Franklin, reportedly the most learned man in the New England of his time, and President of Yale University."[132] While acknowledging the unlikelihood of such aristocratic ancestry and the impossibility of proving it, Kennan, in laying out this prospect, revealed how much it intrigued him.

Probing ultimate origins and meaning figured also in Kennan's recording his dreams in a special diary. He believed that his nighttime visions stemmed from some external force trying to tell him something.

In 1997–1998, a series of dreams "rocked me as nothing" before. They "confronted me with all my sexual emotional delinquencies," particularly those from a "time more than fifty years ago." The dreams underscored how grievously he had "inflicted, or could have inflicted, suffering or injuries to relatively innocent persons of the other sex." Always elusive about the details, he nevertheless also implied the possible victimizing of a child. One dream featured "a weird semi-nocturnal scene of a great, tireless, cold, and deserted plateau, with only one tiny human figure—far away—lost, abandoned, and desperate. The plight was, in some way, my doing."[133]

The night visions reflected his decades-long struggle between sexual creativity and marital obligation. Fifty years earlier, in the 1940s, Kennan had stood at the apex of his prestige and influence. Tall, blue-eyed, and charming, he had women flocking around him. He traveled frequently. His marriage was not the happiest. His belief in Freud's notion that sexual freedom accorded with creativity offered justification. No doubt he had taken advantage of the ample opportunity for extramarital affairs. While guilt now spurred the dreams, rationalization soothed the daytime reasoning. He could not help having a "split personality," he told himself. The division dated, "I am sure, from the day in April 1904 when my infantile relationship to my mother was suddenly torn apart by her sudden and tragic death." Moreover, no matter how deplorable and demanding of regret his "corruption and helplessness" had been, those were sins he shared with "the remainder of humanity."[134]

Guilt about past transgressions did not prevent present-day squabbles with Annelise. With the children gone, she alone bore the fury of his occasional tirades. Their eldest daughter, Grace, recalled that "when my father became angry it felt like a searing white heat that scorched everything in its path. Our brilliant, thoughtful, charismatic father suddenly turned into a petulant, irrational man with whom one could not argue and from whom I longed to escape."[135] Though they had long ago grown comfortable with their marriage, George and Annelise differed over where to live. She encouraged their sojourns to visit friends in Florida, the Caribbean, and Maine. He endured "an agonizing and absurd evening wrangling with Annelise" about the pace of their life. The never-ending engagements to meet people and write this or that were exhausting him. He feared making a fool of himself. But "on the other side of the marital table—no understanding for any of this." You do all right, she insisted.[136] Annelise was right; George did continue to perform. And, after all, he himself had taken on these obligations.

Kennan's diary continued to exaggerate reports of his imminent death. In October 1999, a short walk along Nassau Street in Princeton led him to near collapse. "In the shop, where I bought a book, I was a feeble caricature of my former self. Does so rapid a physical and nervous decline mean the rapid descent to the end?"[137] In June 2001, with nearly four years left to go, he "was struck by a total recognition—total, unquestionable, and susceptible of no doubt or vacillation—that I was a dying man." The end "could not be very far off." Feeling shaky and confused, he nonetheless ventured to his office at the Institute. For the last time, he looked out at the massive trees of the Institute Woods, gathered up a few papers and books, and arranged for the disposal of the remainder.[138]

While the tragedy of the terrorist attacks on September 11, 2001, saddened Kennan, the aggressively military response of the George W. Bush administration infused his life with renewed purpose. He could not help but regard himself as an adviser on call. Though the Bush administration had neither consulted him nor given him reason to believe his opinion would be welcomed, the former strategist nonetheless worried about the "multiple, unnecessary, and grave dangers" incurred by the invasion of Afghanistan in pursuit of the terrorist leader Osama bin Laden. This latest war had turned him into "more of an isolationist than ever" while reinforcing his wish that the United States would develop domestic alternatives to Middle Eastern oil.[139] In 2002, he mused about collecting his thoughts on public issues in a book entitled *An Old Man's Dream*. Then, overwhelmed by all that would require, he dropped the idea. "My mind is a hodgepodge of random, uncoordinated impulses and reflections," he confessed at age ninety-eight. He resolved to "let them flow as they may, like water slowly seeping through a swamp."[140]

Kennan's horror at the Bush administration's push for war against Iraq based on flimsy evidence of weapons of mass destruction and links with terrorists organized those impulses and reflections into cogent analysis. This would prove the strategist's last hurrah as a public critic of U.S. foreign policy. When the couple caring for them in their Hodge Road house in Princeton went on vacation, Annelise and George moved for a month into a nursing home in Washington. He hated it, grousing that the room was alternately too cold or too hot. Arthritis now confined him to a wheelchair. Nevertheless, when President Bush on September 17, 2002, announced that the United States would henceforth exercise preemptive war rather than containment against its enemies, Kennan rallied a response.

At a small press conference held at the apartment of his old friend former Senator Eugene McCarthy, Kennan predicted the disaster that would indeed flow from Bush's invasion of Iraq. The history of American diplomacy demonstrated that while "you might start a war with certain things on your mind . . . in the end you found yourself fighting for entirely different things that you had never thought of before." He charged, correctly as it would turn out, that the administration had no "realistic plans for dealing with the great state of confusion in Iraqian affairs" after the dictator Saddam Hussein was eliminated. U.S. military force would aggravate rather than alleviate the problem. While opposing a switch from the doctrine of containment to that of preemption because it would incur more wars, Kennan, taking the broadest view, announced: "I deplore doctrines." A doctrine "pins you down" to conduct in situations you cannot foresee, "which is a great mistake in principle." Containment had applied to a specific situation in 1946–1947.

He volunteered further advice, none of it new but all of it wise. Even as the world's sole superpower, the United States could not "confront all the painful and dangerous situations that exist in the world. That's beyond our capabilities." Peaceful solutions remained almost always preferable because "war seldom ever leads to good results." Congress had the obligation to check the president's rush to war. Finally, reaching back to the past, Kennan half-defended a former nemesis. While Saddam Hussein admired Stalin, "the streak of adventurism that has marked Saddam's behavior was quite foreign to Stalin."[141]

Kennan's condition, always ailing but never totally failing, worsened in 2003. By midyear, he was "totally confused about time" on the calendar. At year's end, his ability to focus had shrunk to mere hours. "My limit of successful effort is the single 60-minute hour," he scratched in the diary. He resolved to mark the passage of each hour. But then he noticed the clock showed that two hours had elapsed without any notation by him. "Where do we go from there?" he wondered. "And what becomes of my good intentions? To give up? Nothing left, then, than the end." Ever stubborn, ever dutiful, he resolved, "So: struggle along."

Kennan also remained a hypochondriac. In his last years, he wrote detailed letters to his Princeton physician, Dr. Wei, interpreting his symptoms and proffering a diagnosis. He was mobilizing his feelings, intuition, and thinking to probe the underlying realities of his body and mind, just as years before he had tried to discern the murky realities in the Kremlin. Characteristically, he was disciplining his feelings by incorporating them into his analysis. In addition to trying to understand, and so to some extent control, his health, Kennan at the very end also sought to understand and manage his dying. With Mary A. Bundy, who had recently lost Bill, "he wanted to talk about death a lot. He wanted to know how death occurred."[142]

Perhaps Kennan throughout his life sought such control over matters because he had lacked control over the signature trauma of his life, losing his mother. A few days before the April 2003 interview with Doug James, George asked Betsy Barrett, his live-in nurse, to drive him to the Episcopal Church in Princeton. It was precisely ninety-nine years since his mother had died. Although nearly crippled by the arthritis in his knees, he hobbled with a cane to the altar. There he knelt on those painful knees to pray for his mother. Afterward, he told Betsy that he hoped he could finally soothe the sorrow in his heart.[143]

—————

Kennan succeeded in pulling himself together for the 100th birthday celebration in his honor at the Institute for Advanced Study. He did not attend a ceremony sponsored by Princeton University, at which hundreds attended, Secretary of State Colin Powell spoke, and Gaddis gave the keynote address. With his mind slipping, Kennan tried to render the disability into a task. He started a list of the "Reality and Unreality in My Recent Memory." He then tried to stem the engulfing confusion with a time line of his career—only to abandon the effort amid a jumble of inaccuracies. Toward the end, his hearing failed, and his tongue had difficulty forming words. His eloquence was now muffled by his garbled speech and difficulty in writing. But he never gave up trying to hold on to his ability to reason. Shortly before he died on March 17, 2005—one year, one month, and one day after his 101st birthday, and during the always difficult lead-up to the anniversary of his mother's death—George was visited by his friend Bill Riley. Riley recalled that "George indicated he wanted me to come closer, and I put my ear to his mouth." George managed to whisper, "'Bill, I had planned for everything except this.' What I took him to mean was that he was completely prepared to die, but not to lose his ability to think clearly."

Kennan did think clearly. Despite his prejudices and quirks—and despite all the honors accorded him—Kennan remains the underappreciated thinker and activist. He spent four decades trying to ease a Cold War that he had helped instigate. Then he devoted the last years of his life to heading off yet another unwise confrontation with Russia. Kennan ranked not only as a pioneering environmentalist, but also as a clear-eyed critic who appreciated that industrialism itself was the tragic misunderstanding distorting people's relations with each other and with nature.

THE LIMITS OF HONOR

FEW PRIVATE CITIZENS IN U.S. history have received the overt honors heaped upon George F. Kennan in his last year. On February 18, 2004, the Institute for Advanced Study in Princeton celebrated Kennan's 100th birthday with a symposium featuring former Secretary of State Lawrence S. Eagleburger, the top Russian experts of the Ronald Reagan and Bill Clinton administrations, and the last Soviet foreign minister. Though frail and hobbled by arthritis in his knees, Kennan, still acute of mind, was wheeled into the elegant, wood-paneled auditorium at the Institute. His brief remarks demonstrated that he had not lost his ability to command a room or crack a joke. Kennan, emphasizing how much his half-century on the faculty had meant to him, apologized for not having done much scholarship in his late nineties. Two days later, Princeton University paid homage as some seven hundred admirers convened to hear Colin Powell, who had just stepped down as secretary of state, and a roster of other dignitaries. A bit more than a year later, after Kennan died on March 17, 2005, Powell again signaled his esteem by attending a memorial service at the Washington National Cathedral. Also paying their respects were Secretary of State Condoleezza Rice, former National Security Adviser Zbigniew Brzezinski, and an ensemble of family members, foreign diplomats, and friends of Kennan. Although former President Bill Clinton did not attend, he wrote a tribute that was read during the service.

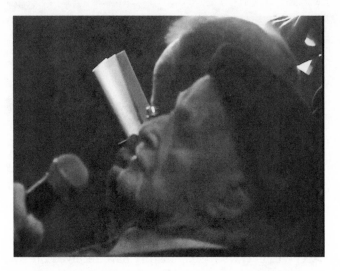

FIGURE 40. From a video of Kennan at his 100th birthday
celebration held at the Institute for Advanced Study.
(Courtesy of Institute for Advanced Study.)

How did this adulation fit with Kennan's frequent complaint that despite all the honor bestowed upon him, he was not listened to in the venues that meant the most to him, the corridors of power in Washington? Did the admiration for him mean that he was wrong about his lack of influence? Or did the idolizing of Kennan ironically contribute to his failure, at least since 1949, to sway U.S. foreign policy and domestic affairs? A close examination of the words and tone at these salutes illustrates how honoring Kennan could substitute for, or actually impede, heeding or even hearing him.

Telling evidence came from the off-the-cuff remarks of Eagleburger, who had worked with Ambassador Kennan in the Belgrade embassy in the 1960s, regarded him as a mentor, and knew him well. The former secretary of state started to say, "George Kennan is a man of . . ." Then he paused, cupped his face with upraised fingers in a gesture of seeming exasperated frustration, and blurted out, "I've never totally understood him. I don't think anybody else can." What Eagleburger was expressing was a common sentiment, rooted in the dissonance between what Kennan was best known for and the full spectrum of his ideas.[1]

Fully understanding Kennan required seriously weighing his beliefs and what he was trying to achieve over the total span of his life, not just when he wrote the long telegram and the "X" article in 1946 and 1947. Like many other pillars of the foreign policy establishment, Eagleburger admired Kennan while remaining skeptical of his efforts to ease or end the Cold War. Even as he praised the author of containment as the best Foreign Service officer in the history of the State Department, Eagleburger felt compelled to reiterate the stock argument that a half-century of huge U.S. military expenditures had been necessary to defeat the Soviet Union. That claim flew in the face of Kennan's thesis that such spending had heightened dangerous tensions that diplomacy could have relieved decades earlier.

To be fair to Eagleburger, his inability to totally understand Kennan stemmed in part from the sage's detachment from his own time. Kennan regarded himself as the child of an earlier epoch. Throughout the twentieth century he would remain shaped by what he had encountered in Milwaukee, Princeton, Washington, Riga, and Berlin in the 1910s and 1920s. He embodied a package deal molded by a bygone era. His racist, misogynistic, and anti-Semitic inclinations could outrage late twentieth century ears. His anachronistic idiosyncrasies, such as championing artisanal over industrial production, could amuse—or prod reflection. Of greatest consequence, however, was his perspective on foreign affairs. Here an old-fashioned sense of limits about America's role in the world, faith in diplomacy, prescience about the future, and appreciation for Moscow's dilemmas fused into incisive criticism of the Cold War. The singularity of Kennan's political viewpoint reinforced the loneliness arising from his personal life. "My mental processes will never be understood by anyone else," he had concluded while still a young man.[2]

Eagleburger did, however, grasp Kennan's fraught relationship with the doctrine that would forever cling to his name. "Kennan was the author of containment and has been running away from it ever since."[3] The strategist had been fleeing his progeny not only because the doctrine had become militarized, but also because he had soon come to believe that it was time to move on from containing the Soviets to compromising with them. A man who loved Russia profoundly, he wanted the United States not to triumph over the Soviet Union, but rather to negotiate an honorable settlement that would reduce tensions, restore active diplomacy, and lead to a mutual pullback from Europe.

Kennan viewed containment as a postulate: first limit Soviet political expansion in Western Europe by deploying economic and political measures, such as the Marshall Plan, then negotiate a deal with Moscow. To Kennan's frustration, containment developed instead into an axiom: an ongoing state of tension that brought a kind of stability to international relations, enabled continued military spending, and enhanced Washington's influence with its allies. To be sure, Kennan bore some blame for what he deplored. In 1946–1947, he had not just launched the containment doctrine, he had done so with frightening language that made a military buildup seem necessary. Almost immediately, he protested that he was being misunderstood. He argued against massive armaments and opposed making nuclear weapons the cornerstone of the U.S. arsenal. The strategist and later historian never regarded the deterrence doctrine of mutual assured destruction as anything but mad. Finally, as Kennan approached what he believed was impending death, he admitted his responsibility in the militarizing of containment. In a 1996 television interview with the political commentator David Gergen, he acknowledged that regarding this misunderstanding of containment, "it's my fault that it was. I should have emphasized [in the "X" article] that I didn't suspect [the Soviets] of any desire to launch an attack on us. I didn't think I needed to explain that, but I should have done it."[4]

Kennan's rejection of so much Cold War theology proved difficult, however, for many officials and commentators to grasp. Cognitive dissonance prevailed. U.S. leaders and opinion makers clung to containment and continued to associate the author with the doctrine. No matter what Kennan did or said after 1950, it remained overshadowed by his manifestos of 1946–1947. After X's prediction came true with the collapse of the Soviet Union in 1991, the storyline of the farsighted young State Department official and his ingenious, ultimately triumphant plan for halting Soviet aggression became even more entrenched. This crowding out from the public memory of what Kennan had heroically worked for during the second half of his life persisted, sadly, with the homage paid to him in 2004–2005.

Before a large crowd in Princeton University's Richardson Auditorium, Colin Powell related that soon after he was sworn in as secretary of state, he received an "unexpected, unsolicited," but nonetheless "wonderful" letter from George F. Kennan. The letter offered detailed tips on how to cope with the demands of his new position. Though startled, Powell graciously replied that he hoped to receive such "letters of advice on a regular basis." To which the elder statesman shot back, "I'm 97 years old. I do not intend to write you letters on a regular basis." Nevertheless, Kennan being Kennan, a few months later he did send Powell another letter. In relating this story, the former secretary of state referred to Kennan's having reached the century mark. What's the secret to such longevity, he asked the audience. "Is it diet? Is it exercise? Is it just being stubborn? What is it? It's hard to say, but in Ambassador Kennan's case I wonder if it just has anything to do with writing letters to people."[5]

While the audience laughed, Powell had a point. Kennan's belief in his responsibility to advise the U.S. government and his confidence that his advice was needed gave him reason to live. Alerted that Powell would honor him with a visit to his Hodge Road home, Kennan mustered his sense of duty and decorum. He insisted on getting out of bed, dressing, and standing erect to greet the former head of the department that he had served for decades and had never stopped loving.[6]

In his keynote address, Powell lauded Kennan not only for having witnessed seminal events but also for having shaped and interpreted that history. The former secretary, who had evidently read or at least been briefed on Kennan's memoir, praised its author for grasping "the link between diplomacy and human nature," for showing "how to get under the human skin of international politics." Powell then reminisced about how, as national security adviser under President Ronald Reagan and as chairman of the Joint Chiefs of Staff under President George H. W. Bush, he had witnessed the end of the Cold War. Powell stressed that the coming true of the prediction by Kennan that the Soviet Union, once contained, would eventually mellow and break up offered still more grounds for honoring him.

Nevertheless, despite the dignitary's respect for the longevity, insight, and prescience of the honoree, he underestimated the significance, indeed the flawed greatness of the man. In praising the conventional Kennan, Powell missed the unconventional Kennan: the marathon critic of the Cold War he had helped launch, the environmentalist who pinpointed industrialism as the root problem, and the skeptic of American society whose vision was alternately clearsighted and blinkered by prejudice.

Though no doubt pleased by all this attention, Kennan was probably also disheartened by what Powell cited as his core beliefs. In spite of what Kennan had argued in policy documents as well as in decades of public testimony, lectures, articles, and books, the former secretary attributed to the iconoclast conventional American ideology. Demonstrating that he had little idea of what Kennan really stood for or what he had been trying to do in the fifty-seven years since publishing the "X" article, Powell asserted that the sage believed not only in power politics but also in the need to "embrace and to be guided by noble ideals," goals "cherished on each and every continent," especially the objective of "human rights for every man, woman, and child on this earth."[7] In actuality, Kennan fumed at the conceit that the rest of the world should or would adopt American ideals. He scoffed at aspirations for universal human rights as a chimera and an assault on national sovereignty.

Kennan did not embrace Powell's ideals of mass democracy, freedom of enterprise, and the pursuit of consumer culture at home along with the management of an informal empire abroad. Rather, he argued for cautious limits to U.S. engagement with other nations. With regard to domestic affairs, Kennan believed in individual responsibility and identity, policy by trained experts, planning of economic activity, restraint of consumption, and preference for artisanal over industrial production. If change were necessary, it should be slow and organic. Most "progress" was suspect. Respecting the environment remained paramount.

The final address on that long day of celebration at Princeton in February 2004 came from someone who knew Kennan far better than Powell or any of the other nine speakers. John Lewis Gaddis, the authorized biographer with exclusive access to the bulk of Kennan's

papers, including the intimate diaries, had, over the course of two decades, conducted eight interviews with George and more than thirty
with his wife, Annelise, his siblings, and personal and professional associates. Moreover, the historian had grown personally close to George,
with whom he exchanged many letters, and perhaps even closer to Annelise. Nevertheless, despite this unparalleled, wholesale access to his
subject, Gaddis retailed the standard narrative. He highlighted the
Kennan of the long telegram while obscuring Kennan the would-be
peacemaker.

As the hundreds of listeners in the huge auditorium settled down
with their buffet dinners, they heard Gaddis heap yet more honor on
the great man. Kennan would not be forgotten, because "greatness is
one of the things that brings about the transition from mortality to im-
mortality." While citing Kennan's work as a historian, his eloquence as
a writer, and his career as a philosopher as further qualifications for
greatness, Gaddis ranked first and foremost the impact of his long telegram and "X" article. "More than any other individual, Kennan illuminated a path away from the self-destruction of the first half of the twentieth century. What Kennan opened up in February 1946 was a way out
of all this." His Grand Strategy of containment had "removed the danger
of a great power war and had revived capitalism."

Removing the danger of a major war was precisely what he had *not*
achieved, Kennan would have protested if not rendered frail by the
weight of his 100 years. While containment in 1946–1947 had offered a
way out of the perceived dilemma of appeasement or war, the subsequent militarization of the Cold War and the buildup of huge nuclear
arsenals had made the danger of a major war far more ghastly. Of Kennan's half-century of efforts to promote negotiations between Washington and Moscow, Gaddis said nothing. Similarly, Kennan's impassioned
environmentalism and his perception of the destructive effects of industrialism on how people interacted with each other and with nature were
barely alluded to, and then as Kennanish oddities. As someone who
would have been happier living in an earlier century, Gaddis noted,
Kennan displayed an "occasional tendency to rant against favorite tar-
gets, such as automobiles, television, the U.S. Congress, and the state of

California." This was Kennan as comic relief, someone whose anachronisms merited a fond chuckle rather than serious consideration.[8]

While Gaddis, U.S. political leaders, and much of the public applauded the containment doctrine in 1946–1947, they balked at following Kennan's subsequent recommendations. Those ideas entailed patience, sacrifice, and restraint—not prominent American traits. While venerating the elderly man as a sage and as a prophet, Americans paid little heed to his message. Ironically, the honor that enveloped Kennan when his predictions came true also encased him.

The containment of Kennan by the containment doctrine chalked the bounds of the memorial service held at the Washington National Cathedral on April 6, 2005, following his death a month earlier. "Memorial for Kennan Recalls Drama of Cold War Tensions," headlined the *New York Times* story of the event attended by hundreds, including Powell and other dignitaries. The Kennan children who spoke tried to move the conversation beyond 1946–1947. Grace Kennan Warnecke noted the address to Congress by the post–Cold War president of Ukraine that very day. Christopher Kennan hoped that his father's relevance had not ended with the Cold War. Rather, "Dad left us with a lot to think about." Nevertheless, the thrust of the media coverage was summed up in the letter from former president Bill Clinton that was read to the congregation. Clinton praised Kennan as the man "who shaped the discourse and guided the policy of this country for more than fifty years," in other words, since the start of the Cold War.[9]

Clinton's message inadvertently pointed out the frustration of Kennan and the loss to presidents such as himself. The far-seeing strategist had wanted nothing more than, as Clinton put it, to shape the conversation and guide the direction of the United States, not just in containing Soviet expansion in Europe, but after that. As early as 1948–1949, with containment largely achieved, Kennan had envisioned pursuing serious diplomacy with Moscow to achieve a political settlement, a lowering of tensions, and containment of the truly horrifying menace: nuclear weapons. In restricting its vision to the success of the first part of Kennan's career as a strategist, the prevailing judgment of history reinscribed the failure of the far longer second phase, when he tried in vain to push for negotiations. As Kennan himself often lamented, despite his legion of admirers, his influence where it counted, in the corridors of power, remained next to nil.

Looking down from Heaven, Kennan probably would have regarded the ceremony, despite the words of tribute, the spring sunshine streaming through the stained-glass windows, and the beautiful music—appropriately, "Vocalise," composed by the Russian aristocrat Sergei Rachmaninoff shortly before the Bolshevik revolution—as nonetheless disappointing. Here was the final demonstration of the limits that had bedeviled his aspirations, despite all his talent and relentless effort.

In his lifetime, Kennan had found such memorial services at the Washington National Cathedral, such as that for Walter Lippmann in 1975, could spur "highly egoistic and improper, but very human thoughts." Listening to praise for the famed commentator on foreign affairs had prompted Kennan to appraise himself. How this proud yet self-critical man judged himself figures appropriately in our own evaluation of him. The tribute to Lippmann, he rued, highlighted "my failure, as great as his success, to make any mark upon the governing establishment of this country." Acknowledging his own "many faults," Kennan nonetheless reckoned he had "an education broader if less deep than [Lippmanns's], a mind no less powerful, [and] a stylistic ability fully as great." His insight appeared "less practical, less adjusted to the contemporary scene, less immediately useful," but also for that very reason, "bolder, more penetrating, and more prophetic than his." Kennan ranked himself as one of the few who matched Lippmann. Nevertheless, and the repetition of the plaint evidenced how painfully it ate at him, his policy recommendations had "fallen in Washington only on deaf ears."[10]

A pair of those deaf ears belonged to Richard Holbrooke, a hard-driving leader of the Democratic Party's foreign policy establishment who had negotiated the Bosnian peace accords in the mid-1990s. Like Eagleburger and others, he "greatly admired" Kennan, "but disagreed with him profoundly" on most issues other than containment. Reflecting on Kennan's passing in an op-ed, Holbrooke could not help but genuflect before the "most famous telegram in U.S. diplomatic history" and the "most influential article ever written on American foreign policy." Nonetheless, he faulted the great man for opposing NATO expansion into former Soviet domains and U.S. intervention in such places as the Balkans.

More telling than disagreement over specific policies, however, was Holbrooke's relish in reviving an old story. It originated with former Secretary of State Dean Acheson, who in 1958 had mobilized the establishment not only to oppose Kennan on disengagement, but also to humiliate him publicly. Acheson once told a Yale student named Bob Woodward "that Kennan reminded him of his father's old horse who, when crossing wooden bridges, would make a lot of noise, then stop, alarmed by the racket he had caused." The underlying logic in what Holbrooke termed this "wonderful description" disparaged Kennan and his politics in multiple ways. Old horses and wooden bridges had no practical role to play in modern America. In giving lectures and in writing articles to drum up support for easing the Cold War, Kennan was in effect making a lot of noise and then growing emotional at the unnecessary racket that he himself had caused. The lesson of the tale: no need to take seriously most of what Kennan had said or written after 1949.

The subtle ways in which honoring Kennan could excuse admirers from heeding him went beyond focusing on nothing but containment. Like Holbrooke, Eagleburger and Strobe Talbott, (formerly the Clinton administration's expert on Russia and subsequently president of the Brookings Institution) both mixed their praise for Kennan with caution about the seductiveness of his words. Talbott esteemed Kennan as "a higher contrarian," he told the gathering at the Institute. Each year in traveling from Washington to New York for the meeting of the United Nations General Assembly, Talbott went by automobile so that he and a couple of Foreign Service officers could stop off in Princeton to talk with Kennan. "I went out of my way to get criticism directly from George," he recounted, "because he was so constructive." He remembered Kennan's warnings against "American triumphalism, American exceptionalism, Wilsonianism." Although neither Talbott nor, probably, Kennan put it that way, the elderly man was challenging prevailing American ideology.

Talbott's fondness and respect for Kennan were palpable. He especially admired his mastery of the English language. All the more significant, then, that Talbott prefaced his story of seeking out Kennan's opinion by quoting Acheson's deflating critique: "The problem with George is that he writes so damned well that he can convince you of *anything*, including some of the *worst* ideas." In emphasizing these two words, Talbott got a knowing laugh—this from an audience of admirers on Kennan's home turf. The very elegance of Kennan's prose rendered him dangerous. The logic of Talbott's remarks was that only by lashing yourself to the mast of orthodoxy could you steer safely past the sirens of Kennan's seductively phrased ideas. In giving Acheson's story such a prominent position in his remarks, Talbott may also have been explaining how he had resisted Kennan's repeated pleas not to expand NATO into Eastern Europe. Listening to Talbott's account, Eagleburger, chuckling, chimed in with his own memory of Acheson's telling a similar story at Kennan's expense.

It was all quite jovial, and Acheson's arrogance was also subject to jest. Nevertheless, most at stake here was Kennan's credibility as a serious critic of U.S. foreign policy. In hearing and in honoring the elderly man over the years, Talbott had also insulated himself from heeding him. Holbrooke, Talbott, and Eagleburger all made a point of invoking Acheson, the gruff symbol of Cold War orthodoxy and the authority figure who had publicly disparaged Kennan, to explain and to reinscribe the sharp limits of the latter's influence. Kennan's words, the emotional force propelling them, and the decades-long perspective that he brought to current events all brought him respect. Nevertheless, he challenged the Cold War and post–Cold War status quo more than those in authority were willing to accept. Honoring George offered a way to square the circle.

One of the few who commented on Kennan's 100th birthday in a more discerning way was Ronald Steel, from the liberal intellectual establishment that often grasped Kennan better than did the political leadership. Such organs as the *New Yorker* and the *New York Review of Books* featured Kennan's writing and favorably reviewed his books. In a 2004 tribute, Steel deplored the chaining of Kennan to containment "as

a great pity, for it is among the least of his accomplishments." The doctrine "distorts the subtlety of his mind and the acuteness of his sensibility." In pointing up sensibility, he was also pointing to the more unconventional Kennan, "our lyric philosopher of loss and nostalgia, our
Ancient Mariner, our traveler in time and space between the worlds of
power and feeling." Steel flashed insight into Kennan's inner world.

———

That Kennan so often used the word "bewildered" offers telling evidence of his own feelings of displacement. He employed the word or a
variant of it when his defenses were down or when he felt overwhelmed
by feeling or events. He used it in reference to a variety of personal and
political matters, as well as to both domestic and foreign issues. As the
literal meaning of "bewilder" suggests, Kennan often felt disconnected,
perplexed, and alienated by the circumstances or people around him.
He responded in different, though not mutually exclusive ways. He
might plunge deeper into the wild in pursuit of what he called the "mystery" and embracing unconvention. Or he would seek connection and
safety in a more conventional route. Or he might pursue both convention and unconvention in his own Kennanish manner. Though impre-
cise and even contradictory, this pattern of behavior and thought was
discernible in how Kennan perceived himself as he struggled to connect
with America and with Russia.

George often pondered where he might fit. He felt bereft of his
mother, hostile toward his stepmother, and distant from his father. He
had to navigate between his male parent and his maternal relatives, who
resented his father. At St. John's, he started out as a boy younger and
smaller than the rest who was consequently bullied. Afraid of snakes, he
had them thrust down his back. At Princeton, he actually adjusted better than he later remembered, but he remained on the social periphery.
In the mid-1920s, the family of his fiancée, Eleanor Hard, snatched back
the promise of inclusion. Though he loved the culture and people of
Russia, the secret police limited his contact with them. Even at the peak
of his influence in Washington from 1947 to 1949, Kennan remained the

outsider, the oddball who never quite fit into the Georgetown set, the midwesterner more cerebral and emotional than the Achesons, Bohens, Alsops, and other Eastern sophisticates. Weekends George and Annelise spent not socializing in Washington, but rather at their farm in East Berlin. Although he cultivated this image of unconvention, being dismissed as eccentric bothered him. When *The Wise Men*, a tell-all portrait of the men who had run America's Cold War establishment from the time of Truman to Vietnam, appeared in 1986, Kennan at first protested that the "shallow, gossipy" book had disparaged him as a "plaintive neurasthenic." Soon thereafter, however, he suffered an "almost nauseous sense of revulsion" in reflecting on his behavior and standing during those years in Washington.[11]

Similarly, while painfully aware of the influence he had not achieved, Kennan was also proud of how far he had come. "It was a long way from the class of 1921 at St. John's Military Academy to such things as the presidency of the American Academy of Arts and Letters and a professorship at the Institute for Advanced Study," he told a young admirer. "I was, Princeton notwithstanding, largely self-educated."[12]

Though he lived into the twenty-first century, Kennan objected to most of the change that had occurred since the eighteenth. He ranted against the primacy of the automobile, which attenuated community, polluted the environment, and penetrated into nature's preserves. He hated advertising, which he saw as based on lying and distortions. He loathed television, aside from his beloved tennis, as the handmaiden of advertising and as the opiate of the masses. He faulted the reliance on machines because they alienated workers from their labor and its products. While this critique of the machine echoed the early Karl Marx and Henry Adams, it stemmed more directly from Anton Chekhov, Kennan's favorite Russian writer. Chekhov meant so much to Kennan that while he spent years researching and thinking about a biography, he could not bring himself to profane the master with actual prose, even that which emerged from Kennan's exquisite penmanship or the clickety-clack of his old-fashioned typewriter. He mourned the abandonment of manual talents and ingenious techniques in the rush to embrace electricity and the internal combustion engine. Appalled at the relentless encroachment of mechanization, Kennan lamented the loss of personal interactions, however perfunctory, when self-dialed phoning replaced operators and when self-wheeled baggage carts replaced porters. A radical environmentalist at heart, he took satisfaction when icy roads halted traffic, a labor strike grounded flights, and stormy seas pounded oil derricks. While certainly quirky, Kennan nevertheless offered insightful criticism of the late twentieth century.

Though he remained a private man who kept secrets even from his diary, Kennan did on occasion expose his inner self. He described moments of transcendence, of tiptoeing into the figurative wild and finding there not only mystery, but also nurturing connection and meaning. This lifelong quest for integration or immersion in some fostering, enveloping, possibly maternal presence, culminated in Kennan's idealizing national unity.

Kennan's yearning for concerted, selfless national action in solving domestic problems influenced his ideas about foreign policy. His manifestos, especially the "Prerequisites" essay of 1938, the long telegram of 1946, and the "X" article of 1947, all emphasized the importance of getting domestic affairs right. Much of the grumbling that filled his diary pointed up problems that he believed could be remedied with concerted national action. He emphasized the external challenge of the Soviet Union in part to mobilize attention to domestic priorities. The long telegram concluded that "much depends on [the] health and vigor of our own society."[13] The "X" essay closed with the assurance that "to avoid destruction the United States need only measure up to its own best traditions." The foreign policy strategist was usually vague about what he meant by "health and vigor" and by "best traditions." At times, however, he revealed how much his political agenda as an adult traced back to his yearning for connection as a youth.

George's early twentieth-century imagined community of white, middle-class, heterosexual, largely Anglo-Saxon, patriotic, and independent though mutually caring and responsible Americans would remain his ideal until his death early in the following century. A yeaning to restore this community helps account for his exaggeration of the Soviet threat in order to mobilize attention to domestic problems. Rebuilding

Western Europe through the Marshall Plan and other ventures, though important in and of themselves, also figured as a means to buttress American culture by revitalizing cultural kin. These values imbued his last major book, *Around the Cragged Hill: A Personal and Political Philosophy*. Despite his estrangement from contemporary America, the sentimentalist never stopped loving the imagined America of his youth.

Did Kennan's idealizing of what he termed "ultimate faith in our country" and a "single national culture" edge into fascism? His skepticism if not hostility to democracy and multiculturalism, his racism, homophobia, patriarchy, opposition to immigration, and his elements of anti-Semitism all would seem to indict him along this line. His children used to squirm at the dinner table as their otherwise brilliant, erudite father would spout racist slurs. His prejudices remain inexcusable and a stain on his reputation.

Nevertheless, George F. Kennan was not a fascist, neither as that term was understood in the 1920s to 1940s nor as it came into use again in the twenty-first century. Most importantly, his love of country did not extend to chauvinism or jingoism. He opposed a bristling, overbuilt American military. Even as the Policy Planning Staff director, he wanted the United States to focus more on tending to its own garden rather than on expanding its global influence. Despite his deplorable disdain for much of Latin America, Africa, and Asia, Kennan was no fan of American empire in those lands. He regarded empires as doomed to fail, whether they were led by Rome, Berlin, Moscow, or Washington. He saw through the self-congratulatory piety and wishful thinking that tripped up Americans wishing to do good in distant nations. As Kennan realized, such missions had perversely ended up with Americans killing perceived enemies in Vietnam, Somalia, Serbia, Afghanistan, and Iraq.

Emotions figured large in how Kennan viewed not only the United States but also Russia. Indeed, his feelings for Russia extended to realms beyond reason or prose. His intimate engagement blended sensory perceptions, knowledge suffused with emotion, and mystery. Returning to Moscow in October 1944, he found himself "fascinated with it every minute." He walked the streets for hours, "without tiring of anything, moved by everything I heard and saw." The embrace extended to his core, where Russia and America came together. Moscow seemed "poignantly familiar and significant to me—as though I had lived here in childhood." Russia shimmered with "that indefinable something—so full of promise and meaning—that I have always felt to be just around the corner."[14]

Despite the ineradicable historical memory chaining Kennan to the containment doctrine, he himself came to oppose America's isolation of Russia. Especially after Stalin was gone, he hoped to bring the two nations together. He asserted that Americans and Russians had a natural affinity for each other. They both lived in big, wide-open, practical-minded nations that hated pretense. The Russophile believed that the cultures of the two nations complemented each other and would benefit from greater contact. Americans would learn from Russian literature and music, and Russians would learn from American efficiency and directness.

Kennan also saw the two nations as coming together in his own person. An impromptu evening talk with students and spouses at the National War College in December 1946 proved one of those occasion when he revealed more of himself than usual. Kennan ventriloquized the Russians as pushing for the reforms to American society that he himself had long sought. In an astonishing recasting of the Cold War, Washington's foremost strategist explained that if the Russians "have been ready to destroy us, it was in reality for our failure to eradicate the weaknesses of our own society, for our failure to be what they thought we should be, to bring out the best they felt was in us."[15] In a similar transposing of domestic and foreign dangers, Kennan, relying on his "profound instinctive conviction," affirmed in 1950 that the Cold War would be determined "less by what we do to the Russians than what we do to ourselves." To the probably puzzled Cincinnati business executives, he explained his Chekhovian diagnosis that "the real disease from which we are suffering" was "the problem of the relationship of human freedom and human spirit to the machine." Russian communists were only "a complication of this disease."[16]

Though he knew vast amounts about Russia, Kennan extrapolated further into what he proudly acknowledged as "sheer intuition."[17] He trusted his "invisible antennae."[18] Much of his analysis of the Kremlin or the Russian people rested not on observation, but rather on hunches—informed conjuncture, but guesses nonetheless. Especially in the halcyon years of 1946 through 1949, much of the U.S. government, the American public, and allied governments accepted as gospel Kennan's pronouncements on matters about which he could only intuit. Few questioned him, because he communicated so persuasively and he was offering up popular Cold War fare. Later, when Kennan employed much the same intuition to argue, probably with greater justification, for negotiation and compromise with the Soviets, his expertise lost its luster, especially with such no-nonsense Cold Warriors as Acheson and John Foster Dulles.[19] Thus the vaunted "Grand Strategist" was dismissed as an impractical visionary. Checked in the present, Kennan looked ahead.

From Gaddis, Kennan hoped for a posthumous biography that would give readers in the future a sympathetic understanding of his ideas and life story. In key ways, Gaddis met those expectations with the book he published in 2011, *George F. Kennan: An American Life*. This 698-page, well-researched, and beautifully written cradle-to-grave account concluded with a chapter entitled "Greatness." His argument for Kennan's exalted rank reiterated the points he had made at the February 2004 Princeton celebration. The book won mostly glowing reviews and snared the Pulitzer Prize in biography. Once again, Kennan's name appeared in the press. Gaddis's encyclopedic approach leaned, however, more toward narrative than analysis. He had slight sympathy for, and devoted scant attention to, Kennan's efforts to tone down the Cold War and to challenge the hegemony of industrialism. On one topic, however, the book offered rich, knowing, sympathetic explication: the impact on U.S. policy in 1946–1949 of Kennan's long telegram, "X" article, lectures at the National War College, and Policy Planning Staff papers. This was the area of expertise that had attracted Kennan to Gaddis decades earlier.

"Annelise had her way with this book," Gaddis explains in the preface, and that's why he dedicated it to her. The tribute reads: "In memory of Annelise Sorensen Kennan, 1910–2008, without whom it would not have been possible." Although Annelise remained largely apolitical, she liked puncturing her husband's balloon. As George and Annelise became what Gaddis would fondly remember as "my companions," the historian took sides in an ancient rift in their marriage. He saw as unequivocally positive "the stabilizing role she played in his life."[20] Gaddis marveled how, when George was going on about this or that, Annelise was very effective in "pulling him right back down to earth." She could "deflate him, very deftly and very gracefully." With a neighbor of the Kennans', Gaddis used an equally telling metaphor: "She pulls him back to reality, or to the center." Gaddis made clear his own attitude toward this dynamic: "It's fun to watch it."[21]

If Annelise helped make it seem normal at times to depreciate George and dismiss his views, Gaddis adopted a similar tone when he dealt with the many parts of Kennan's life he did not agree or sympathize with, such as Kennan's tilting against the Cold War, out-of-control technology, and environmental destruction. One of the ways in which Annelise may have "had her way with this book" was in influencing the author's changing attitudes toward Kennan over the course of their involvement.

———

In 1995, in reply to Gaddis's query as to what he wanted in his obituary, Kennan mentioned that someone had said to him, "'George, you are by nature really a teacher.' I think there's a lot to that."[22] Probably millions of people had learned from Kennan's books, articles, and lectures. In the Foreign Service he was revered as a model. Nevertheless, he had not really succeeded in instructing the American people and their leaders, about ending the arms race, negotiating with the Soviets, repairing the environment, and halting the destructive impact of machines on relations among humans and between humans and their environment. Arthur S. Link and Robert C. Tucker, both professors at Princeton University, observed of Kennan that "he never had much interest in teaching students. That was very clear."[23]

After the comment to Gaddis about teaching, Kennan moved on to evaluate other aspects of his life. He emphasized, first, his intellectual "independence," repeating that word four times in a short paragraph. Second, he stressed that while he had been blessed with insights, these had not gained wide credence. Finally, he was proud of having been honest all his life.[24]

Kennan assessed himself, then, more as the unconventional, stalwart critic than as the teacher bound by convention. Here Ronald Steel's insights seem apt. What Kennan the iconoclast contributed was valuable because he remained an outsider, an organic conservative in a society bent on assumed progress. Kennan is "our conscience and our censorious judge," Steel wrote months before the centenarian died. He is "our Gibbon, the chronicler of our imperial republic. Even more he is our Henry Adams, the despairing witness of our democratic self-gratification."[25]

Kennan was great because he never gave up on three causes that he championed, sometimes almost alone, for decades. He never stopped loving both America and Russia and trying to bring them together. He championed the environment long before it became fashionable. He questioned the reliance on machines and the neglect of nature and manual skills. His greatness was marred by his prejudices. In all of this, Kennan viewed matters as a man outside his time. His era desperately needed that perspective. So does ours.

NOTES

Preface

1. Dorothy Fosdick interview with John Lewis Gaddis, October 29, 1987, folder 14, box 1, John Lewis Gaddis Papers, Seeley G. Mudd Library, Princeton University, Princeton, NJ.

2. Ware Adams interview with C. Ben Wright, September 30, 1970, C. Ben Wright Papers, George C. Marshall Library, Lexington, VA.

3. Kennan to Jeanette Kennan Hotchkiss [n.d. but summer 1942], folder 4, box 328, George F. Kennan Papers, Seeley G. Mudd Library, Princeton University, Princeton, NJ.

4. Kennan lecture at Oxford University, May 13, 1958, folder 22, box 300, Kennan Papers.

5. Christopher Kennan interview with author, September 22, 2012.

6. Kennan to Family, July 4, 1929, folder 10, box 328, Kennan Papers.

7. Undated fragment, probably from the early 1990s, p. 14, folder 17, box 329, Kennan Papers.

8. Timothy Snyder, *Bloodlands: Europe Between Hitler and Stalin* (New York: Basic Books, 2010).

9. Frank Costigliola, ed., *The Kennan Diaries* (New York: W. W. Norton, 2014), 48, 56–57, 59.

Introduction

1. Costigliola, *Kennan Diaries*, 374–75.

2. George and Annelise Kennan interview with Doug James, April 25, 2003. My thanks to Doug James for sharing this document with me.

3. George and Annelise Kennan interview with Doug James, April 25, 2003.

4. Grace Kennan Warnecke interview with author, June 15, 2015.

5. William P. and Mary A. Bundy interview with John Lewis Gaddis, December 6, 1987, pp. 2, 33, folder 7, box 1, Gaddis Papers.

6. See, for example, Dagmar Herzog, *Cold War Freud* (Cambridge, UK: Cambridge University Press, 2016).

7. Kennan diary, September 10, 1958, and October 28, 1952, box 232, Kennan Papers. See Sigmund Freud, *Civilization and Its Discontents*, trans. Joan Riviere (London: Hogarth Press, 1951).

8. Kennan diary, [no date] 1935, box 230, Kennan Papers.

9. Kennan diary, June 25, 1935; and Kennan diary, [no date] 1935, box 230, Kennan Papers.

10. Kennan, Sermon (Palm Sunday), Protestant Church Group, Belgrade, April 15, 1962, folder 27, box 302, Kennan Papers. For Kennan's frustrations as ambassador, see Costigliola, *Kennan Diaries*, 417–19. For the societal context of Kennan's belief in Freud, see Herzog, *Cold War Freud*.

11. Kennan, "Draft of Information Policy on Relations with Russia," July 22, 1946, box 27, Dean Acheson Papers, Harry S. Truman Presidential Library, Independence, MO.

12. George F. Kennan, *Sketches from a Life* (New York: Pantheon, 1989), 90.

13. Kennan, "The XVIII Century," [1942], box 298, Kennan Papers.

14. *Foreign Relations of the United States [hereafter FRUS] 1952–1954, Vol. 8* (Washington: Government Printing Office, 1988), 1024.

15. Gaddis quoted in "Kennan '25 Honored as Hundredth Birthday Nears," *Daily Princetonian*, November 12, 2003.

16. George Kennan, *Siberia and the Exile System*, ed. George F. Kennan (Chicago: University of Chicago Press, 1958), xvi.

17. These paragraphs draw on Kennan interview with Gaddis, August 24, 1982, pp. 8–16, folder 24, box 1, Gaddis Papers.

18. Costigliola, *Kennan Diaries*, 185.

19. Richard H. Immerman and Timothy Andrew Sayle, "The CIA: Its Origin, Transformation, and Crisis of Identity from Harry S. Truman to Barack Obama," in *Origins of the National Security State and the Legacy of Harry S. Truman*, ed. Mary Ann Heiss and Michael J. Hogan (Kirksville, MO: Truman State University Press, 2015), 6–8.

20. Costigliola, *Kennan Diaries*, 204.

21. Christopher McKnight Nichols and Andrew Preston, "Introduction," in *Rethinking American Grand Strategy*, ed. Elizabeth Borgwardt, Christopher McKnight Nichols, and Andrew Preston (New York: Oxford University Press, 2021), 1, 6. See also Hal Brands, "Getting Grand Strategy Right," 36–37; David Greenberg, "The Misanthropy Diaries: Containment, Democracy, and the Prejudices of George Frost Kennan," 254–71.

22. Costigliola, *Kennan Diaries*, 78.

23. Bundy and Bundy interview with Gaddis, December 6, 1987, p. 34, folder 7, box 1, Gaddis Papers.

24. Barklie Griggs interview with author, February 8, 2021.

25. Grace Kennan Warnecke interview with author, June 15, 2015; Wendy Kennan interview with author, November 15, 2015; Christopher Kennan interview with author, September 22, 2012.

26. Joan Kennan email to author, July 10, 2013.

27. Brandon Griggs interview with author, January 17, 2021; Kevin McClatchy interview with author, January 10, 2021; Barklie Briggs interview with author, February 8, 2021.

28. Grace Kennan Warnecke interviews with author, January 8, 2016, and December 1, 2020; Grace Kennan Warnecke, *Daughter of the Cold War* (Pittsburgh: University of Pittsburgh Press, 2018), 104–5.

29. Mary A. Bundy interview with author, May 23, 2011.

30. Grace Kennan Warnecke interviews with author, April 30, 2012, and November 6, 2020.

31. Costigliola, *Kennan Diaries*, 81.

32. Grace Warnecke Kennan interviews with author, June 15, 2015; January 8, 2016; November 6, 2020; December 1, 2020; February 9, 2021.

33. These paragraphs draw on Grace Warnecke Kennan interview with author, November 6, 2020; Christopher Kennan interview with author, September 22, 2012.

34. Arthur S. Link interview with Gaddis, September 5, 1984, p. 9, folder 4, box 6, Gaddis Papers.

35. Christopher Kennan interview with author, March 11–12, 2016; Wayne Lau interview with author, August 2, 2015.

36. Grace Kennan Warnecke interviews with author, June 15, 2015, and January 8, 2016; Gene Hotchkiss interview with author, May 30, 2016.

37. Christopher Kennan interview with author, March 11–12, 2016.

38. Mary A. Bundy interview with author, May 23, 2011.

39. Dorothy Fosdick interview with Gaddis, October 29, 1987, pp. 1–2, folder 14, box 1, Gaddis Papers; Berlin and Berlin interview with Gaddis, November 29, 1992, p. 18, folder 2, box 1, Gaddis Papers.

40. Bundy and Bundy interview with Gaddis, December 6, 1987, p. 13, folder 7, box 1, Gaddis Papers.

41. Wilson D. Miscamble, *George F. Kennan and the Making of American Foreign Policy, 1947–1950* (Princeton, NJ: Princeton University Press, 1992), 353. See also John L. Gaddis, *George F. Kennan: An American Life* (New York: Penguin, 2011), 265–336.

42. Bundy and Bundy interview with Gaddis, December 6, 1987, p. 1, folder 7, box 1, Gaddis Papers.

43. J. Richardson Dilworth interview with Gaddis, December 6, 1987, pp. 1–2, folder 11, box 1, Gaddis Papers.

44. Goodman interview with Gaddis, December 10, 1987, pp. 5–6, 16, folder 16, box 1, Gaddis Papers.

45. Dorothy Fosdick interview with Gaddis, October 29, 1983, pp. 1–2, folder 14, box 1, Gaddis Papers.

46. Wendy Kennan interview with author, November 22, 2015.

47. Kennan, "Medical History," October 20, 1974, folder 11, box 183, Kennan Papers.

48. Frieda Por to Kennan, July 2, 1977, folder 1, box 329, Kennan Papers; Grace Kennan Warnecke interview with author, June 15, 2015.

49. Kennan to Frieda Por, July 14, 1977, folder 1, box 329, Kennan Papers.

50. Por to Kennan, June 22, 1978; Kennan to Por, July 29, 1978, folder 1, box 329, Kennan Papers.

Chapter 1

1. Constance Kennan Bradt interview with John Lewis Gaddis, November 13, 1982, p. 2, box 1, Gaddis Papers.

2. George F. Kennan, *Memoirs 1925–1950* (Boston: Little, Brown, 1967), 2.

3. Frances Kennan Worobec interview with Gaddis, June 28, 1984, p. 11, box 6, Gaddis Papers.

4. Frances Kennan Worobec interview with Gaddis, June 28, 1984, p. 4.

5. Jeanette Kennan Hotchkiss, "My Father and His Family: Kossuth Kent Kennan, 1851–1933," edited by Nancy McCoy Hotchkiss (Hinsdale, Illinois, 2003), p. 25, folder 20, box 329, Kennan Papers.

6. Frances Kennan Worobec interview with Joan Kennan [ca. 1972], p. 1, folder 2, box 330, Kennan Papers.

7. Frances Kennan Worobec interview with Joan Kennan [ca. 1972], p. 12.

8. Hotchkiss, "My Father and His Family."

9. Kennan interview with Gaddis, August 24, 1982, p. 4, folder 24, box 1, Gaddis Papers.

10. Jeanette Kennan Hotchkiss interview with Joan Kennan, November 2, 1972, pp. 13–14, folder 2, box 330, Kennan Papers (emphasis in original).

11. Gene Hotchkiss interview with author, May 30, 2016.

12. George F. Kennan interview with Joan Kennan [n.d., ca. 1972], p. 1, folder 1, box 330, Kennan Papers.

13. Constance Kennan Bradt interview with Gaddis, November 13, 1982, p. 2; Frances Kennan Worobec interview with Joan Kennan, p. 16.

14. Hotchkiss, "My Father and His Family," pp. 29, 27, box 330, Kennan Papers.

15. One of George's cousins, Kathryn, would later marry into the wealthy Vogel family, German Americans who had lived in the United States since 1847.

16. For George and the other Kennan children, instruction in German was also part of their elementary school program.

17. Kennan interview with Gaddis, August 24, 1982, p. 1; Kennan to Roger G. Connor, January 25, 1993, folder 6, box 23, Kennan Papers.

18. Kennan to Jeanette Kennan Hotchkiss, December 14, 1933, box 330, Kennan Papers.

19. Kennan to Father, November 5, 1912, folder 6, box 330, Kennan Papers. For Alfred James, Sr.; see Kennan interview with Gaddis, August 24, 1982, p. 2.

20. Jeanette Hotchkiss Kennan, "My Father and His Family: Kossuth Kent Kennan 1851–1933," p. 23.

21. Kennan interview with Gaddis, August 24, 1982, p. 3.

22. Kossuth Kent Kennan, *Income Taxation: Methods and Results in Various Counties* (Milwaukee: Burdick & Allen, 1910).

23. Jeanette Kennan Hotchkiss, "Memoirs for Two" [n.d., but probably late 1960s to early 1970s], p. 10, box 330, Kennan Papers.

24. Kennan interview with Gaddis, August 24, 1982, p. 4.

25. Constance Kennan interview with Gaddis, p. 3

26. Hotchkiss interview with Gaddis, December 21, 1982, p. 2.

27. "In the Matter of the Guardianship of Constance L. Kennan, Jeanette S. Kennan, and George F. Kennan, Minors," May 3, 1918, records of Milwaukee County Court in Probate, vol. 95, p. 482. While the will of Alfred James provided for distribution upon reaching twenty-one, that of Frances W. Kennan mandated the age of twenty-five. By the date of this petition, in which Kent Kennan was asking for a loan from the principal to fix up the country place at Nagawicka Lake, the eldest child, Frances W. Kennan, had already reached twenty-one years of age. My thanks to legal sleuth Edward Ehrlich for tracking down these records. When Jeanette reached the age of twenty-one, her share amounted to $50,000, a considerable sum that yielded an income of $3,000 a year. Hotchkiss interview with Gaddis, December 21, 1982, p. 8.

28. Kennan interview with Gaddis, August 24, 1982, p. 3.

29. Kennan interview with Joan Kennan, p. 10.

30. Constance Kennan interview with Joan Kennan, p. 3.

31. Hotchkiss, "My Father and His Family," p. 30, box 330, Kennan Papers.

32. Kennan interview with Joan Kennan, p. 6.

33. Kennan interview with Joan Kennan, p. 3.

34. Hotchkiss, "Memoirs for Two," p. 17.

35. Hotchkiss, "My Father and His Family," pp. 33, 51.

36. Hotchkiss interview with Gaddis, December 21, 1982, p. 4.

37. Kennan interview with Joan Kennan, p. 2; Kennan to Gene Hotchkiss [Jeanette's son], February 14, 2003, box 330, Kennan Papers.

38. Kennan interview with Joan Kennan, pp. 2–3.

39. Kennan interview with Gaddis, August 24, 1982, p. 11.

40. Hotchkiss, "Memoirs for Two," p. 15.

41. Quoted in Hotchkiss, "My Father and His Family," pp. 31–32.

42. Kennan interview with Gaddis, August 24, 1982, p. 1.

43. Frances Kennan Worobec interview with Joan Kennan [ca. 1972], p. 8.

44. Jeanette Kennan Hotchkiss interview with Joan Kennan, November 2, 1972, pp. 9, 21.

45. Hotchkiss interview with Gaddis, December 21, 1982, p. 25.

46. Costigliola, *Kennan Diaries*, 6–7.

47. Kennan, *Memoirs 1925–1950*, 4.

48. Hotchkiss, Memoirs for Two," p. 1.

49. Kennan interview with Joan Kennan, p. 26.

50. Jeanette Kennan Hotchkiss interview with Joan Kennan, November 2, 1972, p. 12.

51. Hotchkiss interview with Gaddis, December 21, 1982, p. 4.

52. Jeanette Kennan Hotchkiss interview with Joan Kennan, November 2, 1972, p. 16.

53. Hotchkiss interview with Gaddis, December 21, 1982, p. 11.

54. Jeanette Kennan Hotchkiss interview with Joan Kennan, p. 16 (emphasis in original).

55. Gene Hotchkiss interview with author, May 30, 2016.

56. Kennan interview with Joan Kennan, p. 27.

57. Robert W. Wells, "St. John's Military Academy's Priceless Heritage," (1960, 1994), pp. 148–50, St. John's Northwestern Military Academy Archive, Delafield, WI.

58. Joan Kennan interview with author, June 24, 2015.

59. Kennan interview with Joan Kennan, p. 27.

60. Wells, "St. John's Military Academy's Priceless Heritage," pp. 148–50.

61. Kennan interview with Gaddis, August 24, 1982, p. 14.

62. Kennan interview with Joan Kennan, p. 19.

63. Wells, "St. John's Military Academy's Priceless Heritage," pp. 148–50.

64. Jeanette Hotchkiss interview with Joan Kennan, November 2, 1972, p. 16.

65. Kennan to Jeanette, November 4, 1919, folder 5, box 328, Kennan Papers.

66. Class of 1921 Yearbook, "Kennan, Geo. Frost." Transcript, St. Johns Northwestern Military Academy Archive.

67. Kennan interview with Joan Kennan, pp. 26–29.

68. Hotchkiss, "My Father and His Family," p. 50.

69. The account in the memoir was so grim that it darkened how many historians viewed Kennan's life overall. When his authorized biographer, John L. Gaddis, read those letters and then queried Kennan, the latter protested that he had not been all that depressed. In the memoir, Kennan seems to have pursued a rhetorical strategy he had developed while taking exams at Princeton—namely, spinning an elaborate scenario and making a persuasive argument based more on emotion-evoking language than on strong evidence.

70. Kennan, *Memoirs 1925–1950*, 4, 15.

71. Kennan interview with Joan Kennan, p. 10.

72. Hotchkiss, "My Father and His Family," p. 50, box 330, Kennan Papers.

73. Kennan interview with Gaddis, December 13, 1987, p. 8.

74. Kennan interview with Gaddis, December 13, 1987, p. 8.

75. Kennan to Jeanette Kennan, October 30, 1921, folder 10, box 23, Kennan Papers.

76. Kennan to Jeanette, May 3, 1922, folder 10, box 23.

77. Kennan interview with Gaddis, August 24, 1982, p. 16. In remembering his reaction, Kennan enunciated each word with extra emphasis, and the rising emotion caused his voice to break into a short laugh as he referred to the "marvelous" restraint.

78. F. Scott Fitzgerald, *The Great Gatsby* (New York: Scribner, 1925, 2018), 175–76.

79. Kennan to John Lamberton Harper [1991 or 1992], folder 11, box 18, Kennan Papers.

80. Kennan to Jeanette, May 3, 1922, folder 10, box 23.

81. Kennan to Jeanette Kennan, Thanksgiving Day [November 24] 1921, folder 10, box 23, Kennan Papers.

82. Kennan to Jeanette Kennan, March 1, 1922, folder 10, box 23, Kennan Papers.

83. Kennan to Jeanette Kennan, March 4, 1922, folder 10, box 23, Kennan Papers.

84. "In the Matter of the Guardianship of Jeanette Sinclair Kennan and George Frost Kennan, August 1922," records of Milwaukee County Court in Probate, vol. 95, p. 482. Total income from January to August 1922 amounted to $2,132.81, while total expenses were $1,712.66.

85. Kennan interview with Joan Kennan, p. 9.

86. Kennan to Jeanette, December 6, 1922, folder 10, box 23.

87. Kennan to Jeanette, May 3, 1922, folder 10, box 23.

88. Kennan to Jeanette, October 19, 1922, folder 10, box 23.

89. Kennan to Jeanette, May 20, 1922, folder 10, box 23.

90. Kennan to Jeanette, December 6, 1922, folder 10, box 23.

91. Walter Isaacson and Evan Thomas, *The Wise Men: Six Friends and the World They Made* (New York: Simon & Schuster, 1986), 77.

92. Kennan to Jeanette, November 10, 1922, folder 10, box 23.

93. Kennan to Jeanette, March 8, 1922, folder 10, box 23.

94. Kennan to Jeanette, [April] 1922, folder 10, box 23.

95. Kennan to Jeanette, November 1, 1922, folder 10, box 23.

96. Kennan, *Memoirs 1925–1950*, 10.

97. Transcript on display at Kennan Centennial Conference, February 20, 2004.

98. Kennan to Jeanette, December 6, 1922, folder 10, box 23.

99. Costigliola, *Kennan Diaries*, 9.

100. Costigliola, *Kennan Diaries*, 11.

101. Kennan to Jeanette, February 28, 1923, folder 10, box 23.

102. Kennan to Jeanette, May 1, 1923, folder 10, box 23.

103. Kennan to Jeanette, April 11, 1923, folder 10, box 23.

104. Kennan interview with Joan Kennan [early 1970s], p. 14.

105. Kennan interview with Joan Kennan, p. 13.

106. Harry Kemp, *Tramping on Life: An Autobiographical Narrative* (Garden City, NY: Boni & Liveright, 1922). In August 1911, with Harry Kemp present, Upton Sinclair and his wife, Meta Fuller Sinclair, announced their divorce at a press conference held at the Hotel Imperial in New York City. The three together called for society's establishing trial marriages as the means toward evolving more perfect, monogamous unions. They explained that the prerequisites to such temporary unions were, first, elevating women to "the same economic basis" as men and, second, state subsidies to mothers. In sum, as the trio put it, happy marriages required socialism. *New York Times*, August 29, 1911, p. 1.

107. Kennan to Jeanette, April 11, 1923, folder 10, box 23.

108. Kennan to Jeanette, May 18, 1923, folder 10, box 23.

109. Kennan, *Memoirs 1925–1950*, 12–13.

110. Costigliola, *Kennan Diaries*, 15.

111. Costigliola, *Kennan Diaries*, 16. More than a half-century after describing this put-down technique, Kennan still felt some of the humiliation inflicted on him. "I've never forgotten that the first day I was at college, all freshmen were asked to assemble in a big lecture hall." During an intermission, "I asked the boy next to me the time—did he have the time? He took a puff on his cigarette, and let it all out, and then he looked down at his watch and then gave it to me. And somehow or other, I got the message." Kennan interview with Gaddis, August 24, 1982, p. 1. In relating this incident, Kennan's voice rose, and he enunciated forcefully the phrases "I've never forgotten" and "the first day."

112. Costigliola, *Kennan Diaries*, 19–20.

113. Costigliola, *Kennan Diaries*, 20–21.

114. Costigliola, *Kennan Diaries*, 21.

115. Costigliola, *Kennan Diaries*, 26–27.

116. Costigliola, *Kennan Diaries*, 24–25.

117. Costigliola, *Kennan Diaries*, 28–29.

118. Kennan interview with Joan Kennan, p. 22.

119. Costigliola, *Kennan Diaries*, 35.

120. Kennan to Father, January 19, 1924, folder 7, box 53; Kennan to Father, May 4, 1925, Kennan Papers; Kennan to Father, April 7, 1933, Kennan Papers.

121. Kennan interview with Gaddis, August 24, 1982, pp. 2-3.

Chapter 2

1. Kennan to Family, February 2, 1930, file 10, box 328, Kennan Papers. The State Department was so accommodating because prior conditions in the Berlin consulate were so dire. A report found the office "drifting in the most hopeless, aimless, dangerous manner . . . dissipation, rancor, hatred even, gossip, backbiting and turmoil existed to an alarming degree." Thomas Murray

Wilson, inspection report, May 3, 1928, box 19, Inspection Reports on Foreign Service Posts, 1906–39, Record Group 59, General Records of the Department of State, National Archives, College Park, MD (hereafter RG 59).

2. George S. Messersmith to Secretary of State, "The German Export Trade to Soviet Russia Prepared by Consul George F. Kennan," April 21, 1931, 661.6211/39; Wilbur J. Carr to Messersmith, July 21, 1931, RG 59.

3. Messersmith to Secretary of State, "Citizenship and Protection Cases of Americans residing in Soviet Russia," April 28, 1931, 861.012/31, RG 59; for the pushback, see Wilbur J. Carr to Messersmith, April 12, 1932, RG 59.

4. Kennan to Family, March 19, 1931, file 10, box 328, Kennan Papers.

5. Kennan, *Memoirs 1925–1950*, 28.

6. Kennan interview with Joan Kennan [no date, early 1970s], p. 26, folder 1, box 330, Kennan Papers.

7. Kennan to Jeanette Kennan Hotchkiss, September 3, 1928, folder 10, box 23, Kennan Papers.

8. Kennan interview with Joan Kennan, p. 26; Mrs. Gerald K. Lake [Eleanor Hard] to John Lamberton Harper, February 7, 1992, and July 12, 1992, in private possession. My thanks to John Lamberton Harper for sharing this correspondence with me.

9. Kennan to Hotchkiss, October 28, 1925, folder 10, box 23, Kennan Papers.

10. Kennan to Hotchkiss, September 3, 1928, folder 10, box 23, Kennan Papers.

11. Lake to Harper, July 12, 1990, in private possession.

12. Isaacson and Thomas, *The Wise Men*, 146.

13. Kennan interview with Joan Kennan, p. 25, folder 1, box 330, Kennan Papers; Hotchkiss interview with Gaddis, p. 16.

14. Costigliola, *Kennan Diaries*, 50.

15. Kennan interview with John Lewis Gaddis, December 13, 1987, pp. 7–8, folder 1, box 6, Gaddis Papers.

16. Kennan to Father and Mother, August 26, 1928; Kennan to Family, December 24, 1928, both in folder 10, box 328, Kennan Papers.

17. Kennan interview with Gaddis, December 13, 1987, p. 14; Kennan to Father, April 26, 1933, Kennan Papers.

18. Kennan to Hotchkiss, September 9, 1927, folder 10, box 23, Kennan Papers.

19. Kennan to Secretary of State, November 22, 1927; Kellogg to Kennan, December 9, 1927, 123K36/19, RG 59, National Archives.

20. Lake to Harper, July 12, 1990, in private possession.

21. Costigliola, *Kennan Diaries*, 62.

22. Kennan to Family, October 7, 1928, and November 18, 1928, folder 10, box 328, Kennan Papers.

23. Kennan to Family, January 27, 1929, folder 10, box 328, Kennan Papers.

24. Kennan to Family, October 12, 1929, and November 12, 1929, folder 10, box 328, Kennan Papers.

25. Kennan to Family, February 17, 1930, folder 10, box 328, Kennan Papers.

26. Kennan to Family, November 17, 1929, folder 10, box 328, Kennan Papers.

27. Kennan to Family, November 24, 1929, folder 10, box 328, Kennan Papers.

28. Kennan to Family, December 24, 1928, folder 10, box 328, Kennan Papers.

29. Kennan to Family, December 24, 1928, folder 10, box 328 Kennan Papers.

30. Kennan to Hotchkiss, November 16, 1930, folder 10, box 23, Kennan Papers.

31. Kennan to Family, October 6, 1929, folder 10, box 328, Kennan Papers.

32. Kennan to Family, March 2, 1930, folder 10, box 328, Kennan Papers.

33. Kennan to Family, December 21, 1930, folder 10, box 328, Kennan Papers.

34. Kennan to Family, May 12, 1929, folder 10, box 328, Kennan Papers.

35. Kennan to Family, December 8, 1930, and December 28, 1930, folder 10, box 328, Kennan Papers.

36. Kennan to Family, December 8, 1930, folder 10, box 328, Kennan Papers.

37. Kennan to Family, June 5, 1929, folder 10, box 328, Kennan Papers.

38. Kennan to Family, March 22, 1930, folder 10, box 328, Kennan Papers [emphasis in original].

39. Kennan to Family, November 11, 1930, folder 10, box 328, Kennan Papers.

40. Kennan to Family, February 4, 1929, folder 10, box 328, Kennan Papers.

41. Kennan to Family, April 30, 1930, folder 10, box 328, Kennan Papers.

42. Kennan to Family, December 10, 1928, and September 16, 1929, folder 10, box 328, Kennan Papers.

43. Kennan to Family, September 16, 1929, October 6, 1929, and November 12, 1929, folder 10, box 328, Kennan Papers.

44. Kennan to Family, January 30, 1931, folder 10, box 328, Kennan Papers.

45. Kennan to Family, July 8, 1930, January 30, 1931, and April 30, 1930, folder 10, box 328, Kennan Papers.

46. Kennan to Walt Ferris, January 12, 1931, folder 9, box 53, Kennan Papers.

47. Kennan to Robert F. Kelley, November 14, 1929, and December 6, 1929; Kelley to Kennan, February 17, 1930, 123 K36/68, RG 59.

48. Robert P. Skinner to Secretary of State [with Kennan's request], July 26, 1932; E. L. Packer to Skinner, August 25, 1932, 123 K36/116, RG 59.

49. Messersmith to Secretary of State, "The Soviet Export Trade to Soviet Russia Prepared by Consul George F. Kennan," April 21, 1931; Carr to Messersmith, July 21, 1931.

50. Kennan to Family, March 19, 1931, folder 10, box 328, Kennan Papers.

51. Kennan to Family, March 19, 1931, folder 10, box 328, Kennan Papers.

52. Kennan to Hotchkiss, April 28, 1931, folder 10, box 23, Kennan Papers.

53. Kennan to Hotchkiss, April 28, 1931, folder 10, box 23, Kennan Papers.

54. Kennan to Hotchkiss, January 3, 1931, folder 10, box 23, Kennan Papers.

55. Kennan to Hotchkiss, January 3, 1931, folder 10, box 23, Kennan Papers.

56. Costigliola, *Kennan Diaries*, 68–69.

57. Annelise Sorensen Kennan interview with John Lewis Gaddis, August 26, 1982, pp. 1–6, folder 22, box 1, Gaddis Papers.

58. Annelise to George, Sunday afternoon [July–August 1931], folder 7, box 328, Kennan Papers.

59. Annelise to George, Friday after lunch [July–August 1931], folder 7, box 328, Kennan Papers.

60. Annelise to George, July 24, 1931, folder 7, box 328, Kennan Papers.

61. Kennan, "Flashbacks," in George F. Kennan, *At a Century's Ending: Reflections 1982–1995* (New York: W. W. Norton, 1996), 31.

62. Kennan to Hotchkiss, November 1, 1931, folder 10, box 23, Kennan Papers.

63. Kennan to Father, December 16, 1928, folder 10, box 328, Kennan Papers.

64. Kennan, "Flashbacks (1985)," 31.

65. Kennan to Family, April 18, 1930, folder 10, box 328, Kennan Papers.

66. Kennan to Family, April 18, 1930, folder 10, box 328, Kennan Papers.

67. Costigliola, *Kennan Diaries*, 77, 81; Kennan to Father, June 5, 1932, folder 10, box 328, Kennan Papers.

68. Costigliola, *Kennan Diaries*, 81–82.

69. Costigliola, *Kennan Diaries*, 76–77.

70. Costigliola, *Kennan Diaries*, 82–86.

71. Robert Shaplen, *Kreuger: Genius and Swindler* (New York: Knopf, 1960), 182.

72. For the wills, see Final Decree in the Matter of the Estate of Florence James Kennan, May 2, 1905, Milwaukee County Court in Probate, 23/239/18480; Amended Inventory and Appraisal in the Matter of the Estate of Alfred James, January 3, 1906, Milwaukee County Court in Probate, 24/284/19147, both in Records of Milwaukee County.

73. Kennan to Hotchkiss, April 12, 1932, folder 1, box 24, Kennan Papers.

74. Costigliola, *Kennan Diaries*, 78 (emphasis in original).

75. Costigliola, *Kennan Diaries*, 65.

76. Kennan to Volodia Kozhenikov, October 20, 1930, folder 8, box 53, Kennan Papers.

77. Kennan to Kozhenikov, October 20, 1930, Kennan Papers.

78. Costigliola, *Kennan Diaries*, 79.

79. Costigliola, *Kennan Diaries*, 83.

80. Kennan to Family, February 4, 1933, folder 11, box 328, Kennan Papers.

81. Kennan to Father, April 7, 1933, folder 11, box 328, Kennan Papers.

82. Annelise to Hotchkiss, February 8, 1933, folder 2, box 328; Kennan to Family, March 10, 1933, folder 11, box 328, Kennan Papers.

83. Kennan to Hotchkiss, March 21, 1933, folder 16, box 328, Kennan Papers.

84. Costigliola, *Kennan Diaries*, 86.

85. Kennan to Family October 21, 1933, folder 11, box 328, Kennan Papers.

86. Kennan to Hotchkiss, December 14, 1933, folder 17, box 328, Kennan Papers.

87. Kent Kennan to George Kennan, November 24, 1933, folder 25, box 327, Kennan Papers.

88. "Fair Day, Adieu!" [Memoirs of 1933–1938], pp. 1, 3, folder 2, box 240, Kennan Papers.

89. Kennan to Father, November 28, 1933, folder 11, box 328; Kennan to Jeanette, December 2, 1933, folder 17, box 328, Kennan Papers.

90. Kennan to Jeanette, June 7, 1933, folder 17, box 328, Kennan Papers.

Chapter 3

1. Thayer to Kennan, April 10, 1940, box 3, Charles W. Thayer Papers, Harry S. Truman Presidential Library, Independence, MO.

2. Charles E. Bohlen, *Witness to History 1929–1969* (New York: W. W. Norton, 1973), 29.

3. Robert W. Thurston, *Life and Terror in Stalin's Russia* (New Haven, CT: Yale University Press, 1996), 2.

4. Sheila Fitzpatrick, *Everyday Stalinism* (New York: Oxford University Press, 1999), 68–69.

5. Kennan, "Memorial Service for Louis Fischer," January 23, 1970, folder 7, box 6, Louis Fischer Papers, Seeley G. Mudd Library, Princeton University, Princeton, NJ.

6. Louis Fischer quoted in Marie Ventura, "Honks, Whistles, and Harp: The Transnational Sound of Harpo Marx," *Miranda* 22 (2021), https://doi.org/10.4000/miranda.36228.

7. Bullitt's papers at Yale University include dozens of letters reflecting Missy LeHand's love for Bullitt and her expectation that they would marry. Bullitt's letters to LeHand were destroyed, perhaps by White House officials in the turmoil following her stroke in June 1941. See Frank Costigliola, *Roosevelt's Lost Alliances: How Personal Politics Helped Start the Cold War* (Princeton, NJ: Princeton University Press, 2012), 70–71.

8. For Harpo Marx as courier, see U.S. Department of State, "None Swifter than These: 100 Years of the Diplomatic Courier Service," November 23, 2018, https://www.state.gov/none -swifter-than-these-100-years-of-the-diplomatic-courier-service/dcs.

9. Bullitt's papers include many pages about Wilson in Freud's handwriting. See also Sigmund Freud and William C. Bullitt, *Thomas Woodrow Wilson: A Psychological Study* (Boston: Houghton Mifflin, 1967).

10. Kennan, *At a Century's Ending*, 32.

11. Kennan, "Fair Day, Adieu!", p. 9.

12. Bullitt to Secretary of State, January 4, 1934, 123 Bullitt, Wm. C./32, RG 59.

13. Kennan to Hotchkiss, January 25, 1935, folder 1, box 24, Kennan Papers.

14. Bullitt to Franklin D. Roosevelt, January 1, 1934, published in *For the President, Personal and Secret: Correspondence between Franklin D. Roosevelt and William C. Bullitt*, ed. Orville H. Bullitt (Boston: Houghton Mifflin, 1972), 65.

15. Bullitt, *For the President*, 66–69. For the memory of this kiss in the very different atmosphere of the early Cold War, see *The Price of Vision: The Diary of Henry A. Wallace 1942–1946*, ed. John Morton Blum (Boston: Houghton Mifflin, 1973), 548.

16. Bullitt, *For the President*, 87.

17. Philipps to American Legation, Riga, December 27, 1933, 123 K 36/145, RG 59.

18. Philipps to American Legation, Riga, December 27, 1933, 123 K 36/145, RG 59.

19. MacMurray to Secretary of State, January 2, 1934, 123 K 36/46, RG 59.

20. Kennan to Bullitt, December 27, 1933; Kennan to Bullitt, December 27, 1933, box 44, William C. Bullitt Papers, Sterling Library, Yale University, New Haven, CT.

21. George to Annelise, December 29, 1933; Annelise to George, January 2, 1934, folder 7, box 328, Kennan Papers; Kennan to Hotchkiss, January 6, 1933 [1934], folder 10, box 23, Kennan Papers.

22. Kennan, "Fair Day, Adieu!", p. 9.

23. Charles W. Thayer, *Bears in the Caviar* (Montpelier, VT: Russian Life, 2015), 87–93.

24. Kennan to Charlie James, July 29, 1934, folder 10, box 53, Kennan Papers.

25. Kennan, "Fair Day, Adieu!", pp. 6–9.

26. Kennan to Hotchkiss, April 15, 1934, folder 1, box 24, Kennan Papers.

27. Dietrich Beyrau, "Mortal Embrace: Germans and (Soviet) Russians in the First Half of the Twentieth Century," trans. Mark Keck-Szabel, in *Fascination and Enmity: Russia and Germany as Entangled Histories, 1914–1945*, ed. Michael David-Fox, Peter Holquist, and Alexander M. Martin (Pittsburgh: University of Pittsburgh Press, 2012), 228–40; Dale Pesmen, *Russia and Soul* (Ithaca, NY: Cornell University Press, 2000); Vera Tolz, *Russia: Inventing the Nation* (New York: Oxford University Press, 2001).

28. Thayer diary, February 16, 1934, box 6, Thayer Papers.

29. Kennan, *At a Century's Ending*, 34; Kennan, "Fair Day, Adieu!", p. 18; Kennan to Hotchkiss, January 6, 1933 [1934], Kennan Papers.

30. Kennan, "Fair Day, Adieu!", p. 7.

31. Kennan, "Fair Day, Adieu!", p. 7. The purported insults included: "O sultan, Turkish devil and damned devil's kith and kin, secretary to Lucifer himself." "What the devil kind of knight are you, that can't slay a hedgehog with your naked arse?" "The devil excretes, and your army eats." "You will not, you son of a bitch, make subjects of Christian sons; we've no fear of your army, by land and by sea we will battle with thee, fuck your mother."

32. Kennan, "Fair Day, Adieu!", p. 7.

33. Costigliola, *Kennan Diaries*, 92.

34. John and Patricia Davies interview with Gaddis, December 7, 1982, p. 6. Patricia Davies made the observation.

35. Charles E. Bohlen to Mother, April 15, 1934, box 36, Charles E. Bohlen Papers, Library of Congress, Washington, DC.

36. Thayer to Muzzy, May 9, 1934, box 5, Thayer Papers.

37. Thayer to Muzzy, February 11, 1935, box 5, Thayer Papers.

38. Bohlen to Mother, April 15, 1934, box 36, Bohlen Papers.

39. Thayer to Muzzy, November 8, 1934, box 5, Thayer Papers.

40. Thayer diary, April 14–May 20, 1934, box 6, Thayer Papers; Bohlen to Mother, April 15, 1934, box 36, Bohlen Papers; Bohlen, rough draft of *Witness to History*, box 10, Bohlen Papers.

41. Bohlen, *Witness to History 1929–1969*, 20.

42. Thayer to Kennan, April 10, 1940, box 3, Thayer Papers.

43. Thayer, *Bears in the Caviar*, 118–27.

44. Costigliola, *Kennan Diaries*, 92–93.

45. Costigliola, *Kennan Diaries*, 64.

46. Costigliola, *Kennan Diaries*, 69.

47. Klaus Meinert, *Youth in Soviet Russia*, trans. Michael Davidson (New York: Harcourt, Brace, 1933), 237.

48. Kennan to the Minister, August 19, 1932, published in *New York Review of Books*, April 26, 2001, 23. Kennan copied much of this document from a diary entry penned on June 26, 1931, amid his post-frenzy anomie. Costigliola, *Kennan Diaries*, 72–73.

49. Costigliola, *Kennan Diaries*, 66.

50. Costigliola, *Kennan Diaries*, 79.

51. Kennan, "Anton Chekhov and the Bolsheviks," 1932, folder 14, box 329, Kennan Papers.

52. Edward C. Wynne [Publications Committee of the State Department] to Editors of the *Yale Review*, December 27, 1932; EHF to Editor, *Scribner's* Magazine, July 12, 1933, folder 14, box 329, Kennan Papers.

53. Kennan, "Fair Day, Adieu!", p. 20.

54. Kennan, "Memorial Service for Louis Fischer," January 23, 1970, folder 7, box 6, Fischer Papers.

55. Kennan to Charlie James, July 29, 1934, folder 10, box 53, Kennan Papers.

56. Kennan to Hotchkiss, May 19, 1934, folder 17, box 328, Kennan Papers.

57. Kennan to Hotchkiss, May 19, 1934, folder 17, box 328, Kennan Papers.

58. Costigliola, *Kennan Diaries*, 91.

59. Kennan to Hotchkiss, May 19, 1934, folder 17, box 328, Kennan Papers.

60. Kennan to Hotchkiss, May 19, 1934, folder 17, box 328, Kennan Papers.

61. Kennan to Bullitt, July 6, 1934; Bullitt to Kennan, July 20, 1934; Kennan to Bullitt, July 31, 1934, all in box 44, Bullitt Papers.

62. Kennan to Hotchkiss, July 1, 1934, Kennan Papers.

63. Kennan to Hotchkiss, August 1, 1934, and postscript August 6, 1934, Kennan Papers.

64. "Death of Menzhinski, Head of the O.G.P.U.," May 17, 1934, 861.105/11, RG 59.

65. "Conditions in the Bashkir Republic," October 17, 1934, 861.5017—Living Conditions/770, RG 59.

66. David C. Engerman, *Modernization from the Other Shore: American Intellectuals and the Romance of Russian Development* (Cambridge, MA: Harvard University Press, 2003), especially 252–58.

67. "Report on Non-Aggression Pacts between Russia, Baltic States, and Poland," April 3, 1924, 761.0012 (Aggressor)/66; April 10, 1934, 761.0012 (Aggressor)/68; May 9, 1934; "German Refusal to Join Soviet Russia in Guaranteeing the Integrity of the Baltic Countries," May 4, 1934, 761.62/305, RG 59, National Archives.

68. "The Sale of the Chinese Eastern Railway," October 31, 1934, 861.77 Chinese Eastern/1354, RG 59, National Archives.

69. "Relations between the Second and Third Internationals," November 14, 1934, 800.00B – Communist International/159, RG 59, National Archives.

70. "The Hauptmann Case," October 29, 1934, 311.1111 Lindbergh Baby/346, RG 59, National Archives.

71. "Soviet Attitude towards Alaska," October 29, 1934, 811.Alas 014/10, RG 59, National Archives.

72. "PRAVDA Article Concerning American Elections," November 19, 1934, 811.00/431, RG 59, National Archives.

73. "Possibilities for the Development of Fascism in the United States," December 1, 1934, 811.00F/182, RG 59, National Archives.

74. Kennan, "Fair Day, Adieu!", pp. 14–15.

75. Annelise to Hotchkiss, November 9, 1934, folder 17, box 328, Kennan Papers.

76. Kennan to Hotchkiss, December 2, 1934, folder 1, box 24, Kennan Papers.

77. Annelise to Hotchkiss, November 9, 1934, folder 17, box 328, Kennan Papers.

78. Costigliola, *Kennan Diaries*, 94.

79. Kennan to Hotchkiss, November 24, 1934, folder 1, box 24, Kennan Papers.

80. Kennan, "Fair Day, Adieu!", p. 22.

81. Kennan, "Fair Day, Adieu!", p. 22.

82. Kennan, "Fair Day, Adieu!", pp. 22–24.

83. Kennan to Bullitt, January 4, 1935, box 44, Bullitt Papers.

84. John C. Wiley to Bullitt, December 21, 1934, box 90, Bullitt Papers.

85. Costigliola, *Kennan Diaries*, 94.

86. Kennan to Hotchkiss, December 31, 1934, folder 1, box 24, Kennan Papers.

87. Annelise to Hotchkiss, November 9, 1934, folder 17, box 328, Kennan Papers.

88. Kennan to Hotchkiss, December 31, 1934, folder 1, box 24, Kennan Papers.

89. Bullitt to Kennan, January 7, 1935, box 44, Bullitt Papers.

90. Kennan to Bullitt, February 12, 1935, box 44, Bullitt Papers.

91. Kennan to Hotchkiss, December 2, 1934, folder 1, box 24, Kennan Papers.

92. Kennan to Hotchkiss, January 25, 1935, folder 1, box 24, Kennan Papers.

93. Kennan to Hotchkiss, January 20, 1935, and January 21, 1935, folder 1, box 24, Kennan Papers.

94. Kennan to Hotchkiss, January 25, 1935, folder 1, box 24, Kennan Papers.

95. Kennan interview with Gaddis, December 13, 1987, pp. 21–22, folder 1, box 6, Gaddis Papers. Decades later, Kennan reflected that for a Hungarian "Jewish woman to become a staff physician in Gutenbrunn in those days—a very conservative old Austrian sanatorium with all the other doctors real Viennese—that was quite an achievement. She was an absolutely first-rate doctor." Kennan interview with Gaddis, December 13, 1987, p. 21, folder 1, box 6, Gaddis Papers.

96. Costigliola, *Kennan Diaries*, 99.

97. Costigliola, *Kennan Diaries*, 95–96.

98. Costigliola, *Kennan Diaries*, 103.

99. Costigliola, *Kennan Diaries*, 106.

100. Costigliola, *Kennan Diaries*, 110.

101. Kennan to Hotchkiss, March 6, 1935, folder 1, box 24, Kennan Papers.

102. Costigliola, *Kennan Diaries*, 108.

103. Costigliola, *Kennan Diaries*, 108.

104. Although Kennan did not specify which columns he had read, they likely included Frank Kent's "No Winners in This Fight," May 1, 1935; "An Ideal Duel," March 8, 1935; "Huey Long vs. Jim Farley," March 1, 1935; and "The Huey Problem," February 8, 1935. Kent scorned the many politicians who "relish the slush thrown at them almost as much as the slush they throw at others." Drew Pearson's columns also mocked the State Department. Pearson published a column that seems particularly to have irked Kennan. It poked fun at the spoiled, lazy careerists, such as the venerable Hugh Gibson, currently ambassador to Brazil. Unfortunately for Gibson, his Belgian-born wife despised Brazil as "the wilderness." So he had abandoned his post by taking serial sick leaves and other leaves with pay. To quiet the uproar, the State Department assigned Gibson to Buenos Aires to mediate the Chaco War between Bolivia and Paraguay, a conflict that Pearson ridiculed as a tempest in a teapot. He concluded the column with the snide comment that the State Department "hopes Mrs. Gibson will like" the Argentine capital. "Washington Merry-Go-Round," May 9, 1935.

105. Kennan to Hotchkiss, May 13, 1935, folder 1, box 24, Kennan Papers.

106. Kennan to Hotchkiss, May 13, 1935, folder 1, box 24, Kennan Papers.

107. Bullitt to Kennan, April 27, 1935, box 44, Bullitt Papers.

108. Kennan to Bullitt, February 12, 1935, box 44, Bullitt Papers.

109. Kennan to Hotchkiss, May 13, 1935, folder 1, box 24, Kennan Papers.

110. Kennan to Hotchkiss, May 13, 1935, folder 1, box 24, Kennan Papers.

111. Once Annelise returned from Norway, they took a beautiful, spacious apartment in the park of the Schönbrunn Palace. While the rent was only $80 per month, George's monthly income, with exchange adjustment, amounted to well over $400.

112. Kennan, "Fair Day, Adieu!", p. 30.

113. Kennan to Bullitt, April 15, 1935; Bullitt to Kennan, April 27, 1935, box 44, Bullitt Papers.

114. Annelise to Hotchkiss, May 31, 1935, folder 2, box 328, Kennan Papers.

115. Kennan to Charlie Thayer, May 22, 1935, box 3, Thayer Papers.

116. Messersmith to Bullitt, June 26, 1935, box 56, Bullitt Papers.

117. Bullitt to Messersmith, August 28, 1935, box 56, Bullitt Papers.

118. Messersmith to Bullitt, November 6, 1935, box 56, Bullitt Papers.

119. Kennan to Hotchkiss, June 28, 1935, folder 1, box 24, Kennan Papers.

120. Annelise to Hotchkiss, May 31, 1935, folder 2, box 328, Kennan Papers.

121. Thayer to Muzzy, February 11, 1935, box 5, Thayer Papers.

122. Kennan to Thayer, May 22, 1935, box 3, Thayer Papers.

123. Thayer to Kennan, April 10, 1940, box 3, Thayer Papers.

Chapter 4

1. George F. Kennan to Jeanette Kennan Hotchkiss, September 11, 1935, folder 1, box 24, Kennan Papers; Kennan to William C. Bullitt, November 4, 1935, box 44, Bullitt Papers.

2. Isaiah Berlin interview with John Lewis Gaddis, November 29, 1992, folder 2, box 1, Gaddis Papers.

3. Kennan, *Memoirs 1925–1950*, 70.

4. These last two disappointments, which soured Kennan's outlook while on the Russian desk of the State Department from September 1937 to September 1938, are covered in chapter 5.

5. Kennan to Hotchkiss, June 28, 1935, folder 1, box 24, Kennan Papers.

6. Kennan, "Fair Day, Adieu!", p. 34.

7. Kennan, "Fair Day, Adieu!", p. 35.

8. Costigliola, *Kennan Diaries*, 111.

9. Kennan to Hotchkiss, November 17, 1935, box 24, folder 1, Kennan Papers.

10. Irena Wiley, "Spaso 1935," box 18, Foy D. Kohler Papers, Ward M. Canaday Center, University of Toledo, Toledo, Ohio; Thayer, *Bears in the Caviar*, 168–76.

11. They formed an emotional community—that is, a group of people who interact with each other to sustain a norm for processing, expressing, and valuing emotions. For the concept, see Barbara H. Rosenwein, *Emotional Communities in the Early Middle Ages* (Ithaca, NY: Cornell University Press, 2006).

12. Kennan, *Memoirs 1925–1950*, 61.

13. Fanny S. Chipman interview with Hope Meyers, July 22, 1987, Association for Diplomatic Studies and Training, Foreign Affairs Oral History Program, Foreign Service Spouse Series, p. 44, https://adst.org/OH%20TOCs/Chipman-Fanny-S.pdf.

14. Thayer to Muzzy, April 1, 1935, box 5, Thayer Papers.

15. Fanny Chipman interview with Hope Meyers, pp. 48–49.

16. Fanny Chipman interview with Hope Meyers, pp. 48–49.

17. Thayer to Kennan, April 10, 1940, box 3, Thayer Papers.

18. Thayer to Kennan, April 10, 1940, box 3, Thayer Papers.

19. Thayer to Sissy, January 15, 1936, box 5, Thayer Papers.

20. Kennan, "Fair Day, Adieu!", p. 36.

21. Kennan, "Fair Day, Adieu!", p. 68; Kennan, *Memoirs 1925–1950*, 83.

22. H. W. Brands, *Inside the Cold War: Loy Henderson and the Rise of the American Empire 1918–1961* (New York: Oxford University Press, 1991), 36–37.

23. Loy W. Henderson interview with Gaddis, September 25, 1982, pp. 3, 10, folder 18, box 1, Gaddis Papers.

24. Kennan, "Fair Day, Adieu!", p. 36.

25. Kennan to Hotchkiss, Christmas Day 1935, folder 1, box 24, Kennan Papers; Kennan, "Fair Day, Adieu!", pp. 36–38.

26. Kennan, "Fair Day, Adieu!", p. 37.

27. In 1884, the wealthy James family had purchased extensive shorefront on Nagawicka Lake and subsequently built three houses. One was the summer home of the Kennan children's Uncle Alfred Farragut and Aunt Nellie James, and another was inherited by the children from their mother's estate. See Jeanette Kennan Hotchkiss, "Grandparents, Known and Unknown," unpublished manuscript edited by Eugene Hotchkiss, February 20, 1996, folder 1, box 330, Kennan Papers.

28. Kennan to Hotchkiss, Christmas Day 1935, folder 1, box 24, Kennan Papers; Kennan, "Fair Day, Adieu!", pp. 36–38.

29. Kennan, "Fair Day, Adieu!", p. 38.

30. Kennan to Hotchkiss, Christmas Day 1935, folder 1, box 24, Kennan Papers.

31. Kennan to Hotchkiss, Christmas Day 1935, folder 1, box 24, Kennan Papers.

32. Kennan to Hotchkiss, January 14 postscript on January 10, 1937 letter, folder 1, box 24, Kennan Papers.

33. Bullitt to Secretary of State, April 24, 1936, 861.657/2, General Records of the Department of State, RG 59. While State Department protocol mandated that despatches go out under the name of the presiding officer in the embassy, it was Kennan who wrote this report and nearly all the others cited in this chapter. The documents bear the initials GFK.

34. Henderson to Secretary of State, September 19, 1936, 811.79661-Levanevsky, S. A./22, RG 59.

35. Henderson to Secretary of State, April 15, 1937, 102.1 6/998, RG 59.

36. Davies to Secretary of State, July 9, 1937, 611.6131/448, RG 59.

37. Henderson to Secretary of State, September 4, 1936, 800.00B-Communist International/191, RG 59.

38. Henderson to Secretary of State, December 19, 1935, 765.84/3347, RG 59.

39. Kennan to Secretary of State, January 18, 1936, 761.00/265, RG 59.

40. Henderson to Secretary of State, December 21, 1935, 711.00111 Armament Control/681, RG 59.

41. Henderson to Secretary of State, November 19, 1936, 852.00/3939, RG 59.

42. Henderson to Secretary of State, December 2, 1936; R. Walton Moore to Loy W. Henderson, January 25, 1937, 861.412/25, RG 59.

43. Bullitt to Secretary of State, March 4, 1936, 861.00B/671, RG 59.

44. Bullitt to Secretary of State, March 4, 1936, 861.00B/671, RG 59.

45. Henderson interview with Gaddis, September 25, 1982, p. 3, folder 18, box 1, Gaddis Papers.

46. "Recent Trends in the All-Union Communist Party of the Soviet Union," February 21, 1936, 861.00-Party, All-Union Communist/180, RG 59.

47. "Recent Trends in the All-Union Communist Party of the Soviet Union," February 21, 1936, 861.00-Party, All-Union Communist/180, RG 59; Kennan, "Fair Day, Adieu!", p. 40.

48. Bullitt to Secretary of State, February 26, 1936, 861.44-Bukharin, Nicolai I/1, RG 59.

49. Kennan, "Fair Day, Adieu!", pp. 43–44; Costigliola, Kennan Diaries, 112, 114.

50. Kennan, "Fair Day, Adieu!", p. 44.

51. For the final dispatch, see Bullitt to the State Department, April 20, 1936, Department of State, Foreign Relations of the United States: The Soviet Union 1933–1939 (Washington: GPO, 1952), 291–96. For Kennan's draft, see "Fair Day, Adieu!", pp. 44–46.

52. Kennan, "Fair Day, Adieu!", p. 45.

53. Kennan, "Fair Day, Adieu!", p. 45.

54. Kennan, "Fair Day, Adieu!", p. 46.

55. Kennan, "Fair Day, Adieu!", p. 47; Kennan to Hotchkiss, September 27, 1936, folder 1, box 24, Kennan Papers.

56. Kennan to Bullitt, June 9, 1936, box 44, Bullitt Papers.

57. Kennan, "Fair Day, Adieu!", pp. 47–48.

58. Kennan to Hotchkiss, September 8, 1936, folder 1, box 24, Kennan Papers; Kennan, Memoirs 1925–1950, 78.

59. Kennan, "Fair Day, Adieu!", pp. 49–50.

60. Sheila Fitzpatrick, On Stalin's Team The Years of Living Dangerously in Soviet Politics (Princeton, NJ: Princeton University Press), 116; Stephen Kotkin, Stalin, 1929–1941 (New York: Penguin, 2017), 377–553.

61. Sarah Davies and James Harris, Stalin's World (New Haven, CT: Yale University Press, 2014), 59–91; Fitzpatrick, On Stalin's Team, 114–17.

62. Pierre Broué, "Party Opposition to Stalin (1930–32) and the First Moscow Trial," in Essays on Revolutionary Culture and Stalinism, ed. John W. Strong (Indianapolis, IN: Slavica, 1990), 98–111.

63. Davies and Harris, Stalin's World, 65. See also 59–91.

64. Davies and Harris, Stalin's World, 91. See also 58–90.

65. Davies and Harris, Stalin's World, 76.

66. Fitzpatrick, On Stalin's Team, 119–20; William Chase, "Stalin as Producer: The Moscow Show Trials and the Construction of Moral Threats," in Stalin: A New History, ed. Sarah Davies and James Harris (New York: Cambridge University Press, 2005), 226–48.

67. "The Case of the Trotskyite-Zinovievite Terrorist Centre," transmitted by Henderson to Secretary of State, December 31, 1936, 861.00/11652, RG 59.

68. "The Case of the Trotskyite-Zinovievite Terrorist Centre"; Karl Schlögel, *Moscow 1937* (Malden, MA: Polity Press, 2012), 68–80. Vain about his performance, Vyshinski years later perked up when Bohlen told him that he had attended the show trial of Bukharin in 1938. "As a producer might about a stage set," Vyshinksi asked the American, "'How did it look to you?'" Bohlen, *Witness to History 1929–1969*, 49.

69. Katerina Clark, *Moscow the Fourth Rome* (Cambridge, MA: Harvard University Press, 2011), 226–27.

70. Kennan, "Fair Day, Adieu!", p. 50.

71. Henderson to Secretary of State, September 30, 1936, 861.002/122. See also Henderson to Secretary of State, September 29, 1936, 861.002/121; Henderson to Secretary of State, October 21, 1936, 861.002/124; Henderson to Secretary of State, October 22, 1936, 861.002/126; Henderson to Secretary of State, November 4, 1936, 861.002/128; Henderson to Secretary of State, May 18, 1937, 800.131/139, all RG 59.

72. Henderson to Secretary of State, November 17, 1936, 861.415/51, RG 59. See also Henderson to Secretary of State, September 29, 1936, 861.002/124, RG 59.

73. Henderson to Secretary of State, September 1, 1936, 861.00/11637, RG 59.

74. Kennan to Hotchkiss, December 6, 1936, folder 1, box 24, Kennan Papers.

75. Fanny Chipman interview with Hope Meyers, pp. 44–45.

76. Kennan to Jeanette Hotchkiss, December 6, 1936, folder 1, box 24, Kennan Papers.

77. Kennan to Hotchkiss January 10, 1937, folder 1, box 24, Kennan Papers.

78. Gaddis, *George F. Kennan: An American Life*, 103.

79. Kennan to Hotchkiss, February 17, 1937, folder 1, box 24, Kennan Papers.

80. Bohlen, *Witness to History*, 45.

81. Kennan, *Memoirs 1925–1950*, 82.

82. Joseph E. Davies to Robert F. Kelley, February 10, 1937, box 3, Joseph E. Davies Papers, Library of Congress, Washington, DC.

83. Kennan, *Memoirs 1925–1950*, 82–83.

84. Kennan to Hotchkiss, March 17, 1937, folder 1, box 24, Kennan Papers.

85. Kennan, *Memoirs 1925–1950*, 83.

86. Kennan to Hotchkiss, February 17, 1937, folder 1, box 24, Kennan Papers.

87. Joseph E. Davies, *Mission to Moscow* (New York: Simon and Schuster, 1941), 32–56; Department of State, *Foreign Relations of the United States: The Soviet Union 1933–1939* (Washington: Government Printing Office, 1952), 362–69.

88. See Davies and Harris, *Stalin's World*, 59–91; Kotkin, *Stalin*, 330–33.

89. Costigliola, *Kennan Diaries*, 70–71.

90. S. Uranov, "Concerning Certain Artful Methods of the Recruiting Work of the Foreign Intelligence Services," *Pravda*, May 4, 1937.

91. Henderson to Secretary of State, "Developments Affecting the Position of Foreigners in the Soviet Union," May 12, 1937, 361.00/11, RG 59.

92. Thayer, *Bears in the Caviar*, 155.

93. Memorandum by Bohlen, June 22, 1937, 361.00/11, RG 59.

94. Fanny Chipman interview with Hope Meyers, pp. 50–51.

95. Henderson to Secretary of State, "Developments Affecting the Position of Foreigners in the Soviet Union," May 12, 1937, 361.00/11, RG 59.

96. Henderson to Secretary of State, April 26, 1937, 361.6121 Steiger, Boris S./1; Henderson to Robert F. Kelley, April 29, 1937, 861.00/11702; Henderson to Secretary of State, May 26, 1937, 861.20/396, RG 59.

97. Fanny Chipman interview with Hope Meyers, p. 51.

98. Davies, *Mission to Moscow*, 80–81, 257; Henderson to Secretary of State, April 26, 1937, 361.6121 Steiger, Boris S./1; Henderson to Robert F. Kelley, April 29, 1937, 861.00/11702, RG 59.

99. Davies, *Mission to Moscow*, 266, 270.

100. Henderson to Secretary of State, June 18, 1937, 861.1281/16, RG 59.

101. Peter Whitewood, *The Red Army and the Great Terror* (Lawrence: University Press of Kansas, 2015), 201–85.

102. Henderson to Secretary of State, June 13, 1937, 861.20/390, RG 59.

103. Henderson to Secretary of State, May 26, 1937, 861.20/396, RG 59.

104. Henderson to Secretary of State, "The Establishment of Military Soviets in the Red Army," May 25, 1937, 861.20/395, RG 59.

105. Henderson to Secretary of State, June 1, 1937, 861.20/398, RG 59. For Gamarnik, see Whitewood, *Red Army and the Great Terror*, 245–46.

106. Henderson to Secretary of State, June 9. 1937, 861.20/386, RG 59.

107. Annelise Kennan interview with Gaddis, September 8, 1983, p. 4, folder 23, box 1, Gaddis Papers.

108. Thayer to Sissy, August 18, 1937, box 5, Thayer Papers.

109. Henderson to Secretary of State, June 12, 1937, 861.20/389, RG 59.

110. Kennan to Eugene Hotchkiss, March [n.d.] 1937, folder 11, box 53, Kennan Papers.

111. Kennan to Hotchkiss, March 31, 1937, folder 1, box 24, Kennan Papers.

112. Costigliola, *Kennan Diaries*, 117.

113. Costigliola, *Kennan Diaries*, 117–18.

114. Kennan to Hotchkiss, March 31, 1937, folder 1, box 24, Kennan Papers.

115. Kennan to Hotchkiss, September 11, 1935, folder 1, box 24, Kennan Papers.

116. Kennan, "Fair Day, Adieu!", p. 42; Kennan to Hotchkiss, March 31, 1937, folder 1, box 24, Kennan Papers.

117. Kennan, "Fair Day, Adieu!", pp. 41–43; Kennan to Hotchkiss, March 31, 1937, folder 1, box 24, Kennan Papers. These quotations are drawn from both the 1937 letter to Hotchkiss and from "Fair Day, Adieu!", written sometime in 1939–1940, in which Kennan seems to have mixed together his impressions of two trips to the Crimea, in March 1936 to Sochi and in March 1937 to Yalta. See also Kennan, *Sketches from a Life*, 27–33.

118. Kennan, "Fair Day, Adieu!", p. 50; Kennan, *Memoirs 1925–1950*, 67.

119. Davies and Harris, *Stalin's World*; Fitzpatrick, *On Stalin's Team*.

120. Kennan, "Fair Day, Adieu!", pp. 55–56.

121. Kennan, "Fair Day, Adieu!", pp. 53–54.

122. Kennan, "Fair Day, Adieu!", pp. 59–61 (emphasis in original).

123. Kennan, "Fair Day, Adieu!", p. 62.

Chapter 5

1. Annelise S. Kennan to Jeanette Kennan Hotchkiss, July 28, 1942, folder 2, box 328, Kennan Papers.

2. Kennan, "Fair Day, Adieu!", p. 72.

3. Kennan to Hotchkiss, September 14, 1937, folder 1, box 24, Kennan Papers.

4. Kennan, "Fair Day, Adieu!", p. 28.

5. Kennan, "Fair Day, Adieu!", pp.75–76.

6. Kennan to Hotchkiss, September 14, 1937, folder 1, box 24, Kennan Papers.

7. Kennan to Hotchkiss [n.d. but late 1937], folder 1, box 24, Kennan Papers.

8. Kennan to Hotchkiss, December 20, 1937, folder 28, box 327, Kennan Papers.

9. William R. Castle diary, June 19, 1937, William R. Castle Papers, Houghton Library, Harvard University, Cambridge, MA.

10. Kennan, *Memoirs 1925–1950*, 85.

11. Kennan, *Memoirs 1925–1950*, 83–85; Bohlen, *Witness to History 1929–1969*, 39–41.

12. Anthony Biddle Jr. [in Warsaw] to J. Pierrepont Moffat [n.d. but 1938], vol. 13, Jay Pierrepont Moffat Papers, Houghton Library, Harvard University; Moffat to Biddle, June 23, 1938, Moffat Papers.

13. Kennan, *Memoirs 1925–1950*, 85.

14. Kennan, "Fair Day, Adieu!", pp. 18–19.

15. Kennan, "Fair Day, Adieu!", p. 2.

16. Kennan, "Fair Day, Adieu!", p. 26.

17. Kennan, "Fair Day, Adieu!", p. 18.

18. Costigliola, *Kennan Diaries*, 118.

19. Kennan, "Fair Day, Adieu!", p. 17.

20. Costigliola, *Kennan Diaries*, 119.

21. Kennan, "Fair Day, Adieu!", p. 30.

22. Costigliola, *Kennan Diaries*, 125, 126, 128; Kennan, "Fair Day, Adieu!", p. 31.

23. Costigliola, *Kennan Diaries*, 129.

24. Costigliola, *Kennan Diaries*, 129.

25. Kennan, *Memoirs 1925–1950*, 559.

26. Kennan, *American Democracy*, 128.

27. Kennan, "Fair Day, Adieu!", p. 30.

28. Kennan to Hotchkiss, February 13, 1940, folder 1, box 24, Kennan Papers.

29. Kennan, "Fair Day, Adieu!", pp. 31–32.

30. Kennan, "The Prerequisites: Notes on the Problems of the United States in 1938," folder 4, box 240, Kennan Papers. See also C. Ben Wright, "George F. Kennan, Scholar-Diplomat: 1926–1946," (PhD diss., University of Wisconsin, 1972); David Mayers, *George Kennan and the Dilemmas of U.S. Foreign Policy* (New York: Oxford University Press, 1988).

31. Kennan, "Fair Day, Adieu!", pp. 29–30.

32. Kennan, "The Prerequisites."

33. Kennan, "The Prerequisites."

34. Douglas Irwin, "What Caused the Recession of 1937–38?", September 11, 2011, http://voxeu.org/article/what-caused-recession-1937-38-new-lesson-today-s-policymakers.

35. Kennan, *Memoirs 1925–1950*, 85–86.

36. George S. Messersmith memorandum of conversation with the president, February 1, 1938, folder 59, box 8, George S. Messersmith Papers, University of Delaware Library, Newark, DE.

37. Wright, "George F. Kennan: Scholar-Diplomat, 1926–1946," 133.

38. Messersmith to Henderson, January 5, 1938, box 1, Loy Henderson Papers, Library of Congress, Washington, DC.

39. Davies to Messersmith, March 10, 1938, 124.616/246, RG 59.

40. Kennan to Moffat and Nielsen, March 24, 1938, 124.61/130, RG 59. Kennan also pressed these ideas in conversation.

41. Edward Bennett, *Franklin D. Roosevelt and the Search for Security* (Wilmington, DE: Scholarly Resources, 1985). 143–44.

42. Kennan, "Fair Day, Adieu!", pp. 7–9.

43. Messersmith to Hull, June 24, 1938, box 9, folder 64, Messersmith Papers.

44. J. J. Murphy to Messersmith, April 26, 1938, 124.616/247, RG 59.

45. Kennan to Messersmith, May 4, 1938, 124.616/247, RG 59.

46. Kennan to Messersmith, May 5, 1938, 124.616/247, RG 59.

47. Kennan to Moffat and Nielsen, March 24, 1938, 124.61/130, RG 59.

48. Alexander C. Kirk to Moffat, October 28, 1938, vol. 13, Moffat Papers; Bohlen, *Witness to History*, 46.

49. Franklin D. Roosevelt to Hull and Messersmith, December 22, 1939; Messersmith to Hull, December 16, 1939, 124.61/144 ½, RG 59.

50. Messersmith to Hull, January 3, 1938, box 8, folder 58, Messersmith Papers.

51. Elizabeth Kimball MacLean, *Joseph E. Davies* (Westport, CT: Praeger, 1992), 54–57.

52. Lecture before the Foreign Service School on May 20, 1938, folder 1, box 298, Kennan Papers.

53. Lecture before the Foreign Service School on May 20, 1938, folder 1, box 298, Kennan Papers.

54. Moffat to Wilbur J. Carr, August 12, 1937, vol. 12, Moffat Papers.

55. Moffat to Kirk, August 2, 1938, vol. 13, Moffat Papers.

56. Kennan to Hotchkiss, December 26, 1937, folder 1, box 24, Kennan Papers.

57. Costigliola, *Kennan Diaries*, 124.

58. Kennan to Bullitt, July 15, 1938; Bullitt to Kennan, July 28, 1938, box 44, Bullitt Papers.

59. Kennan to Hotchkiss, November 14, 1938, folder 1, box 24, Kennan Papers.

60. Kennan to Cousin Grace, October 17, 1938, folder 12, box 53, Kennan Papers.

61. Kennan to Hotchkiss, November 14, 1938, folder 1, box 24; Kennan to Cousin Grace, October 17, 1938, folder 12, box 53, Kennan Papers. George learned enough Czech, Slovak, and Ruthenian to read the newspapers.

62. Costigliola, *Kennan Diaries*, 131.

63. Kennan, *Memoirs 1925–1950*, 415.

64. Costigliola, *Kennan Diaries*, 59.

65. Kennan, *Memoirs 1925–1950*, 94.

66. Kennan, *From Prague after Munich*, 224.

67. Kennan, *From Prague after Munich*, 224.

68. Kennan, *From Prague after Munich*, 171.

69. Kennan, *Memoirs 1925–1950*, 94, 118, 90.

70. Kennan, *From Prague after Munich*, 171.

71. Kennan, *From Prague after Munich*, 45–46.

72. Kennan, *From Prague after Munich*, 53–55.

73. Kennan, *From Prague after Munich*, 85–86.

74. Gaddis, *George F. Kennan*, 126.

75. Kennan to Hotchkiss [July 1943], folder 1, box 24, Kennan Papers.

Chapter 6

1. Kennan, *Memoirs 1925–1950*, 108.

2. Kennan to Gordon Craig, July 28, 1998, box 181, Kennan Papers.

3. Kennan, "The Fate of the Kennan Family during World War II" [1998], folder 21, box 311, Kennan Papers.

4. Kennan to Hotchkiss, March 7, 1940, folder 1, box 24, Kennan Papers.

5. Kennan to Hotchkiss, November 14, 1939, folder 1, box 24, Kennan Papers.

6. Annelise Kennan to Hotchkiss, February 12, 1940, folder 2, box 328, Kennan Papers.

7. Kennan, *Memoirs 1925–1950*, 114–15.

8. Kennan, *Memoirs 1925–1950*, 112–15.

9. Kennan to Hotchkiss, August 17, 1941, folder 1, box 24, Kennan Papers.

10. Kennan, *Memoirs 1925–1950*, 120–21; Kennan to Robert Silvers, January 22, 1972, folder 2, box 272, Kennan Papers.

11. Ger van Roon, *German Resistance to Hitler: Count von Moltke and the Kreisau Circle* (London: Van Nostrand Reinhold, 1971), 186–88.

12. Annelise Sorensen Kennan interview with Gaddis, December 14, 1987, p. 23.

13. Warnecke, *Daughter of the Cold War*, 27.

14. Warnecke, *Daughter of the Cold War*, 27–28.

15. Gene Hotchkiss, Jr. interview with author, May 30, 2016.

16. Kennan, "Fate of the Kennan Family during World War II," p. 5.

17. Warnecke, *Daughter of the Cold War*, 27.

18. Kennan to Hotchkiss, February 13, 1940, folder 1, box 24, Kennan Papers.

19. Kennan to Hotchkiss, July 28, 1941, folder 1, box 24, Kennan Papers.

20. Hotchkiss interview with Gaddis, December 21, 1982, pp. 18–19.

21. Kennan to Hotchkiss, November 5, 1940, folder 1, box 24, Kennan Papers (emphasis in original).

22. Kennan to Hotchkiss, October 21, 1940, folder 1, box 24, Kennan Papers.

23. Kennan to Hotchkiss, September 5, 1941, folder 1, box 24, Kennan Papers.

24. Kennan to Hotchkiss, August 17, 1941, folder 1, box 24, Kennan Papers.

25. Kennan to Hotchkiss, October 21, 1940, folder 1, box 24, Kennan Papers (emphasis in original).

26. Kennan to Hotchkiss, April 15, 1940, folder 1, box 24, Kennan Papers.

27. Kennan to Hotchkiss, April 15, 1940, folder 1, box 24, Kennan Papers.

28. Kennan to James W. Riddleberger, November 20, 1941, folder 8, box 140, Kennan Papers.

29. Kennan, *Memoirs 1925–1950*, 133.

30. Kennan, [Report on Internment] July 22, 1942, folder 14, box 329, Kennan Papers.

31. Kennan, "German Activities Concerning Mr. and Mrs. Weidhaas," May 10, May 25, 1942, 862.20211/3516, RG 59; Kennan, "Activities of Mr. Hugo Templeton Speck during Internment of American Official Group at Bad Nauheim," May 5, May 10, May 25, 1942, 862.20211/3523, RG 59.

32. "Drafts and Notes 1942," folder 8, box 298, Kennan Papers.

33. These paragraphs draw from Kennan, "The Russian Aristocracy of the XVIII Century" [1942] folder 7, box 298, Kennan Papers.

34. Costigliola, *Kennan Diaries*, 148.

35. Costigliola, *Kennan Diaries*, 147–48.

36. Morris to Secretary of State, December 8, 1941, 123K36/356, RG 59; Kennan, *Memoirs 1925–1950*, 139.

37. Warnecke, *Daughter of the Cold War*, 29.

38. Sumner Welles to Mrs. George F. Kennan, March 9, 1942, 123K36/366, RG 59.

39. Annelise Sorensen Kennan to George F. Kennan, April 29, 1942, folder 7, box 330, Kennan Papers [underlining in original].

40. Warnecke, *Daughter of the Cold War*, 116.

41. Kennan to Hotchkiss, July 21, 1942, folder 3, box 329, Kennan Papers.

42. Warnecke, *Daughter of the Cold War*, 31–35.

43. G. Howland Shaw to Kennan, August 31, 1942, 123K36/391, RG 59; Kennan, "Problems and Opportunities of the Foreign Service," Lawrenceville School, April 30, 1953, folder 22, box 300, Kennan Papers.

44. G. Howland Shaw to Kennan, August 31, 1942, 123K36/391, RG 59; Kennan, "Problems and Opportunities of the Foreign Service, Lawrenceville School," April 30, 1953, folder 22, box 300, Kennan Papers.

45. Kennan, *Memoirs 1925–1950*, 143.

46. Annelise S. Kennan to Jeanette Hotchkiss, August 1942, folder 2, box 328, Kennan Papers.

47. Annelise S. Kennan to Jeanette Hotchkiss, November 14, 1942, and December 10, 1942, folder 2, box 328, Kennan Papers.

48. Kennan to Hotchkiss, December 2, 1942, folder 1, box 24, Kennan Papers.

49. Kennan, *Memoirs 1925–1950*, 143; Kennan, "Problems and Opportunities of the Foreign Service," Lawrenceville School, April 30, 1953, folder 22, box 300, Kennan Papers.

50. Robert K. Meiklejohn diary, December 23, 1945, box 211, W. Averell Harriman Papers, Library of Congress.

51. G. Howland Shaw to Adolf Berle, October 6, 1942, 811.20252/9-2642.

52. Kennan to Adolf Berle, March 23, 1943, 811.20200(D)/3-2343.

53. Hull to Kennan [from Lyon], November 27, 1943, 103.918/1904B, NARG 59.

54. Kennan to Hull with attached minutes, August 21, 1943, 740.0011 EW/8-2143.

55. Department of State, *Foreign Relations of the United States 1943* (Washington: Government Printing Office, 1964), 527.

56. Norman Herz, *Operation Alacrity: The Azores and the War in the Atlantic* (Annapolis, MD: Naval Institute Press, 2004), 72–90.

57. "Get Tough," *New York Times*, May 7, 1941, p. 12.

58. Kennan, "Problems of Diplomatic-Military Collaboration," National War College lecture, March 7, 1947, folder 29, box 298, Kennan Papers.

59. Alexandre Moreli, "The War of Seduction: The Anglo-American Struggle to Engage with the Portuguese Ruling Elite (1943–1948)," *International History Review* 48. no. 3 (February 2017): 9–10.

60. Kennan to Dunn, September 9, 1943, 711.53/31, RG 59.

61. Grace Kennan Warnecke email to author, June 17, 2017; Warnecke, *Daughter of the Cold War*, 40–44; Kennan, "The Fate of the Kennan Family during World War II," pp. 11–12.

62. Gaddis, *George F. Kennan*, 170.

63. Warnecke, *Daughter of the Cold War*, 52–58; Kennan, "The Fate of the Kennan Family in World War II."

64. Kennan to James Clement Dunn, September 9, 1943; Dunn to Kennan, October 1, 1943, 711.53/31, RG 59.

65. Kennan, "Problems of Diplomatic-Military Collaboration," National War College lecture, March 7, 1947, folder 29, box 298, Kennan Papers.

66. Kennan to Hotchkiss, January 31, 1943, and April 5, 1943, folder 1, box 24, Kennan Papers.

67. Kennan to the Undersecretary and Matthews, October 18, 1943, box 1, entry 3134, RG 84.

68. H. Freeman Matthews to Stettinius, October 22, 1943, Miscellaneous Office Files, 1910–44, Lot 5 EUR-8, entry A1-207, RG 59.

69. Kennan to the Undersecretary and Matthews, October 20, 1943, box 1, entry 3134, RG 84.

70. Kennan, "Problems of Diplomatic-Military Collaboration."

71. Kennan, *Memoirs 1925–1950*, 156.

72. Kennan, "Problems of Diplomatic-Military Collaboration"; Kennan, *Memoirs 1925–1950*, 157–59.

73. Kennan, *Memoirs 1925–1950*, 161; Kennan, "Problems of Diplomatic-Military Collaboration."

74. Kennan to Matthews and Stettinius, November 3, 1943, Lot 5 EUR-8, Entry A1-207, Miscellaneous Office Files, 1910–1944, RG 59.

75. Kennan, "Problems of Diplomatic-Military Collaboration."

76. Gaddis interview with Frank K. Roberts, box 1, Gaddis Papers.

77. Kennan to Matthews, November 19, 1943, 123K36/-, RG 59.

78. Norweb to Hull, December 2, 1943, 123K36/448; Norweb to Stettinius, December 2, 1943, 123K36/464, RG 59.

79. Moreli, "War of Seduction," 11, 13.

80. Kennan, "Problems of Diplomatic-Military Collaboration."

81. Isaiah Berlin interview by Gaddis, November 29, 1992, p. 2, box 1, Gaddis Papers.

82. Kennan to Hotchkiss, April 30, 1943, folder 1, box 24, Kennan Papers.

83. Kennan to Hotchkiss, March 22, 1943, folder 1, box 24, Kennan Papers.

84. Kennan to Hotchkiss, April 30, 1943, folder 1, box 24, Kennan Papers.

85. Kennan to Hotchkiss, July 20, 1943, folder 1, box 24, Kennan Papers.

86. Kennan to Hotchkiss, March 22, 1943, folder 1, box 24, Kennan Papers.

87. Kennan to Hotchkiss, April 5, 1943, folder 1, box 24, Kennan Papers.

88. Promotion notices in Kennan's personal file, March 27, 1940; June 18, 1942; August 15, 1944, 123K36/-, RG 59.

89. Margaret L. Plunkett, "Trend of Earnings Among White-Collar Workers During the War: Bulletin of the United States Bureau of Labor Statistics," No. 783 (Washington: Government Printing Office, 1944), 10, https://fraser.stlouisfed.org/scribd/?title_id=4259&filepath=/files/docs/publications/bls/bls_0783_1944.pdf.

90. Kennan to Hotchkiss, July 2; July 20, 1943, folder 1, box 24, Kennan Papers.

91. Warnecke, *Daughter of the Cold War*, 39–40.

92. Kennan to Hotchkiss, "at sea" [July 1943], folder 1, box 24, Kennan Papers. The next pages draw heavily from this letter.

93. "Remarks to the Officer Staff of the Legation [Embassy] at Lisbon," June 1944, folder 9, box 298, Kennan Papers. The next pages draw heavily from this talk.

94. Kennan to Gene Hotchkiss, April 18, 1944, folder 6, box 140, Kennan Papers.

95. Kennan manuscript diary, May 14, 1944, box 231, Kennan Papers.

96. Kennan to Cyrus Follmer, May 14, 1944, folder 6, box 140, Kennan Papers.

97. Kennan to Hotchkiss [late July 1943], folder 1, box 24; "Remarks to the Officer Staff of the Legation at Lisbon."

98. These paragraphs draw from Kennan's rambling letter to Jeanette Hotchkiss [late July 1943], folder 1, box 24, Kennan Papers.

99. Kennan, *Memoirs 1925–1950*, 168.

100. Kennan, *Memoirs 1925–1950*, 166.

101. "Remarks to the Officer Staff of the Legation at Lisbon," June 1944, folder 9, box 298, Kennan Papers; "George Kennan's Private Memo" [submitted to Admiral William Leahy] [1944], File: France, Europe, European Advisory Commission, Miscellaneous Office Files, 1910–1944, Entry A1-207, RG 59.

102. "George Kennan's Private Memo."

103. "George Kennan's Private Memo."

104. Kennan, *Memoirs 1925–1950*, 170–71.

Chapter 7

1. Kennan to Hotchkiss, October 8, 1944, box 24, Kennan Papers.

2. Kennan, *Memoirs 1925–1950*, 195.

3. Kennan, "The Sources of Soviet Conduct," *Foreign Affairs* 25 (July 1947): 582.

4. Kennan, "Where Do We Stand?" National War College, December 21, 1949, folder 32, box 299, Kennan Papers.

5. Kennan, "Planning of Foreign Policy," June 18, 1947, folder 37, box 298, Kennan Papers.

6. Giles D. Harlow and George C. Maerz, *Measures Short of War: The George F. Kennan Lectures at the National War College 1946–47* (Washington: National Defense University Press, 1990).

7. Kennan, *Memoirs 1925–1950*, 211.

8. Frank Costigliola, *Roosevelt's Lost Alliances: How Personal Politics Helped Start the Cold War* (Princeton, NJ: Princeton University Press, 2012), 304, 500–01.

9. Milovan Djilas, *Conversations with Stalin* (New York: Harcourt, Brace & World, 1962), 95, 110.

10. "George Kennan's Private Memo" [submitted to Admiral William Leahy] [1944].

11. Robert K. Meiklejohn diary, March 17, 1945, Harriman Papers.

12. Frank Costigliola, "'Like Animals or Worse': Narratives of Culture and Emotion by U.S. and British POWs and Airmen Behind Soviet Lines, 1944–1945," *Diplomatic History* 28, no. 5 (November 2004): 749–80.

13. Kennan, *Memoirs 1925–1950*, 203.

14. Rudy Abramson interview with W. Averell Harriman, January 25, 1983, Rudy Abramson collection, in private possession.

15. Gaddis interview with John and Patricia Davies, December 7, 1982, p. 12, folder 10, box 1, Gaddis Papers. See also K. Tolley to Captain Smedberg, February 26, 1946, box 2, James V. Forrestal Papers, Seeley G. Mudd Library, Princeton University, Princeton, NJ.

16. Gaddis interview with Kennan, August 24, 1982, p. 10, folder 24, box 1, Gaddis Papers.

17. Annelise Sorensen Kennan to Hotchkiss, November 24, 1944, folder 2, box 328, Kennan Papers.

18. C. Ben Wright interview with Dorothy Hessman, October 1, 1970, folder 15, box 8, Wright Papers.

19. Kennan to Hotchkiss, December 22, 1944, box 24, Kennan Papers. Kennan would die during his "time of troubles," on March 17, 2005.

20. Kennan to Hotchkiss, March 15, 1945, box 24, Kennan Papers; Kennan to Leland Morris, April 16, 1945, box 178, Harriman Papers.

21. Kennan to Hotchkiss, October 8, 1944, folder 1, box 24, Kennan Papers.

22. Kennan to Hotchkiss, October 8, 1944, folder 1, box 24, Kennan Papers.

23. Gaddis interview with John and Patricia Davies, December 7, 1982, pp. 4–5, folder 10, box 1, Gaddis Papers; John Hersey to Patch, December 25, 1944, box 7, John Hersey Papers, Beinecke Library, Yale University, New Haven, CT.

24. Gaddis interview with John and Patricia Davies, December 7, 1982, p. 1, folder 10, box 1, Gaddis Papers.

25. Costigliola, *Kennan Diaries*, 497, 660.

26. Costigliola, *Roosevelt's Lost Alliances*, 236–37.

27. Gaddis interview with Kennan, August 25, 1982, p. 12.

28. Harry's socially ambitious new wife, Louise Macy, was enthralled with the Bohlens. As Kennan later explained, while Chip's family merely circulated in the upper crust, his wife, Avis (who was Charlie Thayer's sister), came from "a real Philadelphia family." (Gaddis interview with Kennan, August 25, 1982, p. 13.) The Bohlens and the Hopkinses had vacationed together in Maine, and the two men had collaborated in pre-Yalta negotiations in London and Paris.

29. Costigliola, *Roosevelt's Lost Alliances*.

30. Gaddis interview with Elbridge Durbrow, September 24, 1982, p. 6, folder 24, box 1, Gaddis Papers.

31. Kennan to Bohlen, January 26, 1945, box 1, Bohlen Papers, RG 59. The preceding paragraphs draw from this letter.

32. Kennan, *Memoirs 1925–1950*, 241.

33. Wright interview with William A. Crawford, September 29, 1970, pp. 1–2, folder 15, box 8, Wright Papers. The scope of these "absolutely uninhibited" "contacts" remains uncertain. In Crawford's unpublished memoir for his children, he remembered the delirious joy of that day and observing in the embassy's apartments his "colleagues consorting openly with Russian friends," William Avery Crawford, "Letter to My Children" [1997], p. 63, in private possession.

34. Year later, he still mourned the passing of "the original pathos of the revolution." The "old humane Marxists, most of them Jewish, but grand old men, beautifully educated"—intellectuals admired and respected by Kennan—had perished in the purges and the war. Gaddis interview with George and Annelise Kennan, December 13, 1995, p. 8, folder 2, box 6, Gaddis Papers.

35. Kennan, *Memoirs 1925–1950*, 532–46.

36. Kennan, *Memoirs 1925–1950*, 251.

37. "Trip to Novosibirsk and Stalinisk, June 1945," in Kennan to Harriman, July 27, 1945, box 181, Harriman Papers; Kennan, *Memoirs 1925–1950*, 274.

38. Gaddis interview with Martha Mautner, September 24, 1983, p. 1, folder 5, box 6, Gaddis Papers.

39. "Trip to Novosibirsk and Stalinisk, June 1945," in Kennan to Harriman, July 27, 1945, box 181, Harriman Papers.

40. Kennan, *Memoirs 1925–1950*, 273.

41. "Trip to Novosibirsk and Stalinisk, June 1945," in Kennan to Harriman, July 27, 1945, box 181, Harriman Papers.

42. Kennan confided the conversation to his British counterpart, Frank K. Roberts. Roberts to C. F. A. Warner, August 1, 1945, F. O. 371/47933, National Archives, United Kingdom.

43. "Trip to Novosibirsk and Stalinisk, June 1945," in Kennan to Harriman, July 27, 1945, box 181, Harriman Papers.

44. Roberts to Warner, August 1, 1945, F. O. 371/47933.

45. Gaddis interview with John and Patricia Davies, December 7, 1982, p. 11, folder 10, box 1, Gaddis Papers.

46. Annelise to George, July 29, 1945, folder 2, box 328, Kennan Papers.

47. Author interview with Grace Kennan Warnecke, November 6, 2020.

48. Kennan to Doc Matthews, August 21, 1945, folder 5, box 140, Kennan Papers.

49. Kennan to Hotchkiss, November 18, 1944, folder 1, box 24, Kennan Papers.

50. Kennan to Hotchkiss, January 25, 1945, folder 1, box 24, Kennan Papers; Kennan to Hotchkiss, June 6, 1945, folder 1, box 24, Kennan Papers.

51. Donald S. Russell to Mr. Chapin, December 4, 1945, 120.31 Auxiliary/11-3045, RG 59.

52. Gaddis interview with John and Patricia Davies, December 7, 1982, p. 5, folder 10, box 1, Gaddis Papers.

53. Wright interview with William A. Crawford, September 29, 1970, pp. 3–6, Folder 12, box 8, Wright Papers.

54. Gaddis interview with Sir Isaiah Berlin and Lady Berlin, November 29, 1992, pp. 1–2, folder 2, box 1, Gaddis Papers.

55. This was Bohlen's description of Kennan's view in January 1945. Wright interview with Bohlen, September 29, 1970, p. 13, folder 10, box 8, Wright Papers.

56. Kennan to Hotchkiss, June 6, 1945, box 24, Kennan Papers.

57. Adam Watson to Foreign Office, January 20, 1945, F. O. 371/47860, National Archives, United Kingdom.

58. Costigliola, *Kennan Diaries*, 185.

59. Costigliola, *Kennan Diaries*, 188.

60. Gaddis interview with Frank K. Roberts, March 15, 1993, p. 4.

61. Gaddis interview with Isaiah Berlin, November 29, 1992, p. 8, folder 2, box 1, Gaddis Papers.

62. Wright interview with William A. Crawford, September 29, 1970, pp. 3–4, folder 12, box 8, Wright Papers; Gaddis interview with Martha Mautner, September 24, 1983, p. 1.

63. Gaddis, *George F. Kennan*, 208.

64. Costigliola, *Kennan Diaries*, 190–93 (emphasis in original).

65. Kennan diary, December 19 and December 21, 1945, box 231, Kennan Papers.

66. Robert L. Messer, *The End of an Alliance: James F. Byrnes, Roosevelt, Truman, and the Origins of the Cold War*, (Chapel Hill: University of North Carolina Press), 158.

67. Kennan to Elbridge Durbrow, January 21, 1946, folder 4, box 140, Kennan Papers.

68. Kennan to Bohlen, January 23, 1946, 123 Kennan, George F./, RG 59.

69. Kennan to Durbrow, March 15, 1946, 123 Kennan George F./, RG 59; Wright interview with William A. Crawford, September 29, 1970, pp. 7–8, 20–22, folder 12, box 8, Wright Papers.

70. Kennan diary, February 15, 1935, box 231, Kennan Papers.

71. Kennan diary, September 10, 1959, box 231, Kennan Papers.

72. *FRUS 1946*, 6:701.

73. Norman M. Naimark, *Stalin and the Fate of Europe* (Cambridge, MA: Harvard University Press, 2019).

74. Wright interview with William A. Crawford, September 29, 1970, p. 20, folder 12, box 8, Wright Papers.

75. Gaddis interview with Dorothy Hessman, September 24, 1982, pp. 3–4, folder 19, box 1; Gaddis interview with Martha Mautner, September 24, 1983, p. 2, folder 5, box 6, Gaddis Papers.

76. Gaddis interview with Isaiah Berlin, folder 2, box 1, Gaddis Papers; Kennan to Elbridge Durbrow, January 21, 1946, box 186, Harriman Papers.

77. Gaddis interview with Durbrow, folder 12, box 1, Gaddis Papers; Matthews to Kennan, February 13, 1946, 861.00/2-1246, RG 59.

78. Gaddis interview with Mautner, September 24, 1983, p. 2.

79. *FRUS 1946*, 6:707. For a textual analysis, see Frank Costigliola, "'Unceasing Pressure for Penetration': Gender, Pathology, and Emotion in George F. Kennan's Formation of the Cold War," *Journal of American History* 83 (March 1997): 1331–37.

80. For an overview, see Fredrik Logevall, "A Critique of Containment," *Diplomatic History* 28 (September 2004): 473–98.

81. Kennan, *American Diplomacy*, 117, 127.

82. Kennan, *American Diplomacy*, 127–28.

83. *FRUS 1946*, 6:698.

84. For an overview, see Logevall, "A Critique of Containment."

85. Memorandum by Charles E. Bohlen, March 13, 1946, box 7, Charles E. Bohlen files, RG 59.

86. Henry Norweb to Kennan, March 25, 1946, folder 4, box 140, Kennan Papers; Gaddis, *George F. Kennan*, 229.

87. Kennan, *Memoirs 1925–1950*, 295.

88. Kennan to Hotchkiss, September 3, 1928, folder 10, box 23, Kennan Papers.

89. Kennan to Bruce Hopper, April 17, 1946, folder 4, box 140, Kennan Papers.

90. Kennan to Acheson, October 8, 1946, box 27, Acheson Papers; Kennan to Walter Bedell Smith, June 27, 1946, folder 17, box 328, Kennan Papers.

91. In 1949, Forrestal, having resigned as defense secretary and fearful that Communists were taking over everywhere, fell or jumped to his death from a hospital window. Kennan did not mention the death in his memoir.

92. Kennan, *Memoirs 1925–1950*, 354–55, 358; Lloyd C. Gardner, *Architects of Illusion* (Chicago: Quadrangle Books, 1970), 276–77, 282.

93. Kennan, *Memoirs 1925–1950*, 354–55, 358; Gardner, *Architects of Illusion*, 276–77, 282.

94. Gaddis interview with Loy W. Henderson September 25, 1982, p. 7, box 1, Gaddis Papers.

95. Gaddis interview with Kennan, August 25, 1982, p. 20.

96. Kennan to Kent Kennan, January 31, 1947, folder 1, box 328, Kennan Papers.

97. Costigliola, *Kennan Diaries*, 204.

98. Author interview with Grace Kennan Warnecke, June 15, 2015.

99. Kennan, "Planning of Foreign Policy," June 18, 1947, folder 37, box 298, Kennan Papers; Kennan to George F. Franklin, February 2, 1949, folder 22, box 299, Kennan Papers.

100. Kennan, "Foreign Policy Aims and Military Requirements, June 4, 1948, folder 10, box 299, Kennan Papers.

101. Lecture by Kennan and Thompson, September 17, 1946, folder 13, box 298, Kennan Papers.

102. Kennan talk at Yale, October 1, 1946, box 27, Acheson Papers.

103. Kennan, "Sources of Soviet Conduct," 581–82.

104. The preceding paragraphs are based on Kennan's report to State Department official Francis H. Russell, August 23, 1946, folder 11, box 298, Kennan Papers, and John D. Hickerson to Secretary of State, July 8, 1946, 711.61/6-1946, RG 59; Memorandum to FBI Director J. Edgar Hoover, October 23, 1946, Kennan's FBI File, box 181, Kennan Papers. Kennan's report helped fix the gendered assumptions of Cold-War ideology. Durbrow, stationed in Moscow, shared Kennan's account with a friend in the British embassy, who relayed the story to London. Whereas Kennan had grouped women's clubs, foreign affairs associations, and academics, the British diplomat offered a more reductive interpretation. He contrasted the men "engaged in serious study" with the "women emotionally unresponsive" to Kennan's message. Adam Watson to R. M. A. Hankey, October 10, 1946, F. O. 371/56842, National Archives, Kew, United Kingdom.

105. Kennan, "Draft of Information Policy on Relations with Russia," July 22, 1946, box 27, Acheson Papers; Kennan talk at Yale Institute of International Affairs, October 1, 1946, box 27, Acheson Papers.

106. While Kennan, like most of his contemporaries, viewed reason and emotion as polarized opposites, that construction does not match how the brain operates. Reason and emotion, as well as belief, memory, and other aspects of thought, all result from brain-wide processing that draws on culturally inflected past experiences and expectations. Examining the inner life of Kennan entails, first, keeping in mind these tenets of neuroscience and, second, weighing emotion and reason as if they were largely separable because that is how he and other historical actors conceptualized what they were thinking and feeling. This dual approach is key to examining Kennan's ostensibly objective yet deeply emotional thinking about Russia.

107. Kennan, "The Background of Current Russian Diplomatic Moves," December 10, 1946, in *Measures Short of War*, ed. Harlow and Maerz, 86. As the editors were preparing this compilation for publication, they asked Kennan if he wanted to modify any of the lectures. Though he did alter some of the talks, this extraordinary one he kept unchanged.

108. Harlow and Maerz, *Measures Short of War*, 83–87.

109. Harold W. Dodds to Kennan, December 6, 1946, folder 4, box 140, Kennan Papers.

110. Kennan to Hotchkiss, December 25, 1946, folder 28, box 327, Kennan Papers.

111. Gaddis interview with Kennan, August 25, 1982, p. 20, folder 24, box 1, Gaddis Papers; Gaddis interview with Hessman, September 24, 1982, p. 5, folder 19, box 1, Gaddis Papers.

112. Warnecke, *Daughter of the Cold War*, 65–66. 80–83; Kennan to Waldemar J. Gallman, March 14, 1947, folder 3, box 140, Kennan Papers.

113. Farm Diary, May 21, July 3, July 18, September 13, September 28–29, December 22, December 31, 1946, and January 11, January 18, February 14, 1947. My thanks to Joan Kennan for sharing with me this document and her recollections.

114. Kennan talk to Discussion Group on Soviet Foreign Policy, January 7, 1947, folder 21, box 298, Kennan Papers.

115. Kennan talk to Discussion Group on Soviet Foreign Policy, January 7, 1947, folder 21, box 298, Kennan Papers.

116. Hamilton Fish Armstrong to Kennan, January 10, 1947; Kennan to Armstrong, February 4, 1947; Armstrong to Kennan, March 7, 1947; Armstrong to Kennan, May 15,1947; Kennan to Armstrong, May 20, 1947, folder 3, box 140, Kennan Papers.

117. X [Kennan], "The Sources of Soviet Conduct," *Foreign Affairs* (July 1947): 566–82.

118. Robert Tufts interview with Gaddis, February 5, 1987, p. 6, folder 13, box 6, Gaddis Papers; Ware Adams interview with Wright, September 30, 1970, p. 6, folder 2, box 8, Wright Papers; Paul M. Nitze interview with Gaddis, December 13, 1989, p. 3, folder 6, box 6, Gaddis Papers.

119. Miscamble, *George F. Kennan and the Making of American Foreign Policy, 1947–1950*.

120. Jock Balfour to Nevile Butler, June 10, 1947, F. O. 371/62399, National Archives, United Kingdom.

121. Kennan, *American Diplomat: 1900–1950* (Chicago: University of Chicago Press, 1951).

122. Gaddis interview with Dorothy Fosdick, October 29, 1983, pp. 1–2, folder 14, box 1, Gaddis Papers.

123. Jeffrey Herf, *Israel's Moment International Support for and Opposition to Establishing the Jewish State, 1945-1949* (New York: Cambridge University Press, 2022), 270-71.

124. *FRUS Emergence of the Intelligence Establishment* (Washington: Government Printing Office, 1996), 668–72; Gaddis interview with Kennan, September 7, 1983, pp. 20–21, folder 25,

box 1, Gaddis Papers; Gregg Herken, *The Georgetown Set: Friends and Rivals in Cold War Washington* (New York: Knopf, 2014), 100–04.

125. Herken, *Georgetown Set*, 70–85, 99–104; Gaddis, *George F. Kennan*, 294–319; Scott Anderson, *The Quiet Americans* (New York: Doubleday, 2020), 155–56, 205–06; Louis Menand, *The Free World: Art and Thought in the Cold War* (New York: Farrar, Straus and Giroux, 2021), 717–19.

126. Gaddis, *George F. Kennan*, 318.

127. Anna Kasten Nelson (ed.), *The State Department Policy Planning Staff Papers 1948*, vol. 2 (New York: Garland, 1983), 118–19.

128. Naimark, *Stalin and the Fate of Europe*, 160–64; Geoffrey Roberts, *Stalin's Wars* (New Haven, CT: Yale University Press, 2006), 359–61.

129. Roberts, *Stalin's Wars*, 359-61. See also Kennan to Lippmann, April 6, 1948, box 299, Kennan Papers.

130. Gaddis, *George F. Kennan*, 318.

131. Kennan to Walter Lippmann, April 6, 1948 [not sent], folder 7, box 299, Kennan Papers.

132. Hamilton Fish Armstrong diary, September 20, 1948, box 101, Hamilton Fish Armstrong Papers, Seeley G. Mudd library, Princeton University, Princeton, NJ. For a critical view, see Scott Lucas and Kaeten Mistry, "Illusions of Coherence: George F. Kennan, U.S. Strategy and Political Warfare, 1946–1950," *Diplomatic History* 33 (January 2009): 39–66.

133. Hamilton Fish Armstrong diary, September 20, 1948, box 101, Armstrong Papers.

134. "Preamble of the Interrogation Report of Dr. Gustav Hilger," MIS 208596, October 11, 1945, https://www.cia.gov/readingroom/docs/HILGER%2C%20GUSTAV_0005.pdf.

135. Robert Wolfe, "Gustav Hilger: From Hitler's Foreign Office to CIA Consultant," https://fas.org/sgp/eprint/wolfe.pdf; Herken, *Georgetown Set*, 74–75; Anderson, *Quiet Americans*, 195–97.

136. Kennan to George S. Franklin, February 2, 1949, folder 22, box 299, Kennan Papers.

137. Policy Planning Meeting, October 12, 1949, box 27, Policy Planning Staff Papers, RG 59.

138. Costigliola, *Kennan Diaries*, 218.

139. Costigliola *Kennan Diaries*, 213.

140. Costigliola, *Kennan Diaries*, 217.

141. Costigliola, *Kennan Diaries*, 217.

142. Kennan, "An Estimate of the International Situation," November 11, 1948, folder 17, box 299, Kennan Papers.

143. Costigliola, *Kennan Diaries*, 222.

144. Costigliola, *Kennan Diaries*, 226–27.

145. *FRUS 1949*, vol. 1 (Washington: Government Printing Office, 1976), 404.

146. Kennan, "Basic Factors in American Foreign Policy," February 14, 1949, folder 23, box 299, Kennan Papers.

147. The preceding paragraphs are based on this speech. Kennan, "Where Do We Stand?" December 21, 1949, folder 32, box 299, Kennan Papers.

148. Kennan, "Basic Factors in American Foreign Policy," February 14, 1949, folder 23, box 299, Kennan Papers.

149. *FRUS 1949*, vol. 1, 405; Costigliola, *Kennan Diaries*, 232.

150. Costigliola, *Kennan Diaries*, 236, 230, 239.

151. Costigliola, *Kennan Diaries*, 212–13.

152. The preceding paragraphs draw on this talk. Kennan, "Russia and the United States," May 27, 1950, box 251, Kennan Papers.

153. David S. Foglesong, *The American Mission and the "Evil Empire"* (New York, 2007), 114–115.

Chapter 8

1. Harrison E. Salisbury, *A Journey for Our Times* (New York: Carroll & Graf, 1983), 404.

2. Kennan to Frieda Por, February 17, 1952, folder 1, box 329, Kennan Papers.

3. Costigliola, *Kennan Diaries*, 294, 291. For the talks, see 285–96.

4. Kennan to Acheson, September 1, 1951, folder 7, box 139, Kennan Papers.

5. "Summary on Points of Difference with Department of State," never used, September 1951, folder 27, box 164, Kennan Papers. Kennan wrote at the top of the first page: "This is, in my opinion, important." On China, Kennan to K. L. Rankin, August 9, 1950, 611.93/8-950, RG 59.

6. Costigliola, *Kennan Diaries*, 283–85.

7. Costigliola, *Kennan Diaries*, 279–80.

8. Costigliola, *Kennan Diaries*, 296–97, 280.

9. Costigliola, *Kennan Diaries*, 281.

10. Kennan to John R. Bodo, January 18, 1952, folder 15, box 5, Kennan Papers.

11. Truman's daily schedule, April 1, 1952, folder 9, box B 7, C. Ben Wright Kennan Biography Project, George C. Marshall Institute, Lexington, VA.

12. Costigliola, *Kennan Diaries*, 309.

13. Vladislav M. Zubok, *A Failed Empire: The Soviet Union in the Cold War from Stalin to Gorbachev* (Chapel Hill: University of North Carolina Press, 2007), 82–83; Roberts, *Stalin's Wars*, 356–58; Naimark, *Stalin and the Fate of Europe*, 263.

14. "Stalin Sees No Rise in Chances of War," *New York Times*, April 2, 1952, p. 1.

15. Executive Session Testimony, March 12, 1952, U.S. Congress, Senate Committee on Foreign Relations, *Historical Series* 4: 195, 209–10.

16. Press and Radio News Conference, Tuesday, April 1, 1952, folder 18, box 300, Kennan Papers.

17. *FRUS, 1952–1954*, VIII, document 497, https://history.state.gov/historicaldocuments/frus1952-54v08/d497.

18. D. M. Ladd to Hoover, April 18, 1947; Gaddis, *George F. Kennan*, 497; Kennan to Hoover, November 18, 1963; Hoover's reaction appended to Helen W. Gandy to Kennan, November 28, 1963 (emphasis in original), all in Kennan's FBI file, in folders 3–6, box 181, Kennan Papers.

19. Bohlen to Acheson [n.d. but April 1952], box 9, Bohlen Papers.

20. Costigliola, *Kennan Diaries*, 310–13.

21. Cumming interview with Gaddis, April 17, 1984, p. 6, folder 8, box 1, Gaddis Papers.

22. Costigliola, *Kennan Diaries*, 313.

23. Bohlen to Kennan (n.d. but April 1952), box 9, Bohlen Papers (emphasis in original).

24. Isaiah Berlin interview with Gaddis, November 29, 1992, p. 2, folder 2, box 1, Gaddis Papers.

25. Costigliola, *Kennan Diaries*, 313.

26. Salisbury, *Journey for Our Times*, 403.

27. Tom Whitney interview with Harrison E. Salisbury, October 29, 1983, pp. 12–13, box 375; Salisbury to Whitney, January 5, 1961, box 200, Harrison E. Salisbury Papers. Butler Library, Columbia University, New York, New York; Salisbury, *Journey for Our Times*, 392.

28. Grace Kennan Warnecke interview with author, November 6, 2020.

29. Salisbury, *Journey for Our Times*, 392, 399 (emphasis in original).

30. Juli Whitney to Salisbury, n.d., box 200, Salisbury Papers.

31. Salisbury, *Journey for our Times*, 413.

32. George to Annelise, May 31, 1952, folder 17, box 328, Kennan Papers.

33. George F. Kennan, *Memoirs 1950–1963* (Boston: Little, Brown, 1973), 116, 126–28.

34. Kennan, *Memoirs 1950–1963*, 129–30.

35. Costigliola, *Kennan Diaries*, 317.

36. Costigliola, *Kennan Diaries*, 318.

37. Salisbury, *Journey for Our Times*, 409.

38. Salisbury, *Journey for Our Times*, 411–12.

39. Kennan to Pierrepont Moffat, May 10, 1939, volume 13, Moffat Papers.

40. Harrison E. Salisbury interview with Whitman Basso, July 6, 1985, box 4, Whitman Basso Papers, Library of Congress.

41. Salisbury, *Journey for Our Times*, 412.

42. Notes by Salisbury, May 18, 1952 [with later editing], p. 501, box 201, Salisbury Papers.

43. Kennan to Hugh Cumming, December 31, 1951, folder 7, box 139, Kennan Papers.

44. Salisbury note to self, May 6, 1952, box 201, Salisbury Papers.

45. Joseph Gasccoigne to William Strang, June 16, 1952, F.O. 371/100836, National Archives, Kew, England.

46. Cumming interview with Gaddis, April 17, 1984, pp. 4–5, folder 8, box 1, Gaddis Papers.

47. *FRUS 1952–1954*, v. VIII, document 499, https://history.state.gov/historicaldocuments /frus1952-54v08/d499.

48. George to Annelise, May 31, 1952, folder 17, box 328, Kennan Papers.

49. George to Annelise, June 3, 1952, folder 17, box 328, Kennan Papers.

50. George to Annelise, May 25, 1952, folder 17, box 328, Kennan Papers.

51. George to Annelise, May 27, 1952, folder 17, box 328, Kennan Papers.

52. George to Annelise, June 3, 1952, folder 17, box 328, Kennan Papers.

53. George to Annelise, May 25, 1952, folder 17, box 328, Kennan Papers.

54. George to Annelise, June 8, 1952, folder 17, box 328, Kennan Papers.

55. George to Annelise, June 3, 1952, folder 17, box 328, Kennan Papers.

56. George to Annelise, June 12, 1952; Annelise to Cousin Grace, July 18, 1952, folder 17, box 328, Kennan Papers.

57. George to Annelise, June 3, 1952, folder 17, box 328, Kennan Papers.

58. Kennan to Bohlen, July 10, 1952, 761.00/7-1052, RG 59.

59. *FRUS 1952–1954* (Washington: Government Printing Office, 1988)8:981, 987-1000; Kennan to Bohlen, July 16, 1952, 761.00/7-1052, RG 59.

60. *FRUS 1952–1954*, 8:981, 990–96.

61. *FRUS 1952–1954*, 8:981, 995.

62. *FRUS 1952–1954*, 8:981, 997–98 (emphasis in original).

63. *FRUS 1952–1954*, 8:981, 997–98.

64. *FRUS 1952–1954*, 8:981, 999.

65. *FRUS 1952–1954*, 8:981, 999–1000.

66. *FRUS 1952–1954*, 8:987. Opinion in the State Department held that while Kennan's first scenario was "probable" and the second "possible," the third and fourth—that is, the one focused on him—remained "unlikely." Memorandum to Joseph B. Phillips, June 23, 1952, 611.61/6-6521, RG 59.

67. Gascoigne to Oliver Franks, June 17, 1952, F.O. 371/100836 (emphasis in original).

68. Gascoigne to Paul Mason, June 10, 1952; Mason to Strang, June 16, 1952; minute by Dixon, June 24, 1952, all in F. O. 371/110836.

69. Gascoigne to Dixon, July 4, 1952; minutes by Mason and Strang, July 7, 1952, F. O. 371/110836.

70. Gascoigne to William Strang, May 20, 1952, F. O. 371/100836.

71. William Strang to Gascoigne, June 5, 1952, F.O. 371/100836.

72. Gascoigne to Strang, June 16, 1952; minute by Roger Makin Strang, June 23, 1952, F.O. 371/100836.

73. Harrison Salisbury to Cyrus Sulzberger, August 11, 1952, box 9, Salisbury Papers.

74. *FRUS 1952–1954*, 8:981, 1000–02.

75. *FRUS 1952–1954*, 8:981, 1004–07.

76. *FRUS 1952–1954*, 8:981, 1011–12. As relayed to London, Vyshinsky's expression of respect for Kennan was watered down to "the Soviet Government had nothing against him, Kennan, personally." Gascoigne to Paul Mason, June 20, 1952, F.O. 371/100836.

77. Gascoigne to Paul Mason, June 25, 1952, F. O. 371/100836.

78. Cumming interview with Gaddis, April 17, 1984, p. 8, folder 8, box 1, Gaddis Papers.

79. Kennan to Bohlen, July 16, 1952, 761.00/7-1052, RG 59.

80. Hugh S. Cumming, Jr., "Visit of Soviet Citizen to American Embassy Moscow," July 15, 1952, 761.00/7-1552, RG 59.

81. Kennan to Acheson, July 8, 1952, 761.00/7-852, RG 59.

82. For Stalin's remark to Harriman, see Costigliola, *Roosevelt's Lost Alliances: How Personal Politics Helped Start the Cold War* (Princeton, NJ: Princeton University Press, 2012), 382.

83. Kennan to Bohlen, July 16, 1952, 761.00/7-1052, RG 59.

84. Cyrus L. Sulzberger, *A Long Row of Candles* (New York: Macmillan, 1969), 987.

85. Salisbury to Cyrus L. Sulzberger, August 25, 1952, box 187, Salisbury Papers.

86. Zubok, *Failed Empire*, 86.

87. William Taubman, *Khrushchev: The Man and His Era* (New York: W. W. Norton, 2003), 248, 712.

88. Kennan to Jeanette Kennan Hotchkiss, August 8, 1952, folder 28, box 327, Kennan Papers (emphasis in original).

89. Executive Session Testimony, March 12, 1952, *Historical Series* 4: 192; Kennan to Hans Morgenthau, March 21, 1952, folder 3, box 32, ibid. Kennan's planning on a long stay in Moscow was evidenced also by his efforts renovating the embassy's dacha. See Avis Bohlen to Charles Thayer, May 14, 1953, box 1, Thayer Papers. Harry S. Truman Presidential Library, Independence, MO.

90. Kennan to Acheson, July 25, 1952, folder 4, box 139, Kennan Papers.

91. Salisbury to C. L. Sulzberger, August 11, 1952, box 187, Salisbury Papers.

92. *FRUS 1952–1954*, 8:1035–38 (emphasis in original).

93. *FRUS 1952–1954*, 6:981, 1056–57.

94. Kennan, *Memoirs 1950–1963*, 131.

95. Kennan, *Memoirs 1950–1963*, 155–56.

96. Annelise Sorensen Kennan interview with John L. Gaddis, September 8, 1983, p. 6, folder 23, box 1, Gaddis Papers.

97. Gaddis, *George F. Kennan*, 448.

98. Nicholas Thompson, *The Hawk and the Dove* (New York: Henry Holt, 2009), 138.

99. Kennan to Barklie Henry, September 9, 1952, box 43, J. Robert Oppenheimer Papers, Library of Congress. Henry was a friend of Oppenheimer's, and Kennan included a copy of the letter for "Oppie" at the Institute for Advanced Study. He wanted to hear about Princeton—and may have been thinking about returning there sooner than he had planned.

100. George to Annelise, May 8, 1952, folder 17, box 328, Kennan Papers.

101. Kennan, *Memoirs 1950–1963*, 157–58.

102. Annelise to Jeanette Hotchkiss, September 19, 1952, folder 2, box 328, Kennan Papers.

103. Cumming interview with Gaddis, April 17, 1984, p. 6, folder 8, box 1, Gaddis Papers.

104. Salisbury, *Journey for Our Times*, 414; notes [n.d. but September 1952], p. 548, box 200, Salisbury Papers.

105. Costigliola, *Kennan Diaries*, 314–15.

106. Jack Raymond to Salisbury, November 3, 1952, box 187, Salisbury Papers.

107. Cumming interview with Gaddis, April 17, 1984, p. 18, folder 8, box 1, Gaddis Papers.

108. Kennan, *Memoirs 1950–1963*, 158–59.

109. Costigliola, *Kennan Diaries*, 323–24 (emphasis in original).

110. Kennan, *Memoirs 1950–1963*, 162.

111. Bohlen, "Memorandum of Conversation," enclosed in Bohlen to Livingston T. Merchant, September 7, 1955, box 34, Bohlen Papers. At Bohlen's request, Merchant passed to Kennan a copy of the memorandum.

112. Salisbury to Sulzberger, October 22, 1952, box 9, Salisbury Papers; Harrison E. Salisbury, *American in Russia* (New York: Harper Brothers, 1955), 138.

113. Isaiah Berlin interview with Gaddis, November 29, 1992, p. 11, folder 2, box 1, Gaddis Papers.

114. Kennan to Bohlen, September 27, 1952, box 139, Kennan Papers.

115. Kennan diary, March 17, 1985, box 326, Kennan Papers.

116. Elbridge Durbrow interview with Gaddis, September 24, 1982, p. 12, folder 12, box 1, Gaddis Papers. As another former colleague put it about Tempelhof, "That's typical. When things don't go his way, the hell with it!" He knew the Soviets would kick him out after making that statement. "He didn't want to waste his time if he couldn't accomplish anything." Loy W. Henderson interview with Gaddis, September 25, 1982, p. 10, folder 18, box 1, Gaddis Papers.

117. Memorandum by Joseph B. Phillips, [n.d. but September-October 1952], Records Relating to Worldwide Program Objectives, 1948–57, Entry 1587A, File 16-George F. Kennan, RG 59.

118. Minutes by Paul Mason and RM, September 29, 1952, F.O. 371/100836.

119. Sulzberger, *A Long Row of Candles*, 784.

120. Costigliola, *Kennan Diaries*, 325.

121. Kennan diary, January 15, 1953, box 233, Kennan Papers.

122. Durbrow interview with Gaddis, September 24, 1982, folder 12, box 1, Gaddis Papers.

123. Kennan diary, January 15, 1953, box 233, Kennan Papers.

124. *FRUS 1952–1954*, 8:1015.

125. Melvyn P. Leffler, *For the Soul of Mankind: The United States, the Soviet Union, and the Cold War* (New York: Hill and Wang, 2007), 84–150.

Chapter 9

1. E. W. Kenworthy, "Kennan Bids U.S. 'Dig In' and Await Talks in Vietnam," *New York Times*, February 11, 1966, p. 2.

2. Robert C. and Evgenia Tucker interview with John L. Gaddis, September 4, 1984, p. 18, folder 12, box 6, Gaddis Papers.

3. U.S. Senate Foreign Relations Committee, Hearings on "Supplemental Foreign Assistance Fiscal Year 1966—Vietnam" (Washington: Government Printing Office, 1966), 334–36.

4. U.S. Senate Foreign Relations Committee, Hearings on "Supplemental Foreign Assistance," 369.

5. Costigliola, *Kennan Diaries*, 335–36.

6. Costigliola, *Kennan Diaries*, 343.

7. Grace Kennan Warnecke interview with author, November 6, 2020.

8. Costigliola, *Kennan Diaries*, 327. Entry written on March 13, 1953, reflecting back on previous six months.

9. Richard H. Immerman, *Empire for Liberty: A History of American Imperialism from Benjamin Franklin to Paul Wolfowitz* (Princeton, NJ: Princeton University Press, 2010), 179–80.

10. Robert Bowie interview with Richard Challener, August 10, 1964, John Foster Dulles Oral History Project, Mudd Library, Princeton University.

11. Kennan speech, January 16, 1953, folder 10, box 252, Kennan Papers.

12. Gaddis, *George F. Kennan An American Life* (New York: Penguin, 2011), 477.

13. Grace Kennan Warnecke interview with author, December 1, 2020.

14. Annelise Sorensen Kennan to Jeanette Kennan Hotchkiss, January 19, 1953, folder 2, box 328, Kennan Papers.

15. Annelise to Jeanette, February 23, 1953, folder 2, box 328, Kennan Papers.

16. Gaddis, *George F. Kennan*, 485.

17. Kennan, *Memoirs 1950–1963*, 180.

18. Gaddis, *George F. Kennan*, 483.

19. Gaddis, *George F. Kennan*, 485.

20. John Foster Dulles Centennial Conference, "The Challenge of Leadership in Foreign Affairs" [Symposium on the Solarium Exercise, held at Princeton University on February 27, 1988], p. 11–12. My thanks to Richard Immerman for hosting this retrospective event in 1988 and then for sharing with me a transcript of the proceedings. (Hereafter Dulles Centennial Conference.)

21. Dulles Centennial Conference, p. 13.

22. Dulles Centennial Conference, p. 5–6

23. *FRUS 1952–1954*, vol. 2, pt. 1 (Washington: Government Printing Office, 1984): 406–07.

24. Dulles Centennial Conference, p. 22.

25. Dulles Centennial Conference, p. 32. Robert R. Bowie, then director of the Policy Planning Staff also recalled that "judgments were pretty much up in the air at the time, as to whether [Stalin's death] had made a change, and if so what." p. 32.

26. Kennan interview with Gaddis, September 8, 1983, p. 13, folder 25, box 1; Kennan to Oppenheimer, October 14, 1952; Kennan to Oppenheimer, February 27, 1953; Oppenheimer to Kennan, March 13, 1953, all in box 43, Oppenheimer Papers.

27. Amid the McCarthyite "lavender scare" that exposed and terminated homosexuals from the U.S. government, Thayer, who seems to have been bisexual, was fired. Thayer was also a sacrificial lamb of sorts, since Chip Bohlen, Thayer's brother-in-law and Eisenhower's choice for ambassador to Moscow, was falsely rumored to also be gay. See Robert D. Dean, *Imperial Brotherhood: Gender and the Making of Cold War Foreign Policy* (Amherst, MA: University of Massachusetts Press, 2003).

28. Kennan to Charlie Thayer, July 7, 1953; Kennan to Thayer, September 4, 1953; May 3, 1954, all in box 3, Thayer Papers. Grace Kennan Warnecke later recalled that when applying for a scholarship from Radcliffe College, she had put down zero for her family's income. Author interview, December 1, 2020.

29. Richard Polenberg, ed., *In the Matter of J. Robert Oppenheimer: The Security Clearance Hearing* (Ithaca, NY: Cornell University Press, 2002), 140–45; 145 for the quotation.

30. Oppenheimer to Kennan, "Re: Solar Energy," September 29, 1951; Robert G. Hooker Jr. to Kennan, September 19, 1951, enclosed in Kennan to Oppenheimer, September 23, 1951, box 43, Oppenheimer Papers.

31. Jeanette Kennan Hotchkiss interview with Gaddis, December 21, 1982, p. 27, folder 21, box 1, Gaddis Papers.

32. Hans J. Morgenthau to Kennan, March 15, 1954, box 33, Hans J. Morgenthau Papers, Library of Congress.

33. Costigliola, *Kennan Diaries*, 353.

34. Kennan, *Memoirs 1950–1963*, 77–79; Gaddis interview with Kennan, September 8, 1983, pp. 15–17, folder 25, box 1, Gaddis Papers.

35. Kennan, *Memoirs 1950–1963*, 77–79. Kennan interview with Gaddis, September 8, 1983, pp. 15–17, folder 25, box 1, Gaddis Papers. The delight in Kennan's voice when recounting this story is evident in the recording of the interview with Gaddis, folder 5, box 4, Gaddis Papers.

36. J. Richardson Dilworth interview with Gaddis, December 6, 1987, p. 9, folder 11, box 1, Gaddis Papers.

37. Isaiah Berlin interview with Gaddis, November 29, 1992, p. 7, folder 2, box 1, Gaddis Papers.

38. Kennan interview with Gaddis, September 8, 1983, p. 16–17, folder 25, box 1, Gaddis Papers.

39. Costigliola, *Kennan Diaries*, 350.

40. Costigliola, *Kennan Diaries*, 352–53. A year later, "I sat at the head of my parents' graves and wept my heart out, like a child." Kennan diary, August 20, 1956, folder 4, box 233, Kennan Papers.

41. Kossuth Kent Kennan, *Income Taxation: Methods and Results in Various Countries* (Milwaukee: Burdick & Allen, 1910). See also ch. 1.

42. Costigliola, *Kennan Diaries*, 348 (emphasis in original).

43. A. Beurling, K. Gödel, D. Montgomery, and A. Selberg to Colleagues, November 7, 1955, box 19, Shelby White and Leon Levy Archives Center, Institute for Advanced Study, Princeton, NJ.

44. Gordon A. Craig to Llewellyn Woodward, October 16, 1955, box 19, White and Levy Archives Center. See also Craig to Woodward, March 18, 1955, box 19, White and Levy Archives Center.

45. Ernst Kantorowicz to Oppenheimer, September 16, 1955, box 19, White and Levy Archives Center.

46. Isaiah Berlin to Oppenheimer, March 14, 1955, box 19, White and Levy Archives Center.

47. Oppenheimer to Kennan, November 28, 1955, box 19, White and Levy Archives Center. The appointment start date was January 1, 1956.

48. Costigliola, *Kennan Diaries*, 356.

49. Costigliola, *Kennan Diaries*, 347.

50. John F. Fulton to Oppenheimer, December 31, 1955, box 19, Oppenheimer Papers.

51. *American Historical Review* 62, no. 2 (January 1957): 367–68. Perkins was president of the AHA in 1956, when he wrote the review published in the first month of the following year. In 2023, Princeton University Press published a new edition of *Russia Leaves the War* that includes an introduction by Frank Costigliola that discusses Kennan's unpublished epilogue to the book.

52. Kennan interview with Gaddis, September 8, 1983, p. 5, folder 25, box 1, Gaddis Papers.

53. Costigliola, *Kennan Diaries*, 361.

54. Costigliola, *Kennan Diaries*, 366–67.

55. Kennan to Oppenheimer, October 24, 1957, box 43, Oppenheimer Papers.

56. Kennan, *Memoirs 1950–1963*, 262.

57. Christopher Kennan interview with author, March 12, 2016.

58. Annelise to Jeanette, February 3, 1958, folder 2, box 328, Kennan Papers.

59. Kennan, *Memoirs 1950–1963*, 261.

60. Beate von Oppen interview with Gaddis, August 17, 1982, p. 1, folder 15, box 6, Gaddis Papers; Richard H. Ullman interview with Gaddis, September 30, 1987, p. 5., folder 14, box 6, Gaddis Papers.

61. Kennan to Oppenheimer, October 24, 1957, box 43, Oppenheimer Papers.

62. Kennan interview with Gaddis, August 25, 1982, p. 2, folder 24, box 1, Gaddis Papers.

63. M. Gordon Knox to Department of State, January 8, 1958, 811.41 Kennan, George F./1-858, RG 59.

64. BBC Symposium, December 29, 1957, 22:15–23:00 GMT, copy in box 19, Institute for Advanced Study Archives.

65. Kennan, *Memoirs 1950–1963*, 248–49.

66. George F. Kennan, *Russia, the Atom, and the West* (New York: Harper & Brothers, 1958), 65.

67. Kennan, *Memoirs 1950–1963*, 233–34.

68. For the audio of Kennan's third and fourth Reith Lectures, https://www.bbc.co.uk /sounds/play/p00hg1nj; https://www.bbc.co.uk/programmes/p00hg1n.

69. Kennan, *Russia, the Atom and the West*, 54.

70. *FRUS 1955–1957* (Washington: Government Printing Office, 1992) 26: 346–47.

71. M. Gordon Knox to Department of State, January 8, 1958, 811.41 Kennan, George F./1-858, RG 59.

72. Acheson to Hamilton Fish Armstrong, January 23, 1958, box 1, Hamilton Fish Armstrong Papers, Mudd Library, Princeton University.

73. Hamilton Fish Armstrong diary, February 5, 1958, box 102, Armstrong Papers; Dorothy Hessman to Robert Oppenheimer, January 23, 1958, box 43, Oppenheimer Papers.

74. Arthur M. Schlesinger Jr. interview with Gaddis, December 17, 1986, p. 2, folder 9, box 6, Gaddis Papers.

75. Mary A. Bundy interview with author, May 23, 2011; Mary A. Bundy interview with Gaddis, December 6, 1987, p. 12, folder 7, box 1, Gaddis Papers.

76. James Reston, "New Proposals for Old Disposals," *New York Times Book Review*, March 2, 1958, p. 26.

77. John Foster Dulles to Dean Acheson, January 13, 1958, box 9, Acheson Papers.

78. Armstrong to Acheson, February 4, 1958, box 102, Armstrong Papers.

79. William Hard to Acheson, January 14, 1958; Anne Hard to Dean and Alice Acheson, February 20, 1958; Acheson to Anne Hard, March 4, 1958; Anne Hard to Dean Acheson, April 24, 1958, all in box 15, Acheson Papers.

80. Cyrus L. Sulzberger, *Last of the Giants* (New York: MacMillan, 1970), 442, 444.

81. Frank K. Roberts to P. F. Hancock, January 28, 1958, F. O. 371/137080, National Archives, United Kingdom. Roberts was serving with the British delegation to the NATO meeting in Paris.

82. Costigliola, *Kennan Diaries*, 369.

83. Kennan to Dorothy Hessman and Robert Oppenheimer, January 16, 1958, box 43, Oppenheimer Papers.

84. Costigliola, *Kennan Diaries,* 372.

85. Kennan, *Memoirs 1950–1963*, 261.

86. Annelise to Jeanette Hotchkiss, January 13, 1958, folder 2, box 328, Kennan Papers.

87. Costigliola, *Kennan Diaries*, 372–73.

88. Beate von Oppen interview with Gaddis, August 27, 1982, p. 1, folder 15, box 6, Gaddis Papers.

89. Kennan to Oppenheimer, February 21, 1958, box 19, White and Levy Archives Center.

90. Annelise to Jeanette, January 13, 1958, folder 2, box 328, Kennan Papers.

91. Hotchkiss interview with Gaddis, December 21, 1982, p. 18, folder 21, box 1, Gaddis Papers.

92. Oppenheimer to Kennan, February 28, 1958, box 19, White and Levy Archives Center.

93. Grace Kennan Warnecke interview with author, December 1, 2020.

94. Costigliola, *Kennan Diaries*, 363.

95. Kennan to Oppenheimer, February 21, 1958, box 19, White and Levy Archives Center.

96. Oppenheimer to Kennan, February 28, 1958, box 19, White and Levy Archives Center.

97. Kennan to Oppenheimer, December 14, 1959, box 19, White and Levy Archives Center.

98. Kennan to Oppenheimer, December 14, 1959, box 19, White and Levy Archives Center. If nominated as the Democratic candidate, Kennan would have run against a popular incumbent, the liberal Republican Clifford P. Case.

99. Costigliola, *Kennan Diaries*, 373–74.

100. BBC Symposium, December 29, 1958, 22:15–23:00 GMT, copy in box 19, White and Levy Archives Center.

101. Sulzberger, *Last of the Giants*, 440.

102. *FRUS 1958–1960* (Washington: Government Printing Office, 1993) 10:276.

103. Costigliola, *Kennan Diaries*, 403.

104. Costigliola, *Kennan Diaries*, 384.

105. Kennan interview with Louis Fischer, March 23, 1965, John F. Kennedy Presidential Library, pp. 5, 13. Ironically, Kennan would sign off on the final transcript of this oral history interview on February 28, 1966, only days after his Senate testimony against the buildup of military forces in South Vietnam that Kennedy had initiated.

106. Sulzberger, *Last of the Giants*, 698.

107. Costigliola, *Kennan Diaries*, 412–13.

108. Kennan, Article on Kennedy for *Tagesanzeiger*, Zurich, November 30, 1963, folder 21, box 261, Kennan Papers.

109. Kennan, Article on Kennedy for *Tagesanzeiger*, Zurich, November 30, 1963, folder 21, box 261, Kennan Papers.

110. Arthur M. Schlesinger Jr. interview by Gaddis, December 17, 1986, p. 3, folder 9, box 6, Gaddis Papers.

111. McGeorge Bundy interview with Gaddis, December 17, 1986, p. 3, folder 8, box 1, Gaddis Papers.

112. Avis Bohlen to Charlie Thayer, February 22, 1961, box 1, Thayer Papers (emphasis in original).

113. *FRUS 1961–1963* (Washington: Government Printing Office, 1996) 6:34.

114. Kennan interview with Fischer, March 23, 1965, pp. 119–22, Kennedy Library.

115. Kennan to Llewellyn E. Thompson, December 26, 1961; Kennan to Rusk, December 26, 1961; Rusk to Kennan, January 5, 1962, all in Records of Secretary of State Dean Rusk, Entry A1-5378, folder K, RG 59. In his letter to Rusk, Kennan enclosed a copy of his missive to Thompson. He suggested passing it on to the White House, where "Bundy, in any case, would be interested in seeing it," and he emphasized his planned trip to Moscow.

116. Arthur S. Link, interview with Gaddis, September 5, 1984, p. 9, folder 4, box 6, Gaddis Papers.

117. Sulzberger, *Last of the Giants*, 807.

118. Andrew Schlesinger and Stephen Schlesinger, *Journals 1952–2000: Arthur M. Schlesinger, Jr.* (New York: Penguin, 2007), 128.

119. Bundy and Bundy interview with Gaddis, December 6, 1987, p. 6, folder 7, box 1, Kennan Papers.

120. Cresswell to Evelyn Shuckburgh, September 5, 1961, F. O. 371/160840, National Archives, Kew, UK.

121. Sulzberger, *Last of the Giants*, 852.

122. Costigliola, *Kennan Diaries*, 418–19.

123. Costigliola, *Kennan Diaries*, 419.

124. Grace Kennan Warnecke interview with author, December 1, 2020.

125. Kennan, *Memoirs 1950–1963*, 275.

126. Owen T. Jones diary, May 9, 1961, box 5, Owen T. Jones Papers, Truman Presidential Library.

127. Jones diary, November 4–5, 1962, box 6, Jones Papers.

128. Bundy and Bundy, interview with Gaddis, December 6, 1987, p. 7, folder 7, box 1, Gaddis Papers.

129. Gaddis, *George F. Kennan*, 597.

130. Costigliola, *Kennan Diaries*, 419, 438.

131. Costigliola, *Kennan Diaries*, 429–30.

132. Costigliola, *Kennan Diaries*, 431.

133. Kennan diary, April 6, 1966, box 325, Kennan Papers.

Chapter 10

1. Kennan affirmed the significance of this connection in a letter to his grandson, another George F. Kennan, who also had been born on February 16. Kennan to George F. Kennan, February 16, 1996, folder 2, box 26, Kennan Papers.

2. Costigliola, *Kennan Diaries*, 526.

3. William P. and Mary A. Bundy interview with John Lewis Gaddis, December 6, 1987, p. 35, folder 7, box 1, Gaddis Papers.

4. J. Richardson Dilworth interview with Gaddis, December 6, 1987, p. 1, folder 11, box 1, Gaddis Papers.

5. Kennan, *Democracy and the Student Left* (Boston: Little, Brown, 1968), 3–20.

6. Kennan, *Democracy and the Student Left*, 165.

7. Kennan, *Democracy and the Student Left*, 29.

8. Kennan, *Democracy and the Student Left*, 158.

9. Kennan, *Democracy and the Student Left*, 160.

10. Kennan, *Democracy and the Student Left*, 163.

11. Kennan, *Democracy and the Student Left*, 170.

12. Kennan, *Democracy and the Student Left*, 216–17.

13. Kennan, *Democracy and the Student Left*, 229.

14. Kennan, *Democracy and the Student Left*, 229–30.

15. Ronald Sullivan, "Kennan Attacks Vietnam Policy as Massive, Unparalleled Error," *New York Times*, March 1, 1968, p. 25; Kennan, "Introducing Eugene McCarthy," *New York Review of Books*, April 11, 1968.

16. Israel Shenker, "Hit and Myth Gathering of Intellectuals," *New York Times*, December 8, 1968, p. 238.

17. Kennan to Felix Frankfurter, September 19, 1956, reel 43, Felix Frankfurter Papers, Library of Congress, Washington, DC. It made an impression on Kennan's secretary that Williams "was

not very cooperative." (Dorothy Hessman interview with Gaddis, September 24, 1982. Not having access to the papers of Robins until his own book was nearly completed and forced instead to cite Williams's book was particularly galling to Kennan, who identified in some ways with this extraordinary figure. He saw in Robins someone whose efforts to achieve a historic deal with the Bolshevik leaders might have succeeded had he been able to augment his own talents with the diplomatic skills and expertise on Russia that Kennan himself commanded. Kennan explored this fantasy in an unpublished epilogue. See Costigliola's introduction to Kennan, *Russia Leaves the War* (Princeton University Press, 2023).

18. Costigliola, *Roosevelt's Lost Alliances*, 9.

19. Among those from the IAS were Felix Gilbert, Carl E. Schorske, Gerald Stourzh, Jacob L. Talmon, Morton White, and director Carl Kaysen. Those from Princeton University included Louis Fischer, Lawrence Stone, and Robert C. Tucker.

20. Walter LaFeber, *America, Russia, and the Cold War, 1945–1066* (New York: John Wiley and Sons, 1967); Lloyd C. Gardner, *Economic Aspects of New Deal Diplomacy* (New York: Beacon, 1964).

21. Kennan, handwritten notes [n.d. but 1968], "Notes for Seminar on the Origins of the Cold War, Institute for Advanced Study 1968 February 15," folder 5, box 304, Kennan Papers.

22. Transcript of Cold War Seminar Held at the Institute for Advanced Study, February 15, 1968, in author's possession, p. 8. For Kennan's looking away from the speakers, Lloyd C. Gardner to the author, Zoom meeting, March 15, 2021.

23. Transcript of Cold War Seminar Held at the Institute for Advanced Study, February 15, 1968, p. 32; audio recording of the Cold War Seminar, Shelby White and Leon Levy Archives Center, Institute for Advanced Study, Princeton, NJ [hereafter White and Levy Archives Center].

24. Countering LaFeber's argument that not only the Soviet Union, but also the United States behaved as an ideological state, Schlesinger asserted: "I would not regard free elections as an ideology. I really wouldn't even regard the notion that the world ought to be organized in the form of Wilsonian terms as an ideology." Transcript of Cold War Seminar Held at the Institute for Advanced Study, February 15, 1968, p. 21, in author's possession.

25. Kennan to Paul M. Kattenburg, August 11, 1970; Kennan to John F. Campbell [at the Council on Foreign Relations], August 12, 1970, folder 5, box 304, Kennan Papers.

26. Kennan to Theodore Sands, March 16, 1970, box 19, White and Levy Archives Center.

27. WorldCat shows no publication for Theodore Sands in 1970 or thereafter.

28. Elie Abel to Kennan, June 9, 1972, folder 5, box 304, Kennan Papers.

29. Charles E. Bohlen to Kennan, March 23, 1970, folder 16, box 5, Kennan Papers.

30. Costigliola, *Kennan Diaries*, 462–64.

31. Kennan, "Russia's National Objectives," Air War College, Maxwell Field, AL, April 10, 1947, p. 14 of Q&A, folder 32, bos 298, Kennan Papers.

32. Stephen Arbogast to the author, October 24, 2021.

33. Kennan, "The United States and the Soviet Union, 1917–1976," *Foreign Affairs*, 54 (July 1976): 673, 677, 680.

34. John Lewis Gaddis, *The United States and the Origins of the Cold War* (New York: Columbia University Press, 1972). This book won both the Bancroft Prize and the Stuart L. Bernath Prize given by the Society for Historians of American Foreign Relations.

35. John Lewis Gaddis, "Containment: A Reassessment," *Foreign Affairs* 55 (July 1977): 886.

36. Kennan to Michael J. Lacey, October 11, 1977, box 15, Kennan Papers.

37. Gaddis to Kennan, March 31, 1978, with enclosure of essay by Michael H. Hunt and John W. Coogan, "Kennan and Containment: A Comment," *Society for Historians of American Foreign Relations Newsletter* (March 1978): 23–25; Kennan to Gaddis, April 6, 1978; Gaddis to Kennan, April 10, 1978, with enclosure of essay by Gaddis, "Kennan and Containment: A Reply," all in box 15, Kennan Papers.

38. George Urban, "A Conversation with George F. Kennan," *Encounter* (September 1976), 16. He also acknowledged that "for purposes of argument, I am given to overstating a case." Urban, "Conversation with Kennan," 37.

39. George Urban, "Conversation with Kennan," 11.

40. Urban, "Conversation with Kennan," 11.

41. Kennan, "To Prevent a World Wasteland: A Proposal," *Foreign Affairs* 48, no. 3 (April 1970): 401–13.

42. Kennan, "To Prevent a World Wasteland."

43. Kennan, "To Prevent a World Wasteland."

44. Constance Goodman interview with Gaddis, December 10, 1987, p. 8, folder 16, box 1, Gaddis Papers.

45. Kennan Family Farm Diary, March 9, 1967, in private possession.

46. George and Annelise Kennan interview with Gaddis, December 13, 1987, p. 65, folder 1, box 6, Gaddis Papers.

47. Author interview with Joan Kennan, August 1, 2015.

48. Warnecke, *Daughter of the Cold War*, 154.

49. George and Annelise Kennan interview with Gaddis, December 13, 1987, p. 74, folder 1, box 6, Gaddis Papers.

50. Costigliola, *Kennan Diaries*, 452.

51. George and Annelise Kennan interview with Gaddis, December 13, 1987, pp. 66–67, folder 1, box 6, Gaddis Papers.

52. Svetlana Alliluyeva, *Only One Year* (New York: Harper, 1969), 218.

53. Rosemary Sullivan, *Stalin's Daughter The Extraordinary and Tumultuous Life of Svetlana Alliluyeva* (New York: HarperCollins, 2015), 296.

54. Warnecke, *Daughter of the Cold War*, 156.

55. "Transcript of Mrs. Alliluyeva's Statement and Her Replies at News Conference," *New York Times*, April 27, 1967.

56. "Svetlana's Journey," *New York Times*, April 23, 1967, p. 18; "Text of Kennan; Statement on the Role He Played," *New York Times*, April 22, 1967, p. 11.

57. Kennan to Alliluyeva, April 22, 1967, quoted in Alliluyeva, *Only One Year*, 312.

58. Costigliola, *Kennan Diaries*, 462.

59. Alliluyeva, *Only One Year*, 328–29.

60. CIA report, July 14, 1967, CIA-RDP88-01350R000200680031-6, CREST, CIA online documents.

61. Warnecke, *Daughter of the Cold War*, 156–57.

62. Warnecke, *Daughter of the Cold War*, 159.

63. Journal of Simki Mattern Kuznick, August 1, 1967, in private possession.

64. Alliluyeva, *Only One Year*, 340.

65. Farm Diary [n.d., probably August 8, 1967], in private possession. Simki recorded, "This was Carnival Day [in nearby East Berlin]. And Svetlana burned her passport." Journal of Simki Mattern Kuznick, August 8, 1967.

66. Sullivan, *Stalin's Daughter*.

67. Svetlana Alliluyeva to Joan Kennan Griggs, November 17, 1967, in private possession (emphasis in the original).

68. George and Annelise Kennan interview with Gaddis, December 13, 1987, pp. 69–77, folder 1, box 6, Gaddis Papers.

69. Constance Goodman interview with Gaddis, December 10, 1987, p. 15, folder 16, box 1, Gaddis Papers; Kennan to Kent W. Kennan, December 18, 1965, folder 1, box 328, Kennan Papers.

70. Costigliola, *Kennan Diaries*, 463, 502.

71. Costigliola, *Kennan Diaries*, 505.

72. Costigliola, *Kennan Diaries*, 453.

73. Costigliola, *Kennan Diaries*, 481.

74. Costigliola, *Kennan Diaries*, 515, 533.

75. Costigliola, *Kennan Diaries*, 540–41.

76. Kennan interview with Gaddis, August 25, 1982, p. 6, folder 24, box 1, Gaddis Papers.

77. These paragraphs draw from the longer of two letters penned for Christopher in the late 1960s or early 1970s and intended to be read only after Kennan's death. They are in Kennan's diary for 1988–1989, folder 3, box 326, Kennan Papers.

78. Costigliola, *Kennan Diaries*, 478.

79. Kennan, *The Cloud of Danger: Current Realities of American Foreign Policy* (Boston: Little, Brown, 1977).

80. Kennan, *Cloud of Danger*, 215, 233.

81. Constance Goodman interview with Gaddis, December 10, 1987, pp. 16–17, folder 16, box 1, Gaddis Papers.

82. Ronald Steel, "Russia, the West, and the Rest," *New York Review of Books*, July 14, 1977.

83. Gaddis to Kennan, June 24, 1977, box 15, Kennan Papers. Years later, however, in writing the biography, Gaddis's assessment of *Cloud of Danger* changed from glowing to glowering. He quoted extensively from a negative review in the *Washington Post* and disparaged the book as "Kennan's mistake." Gaddis, *George F. Kennan*, 636.

84. Kennan, *Cloud of Danger*, 170.

85. Kennan, *Cloud of Danger*, 202.

86. Kennan, *Cloud of Danger*, 214.

87. Kennan, *Cloud of Danger*, 9–21.

88. Kennan, *Cloud of Danger*, 23.

89. Kennan, *Cloud of Danger*, 24.

90. Kennan, *Cloud of Danger*, 233–34.

91. Costigliola, *Kennan Diaries*, 507–08.

92. Kennan, *The Decline of Bismarck's European Order: Franco-Russian Relations, 1875–1890* (Princeton, NJ: Princeton University Press, 1979), 3 (emphasis in original).

93. Georgi Arbatov to Kennan, May 5, 1977; Kennan to Arbatov, May 1977, folder 3, box 277, Kennan Papers.

94. Kennan, *Decline of Bismarck's European Order*, 4, 424 (emphasis in original).

95. Goodman interview with Gaddis, December 10, 1987, pp. 17–19, folder 16, box 1, Gaddis Papers.

96. Kennan to Frieda Por, Christmas Day 1977, folder 1, box 329, Kennan Papers.

97. Costigliola, *Kennan Diaries*, 472.

98. Costigliola, *Kennan Diaries*, 478.

99. Costigliola, *Kennan Diaries*, 500.

100. Costigliola, *Kennan Diaries*, 521.

101. Costigliola, *Kennan Diaries*, 515–16.

102. Kennan to Gaddis, September 4, 1980, box 15, Kennan Papers.

103. Costigliola, *Kennan Diaries*, 535.

104. John Lewis Gaddis, *Strategies of Containment: A Critical Appraisal of Postwar American National Security Policy* (New York: Oxford University Press, 1982).

105. Kennan to Gaddis, November 21, 1981, box 15, Kennan Papers.

106. Gaddis to Kennan, November 28, 1981, box 15, Kennan Papers.

107. Goodman interview with Gaddis, December 10, 1987, p. 2, folder 16, box 1, Gaddis Papers.

108. Kennan to Gaddis, December 1, 1981, box 15, Kennan Papers.

109. David A. Mayers, *George Kennan and the Dilemmas of U.S. Foreign Policy* (New York: Oxford University Press, 1988). See also C. Ben Wright, "George F. Kennan, Scholar-Diplomat: 1926–1946" (Ph.D. diss., University of Wisconsin, 1972).

110. Kennan to Gaddis, November 3, 1982, box 15, Kennan Papers; Costigliola, *Kennan Diaries*, 544.

111. Gaddis to Kennan, November 17, 1982, box 15, Kennan Papers. This letter followed a phone call between the two.

112. Schlesinger and Schlesinger, *Journals 1952–2000*, 474.

113. Nicholas Thompson, *The Hawk and the Dove: Paul Nitze, George Kennan and the History of the Cold War* (New York: Henry Holt, 2009), 244.

114. *FRUS 1981–88*, 3: document 104, https://history.state.gov/historicaldocuments/frus1981-88v03/d104.

115. Paul M. Nitze interview with Gaddis, December 13, 1989, p. 1, folder 6, box 6, Gaddis Papers.

116. Walter J. Stoessel Jr., "Meeting of Former US Ambassadors to the Soviet Union," May 18, 1981, Department of State files. My thanks to James Graham Wilson for sharing this document with me.

117. Kennan, "A Proposal for International Disarmament," May 19, 1981, in Kennan, *The Nuclear Delusion: Soviet-American Relations in the Atomic Age* (New York: Pantheon Books, 1982), 175–82.

118. Costigliola, *Kennan Diaries*, 535.

119. Costigliola, *Kennan Diaries*, 531–33.

120. Thompson, *Hawk and the Dove*, 270, 280.

121. Costigliola, *Kennan Diaries*, 538.

122. Costigliola, *Kennan Diaries*, 538

123. Kennan, "Nuclear Weapons and Christian Faith," in Kennan, *At a Century's Ending*, 69.

124. Costigliola, *Kennan Diaries*, 540.

125. Costigliola, *Kennan Diaries*, 541–42.

126. Costigliola, *Kennan Diaries*, 544–45.

Chapter 11

1. George F. Kennan, *Sketches from a Life* (New York: Pantheon Books, 1989), 351–52. Kennan did develop a relationship of mutual respect with Jack F. Matlock Jr., U.S. ambassador to Moscow from 1987 to 1991. Years later, he would welcome former ambassador Matlock's appointment as the George F. Kennan chair at the Institute for Advanced Study.

2. Costigliola, *Kennan Diaries*, 551.

3. Costigliola, *Kennan Diaries*, 578.

4. Costigliola, *Kennan Diaries*, 580–81.

5. Costigliola, *Kennan Diaries*, 557.

6. Costigliola, *Kennan Diaries*, 573.

7. Kennan, "Historical Inevitability and World War (1890–1914)," [1985] in Kennan, *At a Century's Ending*, 26.

8. Costigliola, *Kennan Diaries*, 562.

9. Costigliola, *Kennan Diaries*, 554

10. Costigliola, *Kennan Diaries*, 584–85, 593–94.

11. Costigliola, *Kennan Diaries*, 587.

12. Costigliola, *Kennan Diaries*, 564.

13. Costigliola, *Kennan Diaries*, 556.

14. Costigliola, *Kennan Diaries*, 579.

15. John Lewis Gaddis, *The Long Peace* (New York: Oxford University Press, 1987).

16. Costigliola, *Kennan Diaries*, 572.

17. Costigliola, *Kennan Diaries*, 550–51.

18. Costigliola, *Kennan Diaries*, 569.

19. Costigliola, *Kennan Diaries*, 594.

20. Costigliola, *Kennan Diaries*, 594.

21. Mary McGrory, "Kennan—A Prophet Honored," *Washington Post*, April 9, 1989, pp. B1, B5.

22. Kennan, "Just Another Great Power," *New York Times*, April 9, 1989, reprinted in Kennan, *At a Century's Ending*, 167–68.

23. McGrory, "Kennan—A Prophet Honored," p. B5.

24. Don Oberdorfer, "Revolutionary Epoch Ending in Russia, Kennan Declares," *Washington Post*, April 5, 1989, p. A22.

25. Schlesinger and Schlesinger, *Journals 1952–2000*, 672.

26. Costigliola, *Kennan Diaries*, 596, 598.

27. Costigliola, *Kennan Diaries*, 596–97.

28. Mary Elise Sarotte, *The Collapse: The Accidental Opening of the Berlin Wall* (New York: Basic Books, 2014); James Graham Wilson, *The Triumph of Improvisation: Gorbachev's*

Adaptability, Reagan's Engagement, and the End of the Cold War (Ithaca, NY: Cornell University Press, 2014).

29. Costigliola, *Kennan Diaries*, 601. Kennan underestimated the willingness of the Bush administration to support Gorbachev. See Jeffrey A. Engel, *When the World Seemed New: George H. W. Bush and the End of the Cold War* (New York: Houghton Mifflin Harcourt, 2017).

30. Costigliola, *Kennan Diaries*, 601.

31. Costigliola, *Kennan Diaries*, 602.

32. Costigliola, *Kennan Diaries*, 603.

33. Christopher J. Kennan interview with the author, September 12, 2016.

34. Keith Bradsher, "Party Is Little Changed, but Not the Partygoers," *New York Times*, December 22, 1989, p. B4.

35. Keith Bradsher, "Party Is Little Changed, But Not the Partygoers," *New York Times*, December 22, 1989, p. B4.

36. Kennan, "A New Age of European Security," 174–78.

37. Kennan, "A New Age of European Security," 174–78.

38. Kennan, "A New Age of European Security," 174–78.

39. Kennan, "On the Soviet Union and Eastern Europe," *New York Review of Books*, March 1, 1990.

40. Costigliola, *Kennan Diaries*, 640.

41. Costigliola, *Kennan Diaries*, 608.

42. Costigliola, *Kennan Diaries*, 606.

43. Costigliola, *Kennan Diaries*, 609.

44. Costigliola, *Kennan Diaries*, 608.

45. Costigliola, *Kennan Diaries*, 609.

46. Costigliola, *Kennan Diaries*, 609.

47. Costigliola, *Kennan Diaries*, 611; Sermon, Belgrade, July 21, 1963, folder 41, box 302, Kennan Papers.

48. The very first footnote in the published book defied the by-now, decades old women's movement to explain that he was using the words "man" and "he" to refer to all of mankind, and that "I see in this usage no occasion for apology." Kennan, *Around the Cragged Hill* (New York: W. W. Norton, 1993), 18.

49. Costigliola, *Kennan Diaries*, 610–11.

50. Costigliola, *Kennan Diaries*, 562.

51. Costigliola, *Kennan Diaries*, 612.

52. Costigliola, *Kennan Diaries*, 569.

53. Costigliola, *Kennan Diaries*, 612–13.

54. Costigliola, *Kennan Diaries*, 612–13.

55. Costigliola, *Kennan Diaries*, 612.

56. Tucker and Tucker interview with Gaddis, September 4, 1984, pp. 15–16.

57. Conversation between Alexander Yakovlev and George Frost Kennan, 5 October 1990, Moscow, Fond 10063, opis. 2, delo 39, State Archive of the Russian Federation. Translated by Svetlana Savranskaya for the National Security Archives, Washington, DC.

58. Costigliola, *Kennan Diaries*, 614–15.

59. Kennan interview with Gaddis, January 30, 1991, p. 1; Costigliola, *Kennan Diaries*, 621.

60. Kennan interview with Gaddis, January 30, 1991, p. 2.

61. For an analysis of Stalin's speech, see Costigliola, *Roosevelt's Lost Alliances*, 399.

62. Kennan interview with Gaddis, January 30, 1991, p. 5.

63. Kennan interview with Gaddis, January 30, 1991, p. 9.

64. Kennan interview with Gaddis, January 30, 1991, pp. 9, 12–14.

65. Costigliola, *Kennan Diaries*, 619.

66. Costigliola, *Kennan Diaries*, 620–21.

67. Costigliola, *Kennan Diaries*, 621.

68. Costigliola, *Kennan Diaries*, 623.

69. Costigliola, *Kennan Diaries*, 580.

70. Kennan to Gaddis, December 1, 1981, box 15, Kennan Papers.

71. Gaddis to Kennan, December 14, 1981, box 15, Kennan Papers.

72. J. Richardson Dilworth interview with Gaddis, December 6, 1987; William P. and Mary A. Bundy interview with Gaddis, December 6, 1987, pp. 30–31, box 1, Gaddis Papers.

73. Kennan to Gaddis, April 3, 1984, box 15, Kennan Papers.

74. Gellman had corresponded with Kennan.

75. Kennan to Gaddis, February 20, 1985, box 15, Kennan Papers.

76. Kennan to Gaddis, December 23, 1985, box 15, Kennan Papers. Kennan was also impressed with the published book, which interpreted his ideas as those of an organic conservative. See Anders Stephanson, *Kennan and the Art of Foreign Policy* (Cambridge, MA: Harvard University Press, 1989). For a more recent evaluation of Kennan's thought, see David Milne, *Worldmaking: The Art and Science of American Diplomacy* (New York: Farrar, Straus and Giroux, 2015), 217–67.

77. Kennan interview with Gaddis, January 30, 1991, p. 17.

78. Kennan interview with Gaddis, January 30, 1991, p. 18; Kennan to Kent W. Kennan, July 28, 1989, folder 2, box 23, Kennan Papers.

79. Kennan interview with Gaddis, January 30, 1991, pp. 17–18.

80. Peter Grose, "Uncle Sam's Nazis," *Washington Post*, April 24, 1988.

81. Robert Wolfe, "Gustav Hilger: From Hitler's Foreign Office to CIA Consultant," June 1, 2006, https://sgp.fas.org/eprint/wolfe.pdf.

82. Walter Pozen to John Loftus, September 19, 1983, folder 4, box 28, Kennan Papers.

83. Kennan to Gaddis, November 13, 1987; Kennan to Gaddis, November 19, 1987; Gaddis to John Herman, November 20, 1987; Simpson to Gaddis, November 30, 1987, all in box 15, Kennan Papers. Despite Gaddis's letter, the publisher went ahead. See Christopher Simpson, *Blowback: America's Recruitment of Nazis and Its Effects on the Cold War* (New York: Weidenfeld and Nicolson, 1988).

84. Kennan remarks at Ohio University, n.d. [1988], box 15, Kennan Papers.

85. Costigliola, *Kennan Diaries*, 592.

86. Kennan to Gaddis, March 11, 1992, box 15, Kennan Papers.

87. Kennan to Felix Gilbert, April 14, 1983, https://albert.ias.edu/handle/20.500.12111/3161, Albert Digital Repository, Shelby White and Leon Levy Archives Center, Institute for Advanced Study. Aside from containing a brief acknowledgment from Gilbert, the IAS Archives indicate that no one from the Institute appears to have taken any further action with regard to Kennan's

suggestion of appointing Gaddis to a faculty position. Erica Mosner to the author, June 9, 2021. Gaddis, meanwhile, suggested that Kennan's proposal to have him at the Institute failed "probably because I didn't encourage it. I didn't want to give up teaching students." John L. Gaddis to the author, June 3, 2021.

88. Kennan to Gaddis, April 3, 1992, box 15, Kennan Papers.

89. Gaddis to Kennan, April 12, 1992, box 15, Kennan Papers.

90. Kennan to Gaddis, April 18, 1995; Kennan to Gaddis, November 13, 1995, box 15, Kennan Papers.

91. Kennan to Gaddis, April 18, 1995; Kennan to Gaddis, November 13, 1995, box 15, Kennan Papers.

92. Costigliola, *Kennan Diaries*, 657.

93. Kennan to Gaddis, February 2, 1997 (emphasis in original); Gaddis to Kennan, January 26, 1997, box 15, Kennan Papers.

94. Gaddis to Kennan, May 17, 1997; Kennan to Gaddis, May 28, 1997; Gaddis to Kennan, August 10, 1997, box 14, Kennan Papers.

95. Kennan to Gaddis, May 22, 1997, box 14, Kennan Papers.

96. Kennan to Gaddis, May 22, 1997, box 14, Kennan Papers.

97. Gaddis to Kennan, August 10, 1997, box 14, Kennan Papers.

98. Kennan to Gaddis, August 18, 1997, box 14, Kennan Papers.

99. Gaddis to Kennan, January 17, 1999, folder 2, box 16, Kennan Papers.

100. These paragraphs draw from Kennan to Gaddis, February 2, 1999, folder 2, box 16, Kennan Papers (emphasis in original).

101. Costigliola, *Kennan Diaries*, 674.

102. Costigliola, *Kennan Diaries*, 673–74.

103. John Lukacs interview with author, January 30, 2014.

104. Gaddis, *The Long Peace*, especially 215–45.

105. J. Richardson Dilworth interview with Gaddis, December 6, 1987, p. 3.

106. Costigliola, *Kennan Diaries*, 651.

107. Costigliola, *Kennan Diaries*, 653.

108. Costigliola, *Kennan Diaries*, 658.

109. Costigliola, *Kennan Diaries*, 550.

110. Christopher Kennan interview with author, March 12, 2016.

111. Costigliola, *Kennan Diaries*, 626.

112. Costigliola, *Kennan Diaries*, 663.

113. Costigliola, *Kennan Diaries*, 630–31.

114. Costigliola, *Kennan Diaries*, 653–54.

115. Costigliola, *Kennan Diaries*, 633–34.

116. Costigliola, *Kennan Diaries*, 634.

117. Costigliola, *Kennan Diaries*, 637.

118. Costigliola, *Kennan Diaries*, 633.

119. Strobe Talbott, *The Russia Hand* (New York: Random House, 2002), 134.

120. Costigliola, *Kennan Diaries*, 641.

121. Costigliola, *Kennan Diaries*, 644–45.

122. Kennan to Talbott, April 22, 1997, folder 4, box 47, Kennan papers; Costigliola, *Kennan Diaries*, 656–57; Talbott, *Russia Hand*, 232.

123. Costigliola, *Kennan Diaries*, 658–59.

124. Kennan to Dönhoff, September 22, 1997, folder 15, box 11, Kennan Papers.

125. Costigliola, *Kennan Diaries*, 656.

126. Richard Ullman, "The US and the World: An Interview with George Kennan," *New York Review of Books*, August 12, 1999; Kennan to Talbott, January 31, 1997, folder 4, box 47, Kennan papers.

127. Ullman, "The US and the World."

128. Diary of the Princeton House and Property, August 12–17, 1996, in private possession.

129. Costigliola, *Kennan Diaries*, 640, 645–46.

130. Kennan, *An American Family*.

131. Kennan to Oliver Kennan, May 15, 1996, folder 2, box 26; Kennan papers.

132. Kennan to Ted Vogel, November 8, 1992, folder 3, box 26, Kennan papers; Kennan, *American Family*, 51–71.

133. Costigliola, *Kennan Diaries*, 660–61, 664–65.

134. Costigliola, *Kennan Diaries*, 660–61, 664–65.

135. Grace Kennan Warnecke, "My Father's Anger," [2002] in private possession.

136. Costigliola, *Kennan Diaries*, 665.

137. Costigliola, *Kennan Diaries*, 669.

138. Costigliola, *Kennan Diaries*, 676–77.

139. Costigliola, *Kennan Diaries*, 677.

140. Costigliola, *Kennan Diaries*, 678.

141. Albert Eisele, "George F. Kennan at 98, Veteran Diplomat Declares Congress Must Take Lead on War with Iraq," *The Hill*, September 25, 2002, p. 24; Jane Mayer, "A Doctrine Passes," *New Yorker*, October 14, 2002.

142. Mary A. Bundy interview with author, May 23, 2011.

143. Betsy Barrett interview with author, July 2, 2021.

Conclusion

1. Symposium in Honor of George F. Kennan, Institute for Advanced Study, February 18, 2004, Shelby White and Leon Levy Archives Center, Institute for Advanced Study, Princeton, NJ. My thanks to Erica Mosner for finding and sending this video document.

2. Costigliola, *Kennan Diaries*, 78.

3. Symposium in Honor of Kennan, February 18, 2004, Institute for Advanced Study, White and Levy Archives Center, Institute for Advanced Study.

4. Interview on *NewsHour* with Jim Lehrer, April 18, 1996, folder 16, box 311, Kennan Papers.

5. Colin Powell, Remarks on the Occasion of George Kennan's Centenary Birthday, Princeton University, February 20, 2004, https://2001-2009.state.gov/secretary/former/powell/remarks/29683.htm.

6. Warnecke, *Daughter of the Cold War*, 276.

7. Powell, Remarks on the Occasion of George Kennan's Centenary Birthday, Princeton University, February 20, 2004, https://2001-2009.state.gov/secretary/former/powell/remarks/29683.htm.

8. Author's notes at the George F. Kennan Centennial Conference, Princeton University, February 20, 2004.

9. Todd S. Purdum, "Memorial for Kennan Recalls Drama of Cold War Tensions," *New York Times*, April 7, 2005, p. B10.

10. Costigliola, *Kennan Diaries*, 488–89.

11. Costigliola, *Kennan Diaries*, 574; Isaacson and Thomas, *The Wise Men*.

12. Kennan to Barton Gellman, March 28, 1983. My thanks to Barton Gellman for sharing this document.

13. Kennan, *Memoirs 1925–1950*, 559.

14. Kennan to Hotchkiss, October 8, 1944, box 24, Kennan Papers.

15. Kennan, "The Background of Current Russian Diplomatic Moves," in *Measures Short of War*, 86.

16. Kennan, "Russia and the Russians," Commercial Club of Cincinnati, Ohio, January 21, 1950, file 33, box 299, Kennan Papers.

17. Kennan to Bohlen, July 10, 1952, RG 59.

18. Kennan to Bohlen, July 10, 1952, RG 59.

19. For evidence of the Soviets' inclination to negotiate, see Naimark, *Stalin and the Fate of Europe*; Leffler, *For the Soul of Mankind*.

20. Gaddis, *George F. Kennan*, vii, x.

21. Dilworth interview with Gaddis, December 6, 1987, folder 11, p. 3; Bundy and Bundy interview with Gaddis, December 6, 1987, p. 34, folder 7, box 1, Gaddis Papers.

22. Kennan interview with Gaddis, December 13, 1995, folder 2, box 6, pp. 23–24.

23. Arthur S. Link interview with Gaddis, September 5, 1984, folder 4, box 6, Gaddis Papers. In response to Link's statement, Gaddis replied, "Bob Tucker has raised the same point: that Kennan somehow never felt comfortable as a teacher," perhaps because he tended to overprepare for lectures.

24. Kennan interview with Gaddis, December 13, 1995, folder 2, box 6, pp. 23–24.

25. Ronald Steel, "George Kennan at 100," *New York Review of Books*, April 29, 2004, https://www-nybooks-com.ezproxy.lib.uconn.edu/articles/2004/04/29/george-kennan-at-100/ (accessed April 6, 2022).

INDEX